Beginning Linux Programming

Neil Matthew
and
Richard Stones

Wrox Press Ltd. ®

SHROFF PUBLISHERS & DISTRIBUTORS PVT. LTD.
Navi Mumbai *Calcutta*

Beginning Linux Programming

Printing History

August 1996 : First Edition
October 1996: Reprinted with minor corrections
September 1997: Reprinted with further corrections
September 1999: Second Edition , revised and updated with additional material
December 1999: Reprinted

Fifth Indian Reprint: March 2002

ISBN: 81-7366-156-1

Published by Wrox Press Ltd
Arden House, 1102 Warwick Road, Acocks Green,
Birmingham B27 6BH, UK
Originally Printed in Canada
ISBN 1-861002-97-1

Published by **Shroff Publishers and Distributors Pvt. Ltd.** C-103, MIDC, TTC Industrial Area, Pawane, Navi Mumbai 400 701, Tel: (91 22) 763 4290, Fax: (91 22) 768 3337, e-mail: spd@vsnl.com. Printed at Rose Fine Art, Kurla, Mumbai.

Trademark Acknowledgements

Credits

Authors
Neil Matthew
Richard Stones

Contributing Authors
Jens Axboe
Simon Cozens
Andrew Froggatt
Krishna Vedati

Editors
Martin Brooks
Louay Fatoohi
James Hart
Ian Maddison

Editors (First Edition)
Tim Briggs
Jon Hill
Julian Dobson

Managing Editor
Paul Cooper

Development
John Franklin
Richard Collins

Technical Reviewers
Steve Caron
Stefaan Eeckels
Donal Fellows
Chris Harshman
David Hudson
Jonathan Kelly
Giles Lean
Marty Leisner
Ron McCarty
Bill Moss
Gavin Smyth
Chris Ullman
Bruce Varney
James Youngman

Index
Robin Smith

Design / Layout
Tom Bartlett
David Boyce
Mark Burdett
William Fallon
Jonathan Jones
John McNulty

Cover Design
Chris Morris

Thanks to Larry Ewing (lewing@isc.tamu.edu) and the GIMP for the chapter divider.

"Some people have told me they don't think a fat penguin really embodies the grace of Linux, which just tells me they have never seen an angry penguin charging at them in excess of 100mph. They'd be a lot more careful about what they say if they had." Linus Torvalds announcing Linux 2.0

Code License

In recognition of the considerable value of software available for free under the GNU copyright restriction, including the Linux kernel and many of the other programs that are needed to make a usable Linux system, the authors have agreed with Wrox Press that all the example code in this book, although copyright is retained by Wrox Press, may be reused under the terms of the GNU Public License, version 2 or later. Thus for all the code printed in this book, the following license restriction applies:

A copy of the GNU General Public License may be found in Appendix B.

About the Authors

Neil Matthew

Neil Matthew has been interested in and has programmed computers since 1974. A mathematics graduate from the University of Nottingham, Neil is just plain keen on programming languages and likes to explore new ways of solving computing problems. He's written systems to program in BCPL, FP (Function Programming), Lisp, Prolog and a structured BASIC. He even wrote a 6502 microprocessor emulator to run BBC microcomputer programs on UNIX systems.

In terms of UNIX experience, Neil has used almost every flavor since Version 6, including Xenix, SCO flavors, Ultrix, BSD 4.2, Microport, System V, SunOS 4, Solaris and, of course, Linux. He's been a UNIX system administrator on-and-off since 1983. Neil is familiar with the internals of UNIX-like systems and was involved in the design and implementation of a intelligent communications controller for DEC Ultrix.

He can claim to have been using Linux since August 1993, when he acquired a floppy disk distribution of Soft Landing (SLS) from Canada, with kernel version 0.99.11. He's used Linux-based computers for hacking C, C++, Icon, Prolog and Tcl, at home and at work. He also uses and recommends Linux for Internet connections, usually as a proxy caching server for Windows LANs and also as a file server to Windows 3.11/95 using SAMBA. He's sold a number of Internet firewall systems to UK companies (including Wrox!).

Most of Neil's 'home' projects were originally implemented in SCO UNIX, but they've been ported to Linux with little or no trouble. He says Linux is much easier because it supports quite a lot of features from other systems, so that both BSD and System V targeted programs will generally compile with little or no change.

As the head of software and principal engineer at Camtec Electronics in the Eighties, Neil programmed in C and C++ for real-time embedded systems environments. Since then, he's worked on software development techniques and quality assurance both as a consultant in communications software development with Scientific Generics and as a software QA specialist for GEHE UK.

Neil is married to Christine and has two children, Alexandra and Adrian. He lives in a converted barn in Northamptonshire. His interests include computers, music, science fiction, chess, squash, cars and not doing it yourself.

Richard Stones

Rick started programming at school, more years ago than he cares to remember, on a BBC micro, which with the help a few spare parts continued functioning for the next 15 years. He graduated from the University of Nottingham with an Electronic Engineering degree, by which time he had decided that software was more fun than hardware.

Over the years he has worked for a variety of companies, from the very small with just a few dozen employees, to multinationals, including the IT services giant EDS. Along the way he has worked on a wide range of different projects, from embedded real-time communications systems, through accounting systems, to large help desk systems with multi-gigabyte databases. Many of these projects have either been hosted on UNIX, or UNIX was the development environment. On one project the entire embedded software was developed and tested on Linux, and only ported to the target hardware and minimal real-time executive in the final stages. He is currently employed by the IT department of a pan-European wholesale and distribution company as a systems architect.

Rick's first experience of a UNIX style operating system was on a PDP 11/23+, after which BSD4.2 on a VAX came as a pleasant improvement. After spells using UNIX System V.2, Xenix, SCO UNIX, AIX and a few others, he first met Linux back in the kernel .99 days, and has been a fan ever since.

A bit of a programming linguist, he has programmed systems in SL-1, a couple of assemblers, Fortran, Pascal, C, C++, Java, SQL and Perl. Under pressure he has also been known to admit to some familiarity with Visual Basic, but tries not to advertise this aberration.

Rick lives in a Leicestershire village, with his wife Ann, two children, Jennifer and Andrew, and a pair of cats. Outside work his passion is for classical music, especially early church music, and he does his best to find time for some piano practice between lessons. He occasionally does the odd job for Wrox press.

Finally, both authors were co-authors of Instant UNIX (Wrox Press)

Authors Acknowledgements

The authors would like to thank the many people who helped make this book possible.

Neil's wife, Christine, for her understanding of the reasons why we had to write another book, and his children Alexandra and Adrian for not being sad at losing their Dad for too many weekends.

Rick's wife, Ann, and children, Jennifer and Andrew, for their very considerable patience during the evenings and weekends while this book was being written.

Heartfelt thanks are also due to Richard Neill, for his considerable assistance in reviewing early drafts of the first edition, on which he made numerous helpful comments and suggestions. We would also like to pay tribute to his wife, Angie, and son, Gavin, for putting up with us monopolizing his precious time.

As for the publishing team, we wish to thank the folk at Wrox Press, especially Julian, Tim and Jon for their work on getting the first edition to fly, and Paul, Richard, James, Louay, and Martin for their enthusiasm and editing work on the second edition.

We would also like to thank the people who have contributed additional material to the second edition - Andrew, Jens, Krishna and Simon - and all the people who did excellent work reviewing the second edition. It's certainly a better book than it would otherwise have been. Thanks guys!

We would also like to thank our one-time employers, Scientific Generics and Mobicom, for their support during the creation of the first edition.

Neil and Rick would also like to pay homage to two important motivators who have helped make this book possible. Firstly, Richard Stallman, for the excellent GNU tools and the idea of a free software environment. Secondly, Linus Torvalds, for starting, and continuing to inspire the cooperative development that gives us the ever-improving Linux Kernel.

Table of Contents

Chapter 2: Shell Programming 27

Chapter 14: Sockets 487

Chapter 15: Tcl: Tool Command Language 519

Chapter 16: Programming for X 555

Chapter 21: Device Drivers 787

Foreword

by Alan Cox

Every computer programmer has their own pile of notes and scribbles. They have their code examples saved from the past heroic dive into the manuals or from Usenet - where sometimes even fools fear to follow (The other body of opinion is that fools all get free Usenet access and use it non stop.) It is strange perhaps therefore that so few books follow such a style. In the online world there are a lot of short, to the point, documents about specific areas of programming and administration. The Linux documentation project released a whole pile of three to ten page documents covering everything from installing Linux and NT on the same machine to wiring your coffee machine to Linux. Seriously. Take a look in the mini-how-to index on http://sunsite.unc.edu/LDP.

The book world, on the other hand, mostly seems to consist of either learned tomes - detailed and very complete works that you don't have time to read, and dummies-style books - which you buy for friends as a joke. There are very few books that try to cover the basics of a lot of useful areas. This book is one of them, a compendium of those programmers notes and scribbles, deciphered (try reading programmer handwriting), edited and brought together coherently as a book.

This updated second edition of the book has expanded, as Linux has expanded, and now covers writing threaded programs (otherwise known as "how to shoot yourself in both feet at once") and the GTK toolkit which is the basis of the GNOME GUI and probably the easiest way to write X windows applications in C.

Perl has crept into the book too. There are people who think Perl's time has come. There are those of us who think Perl's time should have come and gone again a long time back. Regardless of my views, Perl has become one of the most powerful (and at times arcane) scripting languages. All Linux programmers, particularly anyone programming cgi scripts for the web, will meet Perl sooner or later so what better than a Perl survival kit.

The final chapter is your chance to join the world of kernel programmers. As you will discover it isn't actually that different to writing modules for large application programs. Put on your pointy hat, grow a beard, drink Jolt Cola and come join in the fun.

Alan

Introduction

Welcome

Welcome to *Beginning Linux Programming*, an easy-to-use guide to developing programs for the Linux and other UNIX-style operating systems.

In this book, we aim to give you an introduction to a wide variety of topics important to you as a developer using UNIX. The word *Beginning* in the title refers more to the content than to your skill level. We've structured the book to help you learn more about what UNIX has to offer, however much experience you have already. UNIX programming is a large field and we aim to cover enough about a wide range of topics to give you a good 'beginning' in each subject.

Who's this Book For?

If you're a programmer who wishes to get up to speed with the facilities that UNIX (and Linux) offers software developers, to maximize your programming time and your application's use of the UNIX system, you've picked up the right book. Clear explanations and a tried and tested step-by-step approach will help you progress rapidly and pick up all the key techniques.

We assume that you know the basics of getting around in UNIX and, ideally, you'll already have some C or C++ programming experience in a non-UNIX environment, perhaps MS-DOS or Microsoft Windows. Where direct comparisons exist, these are indicated in the text.

Watch out if you're new to UNIX. This isn't a book on installing or configuring Linux. If you want to learn more about administering a UNIX system, UNIX concepts and UNIX commands in general, you may want to take a look at Instant UNIX, by the same authors and Andrew Evans, also published by Wrox Press (ISBN 1-874416-65-6).

As it aims to be both a tutorial guide to the various tools and sets of functions/libraries available to you on most UNIX systems and also a handy reference to return to, this book is unique in its straightforward approach, comprehensive coverage and extensive examples.

What's Covered in the Book

The book has a number of aims:

- To teach the use of the standard UNIX C libraries and other facilities as specified by the UNIX98 standard created from the earlier IEEE POSIX and X/Open (SPEC 1170) specifications.
- To show how to make the most of advanced development tools.
- To give concise introductions to popular rapid development languages like the shell, Tcl and Perl.
- To show how to build graphical user interfaces for the X Window System. We will use both Tk on vanilla X and GTK+ for GNOME.
- Having given you firm grounding, to progress to topics of real-world applications which you want to program.

As we cover these topics, we aim to introduce the theory and then illustrate it with an appropriate example and a clear explanation. You can learn quickly on a first read, and look back over things to brush up on all the essential elements again if you need to.

While the small examples are designed mainly to illustrate a set of functions, or some new theory in action, behind the book lies a larger sample project: a simple database application for recording audio CD details. As your knowledge expands, you can develop, re-implement and extend the project to your heart's content. Having said that, it doesn't dominate any chapter, so you can skip it if you want to, but we feel that it provides useful additional examples of the techniques that we'll discuss. It certainly provides an ideal way to illustrate each of the steadily more advanced topics as they are introduced.

Our first meeting with the application occurs at the end of the shell programming chapter and shows how a fairly large shell script is organized, how the shell deals with user input and how it can construct menus and store and search data.

After recapping the basic concepts of compiling programs, linking to libraries and accessing the online manuals, we take a soujourn in shells. We then get stuck into C programming, covering working with files, getting information from the UNIX environment, dealing with terminal input and output, and the `curses` library (which makes interactive input and output more tractable). We're then ready to tackle re-implementing the CD application in C. The application design remains the same, but the code uses the `curses` library for a screen-based user interface.

From there, we cover data management. Meeting the `dbm` database library is sufficient cause for us to re-implement the application again, but this time with a design that will last the rest of the book. The application's user interface is held in one file, while the CD database is a separate program. The database information is now relational.

The size of these recent applications means that next, we need to deal with nuts-and-bolts issues like debugging, source code control, software distribution and makefiles.

Chapter 10 marks a watershed in the book. By this point we will have learned a lot about how running programs behave and can be made to do our bidding. Processes can divide and metamorphose, and they begin to send signals to one another. We also cover POSIX threads, and see how we can create several threads of execution inside a single process.

Having multiple processes opens up the prospect of having a client and a server side to the CD application, with some reliable means of communicating between the two. The client/server application is implemented twice, keeping the database and UI the same, but adding intermediate communication layers using two methods: pipes and the System V IPC. To round this section off, we examine sockets, using a TCP/IP network to enable inter-process communication.

There follows Tcl/Tk's finest hour, as we introduce the Tcl shell and build various X user interfaces with Tk. After this we give an introduction to developing applications for GNOME with the GIMP toolkit (GTK+), using the development of a desktop clock as an example.

Next, we look at the Internet, first at HTML and then at the Common Gateway Interface, which allows us to visit the application one last time. This time, we make the application's user interface available on a remote Web browser accessing web pages generated by CGI programs executing behind the Apache web server.

As the book's finishing flourish, we give an introduction to writing device drivers – an important step along the path to understanding the Linux kernel itself.

As you'd expect, there's a fair bit more in between, but we hope that this gives you a good idea of the material we'll be discussing.

What You Need to Use this Book

In this book, we'll give you a taste of programming for UNIX. To help you get the most from the chapters, we would really like you to try out the examples as you read. These also provide a good base for experimentation and will hopefully inspire you to create programs of your own.

An ideal way to get to grips with the UNIX environment in general is with a distribution of Linux, which brings with it a complete development environment including the GNU C/C++ compiler, associated tools and other useful bits and pieces. It's freely available, POSIX-based, robust, continuously developing and very powerful.

Linux is available for many different systems. Its adaptability is such that enterprising souls have persuaded it to run in one form or another on just about anything with a processor in it! Examples include systems based on the Alpha, SPARC, ARM, PowerPC and 68000 CPUs as well as the Intel x86/PentiumX chips (and compatibles) found in today's PCs.

To develop this book we used Intel-based systems, but very little of what we cover is Intel-specific. Although it is possible to run Linux on a 386 with 2Mb RAM and no hard disk (truly!), to run Linux successfully and follow the examples in this book, we would recommend a specification of at least:

- Pentium processor
- 32Mb RAM
- 600Mb free hard disk space, preferably in its own partition
- For the X Window System, a supported video card

Information on supported video cards can be found at http://www.xfree86.org/.

The hardware requirements of the book's code for most of the chapters is fairly minimal. Only the chapters which need the X Window System will require more computing power (or more patience!)

We wrote this book and developed the examples on two Linux systems with different specifications, so we're confident that if you can run Linux, you can make good use of this book. Furthermore, we tested the code on other versions of Linux during the book's technical review.

As for software requirements, you should be aware that a few of the programs need modern versions of the Linux kernel: 2.2 or greater. The Java Development Kit requires up-to-date versions of the GCC and C libraries (glibc 2 or later). When it comes to other tools, always try to get hold of the newest versions you can. For instance, the Tcl and Tk sections require at least versions, 7.5 and 8.0 respectively. The minimum requirements are stated where necessary and if you have problems with code, using newer tools may help. Fortunately, you can easily download all these tools and, in Appendix C, we provide an Internet resource guide to help you find them. If you are using a recent Linux distribution, you should have no problems.

Because Linux and the GNU toolset and others are released under the GPL they have certain properties, one of which is freedom. They will always have the source code available, and no-one can take that freedom away. They are, therefore, examples of Open Source software – a weaker term for other software that may also have the source code available subject to certain conditions. With GNU/Linux, you will always have the option of support – either do-it-yourself with the source code, or hire someone else. There are now a growing number of companies offering commercial support for Linux and associated tools.

Source Code

We have tried to provide example programs and code snippets that best illustrate the concepts being discussed in the text. Please note that, in order to make the new functionality being introduced as clear as possible, we have taken one or two liberties with coding style.

In particular we do not always check that the return results from every function we call are what we expect. In production code for real applications we would certainly do this, and you too should adopt a rigorous approach towards error handling. We discuss some of the ways that errors can be caught and handled in Chapter 3.

The complete source code from the book is available for download from:

http://www.wrox.com

It's available under the terms of the GNU Public License. We suggest you get hold of a copy to save yourself a lot of typing, although all the code you need is listed in the book.

If you don't have Internet access, you can send away for a disk of the source code. All the details are in the back of the book.

Conventions

To help you get the most from the text and keep track of what's happening, we've used a number of conventions throughout the book.

> **These boxes hold important, not-to-be forgotten, Mission Impossible information which is directly relevant to the surrounding text.**

When we introduce them, we **highlight** important words. We show keyboard strokes like this: *Ctrl-A*.

We present code in three different ways:

```
$ grep "command line" introduction
When the command line is shown, it's in the above style, whereas output is in this
style.
```

Prototypes of UNIX-defined functions and structures are shown in the following style:

```
#include <stdio.h>

int printf (const char *format, ...);
```

```
Lastly in our code examples, the code foreground style shows new, important,
    pertinent code;
while code background shows code that's less important in the present context,
    or has been seen before.
```

We'll presage example code with a Try It Out, which aims to split the code up where that's helpful, to highlight the component parts and to show the progression of the application. When it's important, we also follow the code with a "How It Works" to explain any salient points of the code in relation to previous theory. We find these two conventions help break up the more formidable code listings into more palatable morsels.

Tell Us What You Think

We've worked hard to make this book as useful to you as possible, so we'd like to get a feel for what it is you want and need to know, and what you think about how we've presented things to you.

We appreciate feedback on our efforts and take both criticism and praise on board in our future editorial efforts. If you've anything to say, let us know on:

Feedback@wrox.com
or
http://www.wrox.com

Bookmark the site now!

Why Should I Return the Reply Card?

Why not? If you return the reply card in the back of the book, you'll register this copy of Beginning Linux Programming with Wrox Press, which effectively means that you'll receive free information about updates as soon as they happen. You'll also receive errata sheets when they become available or are updated. (They will be updated on the Web page, too.)

As well as having the satisfaction of having contributed to the future line of Wrox books via your much valued comments and suggestions, you will, as a reward, be given a free subscription to the hugely popular Developer's Journal. This bi-monthly magazine, read by all the software development industry, is invaluable to every programmer who wants to keep up with the cutting edge techniques used by the best developers.

Getting Started

In this first chapter, we'll discover what Linux is and how it relates to its inspiration, UNIX. We'll take a guided tour of the facilities provided by a UNIX development system and we shall write and run our first program. Along the way, we'll be looking at:

- UNIX, Linux and GNU
- Programs and programming languages for UNIX
- Locating development resources
- Static and shared libraries
- The UNIX Philosophy

What is UNIX?

The UNIX operating system was originally developed at Bell Laboratories, once part of the telecommunications giant AT&T. Designed in the 1970s for Digital Equipment PDP computers, it has become a very popular multiuser, multitasking operating system for a wide variety of different hardware platforms, from PC workstations right up to multiprocessor servers and supercomputers.

Strictly, UNIX is a trademark administered by X/Open and refers to a computer operating system that conforms to the X/Open specification XPG4.2. This specification, also known as SPEC1170, defines the names of, interfaces to and behaviors of all UNIX operating system functions. The X/Open specification is largely a superset of an earlier series of specifications, the P1003, or POSIX specifications, actively being developed by the IEEE (Institute of Electrical and Electronic Engineers).

Many UNIX-like systems are available, either commercially, such as Sun's Solaris for SPARC and Intel processors, or for free, such as FreeBSD and Linux. Only a few systems currently conform to the X/Open specification, which allows them to be branded UNIX98. In the past, compatibility between different UNIX systems has been a problem, although POSIX was a great help in this respect. With the publication of the X/Open specification, there's hope that UNIX and the many other UNIX-like systems will converge.

What is Linux?

As you may already know, Linux is a freely distributed implementation of a UNIX-like kernel, the low level core of an operating system. Because Linux takes the UNIX system as its inspiration, Linux and UNIX programs are very similar. In fact, almost all programs written for UNIX can be compiled and run under Linux. Also, many commercial applications sold for commercial versions of UNIX can run unchanged in binary form on Linux systems. Linux was developed by Linus Torvalds at the University of Helsinki, with the help of UNIX programmers from across the Internet. It began as a hobby inspired by Andy Tanenbaum's Minix, a small UNIX system, but has grown to become a complete UNIX system in its own right. The Linux kernel doesn't use code from AT&T or any other proprietary source.

Distributions

As we have already mentioned, Linux is actually just a kernel. You can obtain the sources for the kernel to compile and install them and then obtain and install many other freely distributed software programs to make a complete UNIX-like system. These installations are usually referred to as **Linux systems**, although they consist of much more than just the kernel. Most of the utilities come from the GNU project of the Free Software Foundation.

As you can probably appreciate, creating a Linux system from just source code is a major undertaking. Fortunately, many people have put together 'distributions', usually on CD-ROM, that not only contain the kernel, but also many other programming tools and utilities. These often include an implementation of the X Window system, a graphical environment common on many UNIX systems. The distributions usually come with a setup program and additional documentation (normally all on the CD) to help you install your own Linux system. Some well known distributions are Slackware, SuSE, Debian, Red Hat and Turbo Linux, but there are many others.

The GNU Project and the Free Software Foundation

Linux owes its existence to the cooperative efforts of a large number of people. The operating system kernel itself forms only a small part of a usable development system. Commercial UNIX systems traditionally come bundled with applications programs which provide system services and tools. For Linux systems, these additional programs have been written by many different programmers and have been freely contributed.

The Linux community (together with others) supports the concept of free software, i.e. software that is free from restrictions, subject to the GNU General Public License. Although there may be a cost involved in obtaining the software, it can thereafter be used in any way desired, and is usually distributed in source form.

The Free Software Foundation was set up by Richard Stallman, the author of GNU Emacs, one of the best known editors for UNIX and other systems. Stallman is a pioneer of the free software concept and started the GNU project, an attempt to create an operating system and development environment that will be compatible with UNIX. It may turn out to be very different from UNIX at the lowest level, but will support UNIX applications. The name GNU stands for GNU's Not Unix.

The GNU Project has already provided the software community with many applications that closely mimic those found on UNIX systems. All these programs, so called GNU software, are distributed under the terms of the GNU Public License (GPL), a copy of which may be found in Appendix B. This license embodies the concept of 'copyleft' (a pun on 'copyright'). Copyleft is intended to prevent others from placing restrictions on the use of free software.

Software from the GNU Project distributed under the GPL includes:

- GCC — A C compiler
- G++ — A C++ compiler
- GDB — A source code level debugger
- GNU make — A version of UNIX `make`
- Bison — A parser generator compatible with UNIX `yacc`
- Bash — A command shell
- GNU Emacs — A text editor and environment

Many other packages have been developed and released using free software principles and the GNU Public License. These include graphical image manipulation tools, spreadsheets, source code control tools, compilers and interpreters, internet tools and a complete object-based environment: GNOME. We will meet GNOME again in a later chapter.

You can find out more about the free software concept at http://www.gnu.org.

Programming Linux

Many people think that programming UNIX means using C. It's true that UNIX was originally written in C and that the majority of UNIX applications are written in C, but C is not the only option available to UNIX programmers. In the course of the book, we'll introduce you to some of the alternatives which can sometimes provide a neater solution to programming problems.

> **In fact, the very first version of UNIX was written in PDP 7 assembler language in 1969. C was conceived by Dennis Ritchie around that time and in 1973 he and Ken Thompson rewrote essentially the entire UNIX kernel in C, quite a feat in the days when system software was written in assembly language.**

A vast range of programming languages are available for UNIX systems, and many of them are free and available on CD-Rom collections or from FTP archive sites on the Internet. Appendix C contains a list of useful resources. Here's a partial list of programming languages available to the UNIX programmer:

Ada	C	C++
Eiffel	Forth	Fortran
Icon	Java	JavaScript
Lisp	Modula 2	Modula 3
Oberon	Objective C	Pascal
Perl	PostScript	Prolog
Python	Scheme	Smalltalk
SQL	Tcl/Tk	UNIX Bourne Shell (sh)

In this book, we'll concentrate on just a few of these. We'll see how we can use the UNIX shell (`sh`) to develop small to medium-sized applications in the next chapter. We'll direct our attention mostly at exploring the UNIX programming interfaces from the perspective of the C programmer. In later chapters, we'll take a look at some alternatives to low-level C programming, especially in the context of programming for the Internet (HTML, Perl, Java) and under the X Window system (Tcl/Tk, GNOME).

UNIX Programs

Applications under UNIX are represented by two special types of file: executables and scripts. Executable files are programs that can be run directly by the computer and correspond to DOS `.exe` files. Scripts are collections of instructions for another program, an interpreter, to follow. These correspond to DOS `.bat` files, or interpreted BASIC programs.

UNIX doesn't require that executables or scripts have a specific file name nor any particular extension. File system attributes, which we'll meet in Chapter 2, are used to indicate that a file is a program that may be run. In UNIX, we can replace scripts with compiled programs (and vice versa) without affecting other programs or the people who call them. In fact, at the user level, there is essentially no difference between the two.

When you log in to a UNIX system, you interact with a shell program (often `sh`) that undertakes to run programs for you, in the same way DOS uses `COMMAND.COM`. It finds the programs you ask for by name by searching for a file with the same name in a given set of directories. The directories to search are stored in a shell variable, `PATH`, in much the same way as under DOS. The search path (to which you can add) is configured by your system administrator and will usually contain some standard places where system programs are stored. These include:

`/bin`	Binaries, programs used in booting the system.
`/usr/bin`	User binaries, standard programs available to users.
`/usr/local/bin`	Local binaries, programs specific to an installation.

An administrator's login, such as `root`, may use a `PATH` variable that includes directories where system administration programs are kept, such as `/sbin` and `/usr/sbin`.

Optional operating system components and third-party applications may be installed in subdirectories of `/opt`, and installation programs might add to your `PATH` variable by way of user install scripts.

It is probably a good idea not to delete directories from `PATH` unless you are sure that you understand what will result if you do.

Note that UNIX uses the `:` character to separate entries in the `PATH` variable, rather than the MS-DOS `;`. (UNIX chose `:` first, so ask why MS-DOS was different, not why UNIX is different!). Here's an example `PATH` variable:

```
/usr/local/bin:/bin:/usr/bin:.:/home/neil/bin:/usr/X11R6/bin
```

Here the PATH variable contains entries for the standard program locations, the current directory (`.`), a user's home directory and the X Window System.

The C Compiler

Let's start developing for UNIX using C by writing, compiling and running our first UNIX program. It might as well be that most famous of all, Hello World.

Try It Out - Our First UNIX C Program

1. Here's the source code for the file `hello.c`:

```
#include <stdio.h>

int main()
{
    printf("Hello World\n");
    exit(0);
}
```

2. To enter this program, you'll need to use an editor. There are many to choose from on a typical Linux system. Popular with many users is the `vi` editor. Both the authors like `emacs` and so we suggest you take the time to learn some of the features of this powerful editor. To learn `emacs`, after starting it press *Ctrl-H*, followed by *t* for the tutorial. `emacs` has its entire manual available on-line. Try *Ctrl-H* and then *i* for information. Some versions of Emacs may have menus that you can use to access the manual and tutorial.

3. On POSIX-compliant systems, the C compiler is called `c89`. Historically, the C compiler was simply called `cc`. Over the years, different vendors have sold UNIX-like systems with C compilers with different facilities and options, but often still called `cc`.

When the POSIX standard was prepared, it was impossible to define a standard cc command with which all these vendors would be compatible. Instead, the committee decided to create a new standard command for the C compiler, c89. When this command is present, it will always take the same options, independent of the machine.

On Linux systems, you might find that any or all of the commands c89, cc and gcc refer to the system C compiler, usually the GNU C compiler. On UNIX systems, the C compiler is almost always called cc.

In this book, we'll be using GNU C, because it's provided with Linux distributions and because it supports the ANSI standard syntax for C. If you're using a UNIX system without GNU C, we recommend that you obtain and install it. You can find it starting at http://www.gnu.org. Wherever we use cc in the book, simply substitute the relevant command on your system.

4. Let's compile, link and run our program.

```
$ cc -o hello hello.c
$ ./hello
Hello World
$
```

How It Works

We invoked the system C compiler which translated our C source code into an executable file called hello. We ran the program and it printed a greeting. This is just about the simplest example there is, but if you can get this far with your system, you should be able to compile and run the remainder of the examples in the book. If this did not work for you, make sure that the C compiler is installed on your system. Red Hat Linux has an install option called C Development that you should select.

Since this is the first program we've run, it's a good time to point something out. The hello program will probably be in your home directory. If PATH doesn't include a reference to your home directory, the shell won't be able to find hello. Furthermore, if one of the directories in PATH contains another program called hello, that program will be executed instead. This would also happen if such a directory is mentioned in PATH before your home directory

To get around this potential problem, you can prefix program names with ./ (e.g. ./hello). This specifically instructs the shell to execute the program in the current directory with the given name.

If you forget the -o name option which tells the compiler where to place the executable, the compiler will place the program in a file called a.out (meaning assembler output). Just remember to look for an a.out if you think you've compiled a program and you can't find it! In the early days of UNIX, people wanting to play games on the system often ran them as a.out to avoid being caught by system administrators and many large UNIX installations routinely delete all files called a.out every evening.

Getting Help

All UNIX systems are reasonably well-documented with respect to the system programming interfaces and standard utilities. This is because, since the earliest UNIX systems, programmers have been encouraged to supply a manual page with their programs. These manual pages, which are sometimes provided in a printed form, are invariably available online.

The man command provides access to the online manual pages. The pages vary considerably in quality and detail. Some may simply refer the reader to other, more thorough documentation, while others give a complete list of all options and commands that a utility supports. In either case, the manual page is a good place to start.

The GNU software suite and some other free software uses an online documentation system called `info`. You can browse full documentation online using a special program, `info`, or via the `info` command of the `emacs` editor. The benefit of the `info` system is that you can navigate the documentation using links and cross-references to jump directly to relevant sections. For the documentation author, the `info` system has the benefit that its files can be automatically generated from the same source as the printed, typeset documentation.

Try It Out - Manual Pages and `info`

1. Let's look for documentation of the GNU C compiler. First, the manual page.

```
$ man gcc

GCC(1)                      GNU Tools                      GCC(1)

NAME
       gcc, g++ - GNU project C and C++ Compiler (egcs-1.1.2)

SYNOPSIS
       gcc [ option | filename ]...
       g++ [ option | filename ]...

WARNING
       The  information  in  this man page is an extract from the
       full documentation of the GNU C compiler, and  is  limited
       to the meaning of the options.

       This  man  page  is not kept up to date except when volun-
       teers want to maintain it.   If  you  find  a  discrepancy
       between  the  man  page and the software, please check the
       Info file, which is the authoritative documentation.

       If we find that the things in this man page that  are  out
       of date cause significant confusion or complaints, we will
       stop distributing the man page.  The alternative, updating
       the  man  page when we update the Info file, is impossible
       because the rest of the work of maintaining GNU CC  leaves
       us no time for that.  The GNU project regards man pages as
       obsolete and should not let them take time away from other
       things.
```

```
        For  complete and current documentation, refer to the Info
        file 'gcc' or the manual Using and  Porting  GNU  CC  (for
        version  2.0).  Both are made from the Texinfo source file
        gcc.texinfo.
...
```

If we wish, we can read about the options that the compiler supports for each of the target processors that can be used. The manual page in this case is quite long, but forms only a small part of the total documentation for GNU C (and C++).

When reading manual pages you can use the spacebar to read the next page, *Return* to read the next line and *q* to quit altogether.

2. To get more information on GNU C, we can try `info`.

```
$ info gcc

File: gcc.info,  Node: Top,  Next: Copying,  Up: (DIR)

Introduction
************

   This manual documents how to run, install and port the GNU compiler,
as well as its new features and incompatibilities, and how to report
bugs.  It corresponds to EGCS version 1.1.2.

* Menu:

* G++ and GCC::       You can compile C or C++ programs.
* Invoking GCC::      Command options supported by 'gcc'.
* Installation::      How to configure, compile and install GNU CC.
* C Extensions::      GNU extensions to the C language family.
* C++ Extensions::    GNU extensions to the C++ language.
* Trouble::           If you have trouble installing GNU CC.
* Bugs::              How, why and where to report bugs.
* Service::           How to find suppliers of support for GNU CC.
* VMS::               Using GNU CC on VMS.

* Portability::       Goals of GNU CC's portability features.
* Interface::         Function-call interface of GNU CC output.
* Passes::            Order of passes, what they do, and what each file is for.
* RTL::               The intermediate representation that most passes work on.
* Machine Desc::      How to write machine description instruction patterns.
* Target Macros::     How to write the machine description C macros.
* Config::            Writing the 'xm-MACHINE.h' file.
--zz-Info: (gcc.info.gz)Top, 36 lines --Top-- Subfile: gcc.info-1.gz-----------
Welcome to Info version 3.12f.  Type "C-h" for help, "m" for menu item.
```

We're presented with a long menu of options that we can select to move around a complete text version of the documentation. Menu items and a hierarchy of pages allow us to navigate a very large document. On paper, the GNU C documentation runs to many hundreds of pages.

The `info` system also contains its own help page in `info` form pages, of course. If you type *Ctrl-H*, you'll be presented with some help which includes a tutorial on using `info`. The `info` program is available with many Linux distributions and can be installed on other UNIX systems.

Development System Roadmap

For a UNIX developer, it can be important to know a little about where tools and development resources are located. Let's take a brief look at some important directories and files. We'll concentrate on Linux here, but similar principles apply equally to other UNIX-like systems.

Programs

Programs are usually kept in directories reserved for the purpose. Programs supplied by the system for general use, including program development, are found in `/usr/bin`. Programs added by system administrators for a specific host computer or local network are found in `/usr/local/bin`.

Administrators favor `/usr/local`, as it keeps vendor supplied files and later additions separate from the programs supplied by the system. Keeping `/usr` organized in this way may help when the time comes to upgrade the operating system, since only `/usr/local` need be preserved. We recommend that you compile your programs to run and access required files from the `/usr/local` hierarchy.

Additional features and programming systems may have their own directory structures and program directories. Chief among these is the X Window system, which is commonly installed in a directory called `/usr/X11`. Alternative locations include `/usr/X11R6` for Revision 6, also used by the XFree86 variant for Intel processors distributed by the XFree consortium and used by many Linux distributions and `/usr/openwin` for the Sun Open Windows system provided with Solaris.

The GNU compiler system's driver program, `gcc` (which we used in our programming example earlier on), is typically located in `/usr/bin` or `/usr/local/bin`, but it will run various compiler support programs from another location. This location is specified when you compile the compiler itself and varies with the host computer type. For Linux systems, this location might be a version specific subdirectory of `/usr/lib/gcc-lib/`. The separate passes of the GNU C/C++ compiler, and GNU specific header files, are stored here.

Header Files

For programming in C and other languages, we need header files to provide definitions of constants and declarations for system and library function calls. For C, these are almost always located in `/usr/include` and subdirectories thereof. You can normally find header files that depend on the particular form of UNIX or Linux that you are running in `/usr/include/sys` and `/usr/include/linux`.

Other programming systems will also have include files that are stored in directories which get searched automatically by the appropriate compiler. Examples include `/usr/include/X11` for the X Window system and `/usr/include/g++-2` for GNU C++.

You can use include files in subdirectories or non-standard places by specifying the -I flag to the C compiler. For example,

```
$ gcc -I/usr/openwin/include fred.c
```

will direct the compiler to look in the directory /usr/openwin/include, as well as the standard places, for header files included in the fred.c program. Refer to the manual page for your C compiler for more details.

It's often convenient to use the grep command to search header files for particular definitions and function prototypes. Suppose you need to know the name of the defines that are used for returning the exit status from a program. Simply change to the /usr/include directory and grep for a probable part of the name. Like this:

```
$ grep EXIT_ *.h
...
stdlib.h:#define        EXIT_FAILURE    1       /* Failing exit status.  */
stdlib.h:#define        EXIT_SUCCESS    0       /* Successful exit status.  */
...
$
```

Here grep searches all the files in the directory with a name ending in .h for the string EXIT_. In this example, it has found (among others) the definition we need in the file stdlib.h.

Library Files

Libraries are collections of precompiled functions that have been written to be reusable. Typically, they consist of sets of related functions to perform a common task. Examples include libraries of screen handling functions (the curses library) and database access routines (the dbm library). We'll meet these libraries in later chapters.

Standard system libraries are usually stored in /lib and /usr/lib. The C compiler (or more exactly, the linker) needs to be told which libraries to search, as by default, it searches only the standard C library. This is a remnant of the days when computers were slow and CPU cycles expensive. It's not enough to put a library in the standard directory and hope that the compiler will find it; libraries need to follow a very specific naming convention and need to be mentioned on the command line.

A library name always starts with lib. Then follows the part indicating what library this is (like c for the C library, or m for the mathematical library). The last part of the name starts with a dot ., and specifies the type of the library:

.a for traditional, static libraries

.so and .sa for shared libraries (See below.)

Usually, the libraries exist in both static and shared formats, as a quick `ls /usr/lib` will show. You can instruct the compiler to search a library either by giving it the full path name or by using the `-l` flag. For example,

```
$ cc -o fred fred.c /usr/lib/libm.a
```

tells the compiler to compile file `fred.c`, call the resulting program file `fred` and search the mathematical library in addition to the standard C library to resolve references to functions. A similar result is achieved through:

```
$ cc -o fred fred.c -lm
```

The `-lm` (no space between the `l` and the `m`) is shorthand (Shorthand is much valued in UNIX circles.) for the library called `libm.a` in one of the standard library directories (in this case `/usr/lib`). An additional advantage of the `-lm` notation is that the compiler will automatically choose the shared library when it exists.

Although libraries usually are found in standard places in the same way as header files, we can add to the search directories by using the `-L` (uppercase letter) flag to the compiler. For example,

```
$ cc -o x11fred -L/usr/openwin/lib x11fred.c -lX11
```

will compile and link a program called `x11fred` using the version of the library `libX11` found in the directory `/usr/openwin/lib`.

Static Libraries

The simplest form of library is just a collection of object files kept together in a ready-to-use form. When a program needs to use a function stored in the library, it includes a header file that declares the function. The compiler and linker take care of combining the program code and the library into a single executable program. You must use the `-l` option to indicate which libraries, other than the standard C runtime library, are required.

Static libraries, also known as **archives**, conventionally have names that end with `.a`. Examples are `/usr/lib/libc.a` and `/usr/X11/lib/libX11.a` for the standard C library and the X11 library.

We can create and maintain our own static libraries very easily by using the `ar` (for archive) program and compiling functions separately with `cc -c`. You should try to keep functions in separate source files as much as possible. If functions need access to common data, you can place them in the same source file and use 'static' variables declared in that file.

Try It Out - Static Libraries

1. Let's create our own, small library containing two functions and then use one of them in an example program. The functions are called `fred` and `bill` and just print greetings. We'll create separate source files (called imaginatively `fred.c` and `bill.c`) for each of them.

```
#include <stdio.h>

void fred(int arg)
{
    printf("fred: you passed %d\n", arg);
}
```

```
#include <stdio.h>

void bill(char *arg)
{
    printf("bill: you passed %s\n", arg);
}
```

We can compile these functions individually to produce object files ready for inclusion into a library. We do this by invoking the C compiler with the `-c` option that prevents the compiler from trying to create a complete program. This would fail because we haven't defined a function called `main`.

```
$ cc -c bill.c fred.c
$ ls *.o
bill.o   fred.o
```

2. Now let's write a program that calls the function `bill`. First, it's a good idea to create a header file for our library. This will declare the functions in our library and should be included by all programs that wish to use our library.

```
/*
    This is lib.h. It declares the functions fred and bill for users
*/

void bill(char *);
void fred(int);
```

In fact it's a good idea to include the header file in the files `fred.c` and `bill.c` too. This will help the compiler pick up any errors.

3. The calling program (`program.c`) can be very simple. It includes the library header file and calls one of the functions from the library.

```
#include "lib.h"

int main()
{
    bill("Hello World");
    exit(0);
}
```

4. We can now compile the program and test it. For now, we'll specify the object files explicitly to the compiler, asking it to compile our file and link it with the previously compiled object module `bill.o`.

```
$ cc -c program.c
$ cc -o program program.o bill.o
$ ./program
bill: you passed Hello World
$
```

5. Now let's create and use a library. We use the `ar` program to create the archive and add our object files to it. The program is called `ar` because it creates archives or collections of individual files placed together in one large file. Note that we can also use `ar` to create archives of files of any type. (Like many UNIX utilities, it is a very generic tool.)

```
$ ar crv libfoo.a bill.o fred.o
a - bill.o
a - fred.o
```

The library is created and the two object files added. To use the library successfully, some systems, notably those derived from Berkeley UNIX, require that a table of contents be created for the library. We do this with the `ranlib` command. This step isn't necessary (but harmless) when, as in Linux, we're using the GNU software development tools.

```
$ ranlib libfoo.a
```

Our library is now ready to use. We can add to the list of files to be used by the compiler to create our program like this:

```
$ cc -o program program.o libfoo.a
$ ./program
bill: you passed Hello World
$
```

We can also use the `-l` option to access our library, but as it is not in any of the standard places, we have to tell the compiler where to find it by using the `-L` option like this:

```
$ cc -o program program.o -L. -lfoo
```

The `-L.` option tells the compiler to look in the current directory for libraries. The `-lfoo` option tells the compiler to use a library called `libfoo.a` (or a shared library, `libfoo.so` if one is present).

To see which functions are included in an object file, library or executable program, we can use the `nm` command. If we take a look at `program` and `lib.a`, we see that the library contains both `fred` and `bill`, but that `program` contains only `bill`. When the program is created, it only includes functions from the library that it actually needs. Including the header file, which contains declarations for all of the functions in the library, doesn't cause all of the library to be included in the final program.

If you're familiar with MS-DOS or Microsoft Windows software development, there are a number of direct analogies here.

Item	UNIX	DOS
object module	`func.o`	`FUNC.OBJ`
static library	`lib.a`	`LIB.LIB`
program	`program`	`PROGRAM.EXE`

Shared Libraries

One disadvantage of static libraries is that when we run many programs at the same time and they all use functions from the same library, we may end up with many copies of the same functions in memory and indeed many copies in the program files themselves. This can consume a large amount of valuable memory and disk space.

Many UNIX systems support shared libraries that can overcome both of these disadvantages. A complete discussion of shared libraries and their implementation on different systems is beyond the scope of this book, so we'll restrict ourselves to the visible implementation under Linux.

Shared libraries are stored in the same places as static libraries, but have a different extension. On a typical Linux system, the shared version of the standard C library is `/lib/libc.so.N`, where `N` represents a major version number, currently 6.

At the time of writing many Linux distributions were going through a process of updating the versions of both the C/C++ compiler used and the C library. The example outputs shown below are taken from a Redhat 6.0 distribution using GNU libc 2.1. Your output may differ slightly if you are not using this distribution.

When a program uses a shared library, it is linked in such a way that it doesn't contain function code itself, but references to shared code that will be made available at run time. When the resulting program is loaded into memory to be executed, the function references are resolved and calls are made to the shared library, which will be loaded into memory if needed.

In this way, the system can arrange for a single copy of a shared library to be used by many applications at once and stored just once on the disk. An additional benefit is that the shared library can be updated independently of the programs that rely on it. Symbolic links from the file `/lib/libc.so.6` to the actual library revision (`/lib/libc-2.1.1.so` at the time of writing) are used.

For Linux systems, the program (the dynamic loader) that takes care of loading shared libraries and resolving client program function references is `ld.so` or `ld-linux.so.2`. The additional locations searched for shared libraries are configured in the file `/etc/ld.so.conf`, which needs to be processed by `ldconfig` if changed, for example when X11 shared libraries are added.

You can see which shared libraries are required by a program by running the utility `ldd`:

```
$ ldd program
        libc.so.6 => /lib/libc.so.6 (0x4001a000)
        /lib/ld-linux.so.2 => /lib/ld-linux.so.2 (0x40000000)
```

In this case, we see that the standard C library (`libc`) is shared (`.so`). Our program requires major Version 6, which is provided in this case by GNU libc version 2.1.1. Other UNIX systems will make similar arrangements for access to shared libraries. Refer to your system documentation for details.

In many ways, shared libraries are similar to dynamic-link libraries used under Microsoft Windows. The `.so` libraries correspond to `.DLL` files and are required at run time, while the `.sa` libraries are similar to `.LIB` files that get included in the program executable.

UNIX Philosophy

We hope to convey a flavor of UNIX programming in the following chapters. Although programming in C is in many ways the same whatever the platform, it's true to say that UNIX developers have a special view of program and system development.

The UNIX operating system encourages a certain programming style. Here are a few characteristics shared by typical UNIX programs and systems.

Simplicity

Many of the most useful UNIX utilities are very simple and, as a result, small and easy to understand. KISS (Keep It Small and Simple) is a good technique to learn. Larger, more complex systems are guaranteed to contain larger, more complex bugs and debugging is a chore that we'd all like to avoid!

Focus

It's often better to make a program perform one task well. A program with 'feature bloat' can be difficult to use and difficult to maintain. Programs with a single purpose are easier to improve as better algorithms or interfaces are developed. In UNIX, small utilities are often combined to perform more demanding tasks as and when the need arises, rather than trying to anticipate a user's needs in one large program.

Reusable Components

Make the core of your application available as a library. Well-documented libraries with simple but flexible programming interfaces can help others to develop variations or apply the techniques to new application areas. Examples include the `dbm` database library, a suite of reusable functions rather than a single database management program.

Filters

Very many UNIX applications can be used as filters. That is, they transform their input and produce an output. As we'll see, UNIX provides facilities that allow quite complex applications to be developed from other UNIX programs by combining them in new and novel ways. Of course, this kind of re-use is enabled by the development methods that we've just mentioned.

Open File Formats

The more successful and popular UNIX programs use configuration files and data files that are plain ASCII text. If this is an option for your program development, it's a good choice. It enables users to use standard tools to change and search for configuration items and to develop new tools for performing new functions on the data files. A good example of this is the `ctags` source code cross-reference system, which records symbol location information as regular expressions suitable for use by searching programs.

Flexibility

You can't anticipate exactly how ingeniously users will use your program. Try to be as flexible as possible in your programming. Try to avoid arbitrary limits on field sizes or number of records. If you can, write the program so that it's network-aware and able to run across a network as well as on a local machine. Never assume that you know everything that the user might want to do.

Summary

In this introductory chapter, we've taken note of the things in common between Linux and proprietary UNIX systems and the wide variety of programming systems available to us as UNIX developers.

We've written a simple program and library to demonstrate the basic C tools, comparing them with their MS-DOS equivalents. Finally, we've looked at UNIX programming.

2

Shell Programming

Having just started this book on programming UNIX in C, we almost immediately take a detour into shell programming. Why?

Well, the shell leads a double life. While it has similarities to the DOS command processor `Command.com`, it's actually much more powerful, really a programming language in its own right. Not only can you execute commands and call UNIX utilities, you can also write them. It's an interpreted language, which generally makes debugging easier, because you can execute single lines, plus there's no recompile time. However, this can make the shell unsuitable for time-critical or processor-intensive tasks.

Why use it to program? Well, you can program the shell quickly and simply, and a shell is always available even on the most basic UNIX installation. So, for simple prototyping, you can find out if your idea works. It's also ideal for any small utilities that perform some relatively simple task, where efficiency is less important than easy configuration, maintenance and portability. You can use the shell to organize process control, so commands run in a predetermined sequence dependent on the successful completion of each stage.

There are probably loads of examples on your UNIX account already, like package installers, `autoconf` *from the Free Software Foundation (FSF),* `.xinitrc` *and* `startx` *and the scripts in* `/etc/rc.d` *to configure the system on boot-up.*

Here we come to a bit of UNIX philosophy. UNIX is built on and depends upon a high level of code reuse. You build a small and simple utility, and people use it as one link in a string of others to form a command. A simple example is:

```
$ ls -al | more
```

This uses the `ls` and `more` utilities and pipes the output of the file listing to a screen-at-a-time display. Each utility is one more building block. You can often use many small scripts together to create large and complex suites of programs.

For example, if you want to print a reference copy of the `bash` man pages, use: `man bash | col -b | lpr`.

Furthermore, because of UNIX's file handling, the users of these utilities usually don't need to know what language the utilities are written in. If the utility needs to run faster, it's quite usual to prototype UNIX utilities in the shell and re-implement them later in C or C++ when they have proven their worth. Conversely, if they work well enough, leave well alone!

Other interpreted languages that people like to use as an alternative to C or C++ include Perl, Tcl/Tk and Python.

Whether you ever re-implement the script depends on whether it needs optimizing, whether it needs to be portable, whether it should be easy to change and whether (as usually happens) it outgrows its original purpose.

So, whether you're faced with a nightmare of a shell script in your system administration, whether you want to prototype your latest big (but beautifully simple) idea or just want to speed up some repetitive task, this chapter is for you.

Throughout the chapter, we'll be learning the syntax, structures and commands available to you when you're programming the shell, usually making use of interactive (screen-based) examples. These should serve as a useful synopsis of most of the shell's features and their effect. At the end of the chapter, we program a real-life script which is reprogrammed and extended in C throughout the book.

In this chapter, we'll cover:

- What a shell is.
- Basic considerations.
- The subtleties of syntax: variables, conditions and program control.
- Lists.
- Functions.
- Commands and command execution.
- Here documents.
- Debugging.

What is a Shell?

Let's review the shell's function and the different shells available for UNIX.

A shell is a program that acts as the interface between you and the UNIX system, allowing you to enter commands for the operating system to execute. In that respect, it resembles DOS, but it hides the details of the kernel's operation from the user. So, file redirection just uses < and >, a pipe is represented by `|`, output from a subprocess by `$(...)`, and the implementation details are handled for you. In that respect, it's a high-level programming language for UNIX itself.

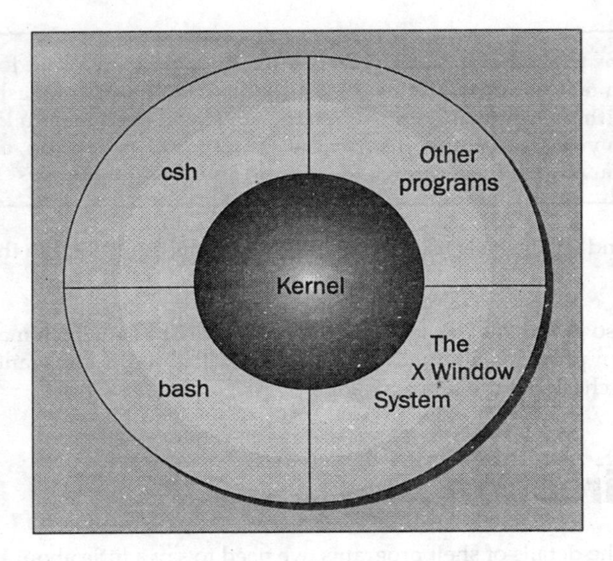

Because UNIX is so modular, you can slot in one of the many different shells in use. Most of them are derived from the original Bourne shell.

Shell Name	A Bit of History
sh (Bourne)	The original shell.
csh, tcsh and zsh	The C shell, created by Bill Joy of Berkeley UNIX fame. Probably the second most popular shell after bash.
ksh, pdksh	The Korn shell and its public domain cousin. Written by David Korn.
bash	The Linux staple, from the GNU project. bash, or Bourne Again Shell, has the advantage that the source code is freely available and even if it's not currently running on your UNIX system, it has probably been ported to it.
rc	More C than csh. Also from the GNU project.

Except for the C shell and a small number of derivatives, all of these are very similar and are closely aligned with the shell specified in the X/Open 4.2 and POSIX 1003.2 specifications. POSIX 1003.2 lays down the minimum specification for a shell, but the extended specification in X/Open provides a more friendly and powerful shell. X/Open is usually the more demanding specification, but also yields a friendlier system. We have only listed here some of the better known shell variants, there are many others.

In this chapter, we'll mostly use those features common to POSIX-compatible shells and we'll assume that the shell has been installed as `/bin/sh` as the default.

> **In many Linux systems the command `/bin/sh` is often no more than a link to the actual shell in use. On many Linux systems it is a link to `/bin/bash`, the bash shell. Check your system with the command `ls -l /bin/sh`. If you ever need to know which version of bash you are running, just invoke `/bin/bash -version`, or `echo $BASH_VERSION` if you are at a bash command prompt, and it will tell you.**

We'll meet the `tclsh` and `wish` shells used by `Tcl` and `Tk` respectively later in the book (Chapters 14 and 15).

The GNU project has also put a set of basic shell utilities, `Shellutils`, which may offer better performance than system-provided alternatives on some installations. If you want to archive text files using only shell scripts, check out the `shar` package.

Pipes and Redirection

Before we get down to the details of shell programs, we need to say a little about how inputs and outputs of UNIX programs (not just shell programs) can be redirected.

Redirecting Output

You may already be familiar with some redirection, such as,

```
$ ls -l > lsoutput.txt
```

which saves the output of the `ls` command into a file called `lsoutput.txt`.

However, there is much more to redirection than this simple example. We'll learn more about the standard file descriptors in a Chapter 3, but for now all we need to know is that file descriptor 0 is the standard input to a program, file descriptor 1 is the standard output and file descriptor 2 is the standard error output. You can redirect each of these independently. In fact, you can also redirect other file descriptors, but it's unusual to want to redirect any other than the standard ones, 0, 1 and 2.

In the above example we redirect the standard output, using the > operator, into a file. By default, if the file already exists, it will be overwritten. If you want to change the default behavior, you can use the command `set -C`, which sets the `noclobber` option to prevent a file being overwritten using redirection. We'll see more options to the `set` command later in the chapter.

To append to the file, we would use the >> operator.

```
$ ps >> lsoutput.txt
```

will append the output of the `ps` command to the file.

To redirect the standard error output, we preface the > operator with the number of the file descriptor we wish to redirect. Since the standard error is on file descriptor 2, we use the 2> operator. This is often useful to discard error information, to prevent it appearing on the screen.

Suppose we want to use the `kill` command to kill a process from a script. There is always a slight risk that the process will die before the `kill` command is executed. If this happens, `kill` will write an error message to the standard error output, which, by default, will appear on the screen. By redirecting both the standard output and error, we can prevent the `kill` command writing any text to the screen.

The command,

```
$ kill -HUP 1234 > killout.txt 2>killerr.txt
```

will put the output and error information into separate files.

If we prefer to capture both sets of output into a single file, we use the >& operator to combine the two outputs. So,

```
$ kill -1 1234 > killouterr.txt 2>&1
```

will put both the output and error outputs into the same file. Notice the order of the operators. This reads as 'redirect standard output to the file `killouterr.txt`, then direct standard error to the same place as the standard output'. If you get the order wrong, the redirect won't work as you expect.

Since we can discover the result of the `kill` command using the return code (of which more later), we probably don't want to save either standard output or standard error. We can use the UNIX universal 'bit bucket' of `/dev/null` to efficiently discard the entire output, like this:

```
$ kill -1 1234 > /dev/null 2>&1
```

Redirecting Input

Rather like redirecting output, we can also redirect input. As a trivial example:

```
$ more < killout.txt
```

Obviously, this is a rather silly example under UNIX, since the UNIX `more` command is quite happy to accept filenames as parameters, unlike the DOS equivalent.

Pipes

We can connect processes together using the pipe | operator. In UNIX, unlike DOS, processes connected by pipes can run simultaneously and are automatically rescheduled as data flows between them.

As a simple example, we could use the `sort` command to sort the output from `ps`.

If we don't use pipes, we must use several steps, like this:

```
$ ps > psout.txt
$ sort psout.txt > pssort.out
```

Much more elegant is to connect the processes with a pipe, like this:

```
$ ps | sort > pssort.out
```

Since we probably want to see the output paginated on the screen, we could connect a third process, `more`, all on the same command line:

```
$ ps | sort | more
```

There's practically no limit to the number of connected processes. Suppose we want to see all the different process names that are running, excluding shells. We could use:

```
$ ps -xo comm | sort | uniq | grep -v sh | more
```

This takes the output of `ps`, sorts it into alphabetical order, extracts processes using `uniq`, then uses `grep -v sh` to remove the process named `sh` and finally displays it paginated on the screen.

Now that we've seen some basic shell operations, it's time to move on to scripts.

The Shell as a Programming Language

There are two ways of writing shell programs. You can type in a sequence of commands and allow the shell to execute them interactively, or you can store those commands in a file which you can then invoke as a program.

Interactive Programs

Just typing in the shell script on the command line is a quick and easy way of trying out small code fragments.

> **To change to a different shell if bash isn't the default on your system, for example, just type in the shell's name (e.g. `/bin/bash`) to run the new shell and change the command prompt. If bash isn't installed on your system, you can download it for free from the GNU web site at `http://www.gnu.org`. The sources are highly portable, and the chances are it will compile on your UNIX straight 'out of the box'.**

Suppose we have a large number of C files and we wish to compile only the files that contain the string `POSIX`. Rather than search using the `grep` command for the string in the files, then compile the files containing the string, we could perform the whole operation in an interactive script like this:

```
$ for file in *
> do
> if grep -l POSIX $file
> then
> more $file
> fi
> done
posix
This is a file with POSIX in it - treat it well
$
```

Note how the normal `$` shell prompt changes to a `>` when you type in shell commands. You can type away, the shell will decide when you're finished and the script will execute immediately.

In this example, the `grep` command prints out the files it finds containing `POSIX` and then `more` prints the contents of the file to the screen. Finally, the shell prompt returns. Note also that we've called the shell variable that deals with each of the files `file` to self-document the script.

The shell also performs wildcard expansion (also called globbing), though you knew that already, right? What you may not know is that you can request single character wildcards using `?`, while `[set]` allows any of a number of single characters to be checked. `[^set]` negates the set - anything but the set you've specified. Brace expansion using `{}` (available on some shells, including `bash`) allows you to group arbitrary strings together in a set which the shell will expand. For example,

```
$ ls my_{finger,toe}s
```

will list those two files which share some common identifier. We've used the shell to check every file in the current directory.

Actually, experienced UNIX users would probably perform this simple operation in a much more efficient way, perhaps with a command such as,

```
$ more `grep -l POSIX *`
```

or the synonymous construction:

```
$ more $(grep -l POSIX *)
```

while

```
$ grep -l POSIX * | more
```

will output the name of the file whose contents matched the pattern `POSIX`. In this script, we see the shell making use of other commands, such as `grep` and `more`, to do the hard work. The shell is simply allowing us to 'glue' several existing commands together in new and powerful ways.

Going through this long rigmarole every time we want to execute a sequence of commands is a bore. We need to store the commands in a file, conventionally referred to as a **shell script**, so we can execute them whenever we like.

Creating a Script

First, using any text editor, we must create a file containing the commands. Create a file called first.sh that looks like this:

```
#!/bin/sh

# first.sh
# This file looks through all the files in the current
# directory for the string POSIX, and then displays those
# files to the standard output.

for file in *
do
  if grep -q POSIX $file
  then
    more $file
  fi
done

exit 0
```

Comments start with a # and continue to the end of a line. Conventionally, though, # is usually kept in the first column. Having made such a sweeping statement, we next note that the first line, #!/bin/sh, is a special form of comment, the #! characters tell the system that the one argument that follows on the line is the program to be used to execute this file. In this case /bin/sh is the default shell program.

Note the absolute path specified in the comment. Since some UNIX implementations have a limit of 32 characters on the interpreter path length, it's wise to keep at least a symbolic link to your favorite shell in /bin. If you try and invoke a command with a very long name or in a deeply nested directory, it may not function correctly.

Because the script is essentially treated as standard input to the shell (something prepared earlier), it can contain any UNIX commands referenced by your PATH environment variable.

The exit command ensures that the script returns a sensible exit code (more on this later in the chapter). This is rarely checked when programs are run interactively, but if you want to invoke this script from another script and check whether it succeeded, returning an appropriate exit code is very important. Even if you never intend to allow your script to be invoked from another, you should still exit with a reasonable code. Such an attitude, though, flies in the face of a very important part of the UNIX philosophy: reuse. Go on, have faith in the usefulness of your script.

A zero denotes success in shell programming. Since the script as it stands can't detect any failures, we always return success. We'll come back to the reasons for using a zero exit code for success later in the chapter, when we look at the exit command in more detail.

Although we have used the extension '.sh' on this example, Linux, and UNIX in general rarely makes use of the file name extension to determine the type of a file. We could have omitted the .sh, or added a different extension if we wished, the shell doesn't care. Most pre-installed scripts will not have any filename extension, and the best way to check if they are a script or not is to use the file command, i.e. file first.sh or file /bin/bash.

Making a Script Executable

Now we have our script file, we can run it in two ways. The simpler way is to invoke the shell with the name of the script file as a parameter, thus:

```
$ /bin/sh first.sh
```

This should work, but it would be much better if we could simply invoke the script by typing its name, giving it the respectability of other UNIX commands.

We do this by changing the file mode to make the file executable for all users using the `chmod` command:

```
$ chmod +x first.sh
```

> **Of course, this isn't the only way to use `chmod` to make a file executable. Use `man chmod` to find out more about octal arguments and other options.**

We can then execute it using the command:

```
$ first.sh
```

This may not work and you may get an error saying the command wasn't found. This is probably because the shell environment variable `PATH` isn't set to look in the current directory. To fix this, either type `PATH=$PATH:. on the command line`, or edit your `.bash_profile` file to add this command to the end of the file, then log out and back in again Alternatively, type `./first.sh` in your scripts directory to give the shell the relative path to the file.

> **You shouldn't change the `PATH` variable like this for the `root` user. It's a security loophole, because the system administrator logged in as `root` can be tricked into invoking a fake version of a standard command. One of the authors admits to doing this once, just to prove a point to the system administrator about security of course! It's a slight risk on ordinary accounts to include the current directory in the path, so if you are particularly concerned just get into the habit of pre-pending ./ to all commands that are in the local directory.**

Once we're confident that our script is executing properly, we can move it to a more appropriate location than the current directory. If the command is just for yourself, you could create a `bin` directory in your home directory and add that to your path. If you want the script to be executable by others, you could use `/usr/local/bin` or another system directory as a convenient location for adding new programs. If you don't have root permissions on your UNIX system, you could ask the system administrator to copy your file for you, although you may have to convince them first. To prevent other users changing the script, perhaps accidentally, you should remove write access from it. The sequence of commands for the administrator to set ownership and permissions would be something like this:

```
# cp first.sh /usr/local/bin
# chown root /usr/local/bin/first.sh
# chgrp root /usr/local/bin/first.sh
# chmod 755 /usr/local/bin/first.sh
```

Notice that, rather than altering a specific part of the permission flags, we use the absolute form of the chmod here, since we know exactly what permissions we require.

If you prefer, you can use the rather longer, but perhaps more obvious form of the chmod command, which would be:

```
# chmod u=rwx,go=rx /usr/local/bin/first.sh
```

Check the manual entry for chmod for more details.

Remember that in UNIX you can delete a file if you have write permission on the directory that contains it. To be safe you should ensure that only root can write to directories containing files that you want to keep safe.

Shell Syntax

Having seen an example of a simple shell program, it's now time to look in more depth at the programming power of the shell. The shell is quite an easy programming language to learn, not least because it's easy to test small program fragments interactively before combining them into bigger scripts. We can use the modern UNIX shell to write quite large, structured programs.

In the next few sections, we'll cover:

- Variables: strings, numbers, environment and parameter.
- Conditions: shell Booleans.
- Program Control: if, elif, for, while, until, case.
- Lists.
- Functions.
- Commands built into the shell.
- Getting the result of a command.
- Here documents.

Variables

We don't usually declare variables in the shell before we use them. Instead, we create them when we first use them, for example, when we assign an initial value to them. By default, all variables are considered and stored as strings, even when they are assigned numeric values. The shell and some utilities will convert 'numeric' strings to their values in order to operate on them as required. UNIX is a case-sensitive system and the shell considers the variable foo to be different from Foo, and both are different from FOO.

Within the shell, we can get at the contents of a variable by preceding its name with a $ character and outputting its contents with the echo command. Whenever we use them, we need to give variables a preceding $, except when an assignment is being made to the variable. On the command line, we can set various values of the variable salutation:

```
$ salutation=Hello
$ echo $salutation
Hello
$ salutation="Yes Dear"
$ echo $salutation
Yes Dear
$ salutation=7+5
$ echo $salutation
7+5
```

Note how a string must be delimited by inverted commas if it contains spaces. Also note that there must be no spaces on either side of the equals sign.

We can assign user input to a variable by using the read command. This takes one parameter, the name of the variable to be read into, then waits for the user to enter some text. The read normally continues when the user presses the *Return* key.

Quoting

Before we move on, we need to be clear about one feature of the shell: the use of quotes.

Normally, parameters are separated by whitespace characters, i.e. a space, a tab, or a newline character. If you want a parameter to contain one or more whitespace characters, you must quote the parameter.

The behavior of variables such as $foo inside quotes depends on the type of quotes you use. If you enclose a $ variable expression in double quotes, it's replaced with its value when the line is executed. If you enclose it in single quotes, no substitution takes place. You can also remove the special meaning of the $ symbol by prefacing it with a \.

Normally, strings are enclosed in double quotes, which protects variables from being separated by whitespace, but allows $ expansion to take place.

Try It Out - Variables

Let's see the effect of quotes on the output of a variable:

```
#!/bin/sh

myvar="Hi there"

echo $myvar
echo "$myvar"
echo '$myvar'
echo \$myvar

echo Enter some text
read myvar

echo '$myvar' now equals $myvar
exit 0
```

This gives the output:

```
Hi there
Hi there
$myvar
$myvar
Enter some text
Hello World
$myvar now equals Hello World
```

How It Works

The variable `myvar` is created and assigned the string `Hi there`. The contents of the variable are displayed with the `echo` command, showing how prefacing the variable with a `$` character expands the contents of the variable. We see how using double quotes doesn't affect the substitution of the variable, while single quotes and the backslash do. We also use the `read` command to get a string from the user.

Environment Variables

When a shell script starts, some variables are initialized from values in the environment. These are normally capitalized to distinguish them from user-defined (shell) variables in scripts, which are conventionally lower case. The variables created will depend on your personal configuration. Many are listed in the manual pages, but the principal ones are:

Environment Variable	Description
`$HOME`	The home directory of the current user.
`$PATH`	A colon-separated list of directories to search for commands.
`$PS1`	A command prompt, usually `$`.
`$PS2`	A secondary prompt, used when prompting for additional input, usually >.
`$IFS`	An input field separator. A list of characters that are used to separate words when the shell is reading input, usually space, tab and new line characters.
`$0`	The name of the shell script
`$#`	The number of parameters passed.
`$$`	The process ID of the shell script, often used inside a script for generating unique temporary filenames, for example `/tmp/tmpfile_$$`

If you want to check out how the program works in a different environment by running `env <command>`, try looking at the `env` manual pages.

Also, we'll see later how to set environment variables in subshells using the `export` command.

Parameter Variables

If your script is invoked with parameters, some additional variables are created. Even if no parameters are passed, the environment variable `$#` listed above does still exist, but has a value of 0.

The parameter variables are:

Parameter Variable	Description
`$1, $2, ...`	The parameters given to the script.
`$*`	A list of all the parameters, in a single variable, separated by the first character in the environment variable `IFS`.
`$@`	A subtle variation on `$*`, that doesn't use the `IFS` environment variable.

As for the difference between the `$*` and `$@` parameters, here's an explanation culled from the X/Open specification.

When the parameter expansion occurs within a double-quoted string, `$*` expands to a single field with the value of each parameter separated by the first character of the `IFS` (internal field separator) variable, or by a space character if `IFS` is unset. If `IFS` is set to a null string, which isn't equivalent to unsetting it, the parameter values will be concatenated. For example:

```
$ IFS=''
$ set foo bar bam
$ echo "$@"
foo bar bam
$ echo "$*"
foobarbam
$ unset IFS
$ echo "$*"
foo bar bam
```

As you can see, within double quotes, `$@` expands the positional parameters as separate fields, regardless of the `IFS` value. In general, if you want access to the parameters, `$@` is the sensible choice.

As well as printing the contents of variables using the `echo` command, we can also read them in using the `read` command.

Try It Out - Parameter and Environment Variables

The following script demonstrates some simple variable manipulation. Once you've typed in the script and saved it as `try_variables`, don't forget to make it executable with `chmod +x try_variables`.

```
#!/bin/sh

salutation="Hello"
echo $salutation
echo "The program $0 is now running"
echo "The second parameter was $2"
echo "The first parameter was $1"
echo "The parameter list was $*"
echo "The user's home directory is $HOME"

echo "Please enter a new greeting"
read salutation

echo $salutation
echo "The script is now complete"
exit 0
```

If we run this script, we get the output:

```
$ ./try_variables foo bar baz
Hello
The program ./try_variables is now running
The second parameter was bar
The first parameter was foo
The parameter list was foo bar baz
The user's home directory is /home/rick
Please enter a new greeting
Sire
Sire
The script is now complete
$
```

How It Works

This script creates the variable `salutation`, displays its contents, then shows how various parameter variables and the environment variable `$HOME` already exist and have appropriate values.

We'll return to parameter substitution in more detail later.

Conditions

Fundamental to all programming languages is the ability to test conditions and perform different actions based on those decisions. Before we talk about that, though, we'll look at the conditional constructs that we can use in shell scripts and then look at the control structures that use them.

A shell script can test the exit code of any command that can be invoked from the command line, including those scripts that you have written yourself. That's why it's important to always include an `exit` command at the end of any scripts that you write.

The test, or [] Command

In practice, most scripts make extensive use of the `[]` or `test` command, the shell's Boolean check. On most systems, these commands are synonymous. Having a command `[]` might seem a little odd, but actually, within the code it does make the syntax of commands look simple, very neat and more like other programming languages.

> **These commands call an external program in some UNIX shells, but they tend to be built in to more modern ones. We'll come back to this when we look at commands in a later section.**
>
> **Since the `test` command is infrequently used outside shell scripts, many UNIX users who have never written shell scripts try to write simple programs and call them `test`. If such a program doesn't work, it's probably conflicting with the shell's `test` command. To find out whether your system has an external command of a given name, try something like `which test`, which will usually yield `/bin/test` or `/usr/bin/test`.**

We'll introduce the `test` command using one of the simplest conditions: checking to see if a file exists. The command for this is `test -f <filename>`, so, within a script, we can write:

```
if test -f fred.c
then
...
fi
```

We can also write it like this:

```
if [ -f fred.c ]
then
...
fi
```

The `test` command's exit code (whether the condition is satisfied) determines whether the conditional code is run.

> **Note that you must put spaces between the `[]` braces and the condition being checked. You can remember this by remembering that `[` is just the same as writing `test`, and would always leave a space after the `test` word.**

If you prefer putting `then` on the same line as the `if`, you must add a semicolon to separate the test from the `then`:

```
if [ -f fred.c ]; then
...
fi
```

The condition types that you can use with the `test` command fall into three types.

String Comparison

String Comparison	Result
`string1 = string2`	True if the strings are equal.
`string1 != string2`	True if the strings are not equal.
`-n string`	True if the string is not null.
`-z string`	True if the string is `null` (an empty string).

Arithmetic Comparison

Arithmetic Comparison	Result
`expression1 -eq expression2`	True if the expressions are equal.
`expression1 -ne expression2`	True if the expressions are not equal
`expression1 -gt expression2`	True if `expression1` is greater than `expression2`.
`expression1 -ge expression2`	True if `expression1` is greater than or equal to `expression2`.
`expression1 -lt expression2`	True if `expression1` is less than `expression2`.
`expression1 -le expression2`	True if `expression1` is less than or equal to `expression2`.
`! expression`	True if the expression is false, and vice versa.

File Conditionals

File Conditional	Result
`-d file`	True if the file is a directory.
`-e file`	True if the file exists.
`-f file`	True if the file is a regular file.
`-g file`	True if `set-group-id` is set on file.
`-r file`	True if the file is readable.
`-s file`	True if the file has non-zero size.
`-u file`	True if `set-user-id` is set on file.
`-w file`	True if the file is writeable.
`-x file`	True if the file is executable.

> **Note that, historically, the `-e` option has not been portable, so `-f` is more usually used**
>
> **You may be wondering what the `set-group-id` and `set-user-id` (also known as `set-gid` and `set-uid`) bits are. The `set-uid` bit gives a program the permissions of its owner, rather than its user, while the `set-gid` bit gives a program the permissions of its group. The bits are set with `chmod`, using the `s` and `g` options.**
>
> **Remember `set-gid` and `set-uid` flags have no effect when set on shell scripts.**

Before the test can be true, all the file conditional tests require that the file also exists. This list is just the commonly used options to the `test` command, so for a complete list refer to the manual entry. If you're using `bash`, where `test` is built in, type `help test` to get more details. We'll use some of these options later in the chapter.

Now we know about conditions, we can look at the control structures that use them.

Control Structures

The shell has a set of control structures, and, once again, they're very similar to other programming languages. For some structures (like the `case` statement), the shell offers more power. Others are just subtle syntax changes.

> **In the following sections, the `statements` are the series of commands to perform when/while/until the `condition` is fulfilled.**

if

The `if` statement is very simple. It tests the result of a command and then conditionally executes a group of statements:

```
if condition
then
  statements
else
  statements
fi
```

Try It Out - Using the `if` Command

A common use is to ask a question, then make a decision based on the answer:

```
#!/bin/sh

echo "Is it morning? Please answer yes or no"
read timeofday

if [ $timeofday = "yes" ]; then
  echo "Good morning"
else
  echo "Good afternoon"
fi

exit 0
```

This would give the following output:

```
Is it morning? Please answer yes or no
yes
Good morning
$
```

This script uses the `[]` command to test the contents of the variable `timeofday`. The result of this is evaluated by the `if` command, which then allows different lines of code to be executed.

> **Notice that we use extra whitespace to indent the statements inside the `if`. This is just a convenience for the human reader, the shell ignores the additional whitespace.**

elif

Unfortunately, there are several problems with this very simple script. It will take any answer except `yes` as meaning `no`. We can prevent this using the `elif` construct, which allows us to add a second condition to be checked when the `else` portion of the `if` is executed.

Try It Out - Doing Further Checks with an `elif`

We can modify our previous script so that we report an error message if the user types in anything other than `yes` or `no`. We do this by replacing the `else` with `elif`, and adding another condition.

```
#!/bin/sh

echo "Is it morning? Please answer yes or no"
read timeofday

if [ $timeofday = "yes" ]
then
  echo "Good morning"
```

```
elif [ $timeofday = "no" ]; then
  echo "Good afternoon"
else
  echo "Sorry, $timeofday not recognized. Enter yes or no"
  exit 1
fi

exit 0
```

How It Works

This is quite similar to the last example, but now uses the `elif` command, which tests the variable again if the first `if` condition was not true. If neither of the tests are successful, an error message is printed and the script exits with the value 1, which the caller can use in a calling program to check if the script was successful.

A Problem with Variables

This fixes the most obvious defect, but a more subtle problem is lurking. Let's try this new script, but just press *Return* rather than answering the question. We get the error message:

```
[: =: unary operator expected
```

What went wrong? The problem is in the first `if` clause. When the variable `timeofday` was tested, it consisted of a blank string, so the `if` clause looks like,

```
if [ = "yes" ]
```

which isn't a valid condition. To avoid this, we must use quotes around the variable,

```
if [ "$timeofday" = "yes" ]
```

so an empty variable gives us the valid test:

```
if [ "" = "yes" ]
```

Our new script is now,

```
#!/bin/sh

echo "Is it morning? Please answer yes or no"
read timeofday

if [ "$timeofday" = "yes" ]
then
  echo "Good morning"
elif [ "$timeofday" = "no" ]; then
  echo "Good afternoon"
else
  echo "Sorry, $timeofday not recognized. Enter yes or no"
  exit 1
fi

exit 0
```

which is safe against just pressing *Return* in answer to the question.

> **If you want the echo command to delete the trailing newline the best choice is to use the `printf` command (see later) rather than the echo command. Some shells allow `echo -e`, but that's not supported on all systems..**

for

We use the `for` construct for looping through a range of values, which can be any set of strings. They could be simply listed in the program or, more commonly, the result of a shell expansion of filenames.

The syntax is simply:

```
for variable in values
do
  statements
done
```

Try It Out - `for` Loop with Fixed Strings

The values are normally strings, so we can write:

```
#!/bin/sh

for foo in bar fud 43
do
  echo $foo
done
exit 0
```

We get the output:

```
bar
fud
43
```

> **What would happen if you changed the first line from `for foo in bar fud 43` to `for foo in "bar fud 43"`? Remember that adding the quotes tells the shell to consider everything between them as a single string. This is one way of getting spaces to be stored in a variable .**

How It Works

This example creates the variable `foo` and assigns it a different value each time around the `for` loop. Since the shell considers all variables to contain strings by default, it's just as valid to use the string `43` as the string `fud`.

Try It Out - `for` Loop with Wildcard Expansion

As we said earlier, it's more common to use the `for` loop with a shell expansion for filenames. By this, we mean using a wildcard for the string value and letting the shell fill out all the values at run time.

We've already seen this in our original example, `first.sh`. The script used shell expansion, the * expanding to the names of all the files in the current directory. Each of these in turn is then used as the variable `$i` inside the `for` loop. Let's quickly look at another wildcard expansion:

Imagine you want to print all the scripts files starting with 'f' in the current directory, and you know that all your scripts end in .sh. You could do it like this:

```
#!/bin/sh

for file in $(ls f*.sh); do
  lpr $file
done
exit 0
```

How It Works

This illustrates the use of the `$(command)` syntax, which we'll review in more detail later (in the section on command execution). Basically, the parameter list for the `for` command is provided by the output of the command enclosed in the `$()` sequence.

The shell expands f*.sh to give the names of all the files matching this pattern.

Remember that all expansion of variables in shell scripts is done when the script is executed, never when it's written. So, syntax errors in variable declarations are only found at execution time, as we saw earlier when we were quoting 'empty' variables.

while

Since all shell values are considered as strings by default, the `for` loop is good for looping through a series of strings, but a little awkward to use for executing commands a fixed number of times.

Look how tedious a script becomes if we want to loop through twenty values using a `for` loop:

```
#!/bin/sh

for foo in 1 2 3 4 5 6 7 8 9 10 11 12 13 14 15 16 17 18 19 20
do
  echo "here we go again"
done
exit 0
```

Even with wildcard expansion, you might be in the situation where you just don't know how many times you'll need to loop. In that case, we can use a `while` loop, which has the syntax:

```
while condition do
  statements
done
```

For example, the ubiquitous password program:

```
#!/bin/sh

echo "Enter password"
read trythis

while [ "$trythis" != "secret" ]; do
  echo "Sorry, try again"
  read trythis
done
exit 0
```

An example of the output from this script is:

```
Enter password
password
Sorry, try again
secret
$
```

Clearly this isn't a very secure way of asking for a password, but it does serve to illustrate the `while` statement! The statements between do and done will be continuously executed until the condition is no longer true. In this case, we're checking that the value of `trythis` isn't equal to `secret`. The loop will continue until `$trythis` equals `secret`. We then continue executing the script at the statement immediately following the done.

Try It Out - Here We Go Again, Again

By combining the `while` construct with arithmetic substitution, we can execute a command a fixed number of times. This is less cumbersome than the `for` loop we saw earlier.

```
#!/bin/sh

foo=1

while [ "$foo" -le 20 ]
do
  echo "Here we go again"
  foo=$(($foo+1))
done

exit 0
```

Note that the `$(( ))` construct was a `ksh` invention, since included in the X/Open specification. Older shells will use `expr` instead, which we'll come across later. However, this is slower and more resource-intensive, where available you should use the `$(( ))` form of the command.

How It Works

This script uses the [] command to test the value of foo against the value 20 and executes the loop body if it's smaller or equal. Inside the while loop the syntax (($foo+1)) is used to perform arithmetic evaluation of the expression inside the braces, so foo is incremented each time around the loop.

Since foo can never be the empty string, we don't need to protect it with double quotes when testing its value. We only do this because it's a good habit to get into.

until

The until statement has the syntax:

```
until condition
do
  statements
done
```

This is very similar to the while loop, but with the condition test reversed. In other words, the loop continues until the condition becomes true, not while the condition is true.

The until statement fits naturally when we want to loop forever until something happens. As an example, we can set up an alarm which works when another user, whose login name we pass on the command line, logs on:

```
#!/bin/sh

until who | grep "$1" > /dev/null
do
   sleep 60
done

# now ring the bell and announce the expected user.

echo -e \\a
echo "**** $1 has just logged in ****"

exit 0
```

case

The case construct is a little more complex than those we have encountered so far. Its syntax is:

```
case variable in
  pattern [ | pattern] ...) statements;;
  pattern [ | pattern] ...) statements;;
  ...
esac
```

While this may look a little intimidating, the case construct allows us to match the contents of a variable against patterns in quite a sophisticated way and then allows execution of different statements depending on which pattern was matched. Notice that each pattern line is terminated with double semicolons (;;). You can put multiple statements between each pattern and the next, so a double semicolon is needed to mark where one statement ends and the next pattern begins.

The ability to match multiple patterns and execute multiple statements makes the `case` construct a good way of dealing with user input. The best way to see how `case` works is with an example. We'll develop it over three Try It Out examples, improving the pattern matching each time.

Try It Out - `case` I: User Input

We can write a new version of our input testing script and, using the `case` construct, make it a little more selective and forgiving of unexpected input.

```
#!/bin/sh

echo "Is it morning? Please answer yes or no"
read timeofday

case "$timeofday" in
    yes)  echo "Good Morning";;
    no )  echo "Good Afternoon";;
    y  )  echo "Good Morning";;
    n  )  echo "Good Afternoon";;
    *  )  echo "Sorry, answer not recognized";;
esac

exit 0
```

How It Works

When the `case` statement is executing, it takes the contents of `timeofday` and compares it to each string in turn. As soon as a string matches the input, the `case` command executes the code following the `)` and finishes.

The `case` command performs normal expansion on the strings that it's using for comparison. You can, therefore, specify part of a string followed by the wildcard, `*`. Using a single `*` will match all possible strings. So, we always put one after the other matching strings to make sure the `case` statement ends with some default action if no other strings are matched. This is possible because the `case` statement compares against each string in turn. It doesn't look for a 'best' match, just the first match. The default condition often turns out to be the 'impossible' condition, so using `*` can help in debugging scripts.

Try It Out - `case` II: Putting Patterns Together

The `case` construct above is clearly more elegant than the multiple `if` statement version, but by putting the patterns together, we can make a much cleaner version:

```
#!/bin/sh

echo "Is it morning? Please answer yes or no"
read timeofday

case "$timeofday" in
    yes | y | Yes | YES ) echo "Good Morning";;
    n* | N* )             echo "Good Afternoon";;
    * )                   echo "Sorry, answer not recognized";;
esac

exit 0
```

How It Works

In this script, we have used multiple strings in each entry of the case so case tests several different strings for each possible statement. This makes the script both shorter and, with practice, easier to read. We also show how *s can be used, although this may match unintended patterns. For example, if the user enters never, this will be matched by n* and Good Afternoon printed, which isn't the intended behavior. Note also that * wildcard expression doesn't work within quotes.

Try It Out - case III: Executing Multiple Statements

Finally to make the script reusable, we need to have a different exit value when the default pattern is used. We also add a set construct to show this in action:

```
#!/bin/sh

echo "Is it morning? Please answer yes or no"
read timeofday

case "$timeofday" in
    yes | y | Yes | YES )
            echo "Good Morning"
            echo "Up bright and early this morning"
            ;;
    [nN]*)
            echo "Good Afternoon"
            ;;
    *)
            echo "Sorry, answer not recognized"
            echo "Please answer yes or no"
            exit 1
            ;;
esac

exit 0
```

How It Works

To show a different way of pattern matching, we change the way in which the 'no' case is matched. We also show how multiple statements can be executed for each pattern in the case statement. Notice that we're careful to put the most explicit matches first and the most general match last. This is important because the case will execute the first match it finds, not the best match. If we put the *) first, it would always be matched, regardless of what was input.

Note that the ;; before esac is optional. Unlike C programming, where leaving out a break is poor programming practice, leaving out the final ;; is no problem if the last case is the default, since no other cases will be considered.

To make the case matching more powerful, we could use something like this:

```
[yY] | [Yy][Ee][Ss] )
```

This restricts the permitted letters, while allowing a variety of answers and gives more control than the * wildcard.

Lists

Sometimes, we want to connect commands together in a series. For instance, we may want several different conditions to be met before we execute a statement like:

```
if [ -f this_file ]; then
    if [ -f that_file ]; then
        if [ -f the_other_file ]; then
            echo "All files present, and correct"
        fi
    fi
fi
```

or you might want at least one of a series of conditions to be true:

```
if [ -f this_file ]; then
   foo="True"
elif [ -f that_file ]; then
   foo="True"
elif [ -f the_other_file ]; then
   foo="True"
else
   foo="False"
fi
if [ "$foo" = "True" ]; then
   echo "One of the files exists"
fi
```

Although these can be implemented using multiple `if` statements, as you can see, the results are awkward. The shell has a special pair of constructs for dealing with lists of commands: the AND list and the OR list. These are often used together, but we'll review their syntax separately.

The AND List

The AND list construct allows us to execute a series of commands, executing the next command only if all the previous commands have succeeded. The syntax is:

```
statement1 && statement2 && statement3 && ...
```

Starting at the left, each statement is executed and, if it returns `true`, the next statement to the right is executed. This continues until a statement returns `false`, when no more statements in the list are executed. The `&&` tests the condition of the preceding command.

Each statement is executed independently, allowing us to mix many different commands in a single list, as the script below shows. The AND list as a whole succeeds if all commands are executed successfully, and it fails otherwise.

Try It Out - AND Lists

In the following script, we `touch file_one` (to check whether it exists and create it if it doesn't) and then remove `file_two`. Then, the AND list tests for the existence of each of the files and echoes some text in between.

```
#!/bin/sh

touch file_one
rm -f file_two

if [ -f file_one ] && echo "hello" && [ -f file_two ] && echo " there"
then
    echo "in if"
else
    echo "in else"
fi

exit 0
```

Try the script and you'll get the following result:

```
hello
in else
```

How It Works

The `touch` and `rm` commands ensure that the files in the current directory are in a known state. The `&&` list then executes the `[ -f file_one ]` statement, which succeeds because we just made sure that the file existed. Since the previous statement succeeded, the `echo` command is executed. This also succeeds (`echo` always returns `true`). The third test, `[ -f file_two ]` is executed. This fails because the file doesn't exist. Since the last command failed, the final `echo` statement isn't executed. The result of the `&&` list is `false`, since one of the commands in the list failed, so the `if` statement executes its `else` condition.

The OR List

The OR list construct allows us to execute a series of commands until one succeeds, then not execute any more. The syntax is:

```
statement1 || statement2 || statement3 || ...
```

Starting at the left, each statement is executed. If it returns `false`, the next statement to the right is executed. This continues until a statement returns `true`, when no more statements are executed.

The `||` list is very similar to the `&&` list, except that the rules for executing the next statement are now that the previous statement must fail.

Try It Out - OR Lists

1. Copy the previous example and change the shaded lines in the following listing:

```
#!/bin/sh

rm -f file_one

if [ -f file_one ] || echo "hello" || echo " there"
then
    echo "in if"
else
    echo "in else"
fi

exit 0
```

This will give you the output:

```
hello
in if
```

How It Works

The first two lines simply set up the files for the rest of the script. The first command, `[ -f file_one ]` fails, since the file doesn't exist. The `echo` statement is then executed. Surprise, surprise, this returns `true` and no more commands in the `||` list are executed. The `if` succeeds, because one of the commands in the `||` list (the `echo`) was `true`.

The result of both of these constructs is the result of the last statement to be executed.

These list type constructs execute in a similar way to those in C when multiple conditions are being tested. Only the minimum number of statements are executed to determine the result. Statements that can't affect the result are not executed. This is commonly referred to as **short circuit evaluation**.

Combining these two constructs is a logician's heaven. Try out:

```
[ -f file_one ] && command for true || command for false
```

This will execute the first command if the test succeeds and the second otherwise. It's always best to experiment with these more unusual lists.

Statement Blocks

If you want to use multiple statements in a place where only one is allowed, such as in an AND or OR list, you can do so by enclosing them in braces `{}` to make a statement block. For example, in the application presented later in this chapter, you'll see the following code:

```
get_confirm && {
    grep -v "$cdcatnum" $tracks_file > $temp_file
    cat $temp_file > $tracks_file
    echo
    add_record_tracks
}
```

Functions

You can define functions in the shell and, if you write shell scripts of any size, you'll want to use them to structure your code.

> **As an alternative, you could break a large script into lots of smaller scripts, each of which performs a small task. This has several drawbacks: executing a second script from within a script is much slower than executing a function. It's more difficult to pass back results and there can be a very large number of small scripts. You should consider the smallest part of your script that sensibly stands alone and use that as your measure of when to break a large script into a collection of smaller ones..**
>
> **If you're appalled at the idea of using the shell for large programs, remember that the FSF `autoconf` program and several UNIX package installation programs are shell scripts. You can always guarantee that a basic shell will be on a UNIX system. In fact, most UNIX systems can't even boot without `/bin/sh`, never mind allowing users to log in, so you can be certain that your script will have a shell available to interpret it on a huge range of UNIX and Linux systems.**

To define a shell function, we simply write its name, followed by empty `()` parentheses and enclose the statements in `{}` braces:

```
function_name () {
  statements
}
```

Try It Out - A Simple Function

Let's start with a really simple function:

```
#!/bin/sh

foo() {
    echo "Function foo is executing"
}

echo "script starting"
foo
echo "script ended"

exit 0
```

Running the script will show:

```
script starting
Function foo is executing
script ending
```

How It Works

This script starts executing at the top, so nothing different there. But when it finds the `foo() {` construct, it knows that a function called `foo` is being defined. It stores the fact that `foo` refers to a function and continues executing after the matching `}`. When the single line `foo` is executed, the shell now knows to execute the previously defined function. When this function completes, execution resumes at the line after the call to `foo`.

You must always define a function before you can invoke it, a little like the Pascal style of function definition before invocation, except there are no forward declarations in the shell. This isn't a problem, since all scripts start executing at the top, so simply putting all the functions before the first call of any function will always cause all functions to be defined before they can be invoked.

When a function is invoked, the positional parameters to the script, `$*`, `$@`, `$#`, `$1`, `$2` and so on are replaced by the parameters to the function. That's how you read the parameters passed to the function. When the function finishes, they are restored to their previous values.

Some older shells may not restore the value of positional parameters after functions execute. It's wise not to rely on this behavior if you want your scripts to be portable.

We can make functions return numeric values using the `return` command. The usual way to make functions return strings is for the function to store the string in a variable, which can then be used after the function finishes. Alternatively you can echo a string and catch the result, like this.

```
foo () { echo JAY;}

...

result="$(foo)"
```

Note that you can declare local variables within shell functions by using the `local` keyword. The variable is then only in scope within the function. Otherwise, the function can access the other shell variables which are essentially global in scope. If a local variable has the same name as a global variable, it overlays that variable but only within the function. For example, we can make the following changes to the above script to see this in action:

```
#!/bin/sh

sample_text="global variable"

foo() {
    local sample_text="local variable"

    echo "Function foo is executing"
    echo $sample_text
}

echo "script starting"
echo $sample_text

foo

echo "script ended"
echo $sample_text

exit 0
```

In the absence of a `return` command specifying a return value, a function returns the exit status of the last command executed.

In the next script, `my_name`, we show how parameters to a function are passed and how functions can return a `true` or `false` result.

Try It Out - Returning a Value

2. After the shell header, we define the function `yes_or_no`:

```
#!/bin/sh

yes_or_no() {
  echo "Is your name $* ?"
  while true
  do
    echo -n "Enter yes or no: "
    read x
    case "$x" in
      y | yes ) return 0;;
      n | no )  return 1;;
      * )       echo "Answer yes or no"
    esac
  done
}
```

3. Then, the main part of the program begins:

```
echo "Original parameters are $*"

if yes_or_no "$1"
then
  echo "Hi $1, nice name"
else
  echo "Never mind"
fi
exit 0
```

Typical output from this script might be:

```
$ ./my_name.sh Rick Neil
Original parameters are Rick Neil
Is your name Rick ?
Enter yes or no: yes
Hi Rick, nice name
$
```

How It Works

As the script executes, the function `yes_or_no` is defined, but not yet executed. In the `if` statement, the script executes the function `yes_or_no`, passing the rest of the line as parameters to the function, after substituting the `$1` with the first parameter to the original script, `Rick`. The function uses these parameters, which are now stored in the positional parameters `$1`, `$2` and so on, and returns a value to the caller. Depending on the return value, the `if` construct executes the appropriate statement.

As we've seen, the shell has a rich set of control structures and conditional statements. We now need to learn some of the commands that are built into the shell and then we'll be ready to tackle a real programming problem with no compiler in sight!

Commands

You can execute two types of command from inside a shell script. There are the 'normal' commands that you could also execute from the command prompt and there are the 'built-in' commands that we mentioned earlier. These 'built-in' commands are implemented internally to the shell and can't be invoked as external programs. Most internal commands are, however, also provided as stand-alone programs - it's part of the POSIX specification. It generally doesn't matter if the command is internal or external, except that internal commands execute more efficiently.

While we're talking about re-implementing commands, it may interest you to see how UNIX can use just a single program for several commands or different files. Look at the `mv`, `cp`, and `ln` commands, with `ls -l`. On many systems, these are actually a single file, having multiple names created using the `ln` (link) command. When the command is invoked, it looks at its first argument, which under UNIX is the name of the command, to discover what action it should perform.

Here we'll cover only the main commands, both internal and external, that we use when we're programming scripts. As a UNIX user, you probably know many other commands that are valid at the command prompt. Always remember that you can use any of these in a script, in addition to the built-in commands we present here.

break

We use this for escaping from an enclosing `for`, `while` or `until` loop before the controlling condition has been met. You can give break and additional numeric parameter, which is the number of loops to break out of. This can make scripts very hard to read and we don't suggest you use it. By default break escapes a single level.

```
#!/bin/sh

rm -rf fred*
echo > fred1
echo > fred2
mkdir fred3
echo > fred4

for file in fred*
do
    if [ -d "$file" ]; then
        break;
    fi
done

echo first directory starting fred was $file

rm -rf fred*
exit 0
```

The : Command

The colon command is a null command. It's occasionally useful to simplify the logic of conditions, being an alias for `true`. Since it's built-in it runs faster than `true`, though it's also much less readable.

You may see it used as a condition for while loops; `while :` implements an infinite loop, in place of the more common `while true`.

The `:` construct is also useful in the conditional setting of variables. For example:

```
: ${var:=value}
```

Without the `:`, the shell would try to evaluate `$var` as a command.

> **In some, mostly older shell scripts, you may see the colon used at the start of a line to introduce a comment, but modern scripts should always use # to start a comment line, since this executes more efficiently.**

```
#!/bin/sh

rm -f fred
if [ -f fred ]; then
    :
else
    echo file fred did not exist
fi

exit 0
```

continue

Rather like the C statement of the same name, this command makes the enclosing `for`, `while` or `until` loop continue at the next iteration, with the loop variable taking the next value in the list.

```
#!/bin/sh

rm -rf fred*
echo > fred1
echo > fred2
mkdir fred3
echo > fred4

for file in fred*
do
    if [ -d "$file" ]; then
            echo "skipping directory $file"
        continue
    fi
    echo file is $file
done

rm -rf fred*
exit 0
```

`continue` can take an optional parameter, the enclosing loop number at which to resume, so you can partially jump out of nested loops. This parameter is rarely used as it often makes scripts much harder to understand. For example:

```
for x in 1 2 3
do
   echo before $x
   continue 1
   echo after $x
done
```

The output will be:

```
before 1
before 2
before 3
```

The . Command

The dot command executes the command in the current shell:

```
. ./shell_script
```

Normally, when a script executes an external command or script, a new environment (a subshell) is created, the command is executed in the new environment and the environment is then discarded, apart from the exit code which is returned to the parent shell. But the external `source` and the dot command (two more synonyms) run the commands listed in a script in the same shell that called the script.

This means that normally, any changes to environment variables that the command makes are lost. The dot command, on the other hand, allows the executed command to change the current environment. This is often useful when you use a script as a 'wrapper' to set up your environment for the later execution of some other command. For example, if you're working on several different projects at the same time, you may find you need to invoke commands with different parameters, perhaps to invoke an older version of the compiler for maintaining an old program.

In shell scripts, the dot command works like the `#include` directive in C or C++. Though it doesn't literally include the script, it does execute the command in the current context, so you can use it to incorporate variable and function definitions into a script.

In the following example, we use the dot command on the command line, but we can just as well use it within a script.

Try It Out - The . Command

1. Suppose we have two files containing the environment settings for two different development environments. To set the environment for the old, classic commands, `classic_set`, we could use:

```
#!/bin/sh

version=classic
PATH=/usr/local/old_bin:/usr/bin:/bin:.
PS1="classic> "
```

2. while for the new commands we use latest_set:

```
#!/bin/sh

version=latest
PATH=/usr/local/new_bin:/usr/bin:/bin:.
PS1=" latest version> "
```

We can set the environment by using these scripts in conjunction with the dot command, as in the sample session below:

```
$ . ./classic_set
classic> echo $version
classic
classic> . latest_set
latest version> echo $version
latest
latest version>
```

echo

Despite the X/Open exhortation to use the `printf` command in modern shells, we've been following 'common practice' by using the `echo` command to output a string followed by a newline character.

A common problem is how to suppress the newline character. Unfortunately, different versions of UNIX have implemented different solutions. The normal method is to use,

```
echo -n "string to output"
```

but you'll often come across:

```
echo -e "string to output\c"
```

> **The second option, `echo -e`, makes sure that the interpretation of backslash escaped characters, such as `\t` for tab and `\n` for carriage returns, is enabled. It's usually set by default. See the `man` pages for details. If you need a portable way to remove the trailing newline, you can use the external `tr` command to get rid of it, but it will execute rather more slowly. In general it's better to stick to `printf` if you need to loose the newline and printf is available on your system.**

eval

The `eval` command allows you to evaluate arguments. It's built into the shell and doesn't normally exist as a separate command. It's probably best demonstrated with a short example borrowed from the X/Open specification itself:

```
foo=10
x=foo
y='$'$x
echo $y
```

This gives the output `$foo`. However,

```
foo=10
x=foo
eval y='$'$x
echo $y
```

gives the output `10`. Thus, `eval` is a bit like an extra `$`: it gives you the value of the value of a variable.

The `eval` command is very useful, allowing code to be generated and run on the fly. It does complicate script debugging, but can let you do things that are otherwise difficult-to-impossible.

exec

The `exec` command has two different uses. It's normally used for replacing the current shell with a different program.

For example,

```
exec wall "Thanks for all the fish"
```

in a script will replace the current shell with the `wall` command. No lines in the script after the `exec` will be processed, because the shell that was executing the script no longer exists.

The second use of `exec` is to modify the current file descriptors.

```
exec 3< afile
```

This causes file descriptor three to be opened for reading from file `afile`. It's rarely used.

exit n

The `exit` command causes the script to exit with exit code `n`. If you use it at the command prompt of any interactive shell, it will log you out. If you allow your script to exit without specifying an exit status, the status of the last command executed in the script will be used as the return value. It's always good practice to supply an exit code.

In shell script programming, exit code 0 is success, codes 1 through 125 inclusive are error codes that can be used by scripts. The remaining values have reserved meanings:

Exit Code	Description
126	The file was not executable
127	A command was not found.
128 and above	A signal occurred.

Using zero as success may seem a little unusual to many C or C++ programmers. The big advantage in scripts is that it allows us to use 125 user-defined error codes, without the need for a global error code variable.

Here's a simple example that returns success if a file called `.profile` exists in the current directory:

```
#!/bin/sh

if [ -f .profile ]; then
    exit 0
fi

exit 1
```

If you're a glutton for punishment, or at least for terse scripts, you can rewrite this using the combined AND and OR list we saw earlier:

```
[ -f .profile ] && exit 0 || exit 1
```

export

The `export` command makes the variable named as its parameter available in subshells. By default, variables created in a shell are not available in further (sub)shells invoked from that shell. The `export` command creates an environment variable from its parameter which can be seen by other scripts and programs invoked from the current program. More technically, the exported variables form the environment variables in any child processes derived from the shell. This is best illustrated with an example of two scripts, `export1` and `export2`.

Try It Out - Exporting Variables

1. We list `export2` first:

```
#!/bin/sh

echo "$foo"
echo "$bar"
```

2. Now for export1. At the end of this script, we invoke export2:

```
#!/bin/sh

foo="The first meta-syntactic variable"
export bar="The second meta-syntactic variable"

export2
```

If we run these, we get:

```
$ export1

The second meta-syntactic variable
$
```

The first blank line occurs because the variable `foo` was not available in `export2`, so `$foo` evaluated to nothing. `echo`ing a null variable gives a newline.

Once a variable has been exported from a shell, it's exported to any scripts invoked from that shell and also to any shell they invoke in turn and so on. If the script `export2` called another script, it would also have the value of `bar` available to it.

> **The commands `set -a` or `set -allexport` will export all variables thereafter.**

expr

The `expr` command evaluates its arguments as an expression. It's most commonly used for simple arithmetic, in the form:

```
x=`expr $x + 1`
```

> **The `` ` ` `` characters make `x` take the result of executing the command `expr $x + 1`. We'll mention more about command substitution later in the chapter.**

In fact, `expr` is a powerful command that can perform many expression evaluations. The principal ones are:

Expression Evaluation	Description
`expr1 | expr2`	`expr1` if `expr1` is non-zero, otherwise `expr2`.
`expr1 & expr2`	Zero if either expression is zero, otherwise `expr1`.
`expr1 = expr2`	Equal.
`expr1 > expr2`	Greater than.
`expr1 >= expr2`	Greater than or equal to.
`expr1 < expr2`	Less than.
`expr1 <= expr2`	Less than or equal to.
`expr1 != expr2`	Not equal.
`expr1 + expr2`	Addition.
`expr1 - expr2`	Subtraction.
`expr1 * expr2`	Multiplication.
`expr1 / expr2`	Integer division.
`expr1 % expr2`	Integer modulo.

In newer scripts, `expr` is normally replaced with the more efficient `$((...))` syntax, which we'll meet later.

printf

The `printf` command is only available in more recent shells. X/Open suggests that we should use it in preference to `echo` for generating formatted output.

The syntax is:

```
printf "format string" parameter1 parameter2 ...
```

The format string is very similar to that used in C or C++, with some restrictions. Principally, floating point isn't supported, because all arithmetic in the shell is performed as integers. The format string consists of any combination of literal characters, escape sequences and conversion specifiers. All characters in the format string other than `%` and `\` appear literally in the output.

The following escape sequences are supported:

Escape Sequence	Description
`\\`	Backslash character.
`\a`	Alert (ring the bell or beep).
`\b`	Backspace character.
`\f`	Form feed character.
`\n`	Newline character.
`\r`	Carriage return.
`\t`	Tab character.
`\v`	Vertical tab character.
`\ooo`	The single character with octal value `ooo`.

The conversion specifier is quite complex, so we'll list only the common usage here. More details can be found in the manual. The conversion specifier consists of a `%` character, followed by a conversion character. The principal conversions are:

Conversion Specifier	Description
d	Output a decimal number.
c	Output a character.
s	Output a string.
%	Output the `%` character.

The format string is then used to interpret the remaining parameters and output the result. For example:

```
$ printf "%s\n" hello
hello
$ printf "%s %d\t%s" "Hi There" 15 people
Hi There 15	people
```

Notice how we must use `" "` to protect the `Hi There` string and make it a single parameter.

return

The `return` command causes functions to return. We mentioned this when we looked at functions earlier. `return` takes a single numeric parameter which is available to the script calling the function. If no parameter is specified, `return` defaults to the exit code of the last command.

set

The `set` command sets the parameter variables for the shell. It can be a useful way of using fields in commands that output space-separated values.

Suppose we want to use the name of the current month in a shell script. The system provides a `date` command, which contains the month as a string, but we need to separate it from the other fields. We can do this using a combination of the `$(...)` construct to execute the date command and return the result (which we'll look at in more detail very soon) and the `set` command. The `date` command output has the month string as its second parameter:

```
#!/bin/sh

echo the date is $(date)
set $(date)
echo The month is $2

exit 0
```

This program sets the parameter list to the `date` command's output and then uses the positional parameter `$2` to get at the month.

Notice that we used `date` command as a simple example to show how to extract positional parameters. Since the `date` command is sensitive to the language local, in reality we would have extracted the name of the month using `date +%B`. The `date` command has many other formatting options, see the manual page for more details.

We can also use the `set` command to control the way the shell executes, by passing it parameters. The most commonly used is `set -x` which makes a script display a trace of its currently executing command.

> **We'll meet `set` and some more of its options when we look at debugging later on in the chapter.**

shift

The `shift` command moves all the parameter variables down by one, so `$2` becomes `$1`, `$3` becomes `$2`, and so on. The previous value of `$1` is discarded, while `$0` remains unchanged. If a numerical parameter is specified in the call to `shift`, the parameters will move that many spaces. The other variables `$*`, `$@` and `$#` are also modified in line with the new arrangement of parameter variables.

`shift` is often useful for scanning through parameters, and if your script requires ten or more parameters, you'll need `shift` to access the tenth and beyond.

Just as an example, we can scan through all the positional parameters like this:

```
#!/bin/sh

while [ "$1" != "" ]; do
    echo "$1"
    shift
done

exit 0
```

trap

The `trap` command is used for specifying the actions to take on receipt of signals, which we'll meet in more detail later in the book. A common use is to tidy up a script when it is interrupted. Historically, shells always used numbers for the signals, but new scripts should use names taken from the `#include` file `signal.h`, with the `SIG` prefix omitted. To see the signals, you can use type `trap -l`.

> **For those not familiar with signals, they are events sent asynchronously to a program. By default, they normally cause the program to terminate.**

The `trap` command is passed the action to take, followed by the signal name (or names) to trap on.

```
trap command signal
```

Remember that the scripts are normally interpreted from 'top' to 'bottom' so you must specify the `trap` command before the part of the script you wish to protect.

To reset a trap condition to the default, simply specify the command as `-`. To ignore a signal, set the command to the empty string `''`. A `trap` command with no parameters prints out the current list of traps and actions.

These are the more important signals covered by the X/Open standard that can be caught (with the conventional signal number in brackets):

Signal	Description
`HUP` (1)	Hang up; usually sent when a terminal goes off line, or a user logs out.
`INT` (2)	Interrupt; usually sent by pressing *Ctrl-C*.
`QUIT` (3)	Quit; usually sent by pressing *Ctrl-*
`ABRT` (6)	Abort; usually sent on some serious execution error.
`ALRM` (14)	Alarm; usually used for handling time-outs.
`TERM` (15)	Terminate; usually sent by the system when it's shutting down.

Try It Out - Trapping Signals

The following script demonstrates some simple signal handling:

```
#!/bin/sh

trap 'rm -f /tmp/my_tmp_file_$$' INT
echo creating file /tmp/my_tmp_file_$$
date > /tmp/my_tmp_file_$$

echo "press interrupt (CTRL-C) to interrupt ...."
while [ -f /tmp/my_tmp_file_$$ ]; do
    echo File exists
    sleep 1
done
echo The file no longer exists

trap - INT
echo creating file /tmp/my_tmp_file_$$
date >  /tmp/my_tmp_file_$$

echo "press interrupt (control-C) to interrupt ...."
while [ -f /tmp/my_tmp_file_$$ ]; do
    echo File exists
    sleep 1
done

echo we never get here
exit 0
```

If we run this script, pressing *Ctrl-C* (or whatever your interrupt keys are) in each of the loops, we get the output:

```
creating file /tmp/my_tmp_file_141
press interrupt (CTRL-C) to interrupt ....
File exists
File exists
File exists
File exists
The file no longer exists
creating file /tmp/my_tmp_file_141
press interrupt (CTRL-C) to interrupt ....
File exists
File exists
File exists
File exists
```

How It Works

This script uses the `trap` command to arrange for the command `rm -f /tmp/my_tmp_file_$$` to be executed when an `INT` (interrupt) signal occurs. The script then enters a `while` loop which continues while the file exists. When the user presses *Ctrl-C*, the statement `rm -f /tmp/my_tmp_file_$$` is executed, then the `while` loop resumes. Since the file has now been deleted, the first `while` loop terminates normally.

The script then uses the `trap` command again, this time to specify that no command be executed when an `INT` signal occurs. It then recreates the file and loops inside the second `while` statement. When the user presses *Ctrl-C* this time, there is no statement configured to execute, so the default behavior occurs, which is to immediately terminate the script. Since the script terminates immediately, the final `echo` and `exit` statements are never executed.

unset

The `unset` command removes variables or functions from the environment. It can't do this to read-only variables defined by the shell itself, such as IFS. It's not often used.

The script,

```
#!/bin/sh

foo="Hello World"
echo $foo

unset foo
echo $foo
```

writes `Hello World` once and a newline the second time.

> **Writing `foo=` has a similar effect in the above program to `unset`, but setting `foo` to `null` isn't the same as removing `foo` from the environment.**

Command Execution

When we're writing scripts, we often need to capture the result of a command's execution for use in the shell script, i.e. we want to execute a command and put the output of the command in a variable. We do this using the `$(command)` syntax, which we met in the earlier `set` command example. There is also an older form, `` `command` ``, which is still in common usage.

> **Note that, with the older form of the command execution, the backquote ` is used, not the single quote ' that we used in earlier shell quoting (to protect against variable expansion). Only use this form for shell scripts that you need to be very portable.**

All new scripts should use the `$(...)` form, which was introduced to avoid some rather complex rules covering the use of the characters $, ` and \ inside the back-quoted command. If a backquote is used within the `` `...` `` construct, it must be escaped with a \ character. These catch programmers out and sometimes even experienced shell programmers are forced to experiment to get the quoting correct in backquoted commands.

The result of the `$(command)` is simply the output from the command. Note that this isn't the return status of the command, but the string output. For example:

```
#!/bin/sh

echo The current directory is $PWD
echo The current users are $(who)

exit 0
```

Because the current directory is a shell environment variable, the first line doesn't need to use this command execution construct. The result of who, however, does need this construct if it is to be available to the script.

The concept of putting the result of a command into a script variable is very powerful, as it makes it easy to use existing commands in scripts and capture their output. If you ever find yourself trying to convert a set of parameters that are the output of a command on standard output, and capture them as arguments for a program, you may well find the command `xargs` can do it for you. Look in the manual for further details.

A problem sometimes arises when the command we want to invoke outputs some whitespace before the text we want, or more output than we actually require. In such a case, we can use the `set` command as we have already shown.

Arithmetic Expansion

We've already used the `expr` command, which allows simple arithmetic commands to be processed, but this is quite slow to execute, since a new shell is invoked to process the `expr` command.

A newer and better alternative is `$((...))` expansion. By enclosing the expression we wish to evaluate in `$((...))`, we can perform simple arithmetic much more efficiently:

```
#!/bin/sh

x=0
while [ "$x" -ne 10 ]; do
    echo $x
    x=$(($x+1))
done

exit 0
```

Parameter Expansion

We've seen the simplest form of parameter assignment and expansion, where we write:

```
foo=fred
echo $foo
```

A problem occurs when we want to append extra characters to the end of a variable. Suppose we want to write a short script to process files called `1_tmp` and `2_tmp`. We could try:

```
#!/bin/sh

for i in 1 2
do
    my_secret_process $i_tmp
done
```

But on each loop, we'll get:

```
my_secret_process: too few arguments
```

What went wrong?

The problem is that the shell tried to substitute the value of the variable `$i_tmp`, which doesn't exist. The shell doesn't consider this an error, it just substitutes a blank, so no parameters at all were passed to `my_secret_process`. To protect the expansion of the `$i` part of the variable, we need to enclose the `i` in `{}` like this:

```
#!/bin/sh

for i in 1 2
do
    my_secret_process ${i}_tmp
done
```

On each loop, the value of `i` is substituted for `${i}`, to give the actual file names. We've substituted the value of the parameter into a string.

We can perform many parameter substitutions in the shell. Often, these provide an elegant solution to many parameter processing problems.

The common ones are:

Parameter Expansion	Description
`${param:-default}`	If `param` is null, set it to the value of `default`.
`${#param}`	Gives the length of `param`.
`${param%word}`	From the end, removes the smallest part of `param` that matches `word` and returns the rest.
`${param%%word}`	From the end, removes the longest part of `param` that matches `word` and returns the rest.
`${param#word}`	From the beginning, removes the smallest part of `param` that matches `word` and returns the rest.
`${param##word}`	From the beginning, removes the longest part of `param` that matches `word` and returns the rest.

These substitutions are often useful when we're working with strings. The last four that remove parts of strings are especially useful for processing filenames and paths, as the example below shows.

Try It Out - Parameter Processing

Each portion of the following script illustrates the parameter matching operators:

```
#!/bin/sh

unset foo
echo ${foo:-bar}

foo=fud
echo ${foo:-bar}

foo=/usr/bin/X11/startx
echo ${foo#*/}
echo ${foo##*/}

bar=/usr/local/etc/local/networks
echo ${bar%local*}
echo ${bar%%local*}

exit 0
```

This gives the output:

```
bar
fud
usr/bin/X11/startx
startx
/usr/local/etc
/usr
```

How It Works

The first statement `${foo:-bar}` gives the value `bar`, since `foo` had no value when the statement was executed. The variable `foo` is unchanged, as it remains unset.

> **`${foo:=bar}`, however, would set the variable to `$foo`. This string operator checks that `foo` exists and isn't null. If it is, it returns its value, but otherwise, it sets `foo` to `bar` and returns that instead.**
>
> **`${foo:?bar}` will print `foo: bar` and abort the command if `foo` doesn't exist or is set to `null`.**
>
> **Lastly, `${foo:+bar}` returns `bar` if `foo` exists and isn't null. What a set of choices!**

The `{foo#*/}` statement matches and removes only the left `/` (remember `*` matches zero or more characters). The `{foo##*/}` matches and removes as much as possible, so removes the rightmost `/`, and all the characters before it.

The {bar%local*} statement matches characters from the right, until the first occurrence of local (followed by any number of characters) is matched, but the {bar%%local*} matches as many characters as possible from the right, until it finds the leftmost local.

Since UNIX is based around filters, the result of one operation must often be redirected manually. Let's say you want to convert a gif file into a jpeg file using the cjpeg program.

```
$ cjpeg image.gif > image.jpg
```

Sometimes, however, you want to perform this type of operation on a large number of files. How do you automate the redirection? As easily as this:

```
#!/bin/sh
for image in  *.gif
do
  cjpeg $image > ${image%%gif}jpg
done
```

This script, giftojpeg, creates a jpeg file for each gif file in the current directory.

Here Documents

One special way of passing input to a command from a shell script is to use a **here document**. This allows a command to execute as though it were reading from a file or the keyboard, whereas in fact it's getting input from the script.

A here document starts with the leader <<, followed by a special sequence of characters that will be repeated at the end of the document. << is the shell's label redirector, which, in this case, forces the command input to be the here document. These act as a marker to tell the shell where the here document ends. The marker characters must not appear in the lines to be passed to the command, so it's best to make them memorable and fairly unusual.

Try It Out - Using Here Documents

The simplest example is simply to feed input to the cat command:

```
#!/bin/sh

cat <<!FUNKY!
hello
this is a here
document
!FUNKY!
```

This gives the output:

```
hello
this is a here
document
```

Here documents might seem a rather curious feature, but they're actually very powerful because they allow us to invoke an interactive program like an editor and feed it some predefined input. However, they're more commonly used for outputting large amounts of text from inside a script, as we saw above, and avoiding having to use `echo` statements for each line. We've used `!` marks on each side of the identifier to ensure that there's no confusion.

If we wish to process several lines in a file in a predetermined way, we could use the ed line editor and feed it commands from a here document in a shell script.

Try It Out - Another Use for a Here Document

1. Let's start with a file, `a_text_file`, containing:

```
That is line 1
That is line 2
That is line 3
That is line 4
```

2. We can edit this file using a combination of a here document and the ed editor:

```
#!/bin/sh

ed a_text_file <<!FunkyStuff!
3
d
.,\$s/is/was/
w
q
!FunkyStuff!

exit 0
```

If we run this script, the file now contains:

```
That is line 1
That is line 2
That was line 4
```

How It Works

The shell script simply invokes the `ed` editor and passes to it the commands that it needs to move to the third line, delete the line and then replace `is` with `was` in the current line (since line three was deleted, the current line is now what was the last line). These `ed` commands are taken from the lines in the script that form the here document, i.e. the lines between the markers `!FunkyStuff!`.

> **Notice the \ inside the here document to protect the $ from shell expansion. The \ escapes the $, so the shell knows not to try to expand `$s/is/was/` to its value, which of course it doesn't have. Instead, the shell passes the text `\$` as `$`, which can then be interpreted by the `ed` editor.**

Debugging Scripts

Debugging shell scripts is usually quite easy, but there are no specific tools to help. We'll quickly summarize the common methods.

When an error occurs, the shell will normally print out the line number of the line containing the error. If the error isn't immediately apparent, we can add some extra echo statements to display the contents of variables and test code fragments by simply typing them into the shell interactively.

Since scripts are interpreted, there's no compilation overhead in modifying and retrying a script.

The main way to trace more complicated errors is to set various shell options. To do this, you can either use command line options after invoking the shell, or you can use the set command. We summarize the options in the following table:

Command Line Option	set Option	Description
sh -n <script>	set -o noexec set -n	Checks for syntax errors only; doesn't execute commands.
sh -v <script>	set -o verbose set -v	Echoes commands before running them.
sh -x <script>	set -o xtrace set -x	Echoes commands after processing on the command line.
	set -o nounset set -u	Gives an error message when an undefined variable is used.

You can set the set option flags on, using -o, and off, using +o, and likewise for the abbreviated versions.

You can achieve a simple execution trace by using the xtrace option. For an initial check, you can use the command line option, but for finer debugging, you can put the xtrace flags (setting an execution trace on and off) inside the script around the problem code. The execution trace causes the shell to print each line in the script, with variables expanded, before executing the line. The level of expansion is denoted (by default) by the number of + signs at the start of each line. You can change the + to something more meaningful by setting the PS4 shell variable in your shell configuration file.

In the shell, you can also find out the program state wherever it exits by trapping the EXIT signal, with a line something like this placed at the start of the script:

```
trap 'echo Exiting: critical variable = $critical_variable' EXIT
```

Putting it All Together

Now that we've seen the main features of the shell as a programming language, it's time to write an example program to put some of what we have learned to use.

Throughout this book, we're going to be building a CD database application to show the techniques we've been learning. We start with a shell script, but pretty soon we'll do it again in C, add a database, and so on. So, let's start.

Requirements

We're going to design and implement a program for managing CDs. Suppose we have an extensive CD collection. An electronic catalogue seems an ideal project to implement as we learn about programming UNIX.

We want, at least initially, to store some basic information about each CD, such as the label, type of music and artist or composer. We would also like to store some simple track information.

We want to be able to search on any of the 'per CD' items, but not on any of the track details.

To make the mini-application complete, we would also like to be able to enter, update and delete all the information from within the application.

Design

The three requirements—updating, searching and displaying the data—suggest that a simple menu will be adequate. All the data we need to store is textual and, assuming our CD collection isn't too big, we have no need for a complex database, so some simple text files will do. Storing information in text files will keep our application simple and if our requirements change, it's almost always easier to manipulate a text file than any other sort of file. As the last resort, we could even use an editor to manually enter and delete data, rather than write a program to do it.

We need to make an important design decision about our data storage: will a single file suffice and, if so, what format should it have? Most of the information we expect to store occurs only once per CD (we'll skip lightly over the fact that some CDs contain the work of many composers or artists), except track information. Just about all CDs have more than one track.

Should we fix a limit on the number of tracks we can store per CD? That seems rather an arbitrary and unnecessary restriction, so let's reject that idea straight away!

If we allow a flexible number of tracks, we have three options:

- Use a single file, use one line for the 'title' type information and then 'n' lines for the track information for that CD.
- Put all the information for each CD on a single line, allowing the line to continue until no more track information needs to be stored.
- Separate the title information from the track information and use a different file for each.

Only the third option allows us to easily fix the format of the files, which we'll need to do if we ever wish to convert our database into a relational form (more on this in Chapter 7), so that's the option we'll choose.

The next decision is what to put in the files.

Initially, for each CD title, we'll choose to store:

- The CD catalog number
- The title
- The type (classical, rock, pop, jazz, etc.)
- The composer or artist

For the tracks, simply:

- Track number
- Track name

In order to 'join' the two files, we must relate the track information to the rest of the CD information. To do this, we'll use the CD catalog number. Since this is unique for each CD, it will appear only once in the titles file and once per track in the tracks file.

Let's look at an example titles file:

Catalog	Title	Type	Composer
CD123	Cool sax	Jazz	Bix
CD234	Classic violin	Classical	Bach
CD345	Hits99	Pop	Various

And its corresponding tracks file:

Catalog	Track No.	Title
CD123	1	Some jazz
CD123	2	More jazz
CD345	1	Dizzy
CD234	1	Sonata in D minor

The two files 'join' using the Catalog field. Remember, there are normally multiple rows in the tracks file for a single entry in the titles file.

The last thing we need to decide is how to separate the entries. Fixed-width fields are normal in a relational database, but are not always the most convenient. Another common method is a comma, which we'll use here (i.e. a comma-separated variable, or CSV, file).

In the following Try It Out, just so you don't get totally lost, we'll be using the following functions:

```
get_return()
get_confirm()
set_menu_choice()
insert_title()
insert_track()
add_record_tracks()
add_records()
find_cd()
update_cd()
count_cds()
remove_records()
list_tracks()
```

Try It Out - A CD Application

1. First in our sample script is, as always, a line ensuring that it's executed as a shell script, followed by some copyright information:

```
#!/bin/sh

# Very simple example shell script for managing a CD collection.
# Copyright (C) 1996-99 Wrox Press.

# This program is free software; you can redistribute it and/or modify it
# under the terms of the GNU General Public License as published by the
# Free Software Foundation; either version 2 of the License, or (at your
# option) any later version.

# This program is distributed in the hopes that it will be useful, but
# WITHOUT ANY WARRANTY; without even the implied warranty of
# MERCHANTABILITY or FITNESS FOR A PARTICULAR PURPOSE. See the GNU General
# Public License for more details.

# You should have received a copy of the GNU General Public License along
# with this program; if not, write to the Free Software Foundation, Inc.
# 675 Mass Ave, Cambridge, MA 02139, USA.
```

2. The first thing to do is to ensure that some global variables that we'll be using throughout the script are set up. We set the title and track files and a temporary file. We also trap *Ctrl-C*, so our temporary file is removed if the user interrupts the script.

```
menu_choice=""
current_cd=""
title_file="title.cdb"
tracks_file="tracks.cdb"
temp_file=/tmp/cdb.$$
trap 'rm -f $temp_file' EXIT
```

3. Now we define our functions, so that the script, executing from the top line, can find all the function definitions before we attempt to call any of them for the first time.

To avoid rewriting the same code in several places, the first two functions are simple utilities.

```
get_return() {
  echo -e "Press return \c"
  read x
  return 0
}

get_confirm() {
  echo -e "Are you sure? \c"
  while true
  do
    read x
    case "$x" in
      y | yes | Y | Yes | YES )
        return 0;;
      n | no  | N | No  | NO )
        echo
        echo "Cancelled"
        return 1;;
      *) echo "Please enter yes or no" ;;
    esac
  done
}
```

4. Here, we come to the main menu function, `set_menu_choice`. The contents of the menu vary dynamically, with extra options being added if a CD entry has been selected.

Note that `echo -e` may not be portable to some shells.

```
set_menu_choice() {
  clear
  echo "Options :-"
  echo
  echo "   a) Add new CD"
  echo "   f) Find CD"
  echo "   c) Count the CDs and tracks in the catalog"
  if [ "$cdcatnum" != "" ]; then
    echo "   l) List tracks on $cdtitle"
    echo "   r) Remove $cdtitle"
    echo "   u) Update track information for $cdtitle"
  fi
  echo "   q) Quit"
  echo
  echo -e "Please enter choice then press return \c"
  read menu_choice
  return
}
```

5. Two more very short functions, `insert_title` and `insert_track`, for adding to the database files. Though some people hate one-liners like these, they help make other functions clearer.

They are followed by the larger `add_record_track` function that uses them. This function uses pattern matching to ensure no commas are entered (since we're using commas as a field separator) and also arithmetic operations to increment the current track number as tracks are entered.

```
insert_title() {
  echo $* >> $title_file
  return
}

insert_track() {
  echo $* >> $tracks_file
  return
}

add_record_tracks() {
  echo "Enter track information for this CD"
  echo "When no more tracks enter q"
  cdtrack=1
  cdttitle=""
  while [ "$cdttitle" != "q" ]
  do
      echo -e "Track $cdtrack, track title? \c"
      read tmp
      cdttitle=${tmp%%,*}
      if [ "$tmp" != "$cdttitle" ]; then
        echo "Sorry, no commas allowed"
        continue
      fi
      if [ -n "$cdttitle" ] ; then
        if [ "$cdttitle" != "q" ]; then
          insert_track $cdcatnum,$cdtrack,$cdttitle
        fi
      else
        cdtrack=$((cdtrack-1))
      fi
    cdtrack=$((cdtrack+1))
  done
}
```

6. The `add_records` function allows entry of the main CD information for a new CD.

```
add_records() {
  # Prompt for the initial information

  echo -e "Enter catalog name \c"
  read tmp
  cdcatnum=${tmp%%,*}

  echo -e "Enter title \c"
  read tmp
  cdtitle=${tmp%%,*}

  echo -e "Enter type \c"
  read tmp
  cdtype=${tmp%%,*}
```

```
    echo -e "Enter artist/composer \c"
    read tmp
    cdac=${tmp%%,*}

    # Check that they want to enter the information

    echo About to add new entry
    echo "$cdcatnum $cdtitle $cdtype $cdac"

    # If confirmed then append it to the titles file

    if get_confirm ; then
      insert_title $cdcatnum,$cdtitle,$cdtype,$cdac
      add_record_tracks
    else
      remove_records
    fi

    return
}
```

7. The `find_cd` function searches for the catalog name text in the CD title file, using the `grep` command. We need to know how many times the string was found, but `grep` only returns a value telling us if it matched zero times or many. To get around this, we store the output in a file, which will have one line per match, then count the lines in the file.

The word count command, `wc`, has whitespace in its output, separating the number of lines, words and characters in the file. We use the `$(wc -l $temp_file)` notation to extract the first parameter from the output to set the `linesfound` variable. If we wanted another, later parameter we would use the `set` command to set the shell's parameter variables to the command output.

We change the `IFS` (Internal Field Separator) to a `,` (comma), so we can separate the comma-delimited fields. An alternative command is `cut`.

```
find_cd() {
  if [ "$1" = "n" ]; then
    asklist=n
  else
    asklist=y
  fi
  cdcatnum=""
  echo -e "Enter a string to search for in the CD titles \c"
  read searchstr
  if [ "$searchstr" = "" ]; then
    return 0
  fi

  grep "$searchstr" $title_file > $temp_file

  set $(wc -l $temp_file)
  linesfound=$1

  case "$linesfound" in
  0)    echo "Sorry, nothing found"
        get_return
        return 0
        ;;
```

```
1)      ;;
2)      echo "Sorry, not unique."
        echo "Found the following"
        cat $temp_file
        get_return
        return 0
esac

IFS=","
read cdcatnum cdtitle cdtype cdac < $temp_file
IFS=" "

if [ -z "$cdcatnum" ]; then
  echo "Sorry, could not extract catalog field from $temp_file"
  get_return
  return 0
fi

echo
echo Catalog number: $cdcatnum
echo Title: $cdtitle
echo Type: $cdtype
echo Artist/Composer: $cdac
echo
get_return

if [ "$asklist" = "y" ]; then
  echo -e "View tracks for this CD? \c"
    read x
  if [ "$x" = "y" ]; then
    echo
    list_tracks
    echo
  fi
fi
return 1
}
```

8. update_cd allows us to re-enter information for a CD. Notice that we search (grep) for lines that start (^) with the $cdcatnum followed by a `,`, and that we need to wrap the expansion of $cdcatnum in {} so we can search for a `,` with no whitespace between it and the catalogue number. This function also uses {} to enclose multiple statements to be executed if get_confirm returns true.

```
update_cd() {
  if [ -z "$cdcatnum" ]; then
    echo "You must select a CD first"
    find_cd n
  fi
  if [ -n "$cdcatnum" ]; then
    echo "Current tracks are :-"
    list_tracks
    echo
    echo "This will re-enter the tracks for $cdtitle"
    get_confirm && {
      grep -v "^${cdcatnum}," $tracks_file > $temp_file
      mv $temp_file $tracks_file
      echo
      add_record_tracks
    }
  fi
  return
}
```

9. `count_cds` gives us a quick count of the contents of our database.

```
count_cds() {
  set $(wc -l $title_file)
  num_titles=$1
  set $(wc -l $tracks_file)
  num_tracks=$1
  echo found $num_titles CDs, with a total of $num_tracks tracks
  get_return
  return
}
```

10. `remove_records` strips entries from the database files, using `grep -v` to remove all matching strings. Notice we must use a temporary file.

If we tried to do this,

```
grep -v "^$cdcatnum" > $title_file
```

11. the $title_file would be set to empty by the > output redirection before the grep had chance to execute, so grep would read from an empty file.

```
remove_records() {
  if [ -z "$cdcatnum" ]; then
    echo You must select a CD first
    find_cd n
  fi
  if [ -n "$cdcatnum" ]; then
    echo "You are about to delete $cdtitle"
    get_confirm && {
      grep -v "^${cdcatnum}," $title_file > $temp_file
      mv $temp_file $title_file
      grep -v "^${cdcatnum}," $tracks_file > $temp_file
      mv $temp_file $tracks_file
      cdcatnum=""
      echo Entry removed
    }
    get_return
  fi
  return
}
```

12. `List_tracks` again uses `grep` to extract the lines we want, `cut` to access the fields we want and then `more` to provide a paginated output. If you consider how many lines of C code it would take to re-implement these 20-odd lines of code, you'll appreciate how powerful a tool the shell can be.

```
list_tracks() {
  if [ "$cdcatnum" = "" ]; then
    echo no CD selected yet
    return
  else
    grep "^${cdcatnum}," $tracks_file > $temp_file
    num_tracks=$(wc -l $temp_file)
    if [ "$num_tracks" = "0" ]; then
      echo no tracks found for $cdtitle
    else {
```

```
        echo
        echo "$cdtitle :-"
        echo
        cut -f 2- -d , $temp_file
        echo
      } | ${PAGER:-more}
    fi
  fi
  get_return
  return
}
```

13. Now all the functions have been defined, we can enter the main routine. The first few lines simply get the files into a known state, then we call the menu function, `set_menu_choice`, and act on the output.

When quit is selected, we delete the temporary file, write a message and exit with a successful completion condition.

```
rm -f $temp_file
if [ ! -f $title_file ]; then
  touch $title_file
fi
if [ ! -f $tracks_file ]; then
  touch $tracks_file
fi

# Now the application proper

clear
echo
echo
echo "Mini CD manager"
sleep 1

quit=n
while [ "$quit" != "y" ];
do
  set_menu_choice
  case "$menu_choice" in
    a) add_records;;
    r) remove_records;;
    f) find_cd y;;
    u) update_cd;;
    c) count_cds;;
    l) list_tracks;;
    b)
      echo
      more $title_file
      echo
      get_return;;
    q | Q ) quit=y;;
    *) echo "Sorry, choice not recognized";;
  esac
done

#Tidy up and leave

rm -f $temp_file
echo "Finished"
exit 0
```

Notes

The `trap` command at the start of the script is intended to trap the user pressing *Ctrl-C*. This may be either the `EXIT` or the `INT` signal, depending on the terminal setup.

There are other ways of implementing the menu selection, notably the `select` construct in `bash` and `ksh` (which, however, isn't specified in X/Open) which is a dedicated menu choice selector. Check it out if your script can afford to be slightly less portable. Multi-line information given to users could also make use of here documents.

You might have noticed that there's no validation of the primary key when a new record is started; the new code just ignores the subsequent titles with the same code, but incorporates their tracks into the first title's listing:

```
1 First CD Track 1
2 First CD Track 2
1 Another CD
2 With the same CD key
```

We'll leave this and other improvements to your imagination and creativity, as you can modify the code under the terms of the GPL.

Summary

In this chapter, we've seen that the shell is a powerful programming language in its own right. Its ability to call other programs easily and then process their output makes the shell an ideal tool for tasks involving the processing of text and files.

Next time you need a small utility program, consider whether you can solve your problem by combining some of the many UNIX commands with a shell script. You'll be surprised just how many utility programs you can write without a compiler.

Working with Files

In this chapter, we'll be looking at UNIX files and directories and how to manipulate them. We'll learn how to create files, open them, read, write and close them. We'll also learn how programs can manipulate directories, to create, scan and delete them, for example. After the last chapter's diversion into shells, we now start programming in C.

Before proceeding to the way UNIX handles file I/O, we'll review the concepts associated with files, directories and devices. To manipulate files and directories, we need to make system calls (the UNIX parallel of the Windows API), but there also exists a whole range of library functions, the standard I/O library (`stdio`), to make file handling more efficient.

We'll spend the majority of the chapter detailing the various calls to handle files and directories. So, this chapter will cover:

- Files and devices
- System calls
- Library functions
- Low-level file access
- Managing files
- The standard I/O library
- Formatted input and output
- File and directory maintenance
- Scanning directories
- Errors
- Advanced topics

UNIX File Structure

"Why," you may be asking, "are we covering file structure? I know about that already." Well, files in the UNIX environment are particularly important, as they provide a simple and consistent interface to the operating system services and to devices. In UNIX, **everything is a file.** Well almost!

This means that, in general, programs can use disk files, serial ports, printers and other devices in exactly the same way as they would use a file. We'll cover some exceptions such as network connections later, but, in the main, you only need to use five basic functions: `open`, `close`, `read`, `write` and `ioctl`.

Directories, too, are special sorts of files. In modern UNIX versions, even the superuser may not write to them directly. All users ordinarily use the high level `opendir/readdir` interface to read directories without needing to know the system specific details of directory implementation. We'll return to special directory functions later in the chapter.

Really, almost everything is represented as a file under UNIX, or can be made available via special files. Even though there are, by necessity, subtle differences from the conventional files we know and love, the general principle still holds. Let's look at the special cases we've mentioned so far.

Directories

As well as its contents, a file has a name and some properties or 'administrative information', i.e. the file's creation/ modification date and its permissions. The properties are stored in the `inode`, which also contains the length of the file and where on the disk it's stored. The system uses the number of the file's inode; the directory structure just names the file for our benefit.

A directory is a file that holds the inode numbers and names of other files. Each directory entry is a link to a file's inode; remove the filename and you remove the link. (You can see the inode number for a file by using `ln -i`.) Using the `ln` command, you can make links to the same file in different directories. If the number of links to a file (the number after the permissions in `ls -l`) reaches zero, the inode and the data it references are no longer in use and are marked as free.

Files are arranged in directories, which may also contain subdirectories. These form the familiar file system hierarchy. A user, **`neil`**, usually has his files stored in a 'home' directory, perhaps `/home/neil`, with subdirectories for electronic mail, business letters, utility programs, and so on. Note that many UNIX shells have an excellent notation for getting straight to your home directory: the tilde ~. For another user, type ~user. As you know, home directories for each user are usually subdirectories of a higher level directory created specifically for this purpose, in this case `/home`. Note though that the standard library functions unfortunately do not understand the tilde notation in file name parameters.

The `/home` directory is itself a subdirectory of the root directory, `/`, which sits at the top of the hierarchy and contains all of the system's files in subdirectories. The root directory normally includes `/bin` for system programs ('binaries'), `/etc` for system configuration files and `/lib` for system libraries. Files that represent physical devices and that provide the interface to those devices are conventionally found in a directory called `/dev`. More information on the Linux file system layout is available in the Linux File System Standard, or you can check out `man hier` for a description of the directory hierarchy.

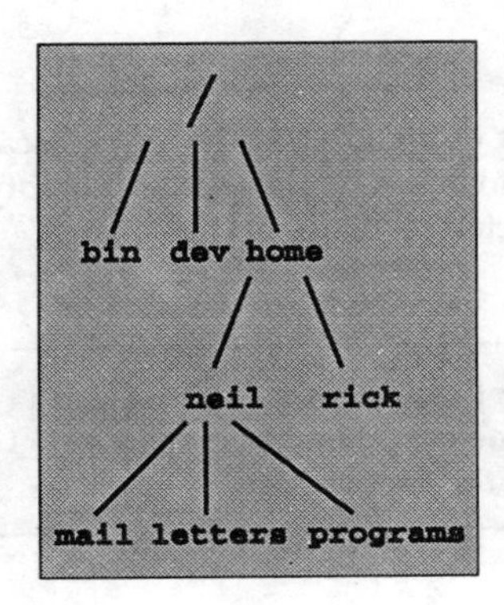

Files and Devices

Even hardware devices are very often represented (mapped) by files in UNIX. For example, as `root`, you mount a CD-ROM drive as a file,

```
$ mount -t iso9660 /dev/hdc /mnt/cd_rom
$ cd /mnt/cd_rom
```

which takes the CD-ROM device (loaded as `hdc` during boot-up) and mounts its current contents as the file structure beneath `/mnt/cd_rom`. You then move around within the CD-ROM's directories just as normal, except, of course, that the contents are read-only.

Three important device files are `/dev/console`, `/dev/tty` and `/dev/null`.

/dev/console

This device represents the system console. Error messages and diagnostics are often sent to this device. Each UNIX system has a designated terminal or screen to receive console messages. At one time, it might have been a dedicated printing terminal. On modern workstations, it's usually the 'active' virtual console, while under X, it will be a special console window on the screen.

/dev/tty

The special file `/dev/tty` is an alias (logical device) for the controlling terminal (keyboard and screen, or window) of a process, if it has one. For instance, processes running from `cron` won't have a controlling terminal, so won't be able to open `/dev/tty`.

Where it can be used, `/dev/tty` allows a program to write directly to the user, without regard to which pseudo-terminal or hardware terminal the user is using. It is useful when the standard output has been redirected. One example of this is in the command `ls -R | more` where the program `more` has to prompt the user for each new page of output. We'll see more of `/dev/tty` in Chapter 5.

Note that while there's only one `/dev/console` device, there are effectively many different physical devices accessed through `/dev/tty`.

/dev/null

This is the null device. All output written to this device is discarded. An immediate end of file is returned when the device is read, and it can be used as a source of empty files by using the cp command. Unwanted output is often redirected to /dev/null.

> **Another way of creating empty files is to use the touch <filename> command, which changes the modification time of a file, or creates a new file if none exists with the given name. It won't empty it of its contents, though.**

```
$ echo do not want to see this >/dev/null
$ cp /dev/null empty_file
```

Other devices found in /dev include hard and floppy disks, communications ports, tape drives, CD-ROMs, sound cards and some devices representing the system's internal state. There's even a /dev/zero which acts as a source of null bytes to create files of zeros. You need superuser permissions to access some of these devices; normal users can't write programs to directly access low-level devices like hard disks. The names of the device files may vary from system to system. Solaris and Linux both have applications that run as superuser to manage the devices which would be otherwise inaccessible, for example, mount for user-mountable file systems.

In this chapter we'll concentrate on disk files and directories. We'll cover another device, the user's terminal, in Chapter 5.

System Calls and Device Drivers

We can access and control files and devices using a small number of functions. These functions, known as **system calls**, are provided by UNIX (and Linux) directly and are the interface to the operating system itself.

At the heart of the operating system, the kernel, are a number of **device drivers**. These are a collection of low-level interfaces for controlling system hardware, which we will cover in detail in chapter 21. For example, there will be a device driver for a tape drive, which knows how to start the tape, wind it forwards and backwards, read and write to it, and so on. It will also know that tapes have to be written to in blocks of a certain size. Because tapes are sequential in nature, the driver can't access tape blocks directly, but must wind the tape to the right place.

Similarly, a low-level hard disk device driver will only write whole numbers of disk sectors at a time, but will be able to access any desired disk block directly, because the disk is a random access device.

To provide a similar interface, device drivers encapsulate all of the hardware-dependent features. Idiosyncratic features of the hardware tend to be made available through ioctl.

Device files in /dev are all used in the same way; they can all be opened, read, written and closed. For example, the same open call that is used to access a regular file is used to access a user terminal, a printer, or a tape drive.

The low-level functions used to access the device drivers, the system calls, include:

- `open` Open a file or device.
- `read` Read from an open file or device.
- `write` Write to a file or device.
- `close` Close the file or device.
- `ioctl` Pass control information to a device driver.

The `ioctl` system call is used to provide some necessary hardware-specific control (as opposed to regular input and output), so its use varies from device to device. For example, a call to `ioctl` can be used to rewind a tape drive or to set the flow control characteristics of a serial port. For this reason, `ioctl` isn't necessarily portable from machine to machine. In addition, each driver defines its own set of `ioctl` commands.

These and other system calls are usually documented in section 2 of the UNIX `man` pages. Prototypes providing the parameter lists and function return types for system calls, and associated `#defines` of constants, are provided in include files. The particular ones required for each system call will be included with the descriptions of individual calls.

Library Functions

The problem with using low-level system calls directly for input and output is that they can be very inefficient. Why? Well:

- There's a performance penalty in making a system call. This is because UNIX has to switch from running your program code to executing its own kernel code and back again and system calls are therefore expensive compared to function calls.
- The hardware has limitations and this can impose restrictions on the size of data blocks that can be read or written by the low-level system call at any one time. For example, tape drives often have a minimum block size, say 10k, that they can write. So, if you attempt to write less than this, the drive will still advance the tape by 10k, leaving gaps on the tape.

To provide a higher level interface to devices and disk files, UNIX provides a number of standard libraries. These are collections of functions that you can include in your own programs to handle these problems. A good example is the standard I/O library that provides buffered output. You can effectively write data blocks of varying sizes and the library functions arrange for the low-level system calls to be provided with full blocks as the data is made available. This dramatically reduces the system call overhead.

Library functions are usually documented in section 3 of the UNIX `man` pages and often have a standard include file associated with them, such as `stdio.h` for the standard I/O library.

To summarize the discussion of the last few sections, here's a figure of the UNIX system showing where the various file functions exist relative to the user, the device drivers, the kernel and the hardware:

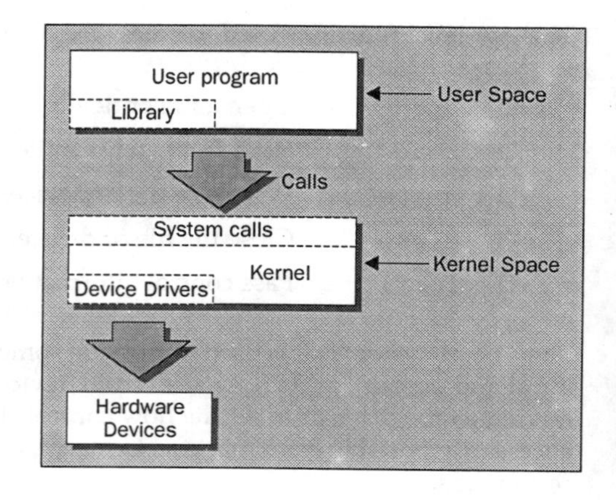

Low-level File Access

Each running program, called a **process**, has associated with it a number of file descriptors. These are sma integers that you can use to access open files or devices. How many of these are available will vary depending on how the UNIX system has been configured. When a program starts, it usually has three of these descriptors already opened. These are:

- 0 Standard input
- 1 Standard output
- 2 Standard error

You can associate other file descriptors with files and devices by using the `open` system call, which we'll be meeting shortly. The file descriptors that are automatically opened, however, already allow us to creat some simple programs using `write`.

write

```
#include <unistd.h>

size_t write(int fildes, const void *buf, size_t nbytes);
```

The `write` system call arranges for the first `nbytes` bytes from `buf` to be written to the file associated with the file descriptor `fildes`. It returns the number of bytes actually written. This may be less than `nbytes` if there has been an error in the file descriptor, or if the underlying device driver is sensitive to block size. If the function returns 0, it means no data was written, if -1, there has been an error in the `write` call and the error will be specified in the `errno` global variable.

With this knowledge, let's write our first program, `simple_write.c`:

```
#include <unistd.h>
#include <stdlib.h>

int main()
{
    if ((write(1, "Here is some data\n", 18)) != 18)
        write(2, "A write error has occurred on file descriptor 1\n",46);

    exit(0);
}
```

This program simply prints a message on the standard output. When a program exits, all open file descriptors are automatically closed, so we don't need to close them explicitly. This won't be the case, however, when we're dealing with buffered output.

```
$ simple_write
Here is some data
$
```

A point worth noting again is that `write` might report that it wrote fewer bytes than you asked it to. This is not necessarily an error. In your programs you will need to check `errno` to detect errors, and call `write` again to write any remaining data.

All the examples in this chapter assume that you have the current directory in your `PATH` and that, consequently, you're not running them while you're a superuser. If you do not have the current directory in your `PATH` (an essential superuser precaution) you can run the program specifying the directory explicitly like this:

```
$ ./simple_write
```

read

```
#include <unistd.h>

size_t read(int fildes, void *buf, size_t nbytes);
```

The `read` system call reads up to `nbytes` bytes of data from the file associated with the file descriptor `fildes` and places them in the data area `buf`. It returns the number of data bytes actually read, which may be less than the number requested. If a `read` call returns 0, it had nothing to read; it reached the end of the file. Again, an error on the call will cause it to return -1.

This program, `simple_read.c`, copies the first 128 bytes of the standard input to the standard output. It copies all of the input if there are less than 128 bytes.

```
#include <unistd.h>
#include <stdlib.h>

int main()
{
    char buffer[128];
    int nread;

    nread = read(0, buffer, 128);
    if (nread == -1)
        write(2, "A read error has occurred\n", 26);

    if ((write(1,buffer,nread)) != nread)
        write(2, "A write error has occurred\n",27);

    exit(0);
}
```

If we run the program, we should see:

```
$ echo hello there | simple_read
hello there
$ simple_read < draft1.txt
Files

In this chapter we will be looking at files and directories and how to manipulate
them. We will learn how to create files, o$
```

Note how the next shell prompt appears at the end of the last line of output because, in this example, the 128 bytes don't form a whole number of lines.

open

To create a new file descriptor we need to use the open system call.

```
#include <fcntl.h>
#include <sys/types.h>
#include <sys/stat.h>

int open(const char *path, int oflags);
int open(const char *path, int oflags, mode_t mode);
```

> *Strictly speaking, we don't need to include `sys/types.h` and `sys/stat.h` to use* open *on POSIX systems, but they may be necessary on some UNIX systems.*

In simple terms, open establishes an access path to a file or device. If successful, it returns a file descriptor that can be used in `read`, `write` and other system calls. The file descriptor is unique and isn't shared by any other processes that may be running. If two programs have a file open at the same time, they maintain distinct file descriptors. If they both write to the file, they will continue to write where they left off. Their data isn't interleaved, but one will overwrite the other. Each keeps its own idea of how far into the file (the offset) it has read or written. We can prevent unwanted clashes of this sort by using file locking, which we'll be looking at in Chapter 7.

The name of the file or device to be opened is passed as a parameter, `path`, and the `oflags` parameter is used to specify actions to be taken on opening the file.

The `oflags` are specified as a bitwise OR of a mandatory file access mode and other optional modes. The `open` call must specify one of the following file access modes:

Mode	Description
O_RDONLY	Open for read-only
O_WRONLY	Open for write-only
O_RDWR	Open for reading and writing

The call may also include a combination (bitwise OR) of the following optional modes in the `oflags` parameter:

- `O_APPEND` Place written data at the end of the file.
- `O_TRUNC` Set the length of the file to zero, discarding existing contents.
- `O_CREAT` Creates the file, if necessary, with permissions given in `mode`.
- `O_EXCL` Used with `O_CREAT`, ensures that the caller creates the file. The `open` is atomic, i.e. it's performed with just one function call. This protects against two programs creating the file at the same time. If the file already exists, `open` will fail.

Other possible values for `oflags` are documented in the `open` manual page, found in section 2 of the manual (use `man 2 open`).

`open` returns the new file descriptor (always a non-negative integer) if successful, or -1 if it fails, when `open` also sets the global variable `errno` to indicate the reason for the failure. We'll be looking at `errno` more closely in a later section. The new file descriptor is always the lowest numbered unused descriptor, a feature that can be quite useful in some circumstances. For example, if a program closes its standard output and then calls `open` again, the file descriptor 1 will be reused and the standard output will have been effectively redirected to a different file or device.

There is also a `creat` call standardized by POSIX, but is not often used. It doesn't only create the file, as one might expect, but also opens it – it's equivalent to calling `open` with `oflags` equal to `O_CREAT|O_WRONLY|O_TRUNC`.

Initial Permissions

When we create a file using the O_CREAT flag with open, we must use the three parameter form. mode, the third parameter, is made from a bitwise OR of the flags defined in the header file sys/stat.h. These are:

- S_IRUSR Read permission, owner.
- S_IWUSR Write permission, owner.
- S_IXUSR Execute permission, owner.
- S_IRGRP Read permission, group.
- S_IWGRP Write permission, group.
- S_IXGRP Execute permission, group.
- S_IROTH Read permission, others.
- S_IWOTH Write permission, others.
- S_IXOTH Execute permission, others.

For example,

```
open ("myfile", O_CREAT, S_IRUSR|S_IXOTH);
```

has the effect of creating a file called myfile, with read permission for the owner and execute permission for others, and only those permissions.

```
$ ls -ls myfile
0 -r-------x   1 neil     software        0 Sep 22 08:11 myfile*
```

There are a couple of factors which may affect the file permissions. Firstly, the permissions specified are only used if the file is being created. Secondly, the user mask (specified by the shell's umask command) affects the created file's permissions. The mode value given in the open call is ANDed with the inverse of the user mask value at run time. For example, if the user mask is set to 001 and the S_IXOTH mode flag is specified, the file won't be created with 'other' execute permission, because the user mask specifies that 'other' execute permission isn't to be provided. The flags in the open and creat calls are in fact requests to set permissions. Whether or not the requested permissions are set depends on the run-time value of umask.

umask

The umask is a system variable that encodes a mask for file permissions to be used when a file is created. You can change the variable by executing the umask command to supply a new value. The value is a three-digit octal value. Each digit is the result of ANDing values from 1, 2 or 4. The separate digits refer to 'user', 'group' and 'other' permissions, respectively. Thus:

Digit	Value	Meaning
1	0	No user permissions are to be disallowed
	4	User read permission is disallowed.
	2	User write permission is disallowed
	1	User execute permission is disallowed
2	0	No group permissions are to be disallowed
	4	Group read permission is disallowed
	2	Group write permission is disallowed
	1	Group execute permission is disallowed
3	0	No other permissions are to be disallowed
	4	Other read permission is disallowed
	2	Other write permission is disallowed
	1	Other execute permission is disallowed

For example, to block 'group' write and execute, and 'other' write, the umask would be:

Digit	Value
1	0
2	2
	1
3	2

Values for each digit are ANDed together; so digit 2 will have `2 & 1`, giving `3`. The resulting umask is `032`.

When we create a file via an `open` or `creat` call, the `mode` parameter is compared with the `umask`. Any bit setting in the `mode` parameter which is also set in the `umask` is removed. The end result of this is that the user can set up their environment to say 'Don't create any files with (say) write permission for others, even if the program creating the file requests that permission.' This doesn't prevent a program or user subsequently using the `chmod` command (or `chmod` system call in a program) to add other write permissions, but it does help protect the user by saving them from having to check and set permissions on all new files.

close

```
#include <unistd.h>

int close(int fildes);
```

We use `close` to terminate the association between a file descriptor, `fildes`, and its file. The file descriptor becomes available for reuse. It returns 0 if successful and -1 on error. Note that it can be important to check the return result from `close`. Some file systems, particularly networked ones, may not report an error writing to a file until the file is closed.

The number of files that any one running program may have open at once is limited. The limit, defined by the constant `OPEN_MAX` in `limits.h`, will vary from system to system, but POSIX requires that it be at least 16. This limit may itself be subject to local system-wide limits.

ioctl

```
#include <unistd.h>

int ioctl(int fildes, int cmd, ...);
```

ioctl is a bit of a rag-bag of things. It provides an interface for controlling the behavior of devices, their descriptors and configuring underlying services. Terminals, file descriptors, sockets, even tape drives may have ioctl calls defined for them and you need to refer to the specific device's man page for details. POSIX only defines ioctl for streams, which are beyond the scope of this book.

ioctl performs the function indicated by cmd on the object referenced by the descriptor fildes. It may take an optional third argument depending on the functions supported by a particular device.

Try It Out - A File Copy Program

We now know enough about the open, read and write system calls to write a low-level program, copy_system.c, to copy one file to another, character by character.

We'll do this in a number of ways during this chapter to compare the efficiency of each method. For brevity, we'll assume that the input file exists and the output file does not and that all reads and writes succeed. Of course, in real-life programs, we would check that these assumptions are valid!

```
#include <unistd.h>
#include <sys/stat.h>
#include <fcntl.h>
#include <stdlib.h>

int main()
{
    char c;
    int in, out;

    in = open("file.in", O_RDONLY);
    out = open("file.out", O_WRONLY|O_CREAT, S_IRUSR|S_IWUSR);
    while(read(in,&c,1) == 1)
        write(out,&c,1);

    exit(0);
}
```

Note that the #include <unistd.h> line must come first as it defines flags regarding POSIX compliance that may affect other include files.

First of all you will need to make a test input file, say 1Mb in size and name it file.in.

Running the program will give something like the following:

```
$ time copy_system
4.67user 146.90system 2:32.57elapsed 99%CPU
...
$ ls -ls file.in file.out
1029 -rw-r---r-   1 neil    users     1048576 Sep 17 10:46 file.in
1029 -rw-------   1 neil    users     1048576 Sep 17 10:51 file.out
```

Here we use the UNIX `time` facility to measure how long the program takes to run. We can see that the 1Mb input file, `file.in`, was successfully copied to `file.out` which was created with read/write permissions for owner only. However, the copy took two and a half minutes and consumed virtually all the CPU time. It was this slow because it had to make over two million system calls.

We can improve matters by copying in larger blocks. Take a look at this modified program, `copy_block.c`, which copies the files in 1k blocks, again using system calls:

```
#include <unistd.h>
#include <sys/stat.h>
#include <fcntl.h>
#include <stdlib.h>

int main()
{
    char block[1024];
    int in, out;
    int nread;

    in = open("file.in", O_RDONLY);
    out = open("file.out", O_WRONLY|O_CREAT, S_IRUSR|S_IWUSR);
    while((nread = read(in,block,sizeof(block))) > 0)
        write(out,block,nread);

    exit(0);
}
```

Now try the program, first removing the old output file:

```
$ rm file.out
$ time copy_block
0.01user 1.09system 0:01.90elapsed 57%CPU
...
$ ls -ls file.in file.out
1029 -rw-r--r--   1 neil    users     1048576 Sep 17 10:46 file.in
1029 -rw-------   1 neil    users     1048576 Sep 17 10:57 file.out
```

Now the program takes a little under two seconds as it only requires around 2000 system calls. Of course, these times are very system-dependent, but they do show that system calls have a measurable overhead, so it's worth optimizing their use.

Other System Calls for Managing Files

There are a number of other system calls that operate on these low-level file descriptors. These allow a program to control how a file is used and to return status information. We reference them here, so you can make use of them, but you may want to miss them out on a first reading.

lseek

```
#include <unistd.h>
#include <sys/types.h>

off_t lseek(int fildes, off_t offset, int whence);
```

The `lseek` system call sets the read/write pointer of a file descriptor, `fildes`, i.e. you can use it to set where in the file the next read or write will occur. You can set the pointer to an absolute location in the file or to a position relative to the current position or the end of file. The `offset` parameter is used to specify the position and the `whence` parameter specifies how the offset is used. `whence` can be one of the following:

- SEEK_SET `offset` is an absolute position
- SEEK_CUR `offset` is relative to the current position
- SEEK_END `offset` is relative to the end of the file

`lseek` returns the `offset` measured in bytes from the beginning of the file that the file pointer is set to, or -1 on failure. The type `off_t`, used for the `offset` in seek operations, is an implementation-dependent type defined in `sys/types.h`.

fstat, stat and lstat

```
#include <unistd.h>
#include <sys/stat.h>
#include <sys/types.h>

int fstat(int fildes, struct stat *buf);
int stat(const char *path, struct stat *buf);
int lstat(const char *path, struct stat *buf);
```

Note that the inclusion of `sys/types.h` is deemed 'optional, but sensible'.

The `fstat` system call returns status information about the file associated with an open file descriptor. The information is written to a structure, `buf`, the address of which is passed as a parameter.

The related functions `stat` and `lstat` return status information for a named file. They produce the same results, except when the file is a symbolic link. `lstat` returns information about the link itself, while `stat` returns information about the file that the link refers to.

The members of the structure, stat, may vary between UNIX systems, but will include:

stat Member	Description
st_mode	File permissions and file type information
st_ino	The inode associated with the file
st_dev	The device the file resides on
st_uid	The user identity of the file owner
st_gid	The group identity of the file owner
st_atime	The time of last access
st_ctime	The time of last change to permissions, owner, group or content
st_mtime	The time of last modification to contents
st_nlink	The number of hard links to the file

The st_mode flags returned in the stat structure also have a number of associated macros defined in the header file sys/stat.h. These macros include names for permission and file type flags and some masks to help with testing for specific types and permissions.

The permissions flags are the same as for the open system call above. File-type flags include:

- S_IFBLK Entry is a block special device.
- S_IFDIR Entry is a directory.
- S_IFCHR Entry is a character special device.
- S_IFIFO Entry is a FIFO (named pipe).
- S_IFREG Entry is a regular file.
- S_IFLNK Entry is a symbolic link.

Other mode flags include:

- S_ISUID Entry has setUID on execution.
- S_ISGID Entry has setGID on execution.

Masks to interpret the st_mode flags include:

- S_IFMT File type.
- S_IRWXU User read/write/execute permissions.
- S_IRWXG Group read/write/execute permissions.
- S_IRWXO Others read/write/execute permissions.

There are some macros defined to help with determining file types. These just compare suitably masked mode flags with a suitable device-type flag. These include:

- S_ISBLK Test for block special file.
- S_ISCHR Test for character special file.
- S_ISDIR Test for directory.
- S_ISFIFO Test for FIFO.
- S_ISREG Test for regular file.
- S_ISLNK Test for symbolic link.

For example, to test that a file doesn't represent a directory and has execute permission set for the owner and no other permissions, we can use the test:

```
struct stat statbuf;
mode_t modes;

stat("filename",&statbuf);
modes = statbuf.st_mode;

if(!S_ISDIR(modes) && (modes & S_IRWXU) == S_IXUSR)
    ...
```

dup and dup2

```
#include <unistd.h>

int dup(int fildes);
int dup2(int fildes, int fildes2);
```

The dup system calls provide a way of duplicating a file descriptor, giving two or more different descriptors that access the same file. These might be used for reading and writing to different locations in the file. The dup system call duplicates a file descriptor, fildes, returning a new descriptor. The dup2 system call effectively copies one file descriptor to another by specifying the descriptor to use for the copy.

These calls can also be useful when you're using multiple processes communicating via pipes. We'll meet the dup system call again in Chapter 11.

The Standard I/O Library

The standard I/O library and its header file stdio.h, provide a versatile interface to low-level I/O system calls. The library, now part of ANSI standard C whereas the system calls we met earlier are not, provides many sophisticated functions for formatting output and scanning input. It also takes care of the buffering requirements for devices.

In many ways, you use this library in the same way that you use low-level file descriptors. You need to open a file to establish an access path. This returns a value that is used as a parameter to other I/O library functions. The equivalent of the low-level file descriptor is called a **stream** and is implemented as a pointer to a structure, a FILE *.

Don't confuse these file streams with either C++ iostreams or with the **STREAMS** *paradigm of inter-process communication introduced in AT&T UNIX System V Release 3, which is beyond the scope of this book. For more information on* **STREAMS**, *check out the X/Open spec and the AT&T* **STREAMS** *Programming Guide that accompanies System V.*

Three file streams are automatically opened when a program is started. They are `stdin`, `stdout` and `stderr`. These are declared in `stdio.h` and represent the standard input, output and error output, respectively, which correspond to the low level file descriptors 0, 1 and 2.

In this next section, we'll look at:

- fopen, fclose
- fread, fwrite
- fflush
- fseek
- fgetc, getc, getchar
- fputc, putc, putchar
- fgets, gets
- printf, fprintf and sprintf
- scanf, fscanf and sscanf

fopen

```
#include <stdio.h>

FILE *fopen(const char *filename, const char *mode);
```

The `fopen` library function is the analog of the low level `open` system call. You use it mainly for files and terminal input and output. Where you need explicit control over devices, you're better off with the low-level system calls, as they eliminate potentially undesirable side effects from libraries, like input/output buffering.

`fopen` opens the file named by the `filename` parameter and associates a stream with it. The `mode` parameter specifies how the file is to be opened. It's one of the following strings:

- `"r"` or `"rb"` — Open for reading only
- `"w"` or `"wb"` — Open for writing, truncate to zero length
- `"a"` or `"ab"` — Open for writing, append to end of file
- `"r+"` or `"rb+"` or `"r+b"` — Open for update (reading and writing)
- `"w+"` or `"wb+"` or `"w+b"` — Open for update, truncate to zero length
- `"a+"` or `"ab+"` or `"a+b"` — Open for update, append to end of file

The `b` indicates that the file is a binary file rather than a text file. Note that, unlike DOS, UNIX doesn't make a distinction between text and binary files. It treats all files exactly the same, effectively as binary files. It's also important to note that the mode parameter must be a string, and not a character. Always use `"r"`, and never `'r'`.

If successful, fopen returns a non-null FILE * pointer. If it fails, it returns the value NULL, defined in stdio.h.

fread

```
#include <stdio.h>

size_t fread(void *ptr, size_t size, size_t nitems, FILE *stream);
```

The fread library function is used to read data from a file stream. Data is read into a data buffer given by ptr from the stream, stream. Both fread and fwrite deal with data records. These are specified by a record size, size, and a count, nitems, of records to transfer. It returns the number of items (rather than the number of bytes) successfully read into the data buffer. At the end of a file, fewer than nitems may be returned, including zero. As with all of the standard I/O functions that write to a buffer, it's the programmer's responsibility to allocate the space for the data and check for errors. See ferror and feof later in this chapter.

fwrite

```
#include <stdio.h>

size_t fwrite (const void *ptr, size_t size, size_t nitems, FILE *stream);
```

The fwrite library call has a similar interface to fread. It takes data records from the specified data buffer and writes them to the output stream. It returns the number of records successfully written.

> **Note that fread and fwrite are not recommended for use with structured data. Part of the problem is that files written with fwrite are potentially non-portable between different machines. We'll discuss further issues of portability in Appendix A.**

fclose

```
#include <stdio.h>

int fclose(FILE *stream);
```

The fclose library function closes the specified stream, causing any unwritten data to be written. It's important to use fclose, because the stdio library will buffer data. If the program needs to be sure that data has been completely written, it should call fclose. Note, however, that fclose is called automatically on all file streams that are still open when a program ends normally, but then of course you do not get a chance to check for errors reported by fclose. The number of available streams is limited, in the same way that file descriptors are limited, with the actual limit, FOPEN_MAX, defined in stdio.h, set to at least eight.

fflush

```
#include <stdio.h>

int fflush(FILE *stream);
```

The fflush library function causes all outstanding data on a file stream to be written immediately. You can use this to ensure that, for example, an interactive prompt has been sent to a terminal before any attempt to read a response. It's also useful for ensuring that important data has been committed to disk before continuing. You can sometimes use it when you're debugging a program to make sure that the program is writing data and not hanging. Note that an implied flush operation is carried out when fclose is called, so you don't need to call fflush before fclose.

fseek

```
#include <stdio.h>

int fseek(FILE *stream, long int offset, int whence);
```

The fseek function is the file stream equivalent of the lseek system call. It sets the position in the stream for the next read or write on that stream. The meaning and values of the offset and whence parameters are the same as those we gave for lseek above. However, where lseek returns an off_t, fseek returns an integer: 0 if it succeeds, -1 if it fails, with errno set to indicate the error. So much for standardization!

fgetc, getc, getchar

```
#include <stdio.h>

int fgetc(FILE *stream);
int getc(FILE *stream);
int getchar();
```

The fgetc function returns the next byte, as a character, from a file stream. When it reaches the end of the file or there is an error, it returns EOF. You must use ferror or feof to distinguish the two cases.

The getc function is equivalent to fgetc, except that you can implement it as a macro, in which case the stream argument must not have side effects (i.e. it can't affect variables that are neither local nor passed to the functions as parameters). Also, you can't then use the address of getc as a function pointer.

The getchar function is equivalent to getc(stdin) and reads the next character from the standard input.

fputc, putc, putchar

```
#include <stdio.h>

int fputc(int c, FILE *stream);
int putc(int c, FILE *stream);
int putchar(int c);
```

The fputc function writes a character to an output file stream. It returns the value it has written, or EOF on failure.

As with fgetc/getc, the function putc is equivalent to fputc, but you may implement it as a macro.

The putchar function is equivalent to putc(c,stdout), writing a single character to the standard output. Note that putchar takes and getchar returns characters as ints, not char. This allows the end of file (EOF) indicator to take the value -1, outside the range of character numbers codes.

fgets, gets

```
#include <stdio.h>

char *fgets(char *s, int n, FILE *stream);
char *gets(char *s);
```

The fgets function reads a string from an input file stream. It writes characters to the string pointed to by s until a newline is encountered, n-1 characters have been transferred or the end of file is reached, whichever occurs first. Any newline encountered is transferred to the receiving string and a terminating null byte, \0, is added. Only a maximum of n-1 characters are transferred in any one call, because the null byte must be added to finish the string, and make up the n bytes.

When it successfully completes, fgets returns a pointer to the string s. If the stream is at the end of a file, it sets the EOF indicator for the stream and fgets returns a null pointer. If a read error occurs, fgets returns a null pointer and sets errno to indicate the type of error.

The gets function is similar to fgets, except that it reads from the standard input and discards any newline encountered. It adds a trailing null byte to the receiving string. Note that gets doesn't limit the number of characters that can be transferred, so it could overrun its transfer buffer. Consequently, you should avoid using it and use fgets instead. Many security issues on the Internet can be traced back to programs that are made to overflow a buffer of some sort or another. This is one such, so be careful!

Formatted Input and Output

There are a number of library functions for producing output in a controlled fashion that you may be familiar with if you've programmed in C. These functions include printf and friends for printing values to a file stream and scanf *et al.* for reading values from a file stream.

printf, fprintf and sprintf

```
#include <stdio.h>

int printf(const char *format, ...);
int sprintf(char *s, const char *format, ...);
int fprintf(FILE *stream, const char *format, ...);
```

The printf family of functions format and output a variable number of arguments of different types. The way each is represented in the output stream is controlled by the format parameter, which is a string that contains ordinary characters to be printed and codes, called **conversion specifiers**, that indicate how and where the remaining arguments are to be printed.

The printf function produces its output on the standard output. The fprintf function produces its output on a specified stream. The sprintf function writes its output and a terminating null character into the string s passed as a parameter. This string must be large enough to contain all of the output. There are other members of the printf family that deal with their arguments in different ways. See the printf manual page for more details,

Ordinary characters are passed unchanged into the output. Conversion specifiers cause `printf` to fetch and format additional arguments passed as parameters. They always start with a `%` character. Here's a simple example,

```
printf("Some numbers: %d, %d, and %d\n", 1, 2, 3);
```

which produces, on the standard output:

```
Some numbers: 1, 2, and 3
```

To print a `%` character, we need to use `%%`, so that it doesn't get confused with a conversion specifier.

Here are some of the most commonly used conversion specifiers:

- `%d, %i` Print an integer in decimal.
- `%o, %x` Print an integer in octal, hexadecimal.
- `%c` Print a character.
- `%s` Print a string.
- `%f` Print a floating point (single precision) number.
- `%e` Print a double precision number, in fixed format.
- `%g` Print a double in a general format.

It's very important that the number and type of the arguments passed to `printf` match the conversion specifiers in the `format` string. An optional size specifier is used to indicate the type of integer arguments. This is either `h`, for example `%hd`, to indicate a `short int`, or `l`, for example `%ld`, to indicate a `long int`. Some compilers can check these `printf` statements, but they aren't infallible. If you are using the GNU compiler `gcc -Wformat` does this.

Here's another example:

```
char initial = 'A';
char *surname = "Matthew";
double age = 10.5;

printf("Hello Miss %c %s, aged %g\n", initial, surname, age);
```

This produces:

```
Hello Miss A Matthew, aged 10.5
```

You can gain greater control over the way items are printed by using field specifiers. These extend the conversion specifiers to include control over the spacing of the output. A common use is to set the number of decimal places for a floating point number, or to set the amount of space around a string.

Field specifiers are given as numbers immediately after the `%` character in a conversion specifier. Here are some more examples of conversion specifiers and resulting output. To make things a little clearer, we'll use vertical bars to show the limits of the output.

Format	Argument	Output
`%10s`	`"Hello"`	`|     Hello|`
`%-10s`	`"Hello"`	`|Hello     |`
`%10d`	`1234`	`|      1234|`
`%-10d`	`1234`	`|1234      |`
`%010d`	`1234`	`|0000001234|`
`%10.4f`	`12.34`	`|   12.3400|`
`%*s`	`10,"Hello"`	`|     Hello|`

All of these examples have been printed in a field width of ten characters. Note that a negative field width means that the item is written left-justified within the field. A variable field width is indicated by using an asterisk, `*`. In this case, the next argument is used for the width. A leading zero indicates the item is written with leading zeros. According to the POSIX specification, `printf` doesn't truncate fields; rather it expands the field to fit. So, for example if we try to print a string longer than the field, the field grows:

Format	Argument	Output
`%10s`	`"HelloTherePeeps"`	`|HelloTherePeeps|`

The `printf` functions return an integer, the number of characters written. This doesn't include the terminating `null` in the case of `sprintf`. On error, these functions return a negative value and set `errno`.

scanf, fscanf and sscanf

```
#include <stdio.h>

int scanf(const char *format, ...);
int fscanf(FILE *stream, const char *format, ...);
int sscanf(const char *s, const char *format, ...);
```

The `scanf` family of functions work in a similar way to the `printf` group, except that they read items from a stream and place values into variables at the addresses they're passed as pointer parameters. They use a format string to control the input conversion in the same way and many of the conversion specifiers are the same.

It's very important that the variables used to hold the values scanned in by the `scanf` functions are of the correct type and that they match the format string precisely. If they don't, your memory could be corrupted and your program could crash. There won't be any compiler errors, but if you're lucky, you might get a warning!

The format string for `scanf` and friends contains both ordinary characters and conversion specifiers, as for `printf`. However, the ordinary characters are used to specify characters that must be present in the input.

Here is a simple example:

```
int num;
scanf("Hello %d", &num);
```

This call to `scanf` will only succeed if the next five characters on the standard input match "`Hello`". Then, if the next characters form a recognizable decimal number, the number will be read and the value assigned to the variable num. A space in the format string is used to ignore all whitespace (spaces, tabs, form feeds and newlines) in the input between conversion specifiers. This means that the call to `scanf` will succeed and place `1234` into the variable num given either of the following inputs.

```
Hello      1234
Hello1234
```

Whitespace is also usually ignored in the input when a conversion begins. This means that a format string of `%d` will keep reading the input, skipping over spaces and newlines until a sequence of digits is found. If the expected characters are not present, the conversion fails and `scanf` returns. This can lead to problems if you are not careful, an infinite loop can occur in your program if you leave a non-digit character in the input while scanning for integers.

Other conversion specifiers are:

- `%d` Scan a decimal integer.
- `%o`, `%x` Scan an octal, hexadecimal integer.
- `%f`, `%e`, `%g` Scan a floating point number.
- `%c` Scan a character (whitespace not skipped).
- `%s` Scan a string.
- `%[]` Scan a set of characters (see below).
- `%%` Scan a % character.

Like `printf`, `scanf` conversion specifiers may also have a field width to limit the amount of input consumed. A size specifier (either `h` for short or `l` for long) indicates whether the receiving argument is shorter or longer than the default. This means that `%hd` indicates a `short int`, `%ld` a `long int`, and `%lg` a double precision floating point number.

A specifier beginning `*` indicates that the item is to be ignored, that is not written into a receiving argument.

We use the `%c` specifier to read a single character in the input. This doesn't skip initial whitespace characters.

We use the `%s` specifier to scan strings, but we must take care. It will skip leading whitespace, but stops at the first whitespace character in the string, so we're better using it for reading words, rather than general strings. Also, without a field-width specifier, there's no limit to the length of string it might read, so the receiving string must be sufficient to hold the longest string in the input stream. It's better to use a field specifier, or to use a combination of `fgets` and `sscanf` to read in a line of input and scan that.

We use the %[] specifier to read a string composed of characters from a set. The format %[A-Z] will read a string of capital letters. If the first character in the set is a caret, ^, the specifier reads a string that consists of characters not in the set. So, to read a string with spaces in it, but stopping at the first comma, we can use %[^,].

Given the input line,

```
Hello, 1234, 5.678, X, string to the end of the line
```

this call to scanf will correctly scan four items:

```
char s[256];
int n;
float f;
char c;

scanf("Hello,%d,%g, %c, %[^\n]", &n,&f,&c,s);
```

The scanf functions return the number of items successfully read, which will be zero if the first item fails. If the end of the input is reached before the first item is matched, EOF is returned. If a read error occurs on the file stream, the stream error flag will be set and the error variable, errno, will be set to indicate the type of error. See the section on stream errors below for more details.

In general, scanf and friends are not highly regarded, for three reasons:

- Traditionally, the implementations have been buggy.
- They're inflexible to use.
- They lead to code where it's very difficult to work out what is being parsed.

Try to use other functions, like fread or fgets to read input lines and the string functions to break the input into the items you need.

Other Stream Functions

There are a number of other stdio library functions that use either stream parameters or the standard streams stdin, stdout, stderr:

- fgetpos Get the current position in a file stream.
- fsetpos Set the current position in a file stream.
- ftell Return the current file offset in a stream.
- rewind Reset the file position in a stream.
- freopen Reuse a file stream.
- setvbuf Set the buffering scheme for a stream.
- remove Equivalent to unlink, unless the path parameter is a directory in which case it's equivalent to rmdir.

These are all library functions documented in section 3 of the UNIX man pages.

You can use the file stream functions to re-implement the file copy program, but using library functions. Take a look at copy_stdio.c.

Try It Out - Another File Copy Program

The program is very similar to earlier versions, but the character-by-character copy is accomplished using calls to the functions referenced in `stdio.h`:

```
#include <stdio.h>
#include <stdlib.h>

int main()
{
    int c;
    FILE *in, *out;

    in = fopen("file.in","r");
    out = fopen("file.out","w");

    while((c = fgetc(in)) != EOF)
        fputc(c,out);

    exit(0);
}
```

Running this program as before, we get:

```
$ time copy_stdio
1.69user 0.78system 0:03.70elapsed 66%CPU
```

This time, the program runs in 3.7 seconds, not as fast as the low level block version, but a great deal better than the other single character at a time version. This is because the `stdio` library maintains an internal buffer within the `FILE` structure and the low level system calls are only made when the buffer fills. Feel free to experiment yourself with testing line-by-line and block `stdio` copying code to see how they perform, relative to the three examples we've tested here.

Stream Errors

To indicate an error, many of the `stdio` library functions return out of range values, such as null pointers or the constant `EOF`. In these cases, the error is indicated in the external variable `errno`:

```
#include <errno.h>

extern int errno;
```

Note that many functions may change the value of `errno`. Its value is only valid when a function has failed. You should inspect it immediately after a function has indicated failure. You should always copy it into another variable before using it, because printing functions, such as `fprintf`, might alter `errno` themselves.

You can also interrogate the state of a file stream to determine whether an error has occurred, or the end of file has been reached.

```
#include <stdio.h>

int ferror(FILE *stream);
int feof(FILE *stream);
void clearerr(FILE *stream);
```

The `ferror` function tests the error indicator for a stream and returns non-zero if it's set, zero otherwise.

The `feof` function tests the end-of-file indicator within a stream and returns non-zero if it is set, zero otherwise. You use it like this:

```
if(feof(some_stream))
    /* We're at the end */
```

The `clearerr` function clears the end-of-file and error indicators for the stream to which `stream` points. It has no return value and no errors are defined. You can use it to recover from error conditions on streams. One example might be to resume writing to a stream after a disk full error has been resolved.

Streams and File Descriptors

Each file stream is associated with a low level file descriptor. You can mix low-level input and output operations with higher level stream operations, but this is generally unwise, as the effects of buffering can be difficult to predict.

```
#include <stdio.h>

int fileno(FILE *stream);
FILE *fdopen(int fildes, const char *mode);
```

We can determine which low-level file descriptor is being used for a file stream by calling the `fileno` function. It returns the file descriptor for a given stream, or -1 on failure. This can be a useful function to use if you need low-level access to an open stream, for example to call `fstat` on it.

We can create a new file stream based on an already opened file descriptor by calling the `fdopen` function. Essentially, this function is providing `stdio` buffers around an already open file descriptor, which might be an easier way to explain it.

The `fdopen` function operates in the same way as the `fopen` function, but, instead of a file name, it takes a low level file descriptor. This can be useful if we have used `open` to create a file, perhaps to get fine control over the permissions, but want to use a stream for writing to it. The `mode` parameter is the same as for the `fopen` function and must be compatible with the file access modes established when the file was originally opened. `fdopen` returns the new file stream or `NULL` on failure.

File and Directory Maintenance

The standard libraries and system calls provide complete control over the creation and maintenance of files and directories.

chmod

You can change the permissions on a file or directory using the chmod system call. This forms the basis of the chmod shell program.

```
#include <sys/stat.h>

int chmod(const char *path, mode_t mode);
```

The file specified by path is changed to have the permissions given by mode. The modes are specified as in the open system call, a bitwise OR of required permissions. Unless the program has been given appropriate privileges, only the owner of the file or a superuser can change its permissions.

chown

A superuser can change the owner of a file using the chown system call.

```
#include <unistd.h>

int chown(const char *path, uid_t owner, gid_t group);
```

The call uses the numeric values of the user and group IDs (culled from getuid and getgid calls) and a constant which can restrict who can change file ownership. The owner and group of a file are changed if the appropriate privileges are set.

POSIX actually allows systems where non-superusers can change file ownerships. All 'proper' POSIX systems won't allow this, but, strictly speaking, it's an extension (for FIPS 151-2). The kind of systems we'll be dealing with in this book are XSI (X/Open System Interface) conformant and they do enforce ownership rules.

unlink, link, symlink

We can remove a file using unlink.

```
#include <unistd.h>

int unlink(const char *path);
int link(const char *path1, const char *path2);
int symlink(const char *path1, const char *path2);
```

The unlink system call removes the directory entry for a file decrements the link count for it. It returns 0 if the unlinking was successful, -1 on an error. You must have write and execute permissions in the directory where the file has its directory entry for this call to function.

If the count reaches zero and no process has the file open, the file is deleted. In actual fact, the directory entry is always removed, but the file's space will not be recovered until the last process (if any) closes it. The rm program uses this call. Additional links represent alternative names for a file, normally created by the ln program. We can create new links to a file programmatically by using the link system call.

Creating a file with open and then calling unlink on it is a trick some programmers use to create transient files. These files are available to the program only while they are open, they will effectively be automatically deleted when the program exits and the file is closed.

The link system call creates a new link to an existing file, path1. The new directory entry is specified by path2. We can create symbolic links using the symlink system call in a similar fashion. Note that symbolic links to a file do not prevent the file from being effectively deleted as normal (hard) links do.

mkdir, rmdir

We can create and remove directories using the mkdir and rmdir system calls.

```
#include <sys/stat.h>

int mkdir(const char *path, mode_t mode);
```

The mkdir system call is used for creating directories and is the equivalent of the mkdir program. mkdir makes a new directory with path as its name. The directory permissions are passed in the parameter mode and are given as in the O_CREAT option of the open system call and, again, subject to umask.

```
#include <unistd.h>

int rmdir(const char *path);
```

The rmdir system call removes directories, but only if they are empty. The rmdir program uses this system call to do its job.

chdir, getcwd

A program can navigate directories in much the same way as a user moves around the UNIX file system. As we use the cd command in the shell to change directory, so a program can use the chdir system call.

```
#include <unistd.h>

int chdir(const char *path);
```

A program can determine its current working directory by calling the getcwd function.

```
#include <unistd.h>

char *getcwd(char *buf, size_t size);
```

The getcwd function writes the name of the current directory into the given buffer, buf. It returns null if the directory name would exceed the size of the buffer (an ERANGE error), given as the parameter size. It returns buf on success.

> getcwd **may also return** null **if the directory is removed (**EINVAL**) or permissions changed (**EACCESS**) while the program is running.**

Scanning Directories

A common problem on UNIX systems is scanning directories, i.e. determining the files that reside in a particular directory. In shell programs, it's easy – just let the shell expand a wildcard expression. In the past, different UNIX variants have allowed programmatic access to the low-level file system structure. We can, still, open a directory as a regular file and directly read the directory entries, but different file system structures and implementations have made this approach non-portable. A standard suite of library functions has now been developed that make directory scanning much simpler.

The directory functions are declared in a header file, `dirent.h`. They use a structure, `DIR`, as a basis for directory manipulation. A pointer to this structure, called a **directory stream** (a `DIR *`), acts in much the same way as a file steam (`FILE *`) does for regular file manipulation. Directory entries themselves are returned in `dirent` structures, also declared in `dirent.h`, as one should never alter the fields in the `DIR` structure directly.

We'll review these functions:

- opendir, closedir
- readdir
- telldir
- seekdir

opendir

The `opendir` function opens a directory and establishes a directory stream. If successful, it returns a pointer to a `DIR` structure to be used for reading directory entries.

```
#include <sys/types.h>
#include <dirent.h>

DIR *opendir(const char *name);
```

`opendir` returns a null pointer on failure. Note that a directory stream uses a low-level file descriptor to access the directory itself; so `opendir` could fail with too many open files.

readdir

```
#include <sys/types.h>
#include <dirent.h>

struct dirent *readdir(DIR *dirp);
```

The `readdir` function returns a pointer to a structure detailing the next directory entry in the directory stream `dirp`. Successive calls to `readdir` return further directory entries. On error, and at the end of the directory, `readdir` returns `NULL`. POSIX compliant systems leave `errno` unchanged when returning `NULL` at end of directory and set it when an error occurs.

Note that readdir scanning isn't guaranteed to list all the files (and subdirectories) in a directory if there are other processes creating and deleting files in the directory at the same time.

The dirent structure containing directory entry details includes the following entries:

- ino_t d_ino The inode of the file.
- char d_name[] The name of the file.

To determine further details of a file in a directory, we need a call to stat.

telldir

```
#include <sys/types.h>
#include <dirent.h>

long int telldir(DIR *dirp);
```

The telldir function returns a value that records the current position in a directory stream. You can use this in subsequent calls to seekdir to reset a directory scan to the current position.

seekdir

```
#include <sys/types.h>
#include <dirent.h>

void seekdir(DIR *dirp, long int loc);
```

The seekdir function sets the directory entry pointer in the directory stream given by dirp. The value of loc, used to set the position, should have been obtained from a prior call to telldir.

closedir

```
#include <sys/types.h>
#include <dirent.h>

int closedir(DIR *dirp);
```

The closedir function closes a directory stream and frees up the resources associated with it. It returns 0 on success and -1 if there is an error.

In the next program, printdir.c, we put together a lot of the file manipulation functions to create a simple directory listing. Each file in a directory is listed on a line by itself. Each subdirectory has its name, followed by a slash and the files in it are listed indented by four spaces.

The program changes directory into the subdirectories so that the files it finds have usable names, i.e. they can be passed directly to opendir. The program will fail on very deeply nested directory structures, because there's a limit on the allowed number of open directory streams.

We could, of course, make it more general by taking a command line argument to specify the start point. Check out the Linux source code of such utilities as ls and find for ideas on a more general implementation.

Try It Out - A Directory Scanning Program

1. We start with the appropriate headers and then a function, `printdir`, which prints out the current directory. It will recurse for subdirectories, using the `depth` parameter for indentation.

```
#include <unistd.h>
#include <stdio.h>
#include <dirent.h>
#include <string.h>
#include <sys/stat.h>
#include <stdlib.h>

void printdir(char *dir, int depth)
{
    DIR *dp;
    struct dirent *entry;
    struct stat statbuf;

    if((dp = opendir(dir)) == NULL) {
        fprintf(stderr,"cannot open directory: %s\n", dir);
        return;
    }
    chdir(dir);
    while((entry = readdir(dp)) != NULL) {
        lstat(entry->d_name,&statbuf);
        if(S_ISDIR(statbuf.st_mode)) {
            /* Found a directory, but ignore . and .. */
            if(strcmp(".",entry->d_name) == 0 ||
                strcmp("..",entry->d_name) == 0)
                continue;
            printf("%*s%s/\n",depth,"",entry->d_name);
            /* Recurse at a new indent level */
            printdir(entry->d_name,depth+4);
        }
        else printf("%*s%s\n",depth,"",entry->d_name);
    }
    chdir("..");
    closedir(dp);
}
```

2. Now we move onto the `main` function:

```
int main()
{
    printf("Directory scan of /home/neil:\n");
    printdir("/home/neil",0);
    printf("done.\n");

    exit(0);
}
```

The program produces output like this (edited for brevity):

```
$ printdir
Directory scan of /home/neil:
.less
.lessrc
.term/
    termrc
.elm/
    elmrc
Mail/
    received
    mbox
.bash_history
.fvwmrc
.tin/
    .mailidx/
    .index/
        563.1
        563.2
posted
attributes
active
tinrc
done.
```

How It Works

Most of the action is within the `printdir` function, so that's where we'll look. After some initial error checking, using `opendir`, to see that the directory exists, `printdir` makes a call to `chdir` to the directory specified. While the entries returned by `readdir` aren't null, the program checks to see whether the entry is a directory. If it isn't, it prints the file entry with indentation `depth`.

If the entry *is* a directory, we meet a little bit of recursion. After the `.` and `..` entries (the current and parent directories) have been ignored, the `printdir` function calls itself and goes through the same process again. How does it get out of these loops? Once the `while` loop has finished, the call `chdir("..")` takes it back up the directory tree and the previous listing can continue. Calling `closedir(dp)` makes sure that the number of open directory streams isn't higher than it needs to be.

As a taster for the discussion of the UNIX environment in Chapter 4, let's look at one way we can make the program more general. The program is limited because it's specific to the directory `/home/neil`. With the following changes to `main`, we could turn it into a more useful directory browser:

```
int main(int argc, char* argv[])
{
    char *topdir = ".";
    if (argc >= 2)
        topdir=argv[1];

    printf("Directory scan of %s\n",topdir);
    printdir(topdir,0);
    printf("done.\n");

    exit(0);
}
```

We've changed three lines and added five, but now it's a general-purpose utility with an optional parameter of the directory name, which defaults to the current directory. You can run it using the command:

```
$ printdir /usr/local | more
```

The output will be paged so that the user can page back and forth through the output. Hence, the user has quite a convenient little general-purpose directory tree browser. With very little effort, you could add space usage statistics, limit depth of display, and so on.

Errors

As we've seen, many of the system calls and functions described in this chapter can fail for a number of reasons. When they do, they indicate the reason for their failure by setting the value of the external variable `errno`. This variable is used by many different libraries as a standard way to report problems. It bears repeating that the program must inspect the `errno` variable immediately after the function giving problems, since it may be overwritten by the next function called, even if that function itself doesn't fail.

The values and meanings of the errors are listed in the header file `errno.h`. They include:

- `EPERM` Operation not permitted
- `ENOENT` No such file or directory
- `EINTR` Interrupted system call
- `EIO` I/O Error
- `EBUSY` Device or resource busy
- `EEXIST` File exists
- `EINVAL` Invalid argument
- `EMFILE` Too many open files
- `ENODEV` No such device
- `EISDIR` Is a directory
- `ENOTDIR` Isn't a directory

There are a couple of useful functions for reporting errors when they occur: `strerror` and `perror`.

```
#include <string.h>

char *strerror(int errnum);
```

The `strerror` function maps an error number into a string describing the type of error that has occurred. This can be useful for logging error conditions.

```
#include <stdio.h>

void perror(const char *s);
```

The perror function also maps the current error, as reported in errno, into a string and prints it on the standard error stream. It's preceded by the message given in the string s (if not null), followed by a colon and a space. For example,

```
perror("program");
```

might give the following on the standard error output:

```
program: Too many open files
```

Advanced Topics

Here, we'll cover a couple of topics that you might like to skip because they're seldom used. Having said that, we've put them here for your reference because they can provide simple solutions to some tricky problems.

fcntl

The fcntl system call provides further ways to manipulate low level file descriptors.

```
#include <fcntl.h>

int fcntl(int fildes, int cmd);
int fcntl(int fildes, int cmd, long arg);
```

You can perform several miscellaneous operations on open file descriptors with the fcntl system call, including duplicating them, getting and setting file descriptor flags, getting and setting file status flags and managing advisory file locking.

The various operations are selected by different values of the command parameter, cmd as defined in fcntl.h. Depending on the command chosen, the system call will require a third parameter, arg.

The call,

```
fcntl(fildes, F_DUPFD, newfd);
```

returns a new file descriptor with a numerical value equal to or greater than the integer newfd. The new descriptor is a copy of the descriptor fildes. Depending on the number of open files and the value of newfd, this can be effectively the same as dup(fildes).

The call,

```
fcntl(fildes, F_GETFD)
```

returns the file descriptor flags as defined in fcntl.h. These include FD_CLOEXEC, which determines whether or not the file descriptor is closed after a successful call to one of the exec family of system calls.

The call,

```
fcntl(fildes, F_SETFD, flags)
```

is used to set the file descriptor flags, usually just FD_CLOEXEC.

The calls,

```
fcntl(fildes, F_GETFL)
fcntl(fildes, F_SETFL, flags)
```

respectively get and set the file status flags and access modes. You can extract the file access modes by using the mask `O_ACCMODE` defined in `fcntl.h`. Other flags include those passed in a third argument to `open` when used with `O_CREAT`. Note that you can't set all flags. In particular, you can't set file permissions using `fcntl`.

You can also implement advisory file locking via `fcntl`. Refer to section 2 of the `man` pages for more information, or wait for Chapter 7, where we'll be discussing file locking.

mmap

UNIX provides a useful facility that allows programs to share memory, and the good news is that it's been included in version 2.0 of the Linux kernel. The `mmap` (for memory map) function sets up a segment of memory that can be read or written by two or more programs. Changes made by one program are seen by the others.

You can use the same facility to manipulate files. You can make the entire contents of a disk file look as if it's an array in memory. If the file consists of records that can be described by C structures, you can update the file using structure array accesses.

This is made possible by the use of virtual memory segments that have special permissions set. Reading from and writing to the segment causes the operating system to read and write the appropriate part of the disk file.

The `mmap` function creates a pointer to a region of memory associated with the contents of the file accessed through an open file descriptor.

```
#include <sys/mman.h>

void *mmap(void *addr, size_t len, int prot, int flags, int fildes, off_t off);
```

You can alter the start of the file data that is accessed by the shared segment by passing the `off` parameter. The open file descriptor is passed as `fildes`. The amount of data that can be accessed (i.e. the length of the memory segment) is set via the `len` parameter.

You can use the `addr` parameter to request a particular memory address. If it's zero, the resulting pointer is allocated automatically. This is the recommended usage as it is difficult to be portable otherwise, systems vary as to the available address ranges.

The `prot` parameter is used to set access permissions for the memory segment. This is a bitwise OR of the following constant values.

- `PROT_READ` The segment can be read.
- `PROT_WRITE` The segment can be written.
- `PROT_EXEC` The segment can be executed.
- `PROT_NONE` The segment can't be accessed.

The `flags` parameter controls how changes made to the segment by the program are reflected elsewhere.

MAP_PRIVATE	The segment is private, changes are local.
MAP_SHARED	The segment changes are made in the file.
MAP_FIXED	The segment must be at the given address, addr.

The `msync` function causes the changes in part or all of the memory segment to be written back to (or read from) the mapped file.

```
#include <sys/mman.h>

int msync(void *addr, size_t len, int flags);
```

The part of the segment to be updated is given by the passed start address, `addr`, and length, `len`. The `flags` parameter controls how the update should be performed.

MS_ASYNC	Perform asynchronous writes.
MS_SYNC	Perform synchronous writes.
MS_INVALIDATE	Read data back in from the file.

The `munmap` function releases the memory segment.

```
#include <sys/mman.h>

int munmap(void *addr, size_t len);
```

The following program, `mmap_eg.c`, shows a file of structures being updated using `mmap` and array-style accesses. Unfortunately, Linux kernels before 2.0 don't fully support this use of `mmap`. The program does work correctly on Sun Solaris and other systems.

Try It Out - Using mmap

1. We start by defining a `RECORD` structure and then create `NRECORDS` versions each recording their number. These are appended to the file `records.dat`.

```
#include <unistd.h>
#include <stdio.h>
#include <sys/mman.h>
#include <fcntl.h>
#include <stdlib.h>

typedef struct {
    int integer;
    char string[24];
} RECORD;

#define NRECORDS (100)

int main()
{
    RECORD record, *mapped;
    int i, f;
    FILE *fp;
```

```
    fp = fopen("records.dat","w+");
    for(i=0; i<NRECORDS; i++) {
        record.integer = i;
        sprintf(record.string,"RECORD-%d",i);
        fwrite(&record,sizeof(record),1,fp);
    }
    fclose(fp);
```

2. We now change the integer value of record 43 to 143, and write this to the 43rd record's string:

```
    fp = fopen("records.dat","r+");
    fseek(fp,43*sizeof(record),SEEK_SET);
    fread(&record,sizeof(record),1,fp);

    record.integer = 143;
    sprintf(record.string,"RECORD-%d",record.integer);

    fseek(fp,43*sizeof(record),SEEK_SET);
    fwrite(&record,sizeof(record),1,fp);
    fclose(fp);
```

3. We now map the records into memory and access the 43rd record in order to change the integer to 243 (and update the record string), again using memory mapping:

```
    f = open("records.dat",O_RDWR);
    mapped = (RECORD *)mmap(0, NRECORDS*sizeof(record),
                          PROT_READ|PROT_WRITE, MAP_SHARED, f, 0);

    mapped[43].integer = 243;
    sprintf(mapped[43].string,"RECORD-%d",mapped[43].integer);

    msync((void *)mapped, NRECORDS*sizeof(record), MS_ASYNC);
    munmap((void *)mapped, NRECORDS*sizeof(record));
    close(f);

    exit(0);
}
```

Later, we'll meet another shared memory facility: System V shared memory.

Summary

In this chapter, we've seen how UNIX provides direct access to files and devices. We've seen how library functions build upon these low-level functions to provide flexible solutions to programming problems. In consequence, we've been able to write a fairly powerful directory-scanning routine in just a few lines of code.

We've also learned enough about file and directory handling to convert the fledgling CD application that we created at the end of Chapter 2 to a C program, using a more structured file-based solution. At this stage, however, we could add no new functionality to the program, so we'll postpone our rewrite until we've learned how to handle the screen and keyboard, which is the subject of the next two chapters.

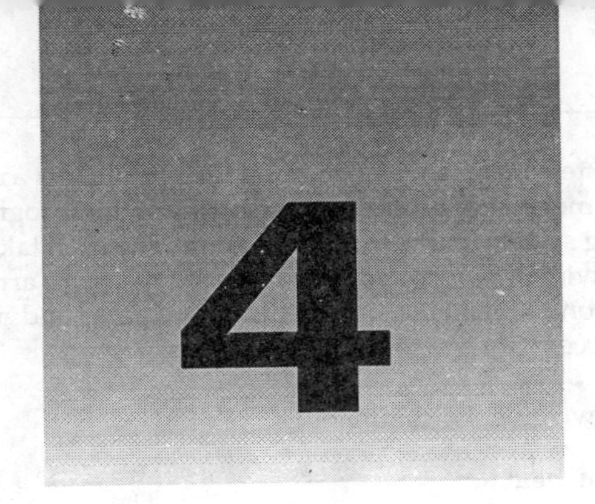

The UNIX Environment

When we write a program for UNIX, we have to take into account that the program will run in a **multitasking environment**. This means that there will be other programs running at the same time sharing the machine resources such as memory, disk space and CPU time. There may even be several instances of the same program running at the same time. It's important that these programs don't interfere with one another, are aware of their surroundings and can act appropriately.

In this chapter, we will consider the environment that programs operate in, how they can use that environment to gain information about operating conditions and how users of the programs can alter their behavior. In particular, we'll be looking at:

- Passing arguments to programs
- Environment variables
- Finding out what the time is
- Temporary files
- Getting information about the user and the host computer
- Causing and configuring log messages
- Discovering the limits imposed by the system

Program Arguments

When a UNIX program written in C runs, it starts at the function `main`. For UNIX programs, `main` is declared as,

```
int main(int argc, char *argv[])
```

where `argc` is a count of the program arguments and `argv` is an array of character strings representing the arguments themselves.

You might also see UNIX programs declaring `main` as:

```
main()
```

This will still work, as the return type will default to `int` and formal parameters that are not used in a function need not be declared. `argc` and `argv` are still there, but if you don't declare them, you can't use them.

Whenever the operating system starts a new program, the parameters argc and argv are set up and passed to main. These parameters are usually supplied by another program, very often the shell that has requested that the operating system start the new program. The shell takes the command line that it's given, breaks it up into individual words and uses these for the argv array. Remember that a UNIX shell performs wild card expansion of file name arguments before argc and argv are set, whereas the DOS shell expects programs to accept arguments with wild cards.

For example, if in the shell, we give the command,

```
$ myprog left right 'and center'
```

the program myprog will be started at main, with parameters:

```
argc: 4
argv: {"myprog", "left", "right", "and center"}
```

Note that the argument count includes the name of the program itself and the argv array contains the program name as its first element, argv[0]. Because we used quotes in the shell command, the fourth argument consists of a string containing spaces.

You'll be familiar with all of this if you've programmed in ISO/ANSI C. The arguments to main correspond to the positional parameters in shell scripts, $0, $1, and so on. Although ISO/ANSI C leaves open the return type of main (it may be void or int), the X/Open specification does contain the explicit declaration given above.

Command line arguments are useful for passing information to programs. We could use them in a database application to pass the name of the database we wish to use. This would allow us to use the same program on more than one database. Many utility programs also use command line arguments to change their behavior or to set options. You would usually set these so-called **flags** or **switches** using command line arguments that begin with a dash. For example, the sort program takes a -r switch to reverse the normal sort order:

```
$ sort -r file
```

Command line options are very common and using them consistently will be a real help to those who use your program. In the past, each utility program adopted its own approach to command line options, which led to some confusion. For example, take a look at the way these commands take parameters:

```
$ tar cvfB /tmp/file.tar 1024
$ dd if=/dev/fd0 of=/tmp/file.dd bs=18k
$ ls -lstr
$ ls -l -s -t -r
```

Another little foible of some programs is to make the option +x (for example) perform the opposite function to -x.

Remembering the order and meaning of all these program options is difficult enough without having to cope with idiosyncratic formats. Often the only recourse is to a -h (help) option or a man page, if the programmer has provided one. As we'll soon see, there's a neat solution to these problems, provided by getopt. For the moment, though, let's just look at dealing with program arguments as they are passed.

Try It Out - Program Arguments

Here's a program, `args.c`, that examines its own arguments:

```
#include <stdio.h>

int main(int argc, char *argv[])
{
    int arg;

    for(arg = 0; arg < argc; arg++) {
        if(argv[arg][0] == '-')
            printf("option: %s\n", argv[arg]+1);
        else
            printf("argument %d: %s\n", arg, argv[arg]);
    }
    exit(0);
}
```

When we run this program, it just prints out its arguments and detects options. The intention is that the program takes a string argument and an optional file name argument introduced by a `-f` option. Other options might also be defined:

```
$ ./args -i -lr 'hi there' -f fred.c
argument 0: args
option: i
option: lr
argument 3: hi there
option: f
argument 5: fred.c
```

How It Works

The program simply uses the argument count, `argc`, to set up a loop to examine all of the program arguments. It detects options by looking for an initial dash.

In this example, if we intended the options `-l` and `-r` to be available, we've missed the fact that the `-lr` perhaps ought to be treated the same as `-l -r`.

The X/Open specification defines a standard usage for command line options (the Utility Syntax Guidelines) and also provides a standard programming interface for providing command line switches in C programs: the `getopt` function.

All command line switches should start with a dash and consist of a single letter or number. Options that take no further argument can be grouped together behind one dash. So, the two `ls` examples we met earlier do follow the guidelines. Each option should be followed by any value it requires as a separate argument. The `dd` example breaks this rule; the `tar` example separates options and their values completely!

getopt

To help us adhere to these guidelines, Linux gives us the `getopt` facility, which supports the use of options with and without values and is simple to use.

```
#include <unistd.h>

int getopt(int argc, char *const argv[], const char *optstring);
extern char *optarg;
extern int optind, opterr, optopt;
```

The getopt function takes the argc and argv parameters as passed to the program's main function and an options specifier string. This string tells getopt what options are defined for the program and whether or not they have associated values. The optstring is simply a list of characters, each representing a single character option. If a character is followed by a colon, it indicates that the option has an associated value which will be taken as the next argument. The getopts command in bash performs a very similar function.

The call,

```
getopt(argc, argv, "if:lr");
```

would be used to handle our example above. It allows for simple options -i, -l , -r and -f, followed by a filename argument. Calling the command with the same parameters but in a different order will alter the behavior. Try it out when we get to the sample code on the following page.

The return result for getopt is the next option character found in the argv array (if there is one). We call getopt repeatedly to get each option in turn. It has the following behavior:

If the option takes a value, that value is pointed to by the external variable optarg.

getopt returns -1 when there are no more options to process. A special argument, --, will cause getopt to stop scanning for options.

It returns ? if there is an unrecognized option, which it stores in the external variable optopt.

If an option requires a value (such as -f in our example) and no value is given, getopt returns :.

The external variable, optind, is set to the index of the next argument to process. getopt uses it to remember how far it's got. Programs would rarely need to set this variable. When all the option arguments have been processed, optind indicates where the remaining arguments can be found at the end of the argv array.

Some versions of getopt will stop at the first non-option argument, returning -1 and setting optind. Others, such as that provided with Linux, can process options wherever they occur in the program arguments. Note that, in this case, getopt effectively rewrites the argv array so that all of the non-option arguments are presented together, starting at argv[optind]. For the GNU version of getopt this behavior is controlled by the POSIXLY_CORRECT environment variable. If set, getopt will stop at the first non-option argument. Additionally, some getopt implementations also print error messages for unknown options. Note that the POSIX specification says that, if the opterr variable is non-zero, getopt will print an error message to stderr. We'll see an example of both these behaviors in a little while.

Try It Out - getopt

Let's use getopt for our example and call the new program argopt.c:

```
#include <stdio.h>
#include <unistd.h>

int main(int argc, char *argv[])
{
    int opt;
```

```
while((opt = getopt(argc, argv, "if:lr")) != -1) {
        switch(opt) {
        case 'i':
        case 'l':
        case 'r':
            printf("option: %c\n", opt);
            break;
        case 'f':
            printf("filename: %s\n", optarg);
            break;
        case ':':
            printf("option needs a value\n");
            break;
        case '?':
            printf("unknown option: %c\n", optopt);
            break;
        }
    }
    for(; optind < argc; optind++)
        printf("argument: %s\n", argv[optind]);
    exit(0);
}
```

Now, when we run the program, we see that all the command line arguments are handled automatically:

```
$ ./argopt -i -lr 'hi there' -f fred.c -q
option: i
option: l
option: r
filename: fred.c
argopt: invalid option--q
unknown option: q
argument: hi there
```

How It Works

The program repeatedly calls `getopt` to process option arguments until none remain, when `getopt` returns `-1`. For each option, the appropriate action is taken, including dealing with unknown options and missing values. Depending on your version of `getopt` you might see slightly different output from that shown above, especially error messages, but the meaning will be clear.

Once all options have been processed, the program simply prints out the remaining arguments as before, but starting from `optind`.

Environment Variables

We met environment variables in Chapter 2. These are variables that can be used to control the behavior of shell scripts and other programs. You can also use them to configure the user's environment. For example, each user has an environment variable, `HOME`, that defines his home directory, the default starting place for his or her session. As we've seen, we can examine environment variables from the shell prompt:

```
$ echo $HOME
/home/neil
```

You can also use the shell's `set` command to list all of the environment variables.

The UNIX specification defines many standard environment variables used for a variety of purposes, including terminal type, default editors, time zones and so on. A C program may gain access to environment variables using the putenv and getenv functions.

```
#include <stdlib.h>

char *getenv(const char *name);
int putenv(const char *string);
```

The environment consists of strings of the form name=value. The getenv function searches the environment for a string with the given name and returns the value associated with that name. It will return null if the requested variable doesn't exist. If the variable exists but has no value, getenv succeeds with a string, the first byte of which is null. The string returned by getenv, and held in static storage provided by getenv, mustn't be overwritten by the application, as it will by any subsequent calls to getenv.

The putenv function takes a string of the form name=value and adds it to the current environment. It will fail and return -1 if it can't extend the environment due to lack of available memory. When this happens, the error variable errno will be set to ENOMEM.

Let's write a program to print out the value of any environment variable we choose. We'll also arrange to set the value if we give the program a second argument.

Try It Out - getenv and putenv0

1. The first few lines after the declaration of main ensure that the program, environ.c, has been called correctly:

```
#include <stdlib.h>
#include <stdio.h>
#include <string.h>

int main(int argc, char *argv[])
{
    char *var, *value;

    if(argc == 1 || argc > 3) {
        fprintf(stderr,"usage: environ var [value]\n");
        exit(1);
    }
```

2. That done, we fetch the value of the variable from the environment, using getenv:

```
    var = argv[1];
    value = getenv(var);
    if(value)
        printf("Variable %s has value %s\n", var, value);
    else
        printf("Variable %s has no value\n", var);
```

3. Next, we check whether the program was called with a second argument. If it was, we set the variable to the value of that argument by constructing a string of the form name=value and then calling putenv:

```
    if(argc == 3) {
        char *string;
        value = argv[2];
        string = malloc(strlen(var)+strlen(value)+2);
        if(!string) {
            fprintf(stderr,"out of memory\n");
            exit(1);
        }
        strcpy(string,var);
        strcat(string,"=");
        strcat(string,value);
        printf("Calling putenv with: %s\n",string);
        if(putenv(string) != 0) {
            fprintf(stderr,"putenv failed\n");
            free(string);
            exit(1);
        }
```

4. Finally, we discover the new value of the variable by calling `getenv` once again:

```
        value = getenv(var);
        if(value)
            printf("New value of %s is %s\n", var, value);
        else
            printf("New value of %s is null??\n", var);
    }
    exit(0);
}
```

When we run this program, we can see and set environment variables:

```
$ environ HOME
Variable HOME has value /home/neil
$ environ FRED
Variable FRED has no value
$ environ FRED hello
Variable FRED has no value
Calling putenv with: FRED=hello
New value of FRED is hello
$ environ FRED
Variable FRED has no value
```

Notice that the environment is only local to the program. Changes that we make within the program are not reflected outside it because variable values are not propagated from the child process (our program) to the parent (the shell).

Use of Environment Variables

Programs often use environment variables to alter the way they work. Users can set the values of these environment variables either in their default environment, via a `.profile` file read by their login shell, a shell-specific startup (`rc`) file or by specifying variables on the shell command line. For example:

```
$ ./environ FRED
Variable FRED has no value
$ FRED=hello environ FRED
Variable FRED has value hello
```

The shell takes initial variable assignments as temporary changes to environment variables. In the second example above, the program `environ` runs in an environment where the variable `FRED` has a value.

For instance, in a future version of our CD database application, we could change an environment variable, say CDDB, to indicate the database to use. Each user could then specify his or her own default, or use a shell command to set it on a run-by-run basis:

```
$ CDDB=mycds; export CDDB
$ cdapp
```

or

```
$ CDDB=mycds cdapp
```

Environment variables are a mixed blessing and you should use them with care. They are more 'hidden' to the user than command line options and, as such, can make debugging harder. In a sense, environment variables are like global variables in that they may alter the behavior of a program, giving unexpected results.

The environ Variable

As we've seen, the program environment is made up of strings of the form `name=value`. This array of strings is made available to programs directly via the `environ` variable which is declared as:

```
#include <stdlib.h>

extern char **environ;
```

Try It Out - environ

Here's a program, `showenv.c`, that uses the `environ` variable to print out the environment variables:

```
#include <stdlib.h>
#include <stdio.h>

extern char **environ;

int main()
{
    char **env = environ;

    while(*env) {
        printf("%s\n",*env);
        env++;
    }
    exit(0);
}
```

When we run this program on a Linux system we get the following output, which has been abbreviated a little:

```
$ ./showenv
HOSTNAME=tilde.provider.com
LOGNAME=neil
MAIL=/var/spool/mail/neil
TERM=console
HOSTTYPE=i386
```

```
PATH=/usr/local/bin:/bin:/usr/bin:
HOME=/usr/neil
LS_OPTIONS=-8bit-color=tty -F -T 0
SHELL=/bin/bash
PS1=\h:\w\$
PS2=>
OSTYPE=Linux
```

How It Works

This program iterates through the `environ` variable, a null-terminated array of strings, to print out the whole environment.

Time and Date

Often it can be useful for a program to be able to determine the time and date. It may wish to log the time for which it's run, or it may need to change the way it behaves at certain times. For example, a game might refuse to run during working hours, or a backup program might want to wait until the early hours before starting an automatic backup.

> *UNIX systems all use the same starting point for times and dates: midnight GMT on the 1st January 1970. This is the 'start of the epoch'. All times in a UNIX system are measured as seconds since then. This is similar to the way MS-DOS handles times, except that the MS-DOS epoch started in 1980. Other systems use other epoch start times.*

Times are handled using a defined type, a `time_t`. This is an integer type large enough to contain dates and times in seconds. On Linux systems, it's a `long` and is defined, together with functions for manipulating time values, in the header file `time.h`.

> **On UNIX and Linux systems using a 32-bit `time_t` type the time will "rollover" in the year 2038. By that time we hope that systems have moved to using a `time_t` that is larger than 32-bits. More information on this Y2K38 problem can be found at `http://www.comlinks.com/mag/ddates.htm`**

```
#include <time.h>

time_t time(time_t *tloc);
```

You can find the low level time value by calling the `time` function, which returns the number of seconds since the start of the epoch. It will also write the returned value to a location pointed to by `tloc`, if this isn't a null pointer.

Try It Out - time

Here's a simple program, `envtime.c` to demonstrate the `time` function:

```
#include <time.h>
#include <stdio.h>
#include <unistd.h>
```

```
int main()
{
    int i;
    time_t the_time;

    for(i = 1; i <= 10; i++) {
        the_time = time((time_t *)0);
        printf("The time is %ld\n", the_time);
        sleep(2);
    }
    exit(0);
}
```

When we run this program, it prints the low-level time value every two seconds for 20 seconds.

```
$ ./envtime
The time is 928663786
The time is 928663788
The time is 928663790
The time is 928663792
The time is 928663794
The time is 928663796
The time is 928663798
The time is 928663800
The time is 928663802
The time is 928663804
```

How It Works

The program calls `time` with a null pointer argument, which returns the time and date as a number of seconds. The program sleeps for two seconds and repeats the call to `time` for a total of ten times.

Using the time and date as a number of seconds since the start of 1970 can be useful for measuring how long something takes to happen. We could consider simply subtracting the values we get from two calls to `time`. However, in its deliberations the ISO/ANSI C standard committee didn't specify that the `time_t` type be used to measure time in seconds, so they invented a function, `difftime`, that will calculate the difference in seconds between two `time_t` values and return it as a `double`:

```
#include <time.h>

double difftime(time_t time1, time_t time2);
```

The `difftime` function calculates the difference between two time values and returns the value `time1-time2` as a floating point number. For UNIX, the return value from `time` is a number of seconds and can be manipulated, but for the ultimate in portability you should use `difftime`.

To present the time and date in a more meaningful way (to humans) we need to convert the time value into a recognizable time and date. There are standard functions to help with this.

The function `gmtime` breaks down a low-level time value into a structure containing more usual fields:

```
#include <time.h>

struct tm *gmtime(const time_t timeval);
```

The structure `tm` is defined to contain at least the following members:

tm	MemberDescription
int tm_sec	Seconds, 0-61.
int tm_min	Minutes, 0-59.
int tm_hour	Hours, 0-23.
int tm_mday	Day in the month, 1-31.
int tm_mon	Month in the year, 0-11. (January= 0)
int tm_year	Years since 1900.
int tm_wday)	Day in the week, 0-6. (Sunday = 0)
int tm_yday	Day in the year, 0-365.
int tm_isdst	Daylight savings in effect.

The range for `tm_sec` allows for the occasional leap second, or double leap second.

Try It Out - gmtime

Here's a program, `gmtime.c`, that prints out the current time and date using the `tm` structure and `gmtime`:

```
#include <time.h>
#include <stdio.h>

int main()
{
    struct tm *tm_ptr;
    time_t the_time;

    (void) time(&the_time);
    tm_ptr = gmtime(&the_time);

    printf("Raw time is %ld\n", the_time);
    printf("gmtime gives:\n");
    printf("date: %02d/%02d/%02d\n",
        tm_ptr->tm_year, tm_ptr->tm_mon+1, tm_ptr->tm_mday);
    printf("time: %02d:%02d:%02d\n",
        tm_ptr->tm_hour, tm_ptr->tm_min, tm_ptr->tm_sec);
    exit(0);
}
```

When we run this program, we get a good approximation of the time and date:

```
$ ./gmtime; date
Raw time is 928663946
gmtime gives:
date: 99/06/06
time: 10:12:26
Sun Jun  6 11:12:26 BST 1999
```

How It Works

The program calls `time` to get the low-level time value and then calls `gmtime` to convert this into a structure with useful time and date values. It prints these out using `printf`. Strictly speaking, we shouldn't print the raw time value in this way, because it isn't guaranteed to be a `long` on all systems. We ran the `date` command immediately after `gmtime` to compare its output.

However, we have a little problem here. If you're running this program in a time zone other than Greenwich Mean Time, or if your local daylight savings time is in effect, you'll notice that the time (and possibly date) is incorrect. This is because `gmtime` returns the time as GMT (now known as UTC—Coordinated Universal Time). UNIX does this so that all programs and systems across the world are synchronized. Files created at the same moment in different time zones will appear to have the same creation time. To see the local time, we need to use the function `localtime` instead.

```
#include <time.h>

struct tm *localtime(const time_t *timeval);
```

The `localtime` function is identical to `gmtime`, except that it returns a structure containing values adjusted for local time zone and daylight savings. If you try the `gmtime` program again, but use `localtime` in place of `gmtime`, you should see a correct time and date reported.

To convert a broken-down `tm` structure into a raw `time_t` value, we can use the function `mktime`:

```
#include <time.h>

time_t mktime(struct tm *timeptr);
```

`mktime` will return `-1` if the structure can't be represented as a `time_t` value.

For 'friendly', as opposed to machine, time and date output provided by the `date` program, we can use the functions `asctime` and `ctime`:

```
#include <time.h>

char *asctime(const struct tm *timeptr);
char *ctime(const time_t *timeval);
```

The `asctime` function returns a string that represents the time and date given by the `tm` structure `timeptr`. The string returned has a format similar to:

```
Sun Jun  6 12:30:34 1999\n\0
```

It's always a fixed format, 26 characters long. The function `ctime` is equivalent to calling:

```
asctime(localtime(timeval))
```

It takes a raw time value and converts it to more readable local time.

Try It Out - ctime

Let's see ctime in action, using the following code:

```
#include <time.h>
#include <stdio.h>

int main()
{
    time_t timeval;

    (void)time(&timeval);
    printf("The date is: %s", ctime(&timeval));
    exit(0);
}
```

Compile and run the surprisingly named ctime.c and you should see:

```
$ ./ctime
The date is: Sun Jun  6 12:50:27 1999
```

How It Works

The ctime.c program calls time to get the low level time value and lets ctime do all the hard work converting it to a readable string, which it then prints.

To gain more control of the exact formatting of time and date strings, modern UNIX systems provide the strftime function. This is rather like a sprintf for dates and times and works in a similar way:

```
#include <time.h>

size_t strftime(char *s, size_t maxsize, const char *format, struct tm *timeptr);
```

The strftime function formats the time and date represented by the tm structure pointed to by timeptr and places the result in the string s. This string is specified as being (at least) maxsize characters long. The format string is used to control the characters written to the string. Like printf, it contains ordinary characters that will be transferred to the string and conversion specifiers for formatting time and date elements. The conversion specifiers include:

Conversion Specifier	Description
%a	Abbreviated weekday name.
%A	Full weekday name.
%b	Abbreviated month name.
%B	Full month name.
%c	Date and time.
%d	Day of the month, 01-31.
%H	Hour, 00-23.

Table Continued on Following Page

Conversion Specifier	Description
%I	Hour in 12 hour clock, 01-12.
%j	Day of the year, 001-366.
%m	Month of the year, 01-12.
%M	Minutes, 00-59.
%p	a.m. or p.m.
%S	Seconds, 00-61.
%u	Day in the week, 1-7. (1 = Monday)
%U	Week in the year, 01-53. (Sunday is theFirst day of the week.)
%V	Week in the year, 01-53. (Monday is the First day of the week.)
%w	Day in the week, 0-6 (0 = Sunday).
%x	Date in local format.
%X	Time in local format.
%y	Last two digits of the year number, 00-99.
%Y	Year.
%Z	Time zone name.
%%	A % character.

So, the usual date as given by the `date` program corresponds to a `strftime` format string of:

```
"%a %b %d %H:%M:%S %Y"
```

To help with reading dates, we can use the `strptime` function, which takes a string representing a date and time and creates a `tm` structure representing the same date and time:

```
#include <time.h>

char *strptime(const char *buf, const char *format, struct tm *timeptr);
```

The `format` string is constructed in exactly the same way as the `format` string for `strftime`. `strptime` acts in a similar way to `sscanf` in that it scans a string, looking for identifiable fields and writes them into variables. Here it's the members of a `tm` structure that are filled in according to the `format` string. However, the conversion specifiers for `strptime` are a little more relaxed than those for `strftime` because `strptime` will allow both abbreviated and full names for days and months. Either representation will match a `%a` specifier in `strptime`. Also, where `strftime` always uses leading zeros on numbers less than ten, `strptime` regards them as optional.

`strptime` returns a pointer to the character following the last one consumed in the conversion process. If it encounters characters that can't be converted, the conversion simply stops at that point. The calling program needs to check that enough of the passed string has been consumed to ensure that meaningful values are written to the `tm` structure.

Try It Out - strftime and strptime

Have a look at the selection of conversion specifiers used in the following program:

```
#include <time.h>
#include <stdio.h>

int main()
{
    struct tm *tm_ptr, timestruct;
    time_t the_time;
    char buf[256];
    char *result;

    (void) time(&the_time);
    tm_ptr = localtime(&the_time);
    strftime(buf, 256, "%A %d %B, %I:%S %p", tm_ptr);

    printf("strftime gives: %s\n", buf);

    strcpy(buf,"Mon 26 July 1999, 17:53 will do fine");

    printf("calling strptime with: %s\n", buf);
    tm_ptr = &timestruct;

    result = strptime(buf,"%a %d %b %Y, %R", tm_ptr);
    printf("strptime consumed up to: %s\n", result);

    printf("strptime gives:\n");
    printf("date: %02d/%02d/%02d\n",
        tm_ptr->tm_year, tm_ptr->tm_mon+1, tm_ptr->tm_mday);
    printf("time: %02d:%02d\n",
        tm_ptr->tm_hour, tm_ptr->tm_min);
    exit(0);
}
```

When we compile and run this program, strftime.c, we get:

```
$ ./strftime
strftime gives: Sunday 06 June, 11:55 AM
calling strptime with: Mon 26 July 1999, 17:53 will do fine
strptime consumed up to:  will do fine
strptime gives:
date: 99/07/26
time: 17:53
```

How It Works

The strftime program obtains the current local time by calling time and localtime. It then converts it to a readable form by calling strftime with an appropriate formatting argument. To demonstrate the use of strptime, the program sets up a string containing a date and time, then calls strptime to extract the raw time and date values and prints them. The conversion specifier %R is a shortcut for %H:%M in strptime.

It's important to note that strptime needs an accurate format string to successfully scan a date. Typically, it won't accurately scan dates read from users unless the format is very much restricted.

It is possible that you will find the compiler issuing a warning when you compile strftime.c. This is because the GNU library does not by default declare strptime. You can work around this by explicitly requesting X/Open standard features by adding the following line before including time.h.

```
#define _XOPEN_SOURCE
```

Temporary Files

Often, programs will need to make use of temporary storage in the form of files. These might hold intermediate results of a computation, or might represent backup copies of files made before critical operations. For example, a database application could use a temporary file when deleting records. The file collects the database entries that need to be retained and then, at the end of the process, the temporary file becomes the new database and the original is deleted.

This popular use of temporary files has a hidden disadvantage. You must take care to ensure that they choose a unique file name to use for the temporary file. If this doesn't happen, because UNIX is a multitasking system, another program could choose the same name and the two will interfere with each other.

A unique file name can be generated by the `tmpnam` function:

```
#include <stdio.h>

char *tmpnam(char *s);
```

The `tmpnam` function returns a valid file name that isn't the same as any existing file. If the string `s` isn't `null`, the file name will also be written to it. Further calls to `tmpnam` will overwrite the static storage used for return values, so it's essential to use a string parameter if `tmpnam` is to be called many times. The string is assumed to be at least `L_tmpnam` characters long. `tmpnam` can be called up to `TMP_MAX` times in a single program and it will generate a different file name each time.

If the temporary file is to be used immediately, you can name it and open it at the same time using the `tmpfile` function. This is important, since another program could create a file with the same name as that returned by `tmpnam`. The `tmpfile` function avoids this problem altogether:

```
#include <stdio.h>

FILE *tmpfile(void);
```

The `tmpfile` function returns a stream pointer that refers to a unique temporary file. The file is opened for reading and writing (via `fopen` with `w+`) and it will be automatically deleted when all references to the file are closed.

`tmpfile` returns a `null` pointer and sets `errno` on error.

Try It Out - tmpnam and tmpfile

Let's see these two functions in action:

```
#include <stdio.h>

int main()
{
    char tmpname[L_tmpnam];
    char *filename;
    FILE *tmpfp;

    filename = tmpnam(tmpname);

    printf("Temporary file name is: %s\n", filename);
```

```
    tmpfp = tmpfile();
    if(tmpfp)
        printf("Opened a temporary file OK\n");
    else
        perror("tmpfile");
    exit(0);
}
```

When we compile and run this program, `tmpnam.c`, we can see the unique file name generated by `tmpnam`:

```
$ ./tmpnam
Temporary file name is: /tmp/filedm9aZK
Opened a temporary file OK
```

How It Works

The program calls `tmpnam` to generate a unique file name for a temporary file. If we wanted to use it, we would have to open it quickly to minimize the risk that another program would open a file with the same name. The `tmpfile` call creates and opens a temporary file at the same time, thus avoiding this risk.

Older versions of UNIX have another way to generate temporary file names using functions `mktemp` and `mkstemp`. These are similar to `tmpnam`, except that you can specify a template for the temporary file name, which gives you a little more control over their location and name:

```
#include <stdlib.h>

char *mktemp(char *template);
int mkstemp(char *template);
```

The `mktemp` function creates a unique file name from the given `template`. The `template` argument must be a string with six trailing `X` characters. The `mktemp` function replaces these `X` characters with a unique combination of valid file name characters. It returns a pointer to the generated string, or a null pointer if it couldn't generate a unique name.

The `mkstemp` function is similar to `tmpfile` in that it creates and opens a temporary file. The file name is generated in the same way as `mktemp`, but the returned result is an open, low-level, file descriptor. In general, you should use `tmpnam` and `tmpfile` rather than `mktemp` and `mkstemp`.

User Information

All UNIX programs, with the notable exception of `init`, are started by other programs or by users. We'll learn more about how running programs, or processes, interact in Chapter 10. Users most often start programs from a shell that responds to their commands. We've seen that a program can determine a great deal about its environment by examining environment variables and reading the system clock. A program can also find out information about the person using it.

When a user logs into a UNIX system, he or she has a user name and password. Once this has been validated, the user is presented with a shell. Internally, the user also has a unique user identifier, known as a **UID**. Each program that UNIX runs is run on behalf of a user and has an associated UID.

You can set up programs to run as if a different user had started them. When a program has its set UID permission set it will run as if started by the owner of the executable file. When the `su` command is executed, it runs as if it had been started by the root user. It then validates the user's access, changes the UID to that of the target account and executes that account's login shell. This also allows a program to be run as if a different user had started it and is often used by system administrators to perform maintenance tasks.

Since the UID is key to the user's identity, let's start with that.

The UID has its own type — `uid_t` — defined in `sys/types.h`. It's normally a small integer. Some are predefined by the system, others are created by the system administrator when new users are made known to the system. Normally, users usually have UID values larger than 100.

```
#include <sys/types.h>
#include <unistd.h>

uid_t getuid(void);
char *getlogin(void);
```

The `getuid` function returns the UID with which the program is associated. This is usually the UID of the user who started the program.

The `getlogin` function returns the login name associated with the current user.

The system file, `/etc/passwd`, contains a database dealing with user accounts. It consists of lines, one per user, that contain the user name, encrypted password, user identifier (UID), group identifier (GID), full name, home directory and default shell. Here's an example line:

```
neil:zBqxfqedfpk:500:4:Neil Matthew:/home/neil:/bin/bash
```

If we write a program that determines the UID of the user who started it, we could extend it to look in the password file to find out the user's login name and full name. We don't recommend this because modern UNIX systems are moving away from using simple password files, in order to improve system security. Many systems have the option to use 'shadow' password files that don't contain any encrypted password information at all (this is often held in `/etc/shadow`, a file that ordinary users cannot read). For this reason a number of functions have been defined to provide a standard and effective programming interface to this user information:

```
#include <sys/types.h>
#include <pwd.h>

struct passwd *getpwuid(uid_t uid);
struct passwd *getpwnam(const char *name);
```

The password database structure, `passwd`, defined in `pwd.h` includes the following members:

`passwd` Member	Description
`char *pw_name`	The user's login name.
`uid_t pw_uid`	The UID number.
`gid_t pw_gid`	The GID number.
`char *pw_dir`	The user's home directory.
`char *pw_shell`	The user's default shell.

Some UNIX systems may include a field for the user's full name, but this isn't standard: on some systems it's `pw_gecos` and on others it's `pw_comment`. This means that we can't recommend its use.

The `getpwuid` and `getpwnam` functions both return a pointer to a `passwd` structure corresponding to a user. The user is identified by UID for `getpwuid` and by login name for `getpwnam`. They both return a null pointer and set `errno` on error.

Try It Out - User Information

Here's a program, `user.c`, that extracts some user information from the password database:

```
#include <sys/types.h>
#include <pwd.h>
#include <stdio.h>
#include <unistd.h>

int main()
{
    uid_t uid;
    gid_t gid;
    struct passwd *pw;

    uid = getuid();
    gid = getgid();

    printf("User is %s\n", getlogin());

    printf("User IDs: uid=%d, gid=%d\n", uid, gid);

    pw = getpwuid(uid);
    printf("UID passwd entry:\n name=%s, uid=%d, gid=%d, home=%s, shell=%s\n",
        pw->pw_name, pw->pw_uid, pw->pw_gid, pw->pw_dir, pw->pw_shell);

    pw = getpwnam("root");
    printf("root passwd entry:\n");
    printf("name=%s, uid=%d, gid=%d, home=%s, shell=%s\n",
        pw->pw_name, pw->pw_uid, pw->pw_gid, pw->pw_dir, pw->pw_shell);
    exit(0);
}
```

It gives the following output, which may differ in minor respects between versions of UNIX:

```
$ ./user
User is neil
User IDs: uid=500, gid=500
UID passwd entry:
 name=neil, uid=500, gid=500, home=/usr/neil, shell=/bin/bash
root passwd entry:
name=root, uid=0, gid=0, home=/root, shell=/bin/bash
```

How It Works

This program calls `getuid` to obtain the UID of the current user. This UID is used in `getpwuid` to obtain detailed password file information. As an alternative, we show how the user name `root` can be given to `getpwnam` to obtain user information.

If you have a copy of the Linux source code, you can see another example of using `getuid` in the `id` command.

To scan all the password file information, we can use the `getpwent` function. This fetches successive file entries:

```
#include <pwd.h>
#include <sys/types.h>

void endpwent(void);
struct passwd *getpwent(void);
void setpwent(void);
```

The `getpwent` function returns each user information entry in turn. When none remain, it returns a null pointer. We can use the `endpwent` function to terminate processing once sufficient entries have been scanned. The `setpwent` function resets the position in the password file to the start so that a new scan can be started with the next call to `getpwent`. These functions operate in a similar way to the directory scanning functions `opendir`, `readdir` and `closedir` that we met in Chapter 3.

Other User Information Functions

User and group identifiers (effective and actual) can be obtained by other, less commonly used functions:

```
#include <sys/types.h>
#include <unistd.h>

uid_t geteuid(void);
gid_t getgid(void);
gid_t getegid(void);
int setuid(uid_t uid);
int setgid(gid_t gid);
```

You should refer to the UNIX system manual pages for details on group identifiers and effective user identifiers, although you'll probably find that you won't need to manipulate these at all.

> Only the superuser may call **setuid** and **setgid**.

Host Information

Just as it can determine information about the user, a program can also establish some details about the computer on which it's running. The `uname(1)` command provides such information. `uname(2)` also exists as a system call to provide the same information within a C program—check it out using `man 2 uname`.

Host information can be useful in a number of situations. We might wish to customize a program's behavior, depending on the name of the machine it's running on in a network, say a student's machine or an administrator's. For licensing purposes, we might wish to restrict a program to running on one machine only. All this means that we need a way to establish which machine the program is running on.

If the UNIX system has the networking component installed, we can obtain its network name very easily with the gethostname function:

```
#include <unistd.h>

int gethostname(char *name, size_t namelen);
```

The gethostname function writes the machine's network name into the string name. This string is assumed to be at least namelen characters long. gethostname returns 0 if successful, -1 otherwise.

You can obtain more detailed information about the host computer from the uname system call:

```
#include <sys/utsname.h>

int uname(struct utsname *name);
```

The uname function writes host information into the structure pointed to by the name parameter. The utsname structure, defined in sys/utsname.h, must contain at least these members:

utsname Member	Description
char sysname[]	The operating system name.
char nodename[]	The host name.
char release[]	The release level of the system.
char version[]	The version number of the system.
char machine[]	The hardware type.

uname returns a non-negative integer on success, -1 otherwise, with errno set to indicate any error.

Try It Out - Host Information

Here's a program, hostget.c, that extracts some host computer information:

```
#include <sys/utsname.h>
#include <unistd.h>
#include <stdio.h>

int main()
{
    char computer[256];
    struct utsname uts;

    if(gethostname(computer, 255) != 0 || uname(&uts) < 0) {
        fprintf(stderr, "Could not get host information\n");
        exit(1);
    }

    printf("Computer host name is %s\n", computer);
    printf("System is %s on %s hardware\n", uts.sysname, uts.machine);
    printf("Nodename is %s\n", uts.nodename);
    printf("Version is %s, %s\n", uts.release, uts.version);
    exit(0);
}
```

It gives the following Linux-specific output. If your machine is networked you may see an extended host name that includes the network:

```
$ ./hostget
Computer host name is tilde
System is Linux on i686 hardware
Nodename is tilde
Version is 2.2.5-15, #2 Mon May 1016:39:40 GMT 1999
```

How It Works

This program calls `gethostname` to obtain the network name of the host computer. In the above examples it gets the name `tilde`. More detailed information about this Intel Pentium-II based Linux computer is returned by the call to `uname`. Note that the format of the strings returned by `uname` is implementation-dependent; in the example the version string contains the date that the kernel was compiled.

For another example of the use of the `uname(2)` function, have a look at the Linux source code for the `uname(1)` command.

Licensing

A unique identifier for each host computer may be available from the `gethostid` function:

```
#include <unistd.h>

long gethostid(void);
```

The `gethostid` function is intended to return a unique value for the host computer. License managers use this to ensure that software programs can only run on machines that hold valid licenses. On Sun workstations, it returns a number that is set in non-volatile memory when the computer is built and so is unique to the system hardware.

Other systems, such as Linux, return a value based on the Internet address of the machine, which isn't secure enough to be used for licensing.

Logging

Many applications need to record their activities. System programs will very often write messages to the console, or a log file. These messages might indicate errors, warnings or more general information about the state of the system. For example, the `su` program might record the fact that a user has tried and failed to gain superuser privileges.

Very often, these log messages are recorded in system files in a directory made available for that purpose. This might be `/usr/adm`, or `/var/log`. On a typical Linux installation, the file `/var/log/messages` contains all system messages, `/var/log/maillog` contains other log messages from the mail system and `/var/log/debug` may contain debug messages. You can check your system's configuration in the file `/etc/syslog.conf`. Here are some sample messages:

```
Nov 21 17:27:00 tilde kernel: Floppy drive(s): fd0 is 1.44M
Nov 21 17:27:00 tilde kernel: snd6 <SoundBlaster 16 4.11> at 0x220
Nov 21 17:27:00 tilde kernel: IP Protocols: ICMP, UDP, TCP
Nov 21 17:27:03 tilde sendmail[62]: starting daemon (8.6.12)
Nov 21 17:27:12 tilde login: ROOT LOGIN ON tty1
```

Here, we can see the sort of messages that are logged. The first few are reported by the Linux kernel itself, as it boots and detects installed hardware. The mail agent, `sendmail`, reports that it's starting up. Finally, the `login` program reports a superuser login.

You may require superuser privilege to view log messages.

Some UNIX systems don't provide a readable messages file in this way, but do provide the administrator with tools to read a database of system events. Refer to your system documentation for details.

Even though the format and storage of system messages may vary, the method of producing the messages is standard. The UNIX specification provides an interface for all programs to produce logging messages, using the `syslog` function:

```
#include <syslog.h>

void syslog(int priority, const char *message, arguments...);
```

The `syslog` function sends a logging message to the logging facility. Each message has a `priority` argument which is a bitwise `OR` of a severity level and a facility value. The severity level controls how the log message is acted upon and the facility value records the originator of the message.

Facility values (from `syslog.h`) include `LOG_USER`, used to indicate that the message has come from a user application, (the default) and `LOG_LOCAL0`, `LOG_LOCAL1`, up to `LOG_LOCAL7`, which can be assigned meanings by the local administrator.

The severity levels in descending order of priority are:

Priority Level	Description
LOG_EMERG	An emergency situation.
LOG_ALERT	High priority problem, such as database corruption.
LOG_CRIT	Critical error, such as hardware failure.
LOG_ERR	Errors.
LOG_WARNING	Warning.
LOG_NOTICE	Special conditions, requiring attention.
LOG_INFO	Informational messages.
LOG_DEBUG	Debug messages.

Depending on system configuration, `LOG_EMERG` messages might be broadcast to all users, `LOG_ALERT` messages might be mailed to the administrator, `LOG_DEBUG` messages might be ignored and the others written to a messages file. We can write a program that uses the logging facility quite simply. All we need to do is call `syslog` when we wish to create a log message.

The log message created by `syslog` consists of a message header and a message body. The header is created from the facility indicator and the date and time. The message body is created from the `message` parameter to `syslog`, which acts like a `printf` format string. Further arguments to `syslog` are used according to `printf` style conversion specifiers in the `message` string. Additionally, the specifier `%m` may be used to insert the error message string associated with the current value of the error variable, `errno`. This can be useful for logging error messages.

Try It Out - syslog

In this program we try to open a non-existent file:

```
#include <syslog.h>
#include <stdio.h>

int main()
{
    FILE *f;

    f = fopen("not_here","r");
    if(!f)
        syslog(LOG_ERR|LOG_USER,"oops - %m\n");
    exit(0);
}
```

When we compile and run this program, `syslog.c`, we see no output, but the file `/var/log/messages` now contains at the end the line:

```
Nov 21 17:56:00 tilde syslog: oops - No such file or directory
```

How It Works

In this program, we try to open a file that doesn't exist. When this fails, we call `syslog` to record the fact in the system logs.

Notice that the log message doesn't indicate which program called the log facility, it just records the fact that `syslog` was called with a message. The `%m` conversion specifier has been replaced by a description of the error, in this case that the file couldn't be found. This is a little more useful than error `17`!

Configuring Logs

Other functions used to alter the behavior of logging facilities are also defined in `syslog.h`. These are:

```
#include <syslog.h>

void closelog(void);
void openlog(const char *ident, int logopt, int facility);
int setlogmask(int maskpri);
```

We can alter the way that our log messages are presented by calling the `openlog` function. This allows us to set up a string, `ident`, that will be prepended to our log messages. We can use this to indicate which program is creating the message. The `facility` parameter records a default facility value to be used for future calls to `syslog`. The default is `LOG_USER`. The `logopt` parameter configures the behavior of future calls to `syslog`. It's a bitwise `OR` of zero or more of the following:

logopt Parameter	Description
LOG_PID	Includes the process identifier, a unique number allocated to each process by the system, in the messages.
LOG_CONS	Sends messages to the console if they can't be logged.
LOG_ODELAY	Opens the log facility at first call to syslog.
LOG_NDELAY	Opens the log facility immediately, rather than at first log.

The openlog function will allocate and open a file descriptor that will be used for writing to the logging facility. You can close this by calling the closelog function. Note that you don't need to call openlog before calling syslog, since syslog will open the logging facility itself, if required.

We can control the priority level of our log messages by setting a log mask using setlogmask. All future calls to syslog with priority levels not set in the log mask will be rejected, so you could, for example, use this to turn off LOG_DEBUG messages without having to alter the body of the program.

We can create the mask for log messages using LOG_MASK(priority) which creates a mask consisting of just one priority level, or LOG_UPTO(priority) which creates a mask consisting of all priorities up to and including the specified priority.

Try It Out - logmask

In this example we'll see logmask in action:

```
#include <syslog.h>
#include <stdio.h>
#include <unistd.h>

int main()
{
    int logmask;

    openlog("logmask", LOG_PID|LOG_CONS, LOG_USER);
    syslog(LOG_INFO,"informative message, pid = %d", getpid());
    syslog(LOG_DEBUG,"debug message, should appear");
    logmask = setlogmask(LOG_UPTO(LOG_NOTICE));
    syslog(LOG_DEBUG,"debug message, should not appear");
    exit(0);
}
```

This program, logmask.c, produces no output, but on a typical Linux system towards the end of /var/log/messages we should see the line:

```
Nov 21 18:19:43 tilde logmask[195]: informative message, pid = 195
```

The file /var/log/debug should contain:

```
Nov 21 18:19:43 tilde logmask[195]: debug message, should appear
```

How It Works

The program initializes the logging facility with its name, `logmask` and requests that log messages contain the process identifier. The informative message is logged to `/var/log/messages` and the debug message to `/var/log/debug`. The second debug message doesn't appear because we call `setlogmask` to ignore all messages with a priority below `LOG_NOTICE`. Note that this may not work on early Linux kernels.

If your installation does not have debug message logging enabled or it is configured differently, you may not see the debug messages appear. To enable all debug messages add the following line to the end of `/etc/syslog.conf` and reboot. (You could also just send a hangup signal to the syslogd process). However, be sure to check your system documentation for the exact configuration details.

```
*.debug /var/log/debug
```

`logmask.c` uses the `getpid` function, which is defined along with the closely related `getppid` as follows:

```
#include <sys/types.h>
#include <unistd.h>

pid_t getpid(void);
pid_t getppid(void);
```

The functions return the process and parent process identifiers of the calling process. For more information on PIDs, see Chapter 10.

Resources and Limits

Programs running on a UNIX system are subject to resource limitations. These might be physical limits imposed by hardware (such as memory), limits imposed by system policies (for example, allowed CPU time) or implementation limits (such as the size of an integer or the maximum number of characters allowed in a file name). The UNIX specification defines some of these limits, which can be determined by an application. For a further discussion of limits and the consequences of breaking them, refer to Chapter 7 on data management.

The header file `limits.h` defines many manifest constants that represent the constraints imposed by the operating system. These include:

Limit Constant	What they're for
NAME_MAX	The maximum number of characters in a file name.
CHAR_BIT	The number of bits in a `char` value.
CHAR_MAX	The maximum `char` value.
INT_MAX	The maximum `int` value.

There will be many others that may be of use to an application, so you should refer to your installation's header files. Note that `NAME_MAX` is file system specific. For more portable code, you should use the `pathconf` function. Refer to the man pages on `pathconf` for more information.

The header file sys/resource.h provides definitions for resource operations. These include functions for determining and setting limits on a program's allowed size, execution priority and file resources:

```
#include <sys/resource.h>

int getpriority(int which, id_t who);
int setpriority(int which, id_t who, int priority);
int getrlimit(int resource, struct rlimit *r_limit);
int setrlimit(int resource, const struct rlimit *r_limit);
int getrusage(int who, struct rusage *r_usage);
```

id_t is an integral type used for user and group identifiers. The rusage structure, defined in sys/resource.h, is used to determine how much CPU time has been used by the current program. It must contain at least these members:

rusage Member	Description
struct timeval ru_utime	The user time used.
struct timeval ru_stime	The system time used.

The timeval structure is defined in sys/time.h and contains fields tv_sec and tv_usec representing seconds and microseconds respectively.

CPU time consumed by a program is separated into **user time** (the time that the program itself has consumed executing its own instructions) and **system time** (the CPU time consumed by the operating system on the program's behalf, i.e. the time spent in system calls performing input and output or other system functions).

The getrusage function writes CPU time information to the rusage structure pointed to by the parameter r_usage. The who parameter can be one of the following constants:

who Constant	Description
RUSAGE_SELF	Returns usage information about current program only.
RUSAGE_CHILDREN	Includes usage information of child processes as well.

We'll meet child processes and task priorities in Chapter 10, but for completeness, we'll cover their implications for system resources here. For now, it's enough to say that each program that's running has a priority associated with it and that higher priority programs are allocated more of the available CPU time. Ordinary users are only able to reduce the priorities of their programs, not increase them.

Applications can determine and alter their (and others') priority with the getpriority and setpriority functions. The process to be examined or changed by the priority functions can be identified either by process identifier, group identifier, or user. The which parameter specifies how the who parameter is to be treated:

which Parameter	Description
PRIO_PROCESS	who is a process identifier.
PRIO_PGRP	who is a process group.
PRIO_USER	who is a user identifier.

So, to determine the priority of the current process, we might call:

```
priority = getpriority(PRIO_PROCESS, getpid());
```

The `setpriority` function allows a new priority to be set, if possible.

The default priority is `0`. Positive priorities are used for background tasks that run when no other higher priority task is ready to run. Negative priorities cause a program to run more frequently, taking a larger share of the available CPU time. The range of valid priorities is `-20` to `+20`. This is often confusing since the higher the numerical value, the lower the execution precedence.

`getpriority` returns a valid priority if successful, and -1 with `errno` set on error. Because `-1` is itself a valid priority, `errno` should be set to zero before calling `getpriority` and checked that it's still zero on return. `setpriority` returns 0 if successful, -1 otherwise.

Limits on system resources can be read and set by `getrlimit` and `setrlimit`. Both of these functions make use of a general purpose structure, `rlimit`, to describe resource limits. It's defined in `sys/resource.h` and has the following members:

rlimit Member	**Description**
`rlim_t rlim_cur`	The current, soft limit.
`rlim_t rlim_max`	The hard limit.

The defined type `rlim_t` is an integral type used to describe resource levels. Typically, the soft limit is an advisory limit that shouldn't be exceeded; doing so may cause library functions to return errors. The hard limit, if exceeded, may cause the system to attempt to terminate the program, by sending a signal to it. Examples would be the signal `SIGXCPU` on exceeding the CPU time limit and the signal `SIGSEGV` on exceeding a data size limit. A program may set its own soft limits to any value less than the hard limit. It may reduce its hard limit. Only a program running with superuser privileges may increase a hard limit.

There are a number of system resources that can be limited. These are specified by the `resource` parameter of the `rlimit` functions and are defined in `sys/resource.h` as:

resource Parameter	**Description**
`RLIMIT_CORE`	The core dump file size limit, in bytes.
`RLIMIT_CPU`	The CPU time limit, in seconds.
`RLIMIT_DATA`	The data (`malloc/sbrk`) segment limit, in bytes.
`RLIMIT_FSIZE`	The file size limit, in bytes.
`RLIMIT_NOFILE`	The limit on the number of open files.
`RLIMIT_STACK`	The limit on stack size, in bytes.
`RLIMIT_AS`	The limit on address space (stack and data), in bytes.

Here's a program, `limits.c`, that simulates a typical application. It also sets and breaks a resource limit.

Try It Out - Resource Limits

1. Make the includes for all the functions we're going to be using in this program:

```
#include <sys/types.h>
#include <sys/resource.h>
#include <sys/time.h>
#include <unistd.h>
#include <stdio.h>
#include <math.h>
```

2. The void function writes a string to a temporary file 10000 times and then performs some arithmetic to generate load on the CPU:

```
void work()
{
    FILE *f;
    int i;
    double x = 4.5;

    f = tmpfile();
    for(i = 0; i < 10000; i++) {
        fprintf(f,"Do some output\n");
        if(ferror(f)) {
            fprintf(stderr,"Error writing to temporary file\n");
            exit(1);
        }
    }
    for(i = 0; i < 1000000; i++)
        x = log(x*x + 3.21);
}
```

3. The main function calls work and then uses the getrusage function to discover how much CPU time it has used. It displays this information on screen:

```
int main()
{
    struct rusage r_usage;
    struct rlimit r_limit;
    int priority;

    work();
    getrusage(RUSAGE_SELF, &r_usage);

    printf("CPU usage: User = %ld.%06ld, System = %ld.%06ld\n",
        r_usage.ru_utime.tv_sec, r_usage.ru_utime.tv_usec,
        r_usage.ru_stime.tv_sec, r_usage.ru_stime.tv_usec);
```

4. Next, it calls getpriority and getrlimit to find out its current priority and file size limits respectively:

```
    priority = getpriority(PRIO_PROCESS, getpid());
    printf("Current priority = %d\n", priority);

    getrlimit(RLIMIT_FSIZE, &r_limit);
    printf("Current FSIZE limit: soft = %ld, hard = %ld\n",
        r_limit.rlim_cur, r_limit.rlim_max);
```

5. Finally, we set a file size limit using setrlimit and call work again, which fails because it attempts to create too large a file:

```
    r_limit.rlim_cur = 2048;
    r_limit.rlim_max = 4096;
    printf("Setting a 2K file size limit\n");
    setrlimit(RLIMIT_FSIZE, &r_limit);

    work();
    exit(0);
}
```

When we run this program, we can see how much CPU resource is being consumed and the default priority at which the program is running. Once a file size limit has been set, the program can't write more than 2048 bytes to a temporary file.

```
$ cc -o limits limits.c -lm
$ ./limits
CPU usage: User = 1.460000, System = 1.040000
Current priority = 0
Current FSIZE limit: soft = 2147483647, hard = 2147483647
Setting a 2K file size limit
File size limit exceeded
```

We can change the program priority by starting it with the `nice` command. Here, we see the priority changes to `+10` and as a result it takes longer to execute the program:

```
$ nice limits
CPU usage: User = 1.310000, System = 0.840000
Current priority = 10
Current FSIZE limit: soft = 2147483647, hard = 2147483647
Setting a 2K file size limit
File size limit exceeded
```

How It Works

The `limits` program calls a function, `work` to simulate the actions of a typical program. It performs some calculations and produces some output, in this case about 150K to a temporary file. It calls the resource functions to discover its priority and file size limits. In this case the file size limits are set to maximum values, allowing us to create a 2GB file, disk space permitting. The program then sets its file size limit to just 2K and tries again to perform some work. This time, the `work` function fails as it can't create such a large temporary file.

Limits may also be placed on a program running under a particular shell with the bash `ulimit` *command.*

In this example the error message 'Error writing to temporary file' may not be printed as we might expect. This is because some systems (such as Linux 2.2) terminate our program when the resource limit is exceeded. It does this by sending a signal, `SIGXFSZ`. We will learn more about signals and how to use them in Chapter 10. Other POSIX compliant systems may simply cause the function that exceeds the limit to return an error.

Summary

In this chapter, we've looked at the UNIX environment and examined the conditions under which programs run. We've covered command line arguments and environment variables, both of which can be used to alter a program's default behavior and provide useful program options.

We've seen how a program can make use of library functions to manipulate date and time values, obtain information about itself and the user and the computer on which it's running.

Since UNIX programs typically have to share precious resources, we've also looked at how those resources can be determined and managed.

Terminals

Let's consider what improvements we might like to make to our basic application from Chapter 2. Perhaps the most obvious failing is the user interface. It's functional, but not very elegant.

In this chapter, we are going to look at how to take more control of the user's terminal, i.e. both keyboard input and screen output. More than this, though, we'll learn how we can 'guarantee' that a variety of user input to the terminal from which the program is run is fed back to the program and that the program's output goes to the right place on the screen. Along the way, we'll lay bare a little more of the thinking of the early UNIX meisters.

Though the re-implemented CD database application won't see the light of day until the end of the next chapter, we'll do much of the groundwork for that chapter here. The next chapter is on `curses`, not some ancient malediction, but a library of functions which provide a higher level of code to control the terminal screen display. You may want to treat this chapter as a build-up to the next, introducing you to some philosophy of UNIX and the concept of terminal input and output. Or the low-level access presented here might be just what you're looking for.

In this chapter, we'll learn about:

- Reading and writing to the terminal
- Terminal drivers and the General Terminal Interface
- `termios`
- Terminal output and `terminfo`
- Detecting keystrokes

Reading from and Writing to the Terminal

In Chapter 3, we learned that when a program is invoked from the command prompt, the shell arranges for the standard input and output streams to be connected to our program. We should be able to interact with the user simply by using the `getchar` and `printf` routines to read and write these default streams

Let's try and rewrite our menu routines in C, using just those two routines, calling it `menu1.c`.

Try It Out – Menu Routines in C

1. Start with the following lines, which define the array to be used as a menu and prototype the `getchoice` function:

```
#include <stdio.h>

char *menu[] = {
    "a - add new record",
    "d - delete record",
    "q - quit",
    NULL,
};

int getchoice(char *greet, char *choices[]);
```

2. The main function calls getchoice with the sample menu, menu:

```
int main()
{
    int choice = 0;

    do
    {
        choice = getchoice("Please select an action", menu);
        printf("You have chosen: %c\n", choice);
    } while(choice != 'q');
    exit(0);
}
```

3. Now for the important code: the function that both prints the menu and reads the user's input:

```
int getchoice(char *greet, char *choices[])
{
    int chosen = 0;
    int selected;
    char **option;

    do {
        printf("Choice: %s\n",greet);
        option = choices;
        while(*option) {
            printf("%s\n",*option);
            option++;
        }
        selected = getchar();
        option = choices;
        while(*option) {
            if(selected == *option[0]) {
                chosen = 1;
                break;
            }
```

```
            option++;
        }
        if(!chosen) {
            printf("Incorrect choice, select again\n");
        }
    } while(!chosen);
    return selected;
}
```

How It Works

`getchoice` prints the program introduction, `greet`, and the sample menu, `choices`, and asks the user to choose the initial character. The program then loops until `getchar` returns a character that matches the first letter of one of the `option` array's entries.

When we compile and run this program, we discover that it doesn't behave as we expected. Here's some dialogue to demonstrate the problem:

```
$ menu1
Choice: Please select an action
a - add new record
d - delete record
q - quit
a
You have chosen: a
Choice: Please select an action
a - add new record
d - delete record
q - quit
Incorrect choice, select again
Choice: Please select an action
a - add new record
d - delete record
q - quit
q
You have chosen: q
$
```

Here the user had to enter *a/Return/q/Return* to make selections. There seem to be at least two problems. The most serious is that we are getting `Incorrect choice` after every correct choice. Plus, we still have to press *Return* before our program reads our input.

Why It Doesn't Quite Work

The two problems are closely related. By default, terminal input is not made available to a program until the user presses *Return*. In most cases this is a benefit, since it allows the user to correct typing mistakes using *Backspace* or *Delete*. Only when they're happy with what they see on the screen do they press *Return* to make the input available to the program.

This behavior is called **canonical**, or **standard**, mode. All the input is processed in terms of lines. Until a line of input is complete (usually when the user presses *Return*) the terminal interface manages all the key presses, including *Backspace*, and no characters may be read by the application.

The opposite of this is **non-canonical** mode, where the application has much greater control over the processing of input characters. We'll come back to these two modes again a little later on.

Amongst other things, the UNIX terminal handler likes translating interrupt characters to signals and can automatically perform *Backspace* and *Delete* processing for you, so you don't have to re-implement it in each program you write. We'll find out more about signals in Chapter 10.

So, what's happening in our program? Well, UNIX is saving the input until the user presses *Return*, then passing both the choice character and the subsequent *Return* to the program. So, each time you enter a menu choice, the program calls `getchar`, processes the character, then calls `getchar` again, which immediately returns with the *Return* character.

The character the program actually sees isn't an ASCII carriage return, `CR` (decimal 13, hex `0D`), but a line feed, `LF` (decimal 10, hex `0A`). This is because, internally, UNIX always uses a line feed to end lines of text, i.e. UNIX uses a line feed alone to mean a newline, where other systems, such as DOS, use a carriage return and a line feed together as a pair. If the input or output device also sends or requires a carriage return, the UNIX terminal processing takes care of it. This might seem a little strange if you're used to DOS or other environments, but one of the very considerable benefits is that there is no real difference between text and binary files on UNIX. Only when you input or output to a terminal or some printers and plotters are carriage returns processed.

We can correct the major deficiency in our menu routine simply by ignoring the additional line feed character with some code such as this:

```
do {
        selected = getchar();
} while(selected == '\n');
```

This solves the immediate problem. We'll return to the second problem of needing to press *Return*, and a more elegant solution to the line feed handling later.

Handling Redirected Output

It's very common for UNIX programs, even interactive ones, to have their input or output redirected, either to files or to other programs. Let's see how our program behaves when we redirect its output to a file.

```
$ menu1 > file
a
q
$
```

We could regard this as successful, since the output has been redirected to a file rather than to the terminal. However, there are cases where we want to prevent this from happening, or where we want to separate prompts that we want the user to see, from other output that can be safely redirected.

We can tell whether the standard output has been redirected by finding out if the low-level file descriptor is associated with a terminal. The `isatty` system call does this. We simply pass it a valid file descriptor and it tests to see if that is currently connected to a terminal.

```
#include <unistd.h>

int isatty(int fd);
```

The `isatty` system call returns `1` if the open file descriptor, `fd`, is connected to a terminal and `0` otherwise.

In our program we are using file streams, but `isatty` operates only on file descriptors. To provide the necessary conversion we need to combine the `isatty` call with the `fileno` routine that we met in Chapter 3.

What are we going to do if `stdout` has been redirected? Just quitting isn't good enough because the user has no way of knowing why the program failed to run. Printing a message on `stdout` won't help either, since it must have been redirected away from the terminal. One solution is to write to `stderr`, which isn't redirected by the shell `> file command`.

Try It Out – Checking for Output Redirection

4. Using the program `menu1.c` you created in the last section, make a new include, change the `main` function to the following and call the new file `menu2.c`.

```
#include <unistd.h>
...
int main()
{
    int choice = 0;

    if(!isatty(fileno(stdout))) {
        fprintf(stderr,"You are not a terminal!\n");
        exit(1);
    }
    do {
        choice = getchoice("Please select an action", menu);
        printf("You have chosen: %c\n", choice);
    } while(choice != 'q');
    exit(0);
}
```

5. Now look at the following sample output:

```
$ menu2
Choice: Please select an action
a - add new record
d - delete record
q - quit
q
You have chosen: q
$ menu2 > file
You are not a terminal!
$
```

How It Works

The new section of code uses the `isatty` function to test whether the standard output is connected to a terminal and halts execution if it isn't. This is the same test the shell uses to decide whether to offer prompts. It's possible, and quite common, to redirect both `stdout` and `stderr` away from the terminal. We can direct the error stream to a different file like this:

```
$ menu2 >file 2>file.error
$
```

Or combine the two output streams into a single file like this:

```
$ menu2 >file 2>&1
$
```

(If you're not familiar with output redirection, take another look at Chapter 2 where we explain this syntax in more detail.) In this case you'll need to send a message to the console.

Talking to the Terminal

If we need to prevent the parts of our program that interact with the user being redirected, but still allow it to happen to other input or output, we need to separate the interaction from `stdout` and `stderr`. We can do this by reading and writing directly to the terminal. Since UNIX is inherently a multiuser system, usually with many terminals either directly connected or connected across a network, how can we discover the correct terminal to use?

Fortunately, UNIX makes things easy for us by providing a special device, `/dev/tty`, which is always the current terminal, or login session. Since UNIX treats everything as a file, we can use normal file operations to read and write to `/dev/tty`.

Let's modify our choice program so that we can pass parameters to the `getchoice` routine, to provide better control over the output. We're up to `menu3.c`.

Try It Out – Using /dev/tty

6. Load up `menu2.c` and change the code to this, so that input and output come from and are directed to `/dev/tty`:

```
#include <stdio.h>
#include <unistd.h>

char *menu[] = {
    "a - add new record",
    "d - delete record",
    "q - quit",
    NULL,
};

int getchoice(char *greet, char *choices[], FILE *in, FILE *out);

int main()
{
    int choice = 0;
    FILE *input;
    FILE *output;

    if(!isatty(fileno(stdout))) {
        fprintf(stderr,"You are not a terminal, OK.\n");
    }

    input = fopen("/dev/tty", "r");
    output = fopen("/dev/tty", "w");
    if(!input || !output) {
        fprintf(stderr,"Unable to open /dev/tty\n");
        exit(1);
    }
    do {
        choice = getchoice("Please select an action", menu, input, output);
        printf("You have chosen: %c\n", choice);
    } while(choice != 'q');
    exit(0);
}
```

```
int getchoice(char *greet, char *choices[], FILE *in, FILE *out)
{
    int chosen = 0;
    int selected;
    char **option;

    do {
        fprintf(out,"Choice: %s\n",greet);
        option = choices;
        while(*option) {
            fprintf(out,"%s\n",*option);
            option++;
        }
        do {
            selected = fgetc(in);
        } while(selected == '\n');
        option = choices;
        while(*option) {
            if(selected == *option[0]) {
                chosen = 1;
                break;
            }
            option++;
        }
        if(!chosen) {
            fprintf(out,"Incorrect choice, select again\n");
        }
    } while(!chosen);
    return selected;
}
```

Now when we run the program with the output redirected, we can still see the prompts and the normal program output is separated:

```
$ menu3 > file
You are not a terminal, OK.
Choice: Please select an action
a - add new record
d - delete record
q - quit
d
Choice: Please select an action
a - add new record
d - delete record
q - quit
q
$ cat file
You have chosen: d
You have chosen: q
```

The Terminal Driver and the General Terminal Interface

Sometimes, a program needs much finer control over the terminal than can be achieved using simple file operations. UNIX provides a set of interfaces that allow us to control the behavior of the terminal driver, to give us much greater control of the processing of terminal input and output.

Overview

As the diagram shows, we can control the terminal through a set of function calls (the General Terminal Interface, or GTI) separate from those used for reading and writing. This keeps the data (read/write) interface very clean, while still allowing detailed control over the terminal behavior. That's not to say that the terminal I/O interface is clean—it's got to deal with a wide variety of different hardware.

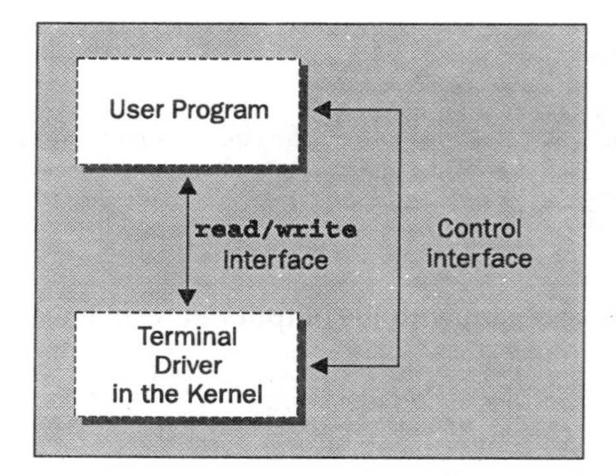

In UNIX terminology, the control interface sets a 'line discipline'. It allows a program considerable flexibility in specifying the behavior of the terminal driver.

The main features that we can control are:

Line editing	Whether to allow *Backspace* for editing.
Buffering	Whether to read characters immediately, or read them after a configurable delay.
Echo	Allows us to control echoing, such as when reading passwords.
`CR/LF`	Mapping for input and output, what happens when you print a `\n`.
Line speeds	Little used on a PC console, but very important for modems and terminals on serial lines.

Hardware Model

Before we look at the General Terminal Interface in detail, it's very important that we understand the hardware model that it's intended to drive.

The conceptual arrangement (and for some UNIX sites it will physically be like this) is to have a UNIX machine connected via a serial port to a modem and then via a telephone line and another modem to a remote terminal. In fact, this is just the kind of setup used by some small Internet service providers. It's a distant relative of the client/server paradigm, used when the program ran on a mainframe and users worked at dumb terminals.

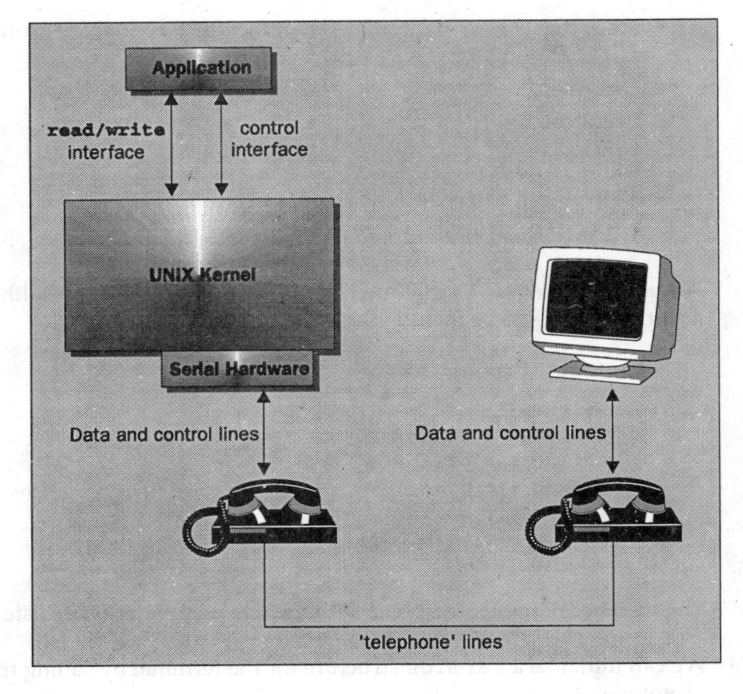

If you're working on a PC running Linux, this may seem an overly complex model. However, as both of the authors have modems, we can, if we choose, use a terminal emulation program like `minicom` to run a remote logon session on each other's machines just like this, using a pair of modems and a telephone line.

The advantage of using such a hardware model is that most 'real world' situations will form a subset of this, the most complex case. Supporting them will be much easier than if the model had omitted such functionality.

The termios Structure

`termios` is the standard interface specified by POSIX and is similar to the System V interface `termio`. The terminal interface is controlled by setting values in a structure of type `termios`, and by using a small set of function calls. Both are defined in the header file `termios.h`.

> **Programs that use the function calls defined in `termios.h` will need to be linked with an appropriate function library. This will normally be the `curses` library, so when compiling the examples in this chapter, you'll need to add `-lcurses` to the end of the compiler command line. On Linux systems, these become `ncurses` and `-lncurses`, respectively.**

The values that can be manipulated to affect the terminal are grouped into various modes:

- Input
- Output
- Control
- Local
- Special control characters

A minimum termios structure is typically declared like this (although the X/Open specification allows additional fields to be included):

```
#include <termios.h>

struct termios {
    tcflag_t c_iflag;
    tcflag_t c_oflag;
    tcflag_t c_cflag;
    tcflag_t c_lflag;
    cc_t     c_cc[NCCS];
};
```

The member names correspond with the five parameter types listed above.

We can initialize a termios structure for the terminal by calling the function tcgetattr, which has the prototype:

```
#include <termios.h>

int tcgetattr(int fd, struct termios *termios_p);
```

This call writes the current values of the terminal interface variables into the structure pointed to by termios_p. If these values are then altered, we can reconfigure the terminal interface with the tcsetattr function:

```
#include <termios.h>

int tcsetattr(int fd, int actions, const struct termios *termios_p);
```

The actions field for tcsetattr controls how any changes are applied. The three possibilities are:

TCSANOW	Change values immediately.
TCSADRAIN	Change values when current output is complete.
TCSAFLUSH	Change values when current output is complete, but discard any input currently available and not yet returned in a read call.

Note that it's very important for programs to restore terminal settings to the values they had before the program started. It's always the responsibility of a program to initially save and restore these settings when it finishes.

We'll now look more closely at the modes and related function calls. Some of the detail of the modes is rather specialized and rarely used, so we'll only cover the main features here. If you need to know more, you should consult your local man pages or a copy of the POSIX or X/Open specification.

The most important mode to take in on your first read is the local mode. The canonical and non-canonical modes are the solution to the second of our problems in the first application. We can instruct the program to wait for a line of input or pounce on input as soon as it is typed.

Input Modes

The input modes control how input (characters received by the terminal driver at a serial port or keyboard) is processed before being passed on to the program. We control them by setting flags in the `c_iflag` member of the `termios` structure. All the flags are defined as macros and can be combined with a bitwise OR. This is the case for all the terminal modes.

The macros that can be used for `c_iflag` are:

- `BRKINT` Generate an interrupt when a break condition is detected on the line.
- `IGNBRK` Ignore break conditions on the line.
- `ICRNL` Convert a received carriage return to a newline.
- `IGNCR` Ignore received carriage returns.
- `INLCR` Convert received newlines to carriage returns.
- `IGNPAR` Ignore characters with parity errors.
- `INPCK` Perform parity checking on received characters.
- `PARMRK` Mark parity errors.
- `ISTRIP` Strip (set to seven bits) all incoming characters.
- `IXOFF` Enable software flow control on input.
- `IXON` Enable software flow control on output.

If neither `BRKINT` nor `IGNBRK` are set, a break condition on the line is read as a `NULL` (`0x00`) character.

You won't very often need to change the input modes, as the default values are usually the most suitable, so we won't discuss them further here.

Output Modes

These modes control how output characters are processed, i.e. how characters sent from a program are processed before being transmitted to the serial port or screen. As you might expect, many of these are counterparts of the input modes. Several additional flags exist, which are mainly concerned with allowing for slow terminals that require time to process characters such as carriage returns. Almost all of these are either redundant (as terminals get faster) or better handled using the `terminfo` database of terminal capabilities, which we'll use later in this chapter.

We control output modes by setting flags in the `c_oflag` member of the `termios` structure. The macros that we can use in `c_oflag` are:

- `OPOST` Turn on output processing.
- `ONLCR` Convert any output newline to a carriage return/line feed pair.
- `OCRNL` Convert any output carriage return to a newline.
- `ONOCR` No carriage return output in column 0.
- `ONLRET` A newline also does a carriage return.
- `OFILL` Send fill characters to provide delays.
- `OFDEL` Use DEL as a fill character, rather then NULL.
- `NLDLY` Newline delay selection.
- `CRDLY` Carriage return delay selection.
- `TABDLY` Tab delay selection.
- `BSDLY` Backspace delay selection.
- `VTDLY` Vertical tab delay selection.
- `FFDLY` Form feed delay selection.

If `OPOST` is not set, all the other flags are ignored.

The output modes are also not commonly used, so we won't consider them further here.

Control Modes

These modes control the hardware characteristics of the terminal. We specify control modes by setting flags in the `c_cflag` member of the `termios` structure, which has the following macros:

- `CLOCAL` Ignore any modem status lines.
- `CREAD` Enable the receipt of characters.
- `CS5` Use five bits in sent or received characters.
- `CS6` Use six bits in sent or received characters.
- `CS7` Use seven bits in sent or received characters.
- `CS8` Use eight bits in sent or received characters.
- `CSTOPB` Use two stop bits per character, rather than one.
- `HUPCL` Hang up modem on close.
- `PARENB` Enable parity generation and detection.
- `PARODD` Use odd parity rather than even parity.

If `HUPCL` is set, when the terminal driver detects that the last file descriptor referring to the terminal has been closed it will set the modem control lines to 'hang-up' the line.

The control modes are mainly used when the serial line is connected to a modem, although they may be used when talking to a terminal. Normally, it's easier to change your terminal's configuration than to change the default line behavior by using the control modes of `termios`.

Local Modes

These modes control various characteristics of the terminal. We specify local modes by setting flags in the `c_lflag` member of the `termios` structure, with the macros:

- `ECHO` Enable local echoing of input characters.
- `ECHOE` Perform a *Backspace, Space, Backspace* combination on receiving ERASE.
- `ECHOK` Perform erase line on the KILL character.
- `ECHONL` Echo newline characters.
- `ICANON` Enable canonical input processing (see below).
- `IEXTEN` Enable implementation specific functions.
- `ISIG` Enable signals.
- `NOFLSH` Disable flush on queue.
- `TOSTOP` Send background processes a signal on write attempts.

The two most important flags here are `ECHO`, which allows you to suppress the echoing of typed characters, and the `ICANON` flag which switches the terminal between two very distinct modes of processing received characters. If the `ICANON` flag is set, then the line is said to be in canonical mode; if not, the line is in non-canonical mode.

We'll explain canonical mode and non-canonical mode in greater detail once we've met the special control characters that are used in both these modes.

Special Control Characters

These are a collection of characters, like *Ctrl-C*, that are acted upon in special ways when the user types them. The `c_cc` array member of the `termios` structure contains the characters mapped to each of the supported functions. The position of each character (its index into the array) is defined by a macro, but there's no limitation that they must be control characters.

The `c_cc` array is used in two very different ways, depending on whether or not the terminal is set to canonical mode (i.e. the setting of the `ICANON` flag in the `c_lflag` member of `termios`).

It's important to realize that there is some overlap in the way the array index values are used for the two different modes. Because of this, you should never mix values from these two modes.

For canonical mode, the array indices are:

- `VEOF` EOF character
- `VEOL` EOL character
- `VERASE` ERASE character
- `VINTR` INTR character
- `VKILL` KILL character
- `VQUIT` QUIT character
- `VSUSP` SUSP character
- `VSTART` START character
- `VSTOP` STOP character

For non-canonical mode, the array indices are:

- `VINTR` INTR character
- `VMIN` MIN value
- `VQUIT` QUIT character
- `VSUSP` SUSP character
- `VTIME` TIME value
- `VSTART` START character
- `VSTOP` STOP character

Since the special characters and non-canonical MIN and TIME values are so important for more advanced input character processing, we'll explain them in some detail.

Characters

Character	Description
INTR	This character will cause the terminal driver to send a `SIGINT` signal to processes connected to the terminal. We'll meet signals in more detail in Chapter 10.
QUIT	This character will cause the terminal driver to send a `SIGQUIT` signal to processes connected to the terminal.
ERASE	This character will cause the terminal driver to delete the last character on the line.
KILL	This character will cause the terminal driver to delete the entire line.
EOF	This character will cause the terminal driver to pass all characters on the line to the application reading input. If the line is empty, a `read` call will return zero characters, as though a `read` had been attempted at the end of a file.
EOL	This character acts as a line terminator, in addition to the more usual newline character.
SUSP	This character will cause the terminal driver to send a `SIGSUSP` signal to processes connected to the terminal. If your UNIX supports job control, the current application will be suspended.
STOP	This character acts to 'flow off', i.e. prevent further output to the terminal. It's used to support XON/XOFF flow control and is usually set to the ASCII XOFF character, *Ctrl-S*.
START	This character restarts output after a `STOP` character, often the ASCII XON character.

The TIME and MIN Values

The values of TIME and MIN are used only in non-canonical mode and act together to control the reading of input. Together, they control what happens when a program attempts to read a file descriptor associated with a terminal.

There are four cases:

MIN = 0 and TIME = 0

In this case, a `read` will always return immediately. If some characters are available they will be returned; if none are available, `read` will return zero and no characters will have been read.

MIN = 0 and TIME > 0

In this case, the `read` will return when any character is available to be read, or when TIME tenths of a second have elapsed. If no character was read because the timer expired, `read` will return zero. Otherwise, it will return the number of characters read.

MIN > 0 and TIME = 0

In this case, the `read` will wait until MIN characters can be read and then return that number of characters. Zero is returned on end of file.

MIN > 0 and TIME > 0

This is the most complex case. When `read` is called, it waits for a character to be received. When the first character and every subsequent time a character is received, an inter-character timer is started (or restarted if it was already running). The `read` will return when either MIN characters can be read or the inter-character time of TIME tenths of a second expires. This can be useful for telling the difference between a single press of the *Escape* key and the start of a function key escape sequence. Be aware, though, that network communications or high processor loads neatly erase such fine timing information.

By setting non-canonical mode and using the MIN and TIME values, programs can perform character-by-character processing of input.

Accessing Terminal Modes from the Shell

If you want to see the `termios` settings that are currently being used while you're using the shell, you can get a list using the command:

```
$ stty -a
```

On our Linux systems, which have some extensions to the standard `termios`, the output is:

```
speed 38400 baud; rows 25; columns 80; line = 0;
intr = ^C; quit = ^\; erase = ^?; kill = ^U; eof = ^D; eol = <undef>;
eol2 = <undef>; start = ^Q; stop = ^S; susp = ^Z; rprnt = ^R; werase = ^W;
lnext = ^V; flush = ^O; min = 1; time = 0;
-parenb -parodd cs8 hupcl -cstopb cread -clocal -crtscts
-ignbrk -brkint -ignpar -parmrk -inpck -istrip -inlcr -igncr icrnl ixon ixoff
-iuclc -ixany -imaxbel
opost -olcuc -ocrnl onlcr -onocr -onlret -ofill -ofdel nl0 cr0 tab0 bs0 vt0 ff0
isig icanon -iexten echo echoe echok -echonl -noflsh -xcase -tostop -echoprt
-echoctl echoke
```

Amongst other things, we can see that the EOF character is *Ctrl-D* and that echoing is enabled. When you're experimenting with terminal control, it's very easy to get the terminal left in a non-standard state, which makes using it very difficult. There are several ways out of this difficulty.

If your version of stty supports it, you can use the command:

```
$ stty sane
```

If you have lost the mapping of the carriage return key to the newline character (which terminates the line), you may need to enter stty sane, but rather than press *Return*, enter *Ctrl-J* (which is the newline character).

The second method is to use the stty -g command to write the current stty setting in a form ready to re-read. On the command line, you can use:

```
$ stty -g > save_stty
..
<experiment with settings>
..
$ stty $(cat save_stty)
```

You may still need to use *Ctrl-J* rather than *Return* for the final stty command. You can use the same technique in a shell script:

```
save_stty="$(stty -g)"
<alter stty settings>
stty $save_stty
```

If you're really stuck, the third method is to go to a different terminal, use the ps command to find the shell you have made unusable and then use kill HUP <process id> to force the shell to terminate. Since stty parameters are always reset before a logon prompt is issued, you should be able to log in normally.

Setting Terminal Modes from the Command Prompt

We can also use the stty command to set the terminal modes directly from the command prompt.

To set a mode in which our shell script could perform single character reads, we need to turn off canonical mode, set MIN to 1 and TIME to 0. The command is:

```
$ stty -icanon min 1 time 0
```

Now that the terminal is set to read characters immediately you can try to run our first program, menu1, again. You should find it works as originally intended.

We could also improve our attempt to check for a password (Chapter 2) by turning echoing off before we prompt for the password. The command to do this is:

```
$ stty -echo
```

Remember to use stty echo to turn echoing back on after you try this!

Terminal Speed

The final function served by the termios structure is manipulating the line speed. No members are defined for terminal speed; instead it's set by function calls. Input and output speeds are handled separately.

The four call prototypes are:

```
#include <termios.h>

speed_t cfgetispeed(const struct termios *);
speed_t cfgetospeed(const struct termios *);
int cfsetispeed(struct termios *, speed_t speed);
int cfsetospeed(struct termios *, speed_t speed);
```

Notice that these act on a termios structure, not directly on a port. This means that, to set a new speed, you must read the current settings with tcgetattr, set the speed using one of the above calls, then write the termios structure back using tcsetattr. Only after the call to tcsetattr will the line speed be changed.

Various values are allowed for speed in the function calls above, the most important are:

- B0 Hang up the terminal
- B1200 1200 baud
- B2400 2400 baud
- B9600 9600 baud
- B19200 19200 baud
- B38400 38400 baud

There are no speeds greater than 38400 defined by the standard and no standard method of supporting serial ports at speeds greater than this.

Some systems, including Linux define B57600, B115200 and B230400 for selecting faster speeds. If you're using an earlier version of Linux and these constants are unavailable, you can use the command setserial to obtain non-standard speeds of 57600 and 115200. In this case, these speeds will be used when B38400 is selected. Both of these methods are non-portable, so be careful when you're using them.

Additional Functions

There are a small number of additional functions for the control of terminals. These work directly on file descriptors, without needing to get and set termios structures. Their definitions are:

```
#include <termios.h>

int tcdrain(int fd);
int tcflow(int fd, int flowtype);
int tcflush(int fd, int in_out_selector);
```

The functions have the following purposes:

- `tcdrain` causes the calling program to wait until all queued output has been sent.
- `tcflow` is used to suspend or restart output.
- `tcflush` can be used to flush input, output or both.

Now that we've covered the rather large subject of the `termios` structure, let's look at a few practical examples. Possibly the simplest is the disabling of echo to read a password. We do this by turning off the `ECHO` flag.

Try It Out – A Password Program with termios

1. Our password program, `password.c`, begins with the following definitions:

```
#include <termios.h>
#include <stdio.h>

#define PASSWORD_LEN 8

int main()
{
    struct termios initialrsettings, newrsettings;
    char password[PASSWORD_LEN + 1];
```

2. Next, add in a line to get the current settings from the standard input and copy them into the termios structure that we created above.

```
    tcgetattr(fileno(stdin), &initialrsettings);
```

3. Make a copy of the original settings to replace them at the end. Turn off the ECHO flag on the newrsettings and ask the user for their password:

```
    newrsettings = initialrsettings;
    newrsettings.c_lflag &= ~ECHO;

    printf("Enter password: ");
```

4. Next, set the terminal attributes to newrsettings and read in the password. Lastly, reset the terminal attributes to their original setting and print the password to render all the previous effort useless.

```
    if(tcsetattr(fileno(stdin), TCSAFLUSH, &newrsettings) != 0) {
        fprintf(stderr,"Could not set attributes\n");
    }
    else {
        fgets(password, PASSWORD_LEN, stdin);
        tcsetattr(fileno(stdin), TCSANOW, &initialrsettings);
        fprintf(stdout, "\nYou entered %s\n", password);
    }
    exit(0);
}
```

How It Works

```
$ password
Enter password:
You entered hello
$
```

In this example, the word `hello` is typed but not echoed at the `Enter password:` prompt. No output is produced until the user presses *Return*.

We're careful only to change the flags we need to change, using the construct `X &= ~FLAG` (which clears the bit defined by `FLAG` in the variable `X`). If needed, we could use `X |= FLAG` to set a single bit defined by `FLAG`, although this wasn't necessary in the above example.

When we're setting the attributes, we use `TCSAFLUSH` to discard any type ahead. This is a good way of encouraging users not to start typing their password until echo has been turned off. We also restore the previous setting before our program terminates.

Another common use of the `termios` structure is to put the terminal into a state where we can read each character as it is typed. We do this by turning off canonical mode and using the `MIN` and `TIME` settings.

Try It Out – Reading Each Character

1. Using our new knowledge, we can make changes to our menu program. The following code bears much resemblance to `password.c`, but needs to be inserted into menu3.c to make our new program, `menu4.c`. For a start, we must include a new header file at the top of the program:

```
#include <stdio.h>
#include <unistd.h>
#include <termios.h>
```

2. Then we need to declare a couple of new variables in the main function:

```
    int choice = 0;
    FILE *input;
    FILE *output;
    struct termios initial_settings, new_settings;
```

3. We need to change the terminal's characteristics before we call the `getchoice` function, so that's where we place these lines:

```
        fprintf(stderr, "Unable to open /dev/tty\n");
        exit(1);
    }
    tcgetattr(fileno(input),&initial_settings);
    new_settings = initial_settings;
    new_settings.c_lflag &= ~ICANON;
    new_settings.c_lflag &= ~ECHO;
    new_settings.c_cc[VMIN] = 1;
    new_settings.c_cc[VTIME] = 0;
    if(tcsetattr(fileno(input), TCSANOW, &new_settings) != 0) {
        fprintf(stderr,"could not set attributes\n");
    }
```

4. We should also return the settings to their original values before exiting:

```
    do {
        choice = getchoice("Please select an action", menu, input, output);
        printf("You have chosen: %c\n", choice);
```

```
    } while (choice != 'q');
    tcsetattr(fileno(input),TCSANOW,&initial_settings);
    exit(0);
}
```

Note that we need to check against carriage returns \r now that we're in non-canonical mode, because the default mapping of CR to LF is no longer being performed.

```
        do {
            selected = fgetc(in);
        } while (selected == '\n' || selected == '\r');
```

5. Unfortunately, if the user now types Ctrl-C at our program, it will terminate. We can disable processing of these special characters by clearing the ISIG flag in the local modes. Add the following line to main.

```
    new_settings.c_lflag &= ~ISIG;
```

How It Works

If we put these changes into our menu program, we now get an immediate response and the character we type isn't echoed:

```
$ menu4
Choice: Please select an action
a - add new record
d - delete record
q - quit
You have chosen: a
Choice: Please select an action
a - add new record
d - delete record
q - quit
You have chosen: q
$
```

If we type *Ctrl-C*, it's passed directly to the program and treated as an incorrect choice.

Terminal Output

Using the `termios` structure, we have control over keyboard input, but it would be good to have the same level of control over the way a program's output is presented on the screen. We used `printf` at the start of the chapter to output characters to the screen, but with no way of placing the output at a particular position on the screen.

Terminal Type

Many UNIX systems are used with terminals, although in many cases today the 'terminal' may actually be a PC running a terminal program. Historically, there have been a very large number of terminals from different manufacturers. Although they nearly all use escape sequences (a string of characters starting with the escape character) to provide control over the position of the cursor and other attributes, such as bold and blinking, they are generally not very well standardized in the way they do this. Some older terminals also have different scrolling capabilities, may or may not erase when backspace is sent, and so on.

There is an ANSI standard set of escape sequences (mostly based on the sequences used in the Digital Equipment Corporation VT series terminals, but not identical). Many PC terminal programs provide an emulation of a standard terminal, often VT100, VT220 or ANSI, and sometimes others as well.

This variety of terminals would be a major problem for programmers wishing to write software that controls the screen and runs on many terminal types. For example, an ANSI terminal uses the sequence *Escape-[-A* to move the cursor up one line. An ADM-3a terminal (very common some years ago), uses the single control character *Ctrl-K*.

Writing a program that can deal with the many different types of terminal that might be connected to a UNIX system would seem to be an extremely daunting task. The program would need different source code for each type of terminal.

Not surprisingly, there is a solution in a package known as `terminfo`. Instead of each program having to cater for every sort of terminal, the program looks up a database of terminal types to get the correct information. In most modern UNIX systems this has been integrated with another package called `curses`, which we will meet in the next chapter.

On Linux, we'll use the implementation of `curses` known as `ncurses`, and include `ncurses.h` to provide prototypes for our `terminfo` functions. The `terminfo` functions themselves are declared in their own header file, `term.h`. Or at least, that used to be the case. With newer Linux versions, there's a blurring of the line between `terminfo` and `ncurses`, to the point where many programs requiring `terminfo` functions must also include the `ncurses` header file.

Identify Your Terminal Type

The UNIX environment contains a variable, `TERM`, that is set to the type of terminal being used. It's usually set automatically by the system at logon time. The system administrator may set a default terminal type for each of the directly connected terminals and may arrange for remote, networked users to be prompted for a terminal type. The value of `TERM` can be negotiated via `telnet` and is passed by `rlogin`.

A user can query the shell to discover the system's idea of the terminal he or she is using.

```
$ echo $TERM
xterm
$
```

In this case, the shell is being run from a program called `xterm`, a terminal emulator for the X Window system.

The `terminfo` package contains a database of capabilities and escape sequences for a large number of terminals and provides a uniform programming interface for using them. A single program can then be written that will take advantage of future terminals as the database is extended, rather than each application having to provide support for the many different terminals.

The terminfo capabilities are described by attributes. These are stored in a set of compiled terminfo files, conventionally found in /usr/lib/terminfo or /usr/share/terminfo. For each terminal (and many printers, which can also be specified in terminfo) there's a file that defines its capabilities and how its features can be accessed. To avoid creating a very large directory, the actual files are stored in subdirectories, where the subdirectory name is simply the first letter of the terminal type. Thus, the VT100 definition is found in ...terminfo/v/vt100.

terminfo files are written one per terminal type in a source format that is (just about!) readable, then compiled using the tic command into a more compact and efficient format for use by application programs. Curiously, the X/Open specification refers to source and compiled format definitions, but fails to mention the tic command for actually getting from source to compiled formats. You can use the infocmp program to print a readable version of a compiled terminfo entry.

Here's an example terminfo file for the VT100 terminal:

```
$ infocmp vt100
vt100|vt100-am|dec vt100 (w/advanced video),
 am, mir, msgr, xenl, xon,
 cols#80, it#8, lines#24, vt#3,
 acsc=``aaffggjjkkllmmnnooppqqrrssttuuvvwwxxyyzz{{||}}~~,
 bel=^G, blink=\E[5m$<2>, bold=\E[1m$<2>,
 clear=\E[H\E[J$<50>, cr=\r, csr=\E[%i%p1%d;%p2%dr,
 cub=\E[%p1%dD, cub1=\b, cud=\E[%p1%dB, cud1=\n,
 cuf=\E[%p1%dC, cuf1=\E[C$<2>,
 cup=\E[%i%p1%d;%p2%dH$<5>, cuu=\E[%p1%dA,
 cuu1=\E[A$<2>, ed=\E[J$<50>, el=\E[K$<3>,
 el1=\E[1K$<3>, enacs=\E(B\E)0, home=\E[H, ht=\t,
 hts=\EH, ind=\n, ka1=\EOq, ka3=\EOs, kb2=\EOr, kbs=\b,
 kc1=\EOp, kc3=\EOn, kcub1=\EOD, kcud1=\EOB,
 kcuf1=\EOC, kcuu1=\EOA, kent=\EOM, kf0=\EOy, kf1=\EOP,
 kf10=\EOx, kf2=\EOQ, kf3=\EOR, kf4=\EOS, kf5=\EOt,
 kf6=\EOu, kf7=\EOv, kf8=\EOl, kf9=\EOw, rc=\E8,
 rev=\E[7m$<2>, ri=\EM$<5>, rmacs=^O, rmkx=\E[?1l\E>,
 rmso=\E[m$<2>, rmul=\E[m$<2>,
 rs2=\E>\E[?3l\E[?4l\E[?5l\E[?7h\E[?8h, sc=\E7,
 sgr=\E[0%?%p1%p6%|%t;1%;%?%p2%t;4%;%?%p1%p3%|%t;7%;%?%p4%t;5%;m%?%p9%t^N%e^O%;,
 sgr0=\E[m^O$<2>, smacs=^N, smkx=\E[?1h\E=,
 smso=\E[1;7m$<2>, smul=\E[4m$<2>, tbc=\E[3g,
```

Each terminfo definition consists of three types of entry. Each entry is called a **capname** and defines a terminal capability.

Boolean capabilities simply indicate whether a terminal supports a particular feature. For example, the Boolean capability xon is present if the terminal supports XON/XOFF flow control, cub1 is present if a 'cursor left' command given while the cursor is in column 0 will put the cursor in the right-most column.

Numeric capabilities define sizes, such as lines, the number of lines on the screen and cols, the number of columns on the screen. The actual number is separated from the capability name by a # character. To define a terminal as having 80 columns and 24 lines, we would write cols#80, lines#24.

String capabilities are slightly more complex. They are used for two distinct types of capability: defining output strings needed to access terminal features and defining the input strings that will be received when the user presses certain keys, normally function keys or special keys on the numeric keypad. Some string capabilities are quite simple, such as el, which is "erase to end of line". On a VT100 terminal, the escape sequence needed to do this is *Esc-[-K*. This is written el=\E[K in terminfo source format.

Special keys are defined in a similar way. For example, function key *f1* on a VT100 sends the sequence *Esc-O-P*. This is defined as `kf1=\EOP`.

Things get slightly more complicated where the escape sequence needs some parameters. Most terminals can move the cursor to a specified row and column location. It's clearly impractical to have a different capability for each possible cursor location, so a generic capability string is used, with parameters defining the values to be inserted when the stings are used. For example, a VT100 terminal uses the sequence *Esc-[-<row>-;-<col>-H* to move the cursor to a specified location. In `terminfo` source format, this is written with the rather intimidating `cup=\E[%i%p1%d;%p2%dH$<5>`.

This means:

- `\E` Send *Escape*.
- `[` Send the `[` character.
- `%i` Increment the arguments.
- `%p1` Put the first argument on the stack.
- `%d` Output the number on the stack as a decimal number.
- `;` Send the `;` character.
- `%p2` Put the second argument on the stack.
- `%d` Output the number on the stack as a decimal number.
- `H` Send the `H` character.

This seems rather more complex than it might be, but allows for the parameters to be in a fixed order, independent of which order the terminal expects them to appear in the final escape sequence. The `%i` to increment the arguments is required because standard cursor addressing is specified as starting from (0,0) at the top left of the screen, but the VT100 addresses this location as (1,1). The final `$<5>` indicates that a delay equivalent to five character output times is required to allow the terminal to process the cursor movement.

We could define many, many capabilities, but, fortunately most UNIX systems come with most terminals predefined. If you need to add a new terminal, you'll find the complete capability list in the manual under `terminfo`. A good starting point is usually to locate a terminal that is similar to your new terminal and define the new terminal as a variation on the existing terminal, or work through the capabilities one at a time, updating them where required.

The standard reference outside the `man` pages is the O'Reilly title *Termcap and Terminfo*, ISBN 0-937175-22-6.

Using terminfo Capabilities

Now that we know how to define terminal capabilities, we need to learn how to access them. When we're using terminfo, the first thing we need to do is to set up the terminal type by calling setupterm. This will initialize a TERMINAL structure for the current terminal type. We'll then be able to ask for capabilities for the terminal and use its facilities. We do this with the setupterm call like this:

```
#include <term.h>

int setupterm(char *term, int fd, int *errret);
```

The setupterm library function sets the current terminal type to that specified by the parameter term. If term is a null pointer, the TERM environment variable will be used. An open file descriptor to be used for writing to the terminal must be passed as fd. The function outcome is stored in the integer variable pointed to by errret, if this isn't a null pointer. The value written will be:

- -1 No terminfo database.
- 0 No matching entry in terminfo database.
- 1 Success.

The setupterm function returns the constant OK if it succeeds and ERR if it fails. If errret is set to a null pointer setupterm will print a diagnostic message and exit the program if it fails, as in this example:

```
#include <stdio.h>
#include <term.h>
#include <ncurses.h>

int main()
{
    setupterm("unlisted",fileno(stdout),(int *)0);
    printf("Done.\n");
    exit(0);
}
```

The output from running this program on your system may not be exactly that given here, but the meaning should be clear enough. Done. isn't printed, since setupterm caused the program to exit when it failed.

```
$ cc -o badterm badterm.c -I/usr/include/ncurses -lncurses
$ badterm
'unlisted': unknown terminal type.
$
```

Notice the compilation line in the example: on this Linux system, the ncurses header file is in the directory /usr/include/ncurses, so we have to specifically instruct the compiler to look there with the -I option. Some Linux systems have arranged for the ncurses library to be available in the standard locations. On these systems we can simply include curses.h, and specify -lcurses for the library.

For our menu choice function, we would like to be able to clear the screen, move the cursor around the screen and write at different locations on the screen. Once we've called setupterm, we can access the terminfo capabilities with three function calls, one for each of the capability types:

```
#include <term.h>

int tigetflag(char *capname);
int tigetnum(char *capname);
char *tigetstr(char *capname);
```

The functions tigetflag, tigetnum and tigetstr return the value of Boolean, numeric and string terminfo capabilities, respectively. On failure (for example if the capability isn't present), tigetflag returns -1, tigetnum returns -2 and tigetstr returns (char *)-1.

Let's use the terminfo database to find out the size of the terminal by retrieving the cols and lines capabilities with this program, sizeterm.c:

```
#include <stdio.h>
#include <term.h>
#include <ncurses.h>

int main()
{
    int nrows, ncolumns;

    setupterm(NULL, fileno(stdout), (int *)0);
    nrows = tigetnum("lines");
    ncolumns = tigetnum("cols");
    printf("This terminal has %d columns and %d rows\n", ncolumns, nrows);
    exit(0);
}
```

```
$ echo $TERM
vt100
$ sizeterm
This terminal has 80 columns and 24 rows
$
```

If we run the program inside a window on a workstation, we'll get answers that reflect the current window's size:

```
$ echo $TERM
xterm
$ sizeterm
This terminal has 88 columns and 40 rows
$
```

If we use tigetstr to retrieve the cursor motion capability (cup) of the xterm terminal type we get a parameterized answer: \E[%p1%d;%p2%dH.

This capability requires two parameters: a row and column to move the cursor to. Both coordinates are measured starting at zero from the top left corner of the screen.

We can substitute the parameters in a capability with actual values using the tparm function. Up to nine parameters can be substituted and a usable escape sequence is returned.

```
#include <term.h>

char *tparm(char *cap, long p1, long p2, ..., long p9);
```

Outputting Control Strings to the Terminal

Once we've constructed the terminal escape sequence with `tparm`, we must send it to the terminal. To process this properly, you shouldn't send the string to the terminal with `printf`. Instead, use one of the special functions provided that correctly process any required delays while the terminal completes an operation. These functions are:

```
#include <term.h>

int putp(char *const str);
int tputs(char *const str, int affcnt, int (*putfunc)(int));
```

On success, `putp` returns `OK`; on failure `ERR`. The `putp` function takes the terminal control string and sends it to `stdout`.

So, to move to row 5, column 30 of the screen, we can use a block of code like this:

```
char *cursor;
char *esc_sequence;
cursor = tigetstr("cup");
esc_sequence = tparm(cursor,5,30);
putp(esc_sequence);
```

The `tputs` function is provided for those situations when the terminal isn't accessed via `stdout` and allows you to specify the function to be used for outputting the characters. It returns the result of the user specified function `putfunc`. The `affcnt` parameter is intended to indicate the number of lines affected by the change. It's normally set to 1. The function used to output the string must have the same parameters and return type as the `putchar` function. Indeed, `putp(string)` is equivalent to the call `tputs(string, 1, putchar)`. We'll see `tputs` used with a user specified output function later.

Be aware that some older Linux distributions define the final parameter of the `tputs` function as `int (*putfunc)(char)`, which would oblige us to alter the definition of the `char_to_terminal` function in our next Try It Out.

> **If you consult the manual pages for information on `tparm` and terminal capabilities, you may come across the `tgoto` function. The reason we haven't used this function, when it apparently offers an easier solution to moving the cursor, is that the X/Open specification (Single UNIX Specification Version 2) does not include them as of the 1997 edition. We therefore recommend that you don't use any of these functions in new programs.**

We're almost ready to add screen handling to our menu choice function. The only thing left to do is to clear the screen, simply using `clear`. Some terminals don't support the `clear` capability which leaves the cursor at the top left corner of the screen. In this case we can position the cursor at the top left corner and use the 'delete to end of display' command, `ed`.

Putting all this information together, we'll write the final version of our sample menu program, `screenmenu.c`, where we 'paint' the options on the screen for the user to pick a valid one.

Try It Out – Total Terminal Control

We can rewrite the `getchoice` function from `menu4.c` to give us total terminal control. In this listing, the main function has been omitted because it isn't changed. Other differences from `menu4.c` are highlighted.

```
#include <stdio.h>
#include <unistd.h>
#include <termios.h>
#include <term.h>
#include <curses.h>

static FILE *output_stream = (FILE *)0;

char *menu[] = {
    "a - add new record",
    "d - delete record",
    "q - quit",
    NULL,
};

int getchoice(char *greet, char *choices[], FILE *in, FILE *out);
int char_to_terminal(int char_to_write);

int main()
{
...
}

int getchoice(char *greet, char *choices[], FILE *in, FILE *out)
{
    int chosen = 0;
    int selected;
    int screenrow, screencol = 10;

    char **option;
    char *cursor, *clear;

    output_stream = out;

    setupterm(NULL,fileno(out), (int *)0);
    cursor = tigetstr("cup");
    clear = tigetstr("clear");

    screenrow = 4;
    tputs(clear, 1, (int *) char_to_terminal);
    tputs(tparm(cursor, screenrow, screencol), 1, char_to_terminal);
    fprintf(out, "Choice: %s", greet);
    screenrow += 2;
    option = choices;
    while(*option) {
        tputs(tparm(cursor, screenrow, screencol), 1, char_to_terminal);
        fprintf(out,"%s", *option);
        screenrow++;
        option++;
    }

    do {
        selected = fgetc(in);
        option = choices;
        while(*option) {
            if(selected == *option[0]) {
                chosen = 1;
                break;
            }
            option++;
        }
```

```
        if(!chosen) {
            tputs(tparm(cursor, screenrow, screencol), 1, char_to_terminal);
            fprintf(out,"Incorrect choice, select again\n");
        }
    } while(!chosen);
    tputs(clear, 1, char_to_terminal);
    return selected;
}

int char_to_terminal(int char_to_write)
{
    if (output_stream) putc(char_to_write, output_stream);
    return 0;
}
```

How It Works

The rewritten `getchoice` function implements the same menu as in previous examples, but the output routines are modified to make use of the `terminfo` capabilities. If you want to see the `You have chosen:` message for more than a moment before the screen is cleared ready for the next selection, add a call to `sleep` in the `main` function:

```
do {
        choice = getchoice("Please select an action", menu, input, output);
        printf("\nYou have chosen: %c\n", choice);
        sleep(1);
    } while (choice != 'q');
```

The last function in this program, `char_to_terminal`, includes a call to the `putc` function, which we mentioned in Chapter 3.

To round off this chapter, we'll look at a quick example of how to detect keystrokes.

Detecting Keystrokes

People who have programmed MS-DOS often look for the UNIX equivalent of the `kbhit` function, which detects whether a key has been pressed without actually reading it. Unfortunately, they fail to find it, since there's no direct equivalent. UNIX programmers don't notice the omission, because UNIX is normally programmed in such a way that programs should rarely, if ever, busy-wait on an event. Since this is the normal use for `kbhit`, it's rarely missed on UNIX.

However, when you're porting programs from MS-DOS, it's often convenient to emulate `kbhit`, which you can do using the non-canonical input mode.

Try It Out – Your Very Own kbhit

1. We begin with the standard headings and declare a couple of structures for the terminal settings. `peek_character` is used in the test of whether or not a key has been pressed. Then we prototype the functions we'll be using later.

```
#include <stdio.h>
#include <termios.h>
#include <term.h>
#include <curses.h>
#include <unistd.h>
static struct termios initial_settings, new_settings;
static int peek_character = -1;
```

```
void init_keyboard();
void close_keyboard();
int kbhit();
int readch();
```

2. The main function calls `init_keyboard` to configure the terminal, then just loops once a second, calling kbhit each time it does so. If the key hit is *q*, `close_keyboard` returns the behavior to normal and the program exits.

```
int main()
{
    int ch = 0;

    init_keyboard();
    while(ch != 'q') {
        printf("looping\n");
        sleep(1);
        if(kbhit()) {
            ch = readch();
            printf("you hit %c\n",ch);
        }
    }
    close_keyboard();
    exit(0);
}
```

3. `init_keyboard` and `close_keyboard` configure the terminal at the start and end of the program.

```
void init_keyboard()
{
    tcgetattr(0,&initial_settings);
    new_settings = initial_settings;
    new_settings.c_lflag &= ~ICANON;
    new_settings.c_lflag &= ~ECHO;
    new_settings.c_lflag &= ~ISIG;
    new_settings.c_cc[VMIN] = 1;
    new_settings.c_cc[VTIME] = 0;
    tcsetattr(0, TCSANOW, &new_settings);
}

void close_keyboard()
{
    tcsetattr(0, TCSANOW, &initial_settings);
}
```

4. Now for the function that checks for the keyboard hit:

```
int kbhit()
{
    char ch;
    int nread;

    if(peek_character != -1)
        return 1;
    new_settings.c_cc[VMIN]=0;
    tcsetattr(0, TCSANOW, &new_settings);
    nread = read(0,&ch,1);
    new_settings.c_cc[VMIN]=1;
    tcsetattr(0, TCSANOW, &new_settings);
```

```
    if(nread == 1) {
        peek_character = ch;
        return 1;
    }
    return 0;
}
```

5. The character pressed is read by the next function, `readch`, which then resets `peek_character` to -1 for the next loop.

```
int readch()
{
    char ch;

    if(peek_character != -1) {
        ch = peek_character;
        peek_character = -1;
        return ch;
    }
    read(0,&ch,1);
    return ch;
}
```

When we run the program, we get:

```
$ kbhit
looping
looping
looping
you hit h
looping
looping
looping
you hit d
looping
you hit q
$
```

How It Works

The terminal is configured in `init_keyboard` to read one character before returning (MIN=1, TIME=0). `kbhit` changes this behavior to check for input and return immediately (MIN=0, TIME=0) and then restores the original settings before exiting.

Notice that we have to read the character that has been pressed, but store it locally ready for returning when it's required.

Pseudo Terminals

Many UNIX systems, and LINUX too, have a feature called pseudo-terminals. These are devices that behave much like the terminals we have been using in this chapter, except that they have no associated hardware. They can be used to provide a terminal-like interface to other programs.

For example, using pseudo-terminals it is possible to make two chess programs play each other, despite the fact that the programs themselves were designed to interact with a human player at a terminal. A application, acting as an intermediary passes one program's moves to the other and vice versa. It uses pseudo-terminals to fool the programs into behaving normally without a terminal being present.

Pseudo-terminals were at one time implemented in a system-specific manner, if at all. They have now been incorporated into the Single UNIX Specification as UNIX98 Pseudo-Terminals or PTYs.

Summary

In this chapter we've learned about three different aspects of controlling the terminal. In the first part of the chapter, we learned about detecting redirection and how to talk directly to a terminal even when the standard file descriptors have been redirected.

We then learned about the General Terminal Interface and the `termios` structure that provides detailed control over UNIX terminal handling.

Finally, we learned how to use the `terminfo` database and related functions to manage screen output in a terminal independent fashion.

Curses

In the last chapter, we saw how to obtain much finer control over the input of characters and how to provide character output in a terminal-independent way. The problem with using the general terminal interface (GTI, or `termios`) and manipulating escape sequences with `tparm` and its related functions is that it requires a lot of lower-level code. For many programs a higher-level interface would be more desirable. We would like to be able to simply draw on the screen and use a library of functions to take care of terminal dependencies automatically.

In this chapter, we'll learn about just such a library, the `curses` library. `curses` is important standard as a halfway house between simple 'line-based' programs and the fully graphical (and generally much harder to program) X Window system programs. Linux does have the svgalib, but that is not a standard UNIX library. The `curses` library is used in many full screen applications as a reasonably easy, and terminal-independent way to write full-screen, albeit character-based, programs. It's generally much easier to write such programs with `curses` than to use escape sequences directly. `curses` can also manage the keyboard, providing an easy to use, non-blocking character input mode. It's used by the people's pet-hate text editor, `vi`. We'll cover:

- Using the `curses` library
- The concepts of `curses`
- Basic input and output control
- Multiple windows
- Keypad
- Color

We will finish by re-implementing the CD Collection program in C, summarizing what we've learned in these last few chapters.

Compiling with curses

Since `curses` is a library, to use it we must include a header file, functions and macros from an appropriate system library. But before that, some history. There have been several different implementations of `curses`. The original version appeared in BSD UNIX and was then incorporated into the System V flavors of UNIX. As we developed the examples for this chapter, we used `ncurses`, a freeware emulation of System V Release 4.0 `curses` that was developed under Linux. This implementation is highly portable to other UNIX versions. There are even versions of curses for MS-DOS and MS-Windows. If you find that the `curses` library bundled with your flavor of UNIX doesn't support some features, we suggest you try and obtain a copy of `ncurses` as an alternative.

The X/Open specification defines two levels of `curses`: base and extended. The version of `ncurses` current when this book was written doesn't yet implement all of the extended features, though it does implement the 'useful' ones, such as multiple windows and color support. Few `curses` programs will need the extended facilities that are not implemented in `ncurses`.

Extended `curses` contains a motley crew of additional routines, including a range of functions for handling multicolumn characters and color manipulation routines.

When you're compiling `curses` programs, you must include the header file `curses.h`, and link against the `curses` library with `-lcurses`. Depending on your system setup, this may already be `ncurses`. You can check how your curses is setup, by doing a `ls -l /usr/include/*curses.h` to look at the header files, and `ls -l /usr/lib/*curses*` to check the library files. If you find that the curses files are links to ncurses files, then (using gcc) you should be able to compile the files in this chapter using a command such as:

```
$ gcc program.c -o program -lcurses
```

If, however, your curses setup is not automatically using ncurses, you may have to explicitly force the use of ncurses by using a compile command such as this.

```
$ gcc -I/usr/include/ncurses program.c -o program -lncurses
```

where the `-I` option specifies the directory in which to search for the header file. The makefile in the downloadable code assumes your setup uses ncurses by default, so you will have to change it, or compile by hand if this is not the case on your system.

If you're unsure how `curses` is set up on your system, refer to the manual pages for `ncurses`.

Concepts

The curses routines work on screens, windows and subwindows. A screen is the device (usually a terminal screen) to which we are writing. It occupies all the available display on that device. Of course, if it's a terminal window inside an X Window, the screen is simply all the character positions available inside the terminal window. There is always at least one curses window, stdscr, which is the same size as the physical screen. You can create additional windows that are smaller than the screen. Windows can overlap each other and can have many subwindows, but each subwindow must always be contained inside its parent window.

The curses library maintains two data structures that act like a map of the terminal screen, stdscr and curscr.

stdscr, the more important, is a structure updated when curses functions produce output. The stdscr data structure is the 'standard screen'. It acts in much the same way as stdout, the standard output, does for the stdio library. It's the default output window in curses programs. This output doesn't appear on the screen until the program calls refresh, when the curses library compares the contents of stdscr (what the screen should look like) with the second structure curscr (what the screen currently looks like). curses then uses the differences between these two structures to update the screen.

Some curses programs need to know that curses maintains a stdscr structure, as it's required as a parameter to a few curses functions. However, the actual stdscr structure is implementation-dependent and should never be accessed directly. curses programs shouldn't need to use curscr.

Thus, the process for the output of characters in a curses program is:

- Use curses functions to update a logical screen.
- Ask curses to update the physical screen with refresh.

The advantage of a two-level approach is that curses screen updates are very efficient and, although this isn't so important on a console screen, it makes a considerable difference if you're running your program over a slow serial or modem link.

A curses program will make many calls to logical screen output functions, possibly moving the cursor all over the screen to get to the right position for writing text and drawing lines and boxes. At some stage, the user will need to see all of this output. When this happens, typically during a call to refresh, curses will calculate the optimum way of making the physical screen correspond to the logical screen. By using appropriate terminal capabilities and by optimizing cursor motions, curses will often be able to update the screen with far fewer characters being output than if all the screen writes had happened immediately. The curses library takes its name from this cursor optimization feature. Although the number of characters output is not as important as it was in the days of dumb terminals and low speed modems, the curses library survives as a useful addition to the programmer's toolkit.

The layout of the logical screen is a character array, arranged by lines and columns with the screen position (0,0) at the top left-hand corner.

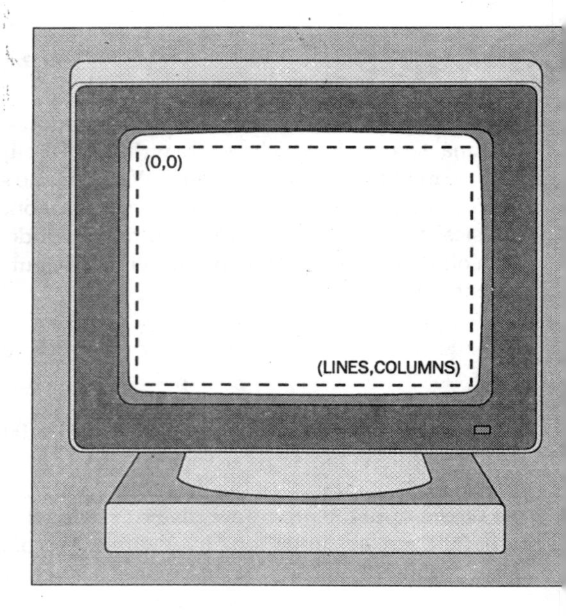

All the curses functions use coordinates with the y value (lines) before the x (columns) value. Each position holds not only the character for that screen location, but also its attributes. The attributes that can be displayed depend on the physical terminal's capabilities, but usually at least bold and underline are available.

Because the curses library needs to create and destroy some temporary data structures, all curses programs must initialize the library before use and then allow curses to restore settings after use. This is done with a pair of function calls, initscr and endwin.

Let's write a very simple curses program, screen1.c, to show these and other basic function calls in action. We'll then describe the function prototypes.

Try It Out - A Simple curses Program

1. We add in the curses.h header file and in the main function we make calls to initialize and reset the curses library.

```
#include <unistd.h>
#include <stdlib.h>
#include <curses.h>

int main() {
    initscr();

...

    endwin();
    exit(EXIT_SUCCESS);
}
```

2. In between, we move the cursor to the point (5,15) on the logical screen, print "Hello World" and refresh the actual screen. Lastly, we use the call `sleep(2)` to suspend the program for two seconds, so we can see the output before the program ends.

```
move(5, 15);
printw("%s", "Hello World");
refresh();

sleep(2);
```

While the program is running, we see "Hello World" in the top left quadrant of an otherwise blank screen.

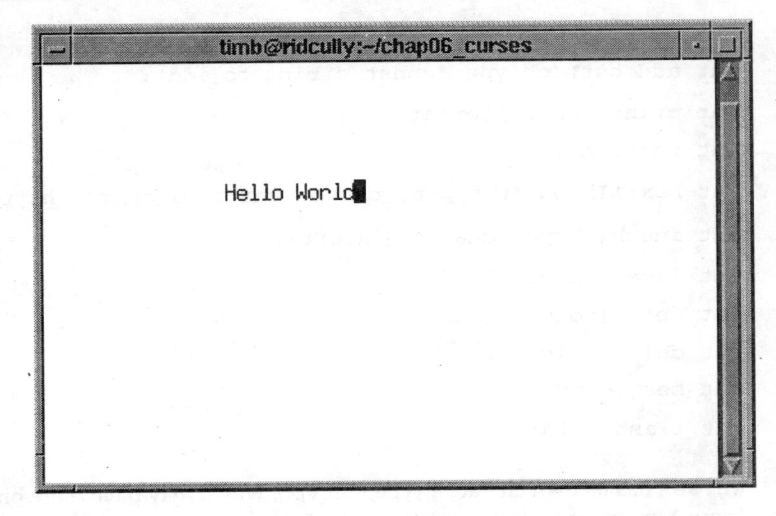

Initialization and Termination

As we've already seen, all `curses` programs must start with `initscr` and end with `endwin`. Here are their header file definitions.

```
#include <curses.h>

WINDOW *initscr(void);
int endwin(void);
```

The `initscr` function should only be called once in each program. The `initscr` function returns a pointer to the `stdscr` structure if it succeeds. If it fails, it simply prints a diagnostic error message and causes the program to exit.

The endwin function returns `OK` on success and `ERR` on failure. You can call `endwin` to leave `curses` and then later resume `curses` operation by calling `clearok(stdscr, 1)` and `refresh`. This effectively makes `curses` forget what the physical screen looks like and forces it to perform a complete redisplay.

The `WINDOW` structure is simply the structure that `curses` uses to store the intended screen display. This structure is opaque, i.e. `curses` doesn't give access to its internals.

Output to the Screen

There are several basic functions provided for updating the screen. These are:

```
#include <curses.h>

int addch(const chtype char_to_add);
int addchstr(chtype *const string_to_add);
int printw(char *format, ...);
int refresh(void);
int box(WINDOW *win_ptr, chtype vertical_char, chtype horizontal_char);
int insch(chtype char_to_insert);
int insertln(void);
int delch(void);
int deleteln(void);
int beep(void);
int flash(void);
```

`curses` has its own character type, `chtype`, which may have more bits than a standard `char`. For the Linux version of `ncurses`, `chtype` is actually an `unsigned long`.

The `add...` functions add the character or string specified at the current location. The `printw` function formats a string in the same way as `printf` and adds it to the current location. The `refresh` function causes the physical screen to be updated, returning `OK` on success and `ERR` if an error occurred. The `box` function allows you to draw a box around a window. In standard `curses`, you may only use 'normal' characters for the vertical and horizontal line characters.

> **In extended `curses`, though, you can use the two defines `ACS_VLINE` and `ACS_HLINE` for a better looking box. For this, your terminal needs to support line drawing characters, though that's pretty much standard now.**

The `insch` function inserts a character, moving existing characters right, though what will happen at the end of a line isn't specified and will depend on the terminal you're using. `insertln` inserts a blank line, moving existing lines down by one. The two `delete` functions are analogous to the two `insert` functions.

To make a sound, you can call `beep`. A very small number of terminals are unable to make any sound, so some `curses` setups will cause the screen to flash when `beep` is called. If you work in a busy office, where beeps can come from any number of machines, you might find you prefer this yourself. As you might expect, `flash` causes the screen to flash, but if this isn't possible, it tries to make a sound on the terminal.

Reading from the Screen

We can read characters from the screen, although this facility isn't commonly used. It's done with the following functions.

```
#include <curses.h>


chtype inch(void);
int instr(char *string);
int innstr(char *string, int number_of_characters);
```

The `inch` function should always be available, but the `instr` and `innstr` functions are not always supported. The `inch` function returns a character and its attribute information from the current screen location of the cursor. Notice that `inch` doesn't return a character, but a `chtype`, whilst `instr` and `innstr` write to arrays of `char`s.

Clearing the Screen

There are four principal ways of clearing an area of the screen. These are:

```
#include <curses.h>


int erase(void);
int clear(void);
int clrtobot(void);
int clrtoeol(void);
```

The `erase` function writes blanks to every screen location. The `clear` function, like `erase`, clears the screen, but enforces a screen redisplay by also calling `clearok`. `clearok` enforces a clear screen sequence and redisplay when the next `refresh` is called.

The `clear` function usually uses a terminal command that erases the entire screen, rather than simply attempting to erase any currently non-blank screen locations. This makes the `clear` function a reliable way of completely erasing the screen. The combination of `clear` followed by `refresh` can provide a useful redraw command.

`clrtobot` clears the screen from the cursor position onwards and `clrtoeol` clears the line from the cursor to the end of the line.

Moving the Cursor

A single function is provided for moving the cursor, with an additional command for controlling where `curses` leaves the cursor after screen updates:

```
#include <curses.h>

int move(int new_y, int new_x);
int leaveok(WINDOW *window_ptr, bool leave_flag);
```

The `move` function simply moves the logical cursor position to the specified location. Remember that the screen coordinates are specified with (0,0) as the top left-hand corner of the screen. In most versions of `curses`, the two `extern` integers `LINES` and `COLUMNS` contain the physical screen size and can be used to determine the maximum allowed values for `new_y` and `new_x`. Calling `move` won't, in itself, cause the physical cursor to move. It only changes the location on the logical screen at which the next output will appear. If you want the screen cursor to move immediately after calling `move`, follow it with a call to `refresh`.

The `leaveok` function sets a flag which controls where `curses` leaves the physical cursor after a screen update. By default, the flag is `false` and, after a refresh, the hardware cursor will be left in the same position on the screen as the logical cursor. If the flag is set to `true`, the hardware cursor may be left randomly, anywhere on the screen. Generally the default option is preferred.

Character Attributes

Each `curses` character can have certain attributes, which control how it's displayed on the screen, assuming that the display hardware can support the requested attribute. The defined attributes are `A_BLINK`, `A_BOLD`, `A_DIM`, `A_REVERSE`, `A_STANDOUT` and `A_UNDERLINE`. You can use these functions to set attributes singly or collectively.

```
#include <curses.h>

int attron(chtype attribute);
int attroff(chtype attribute);
int attrset(chtype attribute);
int standout(void);
int standend(void);
```

The `attrset` function sets the `curses` attributes, `attron` and `attroff` turn on and off specified attributes without disturbing others, while `standout` and `standend` provide a more generic emphasized, or 'stand out' mode. This is commonly mapped to reverse video on most terminals.

Now that we know more about managing the screen, we can try out a more complex example, `moveadd.c`. For the purposes of this example, we'll include several calls to `refresh` and `sleep`, to enable you to see what the screen looks like as each stage. Normally, `curses` programs would refresh the screen as little as possible, because it's not a very efficient operation. The code is slightly contrived for the purposes of illustration.

Try It Out - Moving, Inserting and Attributes

1. We include some header files, define some character arrays and a pointer to those arrays and then initialize the `curses` structures.

```
#include <unistd.h>
#include <stdlib.h>
#include <curses.h>

int main()
{
   const char witch_one[] = " First Witch  ";
   const char witch_two[] = " Second Witch ";
   const char *scan_ptr;

   initscr();
```

2. Now for the three initial sets of text that appear at intervals on the screen. Note the on and off flagging of text attributes.

```
   move(5, 15);
   attron(A_BOLD);
   printw("%s", "Macbeth");
   attroff(A_BOLD);
   refresh();
   sleep(1);

   move(8, 15);
   attron(A_DIM);
   printw("%s", "Thunder and Lightning");
   attroff(A_DIM);
   refresh();
   sleep(1);

   move(10, 10);
   printw("%s", "When shall we three meet again");
   move(11, 23);
   printw("%s", "In thunder, lightning, or in rain ?");
   move(13, 10);
   printw("%s", "When the hurlyburly's done,");
   move(14,23);
   printw("%s", "When the battle's lost and won.");
   refresh();
   sleep(1);
```

3. Lastly, the actors are identified and their names are inserted a character at the time. We also add the reset function at the end of the `main` function.

```
   attron(A_DIM);
   scan_ptr = witch_one + strlen(witch_one);
   while(scan_ptr != witch_one) {
       move(10,10);
       insch(*scan_ptr--);
   }
```

```
    scan_ptr = witch_two + strlen(witch_two);
    while (scan_ptr != witch_two) {
        move(13, 10);
        insch(*scan_ptr--);
    }
    attroff(A_DIM);

    refresh();
    sleep(1);

    endwin();
    exit(EXIT_SUCCESS);
}
```

When we run this program, the final screen looks like this:

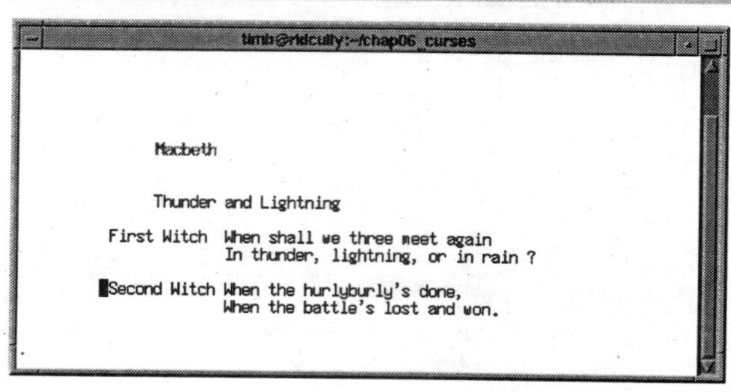

The Keyboard

As well as providing an easier interface to controlling the screen, `curses` also provides an easier method for controlling the keyboard.

Keyboard Modes

The keyboard reading routines are controlled by modes. The functions that set the modes are:

```
#include <curses.h>

int echo(void);
int noecho(void);
int cbreak(void);
int nocbreak(void);
int raw(void);
int noraw(void);
```

The two `echo` functions simply turn the echoing of typed characters on and off. The remaining four function calls control how characters typed on the terminal are made available to the `curses` program.

To explain `cbreak`, we need to understand the default input mode. When a `curses` program starts by calling `initscr`, the input mode is set to what is termed **cooked mode**. This means that all processing is done on a line-by-line basis, i.e. input is only available after the user has pressed *Return*. Keyboard special characters are enabled, so typing the appropriate key sequences can generate a signal in the program Flow control is also enabled. By calling `cbreak`, a program may set the input mode to **cbreak mode** where characters are available to the program immediately they are typed. As in cooked mode, keyboard special characters are enabled , but simple keys, like backspace, are passed directly to the program to be processed, so if you want the backspace key to function as expected, you have to program it yourself.

A call to raw turns off special character processing, so it becomes impossible to generate signals or flow control by typing special character sequences. Calling nocbreak sets the input mode back to Cooked mode, but leaves special character processing unchanged; calling noraw restores both Cooked mode and special character handling.

Keyboard Input

Reading the keyboard is very simple. The principal functions are:

```
#include <curses.h>

int getch(void);
int getstr(char *string);
int getnstr(char *string, int number_of_characters);
int scanw(char *format, ...);
```

These act in a very similar way to their non-curses equivalents getchar, gets and scanf. Note that getstr provides no way of limiting the string length returned, so you should use it only with great caution. If your version of curses supports getnstr, which allows you to limit the number of characters read, you should use it in preference to getstr. This is very similar to the behavior of gets and fgets that we met in Chapter 3.

Here's a short example program, ipmode.c, to show how to handle the keyboard.

Try It Out- Keyboard Modes and Input

1. First, we set up the program and the initial curses calls.

```
#include <unistd.h>
#include <stdlib.h>
#include <curses.h>
#include <string.h>

#define PW_LEN 25
#define NAME_LEN 256

int main() {
    char name[NAME_LEN];
    char password[PW_LEN];
    char *real_password = "xyzzy";
    int i = 0;

    initscr();

    move(5, 10);
    printw("%s", "Please login:");

    move(7, 10);
    printw("%s", "User name: ");
    getstr(name);

    move(9, 10);
    printw("%s", "Password: ");
    refresh();
```

2. When the user enters their password, we need to stop the password being echoed to the screen. Then we check the password against `xyzzy`.

```
    cbreak();
    noecho();

    memset(password, '\0', sizeof(password));
    while (i < PW_LEN) {
        password[i] = getch();
        move(9, 20 + i);
        addch('*');
        refresh();
        if (password[i] == '\n') break;
        if (strcmp(password, real_password) == 0) break;
        i++;
    }
```

3. Finally, we re-enable the keyboard echo and print out success or failure.

```
    echo();
    nocbreak();

    move(11, 10);
    if (strcmp(password, real_password) == 0) printw("%s", "Correct");
    else printw("%s", "Wrong");
    refresh();

    endwin();
    exit(EXIT_SUCCESS);
}
```

Try it and see.

How It Works

Having stopped the echoing of keyboard input and set the input mode to Cbreak, we set up a region of memory ready for the password. Each character of the password entered is processed immediately and a * is shown at the next position on the screen. We need to refresh the screen each time. Then we compare the two strings, entered and real passwords, using `strcmp`.

> **If you're using a very old version of the `curses` library, you may need to make some minor changes to the program to get the screen refreshes correct. In particular, a `refresh` call may need to be added before the `getstr call`. In modern `curses`, `getstr` is defined as calling `getch`, which refreshes the screen automatically.**

Windows

Until now, we have used the terminal as a full screen output medium. This is often sufficient for small and simple programs, but the `curses` library goes a long way beyond that. We can display multiple windows of different sizes concurrently on the physical screen. Many of the functions in this section are only supported by what X/Open terms extended `curses`. However, since they are supported by `ncurses`, there should be little problem in them being made available on most platforms. We're now going to move on and learn how to use multiple windows. We're also going to see how the commands we have used so far are generalized to the multiple window scenario.

The WINDOW Structure

Although we have mentioned stdscr, the standard screen, we have so far had little need to use it, since almost all of the functions that we've met so far assume that they're working on stdscr and it does not need to be passed as a parameter.

The stdscr is just a special case of the WINDOW structure, like stdout is a special case of a file stream. The WINDOW structure is normally declared in curses.h and while it can be instructive to examine it, programs should never access it directly, since the structure can and does change between implementations.

We can create and destroy windows using the newwin and delwin calls:

```
#include <curses.h>

WINDOW *newwin(int num_of_lines, int num_of_cols, int start_y, int start_x);
int delwin(WINDOW *window_to_delete);
```

The newwin function creates a new window, with a screen location of (start_y,start_x) and with the specified number of lines and columns. It returns a pointer to the new window, or null if the creation failed. If you want the new window to have its bottom right-hand corner in the bottom right-hand corner of the screen, you can give the number of lines or columns as zero. All windows must fit within the current screen, so newwin will fail if any part of the new window would fall outside the screen area. The new window created by newwin is completely independent of all existing windows. By default, it will be placed on top of any existing windows, hiding (but not changing) their contents.

The delwin function deletes a window previously created by newwin. Since memory has probably been allocated when newwin was called, you should always delete windows when they are no longer required. Take care never to try and delete curses' own windows, stdscr and curscr!

Having created a new window, how do we write to it? The answer is that almost all the functions that we've seen so far have generalized versions that operate on specified windows, and, for convenience, these also include cursor motion.

Generalized Functions

We've already used the addch and printw functions for adding characters to the screen. Along with many other functions, these can be prefixed, either with a w for window, mv for move, or mvw for move and window. If you look in the curses header file for most implementations of curses, you'll find that many of the functions we've used so far are simply macros (#defines) that call these more general functions.

When the w prefix is added, an additional WINDOW pointer must be prepended to the argument list. When the mv prefix is added, two additional parameters, a y and an x location, must be prepended. These specify the location where the operation will be performed. The y and x are relative to the window rather than the screen, (0,0) being the top left of the window.

When the mvw prefix is added, three additional parameters, a WINDOW pointer, as well as y and x values, must be passed. Confusingly, the WINDOW pointer always comes before the screen coordinates, even though the prefix might suggest the y and x come first.

As an example, here is the full set of prototypes for just the addch and printw sets of functions.

```
#include <curses.h>

int addch(const chtype char);
int waddch(WINDOW *window_pointer, const chtype char)
int mvaddch(int y, int x, const chtype char);
int mvwaddch(WINDOW *window_pointer, int y, int x, const chtype char);
int printw(char *format, ...);
int wprintw(WINDOW *window_pointer, char *format, ...);
int mvprintw(int y, int x, char *format, ...);
int mvwprintw(WINDOW *window_pointer, int y, int x, char *format, ...);
```

Many other functions, such as inch, also have move and window variants available.

Moving and Updating a Window

These commands allow us to move and redraw windows.

```
#include <curses.h>

int mvwin(WINDOW *window_to_move, int new_y, int new_x);
int wrefresh(WINDOW *window_ptr);
int wclear(WINDOW *window_ptr);
int werase(WINDOW *window_ptr);
int touchwin(WINDOW *window_ptr);
int scrollok(WINDOW *window_ptr, bool scroll_flag);
int scroll(WINDOW *window_ptr);
```

The mvwin function moves a window on the screen. Since all parts of a window must fit within the screen area, mvwin will fail if you attempt to move a window so that any part of it falls outside the screen area.

The wrefresh, wclear and werase functions are simply generalizations of the functions we met earlier; they just take a WINDOW pointer so that they can refer to a specific window, rather than stdscr.

The touchwin function is rather special. It informs the curses library that the contents of the window pointed to by its parameter have been changed. This means that curses will always redraw that window next time wrefresh is called, even if you haven't actually changed the contents of the window. This function is often useful for arranging which window to display when you have several overlapping windows stacked on the screen.

The two scroll functions control scrolling of a window. The scrollok function, when passed a Boolean true (usually non-zero) allows a window to scroll. By default, windows can't scroll. The scroll function simply scrolls the window up one line. Some curses implementations also have a wsctl function which additionally takes a number of lines to scroll, which may be a negative number. We'll return to scrolling a little later in the chapter.

Now that we know how to manage more than a single window, let's put these new functions to work in a program, multiw1.c. For the sake of brevity, error checking is omitted.

Try It Out - Multiple Windows

1. As usual let's get our definitions sorted first:

```
#include <unistd.h>
#include <stdlib.h>
#include <curses.h>

int main()
{
    WINDOW *new_window_ptr;
    WINDOW *popup_window_ptr;
    int x_loop;
    int y_loop;
    char a_letter = 'a';

    initscr();
```

2. Then we fill the base window with characters, refreshing the actual screen once the logical screen has been filled.

```
move(5, 5);
    printw("%s", "Testing multiple windows");
    refresh();

    for (y_loop = 0; y_loop < LINES - 1; y_loop++) {
        for (x_loop = 0; x_loop < COLS - 1; x_loop++) {
             mvwaddch(stdscr, y_loop, x_loop, a_letter);
             a_letter++;
             if (a_letter > 'z') a_letter = 'a';
        }
    }

    /* Update the screen */
    refresh();
    sleep(2);
```

3. Now we create a new 10x20 window and add some text to it before drawing it on the screen.

```
    new_window_ptr = newwin(10, 20, 5, 5);
    mvwprintw(new_window_ptr, 2, 2, "%s", "Hello World");
    mvwprintw(new_window_ptr, 5, 2, "%s",
              "Notice how very long lines wrap inside the window");
    wrefresh(new_window_ptr);
    sleep(2);
```

4. We now change the contents of the background window and, when we refresh the screen, the window pointed to by `new_window_ptr` is obscured.

```
    a_letter = '0';
    for (y_loop = 0; y_loop < LINES -1; y_loop++) {
      for (x_loop = 0; x_loop < COLS - 1; x_loop++) {
          mvwaddch(stdscr, y_loop, x_loop, a_letter);
          a_letter++;
          if (a_letter > '9')
              a_letter = '0';
        }
    }

    refresh();
    sleep(2);
```

5. If we make a call to refresh the new window, nothing will change, because we haven't changed the new window.

```
    wrefresh(new_window_ptr);
    sleep(2);
```

6. But if we touch the window first and trick `curses` into thinking that the window has been changed, the next call to `wrefresh` will bring the new window to the front again.

```
    touchwin(new_window_ptr);
    wrefresh(new_window_ptr);
    sleep(2);
```

7. Next, we add another overlapping window with a box around it.

```
    popup_window_ptr = newwin(10, 20, 8, 8);
    box(popup_window_ptr, '|', '-');
    mvwprintw(popup_window_ptr, 5, 2, "%s", "Pop Up Window!");
    wrefresh(popup_window_ptr);
    sleep(2);
```

8. Then we fiddle with the new and pop-up windows before clearing and deleting them.

```
    touchwin(new_window_ptr);
    wrefresh(new_window_ptr);
    sleep(2);
    wclear(new_window_ptr);
    wrefresh(new_window_ptr);
    sleep(2);
    delwin(new_window_ptr);
    touchwin(popup_window_ptr);
    wrefresh(popup_window_ptr);
    sleep(2);
    delwin(popup_window_ptr);
    touchwin(stdscr);
    refresh();
    sleep(2);
    endwin();
    exit(EXIT_SUCCESS);
}
```

Unfortunately, it's not practical to show you this running in the book, but here is a screen shot after the first popup window has been drawn.

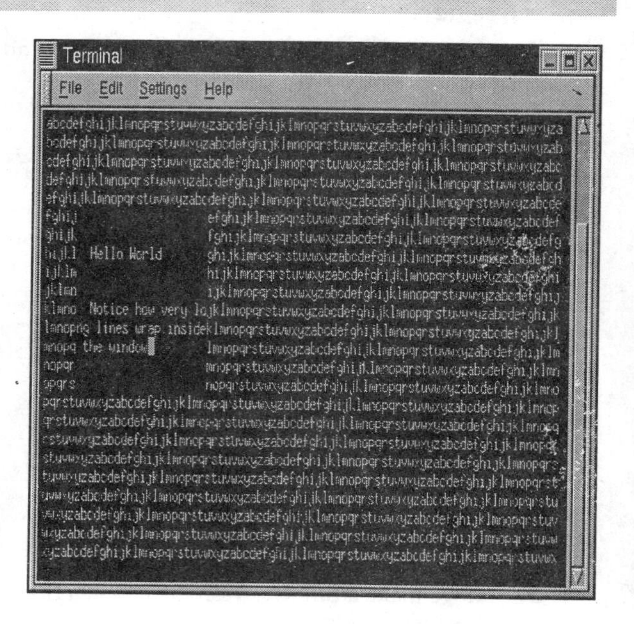

After the background has been changed, and a popup window has been drawn, we see this.

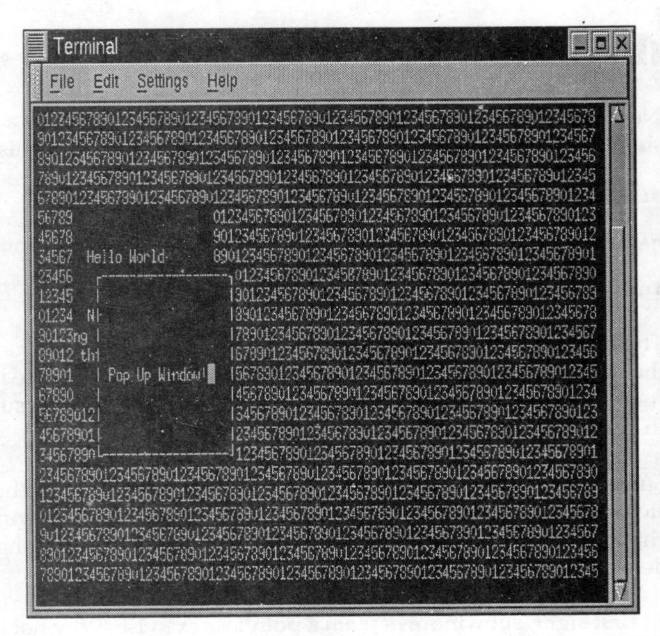

As you can see from the example code, you need to be quite careful about refreshing windows to ensure that they appear on the screen in the correct order. If you ask `curses` to refresh a window, it doesn't store any information about the hierarchy of windows. To ensure that `curses` draws the windows in the correct order, you must refresh them in the correct order. One way of doing this is to store all the pointers to your windows in an array or list, which you maintain in the order they should appear on the screen.

Optimizing Screen Refreshes

As we saw in the example above, refreshing multiple windows can be a little tricky, but not overly onerous. However, a potentially more serious problem arises when the terminal to be updated is on a slow link, perhaps over a modem.

In this case, it's important to minimize the number of characters drawn on the screen, since, on slow links, screen draws can be uncomfortably slow. `curses` provides a special way of doing this, with a pair of functions: `wnoutrefresh` and `doupdate`.

```
#include <curses.h>

int wnoutrefresh(WINDOW *window_ptr);
int doupdate(void);
```

The `wnoutrefresh` function determines which characters would need sending to the screen, but doesn't actually send them. The `doupdate` function actually sends the changes to the terminal. If you simply call `wnoutrefresh`, followed immediately by `doupdate`, the effect is the same as calling `wrefresh`. However, if you wish to redraw a stack of windows, you can call `wnoutrefresh` on each window (in the correct order, of course) and then call `doupdate` only after the last `wnoutrefresh`. This allows `curses` to perform its screen update calculations on each window in turn and only then output the updated screen. This almost always allows `curses` to minimize the number of characters that needs to be sent.

Subwindows

Now that we've looked at multiple windows, we can look at a special case of multiple windows, called **subwindows**. We create and destroy subwindows with the calls:

```
#include <curses.h>

WINDOW *subwin(WINDOW *parent, int num_of_lines, int num_of_cols,
               int start_y, int start_x);
int delwin(WINDOW *window_to_delete);
```

The function `subwin` has almost the same parameter list as `newwin` and subwindows are deleted in just the same way as other windows, with a `delwin` call. Just like new windows, we can use the range of `mvw` functions to write to subwindows. Indeed, most of the time, subwindows behave in a very similar fashion to new windows, with one very important exception:

Subwindows don't themselves store a separate set of screen characters; they share the same character storage space as the parent window specified when the subwindow is created. This means that any changes made in a subwindow are also made in the underlying parent window, so when a subwindow is deleted the screen doesn't change.

At first sight, subwindows seem a pointless exercise. Why not just make the changes to the parent window? The main use for subwindows is to provide a clean way of scrolling parts of another window. The need to scroll a small subsection of the screen is surprisingly common when writing a `curses` program. By making this a subwindow and then scrolling, the subwindow, we achieve the desired result.

> **One restriction imposed by using subwindows is that the application should call `touchwin` on the parent window before refreshing the screen.**

Try It Out - Subwindows

1. First, the initial code section. The base window display is initialized with some text.

```
#include <unistd.h>
#include <stdlib.h>
#include <curses.h>

#define NUM_NAMES 14

int main()
{
    WINDOW *sub_window_ptr;
    int x_loop;
    int y_loop;
    int counter;
    char a_letter = 'A';
```

```
    char *names[NUM_NAMES] = {"David Hudson,", "Andrew Crolla,", "James Jones,",
                              "Ciara Loughran,", "Peter Bradley,", "Nancy Innocenzi,",
                              "Charles Cooper,", "Rucha Nanavati,", "Bob Vyas,",
                              "Abdul Hussain,", "Anne Pawson,", "Alex Hopper,",
                              "Russell Thomas,", "Nazir Makandra,"};

    initscr();

for (y_loop = 0; y_loop < LINES - 1; y_loop++) {
      for (x_loop = 0; x_loop < COLS - 1; x_loop++) {
             mvwaddch(stdscr, y_loop, x_loop, a_letter);
             a_letter++;
             if (a_letter > 'Z') a_letter = 'A';
         }
    }
```

2. We now create the new scrolling subwindow and, as advised, we must 'touch' the parent window before refreshing the screen.

```
    sub_window_ptr = subwin(stdscr, 10, 20, 10, 10);
    scrollok(sub_window_ptr, 1);
    touchwin(stdscr);
    refresh();
    sleep(1);
```

3. Then we erase the contents of the subwindow, print text to it and refresh it. The scrolling text is achieved by a loop.

```
    werase(sub_window_ptr);
    mvwprintw(sub_window_ptr, 2, 0, "%s",
              "This window will now scroll as names are added ");
    wrefresh(sub_window_ptr);
    sleep(1);

    for (counter = 0; counter < NUM_NAMES; counter++) {
        wprintw(sub_window_ptr, "%s ", names[counter]);
        wrefresh(sub_window_ptr);
        sleep(1);
    }
```

4. Having finished this loop, we delete the subwindow. Then we refresh the base screen.

```
    delwin(sub_window_ptr);
    touchwin(stdscr);
    refresh();
    sleep(1);
    endwin();
    exit(EXIT_SUCCESS);
}
```

Towards the end of the program, we see the output:

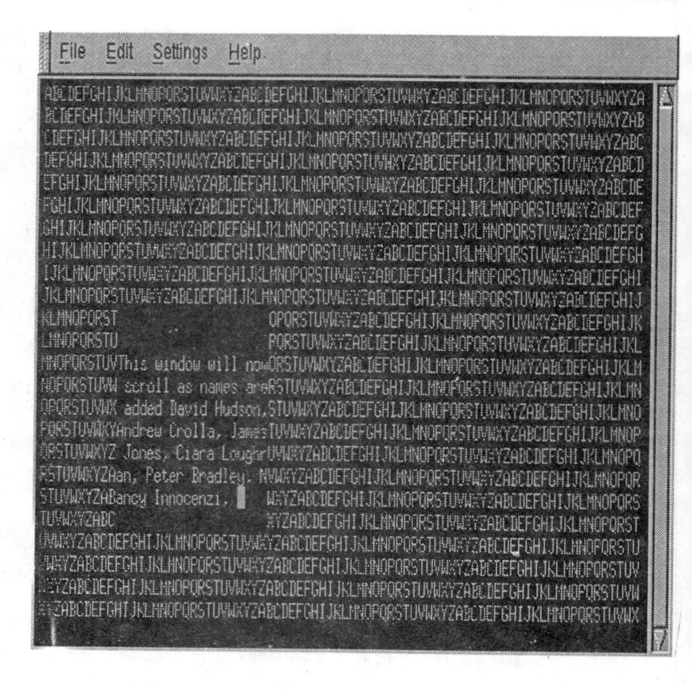

How It Works

After arranging for the `sub_window_ptr` to point to the result of the `subwin` call, we make the subwindow scrollable. Even after the subwindow has been deleted and the base window (`strdcr`) refreshed, the text on the screen remains the same. This is because the subwindow was actually updating the character data for `stdscr`.

The Keypad

We've already seen some of the facilities that `curses` provides for handling the keyboard. Many keyboards have, at the very least, cursor keys and function keys. Many also have a keypad and other keys, such as *Insert* and *Home*.

Decoding these keys is a difficult problem on most terminals, since they normally send a string of characters, starting with the escape character. Not only does the application have the problem of distinguishing between a single press of the *Escape* key and a string of characters caused by pressing a function key, but it must also cope with different terminals using different sequences for the same logical key.

Fortunately, `curses` provides an elegant facility for managing function keys. For each terminal, the sequence sent by each of its function keys is stored, normally in a `terminfo` structure, and the include file `curses.h` has a set of defines prefixed by `KEY_` that define the logical keys.

The translation between the sequences and logical keys is disabled when `curses` starts and has to be turned on by the `keypad` function. If the call succeeds, it returns `OK`, otherwise `ERR`.

```
#include <curses.h>

int keypad(WINDOW *window_ptr, bool keypad_on);
```

Once **keypad mode** has been enabled by calling `keypad` with `keypad_on` set to `true`, `curses` takes over the processing of key sequences, so that reading the keyboard may now not only return the key that was pressed, but also one of the `KEY_` defines for logical keys.

There are three slight restrictions when using Keypad mode.

The first problem is that the recognition of escape sequences is timing-dependent and many network protocols will group characters into packets (leading to improper recognition of escape sequences), or separate them (leading to function key sequences being recognized as *Escape* and individual characters). This behavior is worst over WANs and other busy links. The only workaround is to try to program terminals to send single, unique characters for each function key that you want to use, although this limits the number of control characters.

Secondly, in order for `curses` to separate a press of the *Escape* key from a keyboard sequence starting with *Escape*, it must wait for a brief period of time. Sometimes, a very slight delay on processing of the *Escape* key can be noticed once Keypad mode has been enabled.

The third restriction is that `curses` can't process non-unique escape sequences. If your terminal has two different keys that can send the same sequence, `curses` will simply not process that sequence, since it can't tell which logical key it should return.

> **In our opinion, having escape sequences for some keys and also putting an *Escape* key on the keyboard (heavily used for cancels) was a most unfortunate design decision, but one that we must accept and manage as best we can.**

Here's a short program, `keypad.c`, showing how the keypad mode can be used. When you run this program, try pressing *Escape* and notice the slight delay while the program waits to see if the *Escape* is simply the start of an escape sequence, or a single key press.

Try It Out - Using the Keypad

1. Having initialized the program and the curses library, we set the keypad mode `TRUE`.

```
#include <unistd.h>
#include <stdlib.h>
#include <curses.h>

#define LOCAL_ESCAPE_KEY    27

int main()
{
    int key;

    initscr();
    crmode();
    keypad(stdscr, TRUE);
```

2. Next, we must turn echo off to prevent the cursor being moved when some cursor keys are pressed. The screen is cleared and some text displayed. The program waits for each key stroke and, unless it's *q*, or produces an error, the key is printed. If the key strokes match one of the terminal's keypad sequences, that is printed instead.

```
    noecho();
    clear();
    mvprintw(5, 5, "Key pad demonstration. Press 'q' to quit");
    move(7, 5);
    refresh();
    key = getch();

    while(key != ERR && key != 'q') {
        move(7, 5);
        clrtoeol();

        if ((key >= 'A' && key <= 'Z') ||
            (key >= 'a' && key <= 'z')) {
            printw("Key was %c", (char)key);
        }
        else {
            switch(key) {
            case LOCAL_ESCAPE_KEY: printw("%s", "Escape key"); break;
            case KEY_END: printw("%s", "END key"); break;
            case KEY_BEG: printw("%s", "BEGINNING key"); break;
            case KEY_RIGHT: printw("%s", "RIGHT key"); break;
            case KEY_LEFT: printw("%s", "LEFT key"); break;
            case KEY_UP: printw("%s", "UP key"); break;
            case KEY_DOWN: printw("%s", "DOWN key"); break;
            default: printw("Unmatched - %d", key); break;
            } /* switch */
        } /* else */

        refresh();
        key = getch();
    } /* while */

    endwin();
    exit(EXIT_SUCCESS);
}
```

Color

Originally, very few 'dumb' terminals supported color, so most early versions of curses had no support for it. Now, color is fairly standard and is supported in ncurses and most other modern curses implementations.

Each character cell on the screen can be written in one of a number of different colors, against one of a number of different colored backgrounds. For example, we can write text in green on a red background.

Color support in curses is slightly unusual in that the color for a character isn't defined independently of its background. We must define the foreground and background colors of a character as a pair, called, not surprisingly, a **color pair**.

Before you can use color capability in curses, you must check that the current terminal supports color and then initialize the curses color routines. For this, you use a pair of routines, has_colors and start_color.

```
#include <curses.h>

bool has_colors(void);
int start_color(void);
```

The has_colors routine returns true if color is supported. You should then call start_color, which returns OK if color has been initialized successfully. Once start_color has been called and the colors initialized, the variable COLOR_PAIRS is set to the maximum number of color pairs that the terminal can support. A limit of 64 color pairs is common. The variable COLORS defines the maximum number of colors available, which is often as few as eight.

Before you can use colors as attributes, you must initialize the color pairs that you wish to use. You do this with the init_pair function. Color attributes are accessed with the COLOR_PAIR function.

```
#include <curses.h>

int init_pair(short pair_number, short foreground, short background);
int COLOR_PAIR(int pair_number);
int pair_content(short pair_number, short *foreground, short *background);
```

curses.h usually defines some basic colors, starting with COLOR_. An additional function, pair_content, allows previously defined color pair information to be retrieved.

To define color pair number 1 to be red on green, we would use:

```
init_pair(1, COLOR_RED, COLOR_GREEN);
```

We can then access this color pair as an attribute, using COLOR_PAIR like this:

```
wattron(window_ptr, COLOR_PAIR(1));
```

This would set future additions to the screen to be red on a green background.

Since a `COLOR_PAIR` is an attribute, we can combine it with other attributes. On a PC, we can often access screen high intensity colors by combining the `COLOR_PAIR` attribute with the additional attribute `A_BOLD`, by using a bitwise OR of the attributes:

```
wattron(window_ptr, COLOR_PAIR(1) | A_BOLD);
```

Let's check these functions in an example, `color.c`.

Try It Out - Colors

1. First off, we check whether the program's display terminal supports color. If it does, we start the color display.

```
#include <unistd.h>
#include <stdlib.h>
#include <stdio.h>
#include <curses.h>

int main()
{
    int i;

    initscr();

    if (!has_colors()) {
        endwin();
        fprintf(stderr, "Error - no color support on this terminal\n");
        exit(1);
    }

    if (start_color() != OK) {
        endwin();
        fprintf(stderr, "Error - could not initialize colors\n");
        exit(2);
    }
```

2. We can now print out the allowed number of colors and color pairs. We create seven color pairs and display them one at a time.

```
    clear();
    mvprintw(5, 5, "There are %d COLORS, and %d COLOR_PAIRS available",
             COLORS, COLOR_PAIRS);
    refresh();

    init_pair(1, COLOR_RED, COLOR_BLACK);
    init_pair(2, COLOR_RED, COLOR_GREEN);
    init_pair(3, COLOR_GREEN, COLOR_RED);
    init_pair(4, COLOR_YELLOW, COLOR_BLUE);
    init_pair(5, COLOR_BLACK, COLOR_WHITE);
    init_pair(6, COLOR_MAGENTA, COLOR_BLUE);
    init_pair(7, COLOR_CYAN, COLOR_WHITE);

    for (i = 1; i <= 7; i++) {
        attroff(A_BOLD);
        attrset(COLOR_PAIR(i));
        mvprintw(5 + i, 5, "Color pair %d", i);
        attrset(COLOR_PAIR(i) | A_BOLD);
        mvprintw(5 + i, 25, "Bold color pair %d", i);
        refresh();
        sleep(1);
    }

    endwin();
    exit(EXIT_SUCCESS);
}
```

This example gives the following output:

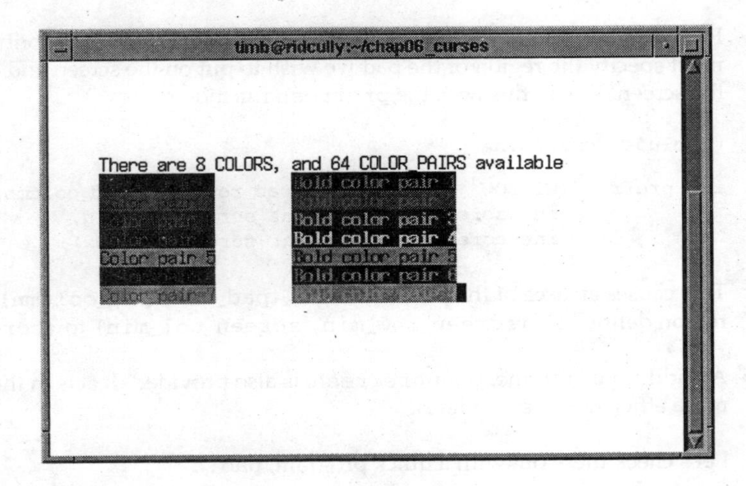

Redefining Colors

A few terminals allow only a limited number of colors on the screen at any one time, but allow us to redefine the colors available. `curses` supports this facility with the `init_color` function.

```
#include <curses.h>

int init_color(short color_number, short red, short green, short blue);
```

This allows an existing color (in the range 0 to `COLORS`) to be redefined with new intensity values, in the range 0 to 1000. This is much like defining color values for a VGA palette for a PC screen.

Pads

When you're writing more advanced `curses` programs, it's sometimes easier to build a logical screen and then output all or part of it to the physical screen later. Occasionally, it's also better to have a logical screen that is actually bigger than the physical screen and only display part of the logical screen at any one time.

It's not easy for us to do this with the `curses` functions that we've met so far, since all windows must be no larger than the physical screen. `curses` does provide a special data structure, a **pad**, for manipulating logical screen information that doesn't fit within a normal window.

A pad structure is very similar to a `WINDOW` structure and all the `curses` routines that write to windows can also be used on pads. However, pads do have their own routines for creation and refreshing.

We create pads in much the same way that we create normal windows:

```
#include <curses.h>

WINDOW *newpad(int number_of_lines, int number_of_columns);
```

Note that the return value is a pointer to a `WINDOW` structure, the same as `newwin`. Pads are deleted with `delwin`, just like windows.

Pads do have different routines for refreshing. Since a pad isn't confined to a particular screen location, we must specify the region of the pad we wish to put on the screen and also the location it should occupy on the screen. We do this with the `prefresh` function:

```
#include <curses.h>

int prefresh(WINDOW *pad_ptr, int pad_row, int pad_column,
             int screen_row_min, int screen_col_min,
             int screen_row_max, int screen_col_max);
```

This causes an area of the pad, starting at `(pad_row, pad_column)` to be written to the screen in the region defined by `(screen_row_min, screen_col_min)` to `(screen_row_max, screen_col_max)`.

An additional routine, `pnoutrefresh`, is also provided. It acts in the same way as `wnoutrefresh`, for more efficient screen updates.

Let's check these out with a quick program, `pad.c`.

Try It Out - Using a Pad

1. At the start of this program, we initialize the pad structure and then create a pad, which returns a pointer to that pad. We add characters to fill the pad structure (which is 50 characters wider and longer than the terminal display.)

```
#include <unistd.h>
#include <stdlib.h>
#include <curses.h>

int main()
{
    WINDOW *pad_ptr;
    int x, y;
    int pad_lines;
    int pad_cols;
    char disp_char;

    initscr();
    pad_lines = LINES + 50;
    pad_cols = COLS + 50;
    pad_ptr = newpad(pad_lines, pad_cols);
    disp_char = 'a';

    for (x = 0; x < pad_lines; x++) {
        for (y = 0; y < pad_cols; y++) {
            mvwaddch(pad_ptr, x, y, disp_char);
            if (disp_char == 'z') disp_char = 'a';
            else disp_char++;
        }
    }
```

2. We can now draw different areas of the pad on the screen at different locations before quitting.

```
    prefresh(pad_ptr, 5, 7, 2, 2, 9, 9);
    sleep(1);
    prefresh(pad_ptr, LINES + 5, COLS + 7, 5, 5, 21, 19);
    sleep(1);
    delwin(pad_ptr);
    endwin();
    exit(EXIT_SUCCESS);
}
```

Running the program, you should see something like this:

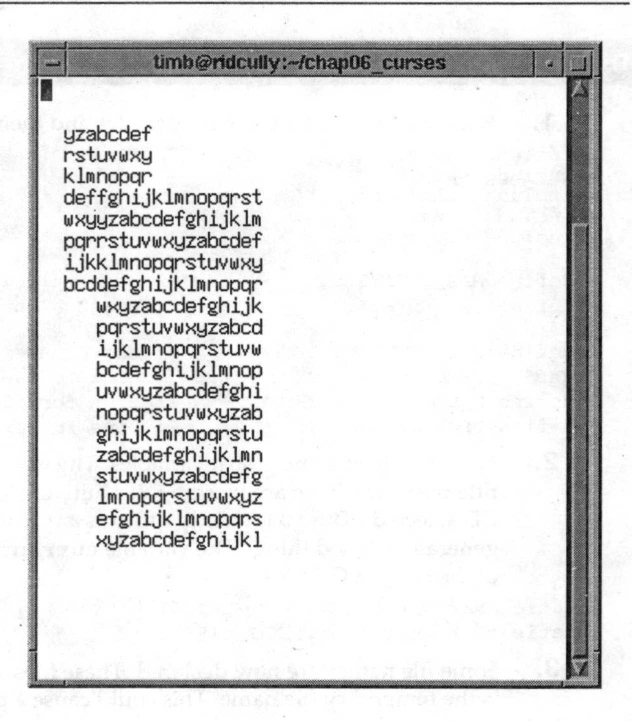

The CD Collection Application

Now that we've learned about the facilities that `curses` has to offer, we can develop our sample application. Here's a version written in C using the `curses` library. It offers some advantages in that the information is more clearly displayed on the screen and a scrolling window is used for track listings.

The whole application is eight pages long, so we've split it up into sections and functions within each section. You can get the full source code from the Wrox web site and, as with all the programs in this book, it's under the Gnu Public License. (See Appendix B.)

> **We've written this version of the CD database application using the information presented in Chapters 5 and 6. It's derived from the shell script presented in Chapter 2. It hasn't been redesigned for the C implementation, so you can still see many features of the shell original in this version.**
>
> **There are some problems with this implementation that we will resolve in later revisions. For example, it doesn't deal with commas in titles and it has a practical limit on tracks per CD to keep them on screen.**

Looking at the code, there are several distinct sections, and these form the "Try It Out" headings. The code conventions used here are slightly different from most of the rest of the book, here code foreground is only used to show where other application functions are called.

Try It Out - A New CD Collection Application

1. First, we include all those header files and then some global constants.

```
#include <unistd.h>
#include <stdlib.h>
#include <stdio.h>
#include <string.h>
#include <curses.h>

#define MAX_STRING 80           /* Longest allowed response       */
#define MAX_ENTRY 1024          /* Longest allowed database entry */

#define MESSAGE_LINE 6            /* Misc. messages on this line    */
#define ERROR_LINE   22           /* Line to use for errors         */
#define Q_LINE       20           /* Line for questions             */
#define PROMPT_LINE  18           /* Line for prompting on          */
```

2. Next, we need some global variables. The variable `current_cd` is used to store the current CD title with which we are working. It's initialized so that the first character is `null` to indicate 'no CD selected'. The `\0` is strictly unnecessary, but it ensures the variable is initialized, which is generally a 'good thing'. The variable `current_cat` will be used to record the catalog number of the current CD.

```
static char current_cd[MAX_STRING] = "\0";
static char current_cat[MAX_STRING];
```

3. Some file names are now declared. These files are fixed in this version to keep things simple, as is the temporary file name. This could cause a problem if the program is run by two users in the same directory.

A better way to obtain database file names would be either by program arguments or from environment variables. We also need an improved method of generating a unique temporary file name, for which we could use the POSIX `tmpnam` function. We'll address many of these issues in later versions.

```
const char *title_file = "title.cdb";
const char *tracks_file = "tracks.cdb";
const char *temp_file = "cdb.tmp";
```

4. Now, finally, we get onto the function prototypes.

```
void clear_all_screen(void);
void get_return(void);
int get_confirm(void);
int getchoice(char *greet, char *choices[]);
void draw_menu(char *options[], int highlight,
               int start_row, int start_col);
void insert_title(char *cdtitle);
void get_string(char *string);
void add_record(void);
void count_cds(void);
void find_cd(void);
void list_tracks(void);
void remove_tracks(void);
void remove_cd(void);
void update_cd(void);
```

5. Before we look at their implementation, we need some structures (actually an array of menu options) for the menus. The first character is the character to return when the choice is selected; the remaining text is to be displayed. The extended menu is displayed when a CD is currently selected.

```
char *main_menu[] =
{
    "add new CD",
    "find CD",
    "count CDs and tracks in the catalog",
    "quit",
    0,
};

char *extended_menu[] =
{
    "add new CD",
    "find CD",
    "count CDs and tracks in the catalog",
    "list tracks on current CD",
    "remove current CD",
    "update track information",
    "quit",
    0,
};
```

That's the initialization done with. Now we move onto the program functions, but first, I reckon we need to summarize the inter-relations of these functions, all sixteen of them. They split into functions to:

- Draw the menu
- Add CDs to the database
- Retrieve and display CD data

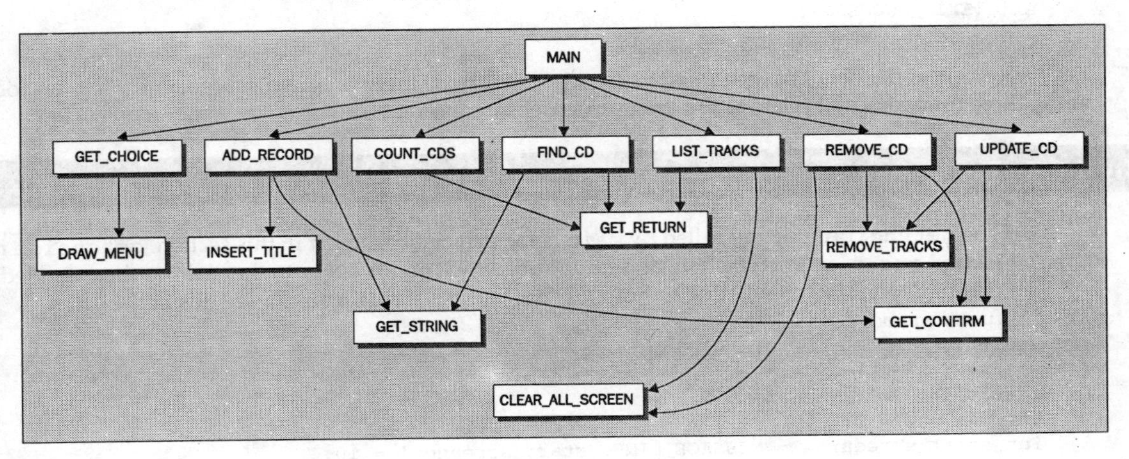

Try It Out - Looking at main

1. main allows us to make selections from the menu until we select quit.

```
int main()
{
    int choice;
    initscr();
    do {
        choice = getchoice("Options:",
                           current_cd[0] ? extended_menu : main_menu);
        switch (choice) {
        case 'q':
            break;
        case 'a':
            add_record();
            break;
        case 'c':
            count_cds();
            break;
        case 'f':
            find_cd();
            break;
        case 'l':
            list_tracks();
            break;
        case 'r':
            remove_cd();
            break;
        case 'u':
            update_cd();
            break;
        }
    } while (choice != 'q');
    endwin();
    exit(EXIT_SUCCESS);
}
```

Let's now look at the detail of the functions associated with the three program subsections. First, we look at the three functions that relate to the program's user interface.

Try It Out - The Menu

1. The getchoice function called by main is the principal function in this section. getchoice is passed greet, an introduction, and choices, which points either to the main or the extended menu (depending on whether or not a CD has been selected). You can see this in the main function above.

```
int getchoice(char *greet, char *choices[])
{
    static int selected_row = 0;
    int max_row = 0;
    int start_screenrow = MESSAGE_LINE, start_screencol = 10;
    char **option;
    int selected;
    int key = 0;

    option = choices;
    while (*option) {
        max_row++;
        option++;
    }
```

```
    /* protect against menu getting shorter when CD deleted */
    if (selected_row >= max_row)
        selected_row = 0;

    clear_all_screen();
    mvprintw(start_screenrow - 2, start_screencol, greet);

    keypad(stdscr, TRUE);
    cbreak();
    noecho();

    key = 0;
    while (key != 'q' && key != KEY_ENTER && key != '\n') {
        if (key == KEY_UP) {
            if (selected_row == 0)
                selected_row = max_row - 1;
            else
                selected_row--;
        }
        if (key == KEY_DOWN) {
            if (selected_row == (max_row - 1))
                selected_row = 0;
            else
                selected_row++;
        }
        selected = *choices[selected_row];
        draw_menu(choices, selected_row, start_screenrow,
                                  start_screencol);
        key = getch();
    }

    keypad(stdscr, FALSE);
    nocbreak();
    echo();

    if (key == 'q')
        selected = 'q';

    return (selected);
}
```

2. Note how there are two more local functions called from within `getchoice`: `clear_all_screen` and `draw_menu`. We'll look at `draw_menu` first:

```
void draw_menu(char *options[], int current_highlight,
               int start_row, int start_col)
{
    int current_row = 0;
    char **option_ptr;
    char *txt_ptr;

    option_ptr = options;
    while (*option_ptr) {
        if (current_row == current_highlight) {
            mvaddch(start_row + current_row, start_col - 3, ACS_BULLET);
            mvaddch(start_row + current_row, start_col + 40, ACS_BULLET);
        } else {
            mvaddch(start_row + current_row, start_col - 3, ' ');
            mvaddch(start_row + current_row, start_col + 40, ' ');
        }

        txt_ptr = options[current_row];
        txt_ptr++;
    }
```

```
    mvprintw(start_row + current_row + 3, start_col,
             "Move highlight then press Return ");
    refresh();
}
```

3. `clear_all_screen`, which, surprisingly enough, clears the screen and rewrites the title. If a CD is selected, its information is displayed.

```
void clear_all_screen()
{
    clear();
    mvprintw(2, 20, "%s", "CD Database Application");
    if (current_cd[0]) {
        mvprintw(ERROR_LINE, 0, "Current CD: %s: %s\n",
                 current_cat, current_cd);
    }
    refresh();
}
```

Now we look at the functions which add to or update the CD database. The functions called from `main` are `add_record`, `update_cd` and `remove_cd`. This function makes several calls to functions that will be defined in the next few sections.

Try It Out - Database File Manipulation

1. First, how do we add a new CD record to the database?

```
void add_record()
{
    char catalog_number[MAX_STRING];
    char cd_title[MAX_STRING];
    char cd_type[MAX_STRING];
    char cd_artist[MAX_STRING];
    char cd_entry[MAX_STRING];

    int screenrow = MESSAGE_LINE;
    int screencol = 10;

    clear_all_screen();
    mvprintw(screenrow, screencol, "Enter new CD details");
    screenrow += 2;

    mvprintw(screenrow, screencol, "Catalog Number: ");
    get_string(catalog_number);
    screenrow++;

    mvprintw(screenrow, screencol, "      CD Title: ");
    get_string(cd_title);
    screenrow++;

    mvprintw(screenrow, screencol, "       CD Type: ");
    get_string(cd_type);
    screenrow++;

    mvprintw(screenrow, screencol, "        Artist: ");
    get_string(cd_artist);
    screenrow++;

    mvprintw(PROMPT_LINE-2, 5, "About to add this new entry:");
    sprintf(cd_entry, "%s,%s,%s,%s",
            catalog_number, cd_title, cd_type, cd_artist);
    mvprintw(PROMPT_LINE, 5, "%s", cd_entry);
    refresh();
```

```
    move(PROMPT_LINE, 0);
    if (get_confirm()) {
        insert_title(cd_entry);
        strcpy(current_cd, cd_title);
        strcpy(current_cat, catalog_number);
    }
}
```

2. `get_string` prompts for and reads in a string at the current screen position. It also deletes any trailing newline.

```
void get_string(char *string)
{
    int len;

    wgetnstr(stdscr, string, MAX_STRING);
    len = strlen(string);
    if (len > 0 && string[len - 1] == '\n')
        string[len - 1] = '\0';
}
```

3. `get_confirm` prompts and reads user confirmation. It reads the user's input string and checks the first character for `Y` or `y`. If it finds any other character, it gives no confirmation.

```
int get_confirm()
{
    int confirmed = 0;
    char first_char;

    mvprintw(Q_LINE, 5, "Are you sure? ");
    clrtoeol();
    refresh();

    cbreak();
    first_char = getch();
    if (first_char == 'Y' || first_char == 'y') {
        confirmed = 1;
    }
    nocbreak();

    if (!confirmed) {
        mvprintw(Q_LINE, 1, "    Cancelled");
        clrtoeol();
        refresh();
        sleep(1);
    }
    return confirmed;
}
```

4. Lastly, we look at `insert_title`. This adds a title to the CD database by appending the title string to the end of the titles file.

```
void insert_title(char *cdtitle)
{
    FILE *fp = fopen(title_file, "a");
    if (!fp) {
        mvprintw(ERROR_LINE, 0, "cannot open CD titles database");
    } else {
        fprintf(fp, "%s\n", cdtitle);
        fclose(fp);
    }
}
```

5. On to the other file manipulation functions called by `main`. We start with `update_cd`. This function uses a scrolling, boxed subwindow and needs some constants, which we define globally, because they will be needed later for the `list_tracks` function. These are:

```
#define BOXED_LINES    11
#define BOXED_ROWS     60
#define BOX_LINE_POS   8
#define BOX_ROW_POS    2
```

6. update_cd allows the user to re-enter the tracks for the current CD. Having deleted the previous tracks record, it prompts for new information.

```
void update_cd()
{
    FILE *tracks_fp;
    char track_name[MAX_STRING];
    int len;
    int track = 1;
    int screen_line = 1;
    WINDOW *box_window_ptr;
    WINDOW *sub_window_ptr;

    clear_all_screen();
    mvprintw(PROMPT_LINE, 0, "Re-entering tracks for CD. ");
    if (!get_confirm())
        return;
    move(PROMPT_LINE, 0);
    clrtoeol();

    remove_tracks();

    mvprintw(MESSAGE_LINE, 0, "Enter a blank line to finish");

    tracks_fp = fopen(tracks_file, "a");
```

7. The listing continues in just a moment. We're making this brief intermission to highlight how we enter the information in a scrolling, boxed window. The trick is to set up a subwindow, draw a box around the edge, then add a new, scrolling, subwindow just inside the boxed subwindow.

```
    box_window_ptr = subwin(stdscr, BOXED_LINES + 2, BOXED_ROWS + 2,
                            BOX_LINE_POS - 1, BOX_ROW_POS - 1);
    if (!box_window_ptr)
        return;
    box(box_window_ptr, ACS_VLINE, ACS_HLINE);

    sub_window_ptr = subwin(stdscr, BOXED_LINES, BOXED_ROWS,
                            BOX_LINE_POS, BOX_ROW_POS);
    if (!sub_window_ptr)
        return;
    scrollok(sub_window_ptr, TRUE);
    werase(sub_window_ptr);
    touchwin(stdscr);

    do {
        mvwprintw(sub_window_ptr, screen_line++, BOX_ROW_POS + 2,
                  "Track %d: ", track);
        clrtoeol();
        refresh();
        wgetnstr(sub_window_ptr, track_name, MAX_STRING);
        len = strlen(track_name);
        if (len > 0 && track_name[len - 1] == '\n')
            track_name[len - 1] = '\0';
```

```
        if (*track_name)
            fprintf(tracks_fp, "%s,%d,%s\n",
                    current_cat, track, track_name);
        track++;
        if (screen_line > BOXED_LINES - 1) {
            /* time to start scrolling */
            scroll(sub_window_ptr);
            screen_line--;
        }
    } while (*track_name);
    delwin(sub_window_ptr);

    fclose(tracks_fp);
}
```

8. The last function called from main is remove_cd.

```
void remove_cd()
{
    FILE *titles_fp, *temp_fp;
    char entry[MAX_ENTRY];
    int cat_length;

    if (current_cd[0] == '\0')
        return;

    clear_all_screen();
    mvprintw(PROMPT_LINE, 0, "About to remove CD %s: %s. ",
             current_cat, current_cd);
    if (!get_confirm())
        return;

    cat_length = strlen(current_cat);

    /* Copy the titles file to a temporary, ignoring this CD */
    titles_fp = fopen(title_file, "r");
    temp_fp = fopen(temp_file, "w");

    while (fgets(entry, MAX_ENTRY, titles_fp)) {
        /* Compare catalog number and copy entry if no match */
        if (strncmp(current_cat, entry, cat_length) != 0)
            fputs(entry, temp_fp);
    }
    fclose(titles_fp);
    fclose(temp_fp);

    /* Delete the titles file, and rename the temporary file */
    unlink(title_file);
    rename(temp_file, title_file);

    /* Now do the same for the tracks file */
    remove_tracks();

    /* Reset current CD to 'None' */
    current_cd[0] = '\0';
}
```

9. We now need only list `remove_tracks`, the function which deletes the tracks from the current CD. It's called by both `update_cd` and `remove_cd`.

```
void remove_tracks()
{
    FILE *tracks_fp, *temp_fp;
    char entry[MAX_ENTRY];
    int cat_length;

    if (current_cd[0] == '\0')
        return;

    cat_length = strlen(current_cat);

    tracks_fp = fopen(tracks_file, "r");
if (!tracks_fp)
  return;
    temp_fp = fopen(temp_file, "w");

    while (fgets(entry, MAX_ENTRY, tracks_fp)) {
        /* Compare catalog number and copy entry if no match */
        if (strncmp(current_cat, entry, cat_length) != 0)
            fputs(entry, temp_fp);
    }
    fclose(tracks_fp);
    fclose(temp_fp);

    /* Delete the tracks file, and rename the temporary file */
    unlink(tracks_file);
    rename(temp_file, tracks_file);
}
```

Try It Out - Querying the CD Database

1. Essential to all acquisitive hobbies is a knowledge of how many of whatever you collect you own. The next function performs this function admirably; it scans the database, counting titles and tracks.

```
void count_cds()
{
    FILE *titles_fp, *tracks_fp;
    char entry[MAX_ENTRY];
    int titles = 0;
    int tracks = 0;

    titles_fp = fopen(title_file, "r");
    if (titles_fp) {
        while (fgets(entry, MAX_ENTRY, titles_fp))
            titles++;
        fclose(titles_fp);
    }
    tracks_fp = fopen(tracks_file, "r");
    if (tracks_fp) {
        while (fgets(entry, MAX_ENTRY, tracks_fp))
            tracks++;
        fclose(tracks_fp);
    }
    mvprintw(ERROR_LINE, 0,
```

```
            "Database contains %d titles, with a total of %d tracks.",
            titles, tracks);
    get_return();
}
```

2. You've lost the sleeve notes from your favorite CD, but don't worry! Having carefully typed the details across, you can now find the track listing using `find_cd`. It prompts for a substring to match in the database and sets the global variable `current_cd` to the CD title found.

```
void find_cd()
{
    char match[MAX_STRING], entry[MAX_ENTRY];
    FILE *titles_fp;
    int count = 0;
    char *found, *title, *catalog;

    mvprintw(Q_LINE, 0, "Enter a string to search for in CD titles: ");
    get_string(match);

    titles_fp = fopen(title_file, "r");
    if (titles_fp) {
        while (fgets(entry, MAX_ENTRY, titles_fp)) {

            /* Skip past catalog number */
            catalog = entry;
            if ((found == strstr(catalog, ","))) {
                *found = '\0';
                title = found + 1;

                /* Zap the next comma in the entry to reduce it to
                   title only */
                if ((found == strstr(title, ","))) {
                    *found = '\0';

                    /* Now see if the match substring is present */
                    if ((found == strstr(title, match))) {
                        count++;
                        strcpy(current_cd, title);
                        strcpy(current_cat, catalog);
                    }
                }
            }
        }
        fclose(titles_fp);
    }
    if (count != 1) {
        if (count == 0) {
            mvprintw(ERROR_LINE, 0, "Sorry, no matching CD found. ");
        }
        if (count > 1) {
            mvprintw(ERROR_LINE, 0,
                     "Sorry, match is ambiguous: %d CDs found. ", count);
        }
        current_cd[0] = '\0';
        get_return();
    }
}
```

Though `catalog` points at a larger array than `current_cat` and could conceivably overwrite memory, the check in `fgets` prevents this.

3. Lastly, we need to be able to list the selected CD's tracks on the screen. We make use of the `#defines` for the subwindows used in `update_cd` in the last section.

```
void list_tracks()
{
    FILE *tracks_fp;
    char entry[MAX_ENTRY];
    int cat_length;
    int lines_op = 0;
    WINDOW *track_pad_ptr;
    int tracks = 0;
    int key;
    int first_line = 0;

    if (current_cd[0] == '\0') {
        mvprintw(ERROR_LINE, 0, "You must select a CD first. ");
        get_return();
        return;
    }
    clear_all_screen();
    cat_length = strlen(current_cat);

    /* First count the number of tracks for the current CD */
    tracks_fp = fopen(tracks_file, "r");
    if (!tracks_fp)
        return;
    while (fgets(entry, MAX_ENTRY, tracks_fp)) {
        if (strncmp(current_cat, entry, cat_length) == 0)
            tracks++;
    }
    fclose(tracks_fp);

    /* Make a new pad, ensure that even if there is only a single
       track the PAD is large enough so the later prefresh() is always
       valid.
    */
    track_pad_ptr = newpad(tracks + 1 + BOXED_LINES, BOXED_ROWS + 1);
    if (!track_pad_ptr)
        return;

    tracks_fp = fopen(tracks_file, "r");
    if (!tracks_fp)
        return;

    mvprintw(4, 0, "CD Track Listing\n");

    /* write the track information into the pad */
    while (fgets(entry, MAX_ENTRY, tracks_fp)) {
        /* Compare catalog number and output rest of entry */
        if (strncmp(current_cat, entry, cat_length) == 0) {
            mvwprintw(track_pad_ptr, lines_op++, 0, "%s",
                      entry + cat_length + 1);
        }
    }
    fclose(tracks_fp);

    if (lines_op > BOXED_LINES) {
        mvprintw(MESSAGE_LINE, 0,
                 "Cursor keys to scroll, RETURN or q to exit");
    } else {
        mvprintw(MESSAGE_LINE, 0, "RETURN or q to exit");
    }
```

```
    wrefresh(stdscr);
    keypad(stdscr, TRUE);
    cbreak();
    noecho();
    key = 0;
    while (key != 'q' && key != KEY_ENTER && key != '\n') {
        if (key == KEY_UP) {
            if (first_line > 0)
                first_line--;
        }
        if (key == KEY_DOWN) {
            if (first_line + BOXED_LINES + 1 < tracks)
                first_line++;
        }
        /* now draw the appropriate part of the pad on the screen */
        prefresh(track_pad_ptr, first_line, 0,
                 BOX_LINE_POS, BOX_ROW_POS,
                 BOX_LINE_POS + BOXED_LINES, BOX_ROW_POS + BOXED_ROWS);
        key = getch();
    }

    delwin(track_pad_ptr);
    keypad(stdscr, FALSE);
    nocbreak();
    echo();
}
```

4. The last two functions call `get_return`, which prompts for and reads a carriage return, ignoring other characters:

```
void get_return()
{
    int ch;
    mvprintw(23, 0, "%s", " Press return ");
    refresh();
    while ((ch = getchar()) != '\n' && ch != EOF);
}
```

If you run this program, you should see something like:

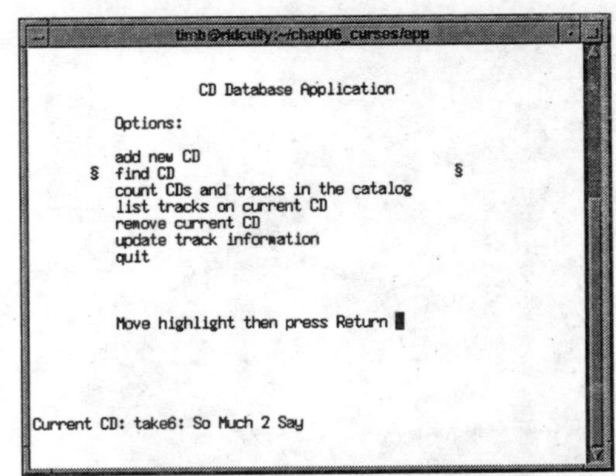

Summary

In this chapter we have explored the `curses` library. `curses` provides a good way for text-based programs to control the screen and read the keyboard. Although the `curses` library doesn't offer as much control as the general terminal interface (GTI) and direct `terminfo` access, it's considerably easier to use. If you're writing a full screen, text-based application, you should consider using the `curses` library to manage the screen and keyboard for you.

Data Management

In Chapter 3, we learned about files and in Chapter 4 we touched on the subject of resource limits. In this chapter, we're going to look initially at ways of managing your resource allocation, then of dealing with files that are accessed by many users more or less simultaneously and lastly at one tool provided in most UNIX systems for overcoming the limitations of data files.

We can summarize these topics as three ways of managing data:

- Dynamic memory management: what to do and what UNIX won't let you do.
- File locking: cooperative locking, locking regions of shared files and avoiding deadlocks.
- The dbm database: a database library featured in UNIX.

Managing Memory

On all computer systems memory is a scarce resource. No matter how much memory is available, it never seems to be enough. It wasn't so long ago that being able to address even a single megabyte of memory was considered more than anyone would ever need, but now sixty four times that is considered a bare minimum for a single-user personal computer, and many systems have much more.

From the earliest versions of the operating system, UNIX has had a very clean approach to managing memory. UNIX applications are never permitted to access physical memory directly. It might appear so to the application, but what the application is seeing is a carefully controlled illusion.

UNIX has always provided processes with a flat, unsegmented memory model—each process 'sees' its own memory area. Almost all versions of UNIX also provide memory protection, which guarantees that incorrect (or malicious) programs don't overwrite the memory of other processes or the operating system. In general, the memory allocated to one process can be neither read nor written to by any other process. Almost all versions of UNIX use hardware facilities to enforce this private use of memory.

Simple Memory Allocation

We allocate memory using the `malloc` call in the standard C library.

```
#include <stdlib.h>

void *malloc(size_t size);
```

Notice that the X/Open specification differs from some UNIX implementations by not requiring a special `malloc.h` include file. Note also that the `size` parameter that specifies the number of bytes to allocate isn't a simple `int`, although it's usually an unsigned integer type.

We can allocate a great deal of memory on most UNIX systems. Let's try.

Try It Out - Simple Memory Allocation

Type in the following program, `memory1.c`:

```
#include <unistd.h>
#include <stdlib.h>
#include <stdio.h>

#define A_MEGABYTE (1024 * 1024)

int main()
{
    char *some_memory;
    int  megabyte = A_MEGABYTE;
    int exit_code = EXIT_FAILURE;

    some_memory = (char *)malloc(megabyte);
    if (some_memory != NULL) {
        sprintf(some_memory, "Hello World\n");
        printf("%s", some_memory);
        exit_code = EXIT_SUCCESS;
    }
    exit(exit_code);
}
```

When we run this program, it outputs:

```
$ memory1
Hello World
```

How It Works

This program asks the `malloc` library to give it a pointer to a megabyte of memory. We check to ensure that `malloc` was successful and then use some of the memory to show that it exists. When you run the program, you should see `Hello World` printed out, showing that `malloc` did indeed return the megabyte of usable memory. We don't check that all of the megabyte is present; we have to put some trust in the `malloc` code!

Notice that since `malloc` returns a `void *` pointer, we cast the result to the `char *` that we need. The `malloc` function is guaranteed to return memory that is aligned so that it can be cast to a pointer of any type.

The simple reason is that most current Linux and UNIX systems use 32-bit integers and use 32-bit pointers for pointing to memory, which allows you to specify up to 4 gigabytes. This ability to address directly with a 32-bit pointer without needing segment registers or other tricks is termed a **flat 32-bit memory model**. This model is also used in Windows NT/2000 and Windows 9x for 32-bit applications. There are a few flavors of UNIX that are restricted to 16-bit, but they are very few and far between. You shouldn't rely on integers being 32-bit, however, as there are also an increasing number of 64-bit versions of Linux and UNIX in use.

Allocating Lots of Memory

Now that we've seen UNIX exceed the limitations of the DOS memory model, let's give it a more difficult problem. The next program will ask to allocate rather more memory than is physically present in the machine, so we might expect `malloc` to start failing somewhere a little short of the actual amount of memory present, since the kernel and all the other running processes will be using some memory.

Try It Out - Asking for all Physical Memory

With `memory2.c`, we're going to ask for all the machine's memory:

```
#include <unistd.h>
#include <stdlib.h>
#include <stdio.h>

#define A_MEGABYTE (1024 * 1024)

int main()
{
    char *some_memory;
    size_t  size_to_allocate = A_MEGABYTE;
    int  megs_obtained = 0;

    while (megs_obtained < 512) {
        some_memory = (char *)malloc(size_to_allocate);
        if (some_memory != NULL) {
            megs_obtained++;
            sprintf(some_memory, "Hello World");
            printf("%s - now allocated %d Megabytes\n", some_memory, megs_obtained);
        }
        else {
            exit(EXIT_FAILURE);
        }
    }
    exit(EXIT_SUCCESS);
}
```

The output, somewhat abbreviated, is:

```
$ memory2
Hello World - now allocated 1 Megabytes
Hello World - now allocated 2 Megabytes
...
Hello World - now allocated 511 Megabytes
Hello World - now allocated 512 Megabytes
```

How It Works

The program is very similar to the previous example. It simply loops, asking for more and more memory. The surprise is that it works at all, because we appear to have created a program that uses every single byte of physical memory on the authors machine. Notice that we use the `size_t` type for our call to `malloc`. This is actually an `unsigned int` in the current Linux implementation.

The other interesting feature, is that, at least on this machine, it ran the program in the blink of an eye. So, not only have we apparently used up all the memory, but we've done it very quickly indeed.

Let's investigate further and see just how much memory we can allocate on this machine with `memory3.c`. Since it's now clear that UNIX can do some very clever things with requests for memory, we'll allocate memory just 1k at a time and write to each block that we obtain.

Try It Out - Available Memory

This is `memory3.c`. By its very nature, it's extremely system-unfriendly and could affect a multi-user machine quite seriously. If you're at all concerned about the risk it's better not to run it at all; it won't harm your understanding if you don't.

```
#include <unistd.h>
#include <stdlib.h>
#include <stdio.h>

#define ONE_K (1024)

int main()
{
    char *some_memory;
    int  size_to_allocate = ONE_K;
    int  megs_obtained = 0;
    int  ks_obtained = 0;

    while (1) {
        for (ks_obtained = 0; ks_obtained < 1024; ks_obtained++) {
            some_memory = (char *)malloc(size_to_allocate);
            if (some_memory == NULL) exit(EXIT_FAILURE);
            sprintf(some_memory, "Hello World");
        }
        megs_obtained++;
        printf("Now allocated %d Megabytes\n", megs_obtained);
    }
    exit(EXIT_SUCCESS);
}
```

This time, the output, again abbreviated, is,

```
$ memory3
Now allocated 1 Megabytes
...
Now allocated 153 Megabytes
Now allocated 154 Megabytes
```

and then the program ends. It also takes quite a few seconds to run and visibly slows down around the same number as the physical memory in the machine. However the program has allocated rather more memory than the author physically has in his machine at the time of writing.

How It Works

The memory that the application is being allocated is managed by the UNIX kernel. Each time the program asks for memory or tries to read or write to memory that it has allocated, the UNIX kernel takes charge to decide how to handle the request.

Initially, the kernel was simply able to use free physical memory to satisfy the application's request for memory, but once physical memory was full, it started using what's called **swap space**. On most versions of UNIX, this is a separate disk area. If you're familiar with MS Windows, the UNIX swap space acts a little like the MS Windows swap file. However, unlike MS Windows, there's no local heap, global heap or any discardable memory segments to worry about—the UNIX kernel does all the management for you.

The kernel moves data and program code between physical memory and the swap space, so that each time you read or write memory, the data always appears to have been in physical memory, wherever it was actually located before you attempted to access it.

In more technical terms, UNIX implements a demand paged virtual memory system. All memory seen by user programs is **virtual**, i.e. it doesn't actually exist at the physical address the program uses. UNIX divides all memory into pages, commonly 4096 bytes per page. When a program tries to access memory, a virtual to physical translation is made, although how this is implemented and the time it takes depend on the particular hardware you're using. When the access is to memory that isn't physically resident, there is a **page fault** and control is passed to the UNIX kernel.

UNIX checks the address being accessed and, if it's a legal address for that program, determines which page of physical memory to make available. It then either allocates it, if it had never been written before, or, if it was stored on the disk in the swap space, reads the memory page containing the data into physical memory (possibly moving an existing page out to disk). Then, after mapping the virtual memory address to match the physical address, it allows the user program to continue. UNIX applications don't need to worry about this activity because the implementation is all hidden in the UNIX kernel.

Eventually, when the application exhausts both the physical memory and the swap space, or when the maximum stack size is exceeded, the UNIX kernel finally refuses the request for further memory.

So, what does this mean to the application programmer? Basically, it's all good news. UNIX is very good at managing memory and will allow application programs to use very large amounts of memory and even very large single blocks of memory. However, you must remember that allocating two blocks of memory won't result in a single continuously addressable block of memory. What you get is what you ask for: two separate blocks of memory.

So does this apparently limitless supply of memory mean that there's no point in checking the return from `malloc`? Definitely not. One of the most common problems in C programs using dynamically allocated memory is to write beyond the end of an allocated block. When this happens, the program may not terminate immediately, but you have probably overwritten some data used internally by the `malloc` library routines.

Usually, the result is that future calls to `malloc` may fail, not because there's no memory to allocate, but because the memory structures have been corrupted. These problems can be quite difficult to track down and, in programs, the sooner the error is detected, the better the chances of tracking down the cause. In Chapter 9 on debugging and optimizing, we'll meet some tools that can help you track down memory problems.

Abusing Memory

Suppose we try and do 'bad' things with memory. Let's allocate some memory and then attempt to write past the end, in memory4.c.

Try It Out - Abuse Your Memory

```
#include <stdlib.h>

#define ONE_K (1024)

int main()
{
    char *some_memory;
    char *scan_ptr;

    some_memory = (char *)malloc(ONE_K);
    if (some_memory == NULL) exit(EXIT_FAILURE);

    scan_ptr = some_memory;
    while(1) {
        *scan_ptr = '\0';
        scan_ptr++;
    }
    exit(EXIT_SUCCESS);
}
```

The output is simply:

```
$ memory4
Segmentation fault (core dumped)
```

How It Works

The UNIX memory management system has protected the rest of the system from this abuse of memory. To ensure that one badly behaved program (this one) can't damage any other programs, UNIX has terminated it.

Each running program on a UNIX system sees its own memory map, which is different from every other program's. Only the operating system knows how physical memory is arranged and not only manages it for user programs, but also protects user programs from each other.

The Null Pointer

Unlike MS-DOS, modern UNIX systems are very protective about writing or reading from a null pointer, although the actual behavior is implementation-specific.

Try It Out - Accessing a Null Pointer

Let's find out what happens when we access a null pointer in memory5a.c:

```
#include <unistd.h>
#include <stdlib.h>
#include <stdio.h>

int main()
{
    char *some_memory = (char *)0;

    printf("A read from null %s\n", some_memory);
    sprintf(some_memory, "A write to null\n");
    exit(EXIT_SUCCESS);
}
```

The output is:

```
$ memory5a
A read from null (null)
Segmentation fault(core dumped)
```

How It Works

The first `printf` attempts to print out a string obtained from a null pointer, then the `sprintf` attempts to write to a null pointer. In this case, Linux (in the guise of the GNU 'C' library) has been forgiving about the read and has simply given us a 'magic' string containing the characters `( n u l l ) \0`. It hasn't been so forgiving about the write and has terminated the program. This can sometimes be helpful in tracking down program bugs.

If we try this again, but this time don't use the GNU 'C' library, we discover that reading from location zero is not permitted:

This is memory5b.c:

```
#include <unistd.h>
#include <stdlib.h>
#include <stdio.h>

int main()
{
        char z = *(const char *)0;
         printf("I read from location zero\n");

        exit(EXIT_SUCCESS);
}
```

The output is:

```
$ memory5b
Segmentation fault(core dumped)
```

How It Works

This time we attempt to read directly from location zero. There is no GNU libc library between us and the kernel this time, and our program is terminated. You should note that some versions of UNIX do permit reading from location zero, but Linux doesn't.

Freeing Memory

Up to now, we've been simply allocating memory and then hoping that when the program ends, the memory we've used hasn't been lost. Fortunately, the UNIX memory management system is quite capable of ensuring that memory is returned to the system when a program ends. However, most programs don't simply want to allocate some memory, use it for a short period, then exit. A much more common use is dynamically using memory as required.

Programs that use memory on a dynamic basis should always release unused memory back to the `malloc` memory manager using the `free` call. This allows separate blocks to be remerged and allows the `malloc` library to look after memory, rather than the application managing it. If a running program (process) uses and then frees memory, that free memory remains allocated to the process. However, if it's not being used, the UNIX memory manager will be able to page it out from physical memory to swap space, where it has little impact on the use of resources.

```
#include <stdlib.h>

void free(void *ptr_to memory);
```

A call to `free` should only be made with a pointer to memory allocated by a call to `malloc`, `calloc` or `realloc`. We'll meet `calloc` and `realloc` very shortly.

Try It Out - Freeing Memory

This program's called `memory6.c`:

```
#include <stdlib.h>

#define ONE_K (1024)

int main()
{
    char *some_memory;
    int exit_code = EXIT_FAILURE;

    some_memory = (char *)malloc(ONE_K);
    if (some_memory != NULL) {
        free(some_memory);
        exit_code = EXIT_SUCCESS;
    }
    exit(exit_code);
}
```

How It Works

This program simply shows how to call `free` with a pointer to some previously allocated memory.

Remember that once you've called `free` on a block of memory, it no longer belongs to the process. It's not being managed by the `malloc` library. Never try to read or write memory after calling `free` on it.

Other Memory Allocation Functions

There are two other memory allocation functions that are not used as often as malloc and free. These are calloc and realloc. The prototypes are:

```
#include <stdlib.h>

void *calloc(size_t number_of_elements, size_t element_size);
void *realloc(void *existing_memory, size_t new_size);
```

Although calloc allocates memory that can be freed with free, it has rather different parameters. It allocates memory for an array of structures and requires the number of elements and the size of each element as its parameters. The allocated memory is filled with zeros and if calloc is successful, a pointer to the first element is returned. Like malloc, subsequent calls are not guaranteed to return contiguous space, so you can't enlarge an array created by calloc by simply calling calloc again and expecting the second call to return memory appended to that returned by the first call.

The realloc function changes the size of a block of memory that has been previously allocated. It's passed a pointer to some memory previously allocated by malloc, calloc or realloc and resizes it up or down as requested. The realloc function may have to move data about to achieve this, so it's important to ensure that once memory has been realloced, you always use the new pointer and never try to access the memory using pointers set up before realloc was called.

Another problem to watch out for is that realloc returns a null pointer if it was unable to resize the memory. This means that, in some applications, you should avoid writing code like this:

```
my_ptr = malloc(BLOCK_SIZE);
....
my_ptr = realloc(my_ptr, BLOCK_SIZE * 10);
```

If realloc fails, it will return a null pointer, my_ptr will point to null and the original memory allocated with malloc can no longer be accessed via my_ptr. It may, therefore, be to your advantage to request the new memory first with malloc and then copy data from the old block to the new block using memcpy before freeing the old block. On error, this would allow the application to retain access to the data stored in the original block of memory, perhaps while arranging a clean termination of the program.

File Locking

File locking is a very important part of multiuser, multitasking operating systems. Programs frequently need to share data, usually through files, and it's very important that those programs have some way of establishing control of a file. The file can then be updated in a safe fashion, or a second program can stop itself from trying to read a file that is in a transient state whilst another program is writing to it.

UNIX has several features that we can use for file locking. The simplest method is a technique to create lock files in an atomic way, so that nothing else can happen while the lock is being created. This gives a program a method of creating files that are guaranteed to be unique and could not have been simultaneously created by a different program.

The second method is more advanced and allows programs to lock parts of a file for exclusive access. In X/Open compliant versions of UNIX, there are two different ways of achieving this second form of locking. We'll look at only one in detail, since the second is very similar—it just has a slightly different programming interface.

Creating Lock Files

Many applications just need to be able to create a lock file for a resource. Other programs can then check the file to see whether they are permitted to access the resource.

Usually, these lock files are in a special place with a name that relates to the resource being controlled. For example, when a modem is in use, Linux creates a lock file in the `/usr/spool/uucp` directory. On many UNIX systems, this directory is used to indicate the availability of serial ports:

```
$ ls /usr/spool/uucp
LCK..ttyS1
```

Remember that lock files act only as indicators; programs need to cooperate to use them. They are termed **advisory**, as opposed to mandatory, locks.

To create a file to use as a lock indicator, we use the `open` system call defined in `fcntl.h` (which we met in Chapter 3) with the `O_CREAT` and `O_EXCL` flags set. This allows us to both check that the file doesn't already exist and then create it in a single, atomic, operation.

Try It Out - Creating a Lock File

Let's see this in action with `lock1.c`:

```
#include <unistd.h>
#include <stdlib.h>
#include <stdio.h>
#include <fcntl.h>
#include <errno.h>

int main()
{
    int file_desc;
    int save_errno;

    file_desc = open("/tmp/LCK.test", O_RDWR | O_CREAT | O_EXCL, 0444);
    if (file_desc == -1) {
        save_errno = errno;
        printf("Open failed with error %d\n", save_errno);
    }
    else {
        printf("Open succeeded\n");
    }
    exit(EXIT_SUCCESS);
}
```

The first time we run the program, the output is,

```
$ lock1
Open succeeded
```

but the next time we try, we get:

```
$ lock1
Open failed with error 17
```

How It Works

The program calls open to create a file called /tmp/LCK.test, using the O_CREAT and O_EXCL flags. The first time we run the program, the file didn't exist, so the open call was successful. Subsequent invocations of the program fail, because the file already exists. To get the program to succeed again we'll have to remove the lock file.

On Linux systems at least, error 17 refers to EEXIST, an error that is used to indicate that a file already exists. Error numbers are defined in the header file errno.h or files included by it. In this case, the definition reads:

```
#define EEXIST          17      /* File exists */
```

This is an appropriate error for an open(O_CREAT | O_EXCL) failure.

If a program simply needs a resource exclusively for a short period of its execution, often termed a **critical section**, it should create the lock file before entering the critical section and use unlink to delete it afterwards, when it exits the critical section.

We can demonstrate how programs can cooperate with this locking mechanism by writing a sample program and running two copies of it at the same time. We're going to use the getpid call that we saw in Chapter 4, which returns the process identifier, a unique number for each currently executing program.

Try It Out - Cooperative Lock Files

1. Here's the source of our test program, lock2.c:

```
#include <unistd.h>
#include <stdlib.h>
#include <stdio.h>
#include <fcntl.h>
#include <errno.h>

const char *lock_file = "/tmp/LCK.test2";

int main()
{
    int file_desc;
    int tries = 10;

    while (tries--) {
        file_desc = open(lock_file, O_RDWR | O_CREAT | O_EXCL, 0444);
        if (file_desc == -1) {
            printf("%d - Lock already present\n", getpid());
            sleep(3);
        }
        else {
```

2. The critical section starts here...

```
            printf("%d - I have exclusive access\n", getpid());
            sleep(1);
            (void)close(file_desc);
            (void)unlink(lock_file);
```

3. ...and ends here:

```
            sleep(2);
        }
    }
    exit(EXIT_SUCCESS);
}
```

To run it, we should first ensure that the lock file doesn't exist, with,

```
$ rm -f /tmp/LCK.test2
```

then run two copies of the program, by using the command:

```
$ lock2 & lock2
```

This is the output that we get:

```
1284 - I have exclusive access
1283 - Lock already present
1283 - I have exclusive access
1284 - Lock already present
1284 - I have exclusive access
1283 - Lock already present
1283 - I have exclusive access
1284 - Lock already present
1284 - I have exclusive access
1283 - Lock already present
1283 - I have exclusive access
1284 - Lock already present
1284 - I have exclusive access
1283 - Lock already present
1283 - I have exclusive access
1284 - Lock already present
1284 - I have exclusive access
1283 - Lock already present
1283 - I have exclusive access
1284 - Lock already present
```

This shows how the two invocations of the same program are cooperating. If you try this, you'll very likely see different process identifiers in the output, but the program behavior will be the same.

How It Works

For the purposes of demonstration, we make the program loop ten times, using the `while` loop. The program then tries to access the critical resource by creating a unique lock file, `/tmp/LCK.test2`. If this fails because the file already exists, the program waits for a short time and tries again. If it succeeds, it can then have access to the resource and, in the part marked 'critical section', can carry out whatever processing is required with exclusive access.

Since this is just a demonstration, we only wait for a short period. When the program has finished with the resource, it releases the lock by deleting the lock file. It can then carry out some other processing (just the `sleep` function in this case) before trying to re-acquire the lock. The lock file acts as a binary semaphore, giving each program a yes or no answer to the question, "Can I use the resource?". We will learn more about semaphores in chapters 12 and 13.

It's important to realize this is a cooperative arrangement and that we must write the programs correctly for this to work. A program failing to create the lock file can't simply delete the file and try again. It might then be able to create the lock file, but the other program that created the lock file has no way of knowing that it no longer has exclusive access to the resource.

Locking Regions

Creating lock files is fine for controlling exclusive access to resources such as serial ports, but isn't so good for access to large shared files. Suppose there exists a large file which is written by one program, but updated by many different programs simultaneously. This might occur if a program is logging some data that is obtained continuously over a long period and is being processed by several other programs. The processing programs can't wait for the logging program to finish—it runs continuously—so they need some way of cooperating to provide simultaneous access to the same file.

We can do this by locking regions of the file, so that a particular section of the file is locked, but other programs may access other parts of the file. UNIX has (at least) two ways to do this: using the `fcntl` system call or the `lockf` call. We'll look primarily at the `fcntl` interface, since that is probably the most common. `lockf` is reasonably similar.

We met the `fcntl` call in Chapter 3. Its definition is:

```
#include <fcntl.h>

int fcntl(int fildes, int command, ...);
```

`fcntl` operates on open file descriptors and, depending on the `command` parameter, can perform different tasks. The three that we're interested in for file locking are:

- `F_GETLK`
- `F_SETLK`
- `F_SETLKW`

When we use these, the third argument must be a pointer to a `struct flock`, so the prototype is effectively:

```
int fcntl(int fildes, int command, struct flock *flock_structure);
```

The `flock` (file lock) structure is implementation-dependent, but will contain at least the following members:

- `short l_type;`
- `short l_whence;`
- `off_t l_start;`
- `off_t l_len;`
- `pid_t l_pid;`

The l_type member takes one of several values, also defined in fcntl.h These are:

Value	Description
F_RDLCK	A shared (or 'read') lock. Many different processes can have a shared lock on the same (or overlapping) regions of the file. If any process has a shared lock then, no process will be able to get an exclusive lock on that region. In order to obtain a shared lock, the file must have been opened with read or read/write access
F_UNLCK	Unlock. Used for clearing locks
F_WRLCK	An exclusive (or 'write') lock. Only a single process may have an exclusive lock on any particular region of a file. Once a process has such a lock, no other process will be able to get any sort of lock on the region. To obtain an exclusive lock, the file must have been opened with write or read/write access

The l_whence, l_start and l_len members define a region, a contiguous set of bytes, in a file. The l_whence must be one of SEEK_SET, SEEK_CUR, SEEK_END (from unistd.h), which correspond to the start, current position and end of a file, respectively. It defines the offset to which l_start, the first byte in the region, is relative. Normally, this would be SEEK_SET, so l_start is counted from the beginning of the file. The l_len parameter defines the number of bytes in the region.

The l_pid parameter is used for reporting the process holding a lock; see the F_GETLK description below.

Each byte in a file can have only a single type of lock on it at any one time and may be locked for shared access, locked for exclusive access or unlocked.

There are quite a few combinations of commands and options to the fcntl call, so let's look at each of them in turn.

The F_GETLK Command

The first command is F_GETLK. This gets locking information about the file that fildes (the first parameter) has open. It doesn't attempt to lock the file. The calling process passes information about the type of lock it might wish to create and fcntl used with the F_GETLK command returns any information that would prevent the lock occurring.

The values used in the flock structure are:

Value	Description
l_type	Either F_RDLCK for a shared (read-only) lock or F_WRLCK for an exclusive (write) lock
l_whence	One of SEEK_SET, SEEK_CUR, SEEK_END LCK
l_start	The start byte of the file region of interest
l_len	The number of bytes in the file region of interest
l_pid	The identifier of the process with the lock

A process may use the F_GETLK call to determine the current state of locks on a region of a file. It should set up the flock structure to indicate the type of lock it may require and define the region it's interested in. The fcntl call returns a value other than -1 if it's successful. If the file already has locks that would prevent a lock request succeeding, it overwrites the flock structure with the relevant information. If the lock would succeed, the flock structure is unchanged. If the F_GETLK call is unable to obtain the information it returns -1 to indicate failure.

If the F_GETLK call is successful (i.e. it returns a value other than -1), the calling application must check the contents of the flock structure to determine whether it was modified. Since the l_pid value is set to the locking process (if one was found), this is a convenient field to check to determine if the flock structure has been changed.

The F_SETLK Command

This command attempts to lock or unlock part of the file referenced by fildes. The values used in the flock structure (and different from those used by F_GETLK) are:

Value	Description
l_type	Either F_RDLCK for a read-only or shared lock; F_WRLCK for an l_type. Either F_RDLCK for a read only, or shared, lock; F_WRLCK for an exclusive, or write,exclusive or write lock; and F_UNLCK to unlock a region
l_pid	Unused

If the lock is successful, fcntl returns a value other than -1; on failure -1 is returned. The function will always return immediately.

The F_SETLKW Command

This is the same as the F_SETLK command above, except that if it can't obtain the lock, the call will wait until it can. Once this call has started waiting, it will only return when the lock can be obtained or a signal occurs. We'll meet signals in Chapter 10.

All locks held by a program on a file are automatically cleared when the relevant file descriptor is closed. This will also happen automatically when the program finishes.

Use of read and write with Locking

When you're using locking on regions of a file, it's very important to use the lower level `read` and `write` calls to access the data in the file, rather than the higher level `fread` and `fwrite`. This is because `fread` and `fwrite` perform buffering of data read or written inside the library, so executing an `fread` call to read the first 100 bytes of a file may (in fact, almost certainly will) read more than 100 bytes and buffer the additional data inside the library. If the program then uses `fread` to read the next 100 bytes, it will actually read data already buffered inside the library and not cause a low level `read` to pull more data from the file.

To see why this is a problem, consider two programs that wish to update the same file. Let's suppose the file consists of 200 bytes of data, all zeros. The first program starts first and obtains a write lock on the first 100 bytes of the file. It then uses `fread` to read in those 100 bytes. However, as we saw in Chapter 3, `fread` will read ahead by up to `BUFSIZ` bytes at a time, so it actually reads the entire file into memory, but only passes the first 100 bytes back to the program.

The second program then starts. It obtains a `write` lock on the second 100 bytes of the program. This is successful, since the first program only locked the first 100 bytes. The second program writes twos to bytes 100 to 199, closes the file, unlocks it and exits. The first program then locks the second 100 bytes of the file and calls `fread` to read them in. Because that data was buffered, what the program actually sees is 100 bytes of zeros, not the 100 twos that actually exist in the file. This problem doesn't occur when we're using `read` and `write`.

That may seem a complex description of file locking, but it's actually more difficult to describe than it is to use. Let's look at an example of how file locking works, `lock3.c`.

To try out locking, we need two programs, one to do the locking and one to test. The first program does the locking.

Try It Out - Locking a File with `fcntl`

1. Start with the `includes` and variable declarations:

```
#include <unistd.h>
#include <stdlib.h>
#include <stdio.h>
#include <fcntl.h>

const char *test_file = "/tmp/test_lock";

int main()
{
    int file_desc;
    int byte_count;
    char *byte_to_write = "A";
    struct flock region_1;
    struct flock region_2;
    int res;
```

2. Open a file descriptor:

```
file_desc = open(test_file, O_RDWR | O_CREAT, 0666);
if (!file_desc) {
    fprintf(stderr, "Unable to open %s for read/write\n", test_file);
    exit(EXIT_FAILURE);
}
```

3. Put some data in the file:

```
for(byte_count = 0; byte_count < 100; byte_count++) {
    (void)write(file_desc, byte_to_write, 1);
}
```

4. Set up region 1 with a shared lock, from bytes 10 to 30:

```
region_1.l_type = F_RDLCK;
region_1.l_whence = SEEK_SET;
region_1.l_start = 10;
region_1.l_len = 20;
```

5. Set up region 2 with an exclusive lock, from bytes 40 to 50:

```
region_2.l_type = F_WRLCK;
region_2.l_whence = SEEK_SET;
region_2.l_start = 40;
region_2.l_len = 10;
```

6. Now lock the file...

```
printf("Process %d locking file\n", getpid());
res = fcntl(file_desc, F_SETLK, &region_1);
if (res == -1) fprintf(stderr, "Failed to lock region 1\n");
res = fcntl(file_desc, F_SETLK, &region_2);
if (res == -1) fprintf(stderr, "Failed to lock region 2\n");
```

7. ...and wait for a while.

```
    sleep(60);

    printf("Process %d closing file\n", getpid());
    close(file_desc);
    exit(EXIT_SUCCESS);
}
```

How It Works

First, the program creates a file, opens it for both reading and writing, then fills the file with data. It then sets up two regions, the first from bytes 10 to 30, for a shared (`read`) lock, the second from bytes 40 to 50 for an exclusive (`write`) lock. It then calls `fcntl` to lock the two regions and waits for a minute before closing the file and exiting.

When the program starts to wait, this is the situation with locks:

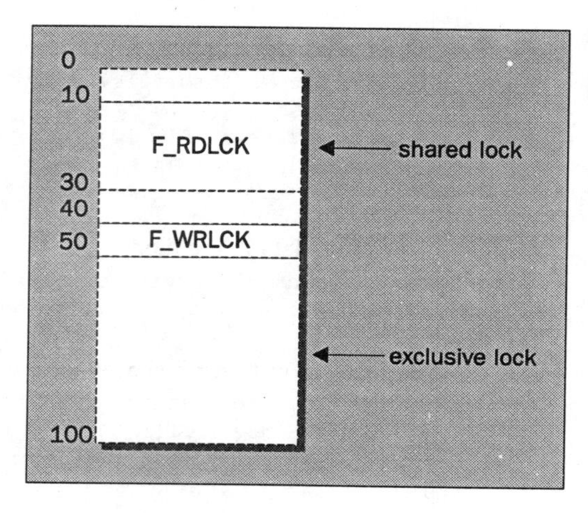

On its own, this program isn't very useful. We need a second program to test the locks, `lock4.c`.

Try It Out - Testing Locks on a File

Let's write a program that tests the different sorts of lock that we could need on different regions of a file.

1. As usual, begin with the `includes` and declarations:

```
#include <unistd.h>
#include <stdlib.h>
#include <stdio.h>
#include <fcntl.h>

const char *test_file = "/tmp/test_lock";
#define SIZE_TO_TRY 5

void show_lock_info(struct flock *to_show);

int main()
{
    int file_desc;
    int res;
    struct flock region_to_test;
    int start_byte;
```

2. Open a file descriptor:

```
    file_desc = open(test_file, O_RDWR | O_CREAT, 0666);
    if (!file_desc) {
        fprintf(stderr, "Unable to open %s for read/write", test_file);
        exit(EXIT_FAILURE);
    }

    for (start_byte = 0; start_byte < 99; start_byte += SIZE_TO_TRY) {
```

3. Set up the region we wish to test:

```
        region_to_test.l_type = F_WRLCK;
        region_to_test.l_whence = SEEK_SET;
        region_to_test.l_start = start_byte;
        region_to_test.l_len = SIZE_TO_TRY;
        region_to_test.l_pid = -1;

        printf("Testing F_WRLCK on region from %d to %d\n",
               start_byte, start_byte + SIZE_TO_TRY);
```

4. Now test the lock on the file:

```
        res = fcntl(file_desc, F_GETLK, &region_to_test);
        if (res == -1) {
            fprintf(stderr, "F_GETLK failed\n");
            exit(EXIT_FAILURE);
        }
        if (region_to_test.l_pid != -1) {
            printf("Lock would fail. F_GETLK returned:\n");
            show_lock_info(&region_to_test);
        }
        else {
            printf("F_WRLCK - Lock would succeed\n");
        }
```

5. Now repeat the test with a shared (read) lock. Set up the region we wish to test again:

```
        region_to_test.l_type = F_RDLCK;
        region_to_test.l_whence = SEEK_SET;
        region_to_test.l_start = start_byte;
        region_to_test.l_len = SIZE_TO_TRY;
        region_to_test.l_pid = -1;

        printf("Testing F_RDLCK on region from %d to %d\n",
               start_byte, start_byte + SIZE_TO_TRY);
```

6. Test the lock on the file again:

```
        res = fcntl(file_desc, F_GETLK, &region_to_test);
        if (res == -1) {
            fprintf(stderr, "F_GETLK failed\n");
            exit(EXIT_FAILURE);
        }
        if (region_to_test.l_pid != -1) {
            printf("Lock would fail. F_GETLK returned:\n");
            show_lock_info(&region_to_test);
        }
        else {
            printf("F_RDLCK - Lock would succeed\n");
        }
    }
    close(file_desc);
    exit(EXIT_SUCCESS);
}

void show_lock_info(struct flock *to_show) {
    printf("\tl_type %d, ", to_show->l_type);
    printf("l_whence %d, ", to_show->l_whence);
    printf("l_start %d, ", (int)to_show->l_start);
    printf("l_len %d, ", (int)to_show->l_len);
    printf("l_pid %d\n", to_show->l_pid);
}
```

To test out locking, we first need to run the lock3 program, then run the lock4 program to test the locked file. We do this by executing the lock3 program in the background, with the command:

```
$ lock3 &
$ process 1534 locking file
```

The command prompt returns, since lock3 is running in the background and we then immediately run the lock4 program with the command:

```
$ lock4
```

The output we get, with some omissions for brevity, is:

```
Testing F_WRLOCK on region from 0 to 5
F_WRLCK - Lock would succeed
Testing F_RDLOCK on region from 0 to 5
F_RDLCK - Lock would succeed
...
Testing F_WRLOCK on region from 10 to 15
Lock would fail. F_GETLK returned:
l_type 0, l_whence 0, l_start 10, l_len 20, l_pid 1534
Testing F_RDLOCK on region from 10 to 15
F_RDLCK - Lock would succeed
Testing F_WRLOCK on region from 15 to 20
Lock would fail. F_GETLK returned:
l_type 0, l_whence 0, l_start 10, l_len 20, l_pid 1534
Testing F_RDLOCK on region from 15 to 20
F_RDLCK - Lock would succeed
...
Testing F_WRLOCK on region from 25 to 30
Lock would fail. F_GETLK returned:
l_type 0, l_whence 0, l_start 10, l_len 20, l_pid 1534
Testing F_RDLOCK on region from 25 to 30
F_RDLCK - Lock would succeed
...
Testing F_WRLOCK on region from 40 to 45
Lock would fail. F_GETLK returned:
l_type 1, l_whence 0, l_start 40, l_len 10, l_pid 1534
Testing F_RDLOCK on region from 40 to 45
Lock would fail. F_GETLK returned:
l_type 1, l_whence 0, l_start 40, l_len 10, l_pid 1534
...
Testing F_RDLOCK on region from 95 to 100
F_RDLCK - Lock would succeed
```

How It Works

For each group of five bytes in the file, lock4 sets up a region structure to test for locks on the file, which it then uses to see if the region could be either write or read locked. The returned information shows the region bytes, offset from byte zero, that would cause the lock request to fail. Since the l_pid part of the returned structure contains the process identifier of the program that currently has the file locked, we set it to -1 (an invalid value) then check whether it has been changed when the fcntl call returns. If the region isn't currently locked, l_pid will be unchanged.

To understand the output, we need to look in the include file fcntl.h (in /usr/include/linux on Linux machines) to find that an l_type of 1 is from the definition of F_WRLCK as 1, and an l_type of 0 is from the definition of F_RDLCK as 0. Thus, an l_type of 1 tells us that the lock would fail because of an existing write lock and an l_type of 0 is because of an existing read lock. On the regions of the file that lock3 has not locked, both shared and exclusive locks will succeed.

From bytes 10 to 30, we can see that it would be possible to have a shared lock, because the existing lock from the lock3 program is a shared, not an exclusive lock. On the region from bytes 40 to 50, both types of lock would fail, since lock3 has an exclusive (F_WRLCK) lock on this region.

Competing Locks

Now that we've seen how to test for existing locks on a file, let's see what happens when two programs compete for locks on the same section of the file. We'll use our lock3 program for locking the file in the first place and a new program to try to lock it again. To complete the example, we'll also add some calls for unlocking.

Here's a program, lock5.c, that tries to lock regions of a file that are already locked, rather than testing the lock status of different parts of the file.

Try It Out - Competing Locks

1. After the #includes and declarations, open a file descriptor:

```
#include <unistd.h>
#include <stdlib.h>
#include <stdio.h>
#include <fcntl.h>

const char *test_file = "/tmp/test_lock";

int main()
{
    int file_desc;
    struct flock region_to_lock;
    int res;

    file_desc = open(test_file, O_RDWR | O_CREAT, 0666);
    if (!file_desc) {
        fprintf(stderr, "Unable to open %s for read/write\n", test_file);
        exit(EXIT_FAILURE);
    }
```

2. The remainder of the program is spent specifying different regions of the file and trying different locking operations on them:

```
    region_to_lock.l_type = F_RDLCK;
    region_to_lock.l_whence = SEEK_SET;
    region_to_lock.l_start = 10;
    region_to_lock.l_len = 5;
    printf("Process %d, trying F_RDLCK, region %d to %d\n", getpid(),
           (int)region_to_lock.l_start, (int)(region_to_lock.l_start +
region_to_lock.l_len));
    res = fcntl(file_desc, F_SETLK, &region_to_lock);
    if (res == -1) {
        printf("Process %d - failed to lock region\n", getpid());
    } else {
        printf("Process %d - obtained lock region\n", getpid());
    }

    region_to_lock.l_type = F_UNLCK;
    region_to_lock.l_whence = SEEK_SET;
    region_to_lock.l_start = 10;
    region_to_lock.l_len = 5;
    printf("Process %d, trying F_UNLCK, region %d to %d\n", getpid(),
```

```
                                (int)region_to_lock.l_start,
(int)(region_to_lock.l_start +
        region_to_lock.l_len));
    res = fcntl(file_desc, F_SETLK, &region_to_lock);
    if (res == -1) {
        printf("Process %d - failed to unlock region\n", getpid());
    } else {
        printf("Process %d - unlocked region\n", getpid());
    }

    region_to_lock.l_type = F_UNLCK;
    region_to_lock.l_whence = SEEK_SET;
    region_to_lock.l_start = 0;
    region_to_lock.l_len = 50;
    printf("Process %d, trying F_UNLCK, region %d to %d\n", getpid(),
                                (int)region_to_lock.l_start,
(int)(region_to_lock.l_start +
        region_to_lock.l_len));
    res = fcntl(file_desc, F_SETLK, &region_to_lock);
    if (res == -1) {
        printf("Process %d - failed to unlock region\n", getpid());
    } else {
        printf("Process %d - unlocked region\n", getpid());
    }

    region_to_lock.l_type = F_WRLCK;
    region_to_lock.l_whence = SEEK_SET;
    region_to_lock.l_start = 16;
    region_to_lock.l_len = 5;
    printf("Process %d, trying F_WRLCK, region %d to %d\n", getpid(),
                                (int)region_to_lock.l_start,
(int)(region_to_lock.l_start +
        region_to_lock.l_len));
    res = fcntl(file_desc, F_SETLK, &region_to_lock);
    if (res == -1) {
        printf("Process %d - failed to lock region\n", getpid());
    } else {
        printf("Process %d - obtained lock on region\n", getpid());
    }

    region_to_lock.l_type = F_RDLCK;
    region_to_lock.l_whence = SEEK_SET;
    region_to_lock.l_start = 40;
    region_to_lock.l_len = 10;
    printf("Process %d, trying F_RDLCK, region %d to %d\n", getpid(),
                                (int)region_to_lock.l_start,
(int)(region_to_lock.l_start +
        region_to_lock.l_len));
    res = fcntl(file_desc, F_SETLK, &region_to_lock);
    if (res == -1) {
        printf("Process %d - failed to lock region\n", getpid());
    } else {
        printf("Process %d - obtained lock on region\n", getpid());
    }

    region_to_lock.l_type = F_WRLCK;
    region_to_lock.l_whence = SEEK_SET;
    region_to_lock.l_start = 16;
    region_to_lock.l_len = 5;
```

```
printf("Process %d, trying F_WRLCK with wait, region %d to %d\n", getpid(),
                                (int)region_to_lock.l_start,
(int)(region_to_lock.l_start +
        region_to_lock.l_len));
    res = fcntl(file_desc, F_SETLKW, &region_to_lock);
    if (res == -1) {
        printf("Process %d - failed to lock region\n", getpid());
    } else {
        printf("Process %d - obtained lock on region\n", getpid());
    }

    printf("Process %d ending\n", getpid());
    close(file_desc);
    exit(EXIT_SUCCESS);
}
```

If we first run our `lock3` program in the background, then immediately run this new program, the output we get is:

```
Process 227 locking file
Process 228, trying F_RDLCK, region 10 to 15
Process 228 - obtained lock on region
Process 228, trying F_UNLCK, region 10 to 15
Process 228 - unlocked region
Process 228, trying F_UNLCK, region 0 to 50
Process 228 - unlocked region
Process 228, trying F_WRLCK, region 16 to 21
Process 228 - failed to lock on region
Process 228, trying F_RDLCK, region 40 to 50
Process 228 - failed to lock on region
Process 228, trying F_WRLCK with wait, region 16 to 21
Process 227 closing file
Process 228 - obtained lock on region
Process 228 ending
```

How It Works

Firstly, the program attempts to lock a region from bytes 10 to 15 with a shared lock. This region is already locked with a shared lock, but simultaneous shared locks are allowed and the lock is successful.

It then unlocks (its own) shared lock on the region, which is also successful. The program then attempts to unlock the first 50 bytes of the file, even though it doesn't have any locks set. This is also successful because, even though this program had no locks in the first place, the final result of the unlock request is that there are no locks held by this program in the first 50 bytes.

Next, the program attempts to lock the region from bytes 16 to 21, with an exclusive lock. This region is also already locked with a shared lock so, this time, the new lock fails, because an exclusive lock could not be created.

After that, the program attempts a shared lock on the region from bytes 40 to 50. This region is already locked with an exclusive lock, so, again, the lock fails.

Finally, the program again attempts to obtain an exclusive lock on the region from bytes 16 to 21, but, this time, it uses the `F_SETLCKW` command to wait until it can obtain a lock. There is then a long pause in the output, until the `lock3` program, which had already locked the region, closes the file, thus releasing all the locks it had acquired. The `lock5` program resumes execution, successfully locking the region, before it also exits.

Other Lock Commands

There is a second method of locking files: the lockf function. This also operates using file descriptors. It has the prototype:

```
#include <unistd.h>

int lockf(int fildes, int function, off_t size_to_lock);
```

It can take the following function values:

- F_ULOCK   Unlock
- F_LOCK   Lock exclusively
- F_TLOCK   Test and lock exclusively
- F_TEST   Test for locks by other processes

The size_to_lock parameter is the number of bytes to operate on, from the current offset in the file.

lockf has a simpler interface than the fcntl interface, principally because it has rather less functionality and flexibility. To use the function, you must seek to the start of the region you wish to lock, then call it with the number of bytes to lock.

Like the fcntl method of file locking, all locks are only advisory; they won't actually prevent reading from or writing to the file. It's the responsibility of programs to check for locks. The effect of mixing fcntl locks and lockf locks is undefined, so you must decide which type of locking you wish to use and stick to it.

Deadlocks

No discussion of locking would be complete without a mention of the dangers of deadlocks. Suppose two programs wish to update the same file. They both need to update byte one and byte two at the same time. Program A chooses to update byte two, then byte one. Program B tries to update byte one first, then byte two.

Both programs start at the same time. Program A locks byte two and program B locks byte one. Program A tries for a lock on byte one. Since this is already locked by program B, program A waits. Program B tries for a lock on byte two. Since this is locked by program A, it too waits.

This situation, when neither program is able to proceed, is called a **deadlock** or **deadly embrace**. Most commercial databases detect deadlocks and break them; the UNIX kernel doesn't. Some external intervention, perhaps forcibly terminating one of the programs, is required to sort out the resulting mess.

Programmers must be wary of this situation. When you have multiple programs waiting for locks, you need to be very careful to consider if a deadlock could occur. In this example it's quite easy to avoid: both programs should simply lock the bytes they require in the same order, or use a larger region to lock.

We don't have the space to consider the difficulties of concurrent programs here. If you're interested in reading further, you might like to consider obtaining a copy of Principles of Concurrent and Distributed Programming , by M. Ben-Ari, Prentice Hall, ISBN 013711821X.

Databases

We've seen how to use files for storing data, so why should we want to use a database? Quite simply, because there are some circumstances where the features of a database provide a better way to solve the problem. Using a database is better than storing files for two reasons. Firstly, you can store data records that vary in size, which can be a little difficult to implement using flat, unstructured files. Secondly, databases store and retrieve data using an index. The big advantage is that this index need not be a simple record number, which would be quite easy to implement in a flat file, but an arbitrary string.

The dbm Database

X/Open compliant versions of UNIX come with a database—not, unfortunately, an ANSI SQL compliant database, but some useful data storage and retrieval routines nonetheless.

Some Linux distributions come with an SQL database called PostgreSQL, which does support SQL, but covering that is beyond the scope of this book.

The `dbm` database is good for storing indexed data which is relatively static. Some database purists would probably argue that `dbm` isn't a database at all, simply an indexed file storage system. The X/Open specification, however, refers to `dbm` as a database, so we'll continue to refer to it as such in this book. Note that many Linux distributions use GNU `gdbm` instead.

The `dbm` database lets you store data structures of variable size, using an index, and then retrieve the structure, either using the index or simply sequentially scanning the database. The `dbm` database is best used for data that is accessed frequently, but updated rarely, since it tends to be rather slow to create entries, but quick to retrieve them.

At this point we come to a minor problem – different Linux distributions ship with different versions of the dbm libraries. Some use the BSD licensed version, which can be found either at ftp://ftp.cs.berkeley.edu/ucb/4bsd/ or from the http://www.openbsd.org sites. Others use the GNU version, which can be found on http://www.gnu.org. To make matters even worse, the GNU flavor can be installed in two modes, the 'normal mode' which is not fully compatible with the X/OPEN dbm specification, or compatibility mode, which is. At the time of writing, Sleepycat Software (http://www.sleepycat.com) has an Open Source product, **The Berkeley Database**, which also supports the Dbm/Ndbm historic interfaces.

This chapter has been written assuming you have an X/OPEN compatible version installed. If you have trouble compiling these examples, either because the `ndbm.h` header file is not present, because the compiler complains `DBM` is undefined, or the link stage of compiling the program fails, the suggested solution is to install an updated version of the GNU version of the `dbm` libraries.

Firstly make yourself a temporary directory. Then go to the http://www.gnu.org site and search for the latest version of the `gdbm` library. This will probably be in a file called something like `gdbm_?_?_tar.gz`. Download the file to your temporary directory, and extract the files using `'tar zxvf <filename>'`. Then read the `README` file, which will tell you how to compile and install it. Generally you first run a command `'./configure'` which checks how your system is configured, then you run `'make'` to compile the programs. Finally you run `'make install'` and `'make install-compat'` to install both the basic files and the additional compatibility files. You may need root permissions to run the install step, and it's often a good idea to use the `'-n'` option to make first, to check what it's going to do, e.g. `'make -n install'`.

You should now have an X/OPEN compatible version of ndbm, normally in the /usr/local part of your system. Your compiler setup may not search these locations by default, in which case you need to add to the gcc command the -I/usr/local/include option to search for headers, and -L/usr/local/lib option to search for libraries.

The dbm Routines

Like curses that we met in the last chapter, the dbm facility consists of a header file and a library that must be linked when the program is compiled. The library is called simply dbm, so we link it by adding the option -ldbm (or occasionally -lgdbm) to the compilation line. The header file is ndbm.h. The reason for the n prefix is that there have been several predecessors to the dbm library, so the n simply separates this 'new' dbm include file from any older versions that may survive.

dbm Concepts

Before we can attempt to explain each of these functions, it's important to understand what the dbm database is trying to achieve. Once we understand this, we'll be in a much better position to understand how to use the dbm functions.

The dbm database basic element is a block of data to store, coupled with a companion block of data that acts as a key for retrieving that data. Each dbm database must have a unique key for each block of data to be stored. There's no restriction on either the keys or the data, nor are any errors defined for using data or keys that are too large. The specification allows an implementation to limit the size of the key/data pair to be 1023 bytes, but generally there is no limit, because implementations have been more flexible than they were required to be. The key value acts as an index into the data stored, like the labels in the diagram.

To manipulate these blocks as data, the ndbm.h include file defines a new type, called datum. The exact contents of this type is implementation-dependent, but it must have at least the following members:

```
void *dptr;
size_t dsize
```

datum will be a type defined by typedef. Also declared in the ndbm.h file is a type definition for dbm, which is a structure used for accessing the database, much like a FILE is used for accessing files. The internals of the dbm type are implementation-dependent and should never be used.

To reference a block of data when we're using the dbm library, we must declare a datum, set dptr to point to the start of the data and set dsize to contain its size. Both the data to store and the index used to access it are always referenced by a datum type.

The dbm type is best thought of as analogous to a FILE type. When we open a dbm database, two physical files are created, one with a .pag extension and one with a .dir extension. A single dbm pointer is returned, which is used to access these two files as a pair. The files should never be read or written to directly, as they are only intended to be accessed via the dbm routines.

If you are using the gdbm library, then the two files have been merged, and only a single new file gets created.

If you're familiar with SQL databases, you'll notice that there are no table or column structures associated with a dbm database. This is because dbm neither imposes a fixed size on each item of data to be stored, nor requires internal structure to the data. The dbm library works on blocks of unstructured binary data.

dbm Access Functions

Now that we've introduced the basis on which the dbm library works, we can take a look at the functions in detail. The prototypes for the main dbm functions are:

```
#include <ndbm.h>

DBM *dbm_open(const char *filename, int file_open_flags, mode_t file_mode);
int dbm_store(DBM *database_descriptor, datum key, datum content, int store_mode);
datum dbm_fetch(DBM *database_descriptor, datum key);
void dbm_close(DBM *database_descriptor);
```

dbm_open

This function is used to open existing databases and can be used to create new databases. The filename argument is a base file name, without a .dir or .pag extension.

The remaining parameters are the same as the second and third parameters to the open function that we met in Chapter 3. We can use the same #defines. The second argument controls whether the database can be read from, written to, or both. To create a new database, the flags must be binary ORed with O_CREAT, to allow the files to be created. The third argument specifies the initial permissions of the files that will be created.

dbm_open returns a pointer to a DBM type. This is used in all subsequent accesses of the database. On failure, a (DBM *)0 is returned.

dbm_store

We use this function for entering data into the database. As we mentioned earlier, all data must be stored with a unique index. To define the data we wish to store and the index used to refer to it, we must set up two datum types: one to refer to the index and one to the actual data. The final parameter, store_mode, controls what happens if an attempt is made to store some data using a key that already exists. If it's set to dbm_insert, the store fails and dbm_store returns 1. If it's set to dbm_replace, the new data overwrites the existing data and dbm_store returns 0. dbm_store will return negative numbers on other errors.

dbm_fetch

This routine is used for retrieving data from the database. It takes a dbm pointer, as returned from a previous call to dbm_open, and a datum type, which must be set up to point to a key. A datum type is returned. If the data relating to the key used was found in the database, the returned datum structure will have dptr and dsize values set up to refer to the returned data. If the key was not found, the dptr will be set to null.

It's important to remember that dbm_fetch is only returning a datum containing a pointer to the data. The actual data may still be held in local storage space inside the dbm library and should be copied into program variables before any further dbm functions are called.

dbm_close

This routine closes a database opened with dbm_open and must be passed a dbm pointer returned from a previous call to dbm_open.

Now that we've met the basic functions of the dbm database, we know enough to write our first dbm program, dbm1.c. In this, we'll use a structure called test_data.

Try It Out - A Simple dbm Database

1. First of all, its include files, #defines, the main function and the declaration of the test_data structure:

```
#include <unistd.h>
#include <stdlib.h>
#include <stdio.h>
#include <fcntl.h>
#include <ndbm.h>
#include <string.h>

#define TEST_DB_FILE "/tmp/dbm1_test"
#define ITEMS_USED 3

struct test_data {
    char misc_chars[15];
    int  any_integer;
    char more_chars[21];
};

int main()
{
```

2. Within main, we set up the items_to_store and items_received structures, the key string and datum types:

```
struct test_data items_to_store[ITEMS_USED];
struct test_data item_retrieved;

char key_to_use[20];
int i, result;

datum key_datum;
datum data_datum;

DBM *dbm_ptr;
```

3. Having declared a pointer to a dbm type structure, we now open our test database for reading and writing, creating it if necessary:

```
dbm_ptr = dbm_open(TEST_DB_FILE, O_RDWR | O_CREAT, 0666);
if (!dbm_ptr) {
    fprintf(stderr, "Failed to open database\n");
    exit(EXIT_FAILURE);
}
```

4. Now we add some data to the items_to_store structure:

```
memset(items_to_store, '\0', sizeof(items_to_store));
strcpy(items_to_store[0].misc_chars, "First!");
items_to_store[0].any_integer = 47;
strcpy(items_to_store[0].more_chars, "foo");

strcpy(items_to_store[1].misc_chars, "bar");
items_to_store[1].any_integer = 13;
strcpy(items_to_store[1].more_chars, "unlucky?");

strcpy(items_to_store[2].misc_chars, "Third");
items_to_store[2].any_integer = 3;
strcpy(items_to_store[2].more_chars, "baz");
```

5. For each entry, we need to build a key for future referencing. This is the first letter of each string and the integer. This key is then identified with the key_datum, while the data_datum refers to the items_to_store entry. Then we store the data in the database.

```
for (i = 0; i < ITEMS_USED; i++) {
    sprintf(key_to_use, "%c%c%d",
            items_to_store[i].misc_chars[0],
            items_to_store[i].more_chars[0],
            items_to_store[i].any_integer);

    key_datum.dptr = (void *)key_to_use;
    key_datum.dsize = strlen(key_to_use);
    data_datum.dptr = (void *)&items_to_store[i];
    data_datum.dsize = sizeof(struct test_data);

    result = dbm_store(dbm_ptr, key_datum, data_datum, DBM_REPLACE);
    if (result != 0) {
        fprintf(stderr, "dbm_store failed on key %s\n", key_to_use);
        exit(2);
    }
}
```

6. Then we see if we can retrieve this new data and, finally, we must close the database:

```
    sprintf(key_to_use, "bu%d", 13);
    key_datum.dptr = key_to_use;
    key_datum.dsize = strlen(key_to_use);

    data_datum = dbm_fetch(dbm_ptr, key_datum);
    if (data_datum.dptr) {
        printf("Data retrieved\n");
        memcpy(&item_retrieved, data_datum.dptr, data_datum.dsize);
        printf("Retrieved item - %s %d %s\n",
               item_retrieved.misc_chars,
               item_retrieved.any_integer,
               item_retrieved.more_chars);
    }
    else {
        printf("No data found for key %s\n", key_to_use);
    }
    dbm_close(dbm_ptr);
    exit(EXIT_SUCCESS);
}
```

When we compile and run the program, the output is simply:

```
$ gcc -o dbm1 dbm1.c -ldbm
$ dbm1
Data retrieved
Retrieved item - bar 13 unlucky?
```

If this fails to compile, you may need to install the GNU gdbm library compatibility files, as described earlier, and/or specify additional directories when you compile, thus:

```
$ gcc -I/usr/local/include -L/usr/local/lib -o dbm1 dbm1.c -ldbm
```

If this still fails, try replacing the `-ldbm` part of the command with `-lgdbm`, thus:

```
$ gcc -I/usr/local/include -L/usr/local/lib -o dbm1 dbm1.c -lgdbm
```

How It Works

First, we open the database, creating it if we need to. We then fill in three members of `items_to_store` that we are using as test data. For each of these three members, we create an index key. To keep it simple, we use the first characters of each of the two strings, plus the integer stored.

We then set up two `datum` structures, one for the key and one for the data to store. Having stored the three items in the database, we construct a new key and set up a `datum` structure to point at it. We then use this key to retrieve data from the database. We check for success by making sure that the `dptr` in the returned `datum` isn't `null`. Provided it isn't, we can then copy the retrieved data (which may be stored internally within the dbm library) into our own structure, being careful to use the size `dbm_fetch` has returned. If we didn't do this and were using variable sized data, we could attempt to copy non-existent data. Finally, we print out the retrieved data to show it was retrieved correctly.

Additional dbm Functions

Now that we've seen the principal dbm functions, we can cover the few remaining functions that are used with dbm. These are:

```
int dbm_delete(DBM *database_descriptor, datum key);
int dbm_error(DBM *database_descriptor);
int dbm_clearerr(DBM *database_descriptor);
datum dbm_firstkey(DBM *database_descriptor);
datum dbm_nextkey(DBM *database_descriptor);
```

dbm_delete

The `dbm_delete` function is used to delete entries from the database. It takes a key `datum` just like `dbm_fetch` but, rather than retrieving the data, it deletes it. It returns 0 on success.

dbm_error

The `dbm_error` function simply tests whether an error has occurred in the database, returning 0 if there is none.

dbm_clearerr

The `dbm_clearerr` clears any error condition flag that may be set in the database.

dbm_firstkey and dbm_nextkey

These routines are normally used as a pair to scan through all the keys of all the items in a database. The loop structure required is:

```
DBM *db_ptr;
datum key;

for(key = dbm_firstkey(db_ptr); key.dptr; key = dbm_nextkey(db_ptr));
```

We'll now amend `dbm1.c` with some of these new functions. Have a look at `dbm2.c`.

Try It Out - Retrieving and Deleting

1. Make a copy of `dbm1.c` and open it for editing. Edit the `#define TEST_DB_FILE` line:

```
#include <unistd.h>
#include <stdlib.h>
#include <stdio.h>
#include <fcntl.h>
#include <ndbm.h>
#include <string.h>

#define TEST_DB_FILE "/tmp/dbm2_test"
#define ITEMS_USED 3
```

2. Then, the only change that we need to make is in the retrieval section:

```
    /* now try and delete some data */
    sprintf(key_to_use, "bu%d", 13);
    key_datum.dptr = key_to_use;
    key_datum.dsize = strlen(key_to_use);

    if (dbm_delete(dbm_ptr, key_datum) == 0) {
        printf("Data with key %s deleted\n", key_to_use);
    }
    else {
        printf("Nothing deleted for key %s\n", key_to_use);
    }

    for (key_datum = dbm_firstkey(dbm_ptr);
           key_datum.dptr;
           key_datum = dbm_nextkey(dbm_ptr)) {
        data_datum = dbm_fetch(dbm_ptr, key_datum);
        if (data_datum.dptr) {
            printf("Data retrieved\n");
            memcpy(&item_retrieved, data_datum.dptr, data_datum.dsize);
            printf("Retrieved item - %s %d %s\n",
                   item_retrieved.misc_chars,
                   item_retrieved.any_integer,
                   item_retrieved.more_chars);
        }
        else {
            printf("No data found for key %s\n", key_to_use);
        }
    }
```

The output is:

```
$ dbm2
Data with key bu13 deleted
Data retrieved
Retrieved item - Third 3 baz
Data retrieved
Retrieved item - First! 47 foo
```

How It Works

The first part of this program is identical to the previous example, simply storing some data in the database. We then build a key to match the second item and delete it from the database.

The program then uses `dbm_firstkey` and `dbm_nextkey` to access each key in the database in turn, retrieving the data. Notice that the data isn't retrieved in order; no order is implied in the keys, it's simply a way of scanning all the entries.

The CD Application

Now that we've learned about the environment and managing data, it's time to update the application. The `dbm` database seems well suited to storing our CD information, so we'll use that as the basis for our new implementation. Since this will involve a significant rewrite, now would be a good time to look at our design decisions to see if they need revising.

Using comma-separated variable files to store the information, whilst it gave an easy implementation in the shell, has turned out to be very restrictive. A lot of CD titles and tracks turn out to have commas in them. Since we can discard this entirely using `dbm`, that's one element of the design that we will change.

The split of the information between 'title' and 'tracks', using a separate file for each, seems to have been a good decision, so we'll stick to the same logical arrangement.

Both the previous implementations have, to some extent, mixed the data access parts of the application with the user interface parts, not least because it was all implemented in a single file. In this implementation, we'll use a header file to describe the data and the routines to access it and split the user interface and data manipulation into separate files.

Although we could have kept the `curses` implementation of the user interface, we'll return to a simple line-based system. This will keep the user interface part of the application small and simple and allow us to concentrate on the other implementation aspects.

Although we can't use SQL with dbm code we can express our new database in more formal terms using SQL terminology. Don't worry if you're not familiar with SQL; you can find the format definition underneath. In code the table can be described by:

```
CREATE TABLE cdc_entry (
    catalog CHAR(30) PRIMARY KEY REFERENCES cdt_entry(catalog),
    title     CHAR(70),
    type      CHAR(30),
    artist    CHAR(70)
);

CREATE TABLE cdt_entry (
    catalog CHAR(30) REFERENCES cdc_entry(catalog),
    track_no  INTEGER CHECK (track_no > 0),
    track_txt CHAR(70),
    PRIMARY KEY(catalog, track_no)
);
```

This very succinct description tells us the names and sizes of the fields. For the `cdc_entry` table, it tells us that there's a unique catalog column for every entry. For the `cdt_entry` table, it tells us that the track number can't be zero and that the combination of catalog and `track_no` columns is unique.

The CD Application Using dbm

We're now going to re-implement our application using the dbm database to store the information we need, with the files `cd_data.h`, `app_ui.c` and `cd_access.c`.

We also rewrite the user interface as a command line program. Later in the book, we'll be reusing the database interface and parts of the user interface as we explore implementing our application using different client/server mechanisms and, finally, as an application that can be accessed across a network using a WWW browser. Converting the interface to a simpler line-driven interface makes it easier for us to focus on the important parts of the application, rather than on the interface.

You'll see the database header file `cd_data.h` and functions from the file `cd_access.c` reused several times in later chapters. We start here with the header file, to define the structure of our data and the routines that we'll use to access it.

Try It Out - cd_data.h

1. This is the data structure definition for the CD database. It defines structures and sizes for the two tables that comprise the database. We start by defining some sizes for the fields that we'll use and two structures: one for the catalog entry and one for the track entry.

```
/* The catalog table */
#define CAT_CAT_LEN       30
#define CAT_TITLE_LEN     70
#define CAT_TYPE_LEN      30
#define CAT_ARTIST_LEN    70

typedef struct {
    char catalog[CAT_CAT_LEN + 1];
    char title[CAT_TITLE_LEN + 1];
    char type[CAT_TYPE_LEN + 1];
    char artist[CAT_ARTIST_LEN + 1];
} cdc_entry;

/* The tracks table, one entry per track */
#define TRACK_CAT_LEN     CAT_CAT_LEN
#define TRACK_TTEXT_LEN   70

typedef struct {
    char catalog[TRACK_CAT_LEN + 1];
    int  track_no;
    char track_txt[TRACK_TTEXT_LEN + 1];
} cdt_entry;
```

2. Now that we have some data structures, we can define some access routines that we'll need. Functions with `cdc_` are for catalog entries; functions with `cdt_` are for track entries.

> **Notice that some of the functions return data structures. We can indicate the failure of these functions by forcing the contents of the structure to be empty.**

```
/* Initialization and termination functions */
int database_initialize(const int new_database);
void database_close(void);

/* two for simple data retrieval */
cdc_entry get_cdc_entry(const char *cd_catalog_ptr);
cdt_entry get_cdt_entry(const char *cd_catalog_ptr, const int track_no);

/* two for data addition */
int add_cdc_entry(const cdc_entry entry_to_add);
int add_cdt_entry(const cdt_entry entry_to_add);

/* two for data deletion */
int del_cdc_entry(const char *cd_catalog_ptr);
int del_cdt_entry(const char *cd_catalog_ptr, const int track_no);

/* one search function */
cdc_entry search_cdc_entry(const char *cd_catalog_ptr, int *first_call_ptr);
```

Try It Out - app_ui.c

1. We now move on to the user interface. This gives us a (relatively) simple program with which to access our database functions, which we'll implement in a separate file. We start, as usual, with some header files:

```
#define _XOPEN_SOURCE

#include <stdlib.h>
#include <unistd.h>
#include <stdio.h>
#include <string.h>

#include "cd_data.h"

#define TMP_STRING_LEN 125 /* this number must be larger than the biggest
                              single string in any database structure */
```

2. We make our menu options `typedef`s. This is in preference to using `#define`d constants, as it allows the compiler to check the types of the menu option variables.

```
typedef enum {
    mo_invalid,
    mo_add_cat,
    mo_add_tracks,
    mo_del_cat,
    mo_find_cat,
    mo_list_cat_tracks,
    mo_del_tracks,
    mo_count_entries,
    mo_exit
} menu_options;
```

3. Now the prototypes for the local functions. Remember that the prototypes for actually accessing the database were included in `cd_data.h`.

```
static int command_mode(int argc, char *argv[]);
static void announce(void);
static menu_options show_menu(const cdc_entry *current_cdc);
static int get_confirm(const char *question);
static int enter_new_cat_entry(cdc_entry *entry_to_update);
static void enter_new_track_entries(const cdc_entry *entry_to_add_to);
static void del_cat_entry(const cdc_entry *entry_to_delete);
static void del_track_entries(const cdc_entry *entry_to_delete);
static cdc_entry find_cat(void);
static void list_tracks(const cdc_entry *entry_to_use);
static void count_all_entries(void);
static void display_cdc(const cdc_entry *cdc_to_show);
static void display_cdt(const cdt_entry *cdt_to_show);
static void strip_return(char *string_to_strip);
```

4. Finally, we get to main. This starts by ensuring the current_cdc_entry that we use to keep track of the currently selected CD catalog entry is initialized. We also parse the command line, announce what program is being run and initialize the database.

```
void main(int argc, char *argv[])
{
    menu_options current_option;
    cdc_entry current_cdc_entry;
    int command_result;

    memset(&current_cdc_entry, '\0', sizeof(current_cdc_entry));

    if (argc > 1) {
        command_result = command_mode(argc, argv);
        exit(command_result);
    }

    announce();

    if (!database_initialize(0)) {
        fprintf(stderr, "Sorry, unable to initialize database\n");
        fprintf(stderr, "To create a new database use %s -i\n", argv[0]);
        exit(EXIT_FAILURE);
    }
```

5. We're now ready to process user input. We sit in a loop, asking for a menu choice and processing it, until the user selects the exit option. Notice that we pass the current_cdc_entry structure to the show_menu function. We do this to allow the menu choices to change if a catalog entry is currently selected.

```
while(current_option != mo_exit) {
        current_option = show_menu(&current_cdc_entry);

        switch(current_option) {
            case mo_add_cat:
                if (enter_new_cat_entry(&current_cdc_entry)) {
                    if (!add_cdc_entry(current_cdc_entry)) {
                        fprintf(stderr, "Failed to add new entry\n");
                        memset(&current_cdc_entry, '\0',
                               sizeof(current_cdc_entry));
                    }
                }
                break;
            case mo_add_tracks:
                enter_new_track_entries(&current_cdc_entry);
                break;
            case mo_del_cat:
                del_cat_entry(&current_cdc_entry);
                break;
            case mo_find_cat:
                current_cdc_entry = find_cat();
                break;
            case mo_list_cat_tracks:
                list_tracks(&current_cdc_entry);
                break;
            case mo_del_tracks:
                del_track_entries(&current_cdc_entry);
                break;
            case mo_count_entries:
                count_all_entries();
                break;
```

```
case mo_exit:
                break;
            case mo_invalid:
                break;
            default:
                break;
        } /* switch */
    } /* while */
```

6. When the main loop exits, we close the database and exit back to the environment. The welcoming sentence is printed by the announce function:

```
    database_close();
    exit(EXIT_SUCCESS);
} /* main */

static void announce(void)
{
    printf("\n\nWelcome to the demonstration CD catalog database \
             program\n");
}
```

7. Here we implement the show_menu function. This checks whether a current catalog entry is selected, using the first character of the catalog name. More options are available if a catalog entry is selected.

> **Note that numbers are now used to select menu items, rather than the initial letters we used in the previous two examples.**

```
static menu_options show_menu(const cdc_entry *cdc_selected)
{
    char tmp_str[TMP_STRING_LEN + 1];
    menu_options option_chosen = mo_invalid;

    while (option_chosen == mo_invalid) {
        if (cdc_selected->catalog[0]) {
            printf("\n\nCurrent entry: ");
            printf("%s, %s, %s, %s\n", cdc_selected->catalog,
                   cdc_selected->title,
                   cdc_selected->type,
                   cdc_selected->artist);

            printf("\n");
            printf("1 - add new CD\n");
            printf("2 - search for a CD\n");
            printf("3 - count the CDs and tracks in the database\n");
            printf("4 - re-enter tracks for current CD\n");
            printf("5 - delete this CD, and all its tracks\n");
            printf("6 - list tracks for this CD\n");
            printf("q - quit\n");
            printf("\nOption: ");
            fgets(tmp_str, TMP_STRING_LEN, stdin);
            switch(tmp_str[0]) {
                case '1': option_chosen = mo_add_cat; break;
                case '2': option_chosen = mo_find_cat; break;
                case '3': option_chosen = mo_count_entries; break;
                case '4': option_chosen = mo_add_tracks; break;
                case '5': option_chosen = mo_del_cat; break;
                case '6': option_chosen = mo_list_cat_tracks; break;
                case 'q': option_chosen = mo_exit; break;
            }
```

```
        }
        else {
            printf("\n\n");
            printf("1 - add new CD\n");
            printf("2 - search for a CD\n");
            printf("3 - count the CDs and tracks in the database\n");
            printf("q - quit\n");
            printf("\nOption: ");
            fgets(tmp_str, TMP_STRING_LEN, stdin);
            switch(tmp_str[0]) {
                case '1': option_chosen = mo_add_cat; break;
                case '2': option_chosen = mo_find_cat; break;
                case '3': option_chosen = mo_count_entries; break;
                case 'q': option_chosen = mo_exit; break;
            }
        }
    } /* while */
    return(option_chosen);
}
```

8. There are several places where we wish to ask the user if they are sure about what they requested. Rather than have several places in the code asking the question, we extract the code as a separate function, `get_confirm`:

```
static int get_confirm(const char *question)
{
    char tmp_str[TMP_STRING_LEN + 1];

    printf("%s", question);
    fgets(tmp_str, TMP_STRING_LEN, stdin);
    if (tmp_str[0] == 'Y' || tmp_str[0] == 'y') {
        return(1);
    }
    return(0);
}
```

9. The function, `enter_new_cat_entry`, allows the user to enter a new catalog entry. We don't want to store the linefeed that `fgets` returns, so we strip it off.

> **Notice that we don't use the `gets` function, since that has no way of checking for an overflow of the buffer. Avoid the `gets` function!**

```
static int enter_new_cat_entry(cdc_entry *entry_to_update)
{
    cdc_entry new_entry;
    char tmp_str[TMP_STRING_LEN + 1];

    memset(&new_entry, '\0', sizeof(new_entry));

    printf("Enter catalog entry: ");
    (void)fgets(tmp_str, TMP_STRING_LEN, stdin);
    strip_return(tmp_str);
    strncpy(new_entry.catalog, tmp_str, CAT_CAT_LEN - 1);

    printf("Enter title: ");
    (void)fgets(tmp_str, TMP_STRING_LEN, stdin);
    strip_return(tmp_str);
    strncpy(new_entry.title, tmp_str, CAT_TITLE_LEN - 1);
```

```
    printf("Enter type: ");
    (void)fgets(tmp_str, TMP_STRING_LEN, stdin);
    strip_return(tmp_str);
    strncpy(new_entry.type, tmp_str, CAT_TYPE_LEN - 1);

    printf("Enter artist: ");
    (void)fgets(tmp_str, TMP_STRING_LEN, stdin);
    strip_return(tmp_str);
    strncpy(new_entry.artist, tmp_str, CAT_ARTIST_LEN - 1);

    printf("\nNew catalog entry entry is :-\n");
    display_cdc(&new_entry);
    if (get_confirm("Add this entry ?")) {
        memcpy(entry_to_update, &new_entry, sizeof(new_entry));
        return(1);
    }
    return(0);
}
```

10. We now come to the function for entering the track information, `enter_new_track_entries`. This is slightly more complex than the catalog entry function, because we allow an existing track entry to be left alone.

```
static void enter_new_track_entries(const cdc_entry *entry_to_add_to)
{
    cdt_entry new_track, existing_track;
    char tmp_str[TMP_STRING_LEN + 1];
    int track_no = 1;

    if (entry_to_add_to->catalog[0] == '\0') return;
    printf("\nUpdating tracks for %s\n", entry_to_add_to->catalog);
    printf("Press return to leave existing description unchanged,\n");
    printf(" a single d to delete this and remaining tracks,\n");
    printf(" or new track description\n");

    while(1) {
```

11. First, we must check whether a track already exists with the current track number. Depending on what we find, we change the prompt.

```
        memset(&new_track, '\0', sizeof(new_track));
        existing_track = get_cdt_entry(entry_to_add_to->catalog,
                                        track_no);
        if (existing_track.catalog[0]) {
            printf("\tTrack %d: %s\n", track_no,
                               existing_track.track_txt);
            printf("\tNew text: ");
        }
        else {
            printf("\tTrack %d description: ", track_no);
        }
        fgets(tmp_str, TMP_STRING_LEN, stdin);
        strip_return(tmp_str);
```

12. If there was no existing entry for this track and the user hasn't added one, we assume that there are no more tracks to be added.

```
        if (strlen(tmp_str) == 0) {
            if (existing_track.catalog[0] == '\0') {
                    /* no existing entry, so finished adding */
                break;
            }
            else {
                /* leave existing entry, jump to next track */
                track_no++;
                continue;
            }
        }
```

13. If the user enters a single d character, this deletes the current and any higher numbered tracks. The del_cdt_entry function will return false if it couldn't find a track to delete.

```
        if ((strlen(tmp_str) == 1) && tmp_str[0] == 'd') {
                /* delete this and remaining tracks */
            while (del_cdt_entry(entry_to_add_to->catalog, track_no)) {
                track_no++;
            }
            break;
        }
```

14. Here we get to the code for adding a new track, or updating an existing one. We construct the cdt_entry structure new_track, then call the database function add_cdt_entry to add it to the database.

```
        strncpy(new_track.track_txt, tmp_str, TRACK_TTEXT_LEN - 1);
        strcpy(new_track.catalog, entry_to_add_to->catalog);
        new_track.track_no = track_no;
        if (!add_cdt_entry(new_track)) {
            fprintf(stderr, "Failed to add new track\n");
            break;
        }
        track_no++;
    } /* while */
}
```

15. The function del_cat_entry deletes a catalog entry. We never allow tracks for a non-existent catalog entry to exist.

```
static void del_cat_entry(const cdc_entry *entry_to_delete)
{
    int track_no = 1;
    int delete_ok;

    display_cdc(entry_to_delete);
    if (get_confirm("Delete this entry and all it's tracks? ")) {
        do {
            delete_ok = del_cdt_entry(entry_to_delete->catalog,
                                      track_no);
            track_no++;
        } while(delete_ok);

        if (!del_cdc_entry(entry_to_delete->catalog)) {
            fprintf(stderr, "Failed to delete entry\n");
        }
    }
}
```

16. The next function is a utility for deleting all the tracks for a catalog:

```
static void del_track_entries(const cdc_entry *entry_to_delete)
{
    int track_no = 1;
    int delete_ok;

    display_cdc(entry_to_delete);
    if (get_confirm("Delete tracks for this entry? ")) {
        do {
            delete_ok = del_cdt_entry(entry_to_delete->catalog, track_no);
            track_no++;
        } while(delete_ok);
    }
}
```

17. Next, we create a very simple catalog search facility. We allow the user to enter a string, then check for catalog entries that contain the string. Since there could be multiple entries that match, we simply offer the user each match in turn:

```
static cdc_entry find_cat(void)
{
    cdc_entry item_found;
    char tmp_str[TMP_STRING_LEN + 1];
    int first_call = 1;
    int any_entry_found = 0;
    int string_ok;
    int entry_selected = 0;

    do {
        string_ok = 1;
        printf("Enter string to search for in catalog entry: ");
        fgets(tmp_str, TMP_STRING_LEN, stdin);
        strip_return(tmp_str);
        if (strlen(tmp_str) > CAT_CAT_LEN) {
            fprintf(stderr, "Sorry, string too long, maximum %d \
                             characters\n", CAT_CAT_LEN);

            string_ok = 0;
        }
    } while (!string_ok);

    while (!entry_selected) {
        item_found = search_cdc_entry(tmp_str, &first_call);
        if (item_found.catalog[0] != '\0') {
            any_entry_found = 1;
            printf("\n");
            display_cdc(&item_found);
            if (get_confirm("This entry? ")) {
                entry_selected = 1;
            }
        }
        else {
            if (any_entry_found) printf("Sorry, no more matches found\n");
            else printf("Sorry, nothing found\n");
            break;
        }
    }
    return(item_found);
}
```

18. `list_tracks` is a utility function that prints out all the tracks for a given catalog entry:

```
static void list_tracks(const cdc_entry *entry_to_use)
{
    int track_no = 1;
    cdt_entry entry_found;

    display_cdc(entry_to_use);
    printf("\nTracks\n");
    do {
            entry_found = get_cdt_entry(entry_to_use->catalog,
                                        track_no);
            if (entry_found.catalog[0]) {
                display_cdt(&entry_found);
                track_no++;
            }
    } while(entry_found.catalog[0]);
    (void)get_confirm("Press return");
} /* list_tracks */
```

19. The `count_all_entries` function counts all the tracks:

```
static void count_all_entries(void)
{
    int cd_entries_found = 0;
    int track_entries_found = 0;
    cdc_entry cdc_found;
    cdt_entry cdt_found;
    int track_no = 1;
    int first_time = 1;
    char *search_string = "";

    do {
        cdc_found = search_cdc_entry(search_string, &first_time);
        if (cdc_found.catalog[0]) {
            cd_entries_found++;
            track_no = 1;
            do {
                cdt_found = get_cdt_entry(cdc_found.catalog, track_no);
                if (cdt_found.catalog[0]) {
                    track_entries_found++;
                    track_no++;
                }
            } while (cdt_found.catalog[0]);
        }
    } while (cdc_found.catalog[0]);

    printf("Found %d CDs, with a total of %d tracks\n", cd_entries_found,
                track_entries_found);
    (void)get_confirm("Press return");
}
```

20. Now we have `display_cdc`, a utility for displaying a catalog entry:

```
static void display_cdc(const cdc_entry *cdc_to_show)
{
    printf("Catalog: %s\n", cdc_to_show->catalog);
    printf("\ttitle: %s\n", cdc_to_show->title);
    printf("\ttype: %s\n", cdc_to_show->type);
    printf("\tartist: %s\n", cdc_to_show->artist);
}
```

and display_cdt, for displaying a single track entry:

```
static void display_cdt(const cdt_entry *cdt_to_show)
{
    printf("%d: %s\n", cdt_to_show->track_no, cdt_to_show->track_txt);
}
```

21. The utility function strip_return removes a trailing linefeed character from a string. Remember that UNIX uses a single linefeed to indicate end of line:

```
static void strip_return(char *string_to_strip)
{
    int len;

    len = strlen(string_to_strip);
    if (string_to_strip[len - 1] == '\n') string_to_strip[len - 1] = '\0';
}
```

22. command_mode is a function for parsing the command line arguments. The getopt function is a good way of ensuring your program accepts arguments conforming to the standard UNIX conventions.

```
static int command_mode(int argc, char *argv[])
{
    int c;
    int result = EXIT_SUCCESS;
    char *prog_name = argv[0];

    /* these externals used by getopt */
    extern char *optarg;
    extern optind, opterr, optopt;

    while ((c = getopt(argc, argv, ":i")) != -1) {
        switch(c) {
            case 'i':
                if (!database_initialize(1)) {
                    result = EXIT_FAILURE;
                    fprintf(stderr, "Failed to initialize database\n");
                }
                break;
            case ':':
            case '?':
            default:
                fprintf(stderr, "Usage: %s [-i]\n", prog_name);
                result = EXIT_FAILURE;
                break;
        } /* switch */
    } /* while */
    return(result);
}
```

Try It Out - cd_access.c

1. Now we come to the functions that access the dbm database. As usual, we start with some #include files. We then use some #defines for specifying the files that we'll use for storing the data.

```
#define _XOPEN_SOURCE

#include <unistd.h>
#include <stdlib.h>
#include <stdio.h>
#include <fcntl.h>
#include <string.h>
#include <ndbm.h>

#include "cd_data.h"

#define CDC_FILE_BASE "cdc_data"
#define CDT_FILE_BASE "cdt_data"
#define CDC_FILE_DIR  "cdc_data.dir"
#define CDC_FILE_PAG  "cdc_data.pag"
#define CDT_FILE_DIR "cdt_data.dir"
#define CDT_FILE_PAG "cdt_data.pag"
```

2. We use these two file scope variables to keep track of the current database:

```
static DBM *cdc_dbm_ptr = NULL;
static DBM *cdt_dbm_ptr = NULL;
```

3. By default, the database_initialize function opens an existing database, but by passing a non-zero (i.e. true) parameter, new_database, we can force it to create a new (empty) database. If the database is successfully initialized, the two database pointers are also initialized, indicating that a database is open.

```
int database_initialize(const int new_database)
{
    int open_mode = O_RDWR;

    /* If any existing database is open then close it */
    if (cdc_dbm_ptr) dbm_close(cdc_dbm_ptr);
    if (cdt_dbm_ptr) dbm_close(cdt_dbm_ptr);

    if (new_database) {
        /* delete the old files */
        (void) unlink(CDC_FILE_PAG);
        (void) unlink(CDC_FILE_DIR);
        (void) unlink(CDT_FILE_PAG);
        (void) unlink(CDT_FILE_DIR);

        open_mode = O_CREAT | O_RDWR;
    }

    /* Open some new files, creating them if required */
    cdc_dbm_ptr = dbm_open(CDC_FILE_BASE, open_mode, 0644);
    cdt_dbm_ptr = dbm_open(CDT_FILE_BASE, open_mode, 0644);
    if (!cdc_dbm_ptr || !cdt_dbm_ptr) {
        fprintf(stderr, "Unable to create database\n");
        cdc_dbm_ptr = cdt_dbm_ptr = NULL;
        return (0);
    }
    return (1);
}
```

4. `database_close` simply closes the database if it was open and sets the two database pointers to `null`, to indicate that no database is currently open.

```
void database_close(void)
{
    if (cdc_dbm_ptr) dbm_close(cdc_dbm_ptr);
    if (cdt_dbm_ptr) dbm_close(cdt_dbm_ptr);

    cdc_dbm_ptr = cdt_dbm_ptr = NULL;
}
```

5. Next, we have a function for retrieving a single catalog entry, when passed a pointer pointing to a catalog text string. If the entry isn't found then the returned data has an empty catalog field.

```
cdc_entry get_cdc_entry(const char *cd_catalog_ptr)
{
    cdc_entry entry_to_return;
    char entry_to_find[CAT_CAT_LEN + 1];
    datum local_data_datum;
    datum local_key_datum;

    memset(&entry_to_return, '\0', sizeof(entry_to_return));
```

6. We start with some sanity checks, to ensure that a database is open and that we were passed reasonable parameters—i.e. the search key contains only the valid string and `nulls`:

```
    if (!cdc_dbm_ptr || !cdt_dbm_ptr) return (entry_to_return);
    if (!cd_catalog_ptr) return (entry_to_return);
    if (strlen(cd_catalog_ptr) >= CAT_CAT_LEN) return (entry_to_return);

    memset(&entry_to_find, '\0', sizeof(entry_to_find));
    strcpy(entry_to_find, cd_catalog_ptr);
```

7. We set up the `datum` structure the `dbm` functions require, then use `dbm_fetch` to retrieve the data. If no data was retrieved, we return the empty `entry_to_return` structure that we initialized earlier.

```
    local_key_datum.dptr = (void *) entry_to_find;
    local_key_datum.dsize = sizeof(entry_to_find);

    memset(&local_data_datum, '\0', sizeof(local_data_datum));
    local_data_datum = dbm_fetch(cdc_dbm_ptr, local_key_datum);
    if (local_data_datum.dptr) {
        memcpy(&entry_to_return, (char *)local_data_datum.dptr,
                    local_data_datum.dsize);
    }
    return (entry_to_return);
} /* get_cdc_entry */
```

8. We'd better be able to get a single track entry as well, which is what the next function does, in the same fashion as `get_cdc_entry`, but with a pointer pointing to a catalog string and a track number as parameters.

```
cdt_entry get_cdt_entry(const char *cd_catalog_ptr, const int track_no)
{
    cdt_entry entry_to_return;
    char entry_to_find[CAT_CAT_LEN + 10];
    datum local_data_datum;
    datum local_key_datum;

    memset(&entry_to_return, '\0', sizeof(entry_to_return));

    if (!cdc_dbm_ptr || !cdt_dbm_ptr) return (entry_to_return);
    if (!cd_catalog_ptr) return (entry_to_return);
    if (strlen(cd_catalog_ptr) >= CAT_CAT_LEN) return (entry_to_return);
    /* set up the search key, which is a composite key of catalog entry
       and track number */
    memset(&entry_to_find, '\0', sizeof(entry_to_find));
    sprintf(entry_to_find, "%s %d", cd_catalog_ptr, track_no);

    local_key_datum.dptr = (void *) entry_to_find;
    local_key_datum.dsize = sizeof(entry_to_find);

    memset(&local_data_datum, '\0', sizeof(local_data_datum));
    local_data_datum = dbm_fetch(cdt_dbm_ptr, local_key_datum);
    if (local_data_datum.dptr) {
        memcpy(&entry_to_return, (char *) local_data_datum.dptr,
                    local_data_datum.dsize);
    }
    return (entry_to_return);
}
```

9. The next function, `add_cdc_entry`, adds a new catalog entry:

```
int add_cdc_entry(const cdc_entry entry_to_add)
{
    char key_to_add[CAT_CAT_LEN + 1];
    datum local_data_datum;
    datum local_key_datum;
    int result;

    /* check database initialized and parameters valid */
    if (!cdc_dbm_ptr || !cdt_dbm_ptr) return (0);
    if (strlen(entry_to_add.catalog) >= CAT_CAT_LEN) return (0);

    /* ensure the search key contains only the valid string and nulls */
    memset(&key_to_add, '\0', sizeof(key_to_add));
    strcpy(key_to_add, entry_to_add.catalog);

    local_key_datum.dptr = (void *) key_to_add;
    local_key_datum.dsize = sizeof(key_to_add);
    local_data_datum.dptr = (void *) &entry_to_add;
    local_data_datum.dsize = sizeof(entry_to_add);

    result = dbm_store(cdc_dbm_ptr, local_key_datum, local_data_datum,
                      DBM_REPLACE);

    /* dbm_store() uses 0 for success */
    if (result == 0) return (1);
    return (0);
}
```

10. add_cdt_entry adds a new track entry. The access key is the catalog string and track number acting as a composite.

```
int add_cdt_entry(const cdt_entry entry_to_add)
{
    char key_to_add[CAT_CAT_LEN + 10];
    datum local_data_datum;
    datum local_key_datum;
    int result;

    if (!cdc_dbm_ptr || !cdt_dbm_ptr) return (0);
    if (strlen(entry_to_add.catalog) >= CAT_CAT_LEN) return (0);

    memset(&key_to_add, '\0', sizeof(key_to_add));
    sprintf(key_to_add, "%s %d", entry_to_add.catalog,
                   entry_to_add.track_no);

    local_key_datum.dptr = (void *) key_to_add;
    local_key_datum.dsize = sizeof(key_to_add);
    local_data_datum.dptr = (void *) &entry_to_add;
    local_data_datum.dsize = sizeof(entry_to_add);

    result = dbm_store(cdt_dbm_ptr, local_key_datum, local_data_datum,
                       DBM_REPLACE);

    /* dbm_store() uses 0 for success and -ve numbers for errors */
    if (result == 0)
        return (1);
    return (0);
}
```

11. If we can add things, we'd better be able to delete them too. This function deletes catalog entries:

```
int del_cdc_entry(const char *cd_catalog_ptr)
{
    char key_to_del[CAT_CAT_LEN + 1];
    datum local_key_datum;
    int result;

    if (!cdc_dbm_ptr || !cdt_dbm_ptr) return (0);
    if (strlen(cd_catalog_ptr) >= CAT_CAT_LEN) return (0);

    memset(&key_to_del, '\0', sizeof(key_to_del));
    strcpy(key_to_del, cd_catalog_ptr);

    local_key_datum.dptr = (void *) key_to_del;
    local_key_datum.dsize = sizeof(key_to_del);

    result = dbm_delete(cdc_dbm_ptr, local_key_datum);

    /* dbm_delete() uses 0 for success */
    if (result == 0) return (1);
    return (0);
}
```

12. Here's the equivalent function for deleting a track. Remember that the track key is a composite index of both the catalog entry string and the track number.

```
int del_cdt_entry(const char *cd_catalog_ptr, const int track_no)
{
    char key_to_del[CAT_CAT_LEN + 10];
    datum local_key_datum;
    int result;

    if (!cdc_dbm_ptr || !cdt_dbm_ptr) return (0);
    if (strlen(cd_catalog_ptr) >= CAT_CAT_LEN) return (0);

    memset(&key_to_del, '\0', sizeof(key_to_del));
    sprintf(key_to_del, "%s %d", cd_catalog_ptr, track_no);

    local_key_datum.dptr = (void *) key_to_del;
    local_key_datum.dsize = sizeof(key_to_del);

    result = dbm_delete(cdt_dbm_ptr, local_key_datum);

    /* dbm_delete() uses 0 for success */
    if (result == 0) return (1);
    return (0);
}
```

13. Last but not least, we have a simple search function. It's not very sophisticated, but it does demonstrate how we can scan through dbm entries without knowing the keys in advance.

Since we don't know in advance how many entries there might be, we implement this function to return a single entry on each call. If nothing is found, the entry will be empty. To scan the whole database, we start by calling this function with a pointer to an integer, `*first_call_ptr`, which should be `1` the first time the function is called. This function then knows it should start searching at the start of the database. On subsequent calls, the variable is `0` and the function resumes searching after the last entry it found.

When we wish to restart our search, probably with a different catalog entry, we must again call this function with `*first_call_ptr` set to true, which re-initializes the search.

In between calls, the function maintains some internal state information. This hides the complexity of continuing a search from the client and preserves the 'secrecy' of how the search function is implemented.

If the search text points to a `null` character then all entries are considered to match.

```
cdc_entry search_cdc_entry(const char *cd_catalog_ptr, int *first_call_ptr)
{
    static int local_first_call = 1;
    cdc_entry entry_to_return;
    datum local_data_datum;
    static datum local_key_datum;     /* notice this must be static */

    memset(&entry_to_return, '\0', sizeof(entry_to_return));
```

14. As usual, we start with sanity checks:

```
    if (!cdc_dbm_ptr || !cdt_dbm_ptr) return (entry_to_return);
    if (!cd_catalog_ptr || !first_call_ptr) return (entry_to_return);
    if (strlen(cd_catalog_ptr) >= CAT_CAT_LEN) return (entry_to_return);

    /* protect against never passing *first_call_ptr true */
    if (local_first_call) {
        local_first_call = 0;
        *first_call_ptr = 1;
    }
```

15. If this function has been called with `*first_call_ptr` set to `true`, we need to start (or restart) searching from the beginning of the database. If `*first_call_ptr` wasn't `true`, we simply move on to the next key in the database:

```
    if (*first_call_ptr) {
        *first_call_ptr = 0;
        local_key_datum = dbm_firstkey(cdc_dbm_ptr);
    }
    else {
        local_key_datum = dbm_nextkey(cdc_dbm_ptr);
    }

    do {
        if (local_key_datum.dptr != NULL) {
            /* an entry was found */
            local_data_datum = dbm_fetch(cdc_dbm_ptr, local_key_datum);
            if (local_data_datum.dptr) {
                memcpy(&entry_to_return, (char *) local_data_datum.dptr,
local_data_datum.dsize);
```

16. Our search facility is a very simple check to see whether the search string occurs in the current catalog entry.

```
                /* check if search string occurs in the entry */
                if (!strstr(entry_to_return.catalog, cd_catalog_ptr))
                    {
                    memset(&entry_to_return, '\0',
                           sizeof(entry_to_return));
                    local_key_datum = dbm_nextkey(cdc_dbm_ptr);
                }
            }
        }
    } while (local_key_datum.dptr &&
        local_data_datum.dptr &&
        (entry_to_return.catalog[0] == '\0'));
    return (entry_to_return);
} /* search_cdc_entry */
```

We're now in a position to be able to put everything together with this `makefile`. Don't worry about it too much right now, because we'll be looking at how it works in the next chapter. For the time being, type it in and save it as `Makefile`.

```
all:    application

app_ui.o: app_ui.c cd_data.h
        gcc -pedantic -Wall -ansi -g -c app_ui.c
```

```
cd_access.o: cd_access.c cd_data.h
        gcc -pedantic -Wall -ansi -g -c cd_access.c

application:    app_ui.o cd_access.o
        gcc -o application -pedantic -Wall -ansi -g app_ui.o cd_access.o -ldbm
```

Remember – you may need to replace `-ldbm` with `-gdbm` if that's how your system is setup.

To compile your new CD application, type this at the prompt:

```
$ make -f Makefile
```

If all has gone well, the `application` executable will be compiled and placed in the current directory.

The first time you run the application, remember to use the '`-i`' option to get the database created.

Summary

In this chapter we've learned about three different aspects of data management. Firstly, we've learned about the UNIX memory system and how simple it is to use, even though the internal implementation of demand paged virtual memory is quite involved. We've also found how it protects both the operating system and other programs from attempts at illegal memory access.

We then moved on to look at how file locking allows multiple programs to cooperate in their access to data. We looked first at a simple binary semaphore scheme and then at a more complex situation where we lock different parts of a file for either shared or exclusive access.

Finally, we've looked at the `dbm` library and its ability to store and efficiently retrieve arbitrary blocks of data using a very flexible indexing arrangement.

Development Tools

In this chapter, we'll look at some of the tools available for developing programs on UNIX systems. In addition to the obvious necessities of compilers and debuggers, UNIX provides a set of tools, each of which does a single job, and then allows the developer to combine these tools in new and innovative ways. Here, we'll look at a few of the more important tools and see some examples of them being used to solve problems including:

- The make command and makefiles
- Source code control using RCS and CVS
- Writing a manual page
- Distributing software using patch and tar

Problems of Multiple Source Files

When they're writing small programs, many people simply rebuild their application after edits by recompiling all the files. However, with larger programs, some problems with this simple approach become apparent. The time for the edit-compile-test cycle will grow. Even the most patient programmer will want to avoid recompiling all the files when only one file has been changed.

A potentially much more difficult problem arises when multiple header files are created and included in different source files. Suppose we have header files a.h, b.h and c.h, and C source files main.c, 2.c and 3.c. (We hope that you choose better names than these for real projects!) We could have the situation shown below.

```
/* main.c */
#include "a.h"
...
```

```
/* 2.c */
#include "a.h"
#include "b.h"
...
```

```
/* 3.c */
#include "b.h"
#include "c.h"
...
```

If the programmer changes `c.h`, the files `main.c` and `2.c` don't need to be recompiled, since they don't **depend** on this header file. The file `3.c` does depend on `c.h` and should therefore be recompiled if `c.h` is changed. However, if `b.h` was changed and the programmer forgot to recompile `2.c`, then the resulting program might no longer function correctly.

The **make** utility can solve both of these problems by ensuring that the files affected by changes are recompiled when necessary.

> **The `make` command is not used only to compile programs. It can be used whenever you produce output files from several input files. Other uses include document processing (such as with `troff` or `TeX`).**

The make Command and Makefiles

Although, as we shall see, the `make` command has a lot of built-in knowledge, it can't know how to build your application all by itself. You must provide a file that tells `make` how your application is constructed. This file is called the **makefile**.

The makefile most often resides in the same directory as the other source files for the project. You can have many different makefiles on your machine at any one time. Indeed, if you have a large project, you may choose to manage it using separate makefiles for different parts of the project.

The combination of the `make` command and a makefile provides a very powerful tool for managing projects. It's often used not only to control the compilation of source code, but also to prepare manual pages and to install the application into a target directory.

The Syntax of Makefiles

A makefile consists of a set of dependencies and rules. A **dependency** has a target (a file to be created) and a set of source files upon which it is dependent. The **rules** describe how to create the target from the dependent files. Commonly, the **target** is a single executable file.

The makefile is read by the `make` command, which determines the target file or files that are to be made and then compares the dates and times of the source files to decide which rules need to be invoked to construct the target. Often, other intermediate targets have to be created before the final target can be made. The `make` command uses the makefile to determine the order in which the targets have to be made and the correct sequence of rules to invoke.

Options and Parameters to make

The make program itself has several options. The three most commonly used are:

- -k, which tells make to 'keep going' when an error is found, rather than stopping as soon as the first problem is detected. You can use this, for example, to find out in one go which source files fail to compile.
- -n, which tells make to print out what it would have done, without actually doing it.
- -f <filename>, which allows you to tell make which file to use as its makefile. If you don't use this option, make looks first for a file called makefile in the current directory. If that doesn't exist, it looks for a file called Makefile. By convention, most UNIX programmers use Makefile.

To make a particular target, which is usually an executable file, you can pass its name to make as a parameter. If you don't, make will try to make the first target listed in the makefile. Many programmers specify all as the first target in their makefile and then list the other targets as being dependent on all. This convention makes it clear which target the makefile should attempt to build by default when no target is specified. We suggest you stick to this convention.

Dependencies

The dependencies specify how each file in the final application relates to the source files. In our example above, we might specify dependencies that say our final application requires (depends on) main.o, 2.o and 3.o; and likewise for main.o (main.c and a.h); 2.o (2.c, a.h and b.h); and 3.o (3.c, b.h and c.h). Thus main.o is affected by changes to main.c and a.h, and it needs to be recreated, by recompiling main.c, if either of these two files changes.

In a makefile, we write these rules by writing the name of the target, a colon, spaces or tabs and then a space or tab-separated list of files that are used to create the target file. The dependency list for our example is:

```
myapp: main.o 2.o 3.o

main.o: main.c a.h

2.o: 2.c a.h b.h

3.o: 3.c b.h c.h
```

This says that myapp depends on main.o, 2.o and 3.o, main.o depends on main.c and a.h, and so on.

This set of dependencies gives a hierarchy showing how the source files relate to one other. We can see quite easily that, if b.h changes, then we need to revise both 2.o and 3.o and, since 2.o and 3.o will have changed, we also need to rebuild myapp.

If we wish to make several files, then we can use the phony target all. Suppose our application consisted of both the binary file myapp and a manual page, myapp.1. We could specify this with the line:

```
all: myapp myapp.1
```

If we don't specify an all target, make simply creates the first target it finds in the makefile.

Rules

This brings us onto the second part of the makefile specifying the rules that describe how to create a target. In our example above, once the make command has determined that 2.o needs rebuilding, what command should be used? It may be that simply using gcc -c 2.c is sufficient (and, as we'll see later, make does indeed know many default rules), but what if we needed to specify an include directory, or set the symbolic information option for later debugging? We can do this by specifying explicit rules in the makefile.

At this point, we have to meet a very strange and unfortunate syntax of makefiles: the difference between a space and a tab.

All rules must be on lines that start with a tab; a space won't do. Since several spaces and a tab look much the same and since almost everywhere else in UNIX programming there's little distinction between spaces and tabs, this can cause problems. Also, a space at the end of a line in the makefile may cause a make command to fail.

However, it's an accident of history and there are far too many makefiles in existence to contemplate changing it now, so take care! Fortunately, it's usually reasonably obvious when the make command isn't working because a tab is missing.

Try It Out - A Simple makefile

Most rules consist of a simple command that could have been typed on the command line. For our example, we will use a makefile, Makefile1.

```
myapp: main.o 2.o 3.o
	gcc -o myapp main.o 2.o 3.o

main.o: main.c a.h
	gcc -c main.c

2.o: 2.c a.h b.h
	gcc -c 2.c

3.o: 3.c b.h c.h
	gcc -c 3.c
```

We invoke the make command with the -f option, since our makefile doesn't have either of the usual default names of makefile or Makefile. If we try this in a directory containing no source code, this happens.

```
$ make -f Makefile1
make: *** No rule to make target 'main.c', needed by 'main.o'.  Stop.
$
```

The make command has assumed that the first target in the makefile, myapp, is the file that we wish to create. It has then looked at the other dependencies and, in particular, has determined that a file called main.c is needed. Since we haven't created this file yet and the makefile does not say how it might be created, make has reported an error. Let's create the source files and try again. Since we're not interested in the result, these files can be very simple. The header files are actually empty, so we can create them with touch.

```
$ touch a.h
$ touch b.h
$ touch c.h
```

main.c contains main, which calls function_two and function_three. The other two files define function_two and function_three. The source files have #include lines for the appropriate headers, so they appear to be dependent on the contents of the included headers. It's not much of an application, but here are the listings.

```
/* main.c */
#include "a.h"

extern void function_two();
extern void function_three();

int main()
{
    function_two();
    function_three();
    exit (EXIT_SUCCESS);
}
```

```
/* 2.c */
#include "a.h"
#include "b.h"

void function_two() {
}
```

```
/* 3.c */
#include "b.h"
#include "c.h"

void function_three() {
}
```

Let's try make again.

```
$ make -f Makefile1
gcc -c main.c
gcc -c 2.c
gcc -c 3.c
gcc -o myapp main.o 2.o 3.o
$
```

This is a successful make.

How It Works

The make command has processed the dependencies section of the makefile and determined the files that need to be created and in which order. Even though we listed how to create myapp first, make has determined the correct order for creating the files. It has then invoked the appropriate commands we gave it in the rules section for creating those files. The make command displays the commands as it executes them. We can now test our makefile to see whether it handles changes to the file b.h correctly.

```
$ touch b.h
$ make -f Makefile1
gcc -c 2.c
gcc -c 3.c
gcc -o myapp main.o 2.o 3.o
$
```

The make command has read our makefile, determined the minimum number of commands required to rebuild myapp and carried them out in the correct order. Let's see what happens if we delete an object file.

```
$ rm 2.o
$ make -f Makefile1
gcc -c 2.c
gcc -o myapp main.o 2.o 3.o
$
```

Again, make correctly determines the actions required.

Comments in a makefile

A comment in a makefile starts with # and continues to the end of the line. As in C source files, comments in a makefile can help both the author and others to understand what was intended when the file was written.

Macros in a makefile

Even if this was all there was to make and makefiles, they would be a powerful tool for managing multifile projects. However, they would also tend to be large and inflexible for projects consisting of a very large number of files. Makefiles allow us to use macros, so we can write them in a more generalized form.

We define a macro in a makefile by writing `MACRONAME=value`, then accessing the value of `MACRONAME` by writing either `$(MACRONAME)` or `${MACRONAME}`. Some versions of make may also accept `$MACRONAME`. We can set a name to blank by leaving the rest of the line after the = blank.

Macros are often used in makefiles for options to the compiler. Often, while an application is being developed it will be compiled with no optimization, but with debugging information included. For a release version the opposite is usually needed; a small binary with no debugging information that runs as fast as possible.

Another problem with `Makefile1` is that it assumes the compiler is called `gcc`. On other UNIX systems, we might be using `cc` or `c89`. If we ever wanted to take our makefile to a different version of UNIX, or even if we obtained a different compiler to use on our existing system, we would have to change several lines of our makefile to make it work. Macros are a good way of collecting together all these system dependent parts, making it easy to change them.

Macros are normally defined inside the makefile itself, but they can be specified by calling `make` with the macro definition, for example, `make CC=c89`. Command line definitions override defines in the makefile.

Try It Out - A Makefile with Macros

Here's an revised version of our makefile, `Makefile2`, using macros.

```
all: myapp

# Which compiler
CC = gcc

# Where are include files kept
INCLUDE = .

# Options for development
CFLAGS = -g -Wall -ansi

# Options for release
# CFLAGS = -O -Wall -ansi

myapp: main.o 2.o 3.o
	$(CC) -o myapp main.o 2.o 3.o

main.o: main.c a.h
	$(CC) -I$(INCLUDE) $(CFLAGS) -c main.c

2.o: 2.c a.h b.h
	$(CC) -I$(INCLUDE) $(CFLAGS) -c 2.c

3.o: 3.c b.h c.h
	$(CC) -I$(INCLUDE) $(CFLAGS) -c 3.c
```

If we delete our old installation and create a new one with this new makefile, we get:

```
$ rm *.o myapp
$ make -f Makefile2
gcc -I. -g -Wall -ansi -c main.c
gcc -I. -g -Wall -ansi -c 2.c
gcc -I. -g -Wall -ansi -c 3.c
gcc -o myapp main.o 2.o 3.o
$
```

How It Works

The `make` command replaces the `$(CC)`, `$(CFLAGS)` and `$(INCLUDE)` with the appropriate definition, rather like the C compiler does with `#define`. Now if we want to change the compile command, we only need to change a single line of the makefile.

In fact, make has several special internal macros that you can use to make makefiles even more succinct. We list the more common ones here, you will see them in use in later examples. Each of these macros is only expanded just before it's used, so the meaning of the macro may vary as the makefile progresses. In fact, macros would be of very little use if they didn't work like this.

`$?`	List of prerequisites changed more recently than the current target.
`$@`	Name of the current target.
`$<`	Name of the current prerequisite.
`$*`	Name of the current prerequisite, without any suffix.

There are two other useful special characters you may see in makefile, preceding the command.

- tells make to ignore any errors. For example if you wanted to make a directory, but wished to ignore any errors, perhaps because the directory might already exist, you just precede mkdir with a minus sign. We will see '-' in use shortly.

@ tells make not to print the command to standard output before executing it. This is handy if you perhaps what to use echo to display some instructions.

Multiple Targets

It's often useful to make more than a single target file, or to collect several groups of commands into a single place. We can extend our makefile to do this. Let's add a 'clean' option that removes unwanted objects and an 'install' option that moves the application to a different directory.

Try It Out - Multiple Targets

Here's the next version of the makefile, Makefile3.

```
all: myapp

# Which compiler
CC = gcc

# Where to install
INSTDIR = /usr/local/bin

# Where are include files kept
INCLUDE = .

# Options for development
CFLAGS = -g -Wall -ansi

# Options for release
# CFLAGS = -O -Wall -ansi

myapp: main.o 2.o 3.o
	$(CC) -o myapp main.o 2.o 3.o

main.o: main.c a.h
	$(CC) -I$(INCLUDE) $(CFLAGS) -c main.c
```

```
2.o: 2.c a.h b.h
	$(CC) -I$(INCLUDE) $(CFLAGS) -c 2.c

3.o: 3.c b.h c.h
	$(CC) -I$(INCLUDE) $(CFLAGS) -c 3.c
```

```
clean:
	-rm main.o 2.o 3.o

install: myapp
	@if [ -d $(INSTDIR) ]; \
		then \
		cp myapp $(INSTDIR);\
		chmod a+x $(INSTDIR)/myapp;\
		chmod og-w $(INSTDIR)/myapp;\
		echo "Installed in $(INSTDIR)";\
	else \
		echo "Sorry, $(INSTDIR) does not exist";\
	fi
```

There are several things to notice in this makefile. Firstly, the special target `all` still only specifies `myapp` as a target. Thus when we execute `make` without specifying a target, the default behavior is to build the target `myapp`. If it was very important that subsequent commands only executed if the previous one had succeeded, then we could have written the commands joined by `&&`, like this.

```
@if [ -d $(INSTDIR) ]; \
	then \
	cp myapp $(INSTDIR) &&\
	chmod a+x $(INSTDIR)/myapp && \
	chmod og-w $(INSTDIR/myapp && \
	echo "Installed in $(INSTDIR)" ;\
else \
	echo "Sorry, $(INSTDIR) does not exist" ; false ; \
fi
```

As you may remember from the shell chapter, this is an 'and' command to the shell and has the effect that each subsequent command only gets executed if the previous one succeeded. Here we don't care too much about ensuring previous commands succeeded, so we stick to the simpler form.

The next important point is the two additional targets, `clean` and `install`. The `clean` target uses the `rm` command to remove the objects. The command starts with - which tells `make` to ignore the result of the command, so `make clean` will succeed even if there are no objects and the `rm` command returns an error. The rules for making the target 'clean' don't specify `clean` as depending on anything; the rest of the line after `clean:` is blank. Thus the target is always considered out of date and its rule is always executed if `clean` is specified as a target.

The `install` target is dependent on `myapp`, so `make` knows that it must create `myapp` before carrying out other commands for making `install`. The rules for making `install` consist of some shell script commands. Since `make` invokes a shell for executing rules and uses a new shell for each rule, we must add backslashes so that all the script commands are on one logical line and are all passed together to a single invocation of the shell for execution. This command starts with an `@` sign, which tells `make` not to print the command on standard output before executing the rule.

You may not have permission as an 'ordinary' user to install new commands in `/usr/local/bin`. You can either change permissions on this directory or change user (with the `su` command) to root before invoking `make install`.

```
$ rm *.o myapp
$ make -f Makefile3
gcc -I. -g -Wall -ansi -c main.c
gcc -I. -g -Wall -ansi -c 2.c
gcc -I. -g -Wall -ansi -c 3.c
gcc -o myapp main.o 2.o 3.o
$ make -f Makefile3
make: Nothing to be done for 'all'.
$ rm myapp
$ make -f Makefile3 install
gcc -o myapp main.o 2.o 3.o
Installed in /usr/local/bin
$ make -f Makefile3 clean
rm main.o 2.o 3.o
$
```

How It Works

First we delete `myapp` and all the objects. The `make` command on its own uses the target `all`, which causes `myapp` to be built. Next we run `make` again, but because `myapp` is up to date, `make` does nothing. We then delete the file `myapp` and do a `make install`. This recreates the binary and copies it to the install directory. Finally, we run `make clean`, which deletes the objects.

Built-in Rules

So far, we've specified in the makefile exactly how to perform each step of the process. In fact, `make` has a large number of built-in rules which can significantly simplify makefiles, particularly if we have many source files. Let's create `foo.c`, a traditional 'Hello World' program.

```
#include <stdlib.h>
#include <stdio.h>

int main()
{
    printf("Hello World\n");
    exit (EXIT_SUCCESS);
}
```

Without specifying a makefile, we'll try and compile it using `make`.

```
$ make foo
cc     foo.c   -o foo
$
```

As you can see, `make` knows how to invoke the compiler, although, in this case, it chose `cc` rather than `gcc`. Sometimes, these built-in rules are referred to as **inference rules**. The default rules use macros, so by specifying some new values for the macros we can change the default behavior.

```
$ rm foo
$ make CC = gcc CFLAGS = "-Wall -g" foo
gcc -Wall -g     foo.c    -o foo
$
```

You can ask make to print its built-in rules with the -p option. There are far too many built-in rules to list them all here, but here's a short extract from the output of make -p for the GNU version of make, showing part of the rules:

```
OUTPUT_OPTION = -o $@

COMPILE.c = $(CC) $(CFLAGS) $(CPPFLAGS) $(TARGET_ARCH) -c

.c.o:
	$(COMPILE.c) $< $(OUTPUT_OPTION)
```

We can now simplify our makefile to take account of these built-in rules by taking out the rules for making objects and just specifying the dependencies, so the relevant section of the makefile reads simply:

```
main.o: main.c a.h
2.o: 2.c a.h b.h
3.o: 3.c b.h c.h
```

You can find this version in the downloadable code as Makefile4.

Suffix Rules

The built-in rules that we've seen, work by using suffixes (similar to DOS extensions), so that when it's given a file with one ending, make knows which rule can be used to create a file with a different ending. The most common rule is the one used to create a file ending in .o from a file ending in .c. The rule is to use the compiler to compile but not to link the source file.

Sometimes, we need to be able to create new rules. The authors commonly work on source files that need to be compiled by several different compilers: two under MS-DOS and gcc under Linux. To keep one of the of MS-DOS compilers happy, the source files, which are C++ rather than C, need to be named with a suffix of .cpp. Unfortunately, the version of make being used with Linux doesn't have a built-in rule for compiling .cpp files. (It does have a rule for .cc, a more common C++ file extension under UNIX.)

Thus either a rule must be specified for each individual source file, or we need to teach make a new rule for creating objects from files with the extension .cpp. Given that there are rather a large number of source files in this project, specifying a new rule saves a lot of typing and also makes adding new source files to the project much easier.

To add a new suffix rule, we first add a line to the makefile telling make about the new suffix; we can then write a rule using this new suffix. make uses the special syntax .<old suffix>.<new suffix>: to define a general rule for creating files with the new suffix from files with the same base name but the old suffix.

Try It Out - Suffix Rules

Here's a fragment of our makefile with a new general rule for converting .cpp files to .o files. You should insert this section at the top of the file, straight after the all: myapp line. Call the new file Makefile5.

```
.SUFFIXES:      .cpp

.cpp.o:
    $(CC) -xc++ $(CFLAGS) -I$(INCLUDE) -c $<
```

Let's try this new rule.

```
$ cp foo.c bar.cpp
$ make -f Makefile5 bar
gcc -xc++ -g -Wall -ansi -I. -c bar.cpp
gcc   bar.o   -o bar
rm bar.o
$
```

How It Works

The special dependency .cpp.o: tells make that the rules that follow are for translating from a file with a suffix of .cpp to a file with a suffix of .o. We use special macro names when we write this dependency, because we don't know the actual names of the files that we'll be translating. To understand this rule you simply need to remember that $< is expanded to the starting filename (with the 'old' suffix). Notice that we only tell make how to get from a .cpp to a .o file; make already knows how to get from an object file to a binary executable file.

When we invoke make, it uses our new rule to get from bar.cpp to bar.o, then uses its built-in rules to get from the .o to an executable file. The extra -xc++ flag is to tell gcc that this is a C++ source file.

Managing Libraries with make

Often, when you're working on larger projects it's convenient to manage several compilation products using a **library**. These are files, conventionally with the extension .a (for **archive**), which contain a collection of object files. The make command has a special syntax for dealing with libraries that makes them very easy to manage.

The syntax is lib(file.o), which means the object file file.o, as stored in the library lib.a. The make command has a built-in rule for managing libraries, which is usually something like this.

```
.c.a:
    $(CC) -c $(CFLAGS) $<
    $(AR) $(ARFLAGS) $@ $*.o
```

The macros $(AR) and $(ARFLAGS) normally default to the command ar and the options rv, respectively. The rather terse syntax tells make that, to get from a .c file to a .a library, it must apply two rules.

The first rule says that it must compile the source file and generate an object. The second one says to use the `ar` command to revise the library, adding the new object file. If we have a library, `fud`, containing the file, `bas.o`, in the first rule, `$<` is replaced by `bas.c`. In the second rule, `$@` is replaced by the library `fud.a` and `$*` is replaced by the name `bas`.

Try It Out - Managing a Library

In practice, this is actually quite simple to use. Let's change our application so that the files `2.o` and `3.o` are kept in a library called `mylib.a`. Our makefile needs very few changes and `Makefile6` looks like this. (We've taken out the rules for dealing with C++ programs, because we won't be needing them again.)

```
all: myapp

# Which compiler
CC = gcc

# Where to install
INSTDIR = /usr/local/bin

# Where are include files kept
INCLUDE = .

# Options for development
CFLAGS = -g -Wall -ansi

# Options for release
# CFLAGS = -O -Wall -ansi

# Local Libraries
MYLIB = mylib.a

myapp: main.o $(MYLIB)
	$(CC) -o myapp main.o $(MYLIB)

$(MYLIB): $(MYLIB)(2.o) $(MYLIB)(3.o)
main.o: main.c a.h
2.o: 2.c a.h b.h
3.o: 3.c b.h c.h

clean:
	-rm main.o 2.o 3.o $(MYLIB)

install: myapp
	@if [ -d $(INSTDIR) ]; \
	then \
		cp myapp $(INSTDIR);\
		chmod a+x $(INSTDIR)/myapp;\
		chmod og-w $(INSTDIR)/myapp;\
		echo "Installed in $(INSTDIR)";\
	else \
		echo "Sorry, $(INSTDIR) does not exist";\
	fi
```

Notice how we allow the default rules to do most of the work. Let's test our new version of the makefile.

```
$ rm -f myapp *.o mylib.a
$ make -f Makefile6
gcc -g -Wall -ansi    -c main.c -o main.o
gcc -g -Wall -ansi    -c 2.c -o 2.o
ar rv mylib.a 2.o
ar: creating mylib.a
```

```
c - 2.o
gcc -g -Wall -ansi   -c 3.c -o 3.o
ar rv mylib.a 3.o
c - 3.o
gcc -o myapp main.o mylib.a
$ touch c.h
$ make -f Makefile6
gcc -g -Wall -ansi   -c 3.c -o 3.o
ar rv mylib.a 3.o
a - 3.o
gcc -o myapp main.o mylib.a
$
```

How It Works

We first delete all the objects and the library and allow make to build myapp, which it does by compiling and creating the library, before linking main.o with the library to create myapp. We then test the dependency rule for 3.o, which tells make that if c.h changes, 3.c must be recompiled. It does this correctly, compiling 3.c and updating the library, before relinking to create a new myapp executable file.

Advanced Topic: Makefiles and Subdirectories

If you're working on a large project, it's sometimes convenient to split some files that comprise a library away from the main files and store them in a subdirectory. There are two ways of doing this with make.

Firstly, you can have a second makefile in the subdirectory to compile the files, store them in a library and then copy the library up a level into the main directory. The main makefile in the higher level directory then has a rule for making the library which invokes the second makefile like this:

```
mylib.a:
    (cd mylibdirectory;$(MAKE))
```

This says that you must always try to make mylib.a When make invokes the rule for building the library, it changes into the subdirectory mylibdirectory and then invokes a new make command to manage the library. Since a new shell is invoked for this, the program using the makefile doesn't execute the cd. Only the shell invoked to carry out the rule to build the library is in a different directory. The brackets ensure that it's all processed by a single shell.

The second way is to use some additional macros in a single makefile. The extra macros are generated by appending a D for directory or an F for filename to those macros we've already met. We could then override the built-in .c.o suffix rule with:

```
.c.o:
        $(CC) $(CFLAGS) -c $(@D)/$(<F) -o $(@D)/$(@F)
```

for compiling files in a subdirectory and leaving the objects in the subdirectory. We then make the library in the current directory with a dependency and rule something like this:

```
mylib.a:   mydir/2.o mydir/3.o
    ar -rv mylib.a $?
```

You need to decide which approach you prefer for your own project. Many projects simply avoid having subdirectories, but this can lead to a source directory with a ridiculous number of files in it. As you can see from the brief overview above, you can use make with subdirectories with only slightly increased complexity.

GNU make and gcc

If you're using GNU make and the GNU gcc compiler, there are two interesting extra options.

The first is the -jN ('jobs') option to make. This allows make to execute N commands at the same time. Where several different parts of the project can be compiled independently, make will invoke several rules simultaneously. Depending on your system configuration, this can give a significant improvement in the time to recompile. If you have many source files, it may be worth trying this option. In general, smaller numbers such as -j3 are a good starting point. If you share your computer with other users, use the 'jobs' option with care. Other users may not appreciate you starting large numbers of processes every time you compile!

The other useful addition is the -MM option to gcc. This produces a dependency list in a form suitable for make. On a project with a significant number of source files, each including different combinations of header files, it can be quite difficult (but very important) to get the dependencies correct. If you make every source file depend on every header file, sometimes you'll compile files unnecessarily. If, on the other hand, you miss some dependencies out, the problem is even worse because you're now failing to compile files that need recompiling.

Try It Out - gcc -MM

```
$ gcc -MM main.c 2.c 3.c
main.o: main.c a.h
2.o: 2.c a.h b.h
3.o: 3.c b.h c.h
$
```

How It Works

The gcc compiler simply outputs the required dependency lines in a format ready for insertion into a makefile. All we have to do is save the output into a temporary file and then insert it into the makefile for a perfect set of dependency rules. There are no excuses for getting your dependencies wrong if you have a copy of gcc!

If you really feel confident about makefiles, you might try using the makedepend tool, which performs a similar function to the -MM option, but actually appends the dependencies at the end of the specified makefile.

Before we leave the topic of makefiles, it's perhaps worth pointing out that you don't have to confine yourself to using makefiles to compile code or create libraries. You can use them to automate any task where there is a sequence of commands that get you from some sort of input file to an output file. A typical 'non compiler' use might be for calling AWK or sed to process some files, or even generating manual pages.

Source Code Control

If you move beyond simple projects, managing changes to source files starts to become important, particularly if more than one person is working on the project. There are two widely used UNIX systems for managing source files: **RCS (Revision Control System)** and **SCCS (Source Code Control System)**.

The RCS utilities, along with their sources, are available from the Free Software Foundation. SCCS was introduced by AT&T in the System V versions of UNIX and is now incorporated in the X/Open standard. In addition, there are many other third party source code control systems, perhaps the best known of which is **CVS (Concurrent Version System)**, which is more advanced than SCCS or RCS, but not (yet) in such common use.

In this chapter, we'll look primarily at RCS, but compare the RCS commands with the SCCS commands. As you'll see, they offer very similar facilities and it's quite painless to change between them. Versions of RCS are also available for MS-DOS, including commercially supported products. We will also take a quick look at CVS a source code control system that is great for multiple developers collaborating using a network.

RCS

The RCS system comprises a number of commands for managing source files. It works by tracking a source file as it's changed by maintaining a single file with a list of changes in sufficient detail to recreate any previous version. It also allows you to store comments associated with every change, which can be very useful if you're looking back through the history of changes to a file.

As a project progresses, you can log each major change or bug fix you make to a source file separately and store comments against each change. This can be very useful for reviewing the changes made to a file, checking where bugs were fixed and occasionally, perhaps, where bugs were introduced!

As the RCS only saves the changes between versions, it's also very space efficient. The system also allows us to retrieve previous revisions in case of an accidental deletion.

The rcs Command

We'll start with an initial version of the file we wish to manage. In this case, we'll use `important.c`, which starts life as a copy of `foo.c` with the following comment at the beginning:

```
/*
  This is an important file for managing this project.
  It implements the canonical "Hello World" program.
*/
```

The first task is to initialize RCS control over the file, using the `rcs` command. The command `rcs -i` initializes the RCS control file.

```
$ rcs -i important.c
RCS file: important.c,v
enter description, terminated with single '.' or end of file:
NOTE: This is NOT the log message!
```

```
>> This is an important demonstration file
>> .
done
$
```

We're allowed multiple comment lines. We terminate the prompting with a single . on a line by itself, or by typing the end of file character, usually *Ctrl-D*.

After this command, `rcs` has created a new read-only file with a `,v` extension:

```
$ ls -l
-rw-r--r--   1 rick     users        226 Feb 11 16:25 important.c
-r--r--r--   1 rick     users        105 Feb 11 16:26 important.c,v
$
```

If you prefer to keep your RCS files in a separate directory, simply create a subdirectory called `RCS` before you use `rcs` for the first time. All the `rcs` commands will automatically use the `RCS` subdirectory for `rcs` files.

The ci Command

We can now check in our file, using the `ci` command to store the current version.

```
$ ci important.c
important.c,v  <--  important.c
initial revision: 1.1
done
$
```

If we had forgotten to do `rcs -i` first, RCS would have asked for a description of the file. One of the advantages of RCS over SCCS is this more relaxed approach to human error. If we now look at the directory, we'll see that `important.c` has been deleted.

```
$ ls -l
-r--r--r--   1 rick     users          442 Feb 11 16:30 important.c,v
$
```

The file contents and control information are all are stored in the RCS file, `important.c,v`.

The co Command

If we wish to change the file, we must first 'check out' the file. If we just want to read the file, we can use `co` to recreate the current version of the file and change the permissions to make it read-only. If we wish to edit it, we must lock the file with `co -l`. The reason for this is that, in a team project, it's important to ensure that only one person at a time is modifying a given file, which is why only one copy of a given version of a file has write permission. When a file is checked out with write permission, the RCS file becomes locked. Let's lock out a copy of the file:

```
$ co -l important.c
important.c,v  -->  important.c
revision 1.1 (locked)
done
$
```

and look at the directory:

```
$ ls -l
-rw-r--r--   1 rick     users          226 Feb 11 16:35 important.c
-r--r--r--   1 rick     users          452 Feb 11 16:35 important.c,v
$
```

There's now a file for us to edit, to put in our new changes. Let's do some edits, store the new version and use the `ci` command again to store the changes. The output section of `important.c` is now:

```
    printf("Hello World\n");
    printf("This is an extra line added later\n");
```

We use `ci` like this.

```
$ ci important.c
important.c,v  <--  important.c
new revision: 1.2; previous revision: 1.1
enter log message, terminated with single '.' or end of file:
>> Added an extra line to be printed out.
>> .
done
$
```

To check in the file and retain the lock so that the user can continue to work on it, you should call `ci` with its `-l` option. The file is automatically checked out again to the same user.

We've now stored the revised version of the file. If we look at the directory, we see that `important.c` has again been removed.

```
$ ls -l
-r--r--r--   1 rick     users          633 Feb 11 16:37 important.c,v
$
```

The rlog Command

It's often useful to look at a summary of changes to a file. We can do this with the `rlog` command.

```
$ rlog important.c

RCS file: important.c,v

Working file: important.c
head: 1.2
branch:
locks: strict
access list:
symbolic names:
comment leader: " * "
keyword substitution: kv
total revisions: 2;     selected revisions: 2
description:
This is an important demonstration file
```

```
----------------------------
revision 1.2
date: 1999/02/11 16:37:35;  author: rick;  state: Exp;  lines: +1 -0
Added an extra line to be printed out.
----------------------------
revision 1.1
date: 1999/02/11 16:30:19;  author: rick;  state: Exp;
Initial revision
=============================================================================
$
```

The first part gives us a description of the file and the options that `rcs` is using. The `rlog` command then lists the revisions of the file, most recent first, along with the text we entered when we checked in the revision. "`lines: +1 -0`" in revision 1.2 tells us that one line was added and none were deleted.

If we now want the first version of the file back, we can ask `co` for it by specifying the revision we require.

```
$ co -r1.1 important.c
important.c,v  -->  important.c
revision 1.1
done
$
```

`ci` also has an `-r` option, which forces the version number to a specified value. For example,

```
ci -r2 important.c
```

would check in `important.c` as version 2.1. Both RCS and SCCS default to using 1 as the first minor version number.

The rcsdiff Command

If we just want to know what was changed between two revisions, we can use the `rcsdiff` command.

```
$ rcsdiff -r1.1 -r1.2 important.c
===================================================================
RCS file: important.c,v
retrieving revision 1.1
retrieving revision 1.2
diff -r1.1 -r1.2
11a12
>       printf("This is an extra line added later\n");

$
```

This tells us that a single line was inserted after the original line 11.

Identifying Revisions

The RCS system can use some special strings (macros) inside the source file to help track the changes. The most common two macros are `$RCSfile$` and `$Id$`. The macro, `$RCSfile$`, is expanded to the name of the file and `$Id$` expands to a string identifying the revision. Consult the manual pages for a full list of the special strings supported. The macros are expanded afresh whenever a file revision is checked out and updated automatically when a revision is checked in.

Let's change our file for a third time and add some of these macros.

```
$ co -l important.c
important.c,v  -->  important.c
revision 1.2 (locked)
done
$
```

We edit the file and it now looks like this.

```
/*
  This is an important file for managing this project.
  It implements the canonical "Hello World" program.

  Filename: $RCSfile$
*/

#include <stdlib.h>
#include <stdio.h>

static char *RCSinfo = "$Id$";

int main() {
    printf("Hello World\n");
    printf("This is an extra line added later\n");
    printf("This file is under RCS control. It's ID is\n%s\n", RCSinfo);
    exit (EXIT_SUCCESS);
}
```

Let's check in this revision and see how RCS manages the special strings.

```
$ ci important.c
important.c,v  <--  important.c
new revision: 1.3; previous revision: 1.2
enter log message, terminated with single '.' or end of file:
>> Added $RCSfile$ and $Id$ strings
>> .
done
$
```

If we look in the directory, we find only the RCS file:

```
$ ls -l
-r--r--r--   1 rick     users          907 Feb 11 16:55 important.c,v
$
```

If we check out (with the co command) and examine the current version of the source file, we can see the macros that have been expanded.

```
/*
  This is an important file for managing this project.
  It implements the canonical "Hello World" program.

  Filename: $RCSfile: important.c,v $
*/

#include <stdlib.h>
#include <stdio.h>

static char *RCSinfo = "$Id: important.c,v 1.3 1999/02/11 16:55:04 rick Exp $";
```

```
int main() {
     printf("Hello World\n");
     printf("This is an extra line added later\n");
     printf("This file is under RCS control. It's ID is\n%s\n", RCSinfo);
     exit (EXIT_SUCCESS);
}
```

Try It Out - GNU make with RCS

GNU make already has some built-in rules for managing RCS files. We will now see how make deals with a missing source file.

```
$ rm -f important.c
$ make important
co  important.c,v important.c
important.c,v --> important.c
revision 1.3
done
cc  -c important.c -o important.o
cc   important.o  -o important
rm important.o important.c
$
```

How It Works

make has a default rule that to make a file with no extension you can compile a file of the same name, but with a .c extension. A second default rule allows make to create important.c from important.c,v by using RCS. Since no file called important.c exists, make has created the .c file by checking out the latest revision with co. After compiling, it tidied up by deleting the file important.c.

The ident Command

We can use the ident command to find the version of a file that contains a Id string . Since we stored the string in a variable, it also appears in the resulting executable. You may find that if you include special strings but never access them in the code, some compilers will optimize them away. You can normally get around this problem by adding some 'dummy' accesses to the string, although as compilers get better this is becoming more difficult!

Try It Out - ident

```
$ important
Hello World
This is an extra line added later
This file is under RCS control. It's ID is
$Id: important.c,v 1.3 1999/02/11 16:55:04 rick Exp $
$ ident important
important:
     $Id: important.c,v 1.3 1999/02/11 16:55:04 rick Exp $
$
```

How It Works

By executing the program we show the string has been incorporated into the executable. Then we show how the ident command can extract Id strings from an executable file.

This technique of using RCS and `$Id$` strings that appear in executables, can be a very powerful tool for checking which version of a file a customer is reporting a problem in. You can also use RCS (or SCCS) as part of a project tracking facility to track problems being reported and how they are fixed. If you're selling software, or even giving it away, it's very important to know what was changed between different releases.

If you'd like some more information, the `rcsinfo` pages in the manual give a thorough introduction to the RCS system, in addition to the standard RCS pages. There are also manual pages for the individual commands `ci`, `co`, etc.

SCCS

SCCS offers very similar facilities to RCS. The advantage of SCCS is that it's specified in X/Open, so all branded versions of UNIX should support it. On a more practical level, RCS is very portable and can be freely distributed. So, if you have a UNIX-like system, whether it's X/Open conformant or not, you should be able to obtain and install RCS for it. For this reason we don't describe SCCS further here, except to provide a brief command comparison for those moving between the two systems.

Comparing RCS and SCCS

It's difficult to provide a direct comparison of commands between the two systems, so the table which follows should only be considered as a quick pointer. The commands listed here don't take the same options to perform the same tasks. If you have to use SCCS, you'll need to find the appropriate options, but at least you'll know where to start looking.

RCS	SCCS
`rcs`	`admin`
`ci`	`delta`
`co`	`get`
`rcsdiff`	`sccsdiff`
`ident`	`what`

In addition to those listed above, the SCCS `sccs` command has some crossover with the `rcs` and `co` commands in RCS. For example, `sccs edit` and `sccs create` are equivalent to `co -l`, and `rcs -i` respectively.

CVS

An alternative to using RCS to manage changes to files is **CVS**, the **Concurrent Versions System**. This is becoming more popular, probably because it has one distinct advantage over RCS. It's practical to use CVS over the Internet, not just on a shared local directory like RCS. CVS also allows for parallel development, i.e. many programmers can work on the same file at once whereas RCS only allows one user to work on one particular file at a time. CVS commands resemble to RCS commands, because CVS was initially developed as a front end to RCS.

Since it can work across a network in a flexible way, CVS is suitable for use if the only network linking the developers is the Internet. Many Linux and GNU projects are using CVS to help the different developers coordinate their work. In general, the way that you use CVS on a remote set of files is almost identical to how you would use it on a local set.

In this chapter, we will look briefly at the basics of CVS, so that you can get started with local repositories and understand how to get a copy of the latest sources of a project when the CVS server is on the Internet. More information is in the CVS manual, written by Per Cederqvist et. al., Copyright Signum Support AB, but distributed under the terms of the GNU General Public License and available on many web sites, where you will also find FAQ files and various other helpful files.

Getting started with CVS

First we need to create a repository, where CVS will store both its control files and the master copies of files that it is managing. A repository has a tree structure, so you can use a single repository to store not just a whole directory structure for a single project, but many projects in the same repository. However you can use separate repositories for separate unrelated projects as well. We will see below how to tell CVS which repository to use.

Using CVS locally

Let's start by creating a repository. To keep it simple, this will be a local repository and, since we will be using only one, a convenient place to put it is somewhere in `/usr/local`. On most Linux distributions all normal users are members of the group `users` so we use this as the group of the repository, so all users can access it.

As superuser, create a directory for the repository.

```
# mkdir /usr/local/repository
# chgrp users /usr/local/repository
```

As a normal user again, initialize it as a CVS repository. You may need to obtain write access to `/usr/local/repositry` to do this.

```
$ cvs -d /usr/local/repository init
```

The `-d` option tells CVS where we want the repository to be created.

Now that the repository has been created, we can store our initial versions of the project in CVS. However, at this point we can save ourselves some typing. All cvs commands have two ways of looking for the CVS directory. Firstly they look for a `-d <path>` on the command line (as we used with the `init` command), if the `-d` option is not present then it looks for an environment variable, `CVSROOT`. Rather than use the `-d` option all the time, we will set up this environment variable. This is the command to use if you use `bash` as your shell.

```
$ export CVSROOT = /usr/local/repository
```

First change to the directory where the project is, then we tell `cvs` to import all the files in the directory.

```
$ cd cvs-sp
$ cvs import -m"Initial version of Simple Project" wrox/chap8-cvs wrox start
```

This bit of magic tells CVS to import all the files in the current directory, and gives it a log message.

The option `wrox/chap8-cvs` tells CVS where, relative to the root of the CVS tree, to store the new project. Remember CVS can store multiple projects in same repository, if you wish. The option `wrox` is a vendor tag used to identify the supplier of the initial version of files being imported and `start` is a release tag. Release tags can be used to identify, as a group, sets of related files - such as those that make up a particular release of an application. CVS responds with:

```
N wrox/chap8-cvs/Makefile
N wrox/chap8-cvs/hello.c

No conflicts created by this import
```

telling us that it imported two files correctly.

Now is a good time to check that we can retrieve our files from CVS. Let's just create a 'junk' directory, and check our files back out again, just to make sure all is well.

```
$ mkdir junk
$ cd junk
$ cvs checkout wrox/chap8-cvs
```

We give CVS the same path as when we checked the files in. CVS creates a directory `wrox/chap8-cvs` in the current directory, and puts the files there for us.

Now we are ready to make some changes to our project. Let's edit `hello.c`, and make a minor change. Let's just add a line.

```
printf("Have a nice day\n");
```

Then recompile and run the program to check all is well.

We can ask CVS what has been changed in the project. We don't have to tell CVS which file we are interested in, it can work on a whole directory at a time.

```
$ cvs diff
```

CVS responds with:

```
cvs diff: Diffing .
Index: hello.c
===================================================================
RCS file: /usr/local/repository/wrox/chap8-cvs/hello.c,v
retrieving revision 1.1.1.1
diff -r1.1.1.1 hello.c
6c6
<
---
>   printf("Have a nice day\n");
```

We are happy with our change, so lets commit it to CVS.

When you commit a change with CVS, it will start an editor to allow you to enter a log message. You may want to set the environment variable `CVSEDITOR` to force a particular editor before you run the `commit` command.

```
$ cvs commit
```

CVS responds by telling us what it is checking.

```
Checking in hello.c;
/usr/local/repository/wrox/chap8-cvs/hello.c,v  <--  hello.c
new revision: 1.2; previous revision: 1.1
done
```

Now we can ask CVS about changes to the project since we first checked it in. We ask for a set of differences since revision 1.1 (the initial version) on project `wrox/chap8-cvs`.

```
$ cvs rdiff -r1.1 wrox/chap8-cvs
```

CVS tells us the details.

```
cvs rdiff: Diffing wrox/chap8-cvs
Index: wrox/chap8-cvs/hello.c
diff -c wrox/chap8-cvs/hello.c:1.1 wrox/chap8-cvs/hello.c:1.2
*** wrox/chap8-cvs/hello.c:1.1  Tue Aug  3 19:54:14 1999
--- wrox/chap8-cvs/hello.c      Tue Aug  3 19:57:19 1999
***************
*** 3,7 ****
--- 3,8 ----
  main(int argc, char* argv[]) {

    printf("Hello World\n");
+   printf("Have a nice day\n");

  }
```

Suppose you have had a copy of code out of CVS for a while in a local directory, and want to refresh files in your local directory that others have changed, but you have not edited. CVS can do this for you, using the `update` command. Move to the top part of the path, in this case to the directory containing `wrox`, and execute the command:

```
$ cvs update -Pd wrox/chap8-cvs
```

and CVS will refresh files for you, extracting from the repository files that others have changed but you have not, and putting them in your local directory. Of course some of the changes might be incompatible with your changes but that is a problem you will have to work on. CVS is good, but it can't perform magic!

You can see by now that using CVS is very like using RCS. However there is one very important difference, that we haven't mentioned yet - the ability to operate over a network without using a mounted file system.

Accessing CVS over a network

We told CVS where the repository was either by using a `-d` option to each command, or by setting the `CVSROOT` environment variable. If we want to operate over a network, we simply use a more advanced syntax for this parameter. For example, at the time of writing the **GNOME (GNU Network Object Model Environment**, a popular open source graphical desktop system) development sources are all accessible on the Internet using CVS. You need only specify where the appropriate CVS repository is by pre-pending some network information to the front of the path specifier.

For example, at the time of writing you point CVS at the GNOME source CVS repository by setting `CVSROOT` to `pserver:anonymous@anoncvs.gnome.org:/cvs/gnome`. This tells CVS that the repository is using password authentication (`pserver`), and is on the server `anoncvs.gnome.org`.

Before we can access the sources, we need to do a login, like this.

```
$ cvs login
```

Press return when prompted for the password.

We are now ready to use `cvs` commands, much as though we where working on a local repository, with one minor exception - we add the `-z3` option to all `cvs` commands to force compression, saving network bandwidth.

If we wanted to fetch the `ORBit` sources for example, then the command is:

```
$ cvs -z3 checkout ORBit
```

If we want to set our own repository to be accessible over the network, then we need to start a CVS server on our machine. This can be done by starting it via `inetd`. We simply add a line to `/etc/inetd.conf` and restart `inetd`. The line we need is:

```
2401 stream tcp nowait root /usr/bin/cvs cvs -b /usr/bin --allow-root =
/usr/local/repository pserver
```

This instructs `inetd` to automatically start a CVS session to clients connecting on port 2401, the standard CVS server port. For more information on starting network services via `inetd` see the manual pages for `inetd` and `inetd.conf`.

In this brief section we have barely had room to scratch the surface of the facilities of CVS. If you want to use CVS seriously, then we strongly urge you to set up a local repository to experiment on, get the extensive CVS documentation, and have fun! Remember, this is open source, so if you ever get seriously stuck about what the code is doing, or (unlikely, but possible!) think you have found a bug - you can always get the source code and have a look for yourself.

There is one other benefit of CVS – not only is there an MS Windows version of the **cvs** client application, for poor users without their own Linux box, there is also a Java client version, for even wider portability.

Writing a Manual Page

If you're writing a new command, as part of the task you should be creating a manual page to go with it. As you've probably noticed, the layout of most manual pages follows a closely set pattern, which is of the form:

- Header
- Name
- Synopsis
- Description
- Options
- Files
- See also
- Bugs

You can leave out sections that aren't relevant. 'Author' also appears often in Linux manual pages.

UNIX manual pages are formatted with a utility called `nroff`, or on most Linux systems the GNU project's equivalent, `groff`. Both these are developments of an earlier `roff` or run-off command. The input to `nroff` or `groff` is plain text, except that, at first glance, the syntax looks impenetrably difficult. Don't panic! As with UNIX programming, where the easiest way of writing a new program is to start with an existing program and adapt it, so it is with manual pages.

It's beyond the scope of this book to explain in detail the many options, commands and macros that the `groff` (or `nroff`) command can use. Rather, we present a simple template that you can borrow and adapt for your own pages.

Here's the source of a simple manual page for our application.

```
.TH MYAPP 1

.SH NAME
Myapp \- A simple demonstration application that does very little.

.SH SYNOPSIS
.B myapp
[\-option ...]

.SH DESCRIPTION
.PP
\fImyapp\fP is a complete application that does nothing useful.

.PP
It was written for demonstration purposes.
```

```
.SH OPTIONS
.PP
It doesn't have any, but let's pretend, to make this template complete:

.TP
.BI \-option
If there was an option, it would not be -option.

.SH RESOURCES
.PP
myapp uses almost no resources.

.SH DIAGNOSTICS
The program shouldn't output anything, so if you find it doing so there's
probably something wrong. The return value is zero.

.SH SEE ALSO
The only other program we know with this this little functionality is the
ubiquitous hello world application.

.SH COPYRIGHT
myapp is Copyright (c) 1999 Wrox Press.

This program is free software; you can redistribute it and/or modify
it under the terms of the GNU General Public License as published by
the Free Software Foundation; either version 2 of the License, or
(at your option) any later version.

This program is distributed in the hope that it will be useful,
but WITHOUT ANY WARRANTY; without even the implied warranty of
MERCHANTABILITY or FITNESS FOR A PARTICULAR PURPOSE.  See the
GNU General Public License for more details.

You should have received a copy of the GNU General Public License
along with this program; if not, write to the Free Software
Foundation, Inc., 59 Temple Place, Suite 330, Boston, MA  02111-1307  USA.

.SH BUGS
There probably are some, but we don't know what they are yet.

.SH AUTHORS
Neil Matthew and Rick Stones
```

As you can see, macros are introduced with a full stop (`.`) at the start of the line and tend to be very abbreviated. The `1` at then end of the top line is the section of the manual in which the command appears. Since commands appear in section 1, that is where we place our new application.

You should be able to generate your own manual pages by modifying this one and inspecting the source for others. You might also take a look at the Linux Man Page mini-HowTo, written by Jens Schweikhardt as part of the Linux Documentation Project archives.

Now we have the source to the manual page, we can process it with `groff`. The `groff` command commonly produces ASCII text (`-Tascii`) or PostScript (`-Tps`) output. We tell `groff` it's a manual page using the `-man` option, which causes special manual page macro definitions to be loaded.

```
$ groff -Tascii -man myapp.1
```

This gives the output:

```
MYAPP(1)                                                    MYAPP(1)
```

```
NAME
       Myapp  - A simple demonstration application that does very
       little.


SYNOPSIS
       myapp [-option ...]

DESCRIPTION
       myapp is a complete application that does nothing  useful.

       It was written for demonstration purposes.

OPTIONS
       It  doesn't  have any, but let's pretend, to make this tem-
       plate complete:


       -option
              If there was an option, it would not be -option.


RESOURCES
       myapp uses almost no resources.


DIAGNOSTICS
       The program shouldn't output anything, so if you  find  it
       doing  so  there's  probably  something  wrong. The return
       value is zero.


SEE ALSO
       The only other program we know with this this little func-
       tionality is the ubiquitous hello world application.


COPYRIGHT
       myapp is Copyright (c) 1999 Wrox Press.

       This  program  is  free  software; you can redistribute it
       and/or modify it under the terms of the GNU General Public
       License  as  published  by  the  Free Software Foundation;
       either version 2 of the License, or (at your  option)  any
       later version.

       This  program  is  distributed in the hope that it will be
       useful, but WITHOUT ANY WARRANTY; without even the implied
       warranty  of  MERCHANTABILITY  or FITNESS FOR A PARTICULAR
       PURPOSE.  See the GNU  General  Public  License  for  more
       details.

                                                                1

MYAPP(1)                                               MYAPP(1)


       You  should have received a copy of the GNU General Public
       License along with this program; if not, write to the Free
       Software  Foundation,  Inc.,   59  Temple Place - Suite 330
       Boston, MA 02111-1307, USA
```

```
BUGS
       There probably are some, but we don't know what  they  are
       yet.

AUTHORS
       Neil Matthew and Rick Stones
```

Now that we've tested our manual page, we need to install it. The man command that shows manual pages uses the MANPATH environment variable to search for manual pages. We can either put our new page in a directory for local manual pages or store it directly in the system /usr/man/man1 directory.

The first time someone asks for this manual page, the man command will automatically format and display it. Some versions of man can automatically generate and store preformatted (and possibly compressed) ASCII text versions of manual pages to speed up subsequent requests for the same page.

Distributing Software

The main problem with program distribution is ensuring that all the files are included and are of exactly the right version. Fortunately, the Internet programming community has evolved a very robust set of methods which go a long way towards removing the problems. These methods include:

- Packaging all component files into a single package file, using standard tools available on all Unix machines.
- Tight version numbering of packages.
- A file naming convention that includes the version number in the package file, so that users can easily see which version they are dealing with.
- Use of subdirectories in the package to ensure that when files are extracted from the package file, they are placed in a separate directory so there's no confusion about what's included in the package and what isn't.

The evolution of these methods has meant that programs can be easily and reliably distributed. The ease with which a program can be installed is another matter, because that depends on the program and the system on which it's being installed, but at least you can be sure that you have the right component files.

The patch Program

When programs have been distributed, it's almost inevitable that users will discover bugs or that the author will want to issue enhancements and updates. When authors distribute programs as binaries, they often simply ship new binaries. Sometimes (all too often), vendors simply release a new version of the program, often with an obscure revision reference and little information about what has changed.

On the other hand, distributing your software as source code is excellent because it allows people to see how you have implemented things and how you have used features. It also allows people to check exactly what programs are doing and to reuse parts of the source code (providing they keep to the licensing agreement).

However, with the source of the Linux kernel weighing in at (very roughly) 13 Mb of compressed source code, shipping an updated set of kernel sources would involve considerable resources, when, in fact, probably only a small percentage of the source has changed between each release.

Fortunately, there is a utility program for solving this problem: `patch`. It was written by Larry Wall, who also wrote the Perl programming language. The `patch` command allows you to distribute just the 'differences', so anyone with version 1 of a file and a difference file for version 1 to version 2 can use the `patch` command to generate version 2 for themselves.

If we start with version 1 of a file:

```
This is file one
line 2
line 3
there is no line 4, this is line 5
line 6
```

and then produce version 2:

```
This is file two
line 2
line 3
line 4
line 5
line 6
a new line 8
```

we can create a difference listing with the `diff` command.

```
$ diff file1.c file2.c > diffs
```

The `diffs` file contains:

```
1c1
< This is file one
—
> This is file two
4c4,5
< there is no line 4, this is line 5
—
> line 4
> line 5
5a7
> a new line 8
```

This is actually a set of editor commands for changing one file into another. Suppose we have `file1.c` and the `diffs` file. We can update our file using `patch`:

```
$ patch file1.c diffs
Hmm...  Looks like a normal diff to me...
Patching file file1.c using Plan A...
Hunk #1 succeeded at 1.
Hunk #2 succeeded at 4.
Hunk #3 succeeded at 7.
done
$
```

The `patch` command has now changed `file1.c` to be the same as `file2.c`.

Patch has an extra 'trick': the ability to unpatch. Suppose we decide we didn't like the changes and wanted our original `file1.c` back? No problem; just use `patch` again, using the `-R` (reverse patch) option.

```
$ patch -R file1.c diffs
Hmm...  Looks like a normal diff to me...
Patching file file1.c using Plan A...
Hunk #1 succeeded at 1.
Hunk #2 succeeded at 4.
Hunk #3 succeeded at 6.
done
$
```

`file1.c` is returned to its original state.

The `patch` command has several other options, but, generally, is very good at deciding from its input what you were trying to do and simply 'doing the right thing'. If `patch` ever fails, it creates a file with the `.rej` extension containing the parts that couldn't be patched.

When you're dealing with software patches, it's a good idea to use the `diff -c` option, which produces a 'context `diff`'. These provide a number of lines before and after each change so that `patch` can verify that the context matches before applying the patch. The patch is also easier to read.

If you find and fix a bug in a program, it's easier, more precise and more polite to send the author a patch than just a description of the fix.

Other Distribution Utilities

UNIX programs and sources are commonly distributed in a file whose name contains the version number, with an extension of `.tar.gz` or `.tgz`. These are `gzip`-ed **TAR** (tape archive) files. If you're using normal `tar`, you must process these files in two steps. Let's create a `gzip` file of our application.

```
$ tar cvf myapp-1.0.tar main.c 2.c 3.c *.h myapp.1 Makefile6
main.c
2.c
3.c
a.h
b.h
c.h
myapp.1
Makefile6
$
```

We now have a TAR file.

```
$ ls -l *.tar
-rw-r--r--   1 rick     users       10240 Feb 11 18:30 myapp-1.0.tar
$
```

We can make this smaller using the compression program `gzip`.

```
$ gzip myapp-1.0.tar
$ ls -l *.gz
-r w - r - - r - -    1 rick     users          1580 Feb 11 18:30 myapp-1.0.tar.gz
$
```

A very impressive reduction in size. This `.tar.gz` may then be renamed to a simple `.tgz` extension.

```
$ mv myapp-1.0.tar.gz myapp_v1.tgz
```

This practice of renaming files to end with a dot and three characters seems to be a concession to MS-DOS and some MS-Windows software, which, unlike UNIX, is heavily dependent on the correct extension being present. To get our file back, we decompress and extract them from the `tar` file again.

```
$ mv myapp_v1.tgz myapp-1.0.tar.gz
$ gzip -d myapp-1.0.tar.gz
$ tar xvf myapp-1.0.tar
main.c
2.c
3.c
a.h
b.h
c.h
myapp.1
Makefile6
$
```

With GNU's version of `tar`, things are even easier We can create the compressed archive in a single step.

```
$ tar zcvf myapp_v1.tgz main.c 2.c 3.c *.h myapp.1 Makefile6
main.c
2.c
3.c
a.h
b.h
c.h
myapp.1
Makefile6
$
```

We can decompress it just as easily.

```
$ tar zxvf myapp_v1.tgz
main.c
2.c
3.c
a.h
b.h
c.h
myapp.1
Makefile6
$
```

If you want to know the contents of the archive without actually extracting them, you should call the `tar` program with the slightly different options, `tar ztvf`.

tar Command Description

We've been using `tar` for the examples above without describing the options any more than absolutely necessary. We'll now take a quick look at the command and a few of its more popular options. As you can see from our examples, the basic syntax is:

```
tar [options] [list of files]
```

The first item in the list is the target and although we've been dealing with files, it could just as well be a device. (`tar` stands for **tape archive**.) The other items in the list are added to a new or existing archive, depending on the options. The list can also include directories, in which case all subdirectories are also included in the file by default. If you're extracting files, there's no need to specify names because full paths are preserved by `tar`.

In this section, we've used combinations of six different options.

`c`	Creates a new archive.
`f`	Specifies that the target is a file rather than a device.
`t`	Lists the contents of an archive without actually extracting them.
`v`	Verbose: `tar` displays messages as it goes.
`x`	Extracts file from an archive.
`z`	Filters the archive through `gzip`, from within GNU `tar`.

There are many more options to `tar` which allow finer control over the operation of the command and the archives it creates. Refer to the tar manual pages for more information.

Summary

In this chapter, we have seen just a few of the UNIX tools that make development and distribution of programs manageable. Firstly and perhaps most importantly, we used `make` and makefiles to manage multiple source files. We then looked at source code control, which lets us track changes as we develop our code. We then looked at `patch`, `tar` and `gzip`, which are used for distributing and updating programs.

Debugging

Every significant piece of software will contain defects, typically 2 to 5 per 100 lines of code. These mistakes lead to programs and libraries that don't perform as required, so that there's a difference between what they do and what they're supposed to do. Bugs and their removal can consume a large amount of a programmer's time during software development.

In this chapter, we'll look at software defects and consider some tools and techniques for tracking down specific instances of erroneous behavior. This isn't the same as testing (the task of verifying the program's operation in all possible conditions), although testing and debugging are, of course, related and many bugs are discovered during the testing process.

Types of Error

A bug usually arises from one of a small number of causes, each of which suggests a method of detection and removal.

Specification Errors

If a program is incorrectly specified, it will inevitably fail to perform as required. The best programmer in the world will simply write the wrong program. Before you start programming (or designing), make sure that you know and understand clearly what your program needs to do. You can detect and remove many (if not all) specification errors by reviewing the requirements and agreeing them with those who will use the program.

Design Errors

Programs of any size need to be designed. It's not usually enough to sit down at a computer keyboard, type in source code directly and expect the program to work first time. Take time to think about how you will construct the program, what data structures you'll need and how they will be used. Try to work out the details in advance, because it can save a lot of rewrites later on.

Coding Errors

Of course, everyone makes typing errors. Creating the source code from your design is an imperfect process. This is where many bugs will creep in. When you're faced with a bug in a program, don't overlook the possibility of simply re-reading the source code, or asking someone else to. It's surprising just how many bugs you can detect and remove by talking through the implementation with someone else.

Languages with compilers, such as C, have an advantage here in that syntax errors can be caught at compile time, whereas interpreted languages such as the UNIX shell might only detect syntax errors when you try to run the program. If the problem is with error handling code, this might not be easy to spot in testing.

Try executing the core of the program on paper, a process sometimes called **dry running**. For the most important routines, write down the values of inputs and calculate the outputs step-by-step. You don't always have to use a computer to debug and sometimes it can be the computer causing the problems. Even the people who write libraries, compilers and operating systems make mistakes! On the other hand, don't be too quick to blame the tools, it is rather more likely that there's a bug in a new program than the compiler.

General Debugging Techniques

There are several distinct approaches to debugging and testing a typical UNIX program. We generally run the program and see what happens. If it doesn't work, we need to decide what to do about it. We can change the program and try again (code inspection, trial and error), we can try to gain more information about what's happening inside the program (instrumentation), or we can inspect the program operation directly (controlled execution). The five stages of debugging are:

- Testing: finding out what defects or bugs exist.
- Stabilization: making the bugs repeatable.
- Localization: identifying the line(s) of code responsible.
- Correction: fixing the code.
- Verification: making sure the fix works.

A Program with Bugs

Let's look at an example program that contains bugs. During the course of this chapter, we can try to debug it. The program has been written during the development of a larger software system. Its purpose is to test out a single function, `sort`, which is intended to implement a bubble sort algorithm on an array of structures of type `item`. The items are sorted in ascending order of the member, `key`. The program calls `sort` on a sample array to test it. In the "real world", we would never seek to use this particular sort of algorithm, it's far too inefficient. We have used it here because it is short, relatively simple to understand, but also easy to get wrong. In fact, the standard C library has a function already, `qsort`.

Unfortunately, the code is not very readable, there are no comments and the original programmer isn't available. We'll have to struggle with it on our own, starting from the basic routine debug1.c.

```
/*   1  */  typedef struct {
/*   2  */      char *data;
/*   3  */      int key;
/*   4  */  } item;
/*   5  */
/*   6  */  item array[] = {
/*   7  */      {"bill", 3},
/*   8  */      {"neil", 4},
/*   9  */      {"john", 2},
/*  10  */      {"rick", 5},
/*  11  */      {"alex", 1},
/*  12  */  };
/*  13  */
/*  14  */  sort(a,n)
/*  15  */  item *a;
/*  16  */  {
/*  17  */      int i = 0, j = 0;
/*  18  */      int s = 1;
/*  19  */
/*  20  */      for(; i < n && s != 0; i++) {
/*  21  */              s = 0;
/*  22  */              for(j = 0; j < n; j++) {
/*  23  */                      if(a[j].key > a[j+1].key) {
/*  24  */                              item t = a[j];
/*  25  */                              a[j] = a[j+1];
/*  26  */                              a[j+1] = t;
/*  27  */                              s++;
/*  28  */                      }
/*  29  */              }
/*  30  */              n--;
/*  31  */      }
/*  32  */  }
/*  33  */
/*  34  */  main()
/*  35  */  {
/*  36  */      sort(array,5);
/*  37  */  }
```

Let's try to compile this program.

```
$ cc -o debug1 debug1.c
```

It compiles successfully with no reported errors or warnings.

Before we run this program, we'll add some code to print out the result. Otherwise, we won't know whether the program has worked. We will add some additional lines to display the array after it's been sorted. We call the new version debug2.c.

```
/*  34  */  main()
/*  35  */  {
/*  36  */          int i;
/*  37  */          sort(array,5);
/*  38  */          for(i = 0; i < 5; i++)
/*  39  */                  printf("array[%d] = {%s, %d}\n",
/*  40  */                          i, array[i].data, array[i].key);
/*  41  */  }
```

This additional code isn't strictly part of the programmer's remit. We've had to put it in just for testing. We'll have to be very careful that we don't introduce further bugs in our test code. Now compile again and, this time, run the program.

```
$ cc -o debug2 debug2.c
$ ./debug2
```

What happens when you do this will depend on your flavor of UNIX (or Linux) and on how it's set up. On one of the authors' systems, we got:

```
array[0] = {john, 2}
array[1] = {alex, 1}
array[2] = {(null), -1}
array[3] = {bill, 3}
array[4] = {neil, 4}
```

But on the other author's system (running a different Linux kernel), we got:

```
Segmentation fault
```

On your UNIX system, you may see either of these outputs, or a different result again. We expected to see:

```
array[0] = {alex, 1}
array[1] = {john, 2}
array[2] = {bill, 3}
array[3] = {neil, 4}
array[4] = {rick, 5}
```

Clearly, there's a serious problem with this code. If it runs at all, it's failing to sort the array correctly and, if it's being terminated with a segmentation fault, the operating system is sending a signal to the program saying that it has detected an illegal memory access and is prematurely terminating the program to prevent memory being corrupted.

The ability of the operating system to detect illegal memory access depends on its hardware configuration and some subtleties of its memory management implementation. On most systems, the memory allocated to the program by the operating system is larger than the memory actually being used. If the illegal memory access occurs in this region of memory, the hardware may not be able to detect the illegal accesss. This is why not all versions of UNIX will generate a segmentation violation.

> **Some library functions, such as `printf`, will also prevent illegal accesses in some special circumstances, such as using a null pointer.**

When you're tracking down array access problems, it's often a good idea to increase the size of array elements, as this increases the size of the error. If we read a single byte beyond the end of an array of bytes, we may 'get away with it' as the memory allocated to the program will be rounded up to an operating system specific boundary, possibly as much as 8K.

If we increase the array element size, in this case by changing the `item` member `data` to be an array of 4096 characters, any access to a non-existent array element will probably be to a memory location beyond that allocated. Each element of the array is 4K in size, so the memory we use incorrectly will be 0-4K off the end.

If we do this, calling the result `debug3.c`, we get a segmentation fault on both the authors' flavors of Linux.

```
/*   2  */        char data[4096];
```

```
$ cc -o debug3 debug3.c
$ ./debug3
Segmentation fault (core dumped)
```

It's possible that some flavors of Linux or UNIX still won't produce a segmentation fault. When the ANSI C standard states that the behavior is 'undefined', it truly does allow the program to do anything. It certainly looks like we have written a non-conforming C program here and a non-conforming C program may exhibit very strange behavior! As we will see the fault does turn out to fall into the category of 'undefined behavior'.

Code Inspection

As we mentioned above, it's often a good idea to re-read your program when it fails to run as expected. For the purposes of this chapter, let's assume that the code has been reviewed and that obvious howlers have been dealt with.

> ***Code inspection* is also a term for the more formal process of a group of developers tracing through a few hundred lines of code in detail, but the scale really doesn't matter; it's still code inspection and it's still a very useful technique.**

There are tools that you can use to help with code reviews, the compiler being an obvious one. It will tell you if you have any syntax errors in your program.

Some compilers also have options to raise warnings on dubious practices, such as failing to initialize variables and using assignments in conditions. For example, the GNU compiler can be run with the options,

```
gcc -Wall -pedantic -ansi
```

which enables many warnings and additional checks for conformance to C standards. We recommend you get into the habit of using these options, *-Wall* especially. It can generate helpful information when tracking down program faults.

We'll others tool, `lint` and `LClint`, a little later on. Like the compiler, they analyse source code and report on code that might be incorrect.

Instrumentation

Instrumentation is the adding of code to a program for the purpose of collecting more information about the behavior of the program as it runs. It's very common to add `printf` calls, as we have done in our example, to print out the values of variables at different stages in a program's execution. We could usefully add several further `printf` calls, but we should be aware that the process entails an additional edit and compile whenever the program is changed and, of course, we will need to remove the code when the bugs are fixed.

There are two instrumentation techniques that can help here. The first uses the C preprocessor to selectively include instrumentation code so that we only need to recompile the program to include or exclude debugging code. We can do this quite simply with constructs like:

```
#ifdef DEBUG
  printf("variable x has value = %d\n", x);
#endif
```

We can compile the program with the compiler flag `-DDEBUG` to define the `DEBUG` symbol and include the extra code, or without to exclude it. We can make more sophisticated use of a numeric debug macro, like this.

```
#define BASIC_DEBUG 1
#define EXTRA_DEBUG 2
#define SUPER_DEBUG 4

#if (DEBUG & EXTRA_DEBUG)
  printf...
#endif
```

In this case, we must always define the `DEBUG` macro, but we can set it to represent a set of debug information, or a level of detail. The compiler flag `-DDEBUG=5` would, in this case, enable `BASIC_DEBUG` and `SUPER_DEBUG`, but not `EXTRA_DEBUG`. The flag `-DDEBUG=0` would disable all debug information. Alternatively, including the following lines eliminates the need to specify `DEBUG` on the command line in the case where no debugging is required:

```
#ifndef DEBUG
#define DEBUG 0
#endif
```

There are several macros defined by the C preprocessor that can help with debug information. These are macros that expand to give information about the current compilation.

Macro	Description
`__LINE__`	A decimal constant representing the current line number.
`__FILE__`	A string representing the current file name.
`__DATE__`	A string of the form `"Mmm dd yyyy"`, the current date.
`__TIME__`	A string of the form `"hh:mm:ss"`, the current time.

Note that these symbols are prefixed and suffixed by two underscores. This is common for standard preprocessor symbols and you should take care to avoid choosing symbols that might clash. The term **current** in the above descriptions refers to the point at which the preprocessing is being performed, i.e. the time and date the compiler was run and the file processed.

Try It Out - Debug Information

Here's a program, `cinfo.c`, that prints information about its compilation date and time, if debugging is enabled.

```
#include <stdio.h>

int main()
{
#ifdef DEBUG
    printf("Compiled: " __DATE__ " at " __TIME__ "\n");
    printf("This is line %d of file %s\n", __LINE__, __FILE__);
#endif
    printf("hello world\n");
    exit(0);
}
```

When we compile this program with debug enabled (using `-DDEBUG`), we see the compilation information.

```
$ cc -o cinfo -DDEBUG cinfo.c
$ ./cinfo
Compiled: Aug  8 1999 at 11:15:21
This is line 7 of file cinfo.c
hello world
$
```

How It Works

The C preprocessor part of the compiler keeps a track of the current line and file when it's compiling. It substitutes the current (compile time) values of these variables whenever it encounters the symbols `__LINE__` and `__FILE__`. The date and time of compilation are made available similarly. Since `__DATE__` and `__TIME__` are strings, we can concatenate them with format strings for `printf` because ANSI C specifies that adjacent strings are treated as one.

Debugging without Recompiling

Before we move on, it's worth mentioning that there's a way of using the `printf` function to help with debugging without using the `#ifdef DEBUG` technique, which requires a program to be recompiled before it can be used.

The method is to add a global variable as a debug flag, allow a `-d` option at the command line, which allows the user to switch debugging on even after the program has been released, and add a debug logging function. Now you can intersperse the program code with things like this:

```
if (debug) {
sprintf(msg, ...)
write_debug(msg)
}
```

You should write debug output to `stderr`, or, if this isn't practical because of the nature of the program, use the logging facilities provided by the `syslog` function.

If you add traces like this to solve problems during development, just leave the code in there. Provided you use a small amount of care, this can be quite safe. The benefit comes when the program has been released; if users encounter a problem, they can run it with debugging on and diagnose the errors for you. Instead of reporting that the program gave the message `segmentation fault`, they can also report exactly what the program was doing at the time, not just what the user was doing. The difference can be immense.

There is, obviously, a downside to this approach; the program is larger than it needs to be. In most cases, this is more an apparent problem than a real one. The program will probably be 20% or 30% larger, but in most cases this doesn't have any real impact on performance. Poor performance comes from increasing size by orders of magnitude, not by a mere doubling.

Controlled Execution

Let's get back to the example program. We have a bug. We can modify the program by adding additional code to print out the values of variables as the program runs, or we can use a debugger to control the program's execution and view its state as execution proceeds.

There are a number of debuggers available on UNIX systems, depending on the vendor. Common ones are `adb`, `sdb`, and `dbx`. The more sophisticated ones allow us to look at the state of the program in some detail, at a source code level. This is true of `sdb`, `dbx` and also of the GNU debugger, `gdb`, that can be used with Linux. There also exist 'front ends' to `gdb` which make it more user-friendly; `xxgdb`, `tgdb` and `DDD` are such programs. The Emacs editor also has a facility(`gdb-mode`) that allows you to run `gdb` on your program, set breakpoints, and see which line in the source code is being executed.

To prepare a program for debugging, you need to compile it with one or more special compiler options. These options instruct the compiler to include extra debugging information into the program. This information includes symbols and line numbers: information the debugger can use to show us where in the source code execution has reached.

The -g flag is the usual one used to compile a program for debugging. We must use it for compiling each source file that needs to be debugged and also for the linker, so that special versions of the standard C library can be used to provide debug support in library functions. The compiler program will pass the flag to the linker automatically. Debugging can be used with libraries that aren't compiled for the purpose, but with less flexibility.

Debug information can make the executable many (up to ten) times larger. Even though the executable may be larger (and take up more disk space) the amount of memory the program needs to run is effectively the same. It is usually a good idea to remove debug information before you release your programs, and only after they have been debugged.

You can remove debug information from an executable file without recompiling by running `strip <file>`.

Debugging with gdb

We'll use the GNU debugger, gdb, to debug this program. It's a very capable debugger which is freely available and can be used on many UNIX platforms. It's also the default debugger on Linux systems. gdb has been ported to many other platforms and can be used to debug embedded real-time systems.

Starting gdb

Let's recompile our example program for debugging and start gdb.

```
$ cc -g -o debug3 debug3.c
$ gdb debug3
GNU gdb 4.17.0.11 with Linux support
Copyright 1998 Free Software Foundation, Inc.
GDB is free software, covered by the GNU General Public License, and you are
welcome to change it and/or distribute copies of it under certain conditions.
Type "show copying" to see the conditions.
There is absolutely no warranty for GDB. Type "show warranty" for details.
This GDB was configured as "i386-redhat-linux"...
(gdb)
```

gdb has extensive online help and the complete manual is available as a set of files which may be viewed with the info program, or from within emacs.

```
(gdb) help
List of classes of commands:

aliases -- Aliases of other commands
breakpoints -- Making program stop at certain points
data -- Examining data
files -- Specifying and examining files
internals -- Maintenance commands
obscure -- Obscure features
running -- Running the program
stack -- Examining the stack
status -- Status inquiries
support -- Support facilities
tracepoints -- Tracing of program execution without stopping the program
user-defined -- User-defined commands

Type "help" followed by a class name for a list of commands in that class.
Type "help" followed by command name for full documentation.
Command name abbreviations are allowed if unambiguous.
(gdb)
```

gdb is itself a text-based application, but it does provide a few short cuts to help with repetitive tasks. Many versions have command line editing, with a history, so you can scroll back and execute the same command again (try using the cursor keys). All versions support an empty command: hitting *Return* will execute the last command again. This is especially useful when stepping through a program line by line with the `step` or `next` commands.

Running a Program

We can execute the program with the `run` command. Any arguments that we give to the `run` command are passed to the program as its arguments. In this case, we don't need any arguments.

We'll assume here that your system, like both the authors', is now generating a segmentation fault. If it isn't, read on. You'll find out what to do when one of your own programs does generate a segmentation violation. If you're not getting a segmentation violation, but want to work though this example as you read the book, you can pick up the program again at `debug4.c`, when the first of the memory access problems has been fixed.

```
(gdb) run
Starting program: /home/neil/debug3

Program received signal SIGSEGV, Segmentation fault.
0x8048488 in sort (a=0x8049684, n=5) at debug3.c:23
23      /*  23  */                          if(a[j].key > a[j+1].key) {

(gdb)
```

The program runs, incorrectly, as before. When the program faults, gdb shows us the reason and the location. We can now investigate the underlying cause of the problem.

Depending on your kernel, C library and compiler version you may see the program fault at a slightly different place, for example on line 25 when array items are exchanged rather than line 23 when array item keys are compared. If this is the case you'll see something like:

```
Program received signal SIGSEGV, Segmentation fault.
0x8000613 in sort (a=0x8001764, n=5) at debug3.c:25
25      /*  25  */                          a[j] = a[j+1];
```

You should still be able to follow the gdb sample session shown below.

Stack Trace

The program has been halted in the `sort` function, at line 23 of the source file `debug3.c`. If we hadn't compiled the program with additional debug information (`cc -g`), we wouldn't be able to see where the program had failed, nor would we be able to use variable names to examine data.

We can see how we got to this position by using the `backtrace` command.

```
(gdb) backtrace
#0  0x8048488 in sort (a=0x8049684, n=5) at debug3.c:23
#1  0x804859e in main () at debug3.c:37
#2  0x40031cb3 in __libc_start_main (main=0x804858c <main>, argc=1,
    argv=0xbffffd64, init=0x8048298 <_init>, fini=0x804863c <_fini>,
    rtld_fini=0x4000a350 <_dl_fini>, stack_end=0xbffffd5c)
    at ../sysdeps/generic/libc-start.c:78
(gdb)
```

This is a very simple program and the trace is short because we haven't called many functions from within other functions. You can see that `sort` was called from `main` at line 37 of the same file, `debug3.c`. Usually, the problem is much more complex and we use `backtrace` to discover the route we took to the error position. This can be very useful when debugging functions that are called from many different places.

The `backtrace` command may be abbreviated `bt` and, for compatibility, with other debuggers, the `where` command has the same function.

Examining Variables

The information printed by `gdb` when it stopped the program and in the stack trace shows us the values of function arguments.

The `sort` function was called with a parameter, `a`, that has the value `0x8049684`. This is the address of the array. It will typically be different on different systems, depending on the compiler used and the operating system.

The offending line, 23, is a comparison of one array element with another.

```
/*  23  */                    if(a[j].key > a[j+1].key) {
```

We can use the debugger to examine the contents of function parameters, local variables and global data. The `print` command shows us the contents of variables and other expressions.

```
(gdb) print j
$1 = 4
```

Here, we can see that the local variable `j` has the value 4. This means that the program has attempted to execute the statement:

```
if(a[4].key > a[4+1].key)
```

The array that we have passed to `sort`, `array`, has only five elements, which will be indexed 0 through 4. So, this statement reads from the non-existent `array[5]`. The loop variable `j` has taken an incorrect value.

If you are working through this example and your program faulted at line 25 this is because your system detected a read past the end of the array only when it got to exchanging elements, executing

```
/*  25  */                             a[j] = a[j+1];
```

which with `j` set to 4 results in

```
a[4] = a[4+1];
```

We can take a look at the elements of the passed array by using an expression with `print`. With gdb we can use almost any legal C expression to print the value of variables, array elements and pointers.

```
(gdb) print a[3]
$2 = {data = "alex", '\000' <repeats 4091 times>, key = 1}
(gdb)
```

gdb keeps the results of commands in pseudo variables, `$<number>`. The last result is always `$` and the one before that is `$$`. This allows one result to be used in another command. For example:

```
(gdb) print j
$3 = 4
(gdb) print a[$-1].key
$4 = 1
```

Listing the Program

We can view the source code of the program from within gdb by using the `list` command. This prints out a portion of the code around the current position. Subsequent uses of `list` will print out more. You can also give `list` a line number or function name as an argument and it will show the code at that position.

```
(gdb) list
18      /*  18  */          int s = -1;
19      /*  19  */
20      /*  20  */          for(; i < n && s != 0; i++) {
21      /*  21  */                  s = 0;
22      /*  22  */                  for(j = 0; j< n; j++) {
23      /*  23  */                          if(a[j].key > a[j+1].key) {
24      /*  24  */                                  item t = a[j];
25      /*  25  */                                  a[j] = a[j+1];
26      /*  26  */                                  a[j+1] = t;
27      /*  27  */                                  s++;
(gdb)
```

We can see that, on line 22, the loop is set to execute while the variable j is less than n. In this case, n is 5, so j will have the final value of 4, which is one too far. A value of 4 causes a comparison of a[4] with a[5] and possibly a swap. One solution to this particular problem is to correct the loop termination condition to be j < n-1.

Let's make that change, call the new program debug4.c, recompile and try again.

```
/*  22  */              for(j = 0; j < n-1; j++) {
```

```
$ cc -g -o debug4 debug4.c
$ ./debug4
array[0] = {john, 2}
array[1] = {alex, 1}
array[2] = {bill, 3}
array[3] = {neil, 4}
array[4] = {rick, 5}
```

The program still doesn't work, as it has printed an incorrectly sorted list. Let's use gdb to step through the program as it runs.

Setting Breakpoints

To find out where the program is failing, we need to be able to see what it's doing as it runs. We can stop the program at any point by setting breakpoints. These cause the program to stop and return control to the debugger. We'll be able to inspect variables and then allow the program to continue.

There are two loops in the sort function. The outer loop, with loop variable i, is run once for each element in the array. The inner loop swaps the element with those further down the list. This has the effect of 'bubbling up' the smaller elements to the top. After each run of the outer loop, the largest element should have made its way to the bottom. We can confirm this by stopping the program at the outer loop and examining the state of the array.

There are a number of commands used for setting breakpoints. These are listed by gdb with help breakpoint:

```
(gdb) help breakpoint
Making program stop at certain points.

List of commands:

awatch -- Set a watchpoint for an expression
break -- Set breakpoint at specified line or function
catch -- Set breakpoints to catch exceptions that are raised
clear -- Clear breakpoint at specified line or function
commands -- Set commands to be executed when a breakpoint is hit
condition -- Specify breakpoint number N to break only if COND is true
delete -- Delete some breakpoints or auto-display expressions
disable -- Disable some breakpoints
enable -- Enable some breakpoints
hbreak -- Set a hardware assisted  breakpoint
ignore -- Set ignore-count of breakpoint number N to COUNT
rbreak -- Set a breakpoint for all functions matching REGEXP
rwatch -- Set a read watchpoint for an expression
tbreak -- Set a temporary breakpoint
thbreak -- Set a temporary hardware assisted breakpoint
watch -- Set a watchpoint for an expression
```

```
Type "help" followed by command name for full documentation.
Command name abbreviations are allowed if unambiguous.
```

Let's set a breakpoint at line 20 and run the program:

```
$ gdb debug4
(gdb) break 20
Breakpoint 1 at 0x80483f1: file debug4.c, line 20.
(gdb) run
Starting program: /home/neil/debug4

Breakpoint 1, sort (a=0x8049684, n=5) at debug4.c:20
20      /*  20  */       for(; i < n && s != 0; i++) {
```

We can print out the array value and then allow the program to continue with the `cont` command. This allows the program to run until it hits the next breakpoint, in this case until it executes line 20 again. We can have many breakpoints active at any time.

```
(gdb) print array[0]
$1 = {data = "bill", '\000' <repeats 4091 times>, key = 3}
```

To print a number of consecutive items, we can use the construction `@<number>` to cause gdb to print a number of array elements. To print all five elements of `array` we can use:

```
(gdb) print array[0]@5
$2 = {{data = "bill", '\000' <repeats 4091 times>, key = 3}, {
    data = "neil", '\000' <repeats 4091 times>, key = 4}, {
    data = "john", '\000' <repeats 4091 times>, key = 2}, {
    data = "rick", '\000' <repeats 4091 times>, key = 5}, {
    data = "alex", '\000' <repeats 4091 times>, key = 1}}
```

Note that the output has been tidied up slightly to make it easier to read. Because this is the first time through the loop, the array is unchanged. When we allow the program to continue, we see successive alterations to `array` as execution proceeds:

```
(gdb) cont
Continuing.

Breakpoint 1, sort (a=0x8049684, n=4) at debug4.c:20
20      /*  20  */       for(; i < n && s != 0; i++) {

(gdb) print array[0]@5
$3 = {{data = "bill", '\000' <repeats 4091 times>, key = 3}, {
    data = "john", '\000' <repeats 4091 times>, key = 2}, {
    data = "neil", '\000' <repeats 4091 times>, key = 4}, {
    data = "alex", '\000' <repeats 4091 times>, key = 1}, {
    data = "rick", '\000' <repeats 4091 times>, key = 5}}
(gdb)
```

We can use the `display` command to set gdb to automatically display the array whenever the program stops at a breakpoint:

```
(gdb) display array[0]@5
1: array[0] @ 5 = {{data = "bill", '\000' <repeats 4091 times>, key = 3}, {
    data = "john", '\000' <repeats 4091 times>, key = 2}, {
    data = "neil", '\000' <repeats 4091 times>, key = 4}, {
    data = "alex", '\000' <repeats 4091 times>, key = 1}, {
    data = "rick", '\000' <repeats 4091 times>, key = 5}}
```

Furthermore, we can change the breakpoint so that, instead of stopping the program, it simply displays the data we have requested and carries on. To do this, we use the `commands` command. This allows us to specify what debugger commands to execute when a breakpoint is hit. Since we have already specified a display, we need only set the breakpoint command to continue execution.

```
(gdb) commands
Type commands for when breakpoint 1 is hit, one per line.
End with a line saying just "end".
> cont
> end
```

Now, when we allow the program to continue it runs to completion, printing the value of the array each time around the outer loop.

```
(gdb) cont
Continuing.

Breakpoint 1, sort (a=0x8049684, n=3) at debug4.c:20
20      /*  20  */         for(; i < n && s != 0; i++) {
1: array[0] @ 5 = {{data = "john", '\000' <repeats 4091 times>, key = 2}, {
     data = "bill", '\000' <repeats 4091 times>, key = 3}, {
     data = "alex", '\000' <repeats 4091 times>, key = 1}, {
     data = "neil", '\000' <repeats 4091 times>, key = 4}, {
     data = "rick", '\000' <repeats 4091 times>, key = 5}}

Breakpoint 1, sort (a=0x8049684, n=2) at debug4.c:20
20      /*  20  */         for(; i < n && s != 0; i++) {
1: array[0] @ 5 = {{data = "john", '\000' <repeats 4091 times>, key = 2}, {
     data = "alex", '\000' <repeats 4091 times>, key = 1}, {
     data = "bill", '\000' <repeats 4091 times>, key = 3}, {
     data = "neil", '\000' <repeats 4091 times>, key = 4}, {
     data = "rick", '\000' <repeats 4091 times>, key = 5}}
array[0] = {john, 2}
array[1] = {alex, 1}
array[2] = {bill, 3}
array[3] = {neil, 4}
array[4] = {rick, 5}

Program exited with code 025.
(gdb)
```

gdb reports that the program exits with an unusual exit code. This is because the program itself doesn't call `exit` and doesn't return a value from `main`. The exit code is effectively meaningless in this case and a meaningful one ought to be provided by a call to `exit`.

The program doesn't seem to execute the outer loop as many times as we expected. We can see that the value of the parameter, n, used in the loop termination condition is reducing at each breakpoint. This means that the loop won't execute enough times. The culprit is the decrement of n on line 30:

```
/*  30  */                   n--;
```

This is an attempt to optimize the program by taking advantage of the fact that at the end of each outer loop the largest element of `array` will be at the bottom and so there is less left to sort. But, as we've seen, this interferes with the outer loop and causes problems. The simplest fix (though there are others) is to delete the offending line. Let's test whether this change will fix the problem by using the debugger to apply a 'patch'.

Patching with the Debugger

We've already seen that we can use the debugger to set breakpoints and examine the value of variables. By using a breakpoint with actions, we can try out a fix, called a **patch**, before changing the source code and recompiling. In this case, we need to break the program on line 30 and increment the variable n. Then, when line 30 is executed, the value will be unchanged.

Let's restart the program from the beginning. First, we must delete our breakpoint and display. We can see what breakpoints and displays we have enabled using the `info` command:

```
(gdb) info display
Auto-display expressions now in effect:
Num Enb Expression
1:   y  array[0] @ 5
(gdb) info break
Num Type           Disp Enb Address    What
1   breakpoint     keep y   0x080483f1 in sort at debug4.c:20
        breakpoint already hit 4 times
        cont
```

We can either disable these or delete them entirely. If we disable them, we retain the option to re-enable them at a later time if we need to:

```
(gdb) disable break 1
(gdb) disable display 1
(gdb) break 30
Breakpoint 2 at 0x8048570: file debug4.c, line 30.
(gdb) commands 2
Type commands for when breakpoint 2 is hit, one per line.
End with a line saying just "end".
>set variable n = n+1
>cont
>end
(gdb) run
Starting program: /home/neil/debug4

Breakpoint 2, sort (a=0x8049684, n=5) at debug4.c:30
30    /*  30  */                   n--;

Breakpoint 2, sort (a=0x8049684, n=5) at debug4.c:30
30    /*  30  */                   n--;

Breakpoint 2, sort (a=0x8049684, n=5) at debug4.c:30
30    /*  30  */                   n--;

Breakpoint 2, sort (a=0x8049684, n=5) at debug4.c:30
30    /*  30  */                   n--;

Breakpoint 2, sort (a=0x8049684, n=5) at debug4.c:30
30    /*  30  */                   n--;
array[0] = {alex, 1}
array[1] = {john, 2}
array[2] = {bill, 3}
array[3] = {neil, 4}
array[4] = {rick, 5}

Program exited with code 025.
(gdb)
```

The program runs to completion and prints the correct result. We could now make the change and move on to test it with more data.

Learning more about gdb

The GNU debugger is an exceptionally powerful tool that can provide a lot of information about the internal state of executing programs. On systems that support a facility called hardware breakpoints, you can use `gdb` to monitor changes to variables in real time. Hardware breakpoints are a feature of some CPUs, these processors are able to stop automatically if certain conditions arise, typically a memory access in a given region. Alternatively, `gdb` can 'watch' expressions. This means that, with a performance penalty, `gdb` can stop a program when an expression takes a particular value, regardless of where in the program the calculation took place.

Breakpoints can be set with counts and conditions so that they only trigger after a fixed number of times or only trigger when a condition is met.

`gdb` is also able to attach itself to programs that are already running. This can be very useful when you're debugging client/server systems, as you can debug a misbehaving server process as it runs, without having to stop and restart it. You can compile programs with (for example) `gcc -O -g` to get the benefit of optimization and debug information. The downside is that optimization may reorder code a bit, so, as you single-step through code, you may find yourself 'jumping around' to achieve the same effect as intended by the original source code.

`gdb` is available under the terms of the GNU Public License and most UNIX systems can support it. We strongly recommend that you get to know it.

More Debugging Tools

Apart from out-and-out debuggers, such as `gdb`, UNIX systems typically provide a number of other tools that you can use to aid the debugging process. Some of these provide static information about a program, others a dynamic analysis.

Static analysis provides information from the program source code alone. Programs like `ctags`, `cxref` and `cflow` work with the source files and provide useful information about function calling and location.

Dynamic analysis provides information about how a program behaves during execution. Programs like `prof` and `gprof` provide information about which functions have been executed and for how long.

Let's take a look at some of these tools and their output. Not all of these tools will be available on all systems, although many of them have freely available versions.

Lint: Removing the Fluff from Your Programs

Original UNIX systems provided a utility called `lint`. It was essentially the front end of a C compiler with added tests designed to apply some 'common sense' and produce warnings. It would detect cases where variables were used before being set and where function arguments were not used, among other things.

More modern C compilers can, at a cost to compile-time performance, produce similar warnings. `lint` itself has been overtaken by the standardization of C. Because the tool was based on an early C compiler, it doesn't cope at all well with ANSI syntax. There are some commercial versions of `lint` available for UNIX and at least one on the Internet for Linux, which is Larch, part of a project at MIT to produce tools for formal specifications. The `lint`-like tool, `lclint` can provide useful code review comments.

> **lclint** can be found at **http://www.sds.lcs.mit.edu/Larch**

Here's a sample output from `lclint` running on an early version of the example program that we debugged earlier:

```
$ lclint debug0.c
LCLint 1.4c — Fri Oct 13 10:28:08 MET 1995

debug0.c:14,22: Old style function declaration.
debug0.c:15,17: **** Processing Params ****
debug0.c:20,24: Unrecognized identifier: n
debug0.c:20,35: Variable s used before set
debug0.c:20,20: if predicate not bool, type int: i < n & s != 0
debug0.c:32,14: Path with no return in function declared to return int
debug0.c:36,14: Return value (type int) ignored: sort(array, 5)
debug0.c:37,14: Path with no return in function declared to return int

Finished LCLint checking — 8 code errors found
$
```

The utility complains about old style (non-ANSI) function declarations and inconsistencies between function return types and the values they do (or do not) return. These don't affect the operation of the program, but ought to be addressed.

It has also detected two real bugs in the following code fragment:

```
/*  18  */       int s;
/*  19  */
/*  20  */       for(; i < n & s != 0; i++) {
/*  21  */               s = 0;
```

The `lclint` tool has determined that the variable `s` is used on line 20, but hasn't been initialized and that the operator `&` has been used in place of the more usual `&&`. In this case, the operator precedence alters the meaning of the test and is a problem for the program.

Both these errors were fixed in a code review before debugging started. Although this example is a little contrived for the purposes of demonstration, these are errors that regularly crop up in real world programs.

Function Call Tools

Three utilities, ctags, cxref and cflow, form part of the X/Open specification and, therefore, must be present on UNIX branded systems with software development capabilities.

> **These utilities, and others mentioned in this chapter may not be present in your Linux distribution. If not, you may like to search for implementations on the Internet. A good place to start (for Linux distributions that support the RPM package format) is http://rufus.w3.org/linux/RPM**

ctags

The ctags program creates an index of functions. For each function, you get a list of the places it's used, like the index of a book.

```
ctags [-a] [-f filename] sourcefile sourcefile ...
ctags -x sourcefile sourcefile ...
```

By default, ctags creates a file, called tags, in the current directory, which contains, for each function declared in any of the input source files, lines of the form:

```
announce        app_ui.c        /^static void announce(void) /
```

Each line in the file consists of a function name, the file it's declared in and a regular expression that can be used to find the function definition within the file. Some editors such as Emacs can use files of this kind to help navigate through source code.

Alternatively, using the -x option to ctags (if available in your version) you can produce lines of a similar form on the standard output:

```
find_cat        403 app_ui.c        static cdc_entry find_cat(
```

You can redirect the output to a different file by using the option -f filename and append it to an existing file by specifying the -a option.

cxref

The cxref program analyses C source code and produces a cross-reference. It shows where each symbol (variable, #define and function) is mentioned in the program. It produces a sorted list with each symbol's definition location marked with an asterisk, as shown on the following page:

```
SYMBOL             FILE       FUNCTION    LINE

BASENID            prog.c        —        *12  *96  124  126  146  156  166
BINSIZE            prog.c        —        *30  197  198  199  206
 BUFMAX            prog.c        —        *44   45   90
 BUFSIZ  /usr/include/stdio.h    —         *4
    EOF  /usr/include/stdio.h    —        *27
   argc            prog.c        —         36
                   prog.c      main       *37   61   81
   argv            prog.c        —         36
                   prog.c      main       *38   61
calldata           prog.c        —         *5
                   prog.c      main        64  188
  calls            prog.c        —        *19
                   prog.c      main        54
```

On the author's machine, the above output was generated with the command,

```
$ cxref *.c *.h
```

but the exact syntax varies from version to version. Consult the documentation for your system or the man pages for more information on whether cxref is available and how to use it.

cflow

The cflow program prints a **function call tree**, a diagram that shows which function calls which others, and which functions are called by them, and so on. It can be useful to find out the structure of a program to understand how it operates and to see what impact changes to a function will have. Some versions of cflow can operate on object files as well as source code. Refer to the manual page for details of operation.

Here's some sample output taken from a version of cflow (cflow-2.0) that is available on the Internet and maintained by Marty Leisner:

```
1        file_ungetc {prcc.c 997}
2        main {prcc.c 70}
3                getopt {}
4                show_all_lists {prcc.c 1070}
5                        display_list {prcc.c 1056}
6                                printf {}
7                        exit {}
8                exit {}
9                usage {prcc.c 59}
10                       fprintf {}
11                       exit {}
```

This sample tells us that main calls (among others) show_all_lists and that show_all_lists in turn calls display_list, which itself calls printf.

One option to this version of cflow is -i to produce an inverted flow graph. For each function, these list the other functions that make a call to that function. It sounds complicated, but it really isn't. Here's a sample.

```
19          display_list {prcc.c 1056}
20                  show_all_lists {prcc.c 1070}
21          exit {}
22                  main {prcc.c 70}
23                  show_all_lists {prcc.c 1070}
24                  usage {prcc.c 59}
...
74          printf {}
75                  display_list {prcc.c 1056}
76                  maketag {prcc.c 487}
77          show_all_lists {prcc.c 1070}
78                  main {prcc.c 70}
...
99          usage {prcc.c 59}
100                 main {prcc.c 70}
```

This shows us that the functions that call `exit`, for example, are `main`, `show_all_lists` and `usage`.

Execution Profiling

A technique that is often useful when you're trying to track down performance problems with a program is **execution profiling**. Normally supported by special compiler options and ancillary programs, a profile of a program shows where it's spending its time.

prof/gprof

The `prof` program (and its GNU equivalent, `gprof`) prints a report from an execution trace file that is produced when a profiled program is run. A profiled executable is created by specifying the `-p` flag (for `prof`) or `-pg` flag (for `gprof`) to the compiler:

```
$ cc -pg -o program program.c
```

The program is linked with a special version of the C library and is changed to include monitoring code. This may vary with specific systems, but is commonly achieved by arranging for the program to be interrupted frequently and the execution location recorded. The monitor data is written to a file in the current directory, `mon.out` (`gmon.out` for `gprof`).

```
$ ./program
$ ls -ls
   2 -rw-r--r--    1 neil     users          1294 Feb  4 11:48 gmon.out
```

The `prof/gprof` program reads this monitoring data and produces a report. Refer to the manual pages for detail on program options. Here is some (abbreviated) `gprof` output as an example.

```
 cumulative    self       self      total
    time     seconds    seconds     calls   ms/call   ms/call          name
    18.5       0.10       0.10       8664      0.01      0.03     _doscan [4]
    18.5       0.20       0.10                                    mcount (60)
    14.8       0.28       0.08      43320      0.00      0.00     _number [5]
     9.3       0.33       0.05       8664      0.01      0.01  _format_arg [6]
     7.4       0.37       0.04     112632      0.00      0.00     _ungetc [8]
     7.4       0.41       0.04       8757      0.00      0.00    _memccpy [9]
     7.4       0.45       0.04          1     40.00    390.02       _main [2]
     3.7       0.47       0.02         53      0.38      0.38       _read [12]
     3.7       0.49       0.02                                      w4str [10]
     1.9       0.50       0.01      26034      0.00      0.00     _strlen [16]
     1.9       0.51       0.01       8664      0.00      0.00     strncmp [17]
```

Assertions

While it's common to introduce debug code such as `printf` calls, possibly by conditional compilation, during the development of a program, it's sometimes impractical to leave these messages in a delivered system. However, it's often the case that problems occur during the program operation that are related to incorrect assumptions, rather than coding errors. These are events that "can't happen". For example, a function may be written with the understanding that its input parameters will be within a certain range. If it's passed incorrect data, it might invalidate the whole system.

For these cases, where the internal logic of the system needs to be confirmed, X/Open provides the `assert` macro which can be used to test that an assumption is correct and halt the program if not.

```
#include <assert.h>

void assert(int expression)
```

The `assert` macro evaluates the expression and, if it's non-zero, writes some diagnostic information to the standard error and calls `abort` to end the program.

The header file `assert.h` defines the macro depending on the definition of `NDEBUG`. If `NDEBUG` is defined when the header file is processed, `assert` is defined to be essentially nothing. This means that you can turn off assertions at compile time by compiling with `-DNDEBUG` or by including the line,

```
#define NDEBUG
```

in each source file before including `assert.h`.

Problems with assert

This method of use is one problem with `assert`. If you use `assert` during testing, but turn if off for production code, potentially, your production code has less safety checking than when you are testing it. Leaving assertions enabled in production code is not normally an option—would you like your code to present a customer with the unfriendly error `assert failed` and a stopped program? You may consider it better to write your own error trapping routine that still checks the assertion, but doesn't need to be completely disabled in production code.

You must also be careful that there are no side-effects in the `assert` expression. For example, if you use a function call with a side-effect, the effect won't happen in the production code if assertions are removed.

Here's a program, `assert.c`, that defines a function that must take a positive value. It protects against the possibility of a bad argument by using an assertion.

Try It Out - assert

Including the `assert.h` header file and a 'square root' function which checks that the parameter is positive, we can then write the `main` function:

```
#include <stdio.h>
#include <math.h>
#include <assert.h>
```

```
double my_sqrt(double x)
{
    assert(x >= 0.0);
    return sqrt(x);
}

int main()
{
    printf("sqrt +2 = %g\n", my_sqrt(2.0));
    printf("sqrt -2 = %g\n", my_sqrt(-2.0));
    exit(0);
}
```

Now, when we run the program, we see an assertion violation when we pass an illegal value. The exact format of the assertion failure message will vary from system to system.

```
$ cc -o assert assert.c -lm
$ ./assert
sqrt +2 = 1.41421
assert.c:7: my_sqrt: Assertion 'x >= 0.0' failed.
Aborted (core dumped)
$
```

How It Works

When we try to call the function, `my_sqrt`, with a negative number, the assertion fails. The `assert` macro provides the file and line number where the assertion violation occurred, as well as the condition that failed. The program terminates with an abort trap. This is the result of `assert` calling `abort`.

If we recompile the program with `-DNDEBUG`, the assertion is compiled out and we get a mathematical error when we call the `sqrt` function from `my_sqrt`.

```
$ cc -o assert -DNDEBUG assert.c -lm
$ ./assert
sqrt +2 = 1.41421
Floating point exception
$
```

Some mathematics library versions will return a NaN value (Not A Number) indicating an invalid result.

```
sqrt -2 = nan
```

Memory Debugging

One area that is a rich source of bugs that are difficult to track down is dynamic memory allocation. If you write a program that uses `malloc` and `free` to allocate memory, it's important that you keep good track of the blocks you allocate and make sure that you don't use a block that you've freed up.

Typically, memory blocks are allocated by `malloc` and assigned to pointer variables. If the pointer variable is changed and there are no other pointers pointing to the memory block, it will become inaccessible. This is a memory leak and it causes your program to grow in size. If you leak a lot of memory, your system will eventually slow down and run out of memory.

If you write beyond the end of an allocated block (or before the beginning of a block), you'll very likely corrupt the data structures used by the malloc library to keep track of allocations. In this case, at some future time, a call to malloc, or even free, will cause a segmentation violation and your program will crash. Tracking down the precise point at which the fault occurred can be very difficult, as it may have been a long time before the event which caused the crash.

Unsurprisingly, there are tools, commercial and free, that can help with these two problem types. There are, for example, many different versions of malloc and free, some of which contain additional code to check on allocations and de-allocations to try to cater for the cases where a block is freed twice and some other types of misuse.

ElectricFence

The ElectricFence library was developed by Bruce Perens and is available as an optional component in some Linux distributions such as RedHat and can be readily found on the Internet. It attempts to use the virtual memory facilities of UNIX to protect the memory used by malloc and free. Its aim is to halt the program at the point of memory corruption.

Try It Out - ElectricFence

Here's a program, efence.c, that allocates a memory block with malloc and then writes beyond the end of the block. Let's see what happens.

```
#include <stdio.h>
#include <stdlib.h>

int main()
{
    char *ptr = (char *) malloc(1024);
    ptr[0] = 0;

    /* Now write beyond the block */
    ptr[1024] = 0;
    exit(0);
}
```

When we compile and run the program, we see no untoward behavior. However, it's likely that the malloc memory area has sustained some corruption and we would eventually run into trouble.

```
$ cc -o efence efence.c
$ ./efence
$
```

However, if we take exactly the same program and link with the ElectricFence library, libefence.a, we get an immediate response.

```
$ cc -o efence efence.c -lefence
$ ./efence

  Electric Fence 2.0.5 Copyright (C) 1987-1998 Bruce Perens.
Segmentation fault
$
```

Running under the debugger pinpoints the problem:

```
$ cc -g -o efence efence.c -lefence
$ gdb efence
(gdb) run
Starting program: /home/neil/efence

  Electric Fence 2.0.5 Copyright (C) 1987-1998 Bruce Perens.

Program received signal SIGSEGV, Segmentation fault.
0x80008e4 in main () at efence.c:11
11          ptr[1024] = 0;
(gdb)
```

How It Works

ElectricFence replaces `malloc` and associated functions with versions that use virtual memory features of the computer's processor to protect against illegal memory access. When such an access occurs, a segmentation violation signal is raised and the program halts.

Checker

Tristan Gingold has developed `Checker`, a modified compiler back end and C library for Linux and UNIX that is capable of detecting many of the problems that we have discussed. In particular, it can detect incorrect pointer references, array access errors and memory leaks. It is usually not included in Linux distributions but can be found at http://www.gnu.org/software/checker/checker.html.

Programs and libraries need to be recompiled to use `Checker`, but, as source code is available for almost all software for Linux, this isn't too much of a restriction, and pre-compiled libraries for use with `Checker` are usually available

Try It Out - Checker

Here's a program, `checker.c`, that allocates some memory, reads from an uninitialized portion of that memory, writes beyond the end of it and then makes it inaccessible.

```
#include <stdio.h>
#include <stdlib.h>

int main()
{
    char *ptr = (char *) malloc(1024);
    char ch;

    /* Uninitialized read */
    ch = ptr[0];

    /* Write beyond the block */
    ptr[1024] = 0;

    /* Orphan the block */
    ptr = 0;
    exit(0);
}
```

To use Checker, we simply have to replace our compiler command with checkergcc, a driver program that takes care of invoking the correct compiler version and linking with special, Checkered, libraries.

When we run the program, we see lots of problems diagnosed:

```
$ checkergcc -o checker checker.c
$ ./checker
Checker version 0.7 Copyright (C) 1993,1994,1995 Tristan Gingold.
This program has been compiled with 'checkergcc' or 'checkerg++'.
Checker is a memory access detector.
Checker is distributed in the hope that it will be useful,
but WITHOUT ANY WARRANTY; without even the implied warranty of
MERCHANTABILITY or FITNESS FOR A PARTICULAR PURPOSE.  See the GNU
General Public License for more details.
For more information, set CHECKEROPTS to '—help'
From Checker (pid:01359): 'checker' is runing (Sun Feb  4 14:54:00 1996)

From Checker (pid:01359): (ruh) read uninitialized byte(s) in a block.
When Reading 1 byte(s) at address 0x0801e12c, inside the heap (sbrk).
0 bytes into a block (start: 0x801e12c, length: 1024, mdesc: 0x0).
The block was allocated from:
        pc=0x080099db in _malloc() at ./l-malloc/malloc.c:211
        pc=0x08009a3d in malloc() at ./l-malloc/malloc.c:232
        pc=0x080001df in main() at checker.c:6
        pc=0x0800010c in _start() at :0
Stack frames are:
        pc=0x08000200 in main() at checker.c:10
        pc=0x0800010c in _start() at :0
From Checker (pid:01359): (bvh) block bounds violation in the heap.
When Writing 1 byte(s) at address 0x0801e52c, inside the heap (sbrk).
0 bytes after a block (start: 0x801e12c, length: 1024, mdesc: 0x0).
The block was allocated from:
        pc=0x080099db in _malloc() at ./l-malloc/malloc.c:211
        pc=0x08009a3d in malloc() at ./l-malloc/malloc.c:232
        pc=0x080001df in main() at checker.c:6
        pc=0x0800010c in _start() at :0
Stack frames are:
        pc=0x08000225 in main() at checker.c:13
        pc=0x0800010c in _start() at :0
```

Here, we can see that the bad reads and writes have been caught and the memory blocks concerned are given, together with the place they were allocated. We can use the debugger to break the program at the point of the error.

There are many options to Checker, including the suppression of certain types of error and memory leak detection. To detect our example leak, we must use one of the options that are passed through the CHECKEROPTS environment variable. To check for memory leaks when the program ends, we need to specify -D=end:

```
$ CHECKEROPTS=-D=end checker

...

From Checker (pid:01407): (gar) garbage detector results.
There is 1 leak and 0 potential leak(s).
Leaks consume 1024 bytes (1 KB) / 131193 KB.
( 0.00% of memory is leaked.)
Found 1 block(s) of size 1024.
```

```
Block at ptr=0x801e40c
        pc=0x08009900 in _malloc() at ./l-malloc/malloc.c:174
        pc=0x08009a3d in malloc() at ./l-malloc/malloc.c:232
        pc=0x080001df in main() at checker.c:6
        pc=0x0800010c in _start() at :0
```

How It Works

We have modified our program by using the `checkergcc` compiler to include additional code to check each pointer reference as it happens. If the access concerns an allocated memory block and is illegal, `Checker` prints a message. At the end of the program, a garbage collection routine is run that determines if any memory blocks have been allocated and not freed. These orphaned blocks are reported.

Resources

The utility programs discussed in this chapter have mostly been made available on FTP servers on the Internet. The authors concerned may, in some cases, retain copyright. Many of the utilities were taken from the Linux archive ftp://metalab.unc.edu/pub/Linux, and we expect new versions will be found there as they are released.

Other Internet resources are listed in Appendix C.

Summary

In this chapter, we've looked at some debugging tools and techniques. UNIX, and especially Linux, provide some powerful aids to help with removing defects from programs.

We eliminated some bugs from a program, using `gdb`, and looked at some static analysis tools such as `cflow` and `lclint`.

Finally, we looked at problems that arise when we use dynamically allocated memory and some utilities that can help diagnose them, such as `ElectricFence` and `Checker`.

Processes and Signals

Processes and signals form a fundamental part of the UNIX operating environment. They control almost all activities performed by a UNIX computer system. An understanding of how UNIX manages processes will hold any systems programmer, applications programmer or system administrator in good stead.

In this chapter, we'll look at how processes are handled in the Linux environment and how to find out exactly what the computer is doing at any given time. We'll also see how to start and stop other processes from within our own programs, how to make processes send and receive messages and how to avoid zombies. In particular, we'll learn about:

- Process structure, type and scheduling
- Starting new processes in different ways
- Parent, child and zombie processes
- What signals are and how to use them

What is a Process?

The Single UNIX Specification, Version 2 (UNIX98) and its predecessor Version 1 (UNIX95), defines a process as "an address space with one or more threads executing within that address space, and the required system resources for those threads." We will look at threads in the next chapter. For now, we will just regard a process as a program that is running.

A multitasking operating system such as UNIX lets many programs run at once. Each instance of a running program constituting a process. This is especially evident with a windowing system such as the X Window system (sometimes simply called X). Like Microsoft Windows, it provides a graphical user interface that allows many applications to be run at once. Each application can display one or more windows. We'll see more of the X Windows system in Chapter 16.

As a multiuser system, UNIX allows many users to access the system at the same time. Each user can run many programs, or even many instances of the same program, at the same time. The system itself runs other programs to manage system resources and control user access.

As we saw in Chapter 4, a program that is running, or process, consists of program code, data, variables (occupying system memory), open files (file descriptors) and an environment. Typically, a UNIX system will share code and system libraries between processes, so that there's only one copy the code in memory at any one time.

Process Structure

Let's have a look at how a couple of processes might be arranged within the operating system. If two users, neil and rick, both run the grep program at the same time to look for different strings in different files, the processes being used might look like this.

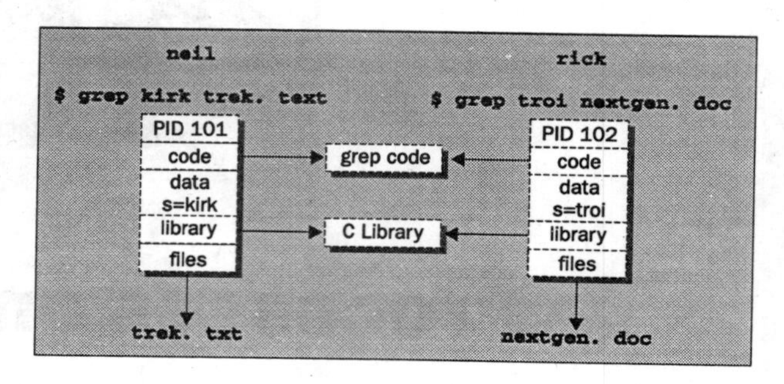

If we run the ps command, described below, the output will look something like this.

```
$ ps -af
UID      PID    PPID  C   STIME   TTY    TIME       CMD
rick     101    96    0   18:24   tty2   00:00:00   grep pid_t /usr/include/sys/*.h
neil     102    92    0   18:24   tty4   00:00:00   grep XOPEN /usr/include/features.h
```

Each process is allocated a unique number, a **process identifier**, or **PID**. This is usually a positive integer between 2 and 32768. When a process is started, the next unused number in sequence is chosen and the numbers restart at 2 so that they wrap around. The number 1 is typically reserved for the special init process, which manages other processes. We will come back to init shortly. Here we see that the two processes started by neil and rick have been allocated the identifiers 101 and 102.

The program code that will be executed by the grep command is stored in a disk file. Normally, a UNIX process can't write to the memory area used to hold the program code, so the code is loaded into memory as read-only. You saw in the diagram that, as this area can't be written, it can safely be shared.

The system libraries can also be shared. Thus there need be only one copy of printf for example in memory, even if many running programs call it. This is a more sophisticated, but similar, scheme to the way dynamic link libraries (DLLs) work in Microsoft Windows.

As you can see in the diagram above, an additional benefit is that the disk file containing the executable program grep is smaller because it doesn't contain shared library code. This might not seem much for a single program, but extracting the common routines for (say) the standard C library saves a significant amount of space over a whole operating system.

Of course, not everything that a program needs to run can be shared. For example, the variables that it uses are distinct for each process. In this example, we see that the search string passed to the grep command appears as a variable, s, in the data space of each process. These are separate and can't normally be read by other processes. The files that are being used in the two grep commands are also different; the processes have their own set of file descriptors used for file access.

Additionally, a process has its own stack space, used for local variables in functions and for controlling function calls and returns. It also has its own environment space, containing environment variables that may be established solely for this process to use, as we saw when we looked at putenv and getenv in Chapter 4. A process must also maintain its own program counter, a record of where it has got to in its execution, which is the execution thread. In the next chapter we will see that when we use threads, processes can have more than one thread of execution.

On many Linux systems, and some UNIX systems, there is a special set of files in a directory called `/proc`. These are rather special files, as they allow you to 'look inside' processes while they are running.

Finally, because UNIX has a virtual memory system that pages code and data out to an area of the hard disk, many more processes can be managed than would fit into the physical memory.

The Process Table

The UNIX **process table** is like a data structure describing all of the processes that are currently loaded with, for example, their PID, status and command string, the sort of information output by `ps`. The operating system manages processes using their PIDs and they are used as an index into the process table. The table is of limited size, so the number of processes a system will support is limited. Ancient UNIX systems were limited to 256 processes. More modern implementations have relaxed this restriction considerably and may be limited only by the memory available to construct a process table entry.

Viewing Processes

The `ps` command shows the processes we're running, the process another user is running or all the processes on the system. Here is some sample output.

```
$ ps -af
UID        PID  PPID  C STIME TTY          TIME CMD
root       433   425  0 18:12 tty1     00:00:00 [bash]
rick       445   426  0 18:12 tty2     00:00:00 -bash
rick       456   427  0 18:12 tty3     00:00:00 [bash]
root       467   433  0 18:12 tty1     00:00:00 sh /usr/X11R6/bin/startx
root       474   467  0 18:12 tty1     00:00:00 xinit /etc/X11/xinit/xinitrc --
root       478   474  0 18:12 tty1     00:00:00 /usr/bin/gnome-session
root       487     1  0 18:12 tty1     00:00:00 gnome-smproxy --sm-client-id def
root       493     1  0 18:12 tty1     00:00:01 [enlightenment]
root       506     1  0 18:12 tty1     00:00:03 panel --sm-client-id default8
root       508     1  0 18:12 tty1     00:00:00 xscreensaver -no-splash -timeout
root       510     1  0 18:12 tty1     00:00:01 gmc --sm-client-id default10
root       512     1  0 18:12 tty1     00:00:01 gnome-help-browser --sm-client-i
root       649   445  0 18:24 tty2     00:00:00 su
root       653   649  0 18:24 tty2     00:00:00 bash
neil       655   428  0 18:24 tty4     00:00:00 -bash
root       713     1  2 18:27 tty1     00:00:00 gnome-terminal
root       715   713  0 18:28 tty1     00:00:00 gnome-pty-helper
root       717   716 13 18:28 pts/0    00:00:01 emacs
root       718   653  0 18:28 tty2     00:00:00 ps -af
```

This shows information about many processes, including the processes involved with the Emacs editor under X Windows on a Linux system. For example, the `TTY` column shows which terminal the process was started from, `TIME` gives the CPU time used so far and the `CMD` column shows the command used to start the process. Let's take a closer look at some of these.

```
neil      655   428  0 18:24 tty4    00:00:00 -bash
```

The initial login was performed on virtual console number four. This is just the console on this machine. The shell program that is running is the Linux default, bash.

```
root      467   433  0 18:12 tty1     00:00:00 sh /usr/X11R6/bin/startx
```

The X Window system was started by the command `startx`. This is a shell script that starts the X Server and runs some initial X Windows programs.

```
root        717    716 13 18:28 pts/0     00:00:01 emacs
```

This process represents a window in the X Windows system running Emacs. It was started by the window manager in response to a request for a new window. A new pseudo terminal, `pts/0`, has been assigned for the shell to read from and write to.

```
root        512      1  0 18:12 tty1      00:00:01 gnome-help-browser --sm-client-i
```

This is the Gnome help browser started by the window manager.

By default, the `ps` program only shows processes that maintain a connection with a terminal, a console, a serial line, or a pseudo terminal. Other processes run without needing to communicate with a user on a terminal. These are typically system processes that UNIX uses to manage shared resources. We can use `ps` to see all such processes using the `-a` option, and to get 'full' information with `-f`. Note that the exact syntax for the `ps` command and the format of the output may vary slightly from system to system. Refer to the manual for more details on the options and output format of `ps`.

System Processes

Here are some of the other processes running on this Linux system. The output has been abbreviated for clarity.

```
$ ps -ax
  PID TTY STAT   TIME COMMAND
    1  ?  S      0:00 init
    7  ?  S      0:00 update (bdflush)
   40  ?  S      0:01 /usr/sbin/syslogd
   46  ?  S      0:00 /usr/sbin/lpd
   51  ?  S      0:00 sendmail: accepting connections
   88 v02 S      0:00 /sbin/agetty 38400 tty2
  109  ?  R      0:41 X :0
  192 pp0 R      0:00 ps -ax
```

Here we can see one very important process indeed.

```
    1  ?  S      0:00 init
```

In general, each process is started by another, known as its parent process. A process so started is known as a child process. When UNIX starts, it runs a single program, the prime ancestor and process number 1, `init`. This is, if you like, the operating system process manager. Other system processes we'll meet soon are started by `init`, or by other processes started by `init`.

One such example is the login procedure. `init` starts the `getty` program once for each serial terminal or dial in modem that we can use to log in. These are shown in the `ps` output like this.

```
   88 v02 S      0:00 /sbin/agetty 38400 tty2
```

The `getty` processes wait for activity at the terminal, prompt the user with the familiar login prompt and then pass control to the login program, which sets up the user environment and finally starts a shell. When the user shell exits, `init` starts another `getty` process.

You can see that the ability to start new processes and to wait for them to finish is fundamental to the system. We'll see later in this chapter how to perform the same tasks from within our own programs with the system calls `fork`, `exec` and `wait`.

Process Scheduling

One further `ps` output example is the entry for the `ps` command itself.

```
192 pp0 R      0:00 ps -ax
```

This indicates that process 192 is in a run state (`R`) and is executing the command `ps -ax`. Thus the process is described in its own output! The status indicator shows only that the program is ready to run, not necessarily that it's actually running. On a single processor computer, only one process can run at a time, while others wait their turn. These turns, known as time slices, are quite short and give the impression that programs are running at the same time. The `R` just shows that the program is not waiting for other processes to finish or waiting for input or output to complete. That is why there are two such processes listed in our example output. (The other is the X display server.)

The UNIX system uses a process scheduler to decide which process will receive the next time slice. It does this using the process priority. We met priorities back in Chapter 4. Processes with a high priority get to run more often, while others, such as low priority background tasks, run less frequently. With UNIX, processes can't overrun their allocated time slice. They are preemptively multitasked, so that they are suspended and resumed without their cooperation. Older systems, such as Microsoft Windows 3.x, generally require processes to explicitly yield so that others may resume.

The operating system determines the priority of a process based on a 'nice' value, which defaults to 10, and on the behavior of the program. Programs that run for long periods without pausing generally get lower priorities. Programs that pause while (for example) waiting for input get rewarded. This helps keep a program that interacts with the user responsive; while it is waiting for some input from the user, the system increases its priority, so that when it's ready to resume, it has a high priority. We can set the process nice value using `nice` and adjust it using `renice`. The `nice` command reduces the nice value of a process by 10. We can view the nice values of active processes using the `-l` or `-f` (for long output) option to `ps`. The value we are interested in is shown in the `NI` (nice) column.

```
$ ps -l
 F    UID   PID  PPID PRI NI SIZE  RSS WCHAN       STAT TTY   TIME COMMAND
  0   501   146     1   1  0   85  756 130b85      S    v01   0:00 oclock
```

Here we can see that the `oclock` program is running with a default nice value. If it had been started with the command:

```
$ nice oclock &
```

it would have been allocated a nice value of +10. If we adjust this value with the command:

```
$ renice 10 146
146: old priority 0, new priority 10
```

the clock program will run less often. We can see the modified nice value with `ps` again.

```
 F    UID   PID  PPID PRI NI SIZE  RSS WCHAN       STAT TTY   TIME COMMAND
  0   501   146     1  20 10   85  756 130b85      S N  v01   0:00 oclock
```

The status column now also contains N to indicate that the nice value has changed from the default. The PPID field of ps output indicates the parent process ID, the PID of either the process that caused this process to start or, if that process is no longer running, init (PID 1).

The UNIX scheduler decides which process to allow to run on the basis of priority. Exact implementations vary, of course, but higher priority processes run more often. In some cases, low priority processes don't run at all if higher priority processes are ready to run.

Starting New Processes

We can cause a program to run from inside another program and thereby create a new process by using the system library function.

```
#include <stdlib.h>

int system (const char *string);
```

The system function runs the command passed to it as string and waits for it to complete. The command is executed as if the command,

```
$ sh -c string
```

has been given to a shell. system returns 127 if a shell can't be started to run the command and -1 if another error occurs. Otherwise, system returns the exit code of the command.

Try It Out - system

We can use system to write a program to run ps for us. While this is not tremendously useful in itself, we'll see how to develop this technique in later examples. We also don't check that the system call actually worked for the sake of simplicity in the example.

```
#include <stdlib.h>
#include <stdio.h>

int main()
{
    printf("Running ps with system\n");
    system("ps -ax");
    printf("Done.\n");
    exit(0);
}
```

When we compile and run this program, system.c, we get the following.

```
$ ./system
Running ps with system
  PID TTY STAT  TIME COMMAND
    1  ?  S     0:00 init
    7  ?  S     0:00 update (bdflush)
...
  146 v01 S N   0:00 oclock
  256 pp0 S     0:00 ./system
  257 pp0 R     0:00 ps -ax
Done.
```

Because the `system` function uses a shell to start the desired program, we could put it in the background by changing the function call in `system.c` to the following.

```
system("ps -ax &");
```

When we compile and run this version of the program, we get:

```
$ ./system2
Running ps with system
Done.
$    PID TTY STAT   TIME COMMAND
      1  ?  S      0:00 init
      7  ?  S      0:00 update (bdflush)
...
    146 v01 S N    0:00 oclock
    266 pp0 R      0:00 ps -ax
```

How It Works

In the first example, the program calls `system` with the string `"ps -ax"`, which executes the `ps` program. Our program returns from the call to `system` when the `ps` command has finished. The `system` function can be quite useful, but is also limited. Because our program has to wait until the process started by the call to `system` finishes, we can't get on with other tasks.

In the second example, the call to `system` returns as soon as the shell command finishes. Because it's a request to run a program in the background, the shell returns as soon as the `ps` program is started, just as would happen if we had typed:

```
$ ps -ax &
```

at a shell prompt. The system program then prints `Done.` and exits before the `ps` command has had a chance to produce any output. The `ps` output follows the shell prompt put out after system exits. This kind of process behavior can be quite confusing for users. To make good use of processes, we need finer control over their actions. Let's look at a lower level interface to process creation, `exec`.

> **In general, using `system` is a far from ideal way to start other processes, because it invokes the desired program using a shell. This is both inefficient, because a shell is started then the program is started, and also quite dependent on the installation for the shell and environment that is used. In the next section we see a much better way of invoking programs, which should almost always be used in preference to the `system` call.**

Replacing a Process Image

There is a whole family of related functions grouped under the exec heading. They differ in the way that they start processes and present program arguments. An exec function replaces the current process with a new process specified by the path or file argument.

```
#include <unistd.h>

char **environ;

int execl(const char *path, const char *arg0, ...,    (char *)0);
int execlp(const char *file, const char *arg0, ...,    (char *)0);
int execle(const char *path, const char *arg0, ...,    (char *)0, const char *envp[]);
int execv(const char *path, const char *argv[]);
int execvp(const char *file, const char *argv[]);
int execve(const char *path, const char *argv[], const char *envp[]);
```

These functions belong to two types. execl, execlp, and execle take a variable number of arguments ending with a null pointer. execv and execvp have as their second argument an array of strings. In both cases, the new program starts with the given arguments appearing in the argv array passed to main. These functions are usually implemented using execve, though there is no requirement for it to be done this way.

The functions with names suffixed with a p differ in that they will search the PATH environment variable to find the new program executable file. If the executable isn't on the path, an absolute file name, including directories, will need to be passed to the function as a parameter.

The global variable environ is available to pass a value for the new program environment. Alternatively, an additional argument to the functions execle and execve is available for passing an array of strings to be used as the new program environment.

If we wish to use an exec function to start the ps program, we have the following choices.

```
#include <unistd.h>

/* Example of an argument list */
/* Note that we need a program name for argv[0] */
const char *ps_argv[] =
    {"ps", "-ax", 0};

/* Example environment, not terribly useful */
const char *ps_envp[] =
    {"PATH=/bin:/usr/bin", "TERM=console", 0};

/* Possible calls to exec functions */
execl("/bin/ps", "ps", "-ax", 0);              /* assumes ps is in /bin */
execlp("ps", "ps", "-ax", 0);                  /* assumes /bin is in PATH */
execle("/bin/ps", "ps", "-ax", 0, ps_envp); /* passes own environment */

execv("/bin/ps", ps_argv);
execvp("ps", ps_argv);
execve("/bin/ps", ps_argv, ps_envp);
```

Try It Out - execlp

Let's modify our example to use an execlp call.

```
#include <unistd.h>
#include <stdio.h>

int main()
{
    printf("Running ps with execlp\n");
    execlp("ps", "ps", "-ax", 0);
    printf("Done.\n");
    exit(0);
}
```

When we run this program, pexec.c, we get the usual ps output, but no Done. message at all. Note also that there is no reference to a process called pexec in the output.

```
$ ./pexec
Running ps with execlp
  PID TTY STAT  TIME COMMAND
    1  ?  S     0:00 init
    7  ?  S     0:00 update (bdflush)
...
  146 v01 S N   0:00 oclock
  294 pp0 R     0:00 ps -ax
```

How It Works

The program prints its first message and then calls execlp, which searches the directories given by the PATH environment variable for a program called ps. It then executes this program in place of our pexec program, starting it as if we had given the shell command:

```
$ ps -ax
```

When ps finishes, we get a new shell prompt. We don't return to pexec, so the second message doesn't get printed. The PID of the new process is the same as the original, as are the parent PID and nice value. In effect, all that has happened is that the running program has started to execute new code from a new executable file specified in the call to exec.

There is a limit on the combined size of the argument list and environment for a process started by exec functions. This is given by ARG_MAX and on Linux systems is 128k bytes. Other systems may set a much reduced limit that can lead to problems. The POSIX specification indicates that ARG_MAX should be at least 4096 bytes.

The exec functions generally don't return unless an error occurs, in which case the error variable errno is set and the exec function returns -1.

The new process started by exec inherits many features from the original. In particular, open file descriptors remain open in the new process, unless their 'close on exec flag' has been set (refer to the fcntl system call in Chapter 3 for more details). Any open directory streams in the original process are closed.

Duplicating a Process Image

To use processes to perform more than one function at a time, we can either use threads, covered in the next chapter, or we need to create an entirely separate process from within a program, as `init` does, rather than replace the current thread of execution, as in the `exec` case.

We can create a new process by calling `fork`. This system call duplicates the current process, creating a new entry in the process table with many of the same attributes as the current process. The new process is almost identical to the original, executing the same code but with its own data space, environment and file descriptors. Combined with the `exec` functions, `fork` is all we need to create new processes.

```
#include <sys/types.h>
#include <unistd.h>

pid_t fork(void);
```

The call to `fork` in the parent returns the PID of the new child process. The new process continues to execute just like the original, with the exception that in the child process the call to `fork` returns 0. This allows both the parent and child to determine which is which.

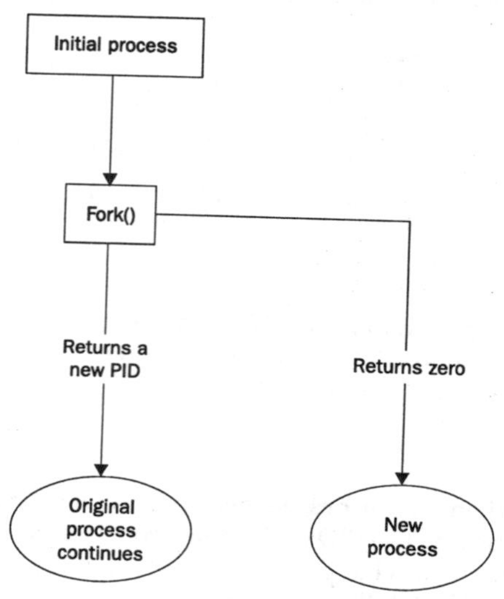

If `fork` fails, it returns -1. This is commonly due to a limit on the number of child processes that a parent may have (`CHILD_MAX`), in which case `errno` will be set to `EAGAIN`. If there is not enough space for an entry in the process table, or not enough virtual memory, the `errno` variable will be set to `ENOMEM`.

A typical code fragment using `fork` is:

```
pid_t new_pid;

new_pid = fork();

switch(new_pid) {
case -1 :       /* Error */
    break;
case 0 :        /* We are child */
    break;
default :       /* We are parent */
    break;
}
```

Try It Out - fork

Let's look at a simple example, fork.c.

```
#include <sys/types.h>
#include <unistd.h>
#include <stdio.h>

int main()
{
    pid_t pid;
    char *message;
    int n;

    printf("fork program starting\n");
    pid = fork();
    switch(pid)
    {
    case -1:
        perror("fork failed");
        exit(1);
    case 0:
        message = "This is the child";
        n = 5;
        break;
    default:
        message = "This is the parent";
        n = 3;
        break;
    }

    for(; n > 0; n--) {
        puts(message);
        sleep(1);
    }
    exit(0);
}
```

This program runs as two processes. A child is created (born?) and prints a message five times. The original process (the parent) prints a message only three times. The parent process finishes before the child has printed all of its messages, so we see the next shell prompt appear mixed in with the output.

```
$ ./fork
fork program starting
This is the parent
This is the child
This is the parent
This is the child
This is the parent
This is the child
$ This is the child
This is the child
```

How It Works

When fork is called, this program divides into two separate processes. The parent process is identified by a non-zero return from fork and is used to set a number of messages to print, each separated by one second.

Waiting for a Process

When we start a child process with `fork`, it takes on a life of its own and runs independently. Sometimes, we would like to find out when a child process has finished. For example, in the previous program, the parent finishes ahead of the child and we get some messy output as the child continues to run. We can arrange for the parent process to wait until the child finishes before continuing by calling `wait`.

```
#include <sys/types.h>
#include <sys/wait.h>

pid_t wait(int *stat_loc);
```

The `wait` system call causes a parent process to pause until one of its child processes is stopped. The call returns the PID of the child process. This will normally be a child process that has terminated. The status information allows the parent process to determine the exit status of the child process, i.e. the value returned from `main` or passed to `exit`. If `stat_loc` is not a null pointer, the status information will be written to the location to which it points.

We can interpret the status information using macros defined in `sys/wait.h`. These include:

Macro	Definition
`WIFEXITED(stat_val)`	Non-zero if the child is terminated normally.
`WEXITSTATUS(stat_val)`	If `WIFEXITED` is non-zero, this returns child exit code.
`WIFSIGNALED(stat_val)`	Non-zero if the child is terminated on an uncaught signal.
`WTERMSIG(stat_val)`	If `WIFSIGNALED` is non-zero, this returns a signal number.
`WIFSTOPPED(stat_val)`	Non-zero if the child has stopped.
`WSTOPSIG(stat_val)`	If `WIFSTOPPED` is non-zero, this returns a signal number.

Try It Out - wait

1. Let's modify our program slightly so we can wait for and examine the child process exit status. Call the new program `wait.c`.

```
#include <sys/types.h>
#include <sys/wait.h>
#include <unistd.h>
#include <stdio.h>

int main()
{
    pid_t pid;
    char *message;
    int n;
    int exit_code;

    printf("fork program starting\n");
    pid = fork();
    switch(pid)
    {
```

```
    case -1:
        perror("fork failed");
        exit(1);
    case 0:
        message = "This is the child";
        n = 5;
        exit_code = 37;
        break;
    default:
        message = "This is the parent";
        n = 3;
        exit_code = 0;
        break;
    }

    for(; n > 0; n--) {
        puts(message);
        sleep(1);
    }
```

This section of the program waits for the child process to finish.

```
    if (pid != 0) {
        int stat_val;
        pid_t child_pid;

        child_pid = wait(&stat_val);

        printf("Child has finished: PID = %d\n", child_pid);
        if(WIFEXITED(stat_val))
            printf("Child exited with code %d\n", WEXITSTATUS(stat_val));
        else
            printf("Child terminated abnormally\n");
    }
    exit(exit_code);
}
```

When we run this program, we see the parent wait for the child.

```
$ ./wait
fork program starting
This is the parent
This is the child
This is the parent
This is the child
This is the parent
This is the child
This is the child
This is the child
Child has finished: PID = 410
Child exited with code 37
$
```

How It Works

The parent process (which got a non-zero return from the `fork` call) uses the `wait` system call to suspend its own execution until status information becomes available for a child process. This happens when the child calls `exit`; we gave it an exit code of 37. The parent then continues, determines that the child terminated normally by testing the return value of the `wait` call and extracts the exit code from the status information.

Zombie Processes

Using `fork` to create processes can be very useful, but you must keep track of child processes. When a child process terminates, an association with its parent survives until the parent in turn either terminates normally or calls `wait`. The child process entry in the process table is therefore not freed up immediately. Although no longer active, the child process is still in the system because its exit code needs to be stored in case the parent subsequently calls `wait`. It becomes what is known as a **zombie process**.

We can see a zombie process being created if we change the number of messages in the fork example program. If the child prints fewer messages than the parent, it will finish first and will exist as a zombie until the parent has finished.

Try It Out - Zombies

`fork2.c` is the same as `fork.c`, except that the number of messages printed by the child and parent processes is reversed. Here are the relevant lines of code.

```
switch(pid)
{
case -1:
    perror("fork failed");
    exit(1);
case 0:
    message = "This is the child";
    n = 3;
    break;
default:
    message = "This is the parent";
    n = 5;
    break;
}
```

How It Works

If we run the above program with `fork2 &` and then call the `ps` program after the child has finished but before the parent has finished, we'll see a line like this. (Non-Linux systems will usually say `<defunct>` rather than `<zombie>`.)

```
PID TTY STAT  TIME COMMAND

420 pp0 Z     0:00 (fork2) <zombie>
```

If the parent then terminates abnormally, the child process automatically gets the process with PID 1 (`init`) as parent. The child process is now a zombie which is no longer running, but which has been inherited by `init` because of the abnormal termination of the parent process. The zombie will remain in the process table until collected by the `init` process, when it's removed from the process table. The bigger the table, the slower this procedure. You need to avoid zombie processes, as they consume resource until `init` cleans them up.

There's another system call that you can use to wait for child processes. It's called `waitpid` and you can use it to wait for a specific process to terminate.

```
#include <sys/types.h>
#include <sys/wait.h>

pid_t waitpid(pid_t pid, int *stat_loc, int options);
```

The pid argument specifies the PID of a particular child process to wait for. If it's -1, waitpid will return information for any child process. Like wait, it will write status information to the location pointed to by stat_loc, if that is not a null pointer. The options argument allows us to modify the behavior of waitpid. The most useful option is WNOHANG, which prevents the call to waitpid from suspending execution of the caller. You can use it to find out whether any child processes have terminated and, if not, to continue. Other options are the same as for wait.

So if we wanted to have a parent process regularly check whether a specific child process has terminated, we could use the call,

```
waitpid(child_pid, (int *) 0, WNOHANG);
```

This will return zero if the child has not terminated or stopped, or child_pid if it has. waitpid will return -1 on error and set errno. This can happen if there are no child processes (errno set to ECHILD), if the call is interrupted by a signal (EINTR), or if the option argument is invalid (EINVAL).

Input and Output Redirection

We can use our knowledge of processes to alter the behavior of programs by exploiting the fact that open file descriptors are preserved across calls to fork and exec. The next example involves a filter program, that is a program that reads from its standard input and writes to its standard output, performing some useful transformation as it does so.

Try It Out - Redirection

Here's a very simple filter program, upper.c, that reads input and converts it to uppercase.

```
#include <stdio.h>
#include <ctype.h>

int main()
{
    int ch;
    while((ch = getchar()) != EOF) {
        putchar(toupper(ch));
    }
    exit(0);
}
```

```
$ ./upper
hello THERE
HELLO THERE
^D
$
```

We can, of course, use it to convert a file to uppercase by using the shell redirection:

```
$ cat file.txt
this is the file, file.txt, it is all lower case.
$ upper < file.txt
THIS IS THE FILE, FILE.TXT, IT IS ALL LOWER CASE.
```

What if we want to use this filter from within another program? This program, `useupper.c`, accepts a file name as an argument and will respond with an error if called incorrectly.

```
#include <unistd.h>
#include <stdio.h>

int main(int argc, char *argv[])
{
    char *filename;

    if (argc != 2) {
        fprintf(stderr, "usage: useupper file\n");
        exit(1);
    }

    filename = argv[1];
```

We reopen the standard input, again checking for any errors as we do so, and then use `execl` to call `upper`.

```
    if(!freopen(filename, "r", stdin)) {
        fprintf(stderr, "could not redirect stdin from file %s\n", filename);
        exit(2);
    }

    execl("./upper", "upper", 0);
```

Don't forget that `execl` replaces the current process; if there is no error, the remaining lines are not executed.

```
    perror("could not exec ./upper");
    exit(3);
}
```

How It Works

When we run this program, we can give it a file to convert to uppercase. The job is done by the program `upper`, which doesn't handle file name arguments. Note that we don't require the source code for `upper`; we can run any executable program in this way.

```
$ ./useupper file.txt
THIS IS THE FILE, FILE.TXT, IT IS ALL LOWER CASE.
```

The `useupper` program uses `freopen` to close the standard input and associate the file stream `stdin` with the file given as a program argument. It then calls `execl` to replace the running process code with that of the upper program. Because open file descriptors are preserved across the call to `execl`, the upper program runs exactly as it would have under the shell command:

```
$ upper < file.txt
```

Threads

UNIX processes can cooperate; they can send each other messages and they can interrupt one another. They can even arrange to share segments of memory between themselves, but they are essentially separate entities within the operating system. They do not readily share variables.

There is a class of process known as a **thread** available in many UNIX and Linux systems. While threads can be difficult to program, they can be of great value in some applications, such as a multithreaded database servers. Programming threads on Linux (and UNIX generally) is not as common as using multiple processes, because UNIX processes are quite light weight, and programming multiple co-operation processes is much easier than programming threads. Threads are covered in the next chapter.

Signals

A **signal** is an event generated by the UNIX system in response to some condition, upon receipt of which a process may in turn take some action. Signals are generated by some error conditions, such as memory segment violations, floating point processor errors or illegal instructions. They are generated by the shell and terminal handlers to cause interrupts. They can also be explicitly sent from one process to another as a way of passing information or modifying behavior. In all these cases, the programming interface is the same. Signals can be generated, caught and acted upon, or (for some at least) ignored. Signal names are defined by including the header file `signal.h`. They all begin with "SIG" and include:

Signal Name	Description
SIGABORT	*Process abort.
SIGALRM	Alarm clock.
SIGFPE	*Floating point exception.
SIGHUP	Hangup.
SIGILL	*Illegal instruction.
SIGINT	Terminal interrupt.
SIGKILL	Kill (can't be caught or ignored).
SIGPIPE	Write on a pipe with no reader.
SIGQUIT	Terminal quit.
SIGSEGV	*Invalid memory segment access.
SIGTERM	Termination.
SIGUSR1	User-defined signal 1.
SIGUSR2	User-defined signal 2.

If a process receives one of these signals without first arranging to catch it, the process will be terminated immediately. For signals marked with a *, implementation-dependent actions may also be taken. Usually, a core dump file is created. This file, called core and placed in the current directory, is an image of the process that can be useful in debugging.

Additional signals include:

Signal Name	Description
SIGCHLD	Child process has stopped or exited.
SIGCONT	Continue executing, if stopped.
SIGSTOP	Stop executing. (Can't be caught or ignored.)
SIGTSTP	Terminal stop signal.
SIGTTIN	Background process trying to read.
SIGTTOU	Background process trying to write.

`SIGCHLD` can be useful for managing child processes. It's ignored by default. The remaining signals cause the process receiving them to stop, except for `SIGCONT` which causes the process to resume. They are used by shell programs for job control and are rarely used by user programs.

We'll look at the first group of signals in a little more detail later, but for now, it's enough to know that if the shell and terminal driver are configured normally, typing the interrupt character (often *Ctrl-C*) at the keyboard will result in the `SIGINT` signal being sent to the foreground process, i.e. the program currently running. This will cause the program to terminate unless it has arranged to catch the signal.

If we want to send a signal to a process other than the current foreground task, we use the `kill` command. This takes an optional signal number or name, and the PID (usually found using the `ps` command) to send the signal too. For example, to send a 'hangup' signal to a shell running on a different terminal with process id 512, we would use the command.

```
kill -HUP 512
```

A useful variant of the `kill` command is `killall`, which allows you to send a signal to all processes running a specified command. Not all versions of UNIX support it, though Linux generally does. This is useful when you do not know the PID, or when you want to send a signal to several different processes executing the same command. A common use is to tell the `inetd` program to re-read it's configuration options. (We will meet `inetd` again in chapter 14.) To do this we can use the command:

```
killall -HUP inetd
```

Programs can handle signals using the signal library function.

```
#include <signal.h>

void (*signal(int sig, void (*func)(int)))(int);
```

This rather complex declaration says that `signal` is a function that takes two parameters, `sig` and `func`. The signal to be caught or ignored is given as argument `sig`. The function to be called when the specified signal is received is given as `func`. This function must be one that takes a single `int` argument (the signal received) and is of type `void`. The signal function itself returns a function of the same type, which is the previous value of the function set up to handle this signal, or one of these two special values:

SIG_IGN	Ignore the signal.
SIG_DFL	Restore default behavior.

An example should make things clear. Let's write a program, `ctrlc.c`, that reacts to *Ctrl-C* by printing an appropriate message rather than terminating. A second *Ctrl-C* will end the program.

Try It Out - Signal Handling

The function `ouch` reacts to the signal which is passed in the parameter `sig`. This function will be called when a signal occurs. It prints a message and then resets the signal handling for `SIGINT` (by default generated by pressing *Ctrl-C*) back to the default behavior.

```
#include <signal.h>
#include <stdio.h>
#include <unistd.h>

void ouch(int sig)
{
    printf("OUCH! - I got signal %d\n", sig);
    (void) signal(SIGINT, SIG_DFL);
}
```

The `main` function has to intercept the `SIGINT` signal generated when we type *Ctrl-C*. For the rest of the time, it just sits in an infinite loop printing a message once a second.

```
int main()
{
    (void) signal(SIGINT, ouch);

    while(1) {
        printf("Hello World!\n");
        sleep(1);
    }
}
```

Typing *Ctrl-C* for the first time causes the program to react and then continue. When we type *Ctrl-C* again, the program ends, because the behavior of `SIG_ING` has returned to the default behavior of causing the program to exit.

```
$ ./ctrlc
Hello World!
Hello World!
Hello World!
Hello World!
^C
OUCH! - I got signal 2
Hello World!
Hello World!
Hello World!
Hello World!
^C
$
```

As you can see from this example, the signal handling function takes a single integer parameter, the signal number that caused the function to be called. This can be useful if the same function is used to handle more than one signal. Here, we print out the value of `SIGINT`, which on this system happens to have the value 2. You shouldn't rely on traditional numeric values for signals; always use signal names in new programs.

> **Normally, when you call `printf` inside a signal handler, you need to set a flag in the signal handler and then check the flag later. Towards the end of the chapter you will find a list of calls than can safely be made inside signal handlers.**

How It Works

The program arranges for the function `ouch` to be called when we give the `SIGINT` signal by typing *Ctrl-C*, which. After the interrupt function `ouch` has completed, the program carries on, but the signal action is restored to the default. (Different versions of UNIX, particularly those derived from Berkley UNIX, have historically had subtly different signal behaviors. If you want the default action to a signal restored after it has occurred, it's always best to specifically code it that way.) When it receives a second `SIGINT` signal, the program takes the default action, which is to terminate the program.

If we wished to retain the signal handler and continue to react to *Ctrl-C*, we would need to re-establish it by calling `signal` again. This leads to a short time when the signal is not handled, from the start of the interrupt function to just before the signal handler is re-established. It's possible for a second signal to be received in this time and terminate the program against our wishes.

> **We don't recommend that you use the `signal` interface. We include it here because you will find it in many older programs. We'll see `sigaction`, a more cleanly defined and reliable interface later, which you should use in all new programs.**

The `signal` function returns the previous value of the signal handler for the specified signal if there is one, or `SIG_ERR` otherwise, in which case, `errno` will be set to a positive value. `errno` will be set to `EINVAL` if an invalid signal is specified or an attempt is made to handle a signal that may not be caught or ignored, such as `SIGKILL`.

Sending Signals

A process may send a signal to another process, including itself, by calling `kill`. The call will fail if the program doesn't have permission to send the signal, commonly because the target process is owned by another user. This is the program equivalent of the shell command of the same name.

```
#include <sys/types.h>
#include <signal.h>

int kill(pid_t pid, int sig);
```

The `kill` function sends the specified signal, `sig`, to the process whose identifier is given by `pid`. It returns 0 on success. To send a signal, the sending process must have permission to do so. Normally, this means that both processes must have the same user ID, i.e. you can only send a signal to one of your own processes, although the superuser may send signals to any process.

kill will fail, return -1 and set errno if the signal given is not a valid one (errno set to EINVAL), if it doesn't have permission (EPERM) or if the specified process doesn't exist (ESRCH).

Signals provide us with a useful alarm clock facility. The alarm function call can be used by a process to schedule a SIGALRM signal at some time in the future.

```
#include <unistd.h>

unsigned int alarm(unsigned int seconds);
```

The alarm call schedules the delivery of a SIGALRM signal in seconds seconds' time. In fact, the alarm will be delivered shortly after that, due to processing delays and scheduling uncertainties. A value of 0 will cancel any outstanding alarm request. Calling alarm before the signal is received will cause the alarm to be rescheduled. Each process can have only one outstanding alarm. alarm returns the number of seconds left before any outstanding alarm call would be sent, or –1 if the call fails.

To see how alarm works, we can simulate its effect by using fork, sleep and signal. A program could start a new process for the sole purpose of sending a signal at some time later.

Try It Out - An Alarm Clock

1. In alarm.c, the first function, ding, simulates an alarm clock.

```
#include <sys/types.h>
#include <signal.h>
#include <stdio.h>
#include <unistd.h>

static int alarm_fired = 0;

void ding(int sig)
{
alarm_fired = 1;
}
```

2. In main, we tell the child process to wait for five seconds before sending a SIGALRM signal to its parent.

```
pid_t pid;

    printf("alarm application starting\n");

    pid = fork();
    switch(pid) {
    case -1:
      /* Failure */
      perror("fork failed");
      exit(1);
    case 0:
        /* child */
        sleep(5);
        kill(getppid(), SIGALRM);
        exit(0);
    }
```

3. The parent process arranges to catch SIGALRM with a call to signal and then waits for the inevitable.

```
    /* if we get here we are the parent process */
    printf("waiting for alarm to go off\n");
    (void) signal(SIGALRM, ding);

    pause();
    if (alarm_fired) printf("Ding!\n");

    printf("done\n");
    exit(0);
}
```

When we run this program, it pauses for five seconds while it waits for the simulated alarm clock.

```
$ ./alarm
alarm application starting
waiting for alarm to go off
<5 second pause>
Ding!
done
$
```

This program introduces a new function, `pause`, which simply causes the program to suspend execution until a signal occurs. When it receives a signal, any established handler is run and execution continues as normal. It's declared as:

```
#include <unistd.h>

int pause(void);
```

and returns -1 (if the next received signal doesn't cause the program to terminate) with `errno` set to `EINTR` when interrupted by a signal. It is more common to use `sigsuspend` when waiting for signals, which we will meet in a minute.

How It Works

The alarm clock simulation program starts a new process via `fork`. This child process sleeps for five seconds and then sends a `SIGALRM` to its parent. The parent arranges to catch `SIGALRM` and then pauses until a signal is received. We do not call `printf` in the signal handler directly, rather we set a flag and then check the flag afterwards.

Using signals and suspending execution is an important part of UNIX programming. It means that a program need not necessarily run all the time. Rather than run in a loop continually checking whether an event has occurred, it can wait for an event to happen. This is especially important in a multiuser environment where processes share a single processor and this kind of busy wait has a large impact on system performance. A particular problem with signals is "what happens if a signal occurs in the middle of a system call?" The answer is rather messily 'it depends'. In general, you only need to worry about 'slow' system calls, such as reading from a terminal, where the system call will return with an error if a signal occurs while it is waiting. If you start using signals in your program you need to be aware that some system calls could now fail because a signal has received, a possible error condition that you may not have considered before signal handling was added.

You must program your signals carefully, as there are a number of 'race conditions' that can occur in programs that use them. For example, if you intend to call pause to wait for a signal and that signal occurs before the call to pause, your program may wait indefinitely for an event that won't occur. These race conditions, critical timing problems, catch many a novice programmer. Always check signal code very carefully.

A Robust Signals Interface

We've covered raising and catching signals using `signal` and friends in some depth, because they are very common in UNIX programs. However, the X/Open and UNIX specifications recommends a newer programming interface for signals that is more robust: `sigaction`.

```
#include <signal.h>

int sigaction(int sig, const struct sigaction *act, struct sigaction *oact);
```

The `sigaction` structure, used to define the actions to be taken on receipt of the signal specified by `sig`, is defined in `signal.h` and has at least the following members.

```
void (*) (int) sa_handler     /*  function, SIG_DFL or SIG_IGN
sigset_t sa_mask              /*  signals to block in sa_handler
int sa_flags                  /*  signal action modifiers
```

The `sigaction` function sets the action associated with the signal `sig`. If `oact` is not null, `sigaction` writes the previous signal action to the location it refers to. If `act` is null, this is all `sigaction` does. If `act` isn't null, the action for the specified signal is set.

As with signal, `sigaction` returns 0 if successful and -1 if not. The error variable `errno` will be set to `EINVAL` if the specified signal is invalid or if an attempt is made to catch or ignore a signal that can't be caught or ignored.

Within the `sigaction` structure pointed to by the argument `act`, `sa_handler` is a pointer to a function called when signal `sig` is received. This is much like the function `func` we saw earlier passed to signal. We can use the special values `SIG_IGN` and `SIG_DFL` in the `sa_handler` field to indicate that the signal is to be ignored or the action is to be restored to its default respectively.

The `sa_mask` field specifies a set of signals to be added to the process' signal mask before the `sa_handler` function is called. These are the set of signals that are blocked and won't be delivered to the process. This prevents the case we saw earlier where a signal is received before its handler has run to completion. Using the `sa_mask` field can eliminate this race condition.

However, signals caught with handlers set by `sigaction` are by default not reset and the `sa_flags` field must be set to contain the value `SA_RESETHAND` if we wish to obtain the behavior we saw earlier with signal. Before we look in any more detail at `sigaction`, let's rewrite the program `ctrlc.c`, using `sigaction` instead of signal.

Try It Out - sigaction

Make the changes shown below so that SIGINT is intercepted by sigaction. We will call the new program ctrlc2.c.

```
#include <signal.h>
#include <stdio.h>
#include <unistd.h>

void ouch(int sig)
{
    printf("OUCH! - I got signal %d\n", sig);
}

int main()
{
    struct sigaction act;

    act.sa_handler = ouch;
    sigemptyset(&act.sa_mask);
    act.sa_flags = 0;

    sigaction(SIGINT, &act, 0);

  while(1) {
    printf("Hello World!\n");
    sleep(1);
  }
}
```

When we run this version of the program, we always get a message when we type *Ctrl-C* because SIGINT is handled repeatedly by sigaction. To terminate the program, we have to type *Ctrl-*, which generates the SIGQUIT signal by default.

```
$ ./ctrlc2
Hello World!
Hello World!
Hello World!
^C
OUCH! - I got signal 2
Hello World!
Hello World!
^C
OUCH! - I got signal 2
Hello World!
Hello World!
^\
Quit
$
```

How It Works

The program calls sigaction instead of signal to set the signal handler for *Ctrl-C* (SIGINT) to the function ouch. It first has to set up a sigaction structure that contains the handler, a signal mask and flags. In this case, we don't need any flags and an empty signal mask is created with the new function sigemptyset.

After running this program you will find a file called core has been created. You can safely delete it.

Signal Sets

The header file signal.h defines the type sigset_t and functions used to manipulate sets of signals. These sets are used in sigaction and other functions to modify process behavior on receipt of signals.

```
#include <signal.h>

int sigaddset(sigset_t *set, int signo);
int sigemptyset(sigset_t *set);
int sigfillset(sigset_t *set);
int sigdelset(sigset_t *set, int signo);
```

These functions perform the operations suggested by their names. sigemptyset initializes a signal set to be empty. sigfillset initializes a signal set to contain all defined signals. sigaddset and sigdelset add and delete a specified signal (signo) from a signal set. They all return 0 if successful and -1 with errno set on error. The only error defined is EINVAL if the specified signal is invalid.

The function sigismember determines whether the given signal is a member of a signal set. It returns 1 if the signal is a member of the set, 0 if it isn't and -1 with errno set to EINVAL if the signal is invalid.

```
#include <signal.h>

int sigismember(sigset_t *set, int signo);
```

The process signal mask is set or examined by calling the function sigprocmask. This signal mask is the set of signals that are currently blocked and will therefore not be received by the current process.

```
#include <signal.h>

int sigprocmask(int how, const sigset_t *set, sigset_t *oset);
```

sigprocmask can change the process signal mask in a number of ways according to the how argument. New values for the signal mask are passed in the argument set, if it isn't null, and the previous signal mask will be written to the signal set oset.

The how argument can be one of:

SIG_BLOCK	The signals in set are added to the signal mask.
SIG_SETMASK	The signal mask is set from set.
SIG_UNBLOCK	The signals in set are removed from the signal mask.

If the set argument is a null pointer, the value of how is not used and the only purpose of the call is to fetch the value of the current signal mask into oset.

If it completes successfully, sigprocmask returns 0, or it returns -1 if the how parameter is invalid, in which case errno will be set to EINVAL.

If a signal is blocked by a process, it won't be delivered, but will remain pending. A program can determine which of its blocked signals are pending by calling the function sigpending.

```
#include <signal.h>

int sigpending(sigset_t *set);
```

This writes a set of signals that are blocked from delivery and are pending into the signal set pointed to by set. It returns 0 if successful, otherwise -1 with errno set to indicate the error. This function can be useful when a program needs to handle signals and to control when the handling function is called.

A process can suspend execution until the delivery of one of a set of signals by calling sigsuspend. This is a more general form of the pause function we met earlier.

```
#include <signal.h>

int sigsuspend(const sigset_t *sigmask);
```

The sigsuspend function replaces the process signal mask with the signal set given by sigmask and then suspends execution. It will resume after the execution of a signal handling function. If the received signal terminates the program, sigsuspend will never return. If a received signal doesn't terminate the program, sigsuspend returns -1 with errno set to EINTR.

sigaction Flags

The sa_flags field of the sigaction structure used in sigaction may contain the following values to modify signal behavior.

SA_NOCLDSTOP	Don't generate SIGCHLD when child processes stop.
SA_RESETHAND	Reset signal action to SIG_DFL on receipt.
SA_RESTART	Restart interruptible functions rather than error with EINTR.
SA_NODEFER	Don't add the signal to the signal mask when caught.

The SA_RESETHAND flag can be used to automatically clear a signal function when a signal is caught, as we saw before.

Many system calls that a program uses are interruptible, i.e. when they receive a signal they will return with an error and errno will be set to EINTR to indicate that the function returned due to a signal. This behavior requires extra care by an application using signals. If SA_RESTART is set in the sa_flags field in a call to sigaction, a function that might otherwise be interrupted by a signal will instead be restarted once the signal handling function has been executed.

Ordinarily, when a signal handling function is being executed, the signal received is added to the process signal mask for the duration of the handling function. This prevents a subsequent occurrence of the same signal, causing the signal handling function to run again. If the function is not re-entrant, having it called by another occurrence of a signal before it finished handling the first may cause problems. If, however, the SA_NODEFER flag is set, the signal mask is not altered when it receives this signal.

A signal-handling function could be interrupted in the middle and called again by something else. When you come back to the first call, it's vital that it still operates correctly. It's not just recursive (calling itself), but re-entrant (can be entered and executed again without problems). Interrupt service routines in the kernel that deal with more than one device at a time need to be re-entrant, as a higher priority interrupt might 'get in' during the execution of the same code.

Functions that are safe to call inside a signal handler, those guaranteed by the X/Open specification either to be re-entrant or not to raise signals themselves are listed below.

All functions not listed below should be considered to be unsafe with respect to signals.

access	alarm	cfgetispeed	cfgetospeed
cfsetispeed	cfsetospeed	chdir	chmod
chown	close	creat	dup2
dup	execle	execve	_exit
fcntl	fork	fstat	getegid
geteuid	getgid	getgroups	getpgrp
getpid	getppid	getuid	kill
link	lseek	mkdir	mkfifo
open	pathconf	pause	pipe
read	rename	rmdir	setgid
setpgid	setsid	setuid	sigaction
sigaddset	sigdelset	sigemptyset	sigfillset
sigismember	signal	sigpending	sigprocmask
sigsuspend	sleep	stat	sysconf
tcdrain	tcflow	tcflush	tcgetattr
tcgetpgrp	tcsendbreak	tcsetattr	tcsetpgrp
time	times	umask	uname
unlink	utime	wait	waitpid
write			

Common Signal Reference

In this section, we list the signals that UNIX programs typically need with their default behaviors.

The default action for the signals in the following table is abnormal termination of the process with all the consequences of `_exit` (which is like `exit` but performs no cleanup before returning to the kernel). However the status is made available to `wait` and `waitpid` indicates abnormal termination by the specified signal.

Signal Name	Description
SIGALRM	Generated by the timer set by the `alarm` function.
SIGHUP	Sent to the controlling process by a disconnecting terminal, or by the controlling process on termination to each foreground process.
SIGINT	Typically raised from the terminal by typing *Ctrl-C* or the configured interrupt character.
SIGKILL	Typically used from the shell to forcibly terminate an errant process as this signal can't be caught or ignored.
SIGPIPE	Generated by an attempt to write to a pipe with no associated reader.
SIGTERM	Sent as a request for a process to finish. Used by UNIX when shutting down to request that system services stop. This is the default signal sent from the kill command.
SIGUSR1, SIGUSR2	May be used by processes to communicate with each other, possibly to cause them to report status information.

By default, the signals in the next table also cause abnormal termination. Additionally, implementation-dependent actions, such as creation of a core file, may occur.

Signal Name	Description
SIGFPE	Generated by a floating point arithmetic exception.
SIGILL	An illegal instruction has been executed by the processor. Usually caused by a corrupt program or invalid shared memory module.
SIGQUIT	Typically raised from the terminal by typing *Ctrl-* or the configured quit character.
SIGSEGV	A segmentation violation, usually caused by reading or writing at an illegal location in memory either by exceeding array bounds or de-referencing an invalid pointer. Overwriting a local array variable and corrupting the stack can cause a `SIGSEGV` to be raised when a function returns to an illegal address.

A process is suspended by default on receipt of one of the signals in the following table.

Signal Name	Description
SIGSTOP	Stop executing (can't be caught or ignored).
SIGTSTP	Terminal stop signal, often raised by typing *Ctrl-Z*.
SIGTTIN, SIGTTOU	Used by the shell to indicate that background jobs have stopped because they need to read from the terminal or produce output.

SIGCONT restarts a stopped process and is ignored if received by a process which is not stopped. The SIGCHLD signal is ignored by default.

Signal Name	Description
SIGCONT	Continue executing, if stopped.
SIGCHLD	Raised when a child process stops or exits.

Summary

In this chapter, we have seen how processes are a fundamental part of the UNIX operating system. We have learned how they can be started, terminated and viewed and how we can use them to solve programming problems.

We've also taken a look at signals, events that can be used to control the actions of running programs. What we have seen is that all UNIX utilities, down to and including `init`, use the same set of system calls available to any programmer.

POSIX Threads

In the previous chapter, we saw how processes are handled in Linux (and indeed in UNIX). These multi-processing features have long been a feature of UNIX type operating systems. Sometimes the overhead of creating a new process with `fork` is considered too great. Then it would be very useful to make a single program do two things at once, or at least to appear to do so. Alternatively, you might want two or more things to happen at the same time in a closely coupled way.

What is a Thread?

Multiple strands of execution in a single program are called **threads**. A more precise definition would be that a thread is 'a sequence of control within a process'. All the programs we have seen so far have executed as a single process, although Linux, like many other operating systems, is quite capable of running multiple processes simultaneously. Indeed all processes have at least one thread of execution. All the processes that we have seen so far have had just one thread of execution.

It's important to be clear about the difference between the `fork` system call and the creation of new threads. When a process executes a `fork` call, a new copy of the process is created with its own variables and its own PID. This new process is scheduled independently, and (in general) executes almost completely independently of the process that created it. When we create a new thread in a process, the new thread of execution gets its own stack (and hence local variables) but shares global variables, file descriptors, signal handlers and its current directory state with its creator.

The idea of threads has been around for some time, but until the IEEE POSIX committee published some standards, they had not been widely available in UNIX type operating systems, and the implementations that did exist tended to vary between different vendors. With the advent of the POSIX 1003.1c specification all that has changed; threads are not only better standardized, but also available on most Linux distributions.

Advantages and Drawbacks of Threads

Creating a new thread has some distinct advantages over creating a new process in certain circumstances. The overhead of creating a new thread is significantly less than that of creating a new process. (Though Linux is particularly efficient at creating new processes compared to some other operating systems.)

Sometimes it is very useful to make a program appear to do two things at once. The classic example is to perform a real-time word count on a document, while still editing the text. One thread can manage the user's input and perform editing. The other, which can still see the same document content, can continuously update a word count variable. The first thread (or even a third one) can use this shared variable to keep the user informed. A perhaps more realistic example is a multithreaded database server, where an apparent single process serves multiple clients, improving the overall data throughput by servicing some requests while others are blocked waiting for disk activity. For a database server, this apparent multitasking is quite hard to do efficiently in different processes, because the requirements for locking and data consistency cause the different processes to be very tightly coupled. This can be done much more easily with multiple threads than multiple processes.

Threads do have drawbacks. Since they are relatively new, they are not as widely available as longer established features. Writing multithreaded programs requires very careful thought. The potential for introducing subtle timing faults, or faults caused by the unintentional sharing of variables, in a multithreaded program is considerable. Debugging a multithreaded program is much harder than a single threaded one.

A program that splits a large calculation into two and runs the two parts as different threads will not necessarily run quicker on a single processor machine, as there are only so many CPU cycles to be had!

However, threads undoubtedly do have their uses. For example, the performance of an application that mixes input, calculation and output may be improved by running these as three separate threads. While the input or output thread is waiting for a connection, one of the other threads can continue. Thus while any application can ultimately only do one thing at a time, threads enable an application to do something useful while it waits for such things as connections.

Switching between threads, at least in theory, requires the operating system to do much less work than switching between processes. Thus threads are much less demanding on resources than processes, and it is more practical to run programs that logically require many threads of executions on single processor systems. In practice this may not always be true. Indeed, on Linux, which implements threads via a `clone` system call, a new thread in a process is very similar 'under the hood' to a new process. To most users of course it doesn't matter how it's implemented so long as it works, but you should be aware that using threads to save the overhead of a process is not a strong argument under Linux.

In this chapter, we are going to look at:

- Checking for thread support on your platform
- Creating new threads within a process
- Synchronizing data access between threads in a single process
- Modifying the attributes of a thread
- Controlling one thread from another in the same process.

Checking for Thread Support

Before using threads, it's sensible to check that the setup actually has support for threads, and is compliant with the POSIX standard. When your C compiler compiles code, it sets some constants internally, and the header files that you include in your program add some more. By checking what definitions are in place in the code when it gets compiled we can check quite a lot about the compiler and libraries, most interestingly in this case their support for threads.

We can do this check in two ways, the difficult way and the easy way. The difficult way is to scour the headers files, such as `limits.h`, `unistd.h` and (more specific to Linux systems) `features.h`. The easy way is to write a very short program, compile it and see what we get.

We are going to do it the easy way! The definition we are interested in is the value `_POSIX_VERSION`. If it's not defined at all, there is no POSIX support at all. If it is defined, it takes one of various values telling us what level of support is present. The value we want for full thread support is `199506L` or higher. However, even if `_POSIX_VERSION` has a lower value, there may still be some thread support and it may still be possible to do most of the examples in this chapter.

Try it out - POSIX compliance test

Let's find out the level of POSIX support. This is `thread1.c`. It doesn't do anything other than test for threads support in the libraries that you use when compiling a program.

```
#include <stdio.h>
#include <unistd.h>
#include <stdlib.h>

int main() {
    printf("POSIX version is set to %ld\n", _POSIX_VERSION);
    if (_POSIX_VERSION < 199506L) {
        if (_POSIX_C_SOURCE >= 199506L) {
            printf("Sorry, you system does not support POSIX1003.1c threads\n");
        }
        else {
            printf("Try again with -D_POSIX_C_SOURCE=199506L\n");
        }
    }
    else {
        printf("Your system supports POSIX1003.1c threads,\n");
        #ifdef _POSIX_THREAD_PRIORITY_SCHEDULING
            printf("including support for priority scheduling\n");
        #else
            printf("but does not support priority scheduling\n");
        #endif
    }
    exit(EXIT_SUCCESS);
}
```

We include some standard headers and check the value of `_POSIX_VERSION`. Normally on Linux systems, the compiler defines `_POSIX_C_SOURCE` as a number greater than or equal to `199506L` automatically, and this causes other definitions to be set. We check that, if the `_POSIX_VERSION` check fails, the compiler has indeed set `_POSIX_C_SOURCE`. On both the authors' machines the result is:

```
$ ./thread1
POSIX version is set to 199506
Your system supports POSIX1003.1c threads,
including support for priority scheduling
```

If your setup did not report support, or failed to compile at all, you should try compiling the program again, setting _POSIX_C_SOURCE on the command line, like this:

```
cc -D_POSIX_C_SOURCE=199506L thread1.c -o thread1
```

If your system still doesn't report support for POSIX1003.1c threads, then you may not be able to test the examples in this chapter, or they may not all work exactly as specified.

How It works

The program simply tests the presence of defines when code is compiled after including some standard headers.

A First Threads Program

There is a whole set of library calls associated with threads, most of whose names start with pthread_. To use these library calls we must define the macro _REENTRANT, include the file pthread.h and link with the threads library using -lpthread.

When the original library routines where designed, it was assumed that there would only be a single thread of execution in any process. An obvious example is errno, the variable used for retrieving error information after a call fails. In a multithreaded program there would by default only be a single errno variable shared between all the threads. The variable could easily be updated by a call in one thread before a different thread has been able to retrieve a previous error code. Similar problems exits with functions such as fputs, which normally use a single global area for buffering output.

We need routines known as **re-entrant**. Re-entrant code can be called more than once, either by different threads, or called by nested invocations in some way, and still function correctly. Thus usually, the re-entrant section of code must only use local variables, in such a way that each and every call to the code gets it's own unique copy of the data.

In multithreaded programs, we tell the compiler that we need this feature by defining the macro _REENTRANT before any #include lines in our program. This does three things for us, and does them so elegantly that usually we don't even need to know what was done. Some functions get prototypes for a re-entrant safe equivalent. These are normally the same function name, but with _r appended so that, for example, gethostbyname is changed to gethostbyname_r. Some stdio.h functions that are normally implemented as macros become proper re-entrant safe functions. The variable errno, from errno.h, is changed to call a function, that can determine the real errno value in a multithread safe way.

Including the file pthread.h provides us with other definitions and prototypes that we will need in our code much like stdio.h for standard input and output routines. Finally, we need to link with the POSIX threads library, that implements the pthread functions.

pthread_create creates a new thread much as fork creates a new process.

```
#include <pthread.h>

int pthread_create(pthread_t *thread, pthread_attr_t *attr, void
*(*start_routine)(void *), void *arg);
```

This may look imposing, but it is actually quite easy to use. The first argument is a pointer to pthread_t. When a thread is created, an identifier is written to the variable to which this pointer points. This identifier enables us to refer to the thread. The next argument sets the thread attributes. You do not usually need any special attributes, and you can simply pass NULL as this argument. Later in the chapter, we will see how to use these attributes. The final two arguments tell the thread the function that it is to start executing and the arguments that are to be passed to this function.

```
void *(*start_routine)(void *)
```

is simply saying we must pass the address of a function taking a pointer to void as a parameter, and returning a pointer to void. Thus we can pass any type of single argument and return a pointer to any type. Using fork causes execution to continue in the same location with a different return code, whereas using a new thread explicitly provides a pointer to a function where the new thread should start execution.

The return value is 0 for success, or an error number if anything goes wrong. The manual pages have details of error conditions for this and other functions used in this chapter.

> **pthread_create, like most pthread_ functions, is among the few UNIX functions that do not follow the convention of using -1 for errors. Unless you are very sure, it's always safest to double check the manual before checking the error code.**

When a thread terminates, it calls the pthread_exit function, much like a process calls exit when it terminates. This function terminates the calling thread, returning a pointer to an object. Never use it to return a pointer to a local variable, which will cease to exist when the thread does causing a serious bug. pthread_exit is declared as follows.

```
#include <pthread.h>

void pthread_exit(void *retval);
```

pthread_join is the thread equivalent of wait that processes use to collect child processes. This function is declared as follows.

```
#include <pthread.h>

int pthread_join(pthread_t th, void **thread_return);
```

The first parameter is the thread for which to wait, the identifier that pthread_create filled in for us. The second argument is a pointer to a pointer to the return value from the thread. Like pthread_create this function returns zero for success and an error code on failure.

Try it out - a simple threaded program.

This program creates a single extra thread, shows that it is sharing variables with the original thread and gets the new thread to return a result to the original thread. Multithreaded programs don't get much simpler than this! Here is `thread2.c`.

```
#include <stdio.h>
#include <unistd.h>
#include <stdlib.h>
#include <pthread.h>

void *thread_function(void *arg);

char message[] = "Hello World";

int main() {
    int res;
    pthread_t a_thread;
    void *thread_result;

    res = pthread_create(&a_thread, NULL, thread_function, (void *)message);
    if (res != 0) {
        perror("Thread creation failed");
        exit(EXIT_FAILURE);
    }
    printf("Waiting for thread to finish...\n");
    res = pthread_join(a_thread, &thread_result);
    if (res != 0) {
        perror("Thread join failed");
        exit(EXIT_FAILURE);
    }
    printf("Thread joined, it returned %s\n", (char *)thread_result);
    printf("Message is now %s\n", message);
    exit(EXIT_SUCCESS);
}

void *thread_function(void *arg) {
    printf("thread_function is running. Argument was %s\n", (char *)arg);
    sleep(3);
    strcpy(message, "Bye!");
    pthread_exit("Thank you for the CPU time");
}
```

To compile this, you need to ensure that `_REENTRANT` is defined and that, if necessary, you have defined `_POSIX_C_SOURCE` yourself. On the authors' systems, we just need to define `_REENTRANT`, so the compile line is simply:

```
$ cc -D_REENTRANT thread2.c -o thread2 -lpthread
```

When you run this program, you should see:

```
$ ./thread2
Waiting for thread to finish...
thread_function is running. Argument was Hello World
Thread joined, it returned Thank you for the CPU time
Message is now Bye!
```

How it works.

We declare a prototype for the function that the thread will call when we create it.

```
void *thread_function(void *arg);
```

As required by `pthread_create`, it takes a pointer to `void` as its only argument and returns a pointer to `void`. We will come to the definition (and the implementation) of this function in a moment.

In `main`, we declare some variables, then call `pthread_create` to cause our new thread to start running.

```
    pthread_t a_thread;
    void *thread_result;

    res = pthread_create(&a_thread, NULL, thread_function, (void *)message);
```

We pass the address of a `pthread_t` object, that we can use to refer to the thread afterwards. We don't wish to modify the default thread attributes, so we pass `NULL` as the second parameter. The final two parameters are the function to call and a parameter to pass to it.

If the call succeeds, two threads are now running. The original thread (`main`) continues and executes the code after `pthread_create`, and a new thread starts executing in our imaginatively named `thread_function`.

The original thread checks that the new thread has started and then calls `pthread_join`.

```
    res = pthread_join(a_thread, &thread_result);
```

Here we pass the identifier of the thread that we are waiting to join and a pointer to a result. This function will wait until the other thread terminates before it returns. It then prints the return value from the thread, the contents of a variable, and exits.

The new thread starts executing in `thread_function`, prints out its arguments, sleeps for a short period, updates global variables and then exits returning a string to the main thread. The new thread writes to the same array, `message`, to which the original thread has access. This would not be so if we had called `fork` rather than `pthread_create`.

Simultaneous Execution

Next, we are going to write a program that checks that the execution of two threads occurs simultaneously (still, of course, on a single processor system, because the CPU is being cleverly switched between the threads). Since we haven't yet met any of the thread synchronization functions we need to do this efficiently, it will be a very inefficient program, that does what is known as a **polling** between the two threads. Again we will make use of the fact that everything except local function variables are shared between the different threads in a process.

Try it out - simultaneous execution of two threads

thread3.c is created by slightly modifying thread2.c. We add an extra file scope variable to test which thread is running.

```
int run_now = 1;
```

We will set run_now to 1 when the main function is executing, and 2 when our new thread is executing.

In the main function, after the creation of the new thread, we add the following code.

```
    int print_count1 = 0;

    while(print_count1++ < 20) {
        if (run_now == 1) {
            printf("1");
            run_now = 2;
        }
        else {
            sleep(1);
        }
    }
```

If run_now is 1, we print "1" and set it to 2. Otherwise, we sleep briefly and check the value again. We are waiting for the value to change to 1 by checking over and over again. This is called a "busy wait", although we have slowed it down by sleeping for a second between checks. We'll see a better way to do this later.

In thread_function, where our new thread is executing, we do much the same but with the values reversed.

```
    int print_count2 = 0;

    while(print_count2++ < 20) {
        if (run_now == 2) {
            printf("2");
            run_now = 1;
        }
        else {
            sleep(1);
        }
    }
```

We have also removed the parameter passing and return value passing, since we are no longer interested in them.

When we run the program, we see the following. (You may find that it takes a few seconds for the program to produce output.)

```
$ cc -D_REENTRANT thread3.c -o thread3 -lpthread
$ ./thread3
12121212121212121212
Waiting for thread to finish...
Thread joined
```

How it works.

Each thread tells the other one to run by setting the `run_now` variable and then waits till the other thread has changed it's value before running again. This shows that execution passes between the two threads automatically and again illustrates the point that both threads are sharing the `run_now` variable.

Synchronization

We saw that both threads are executing together, but our method of switching between them was clumsy and inefficient. Fortunately, there are a set functions specifically for giving us better ways to control the execution of threads and access to critical sections of code.

We will look at two basic methods here. The first is **semaphores**, which act like gatekeepers around a piece of code. The second is **mutexes**, which act as a mutual exclusion (hence mutex) device to protect sections of code.

Both are similar. (Indeed, one can be implemented in terms of the other.) However, there are some cases where the semantics of the problem suggest one is more expressive than the other. For example, controlling access to some shared memory, which only one thread can access it at a time, would most naturally involve a mutex. However, controlling access to a set of identical objects as a whole, such as giving a telephone line to a thread out of a set of five available lines, suits a counting semaphore better. Which one you choose depends on personal preference and the most appropriate mechanism for your program.

Synchronization with Semaphores

There are two sets of interface functions for semaphores. One is taken from POSIX Realtime Extensions and used for threads. The other is known as System V semaphores, which are commonly used for process synchronization. (We will we will meet the second type in a later chapter.) The two are not guaranteed interchangeable and, although very similar, use different function calls.

We are going to look at the simplest type of semaphore, a binary semaphore that takes only values 0 or 1. There is a more general semaphore, a counting semaphore that takes a wider range of values. Normally semaphores are used to protect a piece of code so that only one thread of execution can run it at any one time and, for this job, a binary semaphore is needed. Occasionally, we want to permit a limited number of threads to execute a given piece of code and, for this, we would use a counting semaphore. Since counting semaphores are much less common, we won't consider them further here, except to say that they are just a logical extension of a binary semaphore and that the actual function calls needed are identical.

The semaphore functions do not start with `pthread_`, like most thread specific functions but with `sem_`. There are four basic semaphore functions used in threads. They are all quite simple.

A semaphore is created with the `sem_init` function, which is declared as follows.

```
#include <semaphore.h>

int sem_init(sem_t *sem, int pshared, unsigned int value);
```

This function initializes a semaphore object pointed to by `sem`, sets its sharing option (of which more in a moment), and gives it an initial integer value. The `pshared` parameter controls the type of semaphore. If the value of `pshared` is 0, then the semaphore is local to the current process. Otherwise, the semaphore may be shared between processes. Here we are only interested in semaphores that are not shared between processes. At the time of writing Linux doesn't support this sharing, and passing a non-zero value for `pshared` will cause the call to fail.

The next pair of functions control the value of the semaphore and are declared as follows.

```
#include <semaphore.h>

int sem_wait(sem_t * sem);

int sem_post(sem_t * sem);
```

These both take a pointer to the semaphore object initialized by a call to `sem_init`.

The `sem_post` function atomically increases the value of the semaphore by 1. "**Atomically**" here means that, if two threads simultaneously try and increase the value of a single semaphore by 1, they do not interfere with each other, as might happen if two programs read, increment and write a value to a file at the same time. The semaphore will always be correctly increased in value by 2, since two threads tried to change it.

The `sem_wait` function atomically decreases the value of the semaphore by one, but always waits till the semaphore has a non-zero count first. Thus if you call `sem_wait` on a semaphore with a value of 2, the thread will continue executing but the semaphore will be decreased to 1. If `sem_wait` is called on a semaphore with a value of 0, then the function will wait until some other thread has incremented the value so that it is no longer 0. If two threads are both waiting in `sem_wait` for the same semaphore to become non-zero and it is incremented once by a third process, then only one of the two waiting processes will get to decrement the semaphore and continue; the other will remain waiting.

This atomic 'test and set' ability in a single function is what makes semaphores so valuable. There is another semaphore function, `sem_trywait` that is the non-blocking partner of `sem_wait`. We don't discuss it further here, but you can find more details in the manual pages.

The last semaphore function is `sem_destroy`. This function tidies up the semaphore when we have finished with it. It is declared as follows.

```
#include <semaphore.h>

int sem_destroy(sem_t * sem);
```

Again, this function takes a pointer to a semaphore and tidies up any resources that it may have. If you attempt to destroy a semaphore for which some thread is waiting, you will get an error.

Like most Linux functions, these functions all return 0 on success.

Try it out - a thread semaphore.

This code, `thread4.c` is also based on `thread2.c`. Since a lot has changed, we will present it in full.

```
#include <stdio.h>
#include <unistd.h>
#include <stdlib.h>
#include <string.h>
#include <pthread.h>
#include <semaphore.h>

void *thread_function(void *arg);
sem_t bin_sem;

#define WORK_SIZE 1024
char work_area[WORK_SIZE];

int main() {
    int res;
    pthread_t a_thread;
    void *thread_result;

    res = sem_init(&bin_sem, 0, 0);
    if (res != 0) {
        perror("Semaphore initialization failed");
        exit(EXIT_FAILURE);
    }
    res = pthread_create(&a_thread, NULL, thread_function, NULL);
    if (res != 0) {
        perror("Thread creation failed");
        exit(EXIT_FAILURE);
    }
    printf("Input some text. Enter 'end' to finish\n");
    while(strncmp("end", work_area, 3) != 0) {
        fgets(work_area, WORK_SIZE, stdin);
        sem_post(&bin_sem);
    }
    printf("\nWaiting for thread to finish...\n");
    res = pthread_join(a_thread, &thread_result);
    if (res != 0) {
        perror("Thread join failed");
        exit(EXIT_FAILURE);
    }
    printf("Thread joined\n");
    sem_destroy(&bin_sem);
    exit(EXIT_SUCCESS);
}

void *thread_function(void *arg) {
    sem_wait(&bin_sem);
    while(strncmp("end", work_area, 3) != 0) {
        printf("You input %d characters\n", strlen(work_area) -1);
        sem_wait(&bin_sem);
    }
    pthread_exit(NULL);
}
```

The first important change is the inclusion of `semaphore.h`, to give us access to the semaphore functions. Then we declare a semaphore and some variables and initialize the semaphore **before** we create our new thread.

```
sem_t bin_sem;

#define WORK_SIZE 1024
char work_area[WORK_SIZE];

int main() {
    int res;
    pthread_t a_thread;
    void *thread_result;
    res = sem_init(&bin_sem, 0, 0);
    if (res != 0) {
        perror("Semaphore initialization failed");
        exit(EXIT_FAILURE);
    }
```

Note that we set the initial value of the semaphore to 0.

In the function `main`, after we have started the new thread, we read some text from the keyboard, load our work area and then increment the semaphore with `sem_post`.

```
    printf("Input some text. Enter 'end' to finish\n");
    while(strncmp("end", work_area, 3) != 0) {
        fgets(work_area, WORK_SIZE, stdin);
        sem_post(&bin_sem);
    }
```

In the new thread, we wait for the semaphore and then count the characters from the input.

```
    sem_wait(&bin_sem);
    while(strncmp("end", work_area, 3) != 0) {
      printf("You input %d characters\n", strlen(work_area) -1);
      sem_wait(&bin_sem);
    }
```

While the semaphore is set, we are waiting for keyboard input. When we have some input we release the semaphore allowing the second thread to count the characters before the first thread reads the keyboard again.

Again both threads share the same `work_area` array. Again, we have omitted some error checking, such as the returns from `sem_wait` to make the code samples more succinct and easier to follow. However in production code, you should always check for error returns unless there is a very good reason to omit this check.

Let's give our program a run.

```
$ cc -D_REENTRANT thread4.c -o thread4 -lpthread
$./thread4
Input some text. Enter 'end' to finish
The Wasp Factory
You input 16 characters
Iain Banks
You input 10 characters
end

Waiting for thread to finish...
Thread joined
```

In threaded programs, timing faults are always hard to find, but the program seems resilient to both quick input of text and more leisurely pauses.

How It works.

When we initialize the semaphore, we set its value to 0. Thus, when the threads function starts, the call to `sem_wait` blocks and waits for the semaphore to become non-zero.

In the `main` thread, we wait till we have some text and then increment the semaphore with `sem_post`, which immediately allows the other thread to return from its `sem_wait` and start executing. Once it has counted the characters it again calls `sem_wait` and is blocked until the `main` thread again calls `sem_post` to increment the semaphore.

It is to overlook subtle timing faults. Let's modify the program slightly to `thread4a.c` to pretend that text input from the keyboard is sometime replaced with automatically available text. We modify the reading loop in the `main` to this:

```
printf("Input some text. Enter 'end' to finish\n");
while(strncmp("end", work_area, 3) != 0) {
  if (strncmp(work_area, "FAST", 4) == 0) {
    sem_post(&bin_sem);
    strcpy(work_area, "Wheeee...");
  } else {
    fgets(work_area, WORK_SIZE, stdin);
  }
  sem_post(&bin_sem);
}
```

Now if we enter 'FAST' the program calls `sem_post` to allow the character counter to run, but immediately updates `work_area` with something different.

```
$ cc -D_REENTRANT thread4a.c -o thread4a -lpthread
$ ./thread4a
Input some text. Enter 'end' to finish
Excession
You input 9 characters
FAST
You input 7 characters
You input 7 characters
You input 7 characters
end

Waiting for thread to finish...
Thread joined
```

The problem is that our program was relying on text input from the program taking so long that there was time for the other thread to count the words before the main thread was ever ready to give it more words to count. When we tried to give it two different sets of words to count in quick succession ('`FAST`' from the keyboard, then '`Weeee...`' automatically), there was no time for the second thread to execute. However, the semaphore had been incremented more than once, so the counter thread just kept counting the words and decreasing the semaphore until it became zero again.

This shows just how careful you need to be with timing considerations in multithreaded programs. It's possible to fix the program, by using an extra semaphore to make the main thread wait until the counter thread has had chance to finish its counting.

Synchronization with Mutexes

The other way of synchronizing access in multithreaded programs is with **mutexes**. These act by allowing the programmer to 'lock' an object, so that only one thread can access it. To control access to a critical section of code you lock a mutex before entering the code section and then unlock it when you have finished.

The basic functions required to use mutexes are very similar to those needed for semaphores. They are declared as follows.

```
#include <pthread.h>

int pthread_mutex_init(pthread_mutex_t *mutex, const pthread_mutexattr_t *mutexattr);

int pthread_mutex_lock(pthread_mutex_t *mutex));

int pthread_mutex_unlock(pthread_mutex_t *mutex);

int pthread_mutex_destroy(pthread_mutex_t *mutex);
```

As usual, 0 is returned for success, on failure an error code is returned, but `errno` is not set, you must use the return code.

As with semaphores, they all take a pointer to a previously declared object, this time a `pthread_mutex_t`. The extra attribute parameter `pthread_mutex_init` allows us to provide attributes for the mutex, which control its behavior. The attribute type by default is 'fast'. This has the slight drawback that, if your program tries to call `pthread_mutex_lock` on a mutex that it already has locked, then the program will block. Since the thread that holds the lock is the one that is now blocked, the mutex can never be unlocked and the program is deadlocked. It is possible to alter the attributes of the mutex so that it either checks for this and returns an error or acts recursively and allows multiple locks by the same thread if there are the same number of unlocks afterwards.

Setting the attribute of a mutex is beyond the scope of this book, so we will pass `NULL` for the attribute pointer, and use the default behavior. You can find more about changing the attributes in the manual page for `pthread_mutex_init`.

Try it out - a thread mutex.

Again this is a modification of `thread2.c` but heavily modified. This time, we will be a little paranoid about access to our critical variables and use a mutex to ensure they are only ever accessed by one thread at any one time. To keep the example code easy to read, we have omitted some error checking on the returns from mutex lock and unlock. In production code, we would check these return values. Here is the new program, `thread5.c`.

```
#include <stdio.h>
#include <unistd.h>
#include <stdlib.h>
#include <string.h>
#include <pthread.h>
#include <semaphore.h>

void *thread_function(void *arg);
pthread_mutex_t work_mutex; /* protects both work_area and time_to_exit */
#define WORK_SIZE 1024
char work_area[WORK_SIZE];
```

```
int time_to_exit = 0;

int main() {
    int res;
    pthread_t a_thread;
    void *thread_result;
    res = pthread_mutex_init(&work_mutex, NULL);
    if (res != 0) {
        perror("Mutex initialization failed");
        exit(EXIT_FAILURE);
    }
    res = pthread_create(&a_thread, NULL, thread_function, NULL);
    if (res != 0) {
        perror("Thread creation failed");
        exit(EXIT_FAILURE);
    }
    pthread_mutex_lock(&work_mutex);
    printf("Input some text. Enter 'end' to finish\n");
    while(!time_to_exit) {
        fgets(work_area, WORK_SIZE, stdin);
        pthread_mutex_unlock(&work_mutex);
        while(1) {
            pthread_mutex_lock(&work_mutex);
            if (work_area[0] != '\0') {
                pthread_mutex_unlock(&work_mutex);
                sleep(1);
            }
            else {
                break;
            }
        }
    }
    pthread_mutex_unlock(&work_mutex);
    printf("\nWaiting for thread to finish...\n");
    res = pthread_join(a_thread, &thread_result);
    if (res != 0) {
        perror("Thread join failed");
        exit(EXIT_FAILURE);
    }
    printf("Thread joined\n");
    pthread_mutex_destroy(&work_mutex);
    exit(EXIT_SUCCESS);
}

void *thread_function(void *arg) {
    sleep(1);
    pthread_mutex_lock(&work_mutex);
    while(strncmp("end", work_area, 3) != 0) {
        printf("You input %d characters\n", strlen(work_area) -1);
        work_area[0] = '\0';
        pthread_mutex_unlock(&work_mutex);
        sleep(1);
        pthread_mutex_lock(&work_mutex);
        while (work_area[0] == '\0' ) {
            pthread_mutex_unlock(&work_mutex);
            sleep(1);
            pthread_mutex_lock(&work_mutex);
        }
    }
    time_to_exit = 1;
    work_area[0] = '\0';
    pthread_mutex_unlock(&work_mutex);
    pthread_exit(0);
}
```

```
$ cc -D_REENTRANT thread5.c -o thread5 -lpthread
$ ./thread5
Input some text. Enter 'end' to finish
Whit
You input 4 characters
The Crow Road
You input 13 characters
end

Waiting for thread to finish...
Thread joined
```

How It works.

We start by declaring a mutex, our work area and, this time, an additional variable, `time_to_exit`.

```
pthread_mutex_t work_mutex; /* protects both work_area and time_to_exit */

#define WORK_SIZE 1024
char work_area[WORK_SIZE];
int time_to_exit = 0;
```

Then we initialize the mutex.

```
    res = pthread_mutex_init(&work_mutex, NULL);
    if (res != 0) {
        perror("Mutex initialization failed");
        exit(EXIT_FAILURE);
    }
```

Next we start the new thread. Here is the code that executes in the thread function.

```
    pthread_mutex_lock(&work_mutex);
    while(strncmp("end", work_area, 3) != 0) {
        printf("You input %d characters\n", strlen(work_area) -1);
        work_area[0] = '\0';
        pthread_mutex_unlock(&work_mutex);
        sleep(1);
        pthread_mutex_lock(&work_mutex);
        while (work_area[0] == '\0' ) {
            pthread_mutex_unlock(&work_mutex);
            sleep(1);
            pthread_mutex_lock(&work_mutex);
        }
    }
    time_to_exit = 1;
    work_area[0] = '\0';
    pthread_mutex_unlock(&work_mutex);
```

First the new thread tries to lock the mutex. If this is already locked, the call will block until it is released. Once we have access, we check to see whether we are being requested to exit. If we are requested to exit, we simply set `time_to_exit`, zap the first character of the work area and exit.

If we didn't want to exit, we count the characters and then zap the first character to a null. We use the first character being null as a way of telling the reader program that we have finished the counting. We then unlock the mutex and wait for the main thread to run. Periodically, we attempt to lock the mutex and, when we succeed, check whether the main thread has given us any more work to do. If it hasn't, we unlock the mutex and wait some more. If it has, we count the characters and go round the loop again.

Here is the main thread.

```
    pthread_mutex_lock(&work_mutex);
    printf("Input some text. Enter 'end' to finish\n");
    while(!time_to_exit) {
        fgets(work_area, WORK_SIZE, stdin);
        pthread_mutex_unlock(&work_mutex);
        while(1) {
            pthread_mutex_lock(&work_mutex);
            if (work_area[0] != '\0') {
                pthread_mutex_unlock(&work_mutex);
                sleep(1);
            }
            else {
                break;
            }
        }
    }
    pthread_mutex_unlock(&work_mutex);
```

This is quite similar. We lock the work area so that we can read text into it and then unlock it to allow the other thread access to count the words. Periodically, we re-lock the mutex, check whether the words have been counted (`work_area[0]` set to a null), and release the mutex if we need to wait longer. As we noted earlier, this kind of polling for an answer is generally not good programming and in the real world we would probably have used a semaphore to avoid this. However the code served its purpose as an example.

Thread Attributes

When we first looked at threads, we did not discuss the question of thread attributes. We will now do so. There are quite a few attributes of threads that you can control. However, here we are only going to look at those that you are most likely to need. Details of the others can be found in the manual pages.

In all our previous examples, we have had to re-synchronize our threads using `pthread_join` before we allow the program to exit. We need to do this if we want to allow one thread to return data to the thread that created it. Sometimes, we neither need the second thread to return information to the main thread nor want the main thread to wait for it.

Suppose that we create a second thread to spool a backup copy of a data file that is being edited while the main thread continues to service the user. When the backup has finished the second thread can just terminate. There is no need for it to re-join the main thread.

We can create threads that behave like this. They are called **detached threads**, and we create them by modifying the thread attributes or by calling `pthread_detach`. Since we want to demonstrate attributes, we will use the former method here.

The most important function that we need is `pthread_attr_init`, which initializes a thread attribute object.

```
#include <pthread.h>

int pthread_attr_init(pthread_attr_t *attr);
```

Once again, 0 is returned for success, and an error code is returned on failure.

There is also a destroy function, pthread_attr_destroy, but at the time of writing its implementation in Linux is to do nothing. Its purpose is to allow clean destruction of the attribute object, and you should call it, even though it currently does nothing on Linux, just in case the implementation one day changes and requires it to be called.

When we have a thread attribute object initialized, there are many additional functions that we can call to set different attribute behaviors. We will list them all here but look closely at only two. Here is the list of attribute functions that can be used.

```
int pthread_attr_setdetachstate(pthread_attr_t *attr, int detachstate);

int pthread_attr_getdetachstate(const pthread_attr_t *attr, int *detachstate);

int pthread_attr_setschedpolicy(pthread_attr_t *attr, int policy);

int pthread_attr_getschedpolicy(const pthread_attr_t *attr, int *policy);

int pthread_attr_setschedparam(pthread_attr_t *attr, const struct sched_param *param);

int pthread_attr_getschedparam(const pthread_attr_t *attr, struct sched_param *param);

int pthread_attr_setinheritsched(pthread_attr_t *attr, int inherit);

int pthread_attr_getinheritsched(const pthread_attr_t *attr, int *inherit);

int pthread_attr_setscope(pthread_attr_t *attr, int scope);

int pthread_attr_getscope(const pthread_attr_t *attr, int *scope);

int pthread_attr_setstacksize(pthread_attr_t *attr, int scope);

int pthread_attr_getstacksize(const pthread_attr_t *attr, int *scope);
```

As you can see, there are quite a lot of attributes.

detachedstate

This attribute allows us to avoid the need for threads to re-join. Like most of these _set functions, it takes a pointer to the attribute and a flag to determine the state required. The two possible flag values for pthread_attr_setdetachstate are PTHREAD_CREATE_JOINABLE and PTHREAD_CREATE_DETACHED. By default, the attribute will have value PTHREAD_CREATE_JOINABLE so that we should allow the two threads to join. If the state is set to PTHREAD_CREATE_DETACHED, then you cannot call pthread_join to recover the exit state of another thread.

schedpolicy

This controls how threads are scheduled. The options are SCHED_OTHER, SCHED_RP and SCHED_FIFO. By default, the attribute is SCHED_OTHER. The other two types of scheduling are only available to processes running with superuser permissions, as they both have real time scheduling but with slightly different behavior. SCHED_RR uses a round-robin scheduling scheme, and SCHED_FIFO uses a 'first in, first out' policy. Discussion of these is beyond the scope of this book.

schedparam

This is a partner to schedpolicy and allows control over the scheduling of threads running with schedule policy SCHED_OTHER. We will have a look at an example of this in a short while.

inheritsched

This attribute takes two possible values, PTHREAD_EXPLICIT_SCHED and PTHREAD_INHERIT_SCHED. By default, the value is PTHREAD_EXPLICIT_SCHED, which means scheduling is explicitly set by the attributes. By setting it to PTHREAD_INHERIT_SCHED, a new thread will instead use the parameters that its creator thread was using.

scope

This attribute controls how scheduling of a thread is calculated. Since Linux only currently supports the value PTHREAD_SCOPE_SYSTEM, we will not look at this further here.

stacksize

This attribute controls the thread creation stack size, set in bytes. This is part of the 'optional' section of the specification and is only supported on implementations where _POSIX_THREAD_ATTR_STACKSIZE is defined. Linux implements threads with a large amount of stack by default, so the feature is generally redundant on Linux and consequently not implemented.

Try it out - setting the detached state attribute

For our detached thread example, thread6.c, we create a thread attribute, set it to be detached and then create a thread using the attribute. Now when the child thread has finished, it calls pthread_exit in the normal way. This time, however, the originating thread no longer waits for the thread that it created to rejoin. We use a simple thread_finished flag to allow the main thread to detect whether the child has finished and to show that the threads are still sharing variables.

```
#include <stdio.h>
#include <unistd.h>
#include <stdlib.h>
#include <pthread.h>

void *thread_function(void *arg);

char message[] = "Hello World";
int thread_finished = 0;

int main() {
    int res;
    pthread_t a_thread;

    pthread_attr_t thread_attr;

    res = pthread_attr_init(&thread_attr);
    if (res != 0) {
        perror("Attribute creation failed");
        exit(EXIT_FAILURE);
    }
    res = pthread_attr_setdetachstate(&thread_attr, PTHREAD_CREATE_DETACHED);
    if (res != 0) {
        perror("Setting detached attribute failed");
        exit(EXIT_FAILURE);
    }
    res = pthread_create(&a_thread, &thread_attr, thread_function, (void *)message);
    if (res != 0) {
        perror("Thread creation failed");
        exit(EXIT_FAILURE);
    }
```

```
    (void)pthread_attr_destroy(&thread_attr);
    while(!thread_finished) {
        printf("Waiting for thread to say it's finished...\n");
        sleep(1);
    }
    printf("Other thread finished, bye!\n");
    exit(EXIT_SUCCESS);
}

void *thread_function(void *arg) {
    printf("thread_function is running. Argument was %s\n", (char *)arg);
    sleep(4);
    printf("Second thread setting finished flag, and exiting now\n");
    thread_finished = 1;
    pthread_exit(NULL);
}
```

There are no surprises in the output.

```
$ cc -D_REENTRANT thread6.c -o thread6 -lpthread
$ ./thread6
Waiting for thread to say it's finished...
thread_function is running. Argument was Hello World
Waiting for thread to say it's finished...
Waiting for thread to say it's finished...
Waiting for thread to say it's finished...
Second thread setting finished flag, and exiting now
Other thread finished, bye!
```

How It works.

The two important sections of code are:

```
pthread_attr_t thread_attr;

res = pthread_attr_init(&thread_attr);
if (res != 0) {
    perror("Attribute creation failed");
    exit(EXIT_FAILURE);
}
```

which declares a thread attribute and initializes it, and

```
res = pthread_attr_setdetachstate(&thread_attr, PTHREAD_CREATE_DETACHED);
if (res != 0) {
    perror("Setting detached attribute failed");
    exit(EXIT_FAILURE);
}
```

which sets the attribute values to have the detached state.

The other slight differences are creating the thread, passing the address of the attributes:

```
res = pthread_create(&a_thread, &thread_attr, thread_function, (void *)message);
```

and, for completeness, destroying the attributes when we have used them:

```
pthread_attr_destroy(&thread_attr);
```

Thread Attributes - Scheduling

Let's take a look at a second thread attribute we might wish to change, scheduling. This is very similar to setting the detached state, but there are two more functions that we can use to find the available priority levels, sched_get_priority_max and sched_get_priority_min.

Try is out - scheduling

Since this thread7.c is very similar to the previous example, we'll just look at the differences.

After we have set the detached attribute, we set the scheduling policy.

```
    res = pthread_attr_setschedpolicy(&thread_attr, SCHED_OTHER);
    if (res != 0) {
        perror("Setting scheduling policy failed");
        exit(EXIT_FAILURE);
    }
```

Next we find the range of priorities that are allowed:

```
    max_priority = sched_get_priority_max(SCHED_OTHER);
    min_priority = sched_get_priority_min(SCHED_OTHER);
```

and set one:

```
    scheduling_value.sched_priority = min_priority;
    res = pthread_attr_setschedparam(&thread_attr, &scheduling_value);
    if (res != 0) {
        perror("Setting scheduling priority failed");
        exit(EXIT_FAILURE);
    }
```

How It works

This is very similar to setting a detached state attribute, except that we set the scheduling policy instead.

Canceling a Thread

Sometimes, we want one thread to be able to ask another thread to terminate, rather like sending it a signal. There is a way to do this with threads and, in parallel with signal handling, threads get a way of modifying how they behave when they are asked to terminate.

Let's look first at the function to request a thread to terminate.

```
#include <pthread.h>

int pthread_cancel(pthread_t thread);
```

This is pretty straight forward, given a thread identifier, we can request that it is cancelled. On the receiving end of the cancel request, things are slightly more complicated, but not much. A thread can set its cancel state using pthread_setcancelstate.

```
#include <pthread.h>

int pthread_setcancelstate(int state, int *oldstate);
```

The first parameter is either PTHREAD_CANCEL_ENABLE that allows it to receive cancel requests, or PTHREAD_CANCEL_DISABLE, which causes them to be ignored. The oldstate pointer allows the previous state to be retrieved. If you are not interested, you can simply pass NULL. If cancel requests are accepted, then there is a second level of control the thread can take, the cancel type, which is set with pthread_setcanceltype.

```
#include <pthread.h>

int pthread_setcanceltype(int type, int *oldtype);
```

The type can take one of two values, PTHREAD_CANCEL_ASYNCHRONOUS, which causes cancellation requests to be acted upon immediately, and PTHREAD_CANCEL_DEFERRED, which makes cancellation requests wait until the thread executes one of the functions, pthread_join, pthread_cond_wait, pthread_cond_timedwait, pthread_testcancel, sem_wait, or sigwait.

We have not seen all of these calls in this chapter, as not all are generally needed. More details can be found, as ever, in the manual pages.

According to the POSIX standard, other system calls that may block, such as read, wait and so on should also be cancellation points. At the time of writing Linux does not yet support all of these being cancellation points. However some experimentation suggests that some blocked calls, such as sleep, do allow cancellation to take place. To be on the safe side you may wish to add some pthread_testcancel calls in code that you expect to be canceled.

Again, the oldtype allows the previous state to be retrieved, or a NULL can be passed if you are not interested in knowing the previous state. By default, threads start with the cancellation state PTHREAD_CANCEL_ENABLE and the cancellation type PTHREAD_CANCEL_DEFERRED.

Try it out - canceling a thread.

Our program thread8.c is derived, yet again, from thread2.c. This time, the main thread sends a cancel request to the thread that it has created.

```
#include <stdio.h>
#include <unistd.h>
#include <stdlib.h>
#include <pthread.h>

void *thread_function(void *arg);

int main() {
    int res;
    pthread_t a_thread;
    void *thread_result;

    res = pthread_create(&a_thread, NULL, thread_function, NULL);
    if (res != 0) {
        perror("Thread creation failed");
        exit(EXIT_FAILURE);
    }
```

```
    sleep(3);
    printf("Cancelling thread...\n");
    res = pthread_cancel(a_thread);
    if (res != 0) {
        perror("Thread cancelation failed");
        exit(EXIT_FAILURE);
    }
    printf("Waiting for thread to finish...\n");
    res = pthread_join(a_thread, &thread_result);
    if (res != 0) {
        perror("Thread join failed");
        exit(EXIT_FAILURE);
    }
    exit(EXIT_SUCCESS);
}

void *thread_function(void *arg) {
    int i, res;
    res = pthread_setcancelstate(PTHREAD_CANCEL_ENABLE, NULL);
    if (res != 0) {
        perror("Thread pthread_setcancelstate failed");
        exit(EXIT_FAILURE);
    }
    res = pthread_setcanceltype(PTHREAD_CANCEL_DEFERRED, NULL);
    if (res != 0) {
        perror("Thread pthread_setcanceltype failed");
        exit(EXIT_FAILURE);
    }
    printf("thread_function is running\n");
    for(i = 0; i < 10; i++) {
        printf("Thread is still running (%d)...\n", i);
        sleep(1);
    }
    pthread_exit(0);
}
```

When we run this, we get:

```
$ cc -D_REENTRANT thread8.c -o thread8 -lpthread
$ ./thread8
thread_function is running
Thread is still running (0)...
Thread is still running (1)...
Thread is still running (2)...
Cancelling thread...
Waiting for thread to finish...
Thread is still running (3)...
$
```

How It works

After the new thread has been created in the usual way, the main thread sleeps (to allow the new thread some time to get started) and then issues a cancel request.

```
    sleep(3);
    printf("Cancelling thread...\n");
    res = pthread_cancel(a_thread);
    if (res != 0) {
        perror("Thread cancelation failed");
        exit(EXIT_FAILURE);
    }
```

In the created thread, we first set the cancel state to allow canceling.

```
    res = pthread_setcancelstate(PTHREAD_CANCEL_ENABLE, NULL);
    if (res != 0) {
        perror("Thread pthread_setcancelstate failed");
        exit(EXIT_FAILURE);
    }
```

Then we set the cancel type to be deferred.

```
    res = pthread_setcanceltype(PTHREAD_CANCEL_DEFERRED, NULL);
    if (res != 0) {
        perror("Thread pthread_setcanceltype failed");
        exit(EXIT_FAILURE);
    }
```

Finally, we wait around to be canceled.

```
    for(i = 0; i < 10; i++) {
        printf("Thread is still running (%d)...\n", i);
        sleep(1);
    }
```

Threads in Abundance

Up to now, we have always had the normal thread of execution of a program create just one other thread. However we didn't want you to think that you could only create one extra thread. For our final example in this chapter, `thread9.c`, we show how to create several threads in the same program and then collect them again in a order different from that in which they were started.

Try it out - many threads

```
#include <stdio.h>
#include <unistd.h>
#include <stdlib.h>
#include <pthread.h>

#define NUM_THREADS 6

void *thread_function(void *arg);

int main() {
    int res;
    pthread_t a_thread[NUM_THREADS];
    void *thread_result;
    int lots_of_threads;

    for(lots_of_threads = 0; lots_of_threads < NUM_THREADS; lots_of_threads++) {
        res = pthread_create(&(a_thread[lots_of_threads]), NULL, thread_function,
(void *)&lots_of_threads);
        if (res != 0) {
            perror("Thread creation failed");
            exit(EXIT_FAILURE);
        }
        sleep(1);
    }
```

```
    printf("Waiting for threads to finish...\n");
    for(lots_of_threads = NUM_THREADS - 1; lots_of_threads >= 0; lots_of_threads--) {
        res = pthread_join(a_thread[lots_of_threads], &thread_result);
        if (res == 0) {
            printf("Picked up a thread\n");
        }
        else {
            perror("pthread_join failed");
        }
    }
    printf("All done\n");
    exit(EXIT_SUCCESS);
}

void *thread_function(void *arg) {
    int my_number = *(int *)arg;
    int rand_num;

    printf("thread_function is running. Argument was %d\n", my_number);
    rand_num=1+(int)(9.0*rand()/(RAND_MAX+1.0));
    sleep(rand_num);
    printf("Bye from %d\n", my_number);
    pthread_exit(NULL);
}
```

When we run it, we get:

```
$ cc -D_REENTRANT thread9.c -o thread9 -lpthread
$ ./thread9
thread_function is running. Argument was 0
thread_function is running. Argument was 1
thread_function is running. Argument was 2
thread_function is running. Argument was 3
thread_function is running. Argument was 4
Bye from 1
thread_function is running. Argument was 5
Waiting for threads to finish...
Bye from 5
Picked up a thread
Bye from 0
Bye from 2
Bye from 3
Bye from 4
Picked up a thread
Picked up a thread
Picked up a thread
Picked up a thread
Picked up a thread
All done
```

As you can see, we created many threads and allowed them to finish out of sequence. There is a subtle bug in this program that makes itself evident if you remove the call to `sleep` from the loop that starts the threads. We have included it to show you just how careful you need to be when writing programs that use threads. Can you spot it? We'll explain below.

How It works.

This time we create an array of thread IDs:

```
pthread_t a_thread[NUM_THREADS];
```

and loop round creating several threads:

```
for(lots_of_threads = 0; lots_of_threads < NUM_THREADS; lots_of_threads++) {
    res = pthread_create(&(a_thread[lots_of_threads]), NULL,
                                thread_function, (void *)&lots_of_threads);
    if (res != 0) {
        perror("Thread creation failed");
        exit(EXIT_FAILURE);
    }
    sleep(1);
}
```

The threads themselves then wait for a random time before exiting:

```
void *thread_function(void *arg) {
    int my_number = *(int *)arg;
    int rand_num;

    printf("thread_function is running. Argument was %d\n", my_number);
    rand_num=1+(int)(9.0*rand()/(RAND_MAX+1.0));
    sleep(rand_num);
    printf("Bye from %d\n", my_number);
    pthread_exit(NULL);
}
```

While in the main (original) thread, we wait to pick them up, but not in the order in which we created them.

```
for(lots_of_threads = NUM_THREADS - 1; lots_of_threads >= 0; lots_of_threads--) {
    res = pthread_join(a_thread[lots_of_threads], &thread_result);
    if (res == 0) {
        printf("Picked up a thread\n");
    }
    else {
        perror("pthread_join failed");
    }
}
```

If you try to run the program with no sleep, you might see some strange effects, including some threads being started with the same argument. Did you spot why this could happen? The threads are being started using a local variable for the argument to the thread function. This variable is updated in the loop. The offending lines are:

```
for(lots_of_threads = 0; lots_of_threads < NUM_THREADS; lots_of_threads++) {
    res = pthread_create(&(a_thread[lots_of_threads]), NULL,
                                thread_function, (void *)&lots_of_threads);
```

If the main thread runs fast enough, it might alter the argument (`lots_of_threads`) for some of the threads. Behavior like this arises when not enough care is taken with shared variables and multiple execution paths. To correct the problem, we need to pass the value directly like this:

```
res = pthread_create(&(a_thread[lots_of_threads]), NULL, thread_function, (void *)lots_of_threads);
```

and of course change `thread_function`.

```
void *thread_function(void *arg) {
    int my_number = (int)arg;
```

This is in the downloadable code as `thread9a.c`.

Summary

In this chapter, we have looked at POSIX threads. We have seen how to create several threads of execution inside a process, where each thread shares file scope variables.

We then looked at the two ways threads can control access to critical code and data, using both semaphores and mutexes. After that we moved onto controlling the attributes of threads and, in particular, how we could separate them from the main thread so that it no longer had to wait for threads that it had created to complete. After a quick look at how one thread can request another to finish and at how the receiving thread can manage such requests, we saw a example of a program with many simultaneous threads executing.

We haven't had the space to cover every last function call and nuance associated with threads, but you should now have enough understanding to start writing your own programs with threads and to investigate the more esoteric aspects of threads by reading the manual pages.

Inter-process Communication: Pipes

In the last chapter, we saw a very simple way of sending messages between two processes using signals. We created notification events that could be used to provoke a response, but the information transferred was limited to a signal number.

In this chapter, we'll be looking at pipes, which allow more useful data to be exchanged between processes. By the end of the chapter, we'll be using our new-found knowledge to re-implement the running CD database program as a client/server application.

We'll cover:

- The definition of a pipe
- Process pipes
- Pipe calls
- Parent and child processes
- Named pipes: FIFOs
- Client/server considerations

What is a Pipe?

We use the term **pipe** when we connect a data flow from one process to another. Generally we attach, or pipe, the output of one process to the input of another.

Most UNIX users will already be familiar with the idea of linking shell commands together, so that the output of one process is fed straight to the input of another. For shell commands, this is entered as:

```
cmd1 | cmd2
```

The shell arranges the standard input and output of the two commands, so that:

- The standard input to cmd1 comes from the terminal keyboard.
- The standard output from cmd1 is fed to cmd2 as its standard input.
- The standard output from cmd2 is connected to the terminal screen.

What the shell has done, in effect, is reconnect the standard input and output streams so that data flows from the keyboard input through the two commands and is then output to the screen.

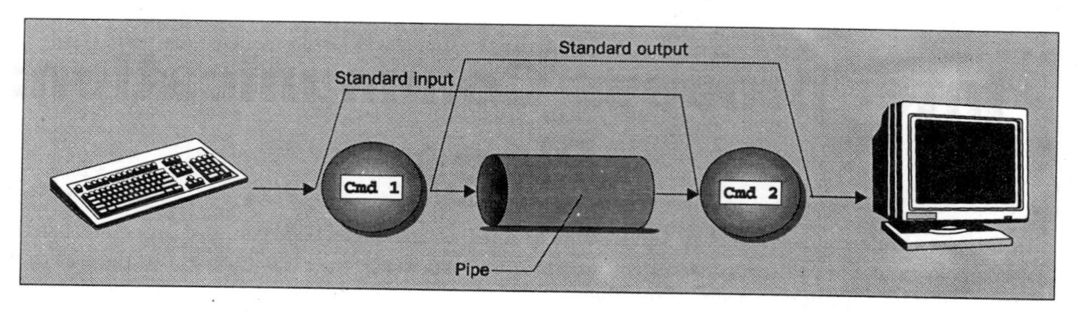

In this chapter, we'll be seeing how to achieve this effect in a program and how we can use pipes to connect multiple processes together to allow us to implement a simple client/server system.

In chapter 5 we mentioned pty's, which have similarities to the pipes described here, but are rather more specialized, so we won't be covering them here.

Process Pipes

Perhaps the simplest way of passing data between two programs is with the popen and pclose functions. These have the prototypes:

```
#include <stdio.h>

FILE *popen(const char *command, const char *open_mode);
int pclose(FILE *stream_to_close);
```

popen

The popen function allows a program to invoke another program as a new process and either pass data to or receive data from it. The command string is the name of the program to run, together with any parameters. open_mode must be either "r" or "w".

If the open_mode is "r", output from the invoked program is made available to the invoking program and can be read from the file stream FILE * returned by popen, using the usual stdio library functions for reading (for example, fread). However, if open_mode is w, the program can send data to the invoked command with calls to fwrite. The invoked program can then read the data on its standard input. Normally, the program being invoked won't be aware that it's reading data from another process; it simply reads its standard input stream and acts on it.

Each call to popen must specify either "r" or "w"; no other option is supported in a standard implementation of popen. This means that we can't invoke another program and both read and write to it. On failure, popen returns a null pointer. If you want bi-directional communication using pipes, then the normal solution is to use two pipes, one for data flow in each direction.

pclose

When the process started with popen has finished, we can close the file stream associated with it using pclose. The pclose call will only return once the process started with popen finishes. If it's still running when pclose is called, the pclose call will wait for the process to finish.

The pclose call normally returns the exit code of the process whose file stream it is closing. If the invoking process has executed a wait statement before calling pclose, the exit status will be lost and pclose will return -1, with errno set to ECHILD.

Let's try a simple popen and pclose example, popen1.c. We'll use popen in a program to access information from uname. The uname -a command prints system information, including the machine type, the OS name, version and release and the machine's network name.

Try It Out - Reading Output From an External Program

Having initialized the program, we open the pipe to uname, making it readable and setting read_fp to point to the output. At the end, the pipe pointed to by read_fp is closed.

```
#include <unistd.h>
#include <stdlib.h>
#include <stdio.h>
#include <string.h>

int main()
{
    FILE *read_fp;
    char buffer[BUFSIZ + 1];
    int chars_read;
    memset(buffer, '\0', sizeof(buffer));
    read_fp = popen("uname -a", "r");
    if (read_fp != NULL) {
        chars_read = fread(buffer, sizeof(char), BUFSIZ, read_fp);
        if (chars_read > 0) {
            printf("Output was:-\n%s\n", buffer);
        }
        pclose(read_fp);
        exit(EXIT_SUCCESS);
    }
    exit(EXIT_FAILURE);
}
```

When we run this program on one of the author's machines, we get:

```
$ popen1
Output was:-
Linux tilde 2.2.5-15 #1 Mon Apr 19 18:20:08 EDT 1999 i686 unknown
```

How It Works

The program uses the popen call to invoke the uname command with the -a parameter. It then uses the returned file stream to read data up to BUFSIZ characters (this being a #define from stdio.h) and then prints it out so it appears on the screen. Since we've captured the output of uname inside a program, it's available for processing.

Sending Output to popen

Now that we've seen an example of capturing output from an external program, let's look at sending output to an external program. Here's a program, popen2.c, that pipes data to another. Here, we'll use od (octal dump).

Try It Out - Sending Output to an External Program

Have a look at the following code, even type it in if you like...

```
#include <unistd.h>
#include <stdlib.h>
#include <stdio.h>

int main()
{
    FILE *write_fp;
    char buffer[BUFSIZ + 1];

    sprintf(buffer, "Once upon a time, there was...\n");
    write_fp = popen("od -c", "w");
    if (write_fp != NULL) {
        fwrite(buffer, sizeof(char), strlen(buffer), write_fp);
        pclose(write_fp);
        exit(EXIT_SUCCESS);
    }
    exit(EXIT_FAILURE);
}
```

When we run this program, we get the output:

```
$ popen2
0000000   O   n   c   e       u   p   o   n       a       t   i   m   e
0000020   ,       t   h   e   r   e       w   a   s   .   .   .  \n
0000037
```

How It Works

The program uses popen with the parameter w to start the od -c command, so that it can send data to it. It then sends a string which the od -c command receives, processes and prints the result of its processing on its standard output.

From the command line, we can get the same output with the command:

```
$ echo "Once upon a time, there was..." | od -c
```

Passing More Data

The mechanism that we've used so far simply sent or received all the data in a single `fread` or `fwrite`. Sometimes, we may want to send the data in smaller pieces, or perhaps we may not know the size of the output. To avoid having to declare a very large buffer, we can just use multiple `fread` or `fwrite` calls and process the data in parts.

Here's a program, `popen3.c`, that reads all of the data from a pipe.

Try It Out - Reading Larger Amounts of Data from a Pipe

In this program, we read data from an invoked `ps -alx` process. There's no way to know in advance how much output there will be, so we must allow for multiple reads of the pipe being required.

```
#include <unistd.h>
#include <stdlib.h>
#include <stdio.h>
#include <string.h>

int main()
{
    FILE *read_fp;
    char buffer[BUFSIZ + 1];
    int chars_read;

    memset(buffer, '\0', sizeof(buffer));
    read_fp = popen("ps -ax", "r");
    if (read_fp != NULL) {
        chars_read = fread(buffer, sizeof(char), BUFSIZ, read_fp);
        while (chars_read > 0) {
                  buffer[chars_read - 1] = '\0';
            printf("Reading:-\n %s\n", buffer);
            chars_read = fread(buffer, sizeof(char), BUFSIZ, read_fp);
        }
        pclose(read_fp);
        exit(EXIT_SUCCESS);
    }
    exit(EXIT_FAILURE);
}
```

The output we get, edited for brevity, is:

```
$ popen3
Reading:-
   PID TTY STAT  TIME COMMAND
    1  ?  S     0:04 init
    2  ?  SW     0:00 [kflushd]
    3  ?  SW     0:00 [kpiod]
    4  ?  SW    0:00 [kswapd]
    5  ?  SW<   0:00 [mdrecoveryd]
...
  240 tty2 S     0:02 emacs draft1.txt
Reading:-
  368 tty1 S     0:00 popen3
  369 tty1 R     0:00 ps -ax
...
```

How It Works

The program uses popen with an r parameter, in a similar fashion to popen1.c. This time, it continues reading from the file stream until there is no more data available. Notice that, although the ps command takes some time to execute, UNIX arranges the process scheduling so that both programs run when they can. If the reader process, popen3, has no input data, it's suspended until some becomes available. If the writer process, ps, produces more output than can be buffered, it's suspended until the reader has consumed some of the data.

In this example, you may not see Reading:- output a second time. This will be the case if BUFSIZ is greater than the length of the ps command output. Some Linux systems set BUFSIZ as high as 8,000 or more.

How popen is Implemented

The popen call runs the program you requested by first invoking the shell, sh, passing it the command string as an argument. This has two effects, one good, the other not so good.

In UNIX, all parameter expansion is done by the shell, so invoking the shell to parse the command string before the program is invoked allows any shell expansion, such as *.c, to be done before the program starts. This is often quite useful and allows complex shell commands to be started with popen. Other process creation functions, such as execl, can be much more complex to invoke, because the calling process has to perform its own shell expansion.

The unfortunate effect of using the shell is that it means for every call to popen, not only is the requested program being invoked, but also a shell. Each call to popen then results in two extra processes being started. This makes the popen function a little expensive in terms of system resources.

Here's a program, popen4.c, that we can use to demonstrate the behavior of popen. We can count the lines in all the popen example source files by cating the files and then piping its output to wc -l, which counts the number of lines. On the command line, we would use:

```
$ cat popen*.c | wc -l
```

Actually, wc -l popen.c is easier to type and more efficient, but the example serves to illustrate the principle...*

Try It Out - popen Starts a Shell

This program uses exactly the command given above, but through popen so that it can read the result:

```
#include <unistd.h>
#include <stdlib.h>
#include <stdio.h>
#include <string.h>

int main()
{
    FILE *read_fp;
    char buffer[BUFSIZ + 1];
    int chars_read;
```

```
    memset(buffer, '\0', sizeof(buffer));
    read_fp = popen("cat popen*.c | wc -l", "r");
    if (read_fp != NULL) {
        chars_read = fread(buffer, sizeof(char), BUFSIZ, read_fp);
        while (chars_read > 0) {
                buffer[chars_read - 1] = '\0';
            printf("Reading:-\n %s\n", buffer);
            chars_read = fread(buffer, sizeof(char), BUFSIZ, read_fp);
        }
        pclose(read_fp);
        exit(EXIT_SUCCESS);
    }
    exit(EXIT_FAILURE);
}
```

When we run this program, the output is:

```
$ popen4
Reading:-
     101
```

How It Works

The program shows that the shell is being invoked to expand `popen*.c` to the list of all files starting `popen` and ending in `.c` and also to process the pipe (`|`) symbol and feed the output from `cat` into `wc`. We invoke the shell, the `cat` program and `wc` and cause an output redirection, all in a single `popen` call. The program that invokes the command sees only the final output.

The Pipe Call

We've seen the high-level `popen` function, but we'll now move on to look at the lower-level `pipe` function. This provides a means of passing data between two programs, without the overhead of invoking a shell to interpret the requested command. It also gives us more control over the reading and writing of data.

The `pipe` function has the prototype:

```
#include <unistd.h>

int pipe(int file_descriptor[2]);
```

`pipe` is passed (a pointer to) an array of two integer file descriptors. It fills the array with two new file descriptors and returns a zero. On failure, it returns `-1` and sets `errno` to indicate the reason for failure. Errors defined in the Linux man pages are:

EMFILE	Too many file descriptors are in use by the process.
ENFILE	The system file table is full.
EFAULT	The file descriptor is not valid.

The two file descriptors returned are connected in a special way. Any data written to `file_descriptor[1]` can be read back from `file_descriptor[0]`. The data is processed in a **first in, first out** basis, usually abbreviated to **FIFO**. This means that if you write the bytes `1, 2, 3` to `file_descriptor[1]`, reading from `file_descriptor[0]` will produce `1, 2, 3`. This is different from a stack, which operates on a **last in, first out** basis, usually abbreviated to **LIFO**.

> **It's important to realize that these are file descriptors, not file streams, so we must use the lower-level `read` and `write` calls to access the data, rather than `fread` and `fwrite`.**

Here's a program, `pipe1.c`, that uses `pipe` to create a pipe.

Try It Out - The `pipe` Function

Type in the following code. Note the `file_pipes` pointer, which is passed to the `pipe` function as a parameter.

```
#include <unistd.h>
#include <stdlib.h>
#include <stdio.h>
#include <string.h>

int main()
{
    int data_processed;
    int file_pipes[2];
    const char some_data[] = "123";
    char buffer[BUFSIZ + 1];

    memset(buffer, '\0', sizeof(buffer));

    if (pipe(file_pipes) == 0) {
        data_processed = write(file_pipes[1], some_data, strlen(some_data));
        printf("Wrote %d bytes\n", data_processed);
        data_processed = read(file_pipes[0], buffer, BUFSIZ);
        printf("Read %d bytes: %s\n", data_processed, buffer);
        exit(EXIT_SUCCESS);
    }
    exit(EXIT_FAILURE);
}
```

When we run this program, the output is:

```
$ pipe1
Wrote 3 bytes
Read 3 bytes: 123
```

How It Works

The program creates a `pipe` using the two file descriptors `file_pipes[]`. It then writes data into the pipe using the file descriptor `file_pipes[1]` and reads it back from `file_pipes[0]`. Notice that the pipe has some internal buffering which stores the data in between the calls to `write` and `read`.

You should be aware that the effect of trying to write, using `file_descriptor[0]`, or read using `file_descriptor[1]` is undefined, so the behavior may differ between UNIX implementations. On the authors' systems, such calls will fail with a -1 return value, which at least ensures that it's easy to catch this mistake.

At first glance, this example of a pipe doesn't seem to offer us anything that we couldn't have done with a simple file. The real advantage of pipes comes when you wish to pass data between two processes. As we saw in the last chapter, when a program creates a new process using the `fork` call, file descriptors that were previously open remain open. By creating a pipe in the original process and then forking to create a new process, we can pass data from one process to the other down the pipe.

Try It Out - Pipes across a `fork`

1. This is `pipe2.c`. It starts rather like the first example, up until we make the call to `fork`.

```
#include <unistd.h>
#include <stdlib.h>
#include <stdio.h>
#include <string.h>

int main()
{
    int data_processed;
    int file_pipes[2];
    const char some_data[] = "123";
    char buffer[BUFSIZ + 1];
    pid_t fork_result;

    memset(buffer, '\0', sizeof(buffer));

    if (pipe(file_pipes) == 0) {
        fork_result = fork();
        if (fork_result == -1) {
            fprintf(stderr, "Fork failure");
            exit(EXIT_FAILURE);
        }
```

2. We've made sure the `fork` worked, so if `fork_result` equals zero, we're in the child process:

```
        if (fork_result == 0) {
            data_processed = read(file_pipes[0], buffer, BUFSIZ);
            printf("Read %d bytes: %s\n", data_processed, buffer);
            exit(EXIT_SUCCESS);
        }
```

3. Otherwise, we must be the parent process:

```
        else {
            data_processed = write(file_pipes[1], some_data,
                                   strlen(some_data));
            printf("Wrote %d bytes\n", data_processed);
        }
    }
    exit(EXIT_SUCCESS);
}
```

When we run this program. the output is, as before:

```
$ pipe2
Wrote 3 bytes
Read 3 bytes: 123
```

How It Works

First, the program creates a pipe with the `pipe` call. It then uses the `fork` call to create a new process. If the `fork` was successful, the parent writes data into the pipe, while the child reads data from the pipe. Both parent and child exit after a single `write` and `read`. If the parent exits before the child you might see the shell prompt between the two outputs.

Although the program is superficially very similar to the first pipe example, we've taken a big step forward by being able to use separate processes for the reading and writing. We can illustrate this with the following diagram:

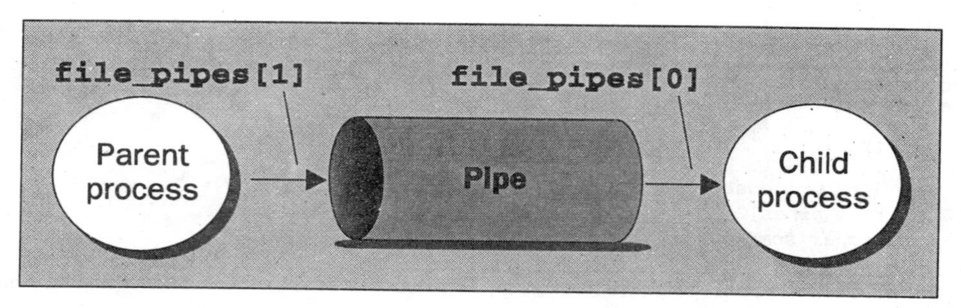

Parent and Child Processes

The next logical step in our investigation of the `pipe` call is to allow the child process to be a different program from its parent, rather than just a different process. We do this using the `exec` call. One difficulty is that the new `exec`ed process needs to know which file descriptor to access. In our previous example, this wasn't a problem, since the child had access to its copy of the `file_pipes` data. After an `exec` call, this will no longer be the case, as the old process has been replaced by the new child process. We can get round this by passing the file descriptor (which is, after all, just a number) as a parameter to the `exec`ed program.

To show how this works, we need two programs. The first is the 'data producer'. It creates the pipe and then invokes the child, the 'data consumer'.

Try It Out - Pipes and `exec`

1. For the first program, we adapt `pipe2.c` to `pipe3.c`. The lines that we've changed are shown shaded:

```
#include <unistd.h>
#include <stdlib.h>
#include <stdio.h>
#include <string.h>

int main()
{
```

```
    int data_processed;
    int file_pipes[2];
    const char some_data[] = "123";
    char buffer[BUFSIZ + 1];
    pid_t fork_result;

    memset(buffer, '\0', sizeof(buffer));

    if (pipe(file_pipes) == 0) {
        fork_result = fork();
        if (fork_result == (pid_t)-1) {
            fprintf(stderr, "Fork failure");
            exit(EXIT_FAILURE);
        }

        if (fork_result == 0) {
            sprintf(buffer, "%d", file_pipes[0]);
            (void)execl("pipe4", "pipe4", buffer, (char *)0);
            exit(EXIT_FAILURE);
        }
        else {
            data_processed = write(file_pipes[1], some_data,
                                   strlen(some_data));
            printf("%d - wrote %d bytes\n", getpid(), data_processed);
        }
    }
    exit(EXIT_SUCCESS);
}
```

2. The 'consumer' program, `pipe4.c`, that reads the data is much simpler:

```
#include <unistd.h>
#include <stdlib.h>
#include <stdio.h>
#include <string.h>

int main(int argc, char *argv[])
{
    int data_processed;
    char buffer[BUFSIZ + 1];
    int file_descriptor;

    memset(buffer, '\0', sizeof(buffer));
    sscanf(argv[1], "%d", &file_descriptor);
    data_processed = read(file_descriptor, buffer, BUFSIZ);

    printf("%d - read %d bytes: %s\n", getpid(), data_processed, buffer);
    exit(EXIT_SUCCESS);
}
```

Remembering that `pipe3` invokes the `pipe4` program for us, when we run `pipe3`, we get the following output:

```
$ pipe3
980 - wrote 3 bytes
981 - read 3 bytes: 123
```

How It Works

The `pipe3` program starts like the previous example, using the `pipe` call to create a pipe and then using the `fork` call to create a new process. It then uses `sprintf` to store the 'read' file descriptor number of the pipe in a buffer that will form an argument of `pipe4`.

A call to `execl` is used to invoke the `pipe4` program. The arguments to `execl` are:

The program to invoke.
`argv[0]`, which takes the program name.
`argv[1]`, which contains the file descriptor number we want the program to read from.
`(char *)0`, which terminates the parameters.

The `pipe4` program extracts the file descriptor number from the argument string and then reads from that file descriptor to obtain the data.

Reading Closed Pipes

Before we move on, we need to look a little more carefully at the file descriptors that are open. Up to this point we have allowed the reading process simply to read some data and then exit, assuming that UNIX will clean up the files as part of the process termination.

Most programs that read data from the standard input do so differently to the examples we've seen so far. They don't usually know how much data they have to read, so they will normally loop, reading data, processing it, then reading more data, until there's no more data to read.

A `read` call will normally block, i.e. cause the process to wait until data becomes available. If the other end of the pipe has been closed, then no process has the pipe open for writing and the `read` blocks. Since this isn't very helpful, a `read` on a pipe that isn't open for writing returns zero, rather than blocking. This allows the reading process to detect the pipe equivalent of end-of-file and act appropriately. Notice that this isn't the same as reading an invalid file descriptor, which `read` considers an error, indicating this by returning -1.

If we use a pipe across a `fork` call, there are two different file descriptors that we can use to write to the pipe, one in the parent and one in the child. We must close the `write` file descriptors of the pipe in both parent and child processes before the pipe is considered closed and a `read` call will fail. We'll see an example of this later when we return to this subject in more detail to look at the `O_NONBLOCK` flag and FIFOs.

Pipes Used as Standard Input and Output

Now that we know how to make a `read` on an empty pipe fail, we can look at a much cleaner method of connecting two processes with a pipe. We arrange for one of the pipe file descriptors to have a known value, usually the standard input, 0, or the standard output, 1. This is slightly more complex to set up in the parent, but allows the child program to be much simpler.

The one big advantage is that we can invoke standard programs, ones that don't expect a file descriptor as a parameter. In order to do this, we need to use the dup function that we met in Chapter 3. There are two closely related versions of dup, that have the prototypes:

```
#include <unistd.h>

int dup(int file_descriptor);
int dup2(int file_descriptor_one, int file_descriptor_two);
```

The purpose of the dup call is to open a new file descriptor, a little like the open call. What is special is that the new file descriptor created by dup refers to the same file (or pipe) as an existing file descriptor. In the case of dup, the new file descriptor is always the lowest number available; while in the case of dup2 it's the same as, or the first available descriptor greater than, the parameter `file_descriptor_two`.

We can get the same effect as `dup` and `dup2` by using the more general `fcntl` call, with a command `F_DUPFD`. Having said that, the `dup` call is easier to use, since it's tailored specifically to the needs of creating duplicate file descriptors. It's also very commonly used, so you'll find it more frequently in existing programs than `fcntl` and `F_DUPFD`.

So how does dup help us in passing data between processes? The trick is knowing that the standard input file descriptor is always zero and that dup always returns a new file descriptor using the lowest available number. By first closing file descriptor 0 and then calling dup, the new file descriptor will have the number zero. Since the new descriptor is a duplicate of an existing one, standard input will have been changed to access the file or pipe whose file descriptor we passed to dup. We will have created two file descriptors that refer to the same file or pipe and one of them will be the standard input.

File Descriptor Manipulation by close and dup

File descriptor number	Initially	After close	After dup
0	Standard input		Pipe file descriptor
1	Standard output	Standard output	Standard output
2	Standard error	Standard error	Standard error
3	Pipe file descriptor	Pipe file descriptor	Pipe file descriptor

Let's return to our previous example, but this time we'll arrange for the child program to have its `stdin` file descriptor replaced with the `read` end of the pipe we create. We'll also do some tidying up of file descriptors so the child program can correctly detect the end of the data in the pipe. As usual, we'll omit some error checking for the sake of brevity.

Try It Out - Pipes and dup

1. Modify pipe3.c to pipe5.c, using the following code:

```
#include <unistd.h>
#include <stdlib.h>
#include <stdio.h>
#include <string.h>

int main()
{
    int data_processed;
    int file_pipes[2];
    const char some_data[] = "123";
    (pid_t) fork_result;

    if (pipe(file_pipes) == 0) {
        fork_result = fork();
        if (fork_result == (pid_t)-1) {
            fprintf(stderr, "Fork failure");
            exit(EXIT_FAILURE);
        }

        if (fork_result == (pid_t)0) {
            close(0);
            dup(file_pipes[0]);
            close(file_pipes[0]);
            close(file_pipes[1]);

            execlp("od", "od", "-c", (char *)0);
            exit(EXIT_FAILURE);
        }
        else {
            close(file_pipes[0]);
            data_processed = write(file_pipes[1], some_data,
                                   strlen(some_data));
            close(file_pipes[1]);
            printf("%d - wrote %d bytes\n", (int)getpid(), data_processed);
        }
    }
    exit(EXIT_SUCCESS);
}
```

The output from this program is:

```
$ pipe5
1239 - wrote 3 bytes
0000000   1   2   3
0000003
```

How It Works

As before, the program creates a pipe and then forks, creating a child process. At this point, both the parent and child have file descriptors that access the pipe, one each for reading and writing, so there are four open file descriptors in total.

Let's look at the child process first. The child closes its standard input with `close(0)`, and then calls `dup(file_pipes[0])`. This duplicates the file descriptor associated with the `read` end of the pipe as file descriptor 0, the standard input. The child then closes the original file descriptor for reading from the pipe, `file_pipes[0]`. Since the child will never write to the pipe, it also closes the `write` file descriptor associated with the pipe, `file_pipes[1]`. It now has a single file descriptor associated with the pipe, file descriptor 0, its standard input.

It can then use `exec` to invoke any program that reads standard input. In this case, we use the `od` command. The `od` command will wait for data to be available to it as if it were waiting for input from a user terminal. In fact, without some special code to explicitly detect the difference, it won't know that the input is from a pipe rather than a terminal.

The parent starts by closing the read end of the pipe `file_pipes[0]`, since it will never read the pipe. It then writes data to the pipe. When all the data has been written, it closes the write end of the pipe and exits. Since there are now no file descriptors open that could write to the pipe, the `od` program will be able to read the three bytes written to the pipe, but subsequent reads will then return 0 bytes, indicating an end of file. When the read returns 0, the `od` program exits. This is analogous to running the `od` command on a terminal, then typing *Ctrl-D* to send end of file to the `od` command.

We can show the sequence pictorially. After the call to `pipe`:

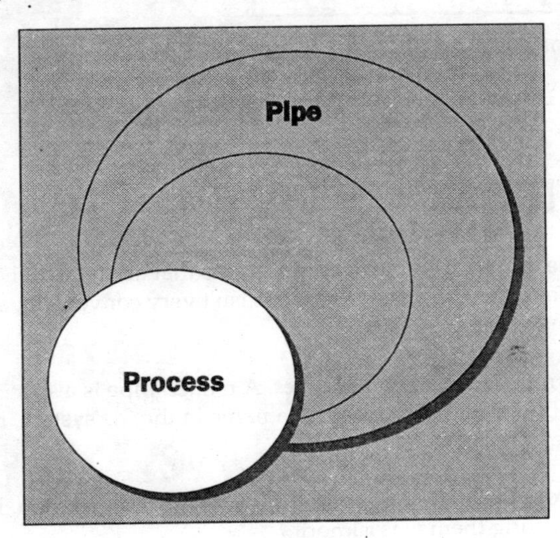

After the call to fork:

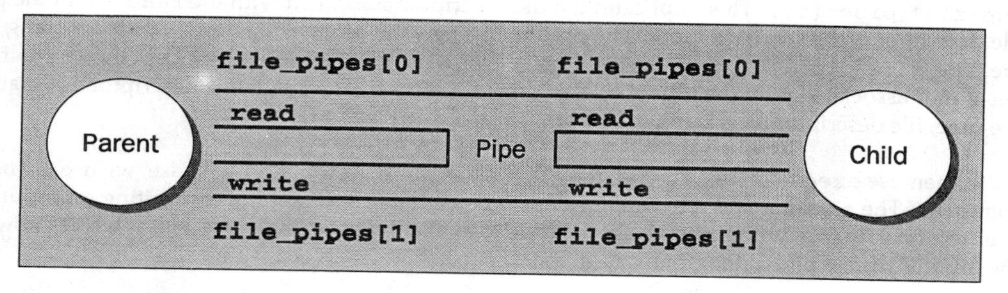

When the program is ready to transfer data:

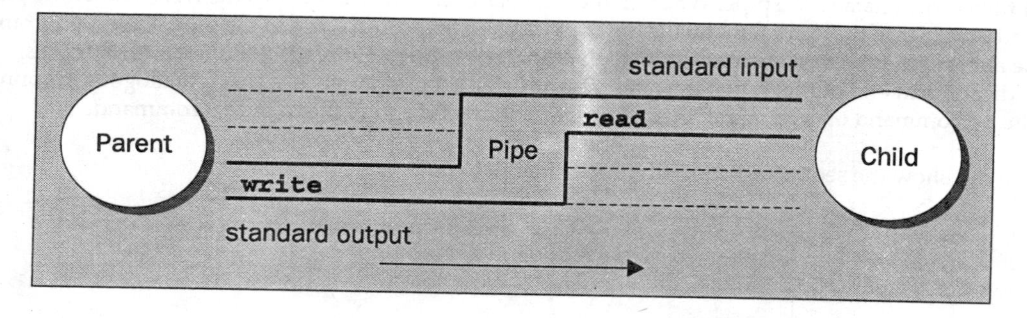

Named Pipes: FIFOs

So far, we have only been able to pass data between programs that are related, i.e. programs that have been started from a common ancestor process. Often, this isn't very convenient, as we would like unrelated processes to be able to exchange data.

We do this with **FIFOs**, often referred to as **named pipes**. A named pipe is a special type of file (remember everything in UNIX is a file!) that exists as a name in the file system, but behaves like the unnamed pipes that we've met already.

We can create named pipes from the command line and from within a program. Historically, the command line program for creating them was mknod:

```
$ mknod filename p
```

However, the mknod command is not in the X/Open command list, so may not be available on all UNIX systems. The preferred command line method is to use:

```
$ mkfifo filename
```

Some older versions of UNIX only have mknod command. X/Open Issue 4 Version 2 has the mknod function call, but not the command. Linux, friendly as ever, supports mknod and mkfifo.

From inside a program, we can use two different calls. These are:

```
#include <sys/types.h>
#include <sys/stat.h>

int mkfifo(const char *filename, mode_t mode);
int mknod(const char *filename, mode_t mode | S_IFIFO, (dev_t) 0);
```

Like the mknod command, you can use the mknod function for making many special types of file. Using a dev_t value of 0 and ORing the file access mode with S_IFIFO is the only portable use of this function which creates a named pipe. We'll use the simpler mkfifo function in our examples.

Try It Out - Creating a Named Pipe

For fifo1.c, just type in the following code:

```
#include <unistd.h>
#include <stdlib.h>
#include <stdio.h>
#include <sys/types.h>
#include <sys/stat.h>

int main()
{
    int res = mkfifo("/tmp/my_fifo", 0777);
    if (res == 0) printf("FIFO created\n");
    exit(EXIT_SUCCESS);
}
```

We can look for the pipe with:

```
$ ls -lF /tmp/my_fifo
prwxr-xr-x   1 rick     users          0 Dec 10 14:55 /tmp/my_fifo|
```

Notice that the first character is a p, indicating a pipe. The | symbol at the end is added by the ls command's -F option and also indicates a pipe.

How It Works

The program uses the mkfifo function to create a special file. Although we ask for a mode of 0777, this is altered by the user mask (umask) setting (in this case 022), just like normal file creation, so the resulting file has mode 755.

We can remove the FIFO by using the rm command, or from within a program by using the unlink system call.

Accessing a FIFO

One very useful feature of named pipes is that, because they appear in the file system, we can use them in commands where we would normally use a file name. Before we do more programming using the FIFO file we've created, we can investigate the behavior of our FIFO file using normal file commands.

Try It Out - Accessing a FIFO File

1. First, let's try reading the (empty) FIFO:

```
$ cat < /tmp/my_fifo
```

2. Now try writing to the FIFO:

```
$ echo "sdsdfasdf" > /tmp/my_fifo
```

3. If we do both at once, we can pass information through the pipe:

```
$ cat < /tmp/my_fifo &
[1] 1316
$ echo "sdsdfasdf" > /tmp/my_fifo
sdsdfasdf

[1]+  Done                    cat </tmp/my_fifo
$
```

With the first two stages, the program simply hangs until we interrupt it, conventionally with *Ctrl-C*. With the third, we get the screen output shown.

How It Works

Since there was no data in the FIFO, the `cat` and `echo` programs block, waiting for some data to arrive and some other process to read the data, respectively.

Looking at the third stage, the `cat` process is initially blocked in the background. When `echo` makes some data available, the `cat` command reads the data and prints it on the standard output. Notice that the `cat` program then exits without waiting for more data. It doesn't block because the pipe will have been closed and calls to `read` in the `cat` program will return 0 bytes, indicating the end of file.

Now that we've seen how the FIFO behaves when we access it using command line programs, let's look in more detail at the program interface, which allows us more control over how `reads` and `writes` behave when we're accessing a FIFO.

> **Unlike a pipe created with the `pipe` call, a FIFO exists as a named file, not as an open file descriptor, and must be opened before it can be read from or written to. You open and close a FIFO using the same `open` and `close` functions that we saw used earlier for files, with some additional functionality. The `open` call is passed the path name of the FIFO, rather than that of a regular file.**

Opening a FIFO with open

The main restriction on opening FIFOs is that a program may not open a FIFO for reading and writing with the mode `O_RDWR`. If a program does this, the result is undefined. This is quite a sensible restriction since, normally, we only use a FIFO for passing data in a single direction, so we have no need for a `O_RDWR` mode. A process would read its own output back from a pipe if it were opened read/write.

If we do wish to pass data in both directions between programs, it's much better to use either a pair of FIFOs or pipes, one for each direction, or (unusually) explicitly change the direction of the data flow by closing and re-opening the FIFO. We'll return to bi-directional data exchange using FIFOs later in the chapter.

The other difference between opening a FIFO and a regular file is the use of the `open_flag` (the second parameter to `open`) with the option `O_NONBLOCK`. Using this `open` mode not only changes how the `open` call is processed, but also changes how `read` and `write` requests are processed on the returned file descriptor.

There are four legal combinations of `O_RDONLY`, `O_WRONLY` and the `O_NONBLOCK` flag. We'll consider each in turn.

```
open(const char *path, O_RDONLY);
```

In this case, the `open` call will block, i.e. not return until a process opens the same FIFO for writing. This is like the first `cat` example above.

```
open(const char *path, O_RDONLY | O_NONBLOCK);
```

The `open` call will now succeed and return immediately, even if the FIFO had not been opened for writing by any process.

```
open(const char *path, O_WRONLY);
```

In this case, the `open` call will block until a process opens the same FIFO for reading.

```
open(const char *path, O_WRONLY | O_NONBLOCK);
```

This will always return immediately, but if no process has the FIFO open for reading, `open` will return an error, -1, and the FIFO won't be opened. If a process does have the FIFO open for reading, the file descriptor returned can be used for writing to the FIFO.

Notice the asymmetry between the use of O_NONBLOCK with O_RDONLY and O_WRONLY, in that a non-blocking open for writing fails if no process has the pipe open for reading, but a non-blocking read doesn't fail. The behavior of the close call isn't affected by the O_NONBLOCK flag.

Let's look at how we can use the behavior of open with the O_NONBLOCK flag to synchronize two processes. Rather than use a number of example programs, we'll write a single test program, fifo2.c, that allows us to investigate the behavior of FIFOs.

Try It Out - Opening FIFO Files

1. Let's start with the header files, a #define and the check that the correct number of command-line arguments have been supplied:

```
#include <unistd.h>
#include <stdlib.h>
#include <stdio.h>
#include <string.h>
#include <fcntl.h>
#include <sys/types.h>
#include <sys/stat.h>

#define FIFO_NAME "/tmp/my_fifo"

int main(int argc, char *argv[])
{
    int res;
    int open_mode = 0;

    if (argc < 2) {
        fprintf(stderr, "Usage: %s <some combination of\
               O_RDONLY O_WRONLY O_NONBLOCK>\n", *argv);
        exit(EXIT_FAILURE);
    }
```

2. Assuming that the program passed the test, we now set the value of open_mode from those arguments:

```
    argv++;
    if (strncmp(*argv, "O_RDONLY", 8) == 0) open_mode |= O_RDONLY;
    if (strncmp(*argv, "O_WRONLY", 8) == 0) open_mode |= O_WRONLY;
    if (strncmp(*argv, "O_NONBLOCK", 10) == 0) open_mode |= O_NONBLOCK;
    argv++;
    if (*argv) {
        if (strncmp(*argv, "O_RDONLY", 8) == 0) open_mode |= O_RDONLY;
        if (strncmp(*argv, "O_WRONLY", 8) == 0) open_mode |= O_WRONLY;
        if (strncmp(*argv, "O_NONBLOCK", 10) == 0) open_mode |= O_NONBLOCK;
    }
```

3. We now check whether the FIFO exists and create it if necessary. Then the FIFO is opened and output given to that effect while the program catches forty winks. Last of all, the FIFO is closed.

```
    if (access(FIFO_NAME, F_OK) == -1) {
        res = mkfifo(FIFO_NAME, 0777);
        if (res != 0) {
            fprintf(stderr, "Could not create fifo %s\n", FIFO_NAME);
            exit(EXIT_FAILURE);
        }
    }

    printf("Process %d opening FIFO\n", getpid());
    res = open(FIFO_NAME, open_mode);
    printf("Process %d result %d\n", getpid(), res);
    sleep(5);
    if (res != -1) (void)close(res);
    printf("Process %d finished\n", getpid());
    exit(EXIT_SUCCESS);
}
```

How It Works

This program allows us to specify on the command line the combinations of O_RDONLY, O_WRONLY and O_NONBLOCK that we wish to use. It does this by comparing known strings with command line parameters and setting (with |=) the appropriate flag if the string matches. The program uses the access function to check whether the FIFO file already exists and will create it if required.

We never destroy the FIFO because we have no way of telling if another program already has the FIFO in use. Anyway, we now have our test program, so let's try out a couple of combinations:

O_RDONLY and O_WRONLY with no O_NONBLOCK

```
$ ./fifo2 O_RDONLY &
[1] 152
Process 152 opening FIFO
$ ./fifo2 O_WRONLY
Process 153 opening FIFO
Process 152 result 3
Process 153 result 3
Process 152 finished
Process 153 finished
```

This is probably the most common use of named pipes. It allows the reader process to start, wait in the open call and then both programs to continue when the second program opens the FIFO. Notice that both the reader and writer processes have synchronized at the open call.

> **When a UNIX process is blocked, it doesn't consume CPU resources, so this method of process synchronization is very CPU-efficient.**

O_RDONLY with O_NONBLOCK and O_WRONLY

```
$ ./fifo2 O_RDONLY O_NONBLOCK &
[1] 160
Process 160 opening FIFO
$ ./fifo2 O_WRONLY
Process 161 opening FIFO
Process 160 result 3
Process 161 result 3
Process 160 finished
Process 161 finished
[1]+  Done                    fifo2 O_RDONLY O_NONBLOCK
```

This time, the reader process executes the open call and continues immediately, even though no writer process is present. The writer also immediately continues past the open call, since the FIFO is already open for reading.

These two examples are probably the most common combinations of open modes. Feel free to use the example program to experiment with some other combinations.

Reading and Writing FIFOs

Using the O_NONBLOCK mode affects how read and write calls behave on FIFOs.

A read on an empty blocking FIFO (i.e. one not opened with O_NONBLOCK) will wait until some data can be read. Conversely, a read on a non-blocking FIFO with no data will return 0 bytes.

A write on a full blocking FIFO will wait until the data can be written. A write on a FIFO that can't accept all of the bytes being written will either:

- Fail if the request is for PIPE_BUF bytes or less and the data can't be written.
- Write part of the data if the request is for more than PIPE_BUF bytes, returning the number of bytes actually written, which could be zero.

The size of a FIFO is an important consideration. There is a system-imposed limit on how much data can be 'in' a FIFO at any one time. This is the #define PIPE_BUF, usually found in limits.h. On Linux and many other UNIX systems, this is commonly 4096 bytes, but could be as low as 512 bytes on some systems. The system guarantees that writes of PIPE_BUF or fewer bytes on a FIFO that has been opened O_WRONLY, i.e. blocking, will either write all or none of the bytes.

Whilst this limit is not very important in the simple case of a single FIFO writer and a single FIFO reader, it's quite common to use a single FIFO to allow many different programs to send requests to a single FIFO reader. If several different programs try to write to the FIFO at the same time, it's usually vital that the blocks of data from different programs don't get interleaved, i.e. each write is 'atomic'. How do you do this?

Well, if you ensure that all your write requests are to a blocking FIFO and are less than PIPE_BUF bytes in size, the system will ensure data never gets interleaved. In general, it's a good idea to restrict the data transferred via a FIFO to blocks of PIPE_BUF bytes, unless you're using only a single writer and a single reader process.

To show how unrelated processes can communicate using named pipes, we need two separate programs, fifo3.c and fifo4.c.

Try It Out - Inter-process Communication with FIFOs

1. The first program is our producer program. This creates the pipe if required, then writes data to it as quickly as possible.

Note that, for illustration purposes, we don't mind what the data is, so we don't bother to initialize buffer. In both listings, shaded lines show the changes from fifo2.c, with all the command line argument code removed.

```
#include <unistd.h>
#include <stdlib.h>
#include <stdio.h>
#include <string.h>
#include <fcntl.h>
#include <limits.h>
#include <sys/types.h>
#include <sys/stat.h>

#define FIFO_NAME "/tmp/my_fifo"
#define BUFFER_SIZE PIPE_BUF
#define TEN_MEG (1024 * 1024 * 10)

int main()
{
    int pipe_fd;
    int res;
    int open_mode = O_WRONLY;
    int bytes_sent = 0;
    char buffer[BUFFER_SIZE + 1];

    if (access(FIFO_NAME, F_OK) == -1) {
        res = mkfifo(FIFO_NAME, 0777);
        if (res != 0) {
            fprintf(stderr, "Could not create fifo %s\n", FIFO_NAME);
            exit(EXIT_FAILURE);
        }
    }

    printf("Process %d opening FIFO O_WRONLY\n", getpid());
    pipe_fd = open(FIFO_NAME, open_mode);
    printf("Process %d result %d\n", getpid(), pipe_fd);

    if (pipe_fd != -1) {
        while(bytes_sent < TEN_MEG) {
            res = write(pipe_fd, buffer, BUFFER_SIZE);
            if (res == -1) {
                fprintf(stderr, "Write error on pipe\n");
                exit(EXIT_FAILURE);
            }
            bytes_sent += res;
        }
        (void)close(pipe_fd);
    }
    else {
        exit(EXIT_FAILURE);
    }

    printf("Process %d finished\n", getpid());
    exit(EXIT_SUCCESS);
}
```

2. Our second program, the consumer, is much simpler. It reads and discards data from the FIFO.

```
#include <unistd.h>
#include <stdlib.h>
#include <stdio.h>
#include <string.h>
#include <fcntl.h>
#include <limits.h>
#include <sys/types.h>
#include <sys/stat.h>
```

```
#define FIFO_NAME "/tmp/my_fifo"
#define BUFFER_SIZE PIPE_BUF

int main()
{
    int pipe_fd;
    int res;
    int open_mode = O_RDONLY;
    char buffer[BUFFER_SIZE + 1];
    int bytes_read = 0;

    memset(buffer, '\0', sizeof(buffer));

    printf("Process %d opening FIFO O_RDONLY\n", getpid());
    pipe_fd = open(FIFO_NAME, open_mode);
    printf("Process %d result %d\n", getpid(), pipe_fd);

    if (pipe_fd != -1) {
        do {
            res = read(pipe_fd, buffer, BUFFER_SIZE);
            bytes_read += res;
        } while (res > 0);
        (void)close(pipe_fd);
    }
    else {
        exit(EXIT_FAILURE);
    }

    printf("Process %d finished, %d bytes read\n", getpid(), bytes_read);
    exit(EXIT_SUCCESS);
}
```

When we run these programs at the same time, using the `time` command to time the reader, the output we get is (with some tidying for clarity):

```
$ ./fifo3 &
[1] 375
Process 375 opening FIFO O_WRONLY
$ time ./fifo4
Process 377 opening FIFO O_RDONLY
Process 375 result 3
Process 377 result 3
Process 375 finished
Process 377 finished, 10485760 bytes read
0.01user 0.02system 0:00.03elapsed 85%CPU (0avgtext+0avgdata 0maxresident)k
0inputs+0outputs (80major+9minor)pagefaults 0swaps
[1]+  Done                    fifo3
```

How It Works

Both programs use the FIFO in blocking mode. We start `fifo3` (the writer/producer) first, which blocks, waiting for a reader to open the FIFO. When `fifo4` (the consumer) is started, the writer is then unblocked and starts writing data to the pipe. At the same time, the reader starts reading data from the pipe.

> **UNIX arranges the scheduling of the two processes so they both run when they can and are blocked when they can't. So, the writer is blocked when the pipe is full and the reader blocked when the pipe is empty.**

The output from the `time` command shows us that it took the reader under 0.1 seconds to run and read ten megabytes of data. This shows us that pipes, at least as implemented in the author's version of Linux, can be an efficient way of transferring data between programs.

Advanced Topic: Client/Server using FIFOs

For our final look at FIFOs, let's consider how we might build a very simple client/server application using named pipes. We want to have a single server process that accepts requests, processes them and returns the resulting data to the requesting party, the client.

We want to allow multiple client processes to send data to the server. In the interests of simplicity, we'll assume that the data to be processed can be broken into blocks, each smaller than `PIPE_BUF` bytes. Of course, we could implement this system in many ways, but we'll consider only one method as an illustration of how named pipes can be used.

Since the server will only process one block of information at a time, it seems logical to have a single FIFO which is read by the server and written to by each of the clients. By opening the FIFO in blocking mode, the server and the clients will be automatically blocked as required.

Returning the processed data to the clients is slightly more difficult. We need to arrange a second pipe, one per client, for the returned data. By passing the process identifier (PID) of the client in the original data sent to the server, both parties can use this to generate the unique name for the return pipe.

Try It Out - An Example Client/Server Application

1. First, we need a header file, `cliserv.h`, that defines the data common to both client and server programs. It also includes the required system headers, for convenience.

```
#include <unistd.h>
#include <stdlib.h>
#include <stdio.h>
#include <string.h>
#include <fcntl.h>
#include <limits.h>
#include <sys/types.h>
#include <sys/stat.h>

#define SERVER_FIFO_NAME "/tmp/serv_fifo"
#define CLIENT_FIFO_NAME "/tmp/cli_%d_fifo"

#define BUFFER_SIZE 20

struct data_to_pass_st {
    pid_t  client_pid;
    char   some_data[BUFFER_SIZE - 1];
};
```

2. Now for the server program, `server.c`. In this section, we create and then open the server pipe. It's set to be read-only, with blocking. After sleeping (for demonstration purposes), the server reads in any data from the client, which has the `data_to_pass_st` structure.

```
#include "cliserv.h"
#include <ctype.h>

int main()
{
    int server_fifo_fd, client_fifo_fd;
    struct data_to_pass_st my_data;
    int read_res;
    char client_fifo[256];
    char *tmp_char_ptr;

    mkfifo(SERVER_FIFO_NAME, 0777);
    server_fifo_fd = open(SERVER_FIFO_NAME, O_RDONLY);
    if (server_fifo_fd == -1) {
        fprintf(stderr, "Server fifo failure\n");
        exit(EXIT_FAILURE);
    }

    sleep(10); /* lets clients queue for demo purposes */

    do {
        read_res = read(server_fifo_fd, &my_data, sizeof(my_data));
        if (read_res > 0) {
```

3. In this next stage, we perform some processing on the data just read from the client: we convert all the characters in `some_data` to uppercase and combine the `CLIENT_FIFO_NAME` with the received `client_pid`.

```
            tmp_char_ptr = my_data.some_data;
            while (*tmp_char_ptr) {
                *tmp_char_ptr = toupper(*tmp_char_ptr);
                tmp_char_ptr++;
            }
            sprintf(client_fifo, CLIENT_FIFO_NAME, my_data.client_pid);
```

4. Then we send the processed data back, opening the client pipe in write-only, blocking mode. Finally, we shut down the server FIFO by closing the file and then `unlink`ing the FIFO.

```
            client_fifo_fd = open(client_fifo, O_WRONLY);
            if (client_fifo_fd != -1) {
                write(client_fifo_fd, &my_data, sizeof(my_data));
                close(client_fifo_fd);
            }
        }
    } while (read_res > 0);
    close(server_fifo_fd);
    unlink(SERVER_FIFO_NAME);
    exit(EXIT_SUCCESS);
}
```

5. Here's the client, `client.c`. The first part of this program opens the server FIFO, if it already exists, as a file. It then gets its own process ID, which forms some of the data that will be sent to the server. The client FIFO is created, ready for the next section.

```
#include "cliserv.h"
#include <ctype.h>

int main()
{
    int server_fifo_fd, client_fifo_fd;
    struct data_to_pass_st my_data;
    int times_to_send;
    char client_fifo[256];

    server_fifo_fd = open(SERVER_FIFO_NAME, O_WRONLY);
    if (server_fifo_fd == -1) {
        fprintf(stderr, "Sorry, no server\n");
        exit(EXIT_FAILURE);
    }

    my_data.client_pid = getpid();
    sprintf(client_fifo, CLIENT_FIFO_NAME, my_data.client_pid);
    if (mkfifo(client_fifo, 0777) == -1) {
        fprintf(stderr, "Sorry, can't make %s\n", client_fifo);
        exit(EXIT_FAILURE);
    }
```

6. For each of the five loops, the client data is sent to the server. Then the client FIFO is opened (read-only, blocking mode) and the data read back. Finally, the server FIFO is closed and the client FIFO removed from memory.

```
    for (times_to_send = 0; times_to_send < 5; times_to_send++) {
    sprintf(my_data.some_data, "Hello from %d", my_data.client_pid);
    printf("%d sent %s, ", my_data.client_pid, my_data.some_data);
    write(server_fifo_fd, &my_data, sizeof(my_data));
    client_fifo_fd = open(client_fifo, O_RDONLY);
    if (client_fifo_fd != -1) {
        if (read(client_fifo_fd, &my_data, sizeof(my_data)) > 0) {
            printf("received: %s\n", my_data.some_data);
        }
        close(client_fifo_fd);
    }
    }
    close(server_fifo_fd);
    unlink(client_fifo);
    exit(EXIT_SUCCESS);
}
```

To test this out, we need to run a single copy of the server and several clients. To get them all started at close to the same time, we use the following shell commands:

```
$ server &
$ for i in 1 2 3 4 5
do
client &
done
```

This starts one server process and five client processes. The output from the clients, edited for brevity, looks like this:

```
531 sent Hello from 531, received: HELLO FROM 531
532 sent Hello from 532, received: HELLO FROM 532
529 sent Hello from 529, received: HELLO FROM 529
530 sent Hello from 530, received: HELLO FROM 530
531 sent Hello from 531, received: HELLO FROM 531
532 sent Hello from 532, received: HELLO FROM 532
```

As you can see, different client requests are being interleaved and each client is getting the suitably processed data returned to it. Note that the interleaving is random and the order in which client requests are received will vary between the machines and possibly between runs on the same machine.

How It Works

In this section, we'll try to explain the sequence of client and server operations as they interact, something that we haven't covered so far.

The server creates its FIFO in read-only mode and blocks. This it does until the first client connects by opening the same FIFO for writing. At that point, the server process is unblocked and the `sleep` is executed, so the `writes` from the clients queue up. (In a real application, the `sleep` would be removed; we're only using it to demonstrate the correct operation of our program with multiple simultaneous clients.)

In the meantime, after the client has opened the server FIFO, it creates its own uniquely-named FIFO for reading data back from the server. Only then does it write data to the server (blocking if the pipe is full or the server's still sleeping) and then blocks on a `read` on its own FIFO, waiting for the reply.

On receiving the data from the client, the server processes it, opens the client pipe for writing and writes the data back, which unblocks the client. When the client is unblocked, it can read from its pipe the data written to it by the server.

The whole process repeats until the last client closes the server pipe, causing the server's `read` to fail (return 0), since no process has the server pipe open for writing. If this were a real server process that needed to wait for further clients, we would need to modify it to either:

- Open a file descriptor to its own server pipe, so `read` always blocks rather than returning 0.
- When `read` returns 0 bytes, close and reopen the server pipe, so the server process blocks in the `open` waiting for a client, just as it did when it first started.

Both these techniques are illustrated in the rewrite of the CD Database application to use named pipes.

The CD Application

Now that we've seen how we can use named pipes to implement a simple client/server system, we can revisit our CD database application and convert it accordingly. We'll also incorporate some signal handling, to allow us to perform some tidy-up actions when the process is interrupted.

Before we get to look in detail at this new version, let's compile the application. If you have the source code from the web site, use the `Makefile` to compile it to `server_app` and `client_app` programs. Typing `server_app -i` allows the program to initialize a new CD database. Needless to say, the client won't run unless the server is up and running. Here's the `Makefile` to show how the programs fit together.

```
all:    server_app client_app

CC=cc
CFLAGS=-I/usr/include/db1 -pedantic -Wall

# For debugging un-comment the next line
# DFLAGS=-DDEBUG_TRACE=1 -g


# Include for systems with dbm, but only as part of the BSD licensed version,
# and not in the standard locations. This is the default...
DBM_INC_PATH=/usr/include/db1
DBM_LIB_PATH=/usr/lib
DBM_LIB_FILE=db

# For systems with dbm in the standard places, comment out the previous
# definitions, and uncomment these
#
#DBM_INC_PATH=/usr/include
#DBM_LIB_PATH=/usr/lib
#DBM_LIB_FILE=ndbm

# For systems where the gdbm libraries have been fetched and installed
# separately in the default locations under /usr/local
# comment out the previous definitions, and uncomment these
#DBM_INC_PATH=/usr/local/include
#DBM_LIB_PATH=/usr/local/lib
#DBM_LIB_FILE=gdbm


.c.o:
        $(CC) $(CFLAGS) -I$(DBM_INC_PATH) $(DFLAGS) -c $<

app_ui.o: app_ui.c cd_data.h
cd_dbm.o: cd_dbm.c cd_data.h
client_if.o: client_if.c cd_data.h cliserv.h
pipe_imp.o: pipe_imp.c cd_data.h cliserv.h
server.o: server.c cd_data.h cliserv.h


client_app: app_ui.o client_if.o pipe_imp.o
        $(CC) -o client_app  $(DFLAGS) app_ui.o client_if.o pipe_imp.o

server_app:    server.o cd_dbm.o pipe_imp.o
        $(CC) -o server_app -L$(DBM_LIB_PATH) $(DFLAGS) server.o cd_dbm.o pipe_imp.o -
l$(DBM_LIB_FILE)

clean:
        rm -f server_app client_app *.o *~
```

Aims

Our aim is to split the part of the application that deals with the database away from the user interface part of the application. We also wish to run a single server process, but allow many simultaneous clients. We also wish to minimize the changes to the existing code. Wherever possible, we'll leave existing code unchanged.

To keep things simple, we also want to be able to create (and delete) pipes within the application, so there's no need for a system administrator to create named pipes before we can use it.

It's also important to ensure that we never busy wait, consuming CPU power, for an event. As we've seen, UNIX allows us to block, waiting for events without using significant resources. We should use the blocking nature of pipes to ensure we use the CPU efficiently. After all, the server could, in theory, wait for many hours for a request to arrive.

Implementation

In the earlier, single process version of the application that we saw in Chapter 7, we used a set of data access routines for manipulating the data. These were:

```
int database_initialize(const int new_database);
void database_close(void);
cdc_entry get_cdc_entry(const char *cd_catalog_ptr);
cdt_entry get_cdt_entry(const char *cd_catalog_ptr, const int track_no);
int add_cdc_entry(const cdc_entry entry_to_add);
int add_cdt_entry(const cdt_entry entry_to_add);
int del_cdc_entry(const char *cd_catalog_ptr);
int del_cdt_entry(const char *cd_catalog_ptr, const int track_no);
cdc_entry search_cdc_entry(const char *cd_catalog_ptr,
                           int *first_call_ptr);
```

These functions provide a convenient place to make a clean separation between client and server.

In the single process implementation, we can view the application as having two parts, even though it was compiled as a single program:

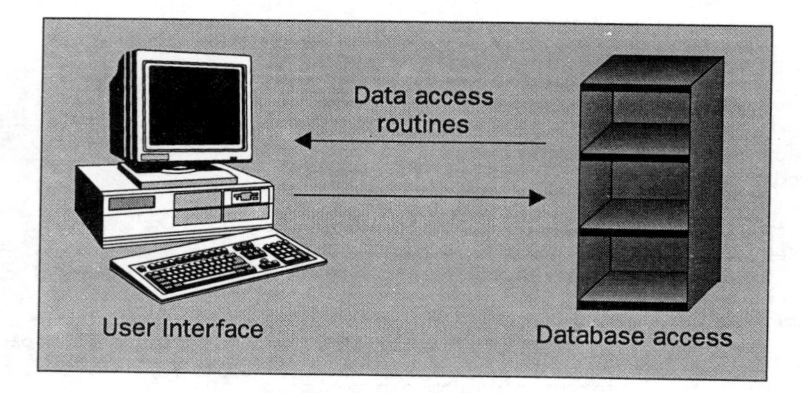

In the client-server implementation, we want to logically insert some named pipes and supporting code between the two major parts of the application.

This is the structure we need:

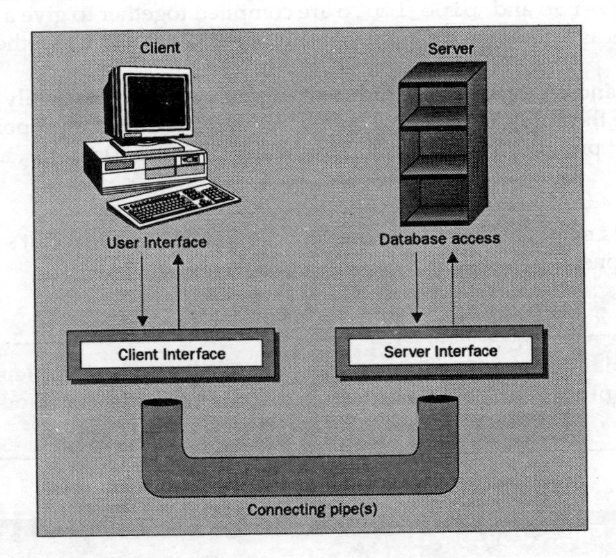

In our implementation, we choose to put both the client and server interface routines in the same file, `pipe_imp.c`. This keeps all the code that depends on the use of named pipes for the client/server implementation in a single file. The formatting and packaging of the data being passed is kept separate from the routines that implement the named pipes. We end up with more source files, but a better logical division between them. The calling structure in the application is:

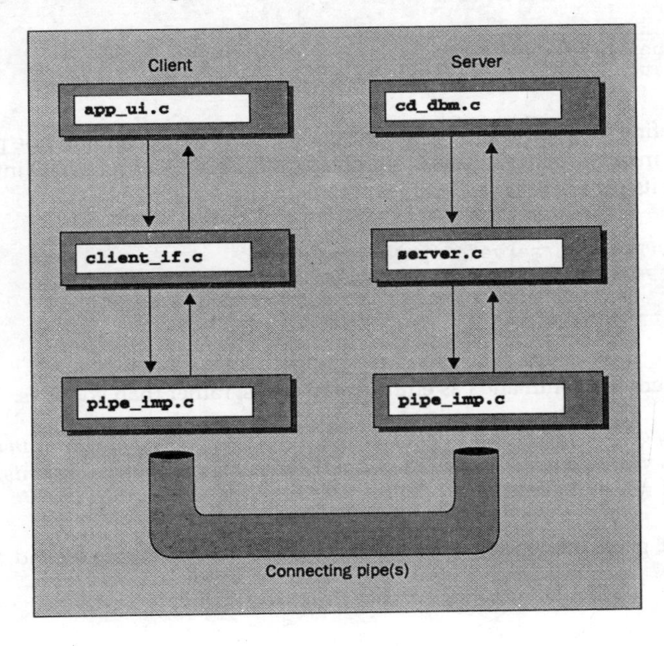

The files app_ui.c, client_if.c and pipe_imp.c are compiled together to give a client program The files cd_dbm.c, server.c and pipe_imp.c are compiled together to give a server program. A header file cliserv.h, acts as a common definitions header file to tie the two together.

The files app_ui.c and cd_dbm.c have only very minor changes, principally to cater for the split into two programs. Since the application is now quite large and a significant proportion of the code is unchanged from that previously seen, we only show here the files cliserv.h, client_if.c and pipe_imp.c.

First, we'll look at cliserv.h. This file defines the client/server interface. It's required by both client and server implementations.

Some parts of this file are dependent on the specific client/server implementation, in this case named pipes. We'll be changing to a different client/server model at the end of the next chapter.

Try It Out - The Header File, cliserv.h

1. There follow the required #include headers:

```
#include <unistd.h>
#include <stdlib.h>
#include <stdio.h>
#include <fcntl.h>
#include <limits.h>
#include <sys/types.h>
#include <sys/stat.h>
```

2. We then define the named pipes. We use one pipe for the server and one pipe for each client. Since there may be multiple clients, the client incorporates a process ID into the name, to ensure that its pipe is unique:

```
#define SERVER_PIPE "/tmp/server_pipe"
#define CLIENT_PIPE "/tmp/client_%d_pipe"

#define ERR_TEXT_LEN 80
```

3. We implement the commands as enumerated types, rather than #defines.

This is a good way of allowing the compiler to do more type checking and also helps in debugging the application, as many debuggers are able to show the name of enumerated constants, but not the name defined by a #define directive.

The first typedef gives the type of request being sent to the server, the second the server response to the client.

```
typedef enum {
    s_create_new_database = 0,
    s_get_cdc_entry,
    s_get_cdt_entry,
    s_add_cdc_entry,
    s_add_cdt_entry,
    s_del_cdc_entry,
    s_del_cdt_entry,
    s_find_cdc_entry
} client_request_e;

typedef enum {
    r_success = 0,
    r_failure,
    r_find_no_more
} server_response_e;
```

4. Next, we declare a structure that will form the message passed in both directions between the two processes.

> **Since we don't actually need to return both a `cdc_entry` and `cdt_entry` in the same response, we could have combined them in a union. For simplicity, we keep them separate. This also makes the code easier to maintain.**

```
typedef struct {
    pid_t               client_pid;
    client_request_e    request;
    server_response_e   response;
    cdc_entry           cdc_entry_data;
    cdt_entry           cdt_entry_data;
    char                error_text[ERR_TEXT_LEN + 1];
} message_db_t;
```

5. Finally, we get to the pipe interface functions that perform data transfer, implemented in `pipe_imp.c`. These divide into server- and client-side functions, in the first and second blocks respectively:

```
int server_starting(void);
void server_ending(void);
int read_request_from_client(message_db_t *rec_ptr);
int start_resp_to_client(const message_db_t mess_to_send);
int send_resp_to_client(const message_db_t mess_to_send);
void end_resp_to_client(void);

int client_starting(void);
void client_ending(void);
int send_mess_to_server(message_db_t mess_to_send);
int start_resp_from_server(void);
int read_resp_from_server(message_db_t *rec_ptr);
void end_resp_from_server(void);
```

We split the rest of the discussion into the client interface functions and details of the server- and client-side functions found in `pipe_imp.c`, and look at the source code as necessary.

Client Interface Functions

Now we look at client_if.c. This provides 'fake' versions of the database access routines. These encod the request in a message_db_t structure, then use the routines in pipe_imp.c to transfer the request to the server. This allows us to make minimal changes to the original app_ui.c.

Try It Out - The Client's Interpreter

1. This file implements the nine database functions prototyped in cd_data.h. It does so by passing requests to the server and then returning the server response from the function, acting as an intermediary.

The file starts with #include files and constants:

```
#define _POSIX_SOURCE

#include <unistd.h>
#include <stdlib.h>
#include <stdio.h>
#include <fcntl.h>
#include <limits.h>
#include <sys/types.h>
#include <sys/stat.h>

#include "cd_data.h"
#include "cliserv.h"
```

2. The static variable mypid reduces the number of calls to getpid that would otherwise be required. We use a local function, read_one_response, to eliminate duplicated code:

```
static pid_t mypid;

static int read_one_response(message_db_t *rec_ptr);
```

3. The database_initialize and close routines are still called, but are now used, respectively, for initializing the client-side of the pipes interface and for removing redundant named pipes when the client exits.

```
int database_initialize(const int new_database)
{
    if (!client_starting()) return(0);
    mypid = getpid();
    return(1);

} /* database_initialize */

void database_close(void) {
    client_ending();
}
```

4. The `get_cdc_entry` routine is called to get a catalog entry from the database, given a CD catalog title. Here we encode the request in a `message_db_t` structure and pass it to the server. We then read the response back into a different `message_db_t` structure. If an entry is found, it's included inside the `message_db_t` structure as a `cdc_entry` structure, so we pass back the appropriate part of the structure:

```
cdc_entry get_cdc_entry(const char *cd_catalog_ptr)
{
    cdc_entry ret_val;
    message_db_t mess_send;
    message_db_t mess_ret;

    ret_val.catalog[0] = '\0';
    mess_send.client_pid = mypid;
    mess_send.request = s_get_cdc_entry;
    strcpy(mess_send.cdc_entry_data.catalog, cd_catalog_ptr);

    if (send_mess_to_server(mess_send)) {
        if (read_one_response(&mess_ret)) {
            if (mess_ret.response == r_success) {
                ret_val = mess_ret.cdc_entry_data;
            } else {
                fprintf(stderr, "%s", mess_ret.error_text);
            }
        } else {
            fprintf(stderr, "Server failed to respond\n");
        }
    } else {
        fprintf(stderr, "Server not accepting requests\n");
    }
    return(ret_val);
}
```

5. Here's the source for the function `read_one_response` that we use to avoid duplicating code:

```
static int read_one_response(message_db_t *rec_ptr) {

    int return_code = 0;
    if (!rec_ptr) return(0);

    if (start_resp_from_server()) {
        if (read_resp_from_server(rec_ptr)) {
            return_code = 1;
        }
        end_resp_from_server();
    }
    return(return_code);
}
```

6. The other get_xxx, del_xxx and add_xxx routines are implemented in a similar way to the get_cdc_entry function and are reproduced here for completeness. First, the function for retrieving CD tracks:

```
cdt_entry get_cdt_entry(const char *cd_catalog_ptr, const int track_no)
{
    cdt_entry ret_val;
    message_db_t mess_send;
    message_db_t mess_ret;

    ret_val.catalog[0] = '\0';
    mess_send.client_pid = mypid;
    mess_send.request = s_get_cdt_entry;
    strcpy(mess_send.cdt_entry_data.catalog, cd_catalog_ptr);
    mess_send.cdt_entry_data.track_no = track_no;

    if (send_mess_to_server(mess_send)) {
        if (read_one_response(&mess_ret)) {
            if (mess_ret.response == r_success) {
                ret_val = mess_ret.cdt_entry_data;
            } else {
                fprintf(stderr, "%s", mess_ret.error_text);
            }
        } else {
            fprintf(stderr, "Server failed to respond\n");
        }
    } else {
        fprintf(stderr, "Server not accepting requests\n");
    }
    return(ret_val);
}
```

7. Next, two functions for adding data, first to the catalog and then to the tracks database:

```
int add_cdc_entry(const cdc_entry entry_to_add)
{
    message_db_t mess_send;
    message_db_t mess_ret;

    mess_send.client_pid = mypid;
    mess_send.request = s_add_cdc_entry;
    mess_send.cdc_entry_data = entry_to_add;

    if (send_mess_to_server(mess_send)) {
        if (read_one_response(&mess_ret)) {
            if (mess_ret.response == r_success) {
                return(1);
            } else {
                fprintf(stderr, "%s", mess_ret.error_text);
            }
        } else {
            fprintf(stderr, "Server failed to respond\n");
        }
    } else {
        fprintf(stderr, "Server not accepting requests\n");
    }
    return(0);
}
```

```
int add_cdt_entry(const cdt_entry entry_to_add)
{
    message_db_t mess_send;
    message_db_t mess_ret;

    mess_send.client_pid = mypid;
    mess_send.request = s_add_cdt_entry;
    mess_send.cdt_entry_data = entry_to_add;

    if (send_mess_to_server(mess_send)) {
        if (read_one_response(&mess_ret)) {
            if (mess_ret.response == r_success) {
                return(1);
            } else {
                fprintf(stderr, "%s", mess_ret.error_text);
            }
        } else {
            fprintf(stderr, "Server failed to respond\n");
        }
    } else {
        fprintf(stderr, "Server not accepting requests\n");
    }
    return(0);
}
```

8. And lastly, two functions for data deletion:

```
int del_cdc_entry(const char *cd_catalog_ptr)
{
    message_db_t mess_send;
    message_db_t mess_ret;

    mess_send.client_pid = mypid;
    mess_send.request = s_del_cdc_entry;
    strcpy(mess_send.cdc_entry_data.catalog, cd_catalog_ptr);

    if (send_mess_to_server(mess_send)) {
        if (read_one_response(&mess_ret)) {
            if (mess_ret.response == r_success) {
                return(1);
            } else {
                fprintf(stderr, "%s", mess_ret.error_text);
            }
        } else {
            fprintf(stderr, "Server failed to respond\n");
        }
    } else {
        fprintf(stderr, "Server not accepting requests\n");
    }
    return(0);
}

int del_cdt_entry(const char *cd_catalog_ptr, const int track_no)
{
    message_db_t mess_send;
    message_db_t mess_ret;

    mess_send.client_pid = mypid;
    mess_send.request = s_del_cdt_entry;
    strcpy(mess_send.cdt_entry_data.catalog, cd_catalog_ptr);
    mess_send.cdt_entry_data.track_no = track_no;
```

```
    if (send_mess_to_server(mess_send)) {
        if (read_one_response(&mess_ret)) {
            if (mess_ret.response == r_success) {
                return(1);
            } else {
                fprintf(stderr, "%s", mess_ret.error_text);
            }
        } else {
            fprintf(stderr, "Server failed to respond\n");
        }
    } else {
        fprintf(stderr, "Server not accepting requests\n");
    }
    return(0);
}
```

Searching the Database

The function for the search on the CD key is rather more complex. The user of this function expects to call it once to start a search. We catered for this in Chapter 7 by setting `*first_call_ptr true` on this first call and the function then to return the first match. On subsequent calls to the search function, `*first_call_ptr` is `false` and further matches are returned, one per call.

Now that we've split the application across two processes, we can no longer allow the search to proceed one entry at a time in the server, because a different client may request a different search from the server whilst our search is in progress. We can't make the server side store the context (where the search had got to) for each client search separately, since the client side can simply stop searching part of the way through a search, when a user finds the CD they are looking for, or if the client 'falls over'.

We can either change the way the search is performed, or, as we have chosen here, hide the complexity in the interface routine. What we've done is to arrange for the server to return all the possible matches to a search and then store them in a temporary file until they are requested by the client.

Our original application functioned in a similar way to a SQL database, which may use a cursor to move through intermediate results. Such a system would have to make a similar design decision about how to return multiple results of a SQL query.

Try It Out - Searching

1. This function looks more complicated than it is because it calls three pipe functions that we'll be looking at in the next section, `send_mess_to_server`, `start_resp_from_server` and `read_resp_from_server`:

```
cdc_entry search_cdc_entry(const char *cd_catalog_ptr, int *first_call_ptr)
{
    message_db_t mess_send;
    message_db_t mess_ret;

    static FILE *work_file = (FILE *)0;
    static int entries_matching = 0;
    cdc_entry ret_val;

    ret_val.catalog[0] = '\0';

    if (!work_file && (*first_call_ptr == 0)) return(ret_val);
```

2. Here's the first call to search, i.e. with `*first_call_ptr` set to `true`. It's set to `false` immediately, lest we forget. A `work_file` is created and the client message structure initialized.

```
if (*first_call_ptr) {
    *first_call_ptr = 0;
    if (work_file) fclose(work_file);
    work_file = tmpfile();
    if (!work_file) return(ret_val);

    mess_send.client_pid = mypid;
    mess_send.request = s_find_cdc_entry;
    strcpy(mess_send.cdc_entry_data.catalog, cd_catalog_ptr);
```

3. Now there's this three-deep condition test, which makes calls to functions in `pipe_imp.c`. If the message is successfully sent to the server, the client waits for the server's response. While `reads` from the server are successful, the search matches are returned to the client's `work_file` and the `entries_matching` counter is incremented.

```
    if (send_mess_to_server(mess_send)) {
        if (start_resp_from_server()) {
            while (read_resp_from_server(&mess_ret)) {
                if (mess_ret.response == r_success) {
            fwrite(&mess_ret.cdc_entry_data, sizeof(cdc_entry), 1, work_file);
                    entries_matching++;
                } else {
                    break;
                }
            } /* while */
        } else {
            fprintf(stderr, "Server not responding\n");
        }
    } else {
        fprintf(stderr, "Server not accepting requests\n");
    }
```

4. The next test checks whether the search had any luck. Then the `fseek` call sets the `work_file` to the next place for data to be written.

```
    if (entries_matching == 0) {
        fclose(work_file);
        work_file = (FILE *)0;
        return(ret_val);
    }
    (void)fseek(work_file, 0L, SEEK_SET);
```

5. If this is not the first call to the search function with this particular search term, the code checks whether there are any matches left. Finally, the next matching entry is read to the `ret_val` structure. The previous checks guarantee that a matching entry exists.

```
    } else {
            /* not *first_call_ptr */
        if (entries_matching == 0) {
            fclose(work_file);
            work_file = (FILE *)0;
            return(ret_val);
        }
    }

    fread(&ret_val, sizeof(cdc_entry), 1, work_file);
    entries_matching--;

    return(ret_val);
}
```

The Server Interface

Just as the client side has an interface to the app_ui.c program, so the server side needs a program to control the (renamed) cd_access.c, now cd_dbm.c. The server's main function is listed here.

Try It Out - server.c

1. Some global variables, a prototype for process_command and a signal catcher to ensure a clean exit.

```
#include <unistd.h>
#include <stdlib.h>
#include <stdio.h>
#include <fcntl.h>
#include <limits.h>
#include <signal.h>
#include <string.h>
#include <errno.h>
#include <sys/types.h>
#include <sys/stat.h>

#include "cd_data.h"
#include "cliserv.h"

int save_errno;
static int server_running = 1;

static void process_command(const message_db_t mess_command);

void catch_signals()
{
    server_running = 0;
}
```

2. Now we come to the main function. After checking that the signal catching routines are all right, the program checks to see whether you passed -i on the command line. If you did, it will create a new database. If the call to the database_initialize routine in cd_dbm.c fails, an error message is shown. If all is well and the server is running, any requests from the client are fed to the process_command function that we'll meet in a moment.

```
int main(int argc, char *argv[]) {
    struct sigaction new_action, old_action;
    message_db_t mess_command;
    int database_init_type = 0;

    new_action.sa_handler = catch_signals;
    sigemptyset(&new_action.sa_mask);
    new_action.sa_flags = 0;
    if ((sigaction(SIGINT, &new_action, &old_action) != 0) ||
        (sigaction(SIGHUP, &new_action, &old_action) != 0) ||
        (sigaction(SIGTERM, &new_action, &old_action) != 0)) {
        fprintf(stderr, "Server startup error, signal catching failed\n");
        exit(EXIT_FAILURE);
    }

    if (argc > 1) {
        argv++;
        if (strncmp("-i", *argv, 2) == 0) database_init_type = 1;
    }
    if (!database_initialize(database_init_type)) {
              fprintf(stderr, "Server error:-\
                     could not initialize database\n");
              exit(EXIT_FAILURE);
    }

    if (!server_starting()) exit(EXIT_FAILURE);

    while(server_running) {
        if (read_request_from_client(&mess_command)) {
            process_command(mess_command);
        } else {
            if(server_running) fprintf(stderr, "Server ended - can not \
                                        read pipe\n");
            server_running = 0;
        }
    } /* while */
    server_ending();
    exit(EXIT_SUCCESS);
}
```

3. Any client messages are fed to the `process_command` function, where they are fed into a `case` statement that makes the appropriate calls to `cd_dbm.c`.

```
static void process_command(const message_db_t comm)
{
    message_db_t resp;
    int first_time = 1;

    resp = comm; /* copy command back, then change resp as required */

    if (!start_resp_to_client(resp)) {
        fprintf(stderr, "Server Warning:-\
                  start_resp_to_client %d failed\n", resp.client_pid);
        return;
    }

    resp.response = r_success;
    memset(resp.error_text, '\0', sizeof(resp.error_text));
    save_errno = 0;
```

```
    switch(resp.request) {
        case s_create_new_database:
            if (!database_initialize(1)) resp.response = r_failure;
            break;
        case s_get_cdc_entry:
            resp.cdc_entry_data =
                        get_cdc_entry(comm.cdc_entry_data.catalog);
            break;
        case s_get_cdt_entry:
            resp.cdt_entry_data =
                        get_cdt_entry(comm.cdt_entry_data.catalog,
                                      comm.cdt_entry_data.track_no);
            break;
        case s_add_cdc_entry:
            if (!add_cdc_entry(comm.cdc_entry_data)) resp.response =
                        r_failure;
            break;
        case s_add_cdt_entry:
            if (!add_cdt_entry(comm.cdt_entry_data)) resp.response =
                        r_failure;
            break;
        case s_del_cdc_entry:
            if (!del_cdc_entry(comm.cdc_entry_data.catalog)) resp.response
                       = r_failure;
            break;
        case s_del_cdt_entry:
            if (!del_cdt_entry(comm.cdt_entry_data.catalog,
                 comm.cdt_entry_data.track_no)) resp.response = r_failure;
            break;
        case s_find_cdc_entry:
            do {
                resp.cdc_entry_data =
                        search_cdc_entry(comm.cdc_entry_data.catalog,
                                         &first_time);
                if (resp.cdc_entry_data.catalog[0] != 0) {
                    resp.response = r_success;
                    if (!send_resp_to_client(resp)) {
                        fprintf(stderr, "Server Warning:-\
                            failed to respond to %d\n", resp.client_pid);
                        break;
                    }
                } else {
                    resp.response = r_find_no_more;
                }
            } while (resp.response == r_success);
        break;
        default:
            resp.response = r_failure;
            break;
    } /* switch */

    sprintf(resp.error_text, "Command failed:\n\t%s\n",
            strerror(save_errno));

    if (!send_resp_to_client(resp)) {
        fprintf(stderr, "Server Warning:-\
                failed to respond to %d\n", resp.client_pid);
    }

    end_resp_to_client();
    return;
}
```

Before we look at the actual pipe implementation, let's discuss the sequence of events that need to occur to pass data between the client and server processes. This diagram shows both client and server processes starting and how both parties loop while processing commands and responses.

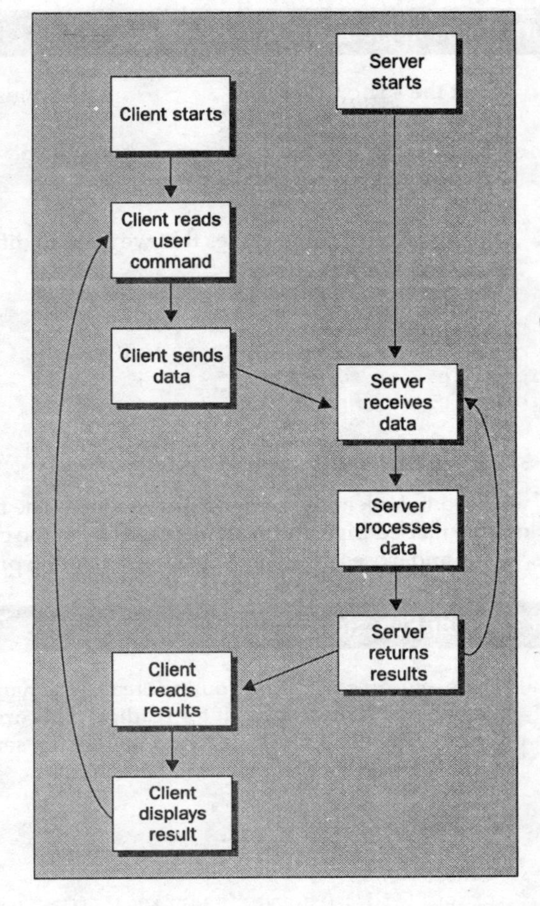

In this implementation, the situation is slightly more difficult, since, for a search request, the client passes a single command to the server and then expects back one or more responses from the server. This leads to some additional complexity, mainly in the client.

The Pipe

Here's the pipes implementation file, `pipe_imp.c`, which has both the client- and server-side functions.

> **As we saw in Chapter 9, the symbol, `DEBUG_TRACE`, can be defined to show the sequence of calls as the client and server processes pass messages between each other.**

Try It Out - Pipes Implementation Header

1. First the #includes:

```
#include "cd_data.h"
#include "cliserv.h"
```

2. We also define some values that we need in different functions within the file:

```
static int server_fd = -1;
static pid_t mypid = 0;
static char client_pipe_name[PATH_MAX + 1] = {'\0'};
static int client_fd = -1;
static int client_write_fd = -1;
```

Server-side Functions

Next, we need to look at the server-side functions. The first section below shows the functions that open and close the named pipe and read messages from the clients. The second Try It Out shows the code that opens, sends and closes the client pipes, based on the process ID the client includes in its message.

Try It Out - Server Functions

1. The server_starting routine creates the named pipe from which the server will read commands. It then opens it for reading. This open will block until a client opens the pipe for writing. We use a blocking mode, so that the server can perform blocking reads on the pipe while waiting for commands to be sent to it.

```
int server_starting(void)
{
    #if DEBUG_TRACE
        printf("%d :- server_starting()\n",  getpid());
    #endif

        unlink(SERVER_PIPE);
    if (mkfifo(SERVER_PIPE, 0777) == -1) {
        fprintf(stderr, "Server startup error, no FIFO created\n");
        return(0);
    }

    if ((server_fd = open(SERVER_PIPE, O_RDONLY)) == -1) {
        if (errno == EINTR) return(0);
        fprintf(stderr, "Server startup error, no FIFO opened\n");
        return(0);
    }
    return(1);
}
```

2. When the server ends, it removes the named pipe, so clients can detect that no server is running.

```
void server_ending(void)
{
    #if DEBUG_TRACE
        printf("%d :- server_ending()\n",  getpid());
    #endif

    (void)close(server_fd);
    (void)unlink(SERVER_PIPE);
}
```

3. The `read_request_from_client` function, shown below, will block reading the server pipe until a client writes a message into it:

```
int read_request_from_client(message_db_t *rec_ptr)
{
    int return_code = 0;
    int read_bytes;

    #if DEBUG_TRACE
        printf("%d :- read_request_from_client()\n",  getpid());
    #endif

    if (server_fd != -1) {
        read_bytes = read(server_fd, rec_ptr, sizeof(*rec_ptr));
...
    }
    return(return_code);
}
```

4. In the special case when no clients have the pipe open for writing, the `read` will return 0, i.e. it detects an `EOF`. Then the server closes the pipe and opens it again, so that it blocks until a client also opens the pipe. This is just the same as when the server first starts; we have re-initialized the server. Insert this code in the function above:

```
        if (read_bytes == 0) {
            (void)close(server_fd);
            if ((server_fd = open(SERVER_PIPE, O_RDONLY)) == -1) {
                if (errno != EINTR) {
                    fprintf(stderr, "Server error, FIFO open failed\n");
                }
                return(0);
            }
            read_bytes = read(server_fd, rec_ptr, sizeof(*rec_ptr));
        }
        if (read_bytes == sizeof(*rec_ptr)) return_code = 1;
```

The server is a single process that may be serving many clients simultaneously. Since each client uses a different pipe to receive its responses, the server needs to write to a different pipe to send responses to different clients. Since file descriptors are a limited resource, the server only opens a client pipe for writing when it has data to send.

We split the opening, writing and closing of the client pipe into three separate functions. We need to do this when we're returning multiple results to a search, so we can open the pipe once, write many responses, then close it again.

Try It Out - Plumbing the Pipes

1. First, we open the client pipe:

```
int start_resp_to_client(const message_db_t mess_to_send)
{
    #if DEBUG_TRACE
        printf("%d :- start_resp_to_client()\n", getpid());
    #endif

    (void)sprintf(client_pipe_name, CLIENT_PIPE, mess_to_send.client_pid);
    if ((client_fd = open(client_pipe_name, O_WRONLY)) == -1) return(0);
    return(1);
}
```

2. The messages are all sent using calls to this function. We'll look at the corresponding client-side functions that field the message soon.

```
int send_resp_to_client(const message_db_t mess_to_send)
{
    int write_bytes;

    #if DEBUG_TRACE
        printf("%d :- send_resp_to_client()\n", getpid());
    #endif

    if (client_fd == -1) return(0);
    write_bytes = write(client_fd, &mess_to_send, sizeof(mess_to_send));
    if (write_bytes != sizeof(mess_to_send)) return(0);
    return(1);
}
```

3. Finally, we close the client pipe:

```
void end_resp_to_client(void)
{
    #if DEBUG_TRACE
        printf("%d :- end_resp_to_client()\n",  getpid());
    #endif

    if (client_fd != -1) {
        (void)close(client_fd);
        client_fd = -1;
    }
}
```

Client-side Functions

Complementing the server are the client functions in `pipe_imp.c`. Very similar, except for the worryingly-named `send_mess_to_server`.

Try It Out - Client Functions

1. After checking that a server is accessible, the `client_starting` function initializes the client-side pipe:

```
int client_starting(void)
{
    #if DEBUG_TRACE
        printf("%d :- client_starting\n",  getpid());
    #endif

    mypid = getpid();
    if ((server_fd = open(SERVER_PIPE, O_WRONLY)) == -1) {
        fprintf(stderr, "Server not running\n");
        return(0);
    }

    (void)sprintf(client_pipe_name, CLIENT_PIPE, mypid);
    (void)unlink(client_pipe_name);
    if (mkfifo(client_pipe_name, 0777) == -1) {
        fprintf(stderr, "Unable to create client pipe %s\n",
                    client_pipe_name);
        return(0);
    }
    return(1);
}
```

2. The `client_ending` function closes file descriptors and deletes the now redundant named pipe:

```
void client_ending(void)
{
    #if DEBUG_TRACE
        printf("%d :- client_ending()\n",  getpid());
    #endif

    if (client_write_fd != -1) (void)close(client_write_fd);
    if (client_fd != -1) (void)close(client_fd);
    if (server_fd != -1) (void)close(server_fd);
    (void)unlink(client_pipe_name);
}
```

3. The `send_mess_to_server` function passes the request through the server pipe:

```
int send_mess_to_server(message_db_t mess_to_send)
{
    int write_bytes;

    #if DEBUG_TRACE
        printf("%d :- send_mess_to_server()\n",  getpid());
    #endif
```

```
    if (server_fd == -1) return(0);
    mess_to_send.client_pid = mypid;
    write_bytes = write(server_fd, &mess_to_send, sizeof(mess_to_send));
    if (write_bytes != sizeof(mess_to_send)) return(0);
    return(1);
}
```

As with the server-side functions we saw earlier, the client gets results back from the server using three functions, to cater for multiple search results.

Try It Out - Getting Server Results

1. This client function starts to listen for the server response. It opens a client pipe as read-only and then reopens this pipe's file as write-only. We'll see why in a moment.

```
int start_resp_from_server(void)
{
    #if DEBUG_TRACE
        printf("%d :- start_resp_from_server()\n",  getpid());
    #endif

    if (client_pipe_name[0] == '\0') return(0);
    if (client_fd != -1) return(1);

    client_fd = open(client_pipe_name, O_RDONLY);
    if (client_fd != -1) {
        client_write_fd = open(client_pipe_name, O_WRONLY);
        if (client_write_fd != -1) return(1);
        (void)close(client_fd);
        client_fd = -1;
    }
    return(0);
}
```

2. Here's the main `read` from the server which gets the matching database entries:

```
int read_resp_from_server(message_db_t *rec_ptr)
{
    int read_bytes;
    int return_code = 0;

    #if DEBUG_TRACE
        printf("%d :- read_resp_from_server()\n",  getpid());
    #endif

    if (!rec_ptr) return(0);
    if (client_fd == -1) return(0);

    read_bytes = read(client_fd, rec_ptr, sizeof(*rec_ptr));
    if (read_bytes == sizeof(*rec_ptr)) return_code = 1;
    return(return_code);
}
```

3. And finally, the client function that marks the end of the server response...

```
void end_resp_from_server(void)
{
    #if DEBUG_TRACE
        printf("%d :- end_resp_from_server()\n", getpid());
    #endif

    /* This function is empty in the pipe implementation */
}
```

How It Works

The second, additional open of the client pipe for writing in `start_resp_from_server`,

```
client_write_fd = open(client_pipe_name, O_WRONLY);
```

is used to prevent a race condition, when the server needs to respond to several requests from the client in quick succession.

To explain this a little more, consider the following sequence of events:

1. The client writes a request to the server.
2. The server reads the request, opens the client pipe and sends the response back, but is suspended before it gets as far as closing the client pipe.
3. The client opens its pipe for reading, reads the first response and closes its pipe.
4. The client then sends a new command and opens the client pipe for reading.
5. The server then resumes running, closing its end of the client pipe.

Unfortunately, at this point the client is trying to read the pipe, looking for a response to its next request, but the `read` will return with 0 bytes, since no process has the client pipe open for writing.

By allowing the client to open its pipe for both reading and writing, thus removing the need for repeatedly re-opening the pipe, we avoid this race condition. Note that the client never writes to the pipe, so there's no danger of reading erroneous data.

Application Summary

We've now separated our CD database application into a client and a server. This will allow us to develop the user interface and the underlying database technology independently. We can see that a well-defined database interface allows each major element of the application to make the best use of computer resources. If we take things a little further, we could change the pipes implementation to a networked one and use a dedicated database server machine. We'll learn more about networking in Chapter 13.

Summary

In this chapter, we've looked at passing data between processes using pipes.

First, we looked at unnamed pipes created with the `popen` or the `pipe` call and discussed how, using a pipe and the `dup` call, we can pass data from one program to the standard input of another.

We then looked at named pipes and saw how we can pass data between unrelated programs.

Finally, we implemented a simple client/server example, using FIFOs to give us not only process synchronization, but also bi-directional data flow.

Semaphores, Message Queues and Shared Memory

In this chapter, we are going to look at a set of interprocess communication facilities that were introduced in the AT&T System V.2 release of UNIX. Since all these facilities appeared in the same release and have a similar programmatic interface, they are often referred to as the IPC (InterProcess Communication) facilities, or System V IPC. As we've already seen, they are by no means the only way of communicating between processes, but the expression System V IPC is usually used to refer to these specific facilities.

Semaphores

When we write programs that use threads, operating in either multiuser systems, multiprocessing systems or a combination of the two, we often discover that we have **critical sections** of code where we need to ensure that a single executing process has exclusive access to a resource.

In our first example application using dbm to access a database in Chapter 7, the data could be corrupted if multiple programs tried to update the database at exactly the same time. There's no trouble with two different programs asking different users to enter data for the database, the only probiem is in the parts of the code that update the database. These are the critical sections.

To prevent problems caused by more than one program accessing a resource, we need a way of generating and using a token that grants access to only one thread of execution in a critical section at a time. We saw briefly in Chapter 11 some thread specific ways we could use a mutex or semaphores to control access to critical sections in a threaded program. In this chapter we return to the topic of semaphores, but look more generally at how they are used between different processes. Be aware that the semaphore functions used with threads are not the ones we will meet here, be careful not to confuse the two types.

It's surprisingly difficult to write code that achieves this without specialist hardware support, although there's a solution known as **Dekker's Algorithm**. Unfortunately, this algorithm relies on a 'busy wait', or 'spin lock', where a process runs continuously, waiting for a memory location to be changed. In a multitasking environment such as UNIX, this is an undesirable waste of CPU resources.

One possible solution that we've already seen is to create files using the `O_EXCL` flag with the `open` function, which provides atomic file creation. This allows a single process to succeed in obtaining a token, the newly created file. This method is fine for simple problems, but rather messy and very inefficient for more complex examples.

An important step forward in this area of concurrent programming occurred when Dijkstra introduced the concept of the **semaphore**. A semaphore is a special variable that takes only whole positive numbers and upon which only two operations are allowed: wait and signal. Since 'wait' and 'signal' already have special meanings in UNIX programming, we'll use the original notation:

- `P(semaphore variable)` for wait,
- `V(semaphore variable)` for signal.

These letters come from the Dutch words for wait (*passeren*: to pass, as in a check point before the critical section) and signal (*vrijgeven*: to give, as in giving up control of the critical section). You may also come across the terms 'up' and 'down' used in relation to semaphores, taken from the use of signaling flags.

Semaphore Definition

The simplest semaphore is a variable that can take only the values 0 and 1, a **binary semaphore**, and this is the most common form. Semaphores that can take many positive values are called **general semaphores**. For the remainder of this chapter, we'll concentrate on binary semaphores.

The definitions of `P` and `V` are surprisingly simple. Suppose we have a semaphore variable, `sv`. The two operations are then defined as:

`P(sv)`	If `sv` is greater than zero, decrement `sv`. If `sv` is zero, suspend execution of this process.
`V(sv)`	If some other process has been suspended waiting for `sv`, make it resume execution. If no process is suspended waiting for `sv`, increment `sv`.

Another way of thinking about semaphores is that the semaphore variable, `sv`, is `true` when the critical section is available, is decremented by `P(sv)` so it's `false` when the critical section is busy, and incremented by `V(sv)` when the critical section is again available. Be aware that simply having a normal variable that you decrement and increment is not good enough, because you can't express in C or C++ the need to make a single, atomic operation of the test to see whether the variable is `true`, or the change of the variable to make it `false`. This is what makes the semaphore operations special.

A Theoretical Example

We can see how this works with a simple theoretical example. Suppose we have two processes `proc1` and `proc2`, both of which need exclusive access to a database at some point in their execution. We define a single binary semaphore, `sv`, that starts with the value 1 and can be accessed by both processes. Both processes then need to perform the same processing to access the critical section of code, indeed the two processes could simply be different invocations of the same program.

The two processes share the `sv` semaphore variable. Once one process has executed `P(sv)`, it has obtained the semaphore and can enter the critical section. The second process is prevented from entering the critical section because, when it attempts to execute `P(sv)`, it's made to wait until the first process has left the critical section and executed `V(sv)` to release the semaphore.

The required pseudo-code is:

```
semaphore sv = 1;

loop forever {
    P(sv);
    critical code section;
    V(sv);
    non-critical code section;
}
```

The code is surprisingly simple because the definition of the `P` and `V` operations is very powerful. Here's a diagram showing how the `P` and `V` operations act as a gate into critical sections of code:

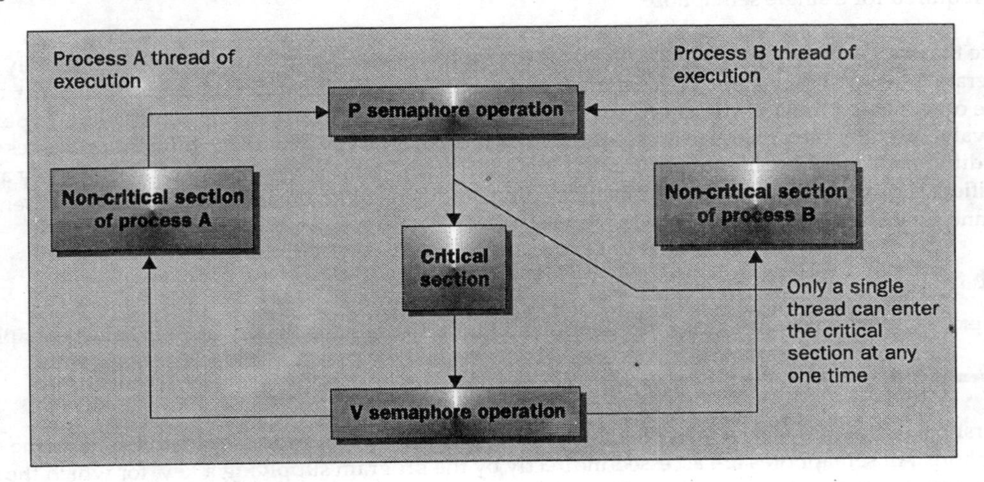

UNIX Semaphore Facilities

Now that we've seen what semaphores are and how they work in theory, we can look at how the features are implemented in UNIX. The interface is rather elaborate and offers far more facilities than are generally required. All the UNIX semaphore functions operate on arrays of general semaphores, rather than a single binary semaphore. At first sight this just seems to make things more complicated, but in complex cases where a process needs to lock multiple resources the ability to operate on an array of semaphores is a big advantage. In this chapter we will concentrate on using single semaphores, since in most cases that's all you will need to use.

The semaphore function definitions are:

```
#include <sys/sem.h>

int semctl(int sem_id, int sem_num, int command, ...);
int semget(key_t key, int num_sems, int sem_flags);
int semop(int sem_id, struct sembuf *sem_ops, size_t num_sem_ops);
```

In practice, the `#include` files `sys/types.h` and `sys/ipc.h` are also usually needed to get some of the `defines` you need for particular operations. There are, however, a few cases when they won't be necessary.

As we work through each function in turn, remember that these functions were designed to work for arrays of semaphore values, which makes their operation significantly more complex than would have been required for a single semaphore.

Notice that `key` acts very much like a file name in that it represents a resource that programs may use and cooperate in using if they agree on a common name. Similarly, the identifier returned by `semget` and used by the other shared memory functions is very much like the `FILE *` file stream returned by `fopen` in that it's a value used by the process to access the shared file. And, just as with files, different processes will have different semaphore identifiers, though they refer to the same semaphore. This use of a key and identifiers is common to all of the IPC facilities discussed here, although each facility uses independent keys and identifiers.

semget

The `semget` function creates a new semaphore or obtains the semaphore key of an existing semaphore.

```
int semget(key_t key, int num_sems, int sem_flags);
```

The first parameter, `key`, is an integral value used to allow unrelated processes to access the same semaphore. All semaphores are accessed indirectly by the program supplying a key, for which the system then generates a semaphore identifier. The semaphore key is only used with `semget`. All other semaphore functions use the semaphore identifier returned from `semget`.

There is a special semaphore `key` value, `IPC_PRIVATE`, that creates a semaphore that only the creating process can access. It must forward this identifier directly to the processes that need it, which are usually child processes it has created. This is rarely used. You should check that you don't accidentally use the value your system declares as `IPC_PRIVATE`. On Linux systems, the value of `IPC_PRIVATE` is usually 0.

The `num_sems` parameter is the number of semaphores required. This is almost always 1.

The `sem_flags` parameter is a set of flags, very much like the flags to the `open` function. The lower nine bits are the permissions for the semaphore, which behave like file permissions. In addition, these can be bitwise ORed with the value `IPC_CREAT` to create a new semaphore. It's not an error to have the `IPC_CREAT` flag set and give the key of an existing semaphore. The `IPC_CREAT` flag is silently ignored if not required. We can use `IPC_CREAT` and `IPC_EXCL` together to ensure that we obtain a new, unique semaphore. It will return an error if the semaphore already exists.

The semget function returns a positive (non-zero) value on success; this is the semaphore identifier used in the other semaphore functions. On error, it returns -1.

semop

The function semop is used for changing the value of the semaphore:

```
int semop(int sem_id, struct sembuf *sem_ops, size_t num_sem_ops);
```

The first parameter, sem_id, is the semaphore identifier, as returned from semget. The second parameter, sem_ops, is a pointer to an array of structures, each of which will have at least the following members:

```
struct sembuf {
    short sem_num;
    short sem_op;
    short sem_flg;
}
```

The first member, sem_num, is the semaphore number, usually 0 unless you're working with an array of semaphores. The sem_op member is the value by which the semaphore should be changed. You can change a semaphore by amounts other than 1. In general, only two values are used, -1, which is our P operation to wait for a semaphore to become available, and +1, which is our V operation to signal that a semaphore is now available.

The final member, sem_flg, is usually set to SEM_UNDO. This causes the operating system to track the changes made to the semaphore by the current process and, if the process terminates without releasing the semaphore, allows the operating system to automatically release the semaphore if it was held by this process. It's good practice to set sem_flg to SEM_UNDO, unless you specifically require different behavior. If you do decide you need a value other than SEM_UNDO, then it's important to be consistent, or you can get very confused as to whether the kernel is attempting to 'tidy up' your semaphores when your process exits.

All actions called for by semop are taken together to avoid a race condition implied by using multiple semaphores. You can find full details of the processing of semop in the man pages.

semctl

The semctl function allows direct control of semaphore information:

```
int semctl(int sem_id, int sem_num, int command, ...);
```

The first parameter, sem_id, is a semaphore identifier, obtained from semget. The sem_num parameter is the semaphore number. You use this when you're working with arrays of semaphores. Usually, this is 0, the first and only semaphore. The command parameter is the action to take and a fourth parameter, if present, is a union semun, which must have at least the following members:

```
union semun {
    int val;
    struct semid_ds *buf;
    unsigned short *array;
}
```

Some versions of Linux have a definition of the semun union in a header file, though X/Open does say that you have to declare your own. If you do find that you need to declare your own, check the manual pages for semctl to see if there is definition given. If there is, we suggest you use exactly the definition given in your manual, even if it differs from that above. This is the semun.h that we used, but you should check the manual pages for your particular Linux system, and change it if necessary:

```
#ifndef _SEMUN_H

#define _SEMUN_H

union semun {
  int val;                    /* value for SETVAL */
  struct semid_ds *buf;       /* buffer for IPC_STAT, IPC_SET */
  unsigned short int *array;  /* array for GETALL, SETALL */
  struct seminfo *__buf;      /* buffer for IPC_INFO */
};

#endif
```

There are many different possible values of command allowed for semctl. Only two, which we describe here, are commonly used. For full details of the semctl function you should consult the manual page.

The two common values of command are:

- SETVAL: used for initializing a semaphore to a known value. The value required is passed as the val member of the union semun. This is required to set the semaphore up before it's used for the first time.
- IPC_RMID: used for deleting a semaphore identifier when it's no longer required.

The semctl function returns different values, depending on the command parameter. For SETVAL and IPC_RMID it returns 0 for success and -1 on error.

Using Semaphores

As you can see from the above descriptions, semaphore operations can be rather complex. This is most unfortunate, since programming multiple processes or threads with critical sections is quite a difficult problem on its own and having a complex programming interface simply adds to the intellectual burden.

Fortunately, we can solve most problems that require semaphores using only a single binary semaphore, the simplest type. In our example, we'll use the full programming interface to create a much simpler P and V type interface for a binary semaphore. We'll then use this much simpler interface to demonstrate how semaphores function.

To experiment with semaphores, we'll use a single program, sem1.c, which we can invoke several times. We'll use an optional parameter to specify whether the program is responsible for creating and destroying the semaphore.

We use the output of two different characters to indicate entering and leaving the critical section. The program invoked with a parameter prints an X on entering and exiting its critical section. Other invocations of the program print an O on entering and exiting their critical sections. Since only one process should be able to enter its critical section at any given time, all X and O characters should appear in pairs.

Try It Out - Semaphores

1. After the #includes, the function prototypes and the global variable, we come to the main function. There the semaphore is created with a call to semget, which returns the semaphore ID. If the program is the first to be called (i.e. it's called with a parameter and argc > 1), a call is made to set_semvalue to initialize the semaphore and op_char is set to X.

```
#include <unistd.h>
#include <stdlib.h>
#include <stdio.h>

#include <sys/types.h>
#include <sys/ipc.h>
#include <sys/sem.h>

#include "semun.h"

static int set_semvalue(void);
static void del_semvalue(void);
static int semaphore_p(void);
static int semaphore_v(void);

static int sem_id;


int main(int argc, char *argv[])
{
    int i;
    int pause_time;
    char op_char = 'O';

    srand((unsigned int)getpid());

    sem_id = semget((key_t)1234, 1, 0666 | IPC_CREAT);

    if (argc > 1) {
        if (!set_semvalue()) {
            fprintf(stderr, "Failed to initialize semaphore\n");
            exit(EXIT_FAILURE);
        }
        op_char = 'X';
        sleep(2);
    }
```

2. Then we have a loop which enters and leaves the critical section ten times. There, we first make a call to semaphore_p which sets the semaphore to wait, as this program is about to enter the critical section.

```
    for(i = 0; i < 10; i++) {

        if (!semaphore_p()) exit(EXIT_FAILURE);
        printf("%c", op_char);fflush(stdout);
        pause_time = rand() % 3;
        sleep(pause_time);
        printf("%c", op_char);fflush(stdout);
```

3. After the critical section, we call `semaphore_v`, setting the semaphore available, before going through the for loop again after a random wait. After the loop, the call to `del_semvalue` is made to clean up the code:

```
        if (!semaphore_v()) exit(EXIT_FAILURE);

        pause_time = rand() % 2;
        sleep(pause_time);
    }

    printf("\n%d - finished\n", getpid());

    if (argc > 1) {
        sleep(10);
        del_semvalue();
    }

    exit(EXIT_SUCCESS);
}
```

4. The function `set_semvalue` initializes the semaphore using the `SETVAL` command in a semctl call. We need to do this before we can use the semaphore:

```
static int set_semvalue(void)
{
    union semun sem_union;

    sem_union.val = 1;
    if (semctl(sem_id, 0, SETVAL, sem_union) == -1) return(0);
    return(1);
}
```

5. The `del_semvalue` function has almost the same form, except that the call to `semctl` uses the command `IPC_RMID` to remove the semaphore's ID:

```
static void del_semvalue(void)
{
    union semun sem_union;

    if (semctl(sem_id, 0, IPC_RMID, sem_union) == -1)
        fprintf(stderr, "Failed to delete semaphore\n");
}
```

6. `semaphore_p` changes the semaphore by -1 (waiting):

```
static int semaphore_p(void)
{
    struct sembuf sem_b;

    sem_b.sem_num = 0;
    sem_b.sem_op = -1; /* P() */
    sem_b.sem_flg = SEM_UNDO;
    if (semop(sem_id, &sem_b, 1) == -1) {
        fprintf(stderr, "semaphore_p failed\n");
        return(0);
    }
    return(1);
}
```

7. semaphore_v is similar except for setting the sem_op part of the sembuf structure to 1, so that the semaphore becomes available.

```
static int semaphore_v(void)
{
    struct sembuf sem_b;

    sem_b.sem_num = 0;
    sem_b.sem_op = 1; /* V() */
    sem_b.sem_flg = SEM_UNDO;
    if (semop(sem_id, &sem_b, 1) == -1) {
        fprintf(stderr, "semaphore_v failed\n");
        return(0);
    }
    return(1);
}
```

Notice that this simple program allows only a single binary semaphore per program, although we could extend it to pass the semaphore variable if we need more semaphores. Normally, a single binary semaphore is sufficient.

We can test our program by invoking it several times. The first time, we pass a parameter to tell the program that it's responsible for creating and deleting the semaphore. The other invocations have no parameter.

Here's some sample output, with two invocations of the program:

```
$ sem1 1 &
[1] 1082
$ sem1
OOXXOOXXOOXXOOXXOOXXOOOOXXOOXXOOXXOOXXXX
1083 - finished
1082 - finished
$
```

As you can see, the Os and Xs are properly paired, indicating that the critical section is being correctly processed. If this doesn't work on your particular system, you may have to use the command `stty -tostop` before invoking the program, to ensure that the background program generating `tty` output does not cause a signal to be generated.

How It Works

The program starts by obtaining a semaphore identity from the (arbitrary) key that we've chosen using the `semget` function. The `IPC_CREAT` flag causes the semaphore to be created if one is required.

If the program has a parameter, it's responsible for initializing the semaphore, which it does with our function `set_semvalue`, a simplified interface to the more general `semctl` function. It also uses the presence of the parameter to determine which character it should print out. The `sleep` simply allows us some time to invoke other copies of the program, before this copy gets to execute too many times round its loop. We use `srand` and `rand` to introduce some pseudo-random timing into the program.

The program then loops ten times, with pseudo-random waits in its critical and non-critical sections. The critical section is guarded by calls to our `semaphore_p` and `semaphore_v` functions, which are simplified interfaces to the more general `semop` function.

Before it deletes the semaphore, the program that was invoked with a parameter then waits to allow other invocations to complete. If the semaphore isn't deleted, it will continue to exist in the system, even though no programs are using it. In real programs, it's very important to ensure you don't unintentionally leave semaphores around after execution. It may cause problems next time you run the program and, also, semaphores are a limited resource which you must conserve.

Semaphore Summary

As we've seen, semaphores have a complex programming interface. Fortunately, we can easily provide ourselves with a much simplified interface, which is sufficient for most semaphore programming problems.

Shared Memory

Shared memory is the second of the three IPC facilities. It allows two unrelated processes to access the same logical memory. Shared memory is a very efficient way of transferring data between two running processes. Although the X/Open standard doesn't require it, it's probable that most implementations of shared memory arrange for the memory being shared between different processes to be the same physical memory.

Overview

Shared memory is a special range of addresses that is created by IPC for one process and appears in the address space of that process. Other processes can then 'attach' the same shared memory segment into their own address space. All processes can access the memory locations just as though the memory had been allocated by `malloc`. If one process writes to the shared memory, the changes immediately become visible to any other process that has access to the same shared memory.

By itself, shared memory doesn't provide any synchronization facilities. There are no automatic facilities to prevent a second process starting to read the shared memory before the first process has finished writing to it. It's the responsibility of the programmer to synchronize access.

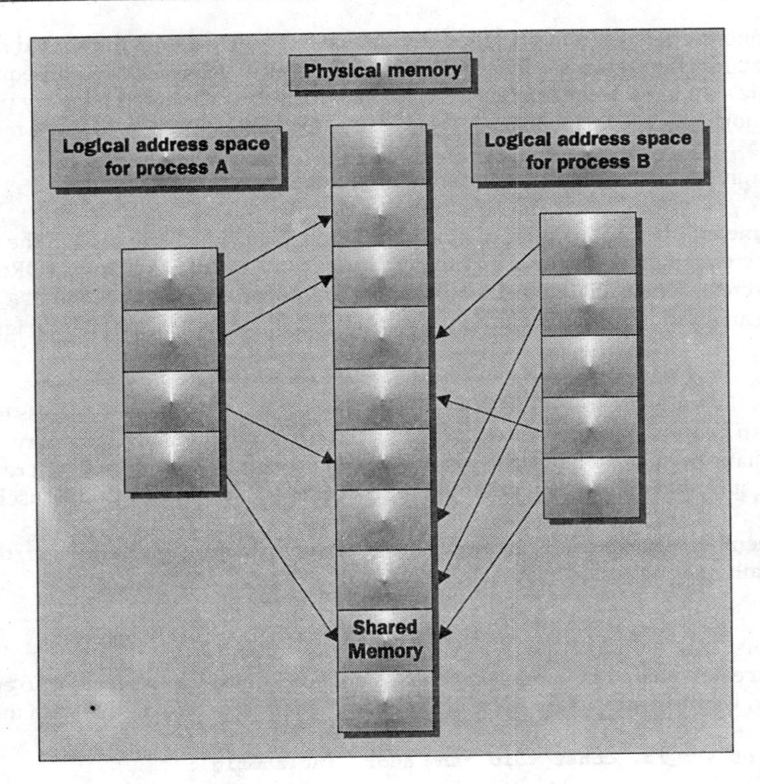

The arrows show the mapping of the logical address space of each process to the physical memory available. In practice, the situation is more complex than this because the available memory actually consists of a mix of physical memory and memory pages that have been swapped out to disk.

Shared Memory Functions

The functions for shared memory resemble those for semaphores:

```
#include <sys/shm.h>

void *shmat(int shm_id, const void *shm_addr, int shmflg);
int shmctl(int shm_id, int cmd, struct shmid_ds *buf);
int shmdt(const void *shm_addr);
int shmget(key_t key, size_t size, int shmflg);
```

As with semaphores, the include files sys/types.h and sys/ipc.h are normally also required.

shmget

We create shared memory using the shmget function:

```
int shmget(key_t key, size_t size, int shmflg);
```

As with semaphores, the program provides key, which effectively names the shared memory segment, and the shmget function returns a shared memory identifier which is used in subsequent shared memory functions. There's a special key value, IPC_PRIVATE, which creates shared memory private to the process. You wouldn't normally use this value, but it *is* possible for a single process to share memory with itself.

The second parameter, size, specifies the amount of memory required, in bytes.

The third parameter, shmflg, consists of nine permission flags, which are used in the same way as the mode flags for creating files. A special bit defined by IPC_CREAT must be bitwise ORed with the permissions to create a new shared memory segment. It's not an error to have the IPC_CREAT flag set and pass the key of an existing shared memory segment. The IPC_CREAT flag is silently ignored if not required.

The permission flags are very useful with shared memory, since they allow a process to create shared memory that can be written by processes owned by the creator of the shared memory, but only read by processes that have been created by other users. We can use this to provide efficient read-only access to data by placing it in shared memory, without the risk of it being changed by other users.

If the shared memory is successfully created, shmget returns a non-negative integer, the shared memory identifier. On failure, it returns -1.

shmat

When we first create a shared memory segment, it's not accessible by any process. To enable access to the shared memory, we must attach it to the address space of a process. We do this with the shmat function:

```
void *shmat(int shm_id, const void *shm_addr, int shmflg);
```

The first parameter, shm_id, is the shared memory identifier returned from shmget.

The second parameter, shm_addr, is the address at which the shared memory is to be attached to the current process. This should normally be a null pointer, which allows the system to choose the address at which the memory appears.

The third parameter, shmflg, is a set of bitwise flags. The two possible values are SHM_RND, which, in conjunction with shm_addr, controls the address at which the shared memory is attached, and SHM_RDONLY, which makes the attached memory read-only. It's very rare to need to control the address at which shared memory is attached; you should normally allow the system to choose an address for you, as doing otherwise will make the application highly hardware-dependent.

If the shmat call is successful, it returns a pointer to the first byte of shared memory. On failure -1 is returned.

The shared memory will have read or write access depending on the owner (the creator of the shared memory), the permissions and the owner of the current process. Permissions on shared memory are similar to the permissions on files.

An exception to this rule arises if `shmflg & SHM_RDONLY` is `true`. Then the shared memory won't be writeable, even if permissions would have allowed write access.

shmdt

The `shmdt` function detaches the shared memory from the current process. It takes a pointer to the address returned by `shmat`. On success, it returns 0, on error -1. Note that detaching the shared memory doesn't delete it, it just makes it unavailable to the current process.

shmctl

The control functions for shared memory are (thankfully) rather simpler than the more complex ones for semaphores:

```
int shmctl(int shm_id, int command, struct shmid_ds *buf);
```

The `shmid_ds` structure has at least the following members:

```
struct shmid_ds {
    uid_t shm_perm.uid;
    uid_t shm_perm.gid;
    mode_t shm_perm.mode;
}
```

The first parameter, `shm_id`, is the identifier returned from `shmget`.

The second parameter, `command`, is the action to take. It can take three values:

Command	Description
`IPC_STAT`	Sets the data in the `shmid_ds` structure to reflect the values associated with the shared memory.
`IPC_SET`	Sets the values associated with the shared memory to those provided in the `shmid_ds` data structure, if the process has permission to do so.
`IPC_RMID`	Deletes the shared memory segment.

The third parameter, `buf` is a pointer to structure containing the modes and permissions for the shared memory.

On success, it returns 0, on failure, -1. X/Open doesn't specify what happens if you attempt to delete a shared memory segment while it's attached. Generally, a shared memory segment that is attached but deleted continues to function until it has been detached from the last process. However, since this behavior isn't specified, it's best not to rely on it.

Now that we've seen the shared memory functions, we can write some code to use them. We'll write a pair of programs, `shm1.c` and `shm2.c`. The first (the consumer) will create a shared memory segment and then display any data that is written into it. The second (the producer) will attach to an existing shared memory segment and allow us to enter data into the segment.

Try It Out - Shared Memory

1. First we create a common header file to describe the shared memory we wish to pass about. We call this `shm_com.h`:

```
#define TEXT_SZ 2048

struct shared_use_st {
    int written_by_you;
    char some_text[TEXT_SZ];
};
```

This defines a structure to use in both the consumer and producer programs. We use an `int` flag `written_by_you` to tell the consumer when data has been written to the rest of the structure, and arbitrarily decide we need to transfer up to 2k of text.

2. Our first program is a consumer. After the headers the shared memory segment (the size of our shared memory structure) is created with a call to `shmget`, with the `IPC_CREAT` bit specified:

```
#include <unistd.h>
#include <stdlib.h>
#include <stdio.h>
#include <string.h>

#include <sys/types.h>
#include <sys/ipc.h>
#include <sys/shm.h>

#include "shm_com.h"

int main()
{
    int running = 1;
    void *shared_memory = (void *)0;
    struct shared_use_st *shared_stuff;
    int shmid;

    srand((unsigned int)getpid());

    shmid = shmget((key_t)1234, sizeof(struct shared_use_st), 0666 | IPC_CREAT);

    if (shmid == -1) {
        fprintf(stderr, "shmget failed\n");
        exit(EXIT_FAILURE);
    }
```

3. We now make the shared memory accessible to the program:

```
    shared_memory = shmat(shmid, (void *)0, 0);
    if (shared_memory == (void *)-1) {
        fprintf(stderr, "shmat failed\n");
        exit(EXIT_FAILURE);
    }

    printf("Memory attached at %X\n", (int)shared_memory);
```

4. The next portion of the program assigns the `shared_memory` segment to `shared_stuff`, which then prints out any text in `written_by_you`. The loop continues until end is found in `written_by_you`. The call to `sleep` forces the consumer to sit in its critical section, which makes the producer wait.

```
    shared_stuff = (struct shared_use_st *)shared_memory;
    shared_stuff->written_by_you = 0;
    while(running) {
        if (shared_stuff->written_by_you) {
            printf("You wrote: %s", shared_stuff->some_text);
            sleep( rand() % 4 ); /* make the other process wait for us ! */
            shared_stuff->written_by_you = 0;
            if (strncmp(shared_stuff->some_text, "end", 3) == 0) {
                running = 0;
            }
        }
    }
```

5. Lastly, the shared memory is detached and then deleted:

```
    if (shmdt(shared_memory) == -1) {
        fprintf(stderr, "shmdt failed\n");
        exit(EXIT_FAILURE);
    }

    if (shmctl(shmid, IPC_RMID, 0) == -1) {
        fprintf(stderr, "shmctl(IPC_RMID) failed\n");
        exit(EXIT_FAILURE);
    }

    exit(EXIT_SUCCESS);
}
```

6. Our second program, `shm2.c`, is the producer and allows us to enter data for consumers. It's very similar to `shm1.c` and looks like this:

```
#include <unistd.h>
#include <stdlib.h>
#include <stdio.h>
#include <string.h>

#include <sys/types.h>
#include <sys/ipc.h>
#include <sys/shm.h>

#include "shm_com.h"

int main()
{
    int running = 1;
    void *shared_memory = (void *)0;
    struct shared_use_st *shared_stuff;
    char buffer[BUFSIZ];
    int shmid;

    shmid = shmget((key_t)1234, sizeof(struct shared_use_st), 0666 | IPC_CREAT);

    if (shmid == -1) {
        fprintf(stderr, "shmget failed\n");
        exit(EXIT_FAILURE);
    }
```

```
    shared_memory = shmat(shmid, (void *)0, 0);
    if (shared_memory == (void *)-1) {
        fprintf(stderr, "shmat failed\n");
        exit(EXIT_FAILURE);
    }

    printf("Memory attached at %X\n", (int)shared_memory);

    shared_stuff = (struct shared_use_st *)shared_memory;
    while(running) {
        while(shared_stuff->written_by_you == 1) {
            sleep(1);
            printf("waiting for client...\n");
        }
        printf("Enter some text: ");
        fgets(buffer, BUFSIZ, stdin);

        strncpy(shared_stuff->some_text, buffer, TEXT_SZ);
        shared_stuff->written_by_you = 1;

        if (strncmp(buffer, "end", 3) == 0) {
                running = 0;
        }
    }

    if (shmdt(shared_memory) == -1) {
        fprintf(stderr, "shmdt failed\n");
        exit(EXIT_FAILURE);
    }
    exit(EXIT_SUCCESS);
}
```

When we run these programs, we get some sample output such as this:

```
$ shm1 &
[1] 294
Memory attached at 50007000
$ shm2
Memory attached at 50007000
Enter some text: hello
You wrote: hello
waiting for client...
waiting for client...
Enter some text: Linux!
You wrote: Linux!
waiting for client...
waiting for client...
waiting for client...
Enter some text: end
You wrote: end
$
```

How It Works

The first program, `shm1`, creates the shared memory segment and then attaches it to its address space. We impose a structure, `shared_use_st` on the first part of the shared memory. This has a flag, `written_by_you`, which is set when data is available. When this flag is set, the program reads the text, prints it out, then clears the flag to show it has read the data. We use the special string, end, to allow a clean exit from the loop. The program then detaches the shared memory segment and deletes it.

The second program, shm2, gets and attaches the same shared memory segment, since it uses the same key, 1234. It then prompts the user to enter some text. If the flag written_by_you is set, it knows that the client process hasn't yet read the previous data and waits for it. When the other process clears this flag, shm2 writes in the new data and sets the flag. It also uses the magic string, end, to terminate and detach the shared memory segment.

Notice that we had to provide our own, rather crude synchronization flag, written_by_you, that involves a very inefficient busy wait (by continuously looping). In real programs we would have passed a message, either using a pipe or IPC messages (which we'll meet shortly), generated a signal, or used a semaphore to provide synchronization between the reading and writing parts of the application.

Shared Memory Summary

Shared memory provides an efficient way of sharing and passing data between multiple processes. Since it provides no synchronization facilities, we usually need to use some other mechanism to synchronize access to the shared memory. Typically, we might use shared memory to provide efficient access to large areas of memory and pass small messages to synchronize access to that memory.

Message Queues

We'll now take a look at the third and final IPC facility: **message queues**.

Overview

In many ways, message queues are like named pipes, but without the complexity associated with opening and closing the pipe. However, using messages doesn't get us away from the problems that we have with named pipes, such as blocking on full pipes.

Message queues provide a way of sending a block of data from one process to another. Additionally, each block of data is considered to have a type, and a receiving process may receive blocks of data having different type values independently. The good news is that we can almost totally avoid the synchronization and blocking problems of named pipes by sending messages. Even better, we can 'look ahead' for messages that are urgent in some way. The bad news is that, just like pipes, there's a maximum size limit imposed on each block of data and also a limit on the maximum total size of all blocks on all queues throughout the system.

Whilst stating that these limits are imposed, the X/Open specification offers no way of discovering what the limits are, except that exceeding them is a valid reason for some message queue functions to fail. Linux does have two defines, MSGMAX and MSGMNB which define the maximum size in bytes of an individual message and maximum size of a queue, respectively. These macros may be different or, for that matter, not even present on other systems.

Message Queue Functions

The message queue function definitions are:

```
#include <sys/msg.h>

int msgctl(int msqid, int cmd, struct msqid_ds *buf);
int msgget(key_t key, int msgflg);
int msgrcv(int msqid, void *msg_ptr, size_t msg_sz, long int msgtype, int msgflg);
int msgsnd(int msqid, const void *msg_ptr, size_t msg_sz, int msgflg);
```

As with semaphores and shared memory, the include files `sys/types.h` and `sys/ipc.h` are normally also required.

msgget

We create and access a message queue using the `msgget` function:

```
int msgget(key_t key, int msgflg);
```

The program must provide a `key` value which, as with other IPC facilities, names a particular message queue. The special value `IPC_PRIVATE` creates a private queue, accessible only by the current process. As before, the second parameter, `msgflg`, consists of nine permission flags. A special bit defined by `IPC_CREAT` must be bitwise ORed with the permissions to create a new message queue. It's not an error to set the `IPC_CREAT` flag and give the key of an existing message queue. The `IPC_CREAT` flag is silently ignored if the message queue already exists.

The `msgget` function returns a positive number, a queue identifier, on success, or -1 on failure.

msgsnd

The `msgsnd` function allows us to add a message to a message queue.

```
int msgsnd(int msqid, const void *msg_ptr, size_t msg_sz, int msgflg);
```

The structure of the message is constrained in two ways. Firstly, it must be smaller than the system limit and, secondly, it must start with a `long int`, which will be used as a message type in the receive function. When you're using messages, it's best to define your message structure something like this:

```
struct my_message {
    long int message_type;
    /* The data you wish to transfer */
}
```

Since the `message_type` is used in message reception, you can't simply ignore it. Not only must you declare your data structure to include it, it's also wise to initialize it, so that it contains a known value.

The first parameter, `msqid`, is the message queue identifier returned from a `msgget` function.

The second parameter, `msg_ptr`, is a pointer to the message to be sent, which must start with a `long int` type as we described above.

The third parameter, msg_sz, is the size of the message pointed to by msg_ptr. This size must not include the long int message type.

The fourth parameter, msgflg, controls what happens if either the current message queue is full, or the system-wide limit on queued messages has been reached. If msgflg has the IPC_NOWAIT flag set, the function will return immediately without sending the message and the return value will be -1. If the msgflg has the IPC_NOWAIT flag clear, the sending process will be suspended waiting for space to become available in the queue.

On success, the function returns 0, on failure -1. If the call is successful, a copy of the message data has been taken and placed on the message queue.

msgrcv

The msgrcv function retrieves messages from a message queue.

```
int msgrcv(int msqid, void *msg_ptr, size_t msg_sz, long int msgtype, int msgflg);
```

The first parameter, msqid, is the message queue identifier returned from a msgget function.

The second parameter, msg_ptr, is a pointer to the message to be received, which must start with a long int type as described above in the msgsnd function.

The third parameter, msg_sz, is the size of the message pointed to by msg_ptr, not including the long int message type.

The fourth parameter, msgtype, is a long int, which allows a simple form of reception priority to be implemented. If msgtype has the value 0, the first available message in the queue is retrieved. If it's greater than zero, the first message with the same message type is retrieved. If it's less than zero, the first message which has a type the same as or less than the absolute value of msgtype is retrieved.

This sounds more complicated than it actually is in practice. If you simply want to retrieve messages in the order in which they were sent, set msgtype to 0. If you want to retrieve only messages with a specific message type, set msgtype equal to that value. If you want to receive messages with a type of n or smaller, set msgtype to -n.

The fifth parameter, msgflg, controls what happens when no message of the appropriate type is waiting to be received. If the IPC_NOWAIT flag in msgflg is set, the call will return immediately with a return value of -1. If the IPC_NOWAIT flag of msgflg is clear, the process will be suspended, waiting for an appropriate type of message to arrive.

On success, msgrcv returns the number of bytes placed in the receive buffer, the message is copied into the user allocated buffer pointed to by msg_ptr, and the data is deleted from the message queue. It returns -1 on error.

msgctl

The final message queue function is msgctl, which is very similar to that of the control function for shared memory.

```
int msgctl(int msqid, int command, struct msqid_ds *buf);
```

The msqid_ds structure has at least the following members:

```
struct msqid_ds {
    uid_t  msg_perm.uid;
    uid_t  msg_perm.gid
    mode_t msg_perm.mode;
}
```

The first parameter, msqid, is the identifier returned from msgget.

The second parameter, command, is the action to take. This can take three values.

Command	Description
IPC_STAT	Sets the data in the msqid_ds structure to reflect the values associated with the message queue.
IPC_SET	If the process has permission to do so, this sets the values associated with the message queue to those provided in the msqid_ds data structure.
IPC_RMID	Deletes the message queue.

0 is returned on success, -1 on failure. If a message queue is deleted while a process is waiting in a msgsnd or msgrcv function, the send or receive function will fail.

Now that we've seen the definitions for message queues, we can see how they work in practice. As before, we'll write two programs, one, msg1.c, to receive and one, msg2.c, to send. We'll allow either program to create the message queue, but use the receiver to delete it after it receives the last message.

Try It Out - Message Queues

1. Here's the receiver program:

```
#include <stdlib.h>
#include <stdio.h>
#include <string.h>
#include <errno.h>
#include <unistd.h>

#include <sys/types.h>
#include <sys/ipc.h>
#include <sys/msg.h>


struct my_msg_st {
    long int my_msg_type;
    char some_text[BUFSIZ];
};

int main()
{
    int running = 1;
    int msgid;
    struct my_msg_st some_data;
    long int msg_to_receive = 0;
```

2. First, we set up the message queue:

```
    msgid = msgget((key_t)1234, 0666 | IPC_CREAT);

    if (msgid == -1) {
        fprintf(stderr, "msgget failed with error: %d\n", errno);
        exit(EXIT_FAILURE);
    }
```

3. Then the messages are retrieved from the queue, until an end message is encountered. Lastly, the message queue is deleted:

```
    while(running) {
        if (msgrcv(msgid, (void *)&some_data, BUFSIZ,
                   msg_to_receive, 0) == -1) {
            fprintf(stderr, "msgrcv failed with error: %d\n", errno);
            exit(EXIT_FAILURE);
        }
        printf("You wrote: %s", some_data.some_text);
        if (strncmp(some_data.some_text, "end", 3) == 0) {
            running = 0;
        }
    }

    if (msgctl(msgid, IPC_RMID, 0) == -1) {
        fprintf(stderr, "msgctl(IPC_RMID) failed\n");
        exit(EXIT_FAILURE);
    }

    exit(EXIT_SUCCESS);
}
```

4. The sender program is very similar to `msg1.c`. In the `main` set up, delete the `msg_to_receive` declaration and replace it with `buffer[BUFSIZ]`, remove the message queue delete and make the following changes to the `running` loop. We now have a call to `msgsnd` to send the entered text to the queue:

```
#include <stdlib.h>
#include <stdio.h>
#include <string.h>
#include <errno.h>
#include <unistd.h>

#include <sys/types.h>
#include <sys/ipc.h>
#include <sys/msg.h>

#define MAX_TEXT 512

struct my_msg_st {
    long int my_msg_type;
    char some_text[MAX_TEXT];
};

int main()
{
    int running = 1;
    struct my_msg_st some_data;
    int msgid;
    char buffer[BUFSIZ];
```

```
msgid = msgget((key_t)1234, 0666 | IPC_CREAT);

    if (msgid == -1) {
        fprintf(stderr, "msgget failed with error: %d\n", errno);
        exit(EXIT_FAILURE);
    }

    while(running) {
        printf("Enter some text: ");
        fgets(buffer, BUFSIZ, stdin);
        some_data.my_msg_type = 1;
        strcpy(some_data.some_text, buffer);

        if (msgsnd(msgid, (void *)&some_data, MAX_TEXT, 0) == -1) {
            fprintf(stderr, "msgsnd failed\n");
            exit(EXIT_FAILURE);
        }
        if (strncmp(buffer, "end", 3) == 0) {
            running = 0;
        }
    }

    exit(EXIT_SUCCESS);
}
```

Unlike in the pipes example, there's no need for the processes to provide their own synchronization method. This is a significant advantage of messages over pipes.

Providing there's room in the message queue, the sender can create the queue, put some data into the queue and then exit before the receiver even starts. We'll run the sender, `msg2`, first. Here's some sample output:

```
$ msg2
Enter some text: hello
Enter some text: How are you today?
Enter some text: end
$ msg1
You wrote: hello
You wrote: How are you today?
You wrote: end
$
```

How It Works

The sender program creates a message queue with `msgget`, then adds messages to the queue with `msgsnd`. The receiver obtains the message queue identifier with `msgget`, then receives messages until the special text end is received. It then tidies up by deleting the message queue with `msgctl`.

Message Queue Summary

Message queues provide a reasonably easy and efficient way of passing data between two unrelated processes. They have the advantage over named pipes that the message queue exists independently of both the sending and receiving processes, which removes some of the difficulties that occur synchronizing the opening and closing of named pipes.

The Application

We're now in a position to modify our CD database application to use the IPC facilities that we've seen in this chapter.

Although we could use many different combinations of the three IPC facilities, since the information we need to pass is quite small, it's sensible to implement the passing of requests and responses directly using message queues.

If the amounts of data that we needed to pass were large, we could have considered passing the actual data in shared memory and using either semaphores or messages to pass a 'token' to inform the other process that data was available in shared memory.

The message queue interface removes the problem that we had in Chapter 11, where we needed both processes to have the pipe open while data was passed. Using message queues allows one process to put messages in the queue, even if that process is currently the only user of the queue.

The only significant decision we need to make is how to return answers to clients. A simple choice would be to have one queue for the server and one queue for each client. If there were a large number of simultaneous clients, this could cause problems by requiring a large number of message queues. By using the message ID field in the message, we can allow all the clients to use a single queue and 'address' response messages to particular client processes by using the client process ID in the message. Each client can then retrieve only messages addressed to itself, leaving messages for other clients in the queue.

To convert our CD application to use IPC facilities, we only need to replace the file `pipe_imp.c`. In the following pages, we'll describe the principal sections of the replacement file, `ipc_imp.c`.

Try It Out - Revising the Server Functions

1. First, we include the appropriate headers, declare some message queue keys and define a structure to hold our message data:

```
#include "cd_data.h"
#include "cliserv.h"

#include <sys/types.h>
#include <sys/ipc.h>
#include <sys/msg.h>

#define SERVER_MQUEUE 1234
#define CLIENT_MQUEUE 4321
```

```
struct msg_passed {
    long int msg_key; /* used for client pid */
    message_db_t real_message;
};
```

2. Two variables with file scope hold the two queue identifiers returned from the `msgget` function:

```
static int serv_qid = -1;
static int cli_qid = -1;
```

3. We make the server responsible for creating both message queues:

```
int server_starting()
{
    #if DEBUG_TRACE
        printf("%d :- server_starting()\n",  getpid());
    #endif

    serv_qid = msgget((key_t)SERVER_MQUEUE, 0666 | IPC_CREAT);
    if (serv_qid == -1) return(0);

    cli_qid = msgget((key_t)CLIENT_MQUEUE, 0666 | IPC_CREAT);
    if (cli_qid == -1) return(0);

    return(1);
}
```

4. The server is also responsible for tidying up if it ever exits. When the server ends, we set our file scope variables to illegal values. This will catch any bugs if the server attempts to send messages after it has called `server_ending`.

```
void server_ending()
{
    #if DEBUG_TRACE
        printf("%d :- server_ending()\n",  getpid());
    #endif

    (void)msgctl(serv_qid, IPC_RMID, 0);
    (void)msgctl(cli_qid, IPC_RMID, 0);

    serv_qid = -1;
    cli_qid = -1;
}
```

5. The server read function reads a message of any type (that is, from any client) from the queue, and returns the data part (ignoring the type) of the message.

```
int read_request_from_client(message_db_t *rec_ptr)
{
    struct msg_passed my_msg;
    #if DEBUG_TRACE
        printf("%d :- read_request_from_client()\n",  getpid());
    #endif

    if (msgrcv(serv_qid, (void *)&my_msg, sizeof(*rec_ptr), 0, 0) == -1) {
        return(0);
    }
    *rec_ptr = my_msg.real_message;
    return(1);
}
```

6. Sending a response uses the client process ID that was stored in the request to address the message:

```
int send_resp_to_client(const message_db_t mess_to_send)
{
    struct msg_passed my_msg;
    #if DEBUG_TRACE
        printf("%d :- send_resp_to_client()\n",  getpid());
    #endif

    my_msg.real_message = mess_to_send;
    my_msg.msg_key = mess_to_send.client_pid;

    if (msgsnd(cli_qid, (void *)&my_msg, sizeof(mess_to_send), 0) == -1) {
        return(0);
    }
    return(1);
}
```

Try It Out - Revising the Client Functions

1. When the client starts, it needs to find the server and client queue identifiers. The client doesn't create the queues. This function will fail if the server isn't running, as the message queues won't exist.

```
int client_starting()
{
    #if DEBUG_TRACE
        printf("%d :- client_starting\n",  getpid());
    #endif

    serv_qid = msgget((key_t)SERVER_MQUEUE, 0666);
    if (serv_qid == -1) return(0);

    cli_qid = msgget((key_t)CLIENT_MQUEUE, 0666);
    if (cli_qid == -1) return(0);
    return(1);
}
```

2. As with the server, when the client ends, we set our file scope variables to illegal values. This will catch any bugs where the client attempts to send messages after it has called `client_ending`.

```
void client_ending()
{
    #if DEBUG_TRACE
        printf("%d :- client_ending()\n",  getpid());
    #endif

    serv_qid = -1;
    cli_qid = -1;
}
```

3. To send a message to the server, we store the data inside our structure. Notice that we must set the message key. As 0 is an illegal value for the key, leaving the key undefined would mean that it takes an (apparently) random value, so this function could occasionally fail if the value happens to be 0.

```
int send_mess_to_server(message_db_t mess_to_send)
{
    struct msg_passed my_msg;
    #if DEBUG_TRACE
        printf("%d :- send_mess_to_server()\n",  getpid());
    #endif

    my_msg.real_message = mess_to_send;
    my_msg.msg_key = mess_to_send.client_pid;

    if (msgsnd(serv_qid, (void *)&my_msg, sizeof(mess_to_send), 0) == -1) {
        perror("Message send failed");
        return(0);
    }
    return(1);
}
```

4. When the client retrieves a message from the server, it uses its process ID to receive only messages addressed to itself, ignoring any messages for other clients.

```
int read_resp_from_server(message_db_t *rec_ptr)
{
    struct msg_passed my_msg;
    #if DEBUG_TRACE
        printf("%d :- read_resp_from_server()\n",  getpid());
    #endif

    if (msgrcv(cli_qid, (void *)&my_msg, sizeof(*rec_ptr), getpid(), 0) == -1) {
        return(0);
    }
    *rec_ptr = my_msg.real_message;
    return(1);
}
```

5. To retain complete compatibility with `pipe_imp.c`, we need to define an extra four functions. In our new program, however, the functions are empty. The operations they implemented when using pipes are simply not needed any more.

```
int start_resp_to_client(const message_db_t mess_to_send)
{
    return(1);
}

void end_resp_to_client(void)
{
}

int start_resp_from_server(void)
{
    return(1);
}

void end_resp_from_server(void)
{
}
```

The conversion of the application to message queues illustrates the power of IPC message queues. We require fewer functions and even those we do need are much smaller than they were previously.

IPC Status Commands

Although they're not required for X/Open compliance, most UNIX systems with semaphores provide a set of commands that allow command line access to IPC information. These are the ipcs and ipcrm commands, which are very useful when you're developing programs.

Semaphores

To examine the state of semaphores on the system, use the ipcs -s command. If any semaphores are present, the output will have the form:

```
$ ipcs -s
—— Semaphore Arrays ——
semid      owner      perms      nsems      status
768        rick       666        1
```

You can use the ipcrm command to remove any semaphores accidentally left by programs. To delete the above semaphore, the command (on Linux) would be:

```
$ ipcrm sem 768
```

Many UNIX systems would use:

```
$ ipcrm -s 768
```

Shared Memory

Like semaphores, many systems provide command line programs for accessing the details of shared memory. These are ipcs -m and ipcrm shm <id> (or ipcrm -m <id>).

Here's some sample output from ipcs:

```
$ ipcs -m

—— Shared Memory Segments ——
shmid      owner      perms      bytes      nattch     status
384        rick       666        4096       2
```

This shows a single shared memory segment of 4Kb attached by two processes.

The ipcrm shm <id> command allows shared memory to be removed. This is sometimes useful when a program has failed to tidy up shared memory.

Message Queues

For message queues the commands are ipcs -q and ipcrm msg <id> (or ipcrm -q <id>).

Here's some sample output from ipcs:

```
$ ipcs -q

—— Message Queues ——
msqid      owner      perms      used-bytes  messages
384        rick       666        2048        2
```

This shows two messages, with a total size of 2048 bytes in a message queue.

The ipcrm msg <id> command allows a message queue to be removed.

Summary

In this chapter, we've looked at the three inter-process communication facilities which first became widely available in UNIX System V.2: semaphores, shared memory, and message queues. We've seen the sophisticated facilities that they offer and how, once these functions are understood, they offer a powerful solution to many inter-process communication requirements.

Sockets

In this chapter, we'll look at yet another method of process communication, but one with a difference. Until now, all the facilities have relied on shared resources on a single computer system. The resource varies; it can be file system space, shared physical memory or message queues, but only processes running on a single machine can use them.

The Berkeley versions of UNIX introduced a new communication tool, the **socket interface**, which is an extension of the pipes concept. You can use sockets in much the same way as pipes, but they include communication across a network of computers. A process on one machine can use sockets to communicate with a process on another, which allows for client/server systems that are distributed across a network. Sockets may also be used between processes on the same machine.

Also, the sockets interface has been made available for Microsoft Windows via a publicly available specification called **Windows Sockets**, or **WinSock**. Socket services are provided by a `Winsock.dll` system file. Thus Microsoft Windows programs can communicate across a network to UNIX computers and vice versa providing client/server systems. Although the programming interface for WinSock isn't quite the same as UNIX sockets, it still has sockets as its basis.

We can't cover the extensive UNIX networking capabilities in a single chapter, so you'll find here a description of the principal programmatic networking interfaces. These should allow you to write your own network programs. We'll look at:

- How a socket connection operates
- Socket attributes, addresses and communications
- Network information and the Internet Daemon
- Clients and servers

What is a Socket?

A socket is a communication mechanism that allows client/server systems to be developed either locally, on a single machine, or across networks. UNIX functions, such as printing, and network utilities, such as `rlogin` and `ftp`, usually use sockets to communicate.

Sockets are created and used in a different way to pipes, because they make a clear distinction between client and server. The socket mechanism can implement multiple clients attached to a single server.

Socket Connections

We can think of socket connections as telephone calls into a busy building. A call comes into an organization and is answered by a receptionist who puts the call through to the correct department (the server process) and then from there to the right person (the server socket). Each incoming call (client) is routed to an appropriate endpoint and the intervening operators are free to deal with further calls. Before we look at the way socket connections are established in UNIX systems, we need to understand how they operate for socket applications that maintain a connection.

First of all, a server application creates a socket, which is just an operating system resource assigned to the server process. As the server creates it using the system call `socket`, it can't be accessed by other processes.

Next, the server process gives the socket a name. Local sockets are given a file name in the UNIX file system, often to be found in `/tmp` or `/usr/tmp`. For network sockets, it will be a service identifier (port number/access point) relevant to the particular network to which the clients can connect. A socket is named using the system call `bind`. The server process then waits for a client to connect to the named socket. The system call, `listen`, creates a queue for incoming connections. The server can accept them using the system call `accept`.

When the server calls `accept`, a new socket is created, distinct from the named socket. This new socket is used solely for communication with this particular client. The named socket remains for further connections from other clients. If the server is written appropriately, it can take advantage of multiple connections. For a simple server, further clients wait on the listen queue until the server is ready again.

The client side of a socket-based system is more straightforward. The client creates an unnamed socket by calling `socket`. It then calls `connect` to establish a connection with the server by using the server's named socket as an address.

Once established, sockets can be used like low-level file descriptors, providing two-way data communications.

Here's an example of a very simple socket client program, `client1.c`. It creates an unnamed socket and connects it to a server socket called `server_socket`. We'll cover the details of the `socket` system call a little later after we've discussed some addressing issues.

Try It Out - A Simple Local Client

1. Make the necessary `includes` and set up the variables.

```
#include <sys/types.h>
#include <sys/socket.h>
#include <stdio.h>
#include <sys/un.h>
#include <unistd.h>

int main()
{
    int sockfd;
    int len;
    struct sockaddr_un address;
    int result;
    char ch = 'A';
```

2. Create a socket for the client.

```
    sockfd = socket(AF_UNIX, SOCK_STREAM, 0);
```

3. Name the socket as agreed with the server.

```
    address.sun_family = AF_UNIX;
    strcpy(address.sun_path, "server_socket");
    len = sizeof(address);
```

4. Now connect our socket to the server's socket.

```
    result = connect(sockfd, (struct sockaddr *)&address, len);

    if(result == -1) {
        perror("oops: client1");
        exit(1);
    }
```

5. We can now read and write via `sockfd`.

```
    write(sockfd, &ch, 1);
    read(sockfd, &ch, 1);
    printf("char from server = %c\n", ch);
    close(sockfd);
    exit(0);
}
```

When we run this program it fails, because we haven't yet created the server side named socket. (The exact error message may differ from system to system.)

```
$ client1
oops: client1: Connection refused
$
```

Here's a very simple server program, `server1.c`, which accepts connections from our client. It creates the server socket, binds it to a name, creates a listen queue and accepts connections.

Try It Out - A Simple Local Server

1. Make the necessary includes and set up the variables.

```
#include <sys/types.h>
#include <sys/socket.h>
#include <stdio.h>
#include <sys/un.h>
#include <unistd.h>

int main()
{
    int server_sockfd, client_sockfd;
    int server_len, client_len;
    struct sockaddr_un server_address;
    struct sockaddr_un client_address;
```

2. Remove any old socket and create an unnamed socket for the server.

```
    unlink("server_socket");
    server_sockfd = socket(AF_UNIX, SOCK_STREAM, 0);
```

3. Name the socket.

```
    server_address.sun_family = AF_UNIX;
    strcpy(server_address.sun_path, "server_socket");
    server_len = sizeof(server_address);
    bind(server_sockfd, (struct sockaddr *)&server_address, server_len);
```

4. Create a connection queue and wait for clients.

```
    listen(server_sockfd, 5);
    while(1) {
        char ch;

        printf("server waiting\n");
```

5. Accept a connection.

```
        client_len = sizeof(client_address);
        client_sockfd = accept(server_sockfd,
            (struct sockaddr *)&client_address, &client_len);
```

6. Read and write to client on `client_sockfd`.

```
        read(client_sockfd, &ch, 1);
        ch++;
        write(client_sockfd, &ch, 1);
        close(client_sockfd);
    }
}
```

The server program in this example can serve only one client at a time. It just reads a character from the client, increments it and writes it back. In more sophisticated systems, where the server has to perform rather more work on the client's behalf, this wouldn't be acceptable, as other clients would be unable to connect until the server had finished. We'll see a couple of ways to allow multiple connections later.

When we run the server program, it creates a socket and waits for connections. If we start it in the background so that it runs independently, we can then start clients in the foreground.

```
$ server1 &
[1] 1094
$ server waiting
```

As it waits for connections, the server prints a message. In the above example, the server waits for a file system socket and we can see it with the normal `ls` command. Remember that it's polite to remove a socket when you've finished with it, even if the program terminates abnormally via a signal.

```
$ ls -lF server_socket
srwxr-xr-x   1 neil     users          0 Jan 14 08:28 server_socket=
```

The device type is socket, shown by the `s` at the front of the permission and the `=` at the end. The socket has been created just as an ordinary file would be, with permissions modified by the current `umask`. If we use the `ps` command, we can see the server running in the background. It's shown sleeping (`STAT` is `S`) and therefore not consuming CPU resources.

```
$ ps -lx
 F   UID   PID  PPID PRI NI SIZE  RSS WCHAN       STAT TTY   TIME COMMAND
 0   501  1094   116   1  0   34  164 116976      S    pp0   0:00 server1
```

Now, when we run the client program, we are more successful. Since the server socket exists, we can connect to it and communicate with the server.

```
$ client1
server waiting
char from server = B
$
```

The output from the server and the client get mixed on our terminal, but you can see that the server has received a character from the client, incremented it and returned it. The server then continues and waits for the next client. If we run several clients together, they will be served in sequence.

```
$ client1 & client1 & client1 &
[2] 1106
[3] 1107
[4] 1108
server waiting
char from server = B
server waiting
char from server = B
server waiting
char from server = B
server waiting
[2]   Done                    client1
[3]-  Done                    client1
[4]+  Done                    client1
$
```

Socket Attributes

To fully understand the system calls used in this example, we need to learn a little about UNIX networking.

A socket is characterized by three attributes, **domain, type** and **protocol**. They also have an address that is used as their name. The formats of the addresses vary depending on the domain, also known as the **protocol family**. Each protocol family can use one or more address families to define the address format.

Socket Domains

Domains specify the network medium that the socket communication will use. The most common socket domain is `AF_INET`, which refers to Internet networking, used on many UNIX local area networks and, of course, the Internet itself. The underlying protocol, **Internet Protocol** (IP), which only has one address family, imposes a particular way of specifying computers on a network. This is the **IP address**.

Although names are almost always refer to networked machines on the Internet, these are translated into lower-level IP addresses. An example IP address is 192.168.1.99. All IP addresses are represented by four numbers, each less than 256, a so-called **dotted quad**. When a client connects across a network via sockets, it needs the IP address of the server computer.

There may be several services available at the server computer. A client can address a particular service on a networked machine by using an IP port. A port is identified within the system by assigning a unique 16-bit integer and externally by the combination of IP address and port number. The sockets are communication 'end points' which must be bound to ports before communication is possible.

Servers wait for connections on particular ports. Well known services have allocated port numbers which are used by all UNIX machines. These are usually, but not always, numbers less than 1024. Examples are the printer spooler (515), `rlogin` (513), `ftp` (21) and `httpd` (80). The last of these is the server for the World Wide Web, (WWW). Usually, ports less than 1024 are reserved for system services and may only be served by processes with superuser privileges. X/Open defines a constant in `netdb.h`, `IPPORT_RESERVED`, to stand for the highest reserved port number.

Because there is a standard set of port numbers for standard services, computers can easily connect to each other without having to establish the correct port. Local services may use non-standard port addresses. The domain in our first example is the UNIX file system domain, `AF_UNIX`, which can be used by sockets based on a single computer that perhaps isn't networked. When this is so, the underlying protocol is file input/output and the addresses are absolute file names. The address which we used for the server socket was `server_socket`, which we saw appear in the current directory when we ran the server application.

Other domains that might be used include `AF_ISO` for networks based on ISO standard protocols and `AF_NS` for the Xerox Network System. We won't cover these here.

Socket Types

A socket domain may have a number of different ways of communicating, each of which might have different characteristics. This isn't an issue with `AF_UNIX` domain sockets, which provide a reliable, two-way communication path. However, in networked domains, we need to be aware of the characteristics of the underlying network.

Internet protocols provide two distinct levels of service, **streams** and **datagrams**.

The first of these, streams (in some ways similar to standard input/output streams), provide a connection that is a sequenced and reliable two-way byte stream. Thus data sent is guaranteed not to be lost, duplicated or re-ordered without an indication that an error has occurred. Large messages are fragmented, transmitted and re-assembled. This is like a file stream as it accepts large amounts of data and writes it to the low-level disk in smaller blocks. Stream sockets have predictable behavior.

Stream sockets, specified by the type `SOCK_STREAM`, are implemented in the `AF_INET` domain by TCP/IP connections. They are also the usual type in the `AF_UNIX` domain. We'll concentrate on `SOCK_STREAM` sockets in this chapter, since they are more commonly used in programming network applications.

> **TCP/IP stands for Transmission Control Protocol/Internet Protocol. IP is the low-level protocol for packets. It provides routing through the network from one computer to another. TCP provides sequencing, flow control and retransmission to ensure that large data transfers arrive as they should.**

In contrast, a datagram socket, specified by the type `SOCK_DGRAM`, doesn't establish and maintain a connection. There is also a limit on the size of a datagram that can be sent. It's transmitted as a single network message that may get lost, duplicated or arrive out of sequence.

Datagram sockets are implemented in the `AF_INET` domain by UDP/IP connections and provide an unsequenced, unreliable service. However, they are relatively inexpensive in terms of resources, since network connections need not be maintained. They're fast because there is no associated connection setup time. UDP stands for User Datagram Protocol.

Datagrams are useful for 'single-shot' inquiries to information services, for providing regular status information or for performing low priority logging. They have the advantage that the 'death' of a server doesn't necessarily require a client restart. Because datagram-based servers usually retain no connection information, they can be stopped and restarted without unduly disturbing their clients.

Socket Protocols

Where the underlying transport mechanism allows for more than one protocol to provide the requested socket type, you can select a specific protocol for a socket. In this chapter, we'll concentrate on UNIX network and file system sockets, which don't require you to choose a protocol other than the default.

Creating a Socket

The `socket` system call creates a socket and returns a descriptor that can be used for accessing the socket.

```
#include <sys/types.h>
#include <sys/socket.h>

int socket(int domain, int type, int protocol);
```

The socket created is one end-point of a communication channel. The `domain` parameter specifies the address family, the `type` parameter specifies the type of communication to be used with this socket and `protocol` specifies the protocol to be employed.

Domains include:

AF_UNIX	UNIX internal (file system sockets)
AF_INET	ARPA Internet protocols (UNIX network sockets)
AF_ISO	ISO standard protocols
AF_NS	Xerox Network Systems protocols
AF_IPX	Novell IPX protocol
AF_APPLETALK	Appletalk DDS

The most common socket domains are `AF_UNIX`, which is used for local sockets implemented via the UNIX file system, and `AF_INET`, which is used for UNIX network sockets. The `AF_INET` sockets may be used by programs communicating across a TCP/IP network including the Internet. The Microsoft Windows Winsock interface also provides access to this socket domain.

The socket parameter `type` specifies the communication characteristics to be used for the new socket. Possible values include `SOCK_STREAM` and `SOCK_DGRAM`.

SOCK_STREAM is a sequenced, reliable, connection-based, two-way byte stream. For an AF_INET domain socket, this is provided by default by a TCP connection that is established between the two end-points of the stream socket when it's connected. Data may be passed in both directions along the socket connection. The TCP protocols include facilities to fragment and re-assemble long messages and to retransmit any parts that may be lost in the network.

SOCK_DGRAM is a datagram service. You can use this socket to send messages of a fixed (usually small) maximum size, but there's no guarantee that the message will be delivered or that messages won't be re-ordered in the network. For AF_INET sockets, this type of communication is provided by UDP datagrams.

The protocol used for communication is usually determined by the socket type and domain. There is normally no choice. The `protocol` parameter is used where there is a choice. 0 selects the default protocol, which we'll use in all our examples.

The `socket` system call returns a descriptor that is, in many ways, similar to a low-level file descriptor. When the socket has been connected to another end-point socket, you may use the `read` and `write` system calls with the descriptor to send and receive data on the socket. The `close` system call is used to end a socket connection.

Socket Addresses

Each socket domain requires its own address format. For an `AF_UNIX` socket, the address is described by a structure, `sockaddr_un`, defined in the include file, `sys/un.h`.

```
struct sockaddr_un {
    sa_family_t    sun_family;    /* AF_UNIX */
    char           sun_path[];    /* pathname */
};
```

So that addresses of different types may be passed to socket handling system calls, each address format is described by a similar structure that begins with a field (in this case, `sun_family`) that specifies the address type (the socket domain). In the `AF_UNIX` domain, the address is specified by a file name in the `sun_path` field of the structure.

On current Linux systems, the type, `sa_family_t`, defined by X/Open as being declared in `sys/un.h` is taken to be a `short`. Also, the `pathname` specified in `sun_path` is limited in size (Linux specifies 108 characters, others may use a manifest constant such as `UNIX_MAX_PATH`). Because address structures may vary in size, many socket calls require or provide as an output a length to be used for copying the particular address structure.

In the `AF_INET` domain, the address is specified using a structure called `sockaddr_in`, defined in `netinet/in.h`, which contains at least these members.

```
struct sockaddr_in {
    short int            sin_family;   /* AF_INET */
    unsigned short int   sin_port;     /* Port number */
    struct in_addr       sin_addr;     /* Internet address */
};
```

The IP address structure, `in_addr`, is defined as:

```
struct in_addr {
    unsigned long int    s_addr;
};
```

The four bytes of an IP address constitute a single 32-bit value. An `AF_INET` socket is fully described by its domain, IP address and port number. From an application's point of view, all sockets act like file descriptors and are addressed by a unique integer value.

Naming a Socket

To make a socket (as created by a call to socket) available for use by other processes, a server program needs to give the socket a name. Thus AF_UNIX sockets are associated with a file system path name, as we saw in our server1 example. AF_INET sockets areassociated with an IP port number.

```
#include <sys/socket.h>

int bind(int socket, const struct sockaddr *address, size_t address_len);
```

The bind system call assigns the address specified in the parameter, address, to the unnamed socket associated with the file descriptor socket. The length of the address structure is passed as address_len.

The length and format of the address depend on the address family. A particular address structure pointer will need to be cast to the generic address type (struct sockaddr *) in the call to bind.

On successful completion, bind returns 0. If it fails, it returns -1 and set errno to one of the following.

EBADF	The file descriptor is invalid.
ENOTSOCK	The file descriptor doesn't refer to a socket.
EINVAL	The file descriptor refers to an already named socket.
EADDRNOTAVAIL	The address is unavailable.
EADDRINUSE	The address has a socket bound to it already.

There are some more values for AF_UNIX sockets.

EACCESS	Can't create the file system name due to permissions.
ENOTDIR, ENAMETOOLONG	Indicates a poor choice of filename.

Creating a Socket Queue

To accept incoming connections on a socket, a server program must create a queue to store pending requests. It does this using the listen system call.

```
#include <sys/socket.h>

int listen(int socket, int backlog);
```

A UNIX system may limit the maximum number of pending connections that may be held in a queue. Subject to this maximum, listen sets the queue length to backlog. Incoming connections up to this queue length are held pending on the socket, further connections will be refused and the client's connection will fail. This mechanism is provided by listen to allow incoming connections to be held pending while a server program is busy dealing with a previous client. A value of 5 for backlog is very common.

The listen function will return 0 on success, or -1 on error. Errors include EBADF, EINVAL and ENOTSOCK, as for the bind system call.

Accepting Connections

Once a server program has created and named a socket, it can wait for connections to be made to the socket by using the `accept` system call.

```
#include <sys/socket.h>

int accept(int socket, struct sockaddr *address, size_t *address_len);
```

The `accept` system call returns when a client program attempts to connect to the socket specified by the parameter `socket`. The client is the first pending connection from that socket's queue. The `accept` function creates a new socket to communicate with the client and returns its descriptor. The new socket will have the same type as the server listen socket.

The socket must have previously been named by a call to `bind` and had a connection queue allocated by `listen`. The address of the calling client will be placed in the `sockaddr` structure pointed to by `address`. A null pointer may be used here if the client address isn't of interest.

The parameter `address_len` specifies the length of the client structure. If the client address is longer than this value, it will be truncated. Before calling `accept` `address_len` must be set to the expected address length. On return, `address_len` will be set to the actual length of the calling client's address structure.

If there are no connections pending on the socket's queue, `accept` will block (so that the program won't continue) until a client makes a connection. You may change this behavior by using the `O_NONBLOCK` flag on the socket file descriptor, using the `fcntl` function like this:

```
int flags = fcntl(socket, F_GETFL, 0);

fcntl(socket, F_SETFL, O_NONBLOCK|flags);
```

The `accept` function returns a new socket file descriptor when there is a client connection pending or `-1` on error. Possible errors are similar to those for `bind` and `listen`, with the addition of `EWOULDBLOCK`, where `O_NONBLOCK` has been specified and there are no pending connections. The error, `EINTR`, will occur if the process is interrupted while blocked in `accept`.

Requesting Connections

Client programs connect to servers by establishing a connection between an unnamed socket and the server listen socket. They do this by calling `connect`.

```
#include <sys/socket.h>

int connect(int socket, const struct sockaddr *address, size_t address_len);
```

The socket specified by the parameter, `socket`, is connected to the server socket specified by the parameter, `address`, which is of length `address_len`. The socket must be a valid file descriptor obtained by a call to `socket`.

If it succeeds, connect returns 0, and -1 on error. Possible errors this time include:

EBADF	An invalid file descriptor was passed in socket.
EALREADY	A connection is already in progress for this socket.
ETIMEDOUT	A connection time has occurred.
ECONNREFUSED	The requested connection is refused by the server.

If the connection can't be set up immediately, connect will block for an unspecified timeout period. Once this timeout has expired, the connection will be aborted and connect will fail. However, if the call to connect is interrupted by a signal that is handled, the connect call will fail (with errno set to EINTR), but the connection attempt won't be aborted, but rather set up asynchronously.

As with accept, the blocking nature of connect may be altered by setting the O_NONBLOCK flag on the file descriptor. In this case, if the connection can't be made immediately, connect will fail with errno set to EINPROGRESS and the connection will be made asynchronously.

While asynchronous connections can be tricky to handle, you can use a call to select on the socket file descriptor to indicate that the socket is ready for writing. We'll cover select later in this chapter.

Closing a Socket

You can terminate a socket connection at the server and client by calling close, just as you would for low-level file descriptors. You should always close the socket at both ends. For the server, you should do this when read returns zero, but the close call could block if the socket has untransmitted data, is of a connection-oriented type and has the SOCK_LINGER option set. We'll learn about setting socket options later in the chapter.

Socket Communications

Now that we have covered the basic system calls associated with sockets, we can take a closer look at the example programs.

We'll try to convert them to use a network socket rather than a file system socket. The file system socket has the disadvantage that, unless the author uses an absolute path name, it's created in the server program's current directory. To make it more generally useful, we need to create it in a globally accessible directory (such as /tmp) that is agreed between the server and its clients. For network sockets, we need only choose an unused port number.

For our example, we'll choose port number 9734. This is an arbitrary choice that avoids the standard services. We can't use port numbers below 1024 as they are reserved for system use. Other port numbers are often listed, with the services provided on them, in the system file /etc/services. When you're writing socket-based applications, always choose a port number not listed in this configuration file.

We'll run our client and server across a network, but network sockets are not only useful on a network. Any machine with an Internet connection (even a modem dial-up) can use network sockets to communicate with others. You can even use a network-based program on an a stand-alone UNIX computer, because a UNIX computer is usually configured to use a loopback network that contains only itself. For illustration purposes, we'll use this loopback network, which can also be useful for debugging network applications as it eliminates any external network problems.

The loopback network consists of a single computer, conventionally called `localhost`, with a standard IP address of 127.0.0.1. This is the local machine. You'll find its address listed in the network hosts file, `/etc/hosts`, with the names and addresses of other hosts on shared networks.

Each network with which a computer communicates has a hardware interface associated with it. A computer may have different network names on each network and certainly will have different IP addresses. For example, my machine, `tilde`, has three network interfaces and therefore three addresses. These are recorded in `/etc/hosts` as:

```
127.0.0.1       localhost             # Loopback
192.168.1.1     tilde.localnet        # Local, private Ethernet
158.152.X.X     tilde.demon.co.uk     # Modem dial-up
```

The first is the simple loopback network, the second a local area network accessed via an Ethernet adapter and the third is the modem link to an Internet service provider. You can write a network socket-based program to communicate with servers accessed via any of these interfaces without alteration.

Here's a modified client program, `client2.c`, to connect to a network socket via the loopback network. It contains a subtle bug concerned with hardware dependency, but we'll discuss that later.

Try It Out - Network Client

1. Make the necessary `includes` and set up the variables.

```
#include <sys/types.h>
#include <sys/socket.h>
#include <stdio.h>
#include <netinet/in.h>
#include <arpa/inet.h>
#include <unistd.h>

int main()
{
    int sockfd;
    int len;
    struct sockaddr_in address;
    int result;
    char ch = 'A';
```

2. Create a socket for the client.

```
    sockfd = socket(AF_INET, SOCK_STREAM, 0);
```

3. Name the socket, as agreed with the server:

```
    address.sin_family = AF_INET;
    address.sin_addr.s_addr = inet_addr("127.0.0.1");
    address.sin_port = 9734;
    len = sizeof(address);
```

The rest of this program is the same as `client1.c`, from earlier in this chapter. When we run this version, it fails to connect because there isn't a server running on port 9734 on this machine.

```
$ client2
oops: client2: Connection refused
$
```

How It Works

The client program used the `sockaddr_in` structure from the include file `netinet/in.h` to specify an `AF_INET` address. It tries to connect to a server on the host with IP address, 127.0.0.1. It uses a function, `inet_addr`, to convert the text representation of an IP address into a form suitable for socket addressing. The manual page for `inet` has more information on other address translation functions.

We also need to modify the server program to wait for connections on our chosen port number. Here's a modified server, `server2.c`.

Try It Out - Network Server

1. Make the necessary `include`s and set up the variables.

```
#include <sys/types.h>
#include <sys/socket.h>
#include <stdio.h>
#include <netinet/in.h>
#include <arpa/inet.h>
#include <unistd.h>

int main()
{
    int server_sockfd, client_sockfd;
    int server_len, client_len;
    struct sockaddr_in server_address;
    struct sockaddr_in client_address;
```

2. Create an unnamed socket for the server.

```
    server_sockfd = socket(AF_INET, SOCK_STREAM, 0);
```

3. Name the socket.

```
    server_address.sin_family = AF_INET;
    server_address.sin_addr.s_addr = inet_addr("127.0.0.1");
    server_address.sin_port = 9734;
    server_len = sizeof(server_address);
    bind(server_sockfd, (struct sockaddr *)&server_address, server_len);
```

From here on, the listing follows `server1.c` exactly.

How It Works

The server program creates an AF_INET domain socket and arranges to accept connections on it. The socket is bound to our chosen port. The address specified determines which computers are allowed to connect. By specifying the loopback address, as in the client program, we are restricting communications to the local machine.

If we want to allow the server to communicate with remote clients, we must specify a set of IP addresses that we are willing to allow. We can use the special value, INADDR_ANY, to specify that we'll accept connections from all of the interfaces our computer may have. If we chose to, we could distinguish between different network interfaces to separate, for example, internal Local Area and external Wide Area Network connections. INADDR_ANY is a 32-bit integer value that we could use in the sin_addr.s_addr field of the address structure. However, we have a problem to resolve first.

Host and Network Byte Ordering

When I run these versions of the server and client programs on my computer, an Intel processor-based Linux machine, I can see the network connections by using the netstat command. This command will also be available on most UNIX systems configured for networking. It shows the client/server connection waiting to close down. The connection closes down after a small timeout. (Again, the exact output may vary between different versions of Linux.)

```
$ server2 &
[4] 1225
$ server waiting
client2
server waiting
char from server = B
$ netstat
Active Internet connections
Proto Recv-Q Send-Q Local Address    Foreign Address   (State)       User
tcp        1      0 localhost:1574   localhost:1174    TIME_WAIT     root
```

> **Before you try out further examples in this book, be sure to terminate running example server programs as they will compete to accept connections from clients and you'll see confusing results. You can kill them all with**
>
> **kill -1 <processid.>**

You can see the port numbers that have been assigned to the connection between the server and the client. The Local Address shows the server and the Foreign Address is the remote client. (Even though it's on the same machine, it's still connected over a network). To ensure that all sockets are distinct, these client ports are typically different to the server listen socket and unique to the computer.

However, the local address (the server socket) is given as 1574, but we chose the port 9734. Why are they different? The answer is that port numbers and addresses are communicated over socket interfaces as binary numbers. Different computers use different byte ordering for integers. For example, an Intel processor stores the 32-bit integer as four consecutive bytes in memory in the order 1-2-3-4, where 1 is the most significant byte. Motorola processors would store the integer in the byte order 4-3-2-1. If the memory used for integers is simply copied byte-by-byte, the two different computers would not be able to agree on integer values.

To enable computers of different types to agree on values for multibyte integers transmitted over a network, you need to define a network ordering. Client and server programs must convert their internal integer representation to the network ordering before transmission. They do this by using functions defined in `netinet/in.h`.

These are:

```
#include <netinet/in.h>

unsigned long int htonl(unsigned long int hostlong);
unsigned short int htons(unsigned short int hostshort);
unsigned long int ntohl(unsigned long int netlong);
unsigned short int ntohs(unsigned short int netshort);
```

These functions convert 16-bit and 32-bit integers between native host format and the standard network ordering. Their names are abbreviations for conversions. For example, 'host to network, long' (`htonl`) and 'host to network, short' (`htons`). For computers where the native ordering is the same as network ordering, these represent null operations.

To ensure correct byte ordering of the 16-bit port number, our server and client need to apply these functions to the port address. The change to `server3.c` is:

```
    server_address.sin_addr.s_addr = htonl(INADDR_ANY);
    server_address.sin_port = htons(9734);
```

We don't need to convert the function call, `inet_addr("127.0.0.1")`, because `inet_addr` is defined to produce a result in network order. The change to `client3.c` is:

```
    address.sin_port = htons(9734);
```

The server has also been changed to allow connections from any IP address by using `INADDR_ANY`.

Now, when we run `server3` and `client3`, we see the correct port being used for the local connection.

```
$ netstat
Active Internet connections
Proto Recv-Q Send-Q Local Address   Foreign Address   (State)     User
tcp        1      0 localhost:9734  localhost:1175    TIME_WAIT   root
```

Remember that if you're using a computer that has the same native and network byte ordering, you won't see any difference. It's still important to always use the conversion functions to allow correct operation with clients and servers on computers with a different architecture.

Network Information

So far, our client and server programs have had addresses and port numbers compiled into them. For a more general server and client program, we can use network information functions to determine addresses and ports to use.

If we have permission to do so, we can add our server to the list of known services in `/etc/services`, which assigns a name to port numbers so that clients can use symbolic services rather than numbers.

Similarly, given a computer's name, we can determine the IP address by calling host database functions that resolve addresses for us. They do this by consulting network configuration files, such as `/etc/hosts`, or network information services, such as NIS (Network Information Services, formerly known as Yellow Pages) and DNS (Domain Name Service).

Host database functions are declared in the interface header file `netdb.h`.

```
#include <netdb.h>

struct hostent *gethostbyaddr(const void *addr, size_t len, int type);
struct hostent *gethostbyname(const char *name);
```

The structure returned by these functions must contain at least these members.

```
struct hostent {
    char *h_name;          /* name of the host */
    char **h_aliases;      /* list of aliases (nicknames) */
    int h_addrtype;        /* address type */
    int h_length;          /* length in bytes of the address */
    char **h_addr_list     /* list of address (network order) */
};
```

If there is no database entry for the specified host or address, the information functions return a null pointer.

Similarly, information concerning services and associated port numbers is available through some service information functions.

```
#include <netdb.h>

struct servent *getservbyname(const char *name, const char *proto);
struct servent *getservbyport(int port, const char *proto);
```

The `proto` parameter specifies the protocol to be used to connect to the service, either `"tcp"` for `SOCK_STREAM` TCP connections or `"udp"` for `SOCK_DGRAM` UDP datagrams.

The structure `servent` contains at least these members:

```
struct servent {
    char *s_name;          /* name of the service */
    char **s_aliases;      /* list of aliases (alternative names) */
    int s_port;            /* The IP port number */
    char *s_proto;         /* The service type, usually "tcp" or "udp" */
};
```

We can gather host database information about a computer by calling gethostbyname and printing the results. Note that the address list needs to be cast to the appropriate address type and converted from network ordering to a printable string, using the inet_ntoa conversion, which has the following definition:

```
#include <arpa/inet.h>

char *inet_ntoa(struct in_addr in)
```

The function converts an Internet host address to a string in dotted quad format. It returns -1 on error, but POSIX doesn't define any errors. The other new function we use is gethostname.

```
#include <unistd.h>

int gethostname(char *name, int namelength);
```

This function writes the name of the current host into the string given by name. The hostname will be null-terminated. The argument namelength indicates the length of the string name and the returned hostname will be truncated if it's too long to fit. gethostname returns 0 on success and -1 on error, but again no errors are defined in POSIX.

This program, getname.c, gets information about a host computer.

Try It Out - Network Information

1. As usual, make the appropriate includes and declare the variables.

```
#include <netinet/in.h>
#include <arpa/inet.h>
#include <unistd.h>
#include <netdb.h>
#include <stdio.h>

int main(int argc, char *argv[])
{
    char *host, **names, **addrs;
    struct hostent *hostinfo;
```

2. Set the host to the argument supplied with the getname call, or by default to the user's machine.

```
    if(argc == 1) {
        char myname[256];
        gethostname(myname, 255);
        host = myname;
    }
    else
        host = argv[1];
```

3. Call gethostbyname and report an error if no information is found.

```
    hostinfo = gethostbyname(host);
    if(!hostinfo) {
        fprintf(stderr, "cannot get info for host: %s\n", host);
        exit(1);
    }
```

4. Display the hostname and any aliases that it may have.

```
    printf("results for host %s:\n", host);
    printf("Name: %s\n", hostinfo -> h_name);
    printf("Aliases:");
    names = hostinfo -> h_aliases;
    while(*names) {
```

```
        printf(" %s", *names);
        names++;
    }
    printf("\n");
```

5. Warn and exit if the host in question isn't an IP host.

```
    if(hostinfo -> h_addrtype != AF_INET) {
        fprintf(stderr, "not an IP host!\n");
        exit(1);
    }
```

6. Otherwise, display the IP address(es).

```
    addrs = hostinfo -> h_addr_list;
    while(*addrs) {
        printf(" %s", inet_ntoa(*(struct in_addr *)*addrs));
        addrs++;
    }
    printf("\n");
    exit(0);
}
```

Alternatively, you could use the function, `gethostbyaddr`, to determine which host has a given IP address. You might use this in a server to find out where the client is calling from.

How It Works

The `getname` program calls `gethostbyname` to extract the host information from the host database. It prints out the hostname, its aliases (other names the computer is known by) and the IP addresses that the host uses on its network interfaces. When I ran the example, specifying `tilde` gave the two interfaces, Ethernet and modem.

```
$ getname tilde
results for host tilde:
Name: tilde.demon.co.uk
Aliases: tilde
192.9.200.4 158.152.38.110
```

When we use the hostname, `localhost`, the loopback network is given.

```
$ getname localhost
results for host localhost:
Name: localhost
Aliases:
127.0.0.1
```

We could now modify our client to connect to any named host. Instead of connecting to our example server, we'll connect to a standard service so that we can also demonstrate extracting the port number.

Most UNIX systems make their system time and date available as a standard service called `daytime`. Clients may connect to this service to discover the server's idea of the current time and date. Here's a client program, `getdate.c`, that does just that.

Try It Out - Connecting to a Standard Service

1. Start with the usual `includes` and declarations.

```
#include <sys/socket.h>
#include <netinet/in.h>
#include <netdb.h>
#include <stdio.h>
#include <unistd.h>
```

```
int main(int argc, char *argv[])
{
    char *host;
    int sockfd;
    int len, result;
    struct sockaddr_in address;
    struct hostent *hostinfo;
    struct servent *servinfo;
    char buffer[128];

    if(argc == 1)
        host = "localhost";
    else
        host = argv[1];
```

2. Find the host address and report an error if none is found.

```
    hostinfo = gethostbyname(host);
    if(!hostinfo) {
        fprintf(stderr, "no host: %s\n", host);
        exit(1);
    }
```

3. Check that the `daytime` service exists on the host.

```
    servinfo = getservbyname("daytime", "tcp");
    if(!servinfo) {
        fprintf(stderr,"no daytime service\n");
        exit(1);
    }
    printf("daytime port is %d\n", ntohs(servinfo -> s_port));
```

4. Create a socket.

```
    sockfd = socket(AF_INET, SOCK_STREAM, 0);
```

5. Construct the address for use with `connect`...

```
    address.sin_family = AF_INET;
    address.sin_port = servinfo -> s_port;
    address.sin_addr = *(struct in_addr *)*hostinfo -> h_addr_list;
    len = sizeof(address);
```

6. then connect and get the information.

```
    result = connect(sockfd, (struct sockaddr *)&address, len);
    if(result == -1) {
        perror("oops: getdate");
        exit(1);
    }

    result = read(sockfd, buffer, sizeof(buffer));
    buffer[result] = '\0';
    printf("read %d bytes: %s", result, buffer);

    close(sockfd);
    exit(0);
}
```

We can use `getdate` to get the time of day from any known host.

```
$ getdate tilde
daytime port is 13
read 26 bytes: Sun Aug  1 11:29:53 1999
$
```

If you receive an error message such as

```
oops: getdate: Connection refused
```

It may be because the computer you are connecting to has not enabled the `daytime` service. This is the default behavior in recent Linux systems. In the next section we will see how to enable this and other services.

How It Works

When we run this program, we can specify a host to connect to. The `daytime` service port number is determined from the network database function `getservbyname`, which returns information about network services in a similar way to host information. The program `getdate` tries to connect to the address given first in the list of alternate addresses for the specified host. If successful, it reads the information returned by the `daytime` service, a character string representing the UNIX time and date.

The Internet Daemon

UNIX systems providing a number of network services often do so by way of a super-server. This program (the Internet Daemon, `inetd`) listens for connections on many port addresses at once. When a client connects to a service, the `inetd` program runs the appropriate server. This cuts down on the need for servers to be running all the time; they can be started by `inetd` as required. Here's an extract from the `inetd` configuration file, `/etc/inetd.conf`, that is used to decide which servers to run:

```
#
# <service_name> <sock_type> <proto> <flags> <user> <server_path> <args>
#
# Echo, discard, daytime, and chargen are used primarily for testing.
#
daytime    stream    tcp    nowait    root    internal
daytime    dgram    udp    wait    root    internal
#
# These are standard services.
#
ftp      stream    tcp    nowait    root    /usr/sbin/tcpd    /usr/sbin/wu.ftpd
telnet   stream    tcp    nowait    root    /usr/sbin/tcpd    /usr/sbin/in.telnetd
#
# End of inetd.conf.
```

The `daytime` service that our `getdate` program connects to is actually handled by `inetd` itself (marked as `internal`) and is available using both `SOCK_STREAM` (`tcp`) and `SOCK_DGRAM` (`udp`) sockets.

The file transfer service, `ftp`, is available only via `SOCK_STREAM` sockets and is provided by an external program, in this case `wu.ftpd`, which `inetd` will start when a client connects to the `ftp` port.

You can change the services provided via `inetd` by editing `/etc/inetd.conf` (a # at the start of a line indicates that the line is a comment) and restarting the `inetd` process. This can be done by sending it a hangup signal using `kill`. To make this easier some systems are configured so that `inetd` writes its process id to a file (on RedHat 6.0 it is `/var/run/inetd.pid`). Alternatively `killall` can be used:

```
# killall -HUP inetd
```

Socket Options

There are many options that you can use to control the behavior of socket connections – too many to detail here. The setsockopt function is used to manipulate options.

```
#include <sys/socket.h>

int setsockopt(int socket, int level, int option_name,
        const void *option_value, size_t option_len);
```

You can set options at various levels in the protocol hierarchy. To set options at the socket level, you must set level to SOL_SOCKET. To set options at the underlying protocol level (TCP, UDP, etc.), set level to the number of the protocol (from either the header file netinet/in.h or as obtained by the function getprotobyname).

The option_name parameter selects an option to set, the option_value is an arbitrary value of length option_len bytes passed unchanged to the underlying protocol handler.

Socket level options defined in sys/socket.h include:

SO_DEBUG	Turn on debugging information.
SO_KEEPALIVE	Keep connections active with periodic transmissions.
SO_LINGER	Complete transmission before close.

SO_DEBUG and SO_KEEPALIVE take an integer option_value used to set the option on (1) or off (0). SO_LINGER requires a linger structure defined in sys/socket.h to define the state of the option and the linger interval.

setsockopt returns 0 if successful, -1 otherwise. The manual pages describe further options and errors.

Multiple Clients

So far in this chapter, we've seen how we can use sockets to implement client/server systems, both locally and across networks. Once established, socket connections behave like low-level open file descriptors and in many ways like bi-directional pipes.

We might need to consider the case of multiple, simultaneous clients connecting to a server. We've seen that when a server program accepts a new connection from a client, a new socket is created and the original listen socket remains available for further connections. If the server doesn't immediately accept further connections, they will be held pending in a queue.

The fact that the original socket is still available and that sockets behave as file descriptors gives us a method of serving multiple clients at the same time. If the server calls fork to create a second copy of itself, the open socket will be inherited by the new child process. It can then communicate with the connecting client while the main server continues to accept further client connections. This is, in fact, a fairly easy change to make to our server program, which is shown here.

Since we're creating child processes but not waiting for them to complete, we must arrange for the server to ignore `SIG_CHLD` signals to prevent zombie processes.

Try It Out - A Server for Multiple Clients

1. This program, `server4.c`, begins in similar vein to our last server, with the notable addition of an `include` for the `signal.h` header file. The variables and the procedure of creating and naming a socket are the same.

```
#include <sys/types.h>
#include <sys/socket.h>
#include <stdio.h>
#include <netinet/in.h>
#include <signal.h>
#include <unistd.h>

int main()
{
    int server_sockfd, client_sockfd;
    int server_len, client_len;
    struct sockaddr_in server_address;
    struct sockaddr_in client_address;

    server_sockfd = socket(AF_INET, SOCK_STREAM, 0);

    server_address.sin_family = AF_INET;
    server_address.sin_addr.s_addr = htonl(INADDR_ANY);
    server_address.sin_port = htons(9734);
    server_len = sizeof(server_address);
    bind(server_sockfd, (struct sockaddr *)&server_address, server_len);
```

2. Create a connection queue, ignore child exit details and wait for clients.

```
    listen(server_sockfd, 5);

    signal(SIGCHLD, SIG_IGN);

    while(1) {
        char ch;

        printf("server waiting\n");
```

3. Accept connection.

```
        client_len = sizeof(client_address);
        client_sockfd = accept(server_sockfd,
            (struct sockaddr *)&client_address, &client_len);
```

4. Fork to create a process for this client and perform a test to see whether we're the parent or the child.

```
        if(fork() == 0) {
```

5. If we're the child, we can now read/write to the client on `client_sockfd`. The five second delay is just for this demonstration.

```
            read(client_sockfd, &ch, 1);
            sleep(5);
            ch++;
            write(client_sockfd, &ch, 1);
            close(client_sockfd);
            exit(0);
        }
```

6. Otherwise, we must be the parent and our work for this client is finished.

```
        else {
            close(client_sockfd);
        }
    }
}
```

We have inserted a five second delay in the processing of the client's request to simulate server calculation or database access. If we had done this with the previous server, each run of `client3` would have taken five seconds. With the new server, we can handle multiple `client3` programs concurrently, with an overall elapsed time of just over five seconds.

```
$ server4&
[7] 1571
$server waiting
client3 & client3 & client3 & ps -ax
[8] 1572
[9] 1573
[10] 1574
server waiting
server waiting
server waiting
PID TTY STAT  TIME COMMAND
 1557 pp0 S     0:00 server4
 1572 pp0 S     0:00 client3
 1573 pp0 S     0:00 client3
 1574 pp0 S     0:00 client3
 1575 pp0 R     0:00 ps -ax
 1576 pp0 S     0:00 server4
 1577 pp0 S     0:00 server4
 1578 pp0 S     0:00 server4
$ char from server = B
char from server = B
char from server = B
ps -ax
PID TTY STAT  TIME COMMAND
 1557 pp0 S     0:00 server4
 1580 pp0 R     0:00 ps -ax
[8]    Done                    client3
[9]-   Done                    client3
[10]+  Done                     client3
$
```

How It Works

The server program now creates a new child process to handle each client, so we see several server waiting messages as the main program continues to wait for new connections. The `ps` output (edited here) shows the main `server4` process, PID 1557, waiting for new clients while the three `client3` processes are being served by three children of the server. After a five second pause, all of the clients get their results and finish. The child server processes exit to leave just the main server alone again.

The server program uses `fork` to handle multiple clients. In a database application, this may not be the best solution, since the server program may be quite large and there is still the problem of coordinating database accesses from multiple server copies. In fact, what we really need is a way for a single server to handle multiple clients without blocking, waiting on client requests to arrive. The solution to this problem involves handling multiple open file descriptors at once and isn't limited to socket applications. Enter `select`.

select

Quite often when you're writing UNIX applications you may need to examine the state of a number of inputs to determine the next action to take. For example, a communication program, such as a terminal emulator, needs to read the keyboard and the serial port effectively at the same time. In a single-user system, it might be acceptable to run in a 'busy wait' loop, repeatedly scanning the input for data and reading it if it arrives. This behavior is expensive in terms of CPU time.

The `select` system call allows a program to wait for input to arrive (or output to complete) on a number of low-level file descriptors at once. This means that the terminal emulator program can block until there is something to do. Similarly, a server can deal with multiple clients by waiting for a request on many open sockets at the same time.

The `select` function operates on data structures, `fd_set`, that are sets of open file descriptors. A number of macros are defined for manipulating these sets:

```
#include <sys/types.h>
#include <sys/time.h>

void FD_ZERO(fd_set *fdset);
void FD_CLR(int fd, fd_set *fdset);
void FD_SET(int fd, fd_set *fdset);
int FD_ISSET(int fd, fd_set *fdset);
```

As suggested by their names, `FD_ZERO` initializes an `fd_set` to the empty set, `FD_SET` and `FD_CLR` set and clear elements of the set corresponding to the file descriptor passed as `fd` and `FD_ISSET` returns non-zero if the file descriptor referred to by `fd` is an element of the `fd_set` pointed to by `fdset`. The maximum number of file descriptors in an `fd_set` structure is given by the constant `FD_SETSIZE`.

The `select` function can also use a timeout value to prevent indefinite blocking. The timeout value is given using a `struct timeval`. This structure, defined in `sys/time.h`, has the following members:

```
struct timeval {
  time_t    tv_sec;     /* seconds */
  long      tv_usec;    /* microseconds */
}
```

The `time_t` type is defined in `sys/types.h` as an integral type.

The `select` system call has the following prototype:

```
#include <sys/types.h>
#include <sys/time.h>

int select(int nfds, fd_set *readfds, fd_set *writefds, fd_set *errorfds, struct
timeval *timeout);
```

A call to `select` is used to test whether any one of a set of file descriptors is ready for reading or writing, or has an error condition pending and optionally block until one is ready.

The `nfds` argument specifies the number of file descriptors to be tested and descriptors from `0` to `nfds-1` are considered. Each of the three descriptor sets may be a null pointer, in which case the associated test isn't carried out.

The `select` function will return if any of the descriptors in the `readfds` set are ready for reading, if any in the `writefds` set are ready for writing, or any in `errorfds` have an error condition. If none of these conditions apply, `select` will return after an interval specified by `timeout`. If the `timeout` parameter is a null pointer and there is no activity on the sockets, then the call will block forever.

When `select` returns, the descriptor sets will have been modified to indicate which descriptors are ready for reading or writing or have errors. You should use `FD_ISSET` to test them, to determine the descriptor(s) needing attention. You can modify the `timeout` value to indicate the time remaining to the next timeout, but this behavior isn't specified by X/Open. In the case of a timeout occurring, all descriptor sets will be empty.

The `select` call returns the total number of descriptors in the modified sets. It returns -1 on failure, setting `errno` to describe the error. Possible errors are `EBADF` for invalid descriptors, `EINTR` for return due to interrupt and `EINVAL` for bad values for `nfds` or `timeout`.

Although Linux modifies the structure pointed to by `timeout` to indicate the time remaining, most versions of UNIX do not. Much existing code that uses the `select` function initializes a `timeval` structure and then continues to use it without ever re-initializing the contents. On Linux, this code may operate incorrectly, since Linux is modifying the `timeval` structure every time a timeout occurs. If you're writing or porting, code that uses the `select` function, you should watch out for this difference and always re-initialize the timeout. Note that both behaviors are correct; they're just different!

Here is a program, `select.c`, to illustrate the use of `select`. We'll see and discuss a more complete example a little later. This program reads the keyboard (standard input—file descriptor 0) with a time-out of 2.5 seconds. It reads the keyboard only when input is ready. It's quite straightforward to extend it to include other descriptors, such as serial lines or pipes and sockets, depending on the application.

Try It Out - select

1. Begin as usual with the `includes` and declarations and then initialize `inputs` to handle input from the keyboard.

```
#include <sys/types.h>
#include <sys/time.h>
#include <stdio.h>
#include <fcntl.h>
#include <sys/ioctl.h>
#include <unistd.h>

int main()
{
    char buffer[128];
    int result, nread;

    fd_set inputs, testfds;
    struct timeval timeout;

    FD_ZERO(&inputs);
    FD_SET(0,&inputs);
```

2. Wait for input on `stdin` for a maximum of 2.5 seconds.

```
while(1) {
    testfds = inputs;
    timeout.tv_sec = 2;
    timeout.tv_usec = 500000;

    result = select(FD_SETSIZE, &testfds, (fd_set *)NULL, (fd_set *)NULL,
                    &timeout);
```

3. After this time, we test `result`. If there has been no input, the program loops again. If there has been an error, the program exits.

```
    switch(result) {
    case 0:
        printf("timeout\n");
        break;
    case -1:
        perror("select");
        exit(1);
```

4. If, during the wait, we have some action on the file descriptor, we read the input on `stdin` and echo it whenever an <end of line> character is received, until that input is *Ctrl-D*.

```
    default:
        if(FD_ISSET(0,&testfds)) {
            ioctl(0,FIONREAD,&nread);
            if(nread == 0) {
                printf("keyboard done\n");
                exit(0);
            }
            nread = read(0,buffer,nread);
            buffer[nread] = 0;
            printf("read %d from keyboard: %s", nread, buffer);
        }
        break;
    }
  }
}
```

When we run this program, it prints `timeout` every two and a half seconds. If we type at the keyboard, it reads the standard input and reports what was typed. With most shells, the input will be sent to the program when the user presses the *Return* key or keys in a control sequence, so our program will print the input whenever we press *Return*. Note that the *Return* itself is read and processed like any other character (try this by not pressing *Return*, but a number of characters followed by *Ctrl-D*).

```
$ ./select
timeout
hello
read 6 from keyboard: hello
fred
read 5 from keyboard: fred
timeout
^D
keyboard done
$
```

How It Works

The program uses the `select` call to examine the state of the standard input. By arranging a timeout value, the program resumes every 2.5 seconds to print a timeout message. This is indicated by `select` returning zero. On end of file, the standard input descriptor is flagged as ready for input, but there are no characters to be read.

Multiple Clients

Our simple server program can benefit by using `select` to handle multiple clients simultaneously, without resorting to child processes. For real applications using this technique we must take care that we do not make other clients wait too long while we deal with the first to connect.

The server can use `select` on both the listen socket and the clients' connection sockets at the same time. Once activity has been indicated, we can use `FD_ISSET` to cycle through all the possible file descriptors to discover which one the activity is on.

If the listen socket is ready for input, this will mean that a client is attempting to connect and we can call `accept` without risk of blocking. If a client descriptor is indicated ready, this means that there's a client request pending that we can read and deal with. A read of zero bytes will indicate that a client process has ended and we can close the socket and remove it from our descriptor set.

Try It Out - An Improved Multiple Client/Server

1. For our final example, `server5.c`, we include the `sys/time.h` and `sys/ioctl.h` headers instead of `signal.h` in our last program and declare some extra variables to deal with `select`.

```
#include <sys/types.h>
#include <sys/socket.h>
#include <stdio.h>
#include <netinet/in.h>
#include <sys/time.h>
#include <sys/ioctl.h>
#include <unistd.h>

int main()
{
    int server_sockfd, client_sockfd;
    int server_len, client_len;
    struct sockaddr_in server_address;
    struct sockaddr_in client_address;
    int result;
    fd_set readfds, testfds;
```

2. Create and name a socket for the server.

```
    server_sockfd = socket(AF_INET, SOCK_STREAM, 0);

    server_address.sin_family = AF_INET;
    server_address.sin_addr.s_addr = htonl(INADDR_ANY);
    server_address.sin_port = htons(9734);
    server_len = sizeof(server_address);

    bind(server_sockfd, (struct sockaddr *)&server_address, server_len);
```

3. Create a connection queue and initialize `readfds` to handle input from `server_sockfd`.

```
    listen(server_sockfd, 5);

    FD_ZERO(&readfds);
    FD_SET(server_sockfd, &readfds);
```

4. Now wait for clients and requests. Since we have passed a null pointer as the `timeout` parameter, no timeout will occur. The program will exit and report an error if `select` returns a value of less than 1.

```
while(1) {
        char ch;
        int fd;
        int nread;

        testfds = readfds;

        printf("server waiting\n");
        result = select(FD_SETSIZE, &testfds, (fd_set *)0,
            (fd_set *)0, (struct timeval *) 0);

        if(result < 1) {
            perror("server5");
            exit(1);
        }
```

5. Once we know we've got activity, we find which descriptor it's on by checking each in turn using `FD_ISSET`:

```
        for(fd = 0; fd < FD_SETSIZE; fd++) {
            if(FD_ISSET(fd,&testfds)) {
```

6. If the activity is on `server_sockfd`, it must be a request for a new connection and we add the associated client_`sockfd` to the descriptor set:

```
                if(fd == server_sockfd) {
                    client_len = sizeof(client_address);
                    client_sockfd = accept(server_sockfd,
                        (struct sockaddr *)&client_address, &client_len);
                    FD_SET(client_sockfd, &readfds);
                    printf("adding client on fd %d\n", client_sockfd);
                }
```

7. If it isn't the server, it must be client activity. If `close` is received, the client has gone away and we remove it from the descriptor set. Otherwise, we 'serve' the client as in the previous examples.

```
                else {
                    ioctl(fd, FIONREAD, &nread);

                    if(nread == 0) {
                        close(fd);
                        FD_CLR(fd, &readfds);
                        printf("removing client on fd %d\n", fd);
                    }

                    else {
                        read(fd, &ch, 1);
                        sleep(5);
                        printf("serving client on fd %d\n", fd);
                        ch++;
                        write(fd, &ch, 1);
                    }
                }
            }
        }
    }
}
```

In a real-world program, it would be advisable to include a variable holding the largest `fd` number connected (not necessarily the most recent fd number connected). This would prevent looping through potentially 1000s of `fds` which aren't even connected and couldn't possibly be ready for reading. We've omitted it here simply for brevity's sake and to make the code simpler.

When we run this version of the server, it deals with multiple clients sequentially in a single process.

```
$ server5 &
[7] 1670
$ server waiting
client3 & client3 & client3 & ps -ax
[8] 1671
[9] 1672
[10] 1673
adding client on fd 4
server waiting
adding client on fd 5
server waiting
adding client on fd 6
server waiting
PID TTY STAT  TIME COMMAND
 1670 pp0 S    0:00 ./server5
 1671 pp0 S    0:00 client3
 1672 pp0 S    0:00 client3
 1673 pp0 S    0:00 client3
 1674 pp0 R    0:00 ps -ax
$ serving client on fd 4
server waiting
char from server = B
serving client on fd 5
char from server = B
serving client on fd 6
server waiting
removing client on fd 4
removing client on fd 5
server waiting
char from server = B
removing client on fd 6
server waiting

[8]   Done                    client3
[9]-  Done                    client3
[10]+  Done                    client3
$
```

Summary

In this chapter, we've covered another method of inter-process communication: sockets. These allow us to develop true distributed client/server applications to run across networks. We briefly covered some of the host database information functions and how UNIX handles standard system services with the Internet Daemon. We developed a number of client/server example programs that demonstrate networking and multiple client handling.

Finally, we learned about the `select` system call that allows a program to be advised of input and output activity on several open file descriptors and sockets at once.

To complete the analogy at the start of the chapter, this table shows the parallels between socket connections and a telephone exchange.

Telephone	Network Sockets
Call company on 555-0828	Connect to IP address 127.0.0.1
Call answered by reception	Connection established to `remote host`
Ask for finance department	Route using specified port (9734)
Call answered by finance administration	Server returns from `select`
Call put through to free account manager	Server calls `accept`, creating new socket on extension 456

Tcl: Tool Command Language

In this chapter, we'll take a look at an exciting development in the UNIX world, that of an extensible, embeddable programming language that is taking the community by storm. Tcl (pronounced *tickle*) has been developed by John Ousterhout and others over a number of years and is now maintained by Scriptics (http://www.scriptics.com). It has become a popular choice of programming language for a diverse range of applications, ranging from fast prototype tools through extension languages to industrial control applications. Tcl is also available on other platforms, including Microsoft Windows and Apple MacOS.

We'll take a look at some of the key features of Tcl, including its extensibility and its use as the interactive interface to new applications and also see some of the extensions and applications that have been created. Some of the things we'll be covering in this chapter are:

- Tcl commands and control structures
- Quoting and substitution
- Strings and lists in Tcl
- Input and output
- Tcl extensions and applications

A Tcl Overview

We begin our look at Tcl with the basics: how to write and execute Tcl programs and the features of the language.

Our First Tcl Program

To see how Tcl programs are created and executed, let's write a very simple "Hello World" program, `hello.tcl`. Here's the source of such a program:

```
set s "Hello World"
puts $s
```

Tcl is an interpreted language and Tcl programs are often referred to as **scripts**. In this respect, Tcl and the UNIX shell have a lot in common. In fact, Tcl scripts need to be executed by a Tcl shell, called `tclsh`.

Let's run our sample script using `tclsh`. Note that running a Tcl program this way only requires file read permission.

```
$ tclsh hello.tcl
Hello World
$
```

Like other UNIX command interpreters, we can run `tclsh` and it will prompt us for Tcl commands to execute immediately. We could have just as well typed in the two lines directly:

```
$ tclsh
% set s "Hello World"
Hello World
% puts $s
Hello World
```

Notice that `tclsh` prompts with `%` and executes our commands immediately they are typed. It keeps reading lines until it gets a complete command. We can use the `source` command to make `tclsh` take commands from a file. Let's make Tcl read our program again:

```
% source hello.tcl
Hello World
% exit
$
```

The `exit` command causes the Tcl shell to end and returns us to the UNIX shell. We can turn our script into a UNIX program by specifying the interpreter to use on the first line, just as we did for the UNIX shell. Save the program in a file, `hello2.tcl`:

```
#!/usr/bin/tclsh

set s "Hello World - 2"
puts $s
```

Now, if we make this script executable, we can run it in the usual way. The location of the Tcl shell, `tclsh`, may vary from system to system. In this case, it has been installed in `/usr/bin`.

> **Generally, you can use the `whereis` or `which` commands to show where `tclsh` is located within the search path.**

```
$ chmod +x hello2.tcl
$ ./hello2.tcl
Hello World - 2
$
```

Tcl Commands

In general, all Tcl commands take the same form. They begin with a keyword and are followed by zero or more arguments. A command is usually terminated by the end of the line, although you can use a backslash (\) at the end of the line to extend a long command over multiple lines.

Quoting and variable substitution (to which we'll come shortly) take place first. Then the resulting command is executed. Some of these commands cause a result to be produced; others cause further commands to be stored for later execution, such as when procedures are defined or loops are encountered.

Because of the fairly simple syntax, Tcl is easy to learn and simple to extend. However, it does mean that some operations, such as assignment and calculations, can seem a little awkward at first.

You can place multiple Tcl commands on the same line if you separate them with semi colons.

In this chapter, when we look at the syntax of Tcl commands, we'll use a notation like this:

```
command argument1 argument2 ?option1? ?option2? …
```

This means that the (fictitious) Tcl command, `command`, takes two mandatory arguments, plus some optional arguments that may be used to change its behavior. You'll find this type of syntax used in the official Tcl/Tk documentation.

Variables and Values

Tcl deals essentially with strings and groups of strings. Most values can be dealt with as strings and, where necessary, Tcl will automatically convert between types, for example to perform arithmetic on numbers. To assign to a variable, creating the variable if necessary, we use the `set` command. You can follow the rest of this section as a walk-through example in the Tcl shell.

```
$ tclsh
% set a 123
123
% set hello there
there
%
```

Variable names are case-sensitive and can be any length. Special characters (such as whitespace) in variable names and values need to be **quoted**, which you do by enclosing the name or value in double quotes. As in the UNIX shell, you need to take care with quoting. We'll learn more about different quoting methods in Tcl shortly.

```
% set "hello there" "fare well"
fare well
%
```

To examine the current value of a variable, use the `set` command again, but this time don't give it a value argument.

```
% set hello
there
% set "hello there"
fare well
%
```

When using Tcl interactively like this, the interpreter prints the result of each command. In the case of the set command, we see the variable's new value printed after an assignment, or the variable's present value if no new value is given. This is because the set command itself returns the current value of the variable.

To use the value of a variable in another command we prefix its name with a $, just as we do in the UNIX shell. In our example program, we assigned a string to the variable s and then used it in the puts command, which wrote it to the screen, by referring to it as $s. You can use braces to quote variable names that contain spaces.

```
% puts $a
123
% puts [expr $a + $a]
246
% puts ${hello there}
fare well
%
```

To use the result of one command in another, we place the command in square brackets, as in the second example above. This causes the Tcl interpreter to execute the command and return a result that is used in its place. This is very like the way we use $(command) in the UNIX shell. In the same example, we use the expr command that evaluates a Tcl expression and returns the result.

We can remove a variable from the Tcl interpreter by using unset.

```
% unset a
% puts $a
can't read "a": no such variable
```

Quoting and Substitution

As it is in the UNIX shell, quoting is crucial in Tcl and there are a number of different quoting and substitution mechanisms in Tcl that you need to understand.

Variable Substitution

In a Tcl command, a variable is replaced with its value whenever its name appears preceded by a dollar sign, $. This is the mechanism we would use to pass parameters to commands and store or use general purpose values.

```
% set apple 5
5
% set orange $apple
5
%
```

Command Substitution

A command contained within square brackets, [], is executed and replaced with its result.

```
% set pear [expr $orange + 1]
6
%
```

Backslash Substitution

We use a backslash, \, to turn off the special meaning of the following character. We can use it to create variables and values with unusual characters (say, dollar signs) in them.

A backslash at the end of a line is used as a continuation marker. (It negates the special meaning of the newline character.)

```
% set fred \$apple
$apple
% set lemon [expr $pear \
+ 1]
7
%
```

String Quoting

We use double quotes to create strings containing white space and other special characters. However, as it does in the UNIX shell, this type of quoting allows substitutions to take place. Variables will be substituted with their values when referenced inside double quoted strings.

```
% set joe "Our fruits are orange: $orange, and pear: $pear"
Our fruits are orange: 5, and pear: 6
%
```

Brace Quoting

Another form of quoting, using braces, {}, doesn't allow variable substitutions and creates a verbatim group of strings. Similar to the use of single quotes in the UNIX shell, braces prevent substitution.

We can also use braces for storing procedure bodies. We want any variable and command substitutions to be performed when the procedure is executed, not when it is defined.

```
% set moe {Our fruits are orange: $orange, and pear: $pear}
Our fruits are orange: $orange, and pear: $pear
%
```

The difference between `joe` and `moe` is clear. The variable substitutions in `moe` have been prevented by the braces.

When a group surrounded by braces is evaluated, the outermost set of braces are effectively removed. If further evaluated, the resulting group will have substitutions performed. Braces can be nested. For example:

```
% set fred 1234
1234
% set cmd1 [puts $fred]
1234
% set cmd2 {[puts $fred]}
[puts $fred]
% set cmd1
% set cmd2
[puts $fred]
```

The variable cmd1 takes a null value, the result of printing the variable fred. The variable cmd2 takes the value of the command itself, not the result. Here, the braces prevent the evaluation of puts and the expansion of $fred.

This can all seem quite confusing, so lets look at what the Tcl shell is actually doing when it encounters different types of quoting.

Tcl Interpreter Substitution

Tcl always performs a single round of substitutions. When a command is executed, the line is broken up into a series of 'words' by separating on white spaces (except new lines, which are command separators). Anything contained by two double quotes "...", two square brackets [...], or two braces {...} is viewed as a single 'word'. Each 'word' is then processed by the interpreter as follows:

- If the 'word' starts with a $, Tcl performs variable substitution.
- If the 'word' starts with an open square bracket ([), Tcl performs 'command substitution', invoking the Tcl interpreter again and processing this 'word' as a new Tcl script. The results replace the original 'word'.
- If the 'word' starts with an open brace ({), everything within the word (minus the opening and closing braces) is left as is. This includes white space, $, etc.
- If the 'word' contains a back slash \, Tcl performs 'backslash substitution'.

So to summarize:

Word	Substitution	Result
$a	variable	value of a
[commands]	command	result of interpreting commands
{the formatted text}	none	the formatted text
\$word	backslash	$word

If the results contain further variable references or nested commands, these are not expanded. This consistency means that the execution of a Tcl command is predictable. However, you do need to carefully consider your choice of quoting method. Let's try to make it clearer with an example or two.

```
% set age 35
35
% set str {I'm $age years old}
I'm $age years old
% set cmd {puts "$str"}
puts "$str"
%
```

These assignments set up two levels of indirection. The variable cmd refers to the variable str, which, in turn, refers to the variable age which has the value 35. If we wish to use cmd to get at the value of age, we must arrange for additional substitutions.

We can gain additional rounds of substitutions using eval or explicitly by calling the subst command, which is implemented in Tcl versions 7.4 and above. The eval command takes its arguments, gathers them together as a single string and then passes this to the Tcl interpreter which executes it.

```
% eval $cmd
I'm $age years old
%
```

The value of cmd, the command puts "$str", is executed. The string, str, has the value I'm $age years old. If we want to expand this string before performing the puts command, we need to use subst. The subst command performs variable, command and backslash substitutions on strings and then returns the newly formed string. The difference is that the argument to eval must be a command, which is executed. subst performs substitution but doesn't evaluate the result.

```
% subst $cmd
puts "I'm $age years old"
%
```

Here, the subst command returns a valid command, which will output a string containing the current value of age at the time it is evaluated.

```
% eval [subst $cmd]
I'm 35 years old
%
```

The control of substitution and execution makes Tcl a very powerful tool. Because the eval command can execute an arbitrary string, Tcl programs can communicate and pass commands for execution to one another. You could use this technique to develop Tcl debuggers in Tcl itself which control the execution of other Tcl programs. You could also use it in Internet programming, where a server application may wish to send a program to the client for execution, or may generate a Tcl script on the fly.

Comments

Tcl programs may contain comments. Comments act almost as if they were a Tcl command with the name #, which has no effect. This means that, unlike some other similar languages, we can continue across many lines by ending each line with a trailing backslash. One peculiarity is that semi colons are not significant in comments, so they can continue after one.

```
# This is a comment
set a 123 ; # This is a trailing comment, note the semi-colon is needed to separate it
\
but the comment continues onto this line; and this is still comment
```

Calculation

Tcl provides a command, expr, to perform arithmetic calculations. This is because the Tcl interpreter itself doesn't contain mathematical functions, rather it relies on additional functionality provided by commands. Although Tcl can perform limited arithmetic, such as that required for loop termination, the bulk of calculation is carried out by expr.

The expr command takes one or more arguments and calculates a result. The arguments may be operands, operators and parentheses. Operands may be specified as numbers (integers or floating point), logical expressions, strings that will be converted to numeric values (including substitutions), variable references and nested commands.

Examples are:

```
% expr 5 + 5
10
% set a 5
5
% set b 6
6
% expr $a+$b
11
% expr 2*"$a.$b"
11.2
% expr 3*(1+[string length "hello"])
18
%
```

Valid operators for expr are listed below, in decreasing order of precedence. Comparison operators produce 1 for true, 0 for false.

Operator Precedence	Description
- + ~ !	Unary minus and plus, bitwise NOT, logical NOT.
* / %	Multiply, divide, remainder.
+ -	Add, subtract.
<< >>	Shift left, shift right (both signed).
< > <= >=	Less than, greater than, less than or equal, greater than or equal.
== !=	Equal, not equal.
&	Bit-wise AND.
^	Bit-wise XOR.
|	Bit-wise OR.
&&	Logical AND.
||	Logical OR.
cond?yes:no	Ternary conditional, as in C. If cond is non-zero return the value of yes, else return the value of no.

As an example of the last operator, consider the following:

```
% set k "foo"
foo
% set result [expr {($k == "foo") ? "pass" : "fail"}]
pass
%
```

Tcl also supports the following mathematical functions in expressions, each of which invokes the math library function of the same name:

acos	asin	atan	atan2
ceil	cos	cosh	exp
floor	fmod	hypot	log
log10	pow	sin	sinh
sqrt	tan	tanh	

Because the construct,

```
set a [expr $a + 1]
```

occurs so often, the `incr` command was introduced. By default, it increments a variable's value by 1. It can also be given an explicit increment.

```
% set a 5
5
% incr a
6
% incr a 5
11
% set a
11
%
```

Control Structures

Tcl supports a wide range of control structures for program flow, including conditionals, loops and selections.

if

```
if expr1 ?then? body1
if expr1 ?then? body1 ?else? body2
if expr1 ?then? body1 elseif expr2 ?then? body2 ?elseif? ... ?else? ?bodyN?
```

The `if` command evaluates `expr1` in the same way as `expr`. If the result is a Boolean `true` (a non-zero numeric value, or a string with the value `true` or `yes`), `body1` is executed and its value returned. Otherwise, the process repeats with the next `elseif` clause if there is one (there may be zero). If none of the expressions evaluate to a Boolean `true`, the `else` clause (if present) is executed and its result returned. If no body is executed, the `if` command returns an empty string. A Boolean `false` would be represented by numeric zero or the string values `false` or `no`.

The body sections need to be single items: a single 'word' or a bracketed command. Note that the then and else keywords are not necessary, but make things easier to read. It's recommended practice to build the construct like this:

```
if {expr1} {
    body1
} else {
    body2
}
```

The reason for the odd layout of braces, especially having the brace and else on the same line, is to make sure the interpreter knows that there's more coming. Without it, we have a complete if statement. Tcl would execute it, assume the next line started with the command else, and give you a syntax error.

switch

```
switch ?options? string pattern body ?pattern body ...?
switch ?options? string {pattern body ?pattern body ...?}
```

The Tcl switch command is the direct analog of the UNIX shell case statement and the C switch (which only works on integer values). The given string is compared in turn with each of the patterns (See the later sections on matching.) When a match is found, the associated body is executed and its result returned. A pattern of default acts as a 'catch all', matching all strings not matched by any other pattern.

Options control the matching technique to be used. These may be:

switch option	Description
-exact	Match the string to the pattern exactly.
-glob	Use glob (shell-style) matching (as in UNIX file name matching).
-regexp	Use regular expression matching as in the UNIX egrep utility.
--	An option used to mark the end of options, in case a string starts with a hyphen.

You can use the two different ways of specifying the patterns and bodies to gain fine control over substitutions in the arguments to switch. Placing patterns and bodies in braces {} has two effects: it prevents substitutions and it allows you to spread the patterns and bodies over several lines without having to quote the end of lines with backslashes.

Here's an example we'll meet again later that illustrates how switch can be used to process program arguments:

```
foreach arg $argv {
    switch -glob -- $arg {
        -v      {set VerboseFlag true}
        -f*     {set FileToRead [string range $arg 2 end]}
        -h      {puts stderr $Usage; exit 1}
        default {error "bad argument: $arg\n$Usage"; exit 1}
    }
}
```

for

```
for start test next body
```

The Tcl for statement is very similar to the for statement in C. The start, next and body arguments must be Tcl command strings and test must yield a Boolean expression. The for command executes the start string and then repeatedly evaluates the test expression. If it yields a Boolean true value, the body string is executed. If a break command is encountered in the body, the loop is terminated immediately. A continue command in the body causes the for loop to be restarted. Each time the loop is completed, the next expression is evaluated.

```
% set n 5
5
% set result 1
1
% for {set i $n} {$i} {incr i -1} {
    set result [expr $result * $i]
}
% set result
120
```

You may recognize this as calculating a factorial. We'll see a little later how to create a Tcl procedure to perform this function.

while

```
while test body
```

The while command acts in a similar way to the while statement in C. It repeatedly evaluates the test string and executes the Tcl command body until test yields a Boolean false value. As with the for command, a break or continue command causes the loop to be terminated or restarted respectively. As an example, this code emulates the UNIX cat command on the file foo. See the section on input and output for more about file handling.

```
% set fd [open "foo" "r"]
file3
% while {[gets $fd line] != -1} {
    puts "$line"
}

<The file "foo" is displayed at this point>

% close $fd
```

Error Handling

When the Tcl interpreter encounters an error, it usually prints a message and halts. This is not always the desired result from within a program, so Tcl provides a facility to raise and trap errors and to recover from them.

error

error message *?info? ?code?*

The `error` command generates an error and terminates execution unless the error is caught or trapped. The message, `message`, is provided as an indication to the application as to what went wrong. It is printed if the interpreter default error action is taken.

If present, the `info` argument is added to the global variable `errorInfo`. This variable accumulates information about command nesting when errors occur. As each Tcl command unwinds, it adds to `errorInfo` to provide a stack trace. Similarly, the `code` argument is intended to add machine readable information to the global variable `errorCode`. Refer to the Tcl documentation for further details.

catch

catch script *?varname?*

The `catch` command evaluates the given `script`, trapping any errors that occur. If present, the variable `varname` will be set to the return value of the script or any error message returned.

Here's an example taken from the Tcl program, `concord`, that we'll see later:

```
if [catch {set Input [open $FileToRead r]} res ] {
    puts stderr "$res"
```

If the attempt to open the input file fails, the program can carry on, rather than stopping with an error. `catch` is extremely useful in this regard, as there are many instances of programs that would not run successfully without trapping the error in this fashion.

String Operations

As Tcl is essentially a string-based language interpreter, it's no surprise that it provides a rich set of commands for manipulating strings and string values.

The main string manipulation command is `string`. It takes one option and a number of arguments, depending on the operation required.

string

string option arg *?arg? ...*

The options (and associated arguments) to `string` are given below. Where a string index is used or returned, it is always base zero, that is, the first character is given an index of 0, the second an index of 1, and so on.

first, last, compare

string first string1 string2
string last string1 string2
string compare string1 string2

first and last search for the appropriate occurrence of string1 in string2 and return the index into string2 of the start of the match found, or -1 if string1 doesn't occur in string2.

```
% string first "o" "foobar"
1
% string last "o" "foobar"
2
```

compare performs a character-by-character comparison. Returns -1, 0 or 1 if string1 is less than, equal to, or greater than string2, in the same way as strcmp in C.

```
% string compare "foo" "bar"
1
```

index

string index string num

index returns a single character from string. The character at index position num is returned, where the first character is deemed to be index 0.

```
% string index "ABC" 1
B
```

length

string length string

length returns the length of string.

```
% string length "ABC"
3
```

match

string match pattern string

match returns 1 if string matches pattern, 0 otherwise. The matching performed is similar to that of the UNIX shell, where so-called glob matching is used in filename expansion.

```
% string match "*B*" "ABC"
1
% string match "*B*" "ZZZ"
0
```

range

string range string first last

range returns a substring of string from index position first (starting at zero) to last, which may be the keyword end to specify the end of the string.

```
% string range "ABCDEF" 3 end
DEF
```

tolower, toupper

```
string tolower string
string toupper string
```

These arguments return a string made from the characters of `string` converted to the appropriate case.

```
% string tolower "ABC"
abc
% string toupper "abc"
ABC
```

trim, trimleft, trimright

```
string trim string ?chars?
string trimleft string ?chars?
string trimright string ?chars?
```

These arguments return a substring of `string`, but with certain characters from the set `chars` removed. `trim` removes leading and trailing characters, while `trimleft` and `trimright` remove leading and trailing characters, respectively. If `chars` is not specified, white space is removed.

```
% string trim "foobar" "for"
ba
% string trimleft "foobar" "for"
bar
% string trimright "foobar" "for"
fooba
```

wordstart, wordend

```
string wordstart string index
string wordend string index
```

These return the index in `string` of the first character of/after the word containing the position `index`.

```
% string wordstart "Tcl is Cool" 5
4
% string wordend "Tcl is Cool" 5
6
```

Glob Matching

In the `string match` and the `switch -glob` commands, a form of pattern matching is used. This involves wild cards that will be familiar to you if you've used the UNIX shell, as they are the same as those used for the shell `case` statement and for matching file names.

For a string to match a pattern, they must be identical, except for special sequences that may appear in the pattern. These are:

*	Matches any sequence of characters.
?	Matches any single character.
[...]	Matches any character in a set.
\<char>	Matches the otherwise special character <char>, e.g. * matches a *.

regexp and regsub Matching

In the `regexp` and `regsub` commands that we'll meet a little later and the `-regexp` option of the `switch` command, patterns are used to match strings. These patterns may contain complex matches, specified by regular expressions, which will be familiar to you if you've used the `egrep` utility and the `ed/vi/emacs` editors.

For a string to match a regular expression, they must be identical, with the exception of special sequences that may occur in the pattern specifier. These are:

.	Matches any character.
*	Indicates zero or more matches of the previous item.
+	Indicates one or more matches of the previous item.
|	Indicates a choice between two expressions.
[...]	Matches any character in a set.
^	Matches the start of the string.
$	Matches the end of the string.
\<char>	matches the otherwise special character <char>, e.g. * matches a *.

You can identify submatches in the regular expression by surrounding them in parentheses, `()`. You can use these for extracting submatches in a match or for substitutions in `regsub`.

append

```
append varname ?value value ...?
```

The append command adds the `value` arguments to the end of the current value of the variable `varname`. This is more efficient than an equivalent assignment if the argument values are long—why copy a string and throw the original away when you can just add to the original?

Given,

```
% set a "This is: "
This is:
% set b "a long string"
a long string
```

the following two Tcl fragments are equivalent (giving `"This is: a long string"`), but the second can be more efficient:

```
% set a $a$b
% append a $b
```

regexp

regexp *?options?* `expression string` *?match? ?submatch submatch ...?*

The `regexp` command uses regular expressions to look for a match in `string`. It returns `1` if it finds a match, `0` otherwise. The `expression` is of a form given above for `regexp` matching. If the regular expression is found in the string, the variable `match` is set to that part of the string that matches the expression. The optional `submatch` variables are set to those parts of the string that match parenthesized submatches in the expression. This example looks for a number starting with a 3:

```
% regexp {3[0-9]*} 3112
1
% regexp {3[0-9]*} 5112
0
```

or

```
% regexp 3\[0-9]* 3112
1
% regexp 3\[0-9]* 5112
0
```

Note we have to use braces or backslashes to prevent Tcl interpreting the square bracket as the start of a command. Options that may be used to control the matching are:

`-nocase`	Causes the match to be case-insensitive.
`-indices`	Causes the `submatch` variables to be set to pairs of indices delimiting the match substrings.

regsub

regsub *?options?* `expression string subst varname`

The `regsub` command matches `string` against a given regular expression and writes a new string to the variable `varname`. The new string is a copy of the `subst` argument with substitutions carried out. These are as follows:

- `&` or `\0` is replaced by the matching string.
- `\1, ... \9` is replaced by the first, ... ninth submatch (parenthesized subexpression).

This example changes a leading 3 to a 5:

```
% regsub {3([0-9]*)} 3112 {5\1} res
1
% set res
5112
```

Try It Out - String Matching and Substitution

Here's an example of string matching and substitution:

```
% set date1 "Wednesday August 11 1999"
Wednesday August 11 1999
% set date2 "Saturday April 1 2000"
Saturday April 1 2000
% set weekend "(Saturday|Sunday)"
(Saturday|Sunday)
% regexp $weekend $date1
0
% regexp $weekend $date2 day
1
% puts $day
Saturday
% set parsedate "(\[A-Z]\[a-z]+) +(\[A-Z]\[a-z]+) +(\[0-9]+) +(\[0-9]+)"
([A-Z][a-z]+) +([A-Z][a-z]+) +([0-9]+) +([0-9]+)
% regexp $parsedate $date2 date day month dom year
1
% puts "$date breaks into $day, $month, $dom, $year"
Saturday April 1 2000 breaks into Saturday, April, 1, 2000
% regsub $parsedate $date2 {\4 \2 \3} newdate
1
% puts $newdate
2000 April 1
%
```

How It Works

Several calls to `regexp` are shown matching dates to days in the weekend and extracting information from a date. A substitution is used to reorder the format of the date. The variable `parsedate` is set to an expression that describes a value date. It uses several key forms:

- `[A-Z][a-z]+` matches a capitalized word of two or more letters, such as the day or month name.
- <space>+ matches a sequence of one or more spaces, as occurs between date elements.
- `[0-9]+` matches a decimal number, such as the date of year number.

Note that when you use backslashes or square brackets in matches or substitutions, you need to protect them against expansion when they're inside double quotes. Alternatively, using braces prevents all expansions.

Arrays

Arrays are special variables accessed with an index in parentheses following the array name. You can't manipulate arrays as an entity by using their name alone.

Tcl supports a form of array known as an **associative array**. This powerful concept is implemented by allowing arrays with arbitrary indices, i.e. arrays can use strings to address their elements. This allows us to store information about general objects in an array, using the object itself as the array index. An example will make things clearer.

> **When we're dealing with associative arrays, indices and elements are often referred to instead as *keys* and *values*.**

```
% set myarray(0) 123
123
% puts $myarray
can't read "myarray": variable is array
% puts $myarray(0)
123
%
```

Array indices are not limited to numeric values, but it's sensible to limit them to either numbers or a string without spaces or special characters, as quoting and variable substitution can become difficult. A common technique is to employ a variable to contain the value of the index and set the variable to the desired value. This eliminates the difficulties with special characters.

```
% set myarray(orange) 1
1
% set myarray(apple) jim
jim
%
```

array

```
array option arrayname ?arg arg ...?
```

Arrays may be manipulated by the `array` command, which takes a number of options. The options to `array` (and associated arguments are):

exists

```
array exists arrayname
```

This returns `1` if `arrayname` is an array, `0` otherwise.

get

```
array get arrayname ?pattern?
```

This returns a list of pairs of elements containing array indices and associated values. If the optional `pattern` is given, it returns only those array elements whose indices match the (glob style) pattern.

names

array names arrayname *?pattern?*

This returns a lists of array index names, optionally only those that match `pattern`.

set

array set arrayname list

This sets the elements of the array `arrayname`. The `list` must be like the one returned by `get`, with a series of indices and their values.

size

array size arrayname

This returns the size of an array.

```
% array exists myarray
1
% array size myarray
3
% array names myarray
orange 0 apple
% array get myarray
orange 1 0 123 apple jim
%
```

We can also perform a search of arrays element-by-element with `array` command options `startsearch`, `anymore`, `nextelement` and `donesearch`. See the Tcl documentation for further details.

Lists

In addition to strings and arrays, Tcl also has full support for lists. These are groups of Tcl objects, numbers, strings and other lists that can be grouped together and manipulated. Tcl allows lists to be created, added to, converted to and from strings and used for controlling loops. We'll outline a number of list manipulation commands below.

The syntax for Tcl lists is the brace group. In fact, we've already seen lists in action with the bodies for loops.

```
% set mylist {bob {1 2 3 {4 5}} fred}
bob {1 2 3 {4 5}} fred
```

This assignment has created a list of three elements. The second element is itself a list of four elements. Notice that Tcl displays braces around lists only when necessary, to show the correct structure. As with arrays and strings, list elements can be accessed by position with an index, starting from zero.

If you have a need for an array, but will only be using numeric indices you should consider using a list instead. They can often prove to be more efficient than the more general arrays.

list

list *?arg arg arg ...?*

We can create lists programmatically in a number of ways, but perhaps the easiest is with the `list` command. `list` takes all of its arguments and creates a list, each element of which is a copy of an argument. If no arguments are given, `list` produces an empty list.

We need to add braces and backslashes as necessary, so that the original arguments may be extracted using `lindex` (see below) and the list can be evaluated by `eval` (if the first argument is the name of a command).

```
% set elist [list puts "Hello World"]
puts {Hello World}
% eval $elist
Hello World
```

split

split string *?delimiters?*

The `split` command is used to create a list from a string. By default, `split` creates a list containing the distinct words (delimited by white space) in `string`. The optional `delimiters` argument is a list of characters used to determine the places to split the string. If the delimiters list is empty, rather than omitted altogether, all characters in the string are individually included as list elements.

```
% split "hello there jim"
hello there jim
% split "hi there everyone" {e}
{hi th} r { } v ryon {}
```

Notice that the delimiters don't appear in the list, but that empty elements will be created if there are adjacent delimiters in the string.

When you're using `split`, you should take care with backslash substitutions. `\$` will be converted to a `$`, not a \ and a `$`. In other words, to get \ included as an element in a list, you'd have to use `\\`. To include the literal `$foo`, you'd need to use `\$foo`.

join

join list *?delimiter?*

The `join` command is the opposite of `split`. It creates a string by recursively joining together elements of a list. It uses the optional `delimiter` string (if there is one) to separate elements. It defaults to a space.

```
% join {1 2 fred {bill bob} 37} ","
1,2,fred,bill bob,37
%
```

concat

```
concat ?arg arg arg ...?
```

The `concat` command takes several arguments, treats them as lists and concatenates them. If you supply no arguments, you'll get an empty result, not an error. When it joins lists, `concat` will effectively strip off one level of braces so that top level members of list arguments become top level members of the resulting list.

Arguments have leading and trailing spaces removed. Each list element is separated by a single space.

```
% concat {1 2} {3 {4 5} 6} 7 8
1 2 3 {4 5} 6 7 8
```

lappend

```
lappend listvar ?arg arg arg ...?
```

We can use the `lappend` command to add further elements to a list. It's more efficient than creating a new list with, for example, `concat`.

Each of the arguments to `lappend` is added as a list element to the existing list `listvar`. Each element added is separated by a single space. Note that, unlike `concat`, no level of braces is removed; each argument is added as is.

```
% set alist {1 2 3 {4 5}}
1 2 3 {4 5}
% lappend alist 6 {7 8}
1 2 3 {4 5} 6 {7 8}
%
```

lindex

```
lindex list index
```

We use the `lindex` command to retrieve an element at position `index` from a list. The list elements are numbered starting from zero. If the requested element is not in the list, an empty string is returned. We can use the keyword end in place of an index to refer to the last element in the list.

```
% set alist {1 2 3 {4 5}}
1 2 3 {4 5}
% lindex $alist 3
4 5
%
```

linsert

linsert list index arg *?arg arg ...?*

We can use the `linsert` command to insert elements into a list. The new list created by `linsert` comprises `list`, with the `arg` arguments inserted just after the element referred to by `index`. If `index` is zero (or negative), the new elements are placed at the beginning of the new list. If the index is greater than or equal to the length of the list, or is the keyword `end`, the new elements are added at the end of the list. Notice that the original list is not itself affected by the `linsert` command.

```
% set alist {{4 5}}
{4 5}
% linsert $alist 0 1 2 3
1 2 3 {4 5}
% linsert [linsert $alist 0 1 2 3] end {6 7 8}
1 2 3 {4 5} {6 7 8}
%
```

llength

llength list

We can obtain the length of a list by the `llength` command, which returns a string containing a decimal number corresponding to the length of the list `list`. An empty list returns a length of zero.

```
% llength hello
1
% llength "1 2 3"
3
% llength {a b {c d}}
3
```

Note that Tcl will try to interpret many different arguments as lists automatically, in which case, quoted and unquoted strings and brace groups are all treated as lists. Each 'word' within a string is interpreted as an individual element.

lrange

lrange list first last

A consecutive subset of a list may be extracted by the `lrange` command. The elements in positions `first` through `last` in the list `list` are extracted and a new list with just those elements is returned.

```
% set alist {1 2 3 {4 5} 6 7 8}
1 2 3 {4 5} 6 7 8
% lrange $alist 2 4
3 {4 5} 6
%
```

lreplace

lreplace list first last *?arg arg arg …?*

We can replace elements in a list by the `lreplace` command. The elements in positions `first` through `last` in the list `list` are replaced with the given arguments. Elements are deleted and new ones inserted. The element in position `first` must exist, although the number of elements to be deleted and the number to be inserted need not be the same. We can use the keyword end for `first` or `last` to specify the last element in the list.

```
% set alist {1 2 3 {4 5} 6 7 8}
1 2 3 {4 5} 6 7 8
% lreplace $alist 2 end bill {bob joe}
1 2 bill {bob joe}
%
```

lsearch

lsearch *?option?* list pattern

We can use `lsearch` to search a list for elements that match a pattern. The options are `-exact`, `-glob` (the default), and `-regexp`, which determine the type of matching to be undertaken. See the section on strings above for more details of Tcl matching.

The given `list` is searched for elements that match the specified `pattern`. The index of the first matching element is returned, or `-1` if no such element is found.

```
% lsearch {apple pear banana orange} b*
2
```

lsort

lsort *?option?* list

We can use the `lsort` command to sort a list according to a number of criteria. The default action is for the elements of the list to be sorted into ascending alphabetical order by ASCII collating sequence, which is the order of alphanumeric characters, plus punctuation. As far as the computer's concerned, it's the numerical order of the byte values of the characters. For example:

```
% lsort {apple pear banana orange}
apple banana orange pear
```

The options to `lsort` that change the type of sort performed include:

lsort option	**Description**
-ascii	Normal string comparison, the default.
-integer	Elements are converted to integers and compared.
-real	Elements are converted to floating point and compared.
-increasing	Sorts in ascending order.
-decreasing	Sorts in descending order.
-command	Use command as a sort function. This must be a procedure taking two list elements as arguments and returning an integer less than zero, zero, or greater than zero depending on whether the first element is to be considered smaller, equal or larger than the second.

foreach

foreach varname list body

We can use `foreach` to separately evaluate or use each element in a list. The command assigns to `varname` each element of the `list` argument in turn and executes `body`. Here's an example:

```
% foreach i {1 2 3 bill bob joe} {
    puts "i is $i "
}
i is 1
i is 2
i is 3
i is bill
i is bob
i is joe
%
```

This is a simplification of the `foreach` command; in the general case, `foreach` can take a list of variable names and a number of lists. In this case, the lists are traversed at the same time. Each time around the loop, each of the variables is assigned for the next element in the corresponding list.

```
% foreach {a b} {1 2 3 4 5 6} {puts "a is $a, b is $b"}
a is 1, b is 2
a is 3, b is 4
a is 5, b is 6
% foreach a {1 2 3} b {4 5 6} {puts "a is $a, b is $b"}
a is 1, b is 4
a is 2, b is 5
a is 3, b is 6
%
```

A `break` or `continue` command in a `foreach` body has the same effect as in a `for` command. If a `break` command is encountered in the body, the loop is terminated immediately. A `continue` command in the body skips the remainder of the loop for the present iteration.

A `foreach` loop in conjunction with `array names` can make a useful way to scan an array:

```
% set myarray(orange) 1
1
% set myarray(apple) 2
2
% set myarray(banana) 3
3
% foreach fruit [array names myarray] { puts "fruit is $fruit" }
fruit is orange
fruit is apple
fruit is banana
%
```

Procedures

Procedures in Tcl are similar to those of other languages, but with some interesting differences. Procedures are introduced to the Tcl interpreter with the `proc` command. We must define all procedures with `proc` before they can be called.

```
proc name args body
```

The `proc` command defines the procedure name. It stores the `body` (a list of executable commands) to be run when the procedure is called. Arguments passed to the procedure when it is executed are substituted for the list of variables, `args`.

Procedures exit when the last command in the body is executed. The value of a procedure is the value of the last command executed. We can prematurely terminate procedures with the `return` command.

```
return ?option? ?string?
```

The optional value `string` is returned as the value of the enclosing procedure. If string is omitted, an empty string is returned. We can specify the action taken when a procedure needs to return an error by one of several options to `return`. See the Tcl documentation for details.

Try It Out - Procedures

Here's a simple procedure for calculating a factorial:

```
% proc fact {n} {
    set result 1
    while {$n > 1} {
        set result [expr $result * $n]
        set n [expr $n - 1]
    }
    return $result
}
% fact 7
5040
```

How It Works

The procedure `fact` builds up the required factorial by iteration. Note that the procedure uses a local variable: `result`. As we don't need to declare variables before they are first used in Tcl, all new variables encountered in Tcl procedures are assumed to be local, i.e. new variables created inside a Tcl procedure don't exist outside of the procedure.

upvar

```
upvar ?level? oldname newname
```

To gain access to a global variable, we must use the command `upvar`, which allows access to variables at a higher level in the call stack. At its simplest, it allows a procedure to use a variable declared in an enclosing scope (possibly the procedure that called it), or a global variable.

The `upvar` command creates a new variable, newname, within the procedure. Accesses and assignments to it are equivalent to using the variable `oldname`, which exists outside the procedure. We can use the `level` argument to determine precisely which stack frame the `oldname` variable is from.

The most common case is simply to provide access to global variables with:

```
upvar variable variable
```

Below is an example of the proper usage of `upvar`:

```
% set result 1
1
% proc badset2 {} {
    set result 2
}
% badset2
2
% set result
1
% proc goodset2 {} {
    upvar result result
    set result 2
}
% goodset2
2
% set result
2
%
```

Input and Output

Tcl provides a sophisticated system for input and output. In this section, we'll cover some of the basic facilities. Refer to the Tcl documentation for further details.

open

```
open filename ?access? ?permissions?
```

The open command establishes a connection to a file or a command pipeline. It combines the functionality of `fopen` and `popen` in C.

open returns a channel identifier (the Tcl equivalent of a file stream) that can be used in future calls to other input and output commands like `gets`, `puts` and `close`. Standard streams are automatically available to Tcl programs as `stdin`, `stdout` and `stderr`.

If present, the `access` argument determines how the file is to be opened. It's a string value and takes the same values as the modes used by `fopen` in C. These are:

access modes	Description
r	Opens `filename` for reading. The file must exist. This is the default.
r+	Opens `filename` for reading and writing. The file must exist.
w	Opens `filename` for writing. The file will be created or truncated.
w+	Opens `filename` for writing and reading. The file will be created or truncated.
a	Opens `filename` for writing. New data will be written at the end of the file.
a+	Opens `filename` for reading and writing. The initial file position is set to the end of the file.

Alternatively, we can set the access modes using a Tcl list of POSIX flags, including `RDONLY`, `WRONLY`, `RDWR`, `APPEND`, `CREAT`, `EXCL`, `NOCTTY`, `NONBLOCK`, `TRUNC`.

The `permissions` argument, if present, is an integer value (default octal 666) used to set the initial permissions on any file created by the call to open.

If the `filename` argument has a pipe symbol (|) as its first character, it's treated as a command pipeline. The UNIX command is executed and its output made available for reading via the returned channel identifier.

close

```
close channelID
```

The `close` command closes the channel given by `channelID`, which must have been obtained from a previous call to open (or in Tcl 7.5 or later, `socket`). The channel is the equivalent of a C file descriptor.

read

```
read ?-nonewline? channel ?bytes?
```

The read command reads all of the input available (or, if bytes is set, a specified number of bytes) on a channel identifier.

If the -nonewline option is specified, read doesn't return the last character in the input if it's a newline. The read command translates end of line sequences into single newlines.

gets

```
gets channel ?varname?
```

The gets command reads the first line of input and stores it in a variable varname if this has been specified. Each subsequent use of gets on a channel results in the next line of data being read, stopping when an end of file character is found. The value returned by gets is the number of characters read into varname, -1 on error, or the string itself if varname is not specified.

```
% set myfile [open "|date" r]
file3
% gets $myfile fred
28
% close $myfile
% set fred
Wed Aug 11 15:03:35 BST 1999
```

puts

```
puts ?-nonewline? ?channel? string
```

The puts command writes output to a channel (defaults to the standard output). The string is written to the channel followed by a newline, unless the option -nonewline is specified. New lines are translated to end of line sequences automatically.

Note that Tcl performs internal buffering so output from puts may not appear in an output file immediately. We can force output with the flush command. Refer to the Tcl documentation for information beyond this simple example:

```
% open "fred.txt" w
file3
% puts file3 "Hello World"
% close file3
% open "fred.txt" r
file3
% gets file3
Hello World
% close file3
%
```

format

```
format formatstring ?arg arg ...?
```

The `format` command is the Tcl equivalent of the C library function `sprintf` and shares many conversion specifiers. In fact, `sprintf` is used in the implementation of `format`.

The format command generates a formatted string. Refer to the Tcl manual page (`man format`) or the C library documentation for `printf/sprintf` for details of conversion specifiers.

scan

```
scan string formatstring var ?var var ...?
```

The `scan` command is the Tcl equivalent of the C library function `sscanf`. The variables specified as arguments are set to values extracted from `string`, according to conversion specifiers given in `formatstring`. As with `format` above, the implementation of `scan` is very similar to ANSI C `sscanf` and readers are directed to the C library documentation for further details of conversion specifiers.

file

```
file option name ?arg arg ... ?
```

File manipulations are carried out in Tcl by the `file` command. It accepts a number of options for changing and inspecting file characteristics. Options used by the `file` command include:

atime, mtime

```
file atime name
file mtime name
```

This returns a string describing the last access time/modified time of the file `name`.

dirname

```
file dirname name
```

This returns the directory part of the file `name`, i.e. all the characters before the last / character.

```
% file dirname "/bin/fred.txt"
/bin
```

exists, executable

```
file executable name
file exists name
```

This returns 1 if the file exists/is executable, 0 otherwise.

```
% file exists "fred.txt"
1
% file executable "fred.txt"
0
```

extension, rootname

```
file extension name
file rootname name
```

This returns the file extension (part of name after last dot) / file root name (part up to last dot).

```
% file extension "fred.txt"
.txt
```

isdirectory, isfile

```
file isdirectory name
file isfile name
```

Returns `1` if name refers to a directory/regular file, `0` otherwise.

owned

```
file owned name
```

This returns `1` if the file is owned by the current user, `0` otherwise.

readable, writeable

```
file readable name
file writeable name
```

This returns `1` if the file is readable/writeable, `0` otherwise.

size

```
file size name
```

This returns the file size, in bytes.

Depending on the operating system that you're using, you have other options available. These include options to retrieve the result of a `stat` or `lstat` system call in a Tcl array. Refer to the system specific Tcl documentation for details.

A Tcl Program

Here's a sample program to demonstrate some Tcl features. It generates a list of the frequencies of word usage in a text file. This might form part of a concordance.

Try It Out - A Concordance Program

1. Type in the listing, `concord.tcl`, below. We begin by specifying the shell to run under and initializing some variables.

```
#!/usr/bin/tclsh

set VerboseFlag false
set FileToRead "-"
set Usage "Usage: concord \[-v] \[-f<filename>]"
```

2. Remembering that `argv` is the program arguments array, parse the command line arguments. Set `FileToRead` and give help.

```
foreach arg $argv {
    switch -glob -- $arg {
        -v      {set VerboseFlag true}
        -f*     {set FileToRead [string range $arg 2 end]}
        -h      {puts stderr $Usage; exit 1}
        default {error "bad argument: $arg\n$Usage"; exit 1}
    }
}
```

3. Set the default input source to the standard input. If a file has been specified, open it 'safely'.

```
set Input stdin

if {$FileToRead != "-"} {
    if [catch {set Input [open $FileToRead r]} res ] {
        puts stderr "$res"
        exit 1
    }
}
```

4. Initialize the word and line counters, then read each line in the input, split the line according to punctuation and increment a concordance array.

```
set NumberOfLines 0
set NumberOfWords 0

while {[gets $Input line] >= 0} {
    incr NumberOfLines
    set words [split $line " \t.,\{\}\(\)\[\]\;\""]
    foreach word $words {
        if {[info exists concord("$word")]} {
            incr concord("$word")
        } else {
            set concord("$word") 1
        }
        incr NumberOfWords
    }
}
```

5. Output a summary, then all the words found, then each word accompanied by its count.

```
puts stdout [format "File contained %d/%d words/lines\n" \
        $NumberOfWords $NumberOfLines]

puts stdout [array names concord]

foreach word [array names concord] {
    puts "$word: $concord($word)"
}
```

Let's try this program out on a text file, such as its own source code. When we run the program with the commands,

```
$ chmod +x concord.tcl
$ ./concord.tcl -fconcord.tcl
```

we get output like this (edited for brevity):

```
File contained 404/48 words/lines

{"$Input"} {"if"} {"exists"} {"%d/%d"} {"$word:"} {"--"} {"error"} {"$words"}
{"$FileToRead"} {"info"} {"set"} {"$argv"} {"contained"} {"NumberOfWords"} {"range"}
{"argument:"} {"!="} {"bad"} {"VerboseFlag"} {"Input"} {"catch"} {"cannot"}
{"$concord"} {"words"} {"File"} {""} {"0"} {"else"} {"while"} {"-v"} {"word"}
{"split"} {"-h"} {"-f<filename>"} {"line"} {"concord"} {"format"} {"1"} {"switch"}
{"exit"} {"stdin"} {"stdout"} {"\"} {"stderr"} {"$NumberOfLines"} {"default"} {"$arg"}
{"\t"} {"$Usage"} {"#!/usr/bin/tclsh"} {"2"} {"open"} {"r"} {"names"} {"-f*"}
{"string"} {"$word"} {"$arg\n$Usage"}
...

"names": 2
"-f*": 1
"string": 1
"$word": 4
"$arg\n$Usage": 1
"NumberOfLines": 2
"arg": 1
"$line": 1
"incr": 3
"puts": 5
"Usage": 1
"array": 2
"Usage:": 1
"FileToRead": 2
"end": 1
"foreach": 3
"oops": 1
">=": 1
"gets": 1
"false": 1
"-": 2
"true": 1
"$NumberOfWords": 1
"-glob": 1
"words/lines\n": 1
```

How It Works

For demonstration purposes, the program prints out the list of words that it found before the frequency listing. The order of the words in the array is undefined; it depends on the Tcl implementation of associative arrays. If we had wanted the output sorted, we could have copied the array elements into a list and used `lsort`, or we could have piped the output through the UNIX `sort` program.

The program works by splitting input lines into individual words, excluding punctuation, and using these words as indices to an associative array. This array, `concord`, is used to collect the word frequencies. We used a quoted string as an index to the array to prevent possible problems with special characters occurring in the words.

Network Support

With Tcl 7.5 and later, Tcl has direct support for networking, where previously third party add-ons were required. The flexibility and concise nature of Tcl combined with a network programming paradigm gives Tcl an exceptionally wide range of uses. In fact, there are even World Wide Web browsers written entirely in Tcl. The key command is `socket`.

```
socket host port
```

By default, the `socket` command opens a `SOCK_STREAM` connection to the specified computer, `host`, and service number, `port`. It returns a channel identifier that can be used in the normal Tcl input/output commands.

Try It Out -

To demonstrate the use of sockets with Tcl, let's revisit a small example from Chapter 14 to compare. Here's a complete program, `socket.c`, in Tcl to display the time of day from a networked computer.

> **To get this to work properly, replace the hostname `tilde` with an appropriate system name on your internal network, or alternatively use `localhost`.**

```
#!/usr/bin/tclsh

set sockid [socket tilde 13]
gets $sockid date
puts "Tilde says the date is: $date"
```

How It Works

Tcl (from Version 7.5) has built-in support for UNIX networking. This program uses the `socket` command to create a communication path to the host `tilde`, port 13, which is the `daytime` service. It reads a string from the socket connection and prints it.

Compare this three line solution with the program from Chapter 14!

> **Using `gets` here reveals a potential pitfall. An unscrupulous system administrator might configure their `daytime` service to return an extremely long string that could give your machine problems. These kinds of antics have been known to occur on the Internet and are known as Denial of Service attacks.**

Creating a New Tcl

One of the design objectives of the Tcl language was that it should be embeddable, so that we can include scripts written in Tcl in other command line programs, and even in C. Indeed, that is how Tcl got started, and why it is called Tool Command Language. And, in this respect, it is very similar to Perl.

It's quite easy to incorporate Tcl into your own command line programs by writing one simple function that initializes the Tcl interpreter. You can link your own functions with the Tcl library to create your own Tcl interpreter that is tailored to your specific needs.

The precise mechanism for this is beyond the scope of this chapter. In fact, many Tcl programmers never have to create their own interpreters. They find that the basic Tcl system, together with Tcl extensions provided by third parties, satisfies all their needs.

Tcl Extensions

Over the years, there have been a large number of extensions to Tcl. These most often take the form of versions of Tcl with additional functionality to serve a particular purpose. We'll cover just a few of them here.

expect

The `expect` program is a Tcl interpreter extended with additional functions aimed particularly at automatic control of interactive programs. We can use it for testing software, because we can write `expect` scripts to send commands to a program, wait for responses and then react to those responses. It has built-in capabilities for time-outs and error recovery. It can run Tcl functions on receipt of a number of different events.

> **`expect` was created by Don Libes of NIST (National Institute of Standards and Technology) shortly after the release of Tcl on the Internet. It is the first major program built around Tcl.**

The extension gets its name from the two principal functions it adds. These are `send`, for sending interactive input to a program under test, and `expect` for arranging for actions to be taken on receipt of different responses, or lack of them.

[incr Tcl]

This extension, the name of which is a pun on C++, adds object oriented features to Tcl.

TclX

`TclX` is 'extended Tcl'. It's a commonly used extension in the UNIX environment as it contains many additional functions that mirror the UNIX system calls. `TclX` programs enjoy greater low-level access to the operating system at the expensive of a certain amount of portability.

Graphics

Many Tcl extensions have been developed to support graphics and additional operations.

Tk

A major Tcl extension, also developed by John Ousterhout, is Tk (for Tool Kit). It bestows on Tcl the ability to create and manipulate graphical user interface objects. Using Tk makes it easy for us to write sophisticated graphical programs.

Initially developed for The X Window System, there are now versions of Tk (and of course Tcl) for Microsoft Windows and Apple MacOS, so a Tcl/Tk program has the potential to run unchanged on several different hardware platforms.

We'll cover the subject of programming with Tk in the next chapter.

Summary

In this chapter, we've taken a look at the Tool Command Language, Tcl. We've seen that it's an extensive and extensible interpreted programming language with support for many high-level programming language features, such as associative arrays and lists.

We've briefly covered the fact that Tcl has been extended in many ways to create new interpreters tailored for specific application areas.

In the next chapter we will take a look at Tk, the graphical toolkit for Tcl that has resulted in many applications being developed and distributed among the UNIX community.

Programming for X

In this chapter and the next, we'll take a look at writing programs to run in the usual UNIX graphical environment, the **X Window System**, or **X**. Modern UNIX systems and nearly all Linux distributions are shipped with a version of X.

We'll be concentrating on the programmer's view of X and we'll assume that you are already comfortable with configuring, running and using X on your system.

We'll cover:

- X Concepts
- X Windows managers
- X programming model
- Tk; its widgets, bindings and geometry managers

In the next chapter, we'll move on to the GTK+ toolkit, which will allow us to program user interfaces in C for the GNOME system.

What is X?

X was created at MIT as a way of providing a uniform environment for graphical programs. It should nowadays be fair to assume that if you've used computers, you've come across either Microsoft Windows, X, or Apple MacOS before, so you'll be familiar with the general concepts underlying a graphical user interface, or GUI. Unfortunately, although a Windows user might be able to navigate around the Mac interface, it's a different story for programmers.

Each windowing environment on each system is programmed differently. The ways that the display is handled and the programs communicate with the user are different. Although each system provides the programmer with the ability to open and manipulate windows on the screen, the functions used will be different. Writing applications that can run on more than one system (without using additional toolkits) is a daunting task.

To overcome the problems associated with proprietary interface systems on mainframes, mini-computers and workstations, the X Windows system was made publicly available and has been implemented on many systems. It defines a programming style based on a client/server model with a clean separation of hardware-dependent components and application programs.

The X Windows system comprises four major components that we'll briefly mention in turn. These are:

- X Server — Interacting with the user
- X Protocol — Client/server communications
- X Library — The programming interface
- X Clients — The applications

X Server

The X server, or X display server, is a program that runs on the application user's computer and is responsible for controlling the graphical display hardware and looking after input and output. The X server responds to requests from X client applications to draw on the screen or read from the keyboard or mouse. It passes input and indications of things like mouse movements and button presses to the client programs.

Typically, there will be a different X server for each distinct hardware combination that X can run on. The most common implementation of X for Linux and other PC-based systems is XFree86 (http://www.xfree86.org). This package ships with X servers specially created for the many different video cards that can be used in PCs, for instance the `XF86_S3` version for S3-based cards. Linux users have much to thank these guys for.

X Protocol

All interactions between X client applications and the X display server take place via message exchanges. The types and uses of the messages form the X protocol. One particularly useful feature of the X Windows system is that the X protocol can be carried across a network as well as between clients and a server running on the same machine. This means that a user with a fairly low-powered personal computer or an X terminal (a machine dedicated to running just an X server) can run X client programs on more powerful networked computers, but conduct the interaction and display the output on his/her own local machine.

Xlib

The X protocol is really only of interest to the programmers that actually implement X servers. Most X applications ultimately use a C function library as a programming interface. This is Xlib, which provides an API for X protocol exchanges. Xlib doesn't add very much on its own – it can just about draw on the screen and respond to a mouse. If you want menus, buttons, scrollbars and all the other goodies, you have to write them yourself.

On the other hand, neither does Xlib impose any particular GUI style. It acts as a medium through which you can create any style you choose.

X Clients

X clients are application programs that use the display and input resources of a computer that may not be the one they're running on. They do this by requesting access to these resources from the X server that manages them. The server can typically handle requests from many clients at once and it must arbitrate use of the keyboard and mouse between clients. The client programs communicate with the server using X protocol messages which are sent and received using Xlib functions.

X Toolkits

We won't linger in the Xlib programming interface, as it's not the best tool for creating programs quickly and easily. Because of its low-level interface, like the Microsoft Windows SDK, it can make for some very complex programs that apparently achieve very little. One book on the author's shelves contains a version of the 'Hello World' program written for Xlib. It does nothing other than display 'Hello World' in a window, together with a button marked 'Exit', which does the obvious thing when you press it. The program listing runs to five pages!

Any programmer who has written an Xlib program like this will surely have wondered if there's a better way. Of course there is! Common user interface elements like buttons, scrollbars and menus have been implemented many times. Collections of these elements, also known as **widgets**, are generally called **X toolkits**. Of these, the best known are the Xt Intrinsics suite that comes with X and two commercial products: Sun's OpenLook and OSF/Motif.

- **Xt** is a free library written on top of X to give it some functionality: an intermediate layer that simplifies application programming.
- **OpenLook** is a free toolkit from Sun that enforces a different look and feel. It's built on top of library called Xview which is similar to Xt.
- **Motif** is an OSF standard designed to bring a common look and feel to the UNIX desktop. It's built on top of Xt. Motif has two main components: a set of include files that define constants used in Xt functions and a library of convenient functions to simplify the creation of elements like dialogs and menus. Motif also defines a programming style that any programmer can follow, whether they are actually using the Motif toolkit or not.
- **Qt** is a library built by trolltech which forms the basis of the **KDE** Desktop environment, which is found with most Linux distributions.
- **GTK+** is the GIMP toolkit, and the basis of the **GNOME** system. We'll look at how to program this high level environment in the next chapter.

Along with all the other commercial UNIX vendors, Sun has adopted the CDE (Common Desktop Environment) which uses Motif. This has spelled the end of OpenLook, which will disappear slowly. Parts of OpenLook have been made available for free and can be seen in Linux distributions.

Each X toolkit implements a set of widgets, usually with a distinctive look and feel. Display elements might have a flat, plain implementation (as with Xt) or a sculpted, 3D effect (like Motif).

To illustrate the difference a toolkit can make, take a look at two different text editors available for Linux, `xedit` and `textedit`. The first, `xedit`, is a very simple editor with hardly any user interface sophistication. To load a file, you need to type a file name into a box and press a button marked `Load`.

In contrast, the `textedit` editor provided by Sun's OpenWindows and written with the OpenLook toolkit provides a dialog box for opening files. This allows the user to browse the file system for the appropriate file to open. The toolkit also provides the familiar look and feel of 3D buttons.

X Window Manager

Another important element of any X system is the **window manager**. This is a special X client that is responsible for dealing with other clients. It looks after the placement of client windows on the display and handles management tasks like moving and resizing windows. It also imposes a distinctive look and feel, depending on the X toolkit it uses.

Examples of window managers are:

Window Manager	Description
`twm`	Tom's (or Tabbed) Window Manager, a small, fast manager that comes with X.
`fvwm`	An alternative window manager by Robert Nation. The favorite under Linux. It supports virtual desktops and has configuration files that allow it to emulate other window managers.
`Fvwm95`	A version of `fvwm` that emulates the Windows 95 interface.
`Gwm`	The generic window manager, programmable in a LISP dialect.
`Olwm`	The OpenLook window manager.
`Mwm`	The Motif window manager.

All of these are available for most UNIX and Linux systems, although `mwm` requires a license.

The X Programming Model

We've seen that the X Windows system separates responsibilities between client applications and X display servers using a communications protocol. This method of programming gives rise to a typical structure for an X application which we'll outline briefly below.

Start Up

A typical X application will start by initializing any resources it may need. It will establish a connection with the X display server, choose which colors and fonts to use and then create a window on the display.

`XOpenDisplay` and `XCloseDisplay` are used by client programs for connecting to and disconnecting from an X server.

```
Display *XOpenDisplay(char *display_name);
void XCloseDisplay(Display *display);
```

The `display_name` specifies the display to which we want to connect. If it's `null`, the environment variable `DISPLAY` is used. This is of the form `hostname:server[.display]`, allowing one or more X servers on a host, each of which can control more than one display. The default display is normally `:0.0`, the first available server on the local machine. To specify a second screen, for a truly awesome desktop, you would use `:0.1`.

`XOpenDisplay` returns a `Display` structure containing information about the X server selected, or `null` if no X server could be opened. After a successful return from `XOpenDisplay`, the client program may start using the X server.

When the client program has finished using the X server, it must call `XCloseDisplay` with the display structure returned from the `XOpenDisplay` call. This will destroy all windows and other resources that the client has created on the display, unless (unusually) `XSetCloseDownMode` has been called to modify the shutdown behavior. Programs should always call `XCloseDisplay` before exiting to allow any pending errors to be reported.

The user can control most of the activities at start-up. Many X applications respond to command line arguments, environment variables and configuration file entries to allow the user to customize the application. We'll give you some examples.

As we've seen, the environment variable `DISPLAY` is used to direct the application to a particular display server, which may be on a different networked computer. The following command would cause the `xedit` program to run, but to open its display on the machine called `alex`.

```
$ DISPLAY=alex:0.0 xedit &
```

The file `.Xresources` (or sometimes `.Xdefaults`) is used to configure the X application. Each application will use configuration entries in the X resources database, typically created when an X system starts up and including the user's own, local preferences. A typical entry in a user's `.Xresources` file, stored in his or her home directory might be:

```
xedit*enableBackups: on
```

This entry changes the behavior of `edit` with respect to making backup files while editing. Each entry has the general format:

```
Class*Resource: Value
```

The command line,

```
$ xedit -geometry 400x200
```

causes xedit to start in a window 400 pixels wide by 200 high. Note that other programs may use the geometry differently. For example,

```
$ xterm -geometry 80x50
```

starts a terminal emulator that has 50 lines, each with 80 columns. Refer to your system documentation and application manual pages for more details on ways to affect X application behavior.

Main Loop

The bulk of an X application is made up of a main loop and code written to react to events. After starting, a typical X program waits for the X display server to which it's connected to send it events. It does this by calling XNextEvent in a loop.

There are over 30 events that an application may have to deal with. We won't cover them here because there are many (very fat) books on the topic of X Windows programming that cover the topic in great depth. However, we'll get a flavor of the kinds of events that X uses from this partial list:

Keyboard events	Key pressed, key released.
Mouse events	Button pressed, button released, mouse moving, mouse entering/leaving a window.
Window events	Window created/destroyed, window gained/lost focus, window exposed.

A low-level X program must respond to these events and more. A program that uses an advanced toolkit or application framework will be able to concentrate on the main business of the application and use sophisticated interface elements like dialog boxes without needing to deal with low-level events like these explicitly. Of course, that doesn't mean that the events aren't still taking place.

Clean Up

When it exits, a well-behaved X program will free up any X display resources it has allocated while it was running. It's often sufficient to simply break the connection with the server, but this can result in the server consuming more memory than required. Also, it's considered a little rude not to say goodbye!

Fast Track X Programming

In the rest of this chapter, we'll leave the low-level considerations of X programming to those who need to squeeze the ultimate performance from and have the finest control over their applications.

For the rest of us who are simply keen to see immediate results and to produce good-looking highly functional X applications, we'll concentrate on a couple of recent innovations in the X programming world.

With the rise of very fast personal computers and workstations, it has become feasible to write at least the user interface part of programs in an interpreted language. We've seen a couple of these already in the shell and Tcl. We've got the power of Perl to look forward to in chapter eighteen.

We'll now take a look at Tk (for Tool Kit), an extension to Tcl for graphical programming, and in the next chapter, GTK+, developed originally as a toolkit for controlling the GIMP (GNU Image Processor), but which forms the underlying graphical language in the GNOME desktop.

The Tk approach to X programming also brings a benefit of portability. It is available for non-X graphical environments (including Microsoft Windows) and is hardware-independent. Tk programs written for one machine should run unchanged on another.

If you are interested in the benefits of a platform independent programming system, and are also looking for the power of a compiled language, then Java provides an interesting solution. The topic of Java programming is too vast to cover here, but Ivor Horton's "Beginning Java 2", also from Wrox (ISBN 1-861002-23-8), is an excellent place to start.

The Tk Toolkit

Tk, created by John Ousterhout to be the companion of Tcl, is a rich collection of graphical user interface (GUI) abstractions (widgets), designed to simplify the essential components of graphical front-end programming under X, Microsoft Windows and Apple MacOS.

Tk is an action-oriented, composition-based, embeddable, extensible, highly portable, event-based toolkit whose widgets are written in C and use Tcl bindings for event handlers. Tk has already been ported to use many other languages like Perl and Python for command bindings.

The current releases of Tk 8.1 and Tk 8.2 work consistently on all the three platforms: Unix, Windows and Macintosh.

By default, Tk's widgets have the native look and feel of the widgets of the platform they run on, but they are highly-configurable. You can operate Tk's widgets in strict Motif mode by checking one of toolkit's global variables. Because Tk's interface is consistent, most scripts written for one platform will run without any modifications on the other two platforms.

All the examples in this section need at least version 8.0 of Tcl and 8.0 of Tk to work. You can download the latest versions of the software from http://www.scriptics.com/resource/software/. Most of the programs in this section are written using Tcl8.0 and Tk8.0 because the latest releases of Jacl and Tcl Blend work only with Tcl8.0 version. Jacl is the complete rewrite of Tcl interpreter in pure Java and Tcl Blend is a dynamically loadable C extension to Tcl to interact with a Java Virtual Machine.

Before we dive into Tk programming, you need to make sure that the Tk windowing shell, `wish`, is installed on your system with the executable in your `PATH`. If Tk is not installed at the default location, you'll need to set the environment variables `TK_LIBRARY` and `TCL_LIBRARY` to point to the right locations. If you have multiple versions of Tcl installed on your machine, you might want to make sure that you point the above-mentioned environmental variables correctly. For example, here is the shell script I use to invoke `wishf` for version 8.2b3 of Tk.

```
#!/bin/sh
LD_LIBRARY_PATH=$LD_LIBRARY_PATH:/usr/local/tcl8.2b3/unix:/usr/local/tk8.2b3/
uni
x:
PATH=$PATH:/usr/local/bin:/usr/local/tcl8.2b3/unix:/usr/local/tk8.2b3/unix:
TCL_LIBRARY=/usr/local/tcl8.2b3/library
TK_LIBRARY=/usr/local/tk8.2b3/library
export LD_LIBRARY_PATH PATH TCL_LIBRARY TK_LIBRARY
/usr/local/tk8.2b3/unix/wish $*
```

When you type `wish` at the shell prompt, a small and, by default, gray window should pop up. To suppress this interactive `wish` window, for example when running scripts, invoke Tk using `wish -f`. `wish` is basically `tclsh` with the Tk functions built in.

Over the next few sections, we'll take a look at:

- Basic concepts of Windows programming
- Writing our first Tk program
- Touring the Tk widget set, with some of their configuration options
- Bindings
- Geometry managers
- Application resource management
- Inter-application communication
- Window management and application embedding
- A mega-widget completely wrtten in Tcl using existing Tk components
- A real Tk example for every day use using Tcl events

Though by no means extensive, these pages should show you how to get started with Tk, how to program using its built-in widget set and where to find out more about Tk, as you need it.

Windows Programming

Using Tk, you can quickly create a graphical interface, using the widgets provided to deal with the underlying window system. You then attach event handlers to these widgets (usually using the Tcl language), so that they react as required to the user's commands. This fits in with usual visual programming practice.

First, create the look of your program, adding in components to access the functionality you eventually want to include. Select a widget from the Tk toolkit, initialize its look and then use Tk's geometry manager to arrange it in relation to other widgets within the screen window. Then, code the response of each GUI component to user commands. What will clicking the `load` button do? How will clicking it load an image into the canvas widget?

This is rather different from the procedural programming we've been looking at throughout the rest of the book. As a programmer, you can never control the order in which the user interacts with the program; the whole point of GUIs is to provide a more natural and intuitive user interface. The program must wait for and then act on user-initiated events.

Every time you create a widget in Tk using its `class` command, the GUI primitive known as the **widget** is created, as is a new Tcl **command**, whose name is the name of the widget. You can then invoke methods (Tk calls them **configuration options**) on this newly created widget using its widget command. Widget commands are like objects in an object-oriented system - when the widget is deleted, the widget command is also deleted.

For example, the widget command,

```
button .b
```

creates a new widget and a widget command named `.b`. You can use this new command to communicate with the widget, so,

```
.b configure -text "Hello"
```

will set the title of the button `.b` to `Hello`. If you think of `.b` as an object, you are invoking the `configure` method on the object to set its `text` attribute to `Hello`.

Tk widgets are not completely object-oriented as they don't support inheritance, polymorphism etc. Their only similarity to OOP principles is the way methods are invoked.

The widget creation and initialization parts of a Tk program will contain Tcl commands to create and arrange the widgets on the user screen. Once you've created and arranged the widgets, they interact with the user using Tcl scripts known as **event handlers**.

We'll try to present all the examples using this approach, although it's sometimes difficult to separate the two stages completely, because event handlers are sometimes bound when you create the widget. For example, most widgets in Tk support the `command` widget handler, which is usually set immediately. Also, it sometimes makes sense to bind the event handlers as soon as you create the widget and manage the screen layout of the widgets later. No single approach is the best. To manage your design, use whichever is appropriate or is easier to understand.

To get us started and make more sense of this introduction, let's look at a program, `hello1.tk`, probably the smallest multiline label program ever created!

Try It Out - Saying Hello

Type in the following script file:

```
#!/usr/bin/wish -f

pack [button .b -text "Hello\nWorld!!!" \
                -justify center \
                -width 20 \
                -command {puts "Hi"}]
```

Make the script executable and run the `hello1.tk` program:

```
$ ./hello1.tk
```

This program creates the window shown in the figure and outputs the string `Hi` each time you click on the button.

How It Works

Let's dissect the program and see what's going on in this ubiquitous masterpiece.

After invoking `wish -f`, we get to the single line that does all the work. It's remarkably terse and we've expanded it to make the specified options more obvious. Ignoring the `pack` command for now, we see that `button...` creates a button named `.b` whose multiline label `Hello World` is centered. The button is set to a width of twenty characters. The `-command` option attaches an event handler to the button to output the string "`Hi`" in the parent window when the user clicks on the button. Note the backslashes that allow you to write the command over several lines.

The `pack` command packs the widget `.b` into the default top-level window created by the application, so that it occupies the window. Note that `pack [button .b ...]` would work just as well if we initialized the button `.b` first and then called `pack .b`.

There's no particular reason for calling the widget `.b`. You can name it `.foo`, or anything else, provided the name begins with a full-stop. An application's widgets are arranged in a hierarchy and the default, top-level, 'application' widget and its corresponding widget command are named '`.`'. Each widget's name is a dot-separated list describing its position in the application's hierarchy. For example, the path name `.a.b.c` implies that widget `.c` is a child of `.a.b`, a grandchild of `.a`, and a great-grandchild of the application widget. Currently, all the widgets in Tk can have any number of children provided all the path names are listed in this way.

Configuration Files

Now let's add one more line before the widget's creation:

```
option add *b.activeForeground brown
```

The program creates the widget `.b` and sets up its default `activeForeground` color to brown. The asterisk before `b` means that any widget called `b` should have the option set, no matter what its parentage.

We can also make it into a more realistic X application by saving the line,

```
*b.activeForeground: brown
```

into a file called `hello.def`, and then adding the following line into the `hello3.tk` script before we create the widget:

```
option readfile hello.def
```

This line reads the application defaults from the file `hello.def` before creating the widget.

More Commands

You might be thinking, "Can't I create more user interactions to the widget than `-command`?" We'll go right ahead and create one such simple **event binding**. If the user presses *Ctrl* along with the mouse button, the widget will output the string "`Help!`".

Here's how to do this:

```
bind .b <Control-Button-1> {puts "Help!"}
```

Our final Hello World program, `hello4.tk`, with all these modifications, reads:

```
#!wish -f

option readfile hello.def
pack [button .b -text "Hello\nWorld!!!" \
               -justify center \
               -width 20 \
               -command {puts "Hi"}]
bind .b <Control-Button-1> {puts "Help!"}
```

This is a simple three line program which can do the same job as a 500 line Xlib program or 100+ lines of Motif code. It has all the features of a basic X application and is still very simple. That's what Tk is all about. It removes all the complexity and fear involved in graphical user interface programming.

Tk Widgets

It's time to look more closely at the set of widgets Tk provides. Before we review the widgets Tk supports, though, here's a simple way to find out all the methods and arguments a widget provides. Note that the symbol `%` denotes Tk's `wish` command shell prompt.

Try It Out - Learning More

First, interactively create a scale widget `.s`:

```
$ wish
% scale .s
.s
```

Call the `config` method of the widget and see its output to check out what the widget offers:

```
% .s config
```

You should see this output:

```
{-activebackground activeBackground Foreground SystemButtonFace SystemButtonFace} {-
background background Background SystemButtonFace SystemButtonFace} {-bigincrement
bigIncrement BigIncrement 0 0.0} {-bd -borderwidth} {-bg -background} {-borderwidth
borderWidth BorderWidth 2 2} {-command command Command {} {}} {-cursor cursor Cursor
{} {}} {-digits digits Digits 0 0} {-fg -foreground} {-font font Font {{MS Sans Serif}
8} {{MS Sans Serif} 8}} {-foreground foreground Foreground SystemButtonText
SystemButtonText} {-from from From 0 0.0} {-highlightbackground highlightBackground
HighlightBackground SystemButtonFace SystemButtonFace} {-highlightcolor highlightColor
HighlightColor SystemWindowFrame SystemWindowFrame} {-highlightthickness
highlightThickness HighlightThickness 2 2} {-label label Label {} {}} {-length length
Length 100 100} {-orient orient Orient vertical vertical} {-relief relief Relief flat
flat} {-repeatdelay repeatDelay RepeatDelay 300 300} {-repeatinterval repeatInterval
RepeatInterval 100 100} {-resolution resolution Resolution 1 1.0} {-showvalue
showValue ShowValue 1 1} {-sliderlength sliderLength SliderLength 30 30} {-
sliderrelief sliderRelief SliderRelief raised raised} {-state state State normal
normal} {-takefocus takeFocus TakeFocus {} {}} {-tickinterval tickInterval
TickInterval 0 0.0} {-to to To 100 100.0} {-troughcolor troughColor Background
SystemScrollbar SystemScrollbar} {-variable variable Variable {} {}} {-width width
Width 15 15}
```

Each list pair follows this combination:

`option-switch option-name option-class option-default-value option-actual-value.`

You can interactively experiment and learn about the widget's options and their default values. There is, however, no easy way to learn a widget's methods without perusing its manual page.

Frames

Frames are the simplest of all the Tk widgets. They are only used as containers, as you can see in the following example:

```
#!usr/bin/wish -f

. config -bg steelblue

foreach frame {sunken raised flat ridge groove} {
   frame .$frame -width 0.5i -height 0.5i -relief $frame  -bd 2
   pack .$frame -side left -padx 10 -pady 10
}
```

This script creates five frames with different 3D borders:

Frames are often invisible and are almost always used to create nested layouts.

How It Works

In the above example, the `-relief` option is used to set the border relief of the frame, while the `-bd 2` option sets the widget border width to two pixels. This option is supported by all the Tk widgets and gives the 3D effect.

As for the rest of the code, you can see the use of a Tcl list to create the five frames. The frames are sized by setting the `-height` and `-width` options to `0.5i` (half an inch), they're packed to the left and padded ten pixels on each side by the `-padx` and `-pady` options.

Toplevel

Toplevel widgets are like frames, except they have their own toplevel windows, whereas frames are internal windows within a toplevel.

```
% toplevel .t -width 1.5i -height 1i  -relief ridge -bd 4
```

will create a toplevel window that looks like the following:

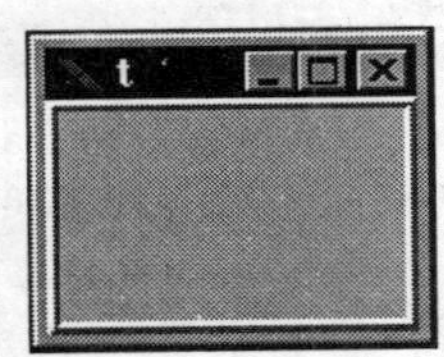

Labels

A label is simple widget which can display multiline text. We can create a label using the `label` command:

```
% label .l -wraplength 1i -justify right -text "Hello Tk World!"
```

This creates a multiline label widget with a text length of one inch for each line. Once you pack the label using,

```
% pack .l
```

it will create a widget which looks like this:

When you've created the label, you can use the widget command to communicate with it. For example, the following command will query the foreground color of the label widget:

```
% .l cget -fg
Black
```

All the Tk widgets support the `cget` widget command, which retrieves any widget configuration option. We can also use the `configure` method of the Tk widgets to set configuration options interactively. For example,

```
% .l configure -fg yellow -bg blue
```

will set the label's foreground to yellow and background to blue.

Buttons

Tk provides three kinds of buttons, ordinary push buttons, check boxes and radio buttons.

Pressing a push button performs an action. We use check boxes to select or deselect a number of options. Radio buttons are similar, but they exclusively select one choice from a group of options. You'll most likely be familiar with the widgets, if not the terminology.

Let's look at the following example, which illustrates most of the uses of Tk buttons.

Try It Out - A Choice of Buttons

1. After the script header and a couple of global variables, we create a check button to control the selection of a favorite programming language.

```
#!/usr/bin/wish -f

set lang tcl
set state 1

checkbutton .lan -text "Language" -command {changeState} -relief flat \
           -variable state -onvalue 1 -offvalue 0
```

2. Next, we create a radio button panel, with one button for each language:

```
radiobutton .c -text "C" -variable lang -value c -justify left
radiobutton .tcl -text "Tcl" -variable lang -value tcl -justify left
radiobutton .perl -text "Perl" -variable lang -value perl -justify left
```

3. We need two push buttons to control the output:

```
button .show -text "Show Value" -command showVars
button .exit -text "Exit" -command {exit}
```

4. Having configured the buttons, we need to arrange them on screen. It's time for a bit of geometry management.

```
grid .lan  -row 1 -column 0 -sticky "w"
grid .c    -row 0 -column 1 -sticky "w"
grid .tcl  -row 1 -column 1 -sticky "w"
grid .perl -row 2 -column 1 -sticky "w"
grid .show -row 3 -column 0 -sticky "w"
grid .exit -row 3 -column 1 -sticky "w"
```

5. The check button needs a callback procedure, `changeState`. This is registered by the check button's `-command` option.

```
proc changeState args {
    global state
    if {$state == "0"} {
        catch {
            .c config -state disabled
            .tcl config -state disabled
            .perl config -state disabled
        }
    } else {
        .c config -state normal
        .tcl config -state normal
        .perl config -state normal
    }
}
```

6. The push buttons need a similar procedure, `showVars`:

```
proc showVars args {
    global state lang
    if {$state == "0"} {
        puts "No Language is selected"
    } else {
        puts "The Language selected is $lang"
    }
}
```

When you run the program, you should see this:

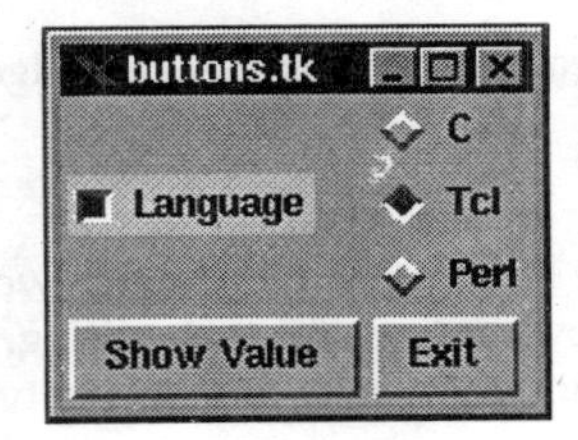

How It Works

The program starts off by setting up two global variables, `lang` and `state`, to serve as the initial values of the check boxes and radio buttons.

A check box is declared to select/deselect the 'language' option. Every time it's invoked, its command will call the `changeState` procedure. It also sets the global variable `state` to 1 or 0, depending upon the selection before executing the command.

Then the program composes the radio button, which is there to select just one of three languages (C, Tcl, Perl). If you look at the code, these buttons all share the same global variable, `lang`, which holds the value of the current selection. This makes sure that the user can only select one radio button at a time.

Lastly, we declare two push buttons, one of which exits the application when the user presses it, while the other will output the selection by calling the procedure `showVars`.

The command `changeState` is used by the check box to change the state of all three radio buttons between active and inactive, depending upon whether it's selected or deselected. `showVars` is used by the `Show Value` push button to output the value of the current selection.

Buttons also support many other options, like flash invoke methods. For more information, look at the `button`, `checkbutton`, `radiobutton` and `options` man pages. Labels and buttons also support bitmaps and images as their labels. We'll learn about images later.

> **The lines in the example which start with `grid...` are used for geometry management of the created widgets. We'll cover geometry management later in this chapter.**

Messages

Messages are similar to labels and are used to display multiline text. They differ from labels in that they will automatically break up text to display it in a multiline format, using word boundaries and aspect ratio. Message widgets can justify the text displayed and they can also handle non-printable characters.

```
#!/usr/bin/wish -f

message .m -aspect 400 -justify center \
        -text "This is a message widget with aspect ratio 400 and \
               center justification. Message widgets can also to \
               display control characters \240 \241 \242 \243 \251 \
               \256 \257 \258  and tabs \t  etc..."
pack .m
```

This example will create a simple message widget containing control characters.

Entrys

Entrys (sic) are single line text widgets which we can use to type in and display a single line of text. Entrys also support many key bindings for text editing. For example, here's a small program, `login.tk`, to handle user logins, though it lacks code to verify the user's password.

Try It Out - Gaining Entry

1. First, set up the look of the login window. We also define a global `loginName` variable:

```
#!/usr/bin/wish -f

set loginName "timB"

label .name -text "Login:"
entry .nameEntry -textvariable loginName
label .passwd -text "Password:"
entry .passwdEntry -textvariable passwd -show *
```

2. Then we select all the text from `.nameEntry`:

```
.nameEntry selection from 1
.nameEntry selection to end
```

3. Lastly, we arrange the widgets on the screen - we'll explain it later!

```
grid .name  -row 0 -column 0 -sticky "w"
grid .passwd -row 1 -column 0 -sticky "w"
grid .nameEntry -row 0 -column 1 -columnspan 2 -sticky "W"
grid .passwdEntry -row 1  -column 1 -columnspan 2 -sticky "W"
```

If you run the program, you'll see this:

How It Works

After the first five lines, which create two label and two entry widgets, the next two lines show how to select the text inside the entry. The `selection` command is Tk's method for moving information between widgets. The last four lines arrange the created widgets on the screen in a grid.

> **X defines a standard mechanism for supplying and retrieving the selection and the `selection` command is Tk's way of managing Inter-Client-Communication. It obeys X's Inter-Client Communication Conventions Manual (ICCCM) rules. The reason we introduce `selection` here is to show that you can programmatically set the selection so that another, non-Tk, X client can retrieve the selection using normal X Windows conventions.**

Entry widgets use key bindings for internal navigation through the text. If you read the `man` page, you'll find that the entry widget supports lots of EMACS bindings, along with all the Motif bindings dictated by the OSF Motif style guide. Meanwhile, here are a few of the more common ones:

Key Binding	Description
Ctrl-a	Moves the insertion cursor to the beginning of the entry text.
Ctrl-e	Moves the cursor to the end of the entry text.
Ctrl-/	Selects all the text in the entry.

List Boxes

A list box widget can display a collection of strings and allows the user to select one or more items. The following program shows a way to use a list box to design a Motif-like prompt dialog.

Try It Out - Lists

1. First we create the user-interface elements:

```
#!/usr/bin/wish -f

scrollbar .h -orient horizontal -command ".list xview"
scrollbar .v  -command ".list yview"
listbox .list -selectmode single -width 20 -height 10 \
              -setgrid 1 -xscroll ".h set" -yscroll ".v set"
label .label -text "File Selected:" -justify left
entry .e -textvariable fileSelected
```

2. To give widgets that Motif-ish look and feel, we use the `grid` geometry manager:

```
grid .list -row 0 -column 0 -columnspan 2 -sticky "news"
grid .v -row 0 -column 2 -sticky "ns"
grid .h -row 1 -column 0 -columnspan 2 -sticky "we"
grid .label -row 2 -column 0
grid .e -row 3 -column 0  -columnspan 3 -sticky "we"

grid columnconfigure . 0 -weight 1
grid rowconfigure . 0 -weight 1
```

3. We initialize the list box with the contents of the current directory:

```
foreach file [glob *] {
    .list insert end $file
}
```

4. Lastly, we bind an event handler to the list box to make it react to the release of the mouse-button 1. This corresponds to the left mouse-button for right-handed users, and vice versa for left-handed users. We'll continue to call it mouse button 1 in this section as this is the convention used in the code.

```
bind .list <ButtonRelease-1> \
    {global fileSelected;set fileSelected [%W get [%W curselection]]}
```

If you run the program, you'll see this:

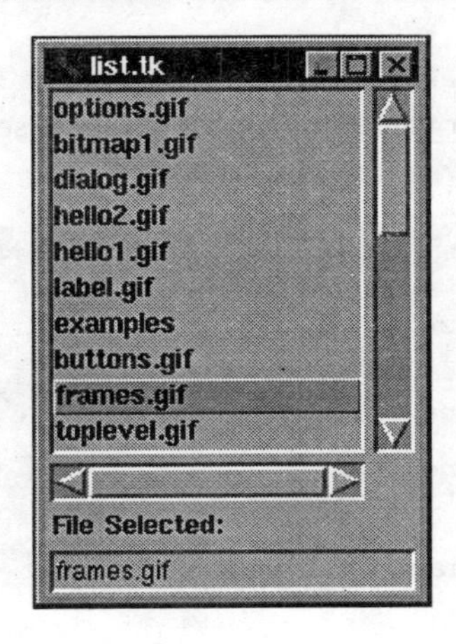

How It Works

The program first creates two scrollbars and then attaches them to the list box it creates. The widgets are inter-connected using `-command` for the scrollbars and `-xview` and `-yview` commands for the list box. This is the way we tell two widgets how to communicate and react to one another's geometry or state. We'll explore more interconnection later in the chapter.

Next, we initialize the list box with the contents of the current directory using the `foreach` loop. The Tcl command `glob` performs pattern matching to return these filenames.

The list box provides many more configuration methods such as `delete`, `get`, `index`, `insert` and `scan` to manipulate the displayed contents.

Scrollbars

As we saw in the previous example, scrollbars are usually connected to other widgets, so that the widget's viewing area will be expanded. In the list box example, the viewing area is controlled by the two scrollbars, `.h` and `.v`, like this:

```
scrollbar .h -orient horizontal -command ".list xview"
scrollbar .v  -command ".list yview"
```

`.h` controls the horizontal viewing area of the list box using the command `.list xview`, and similarly for the vertical scrollbar, `.v`. The list box is also informed about the interconnection using the command:

```
listbox .list ... -xscroll ".h set" -yscroll ".v set"
```

That, then, is how we make two widgets communicate with each other by binding them together and informing each of them about the other's behavior. You can also use implicit interconnection, as we'll see in the next section.

Scales

Scales display an integer value and allow the user to select that value by moving a slider. Let's look at a simple example:

```
#!/usr/bin/wish -f

set foo 100
label .l -text "Choose a Value:" -justify left
scale .s -orient horizontal -from 0 -to 2000 -tickinterval 500 \
       -showvalue true -length 3i  -variable foo
entry .e -width 6 -justify left -textvariable foo

pack .l -side top -anchor nw
pack .s .e -side left -padx 4m -fill x
```

When you run this program, you'll see this screen:

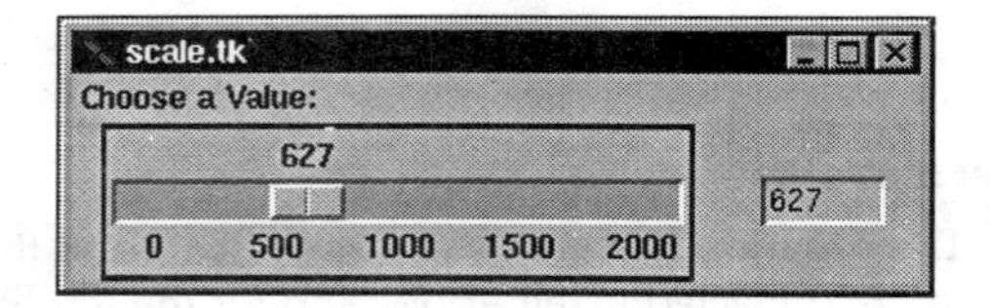

Here, the scale and the entry share an implicit interconnection through the global variable `foo`. If you update the value of the scale, the value in the entry is automatically updated.

> **All the variables used explicitly in Tk's widget event handlers are of global scope. If the bound variable doesn't exist, Tk will automatically create one for you. So, in the above example the variable `foo` is a global variable and both `scale` and `entry` share the same variable, creating an implicit interconnection in their behavior.**

Text

Tk's very versatile text widgets are used to create multiline, editable text. They support three types of annotations, **tags**, **marks** and **embedded windows**, which affect what is displayed.

- **Tags** allow different portions of text to be displayed with different fonts, colors and reliefs. Tcl commands can be associated with tags to make them react to user actions.
- **Marks** are used to keep track of various interesting positions in the text as it's edited.
- **Embedded window** annotations are used to insert widgets (windows) at particular points in the text. You can have any number of embedded windows in the text. All the embedded windows in the text require the text to be the parent of embedded windows.

Let's look at a demonstration of some of the text widget features.

> **Tk's text widget is so powerful that we can use it as an HTML widget without much effort. The well known hypertext man page viewer `TkMan` uses Tk's text widget to display normal UNIX `man` pages in hyper-linked form.**

Try It Out - Manipulating Text

1. First of all, we create a vertical scrollbar which we attach to the text widget. Then we pack them side by side and tell the text window to expand to fill the available window space.

We make sure that the text window continues to fill the window even when resizing occurs by telling the packer, if there's extra vertical space, to expand both the widgets to occupy that space. However, if some extra horizontal space is made available, only the text widget will be expanded.

```
#!/usr/bin/wish -f

scrollbar .y -command ".t yview"
text .t -wrap word -width 80 -spacing1 1m -spacing2 0.5m -spacing3 1m \
        -height 25 -yscrollcommand ".y set"

pack .t -side left -fill both -expand yes
pack .y -side left -fill y
```

2. Next, we want to create embedded windows. We don't have to worry about managing them because the text widget will look after them internally.

```
set image [image create photo -file mickey.gif -width 200 -height 200]
label .t.l -image $image
button .t.b -text "Hello World!" -command "puts Hi"
```

3. Then we configure all the tags that we're going to associate with the text window:

```
.t tag configure bold -font -*-Courier-Bold-O-Normal--*-120-*-*-*-*-*-*
.t tag configure yellowBg -background yellow
.t tag configure blueFg -foreground blue
.t tag configure yellowBgBlueFg -background yellow -foreground red
.t tag configure underline -underline 1
.t tag configure raised -relief raised -borderwidth 2
.t tag configure sunken -relief sunken -borderwidth 2
.t tag configure center -justify center
.t tag configure left  -justify left
.t tag configure right -justify right
.t tag configure super -offset 4p
.t tag configure sub -offset -2p
.t tag bind colorOnEnter <Any-Enter> ".t tag configure colorOnEnter \
                                    -background yellow"
.t tag bind colorOnEnter <Any-Leave> ".t tag configure colorOnEnter \
                                    -background {}"
```

4. Having configured the tags, we now insert text with those tags to show off the widget's potential, if not our graphic design.

```
.t insert end "Tk text widget is so versatile that it can support many \
              display styles:\n"
.t insert end "Background: " bold
.t insert end " You can change the "
.t insert end "background"  yellowBg
.t insert end " or "
.t insert end "foreground" blueFg
.t insert end " or "
.t insert end "both" yellowBgBlueFg
.t insert end "\nUnderlining. " bold
.t insert end "You can "
.t insert end "underline" underline
.t insert end "\n3-D effects: " bold
.t insert end "You can make the text appear "
.t insert end "raised" raised
.t insert end " or "
.t insert end "sunken" sunken
.t insert end " Text"
.t insert end "\nJustification" bold
.t insert end "\nright justification" right
.t insert end "\n center justification " center
.t insert end "\nleft justification " left
.t insert end "\nSuper and Subscripts: " bold
.t insert end "Text can be "
.t insert end "super" super
.t insert end " or "
.t insert end "sub" sub
.t insert end " scripted"
.t insert end "\nBindings: " bold
.t insert end "Text can be made to react to the user interactions" colorOnEnter
.t insert end "\nEmbedded Windows: " bold
.t insert end "You can insert labels "
.t window create end -window .t.l
.t insert end " or any kind of windows "
.t window create end -window .t.b
```

If you run this program, this is what you'll see:

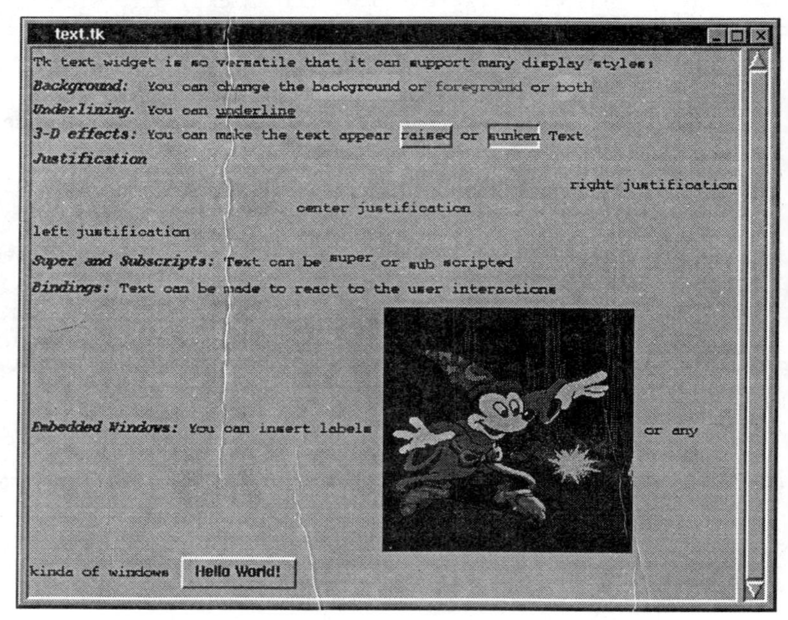

How It Works

In this example, the first text window and a scrollbar are created and managed to create the basic interface. All the internal windows (`.t.l` and `.t.b`) are created, but not explicitly managed, because we're going to insert them into the text widget. Next, all the binding tags that we're going to use are configured using various configuration options. For example,

```
.t tag configure bold -font -*-Courier-Bold-O-Normal--*-120-*-*-*-*-*-*
```

will create a tag called `bold`. The characters inserted with the tag will have the font `-*-Courier-Bold-O-Normal--*-120-*-*-*-*-*-*`. We'll look at the way Tk handles fonts later on. Similarly, characters inserted with `blueFg` will be displayed in blue.

> **We don't need to create the text tag explicitly. When we insert a piece of text with tag `foo`, `foo` will be created automatically. Here, we've configured the tags beforehand and the program has created them.**

We then insert text using tags with the following format:

```
text_widget insert index chars taglist chars taglist...
```

An index is a string used to indicate a particular place within a text, such as a place to insert characters, or one endpoint of a range of characters with blue background. Indices have the syntax:

```
base modifier modifier modifier...
```

`base` gives the starting point and the modifiers shift or adjust the index from the starting point. Modifiers can move the index in either direction from the starting point.

The `base` for the index must have one of the following forms:

Index Base	Description
`line.char`	Indicates the `char`th character of the line `line`.
`@x,y`	Indicates the character that covers the pixel within the text window whose co-ordinates are `x` and `y`.
`mark`	Indicates the character just after the mark.
`tag.first`	Indicates the first character in the text that has been tagged `tag`. Similarly for `tag.last`.
`pathname`	Indicated the position of the embedded window whose path name is `pathname`.

Modifiers can have these forms:

Modifier	Description
`+count chars`	Adjusts the index forward by `count chars`.
`-count chars`	Adjusts the index backward by `count chars`.
`+count lines`	Adjusts the index forward by `count lines`.
`-count lines`	Adjusts the index backward by `count lines`.
`Linestart`	Adjusts the index to refer to the first `char` on the line.
`Lineend`	Adjusts the index to refer to the last `char` on the line.
`Wordstart`	Adjusts the index to first `char` of the word containing the current index.
`Wordend`	Adjusts the index to last `char` of the word containing the current index.

We can associate a particular piece of text with more than one tag. For example, text can be bold and italic at the same time. When you insert text, you need to specify the location. In our last example, end means 'insert after the last character displayed'. In text, indices can also be tags and marks, so the text command:

```
.t insert end "right justification" right
```

will insert the text `right justification` at the end of all the text in text widget and will right justify it.

Text supports lots of features and we recommend that you read the text `man` page and take a look at the text demos that come with Tk distribution. Before we finish text, though, think about what it takes to implement the last example in Motif or Xlib. In Motif, it would take a couple of hundred lines and, in Xlib, perhaps several thousand. The power of Tk can be pretty Mind boggling!

Canvases

Tk's canvas widget is used to implement structured graphics. Canvases can display any number of items, including rectangles, circles, lines, text and embedded windows, which can be manipulated (moved or colored) and bound to user interactions. For example, we can make a particular item change its background color when the user clicks the mouse button over it.

Before we play with the canvas widget, we need to cover some theory: **identifiers** and **tags**.

When we create each item in the canvas, it's assigned a unique integer identifier. Items can have any number of tags associated with them. A tag is a string of characters, which can take any form except an integer. Tags are used for item grouping, identifying and manipulating purposes. The same tag can be associated with many items to group them under one category. Every item inside the canvas can be identified by its ID, or a tag associated with it. The tag `all` is implicitly associated with every item in the canvas. The tag `current` is automatically managed by Tk. It refers to the topmost item whose drawn area lies at the position of the mouse cursor.

When we're specifying items in canvas widget commands, if the specifier is an integer, we assume that it refers to a single item with that ID. If the specifier isn't an integer, we assume that it refers to all the items in the canvas that have the tag matching the specifier. In the next example, we use the `tagOrId` symbol to specify either an ID that selects a single item or a tag that selects zero or more items.

When we create any item on the canvas, we specify its location. The locations are floating point numbers optionally suffixed with one of the letters `m`, `c`, `i`, `p`:

- `m` stands for millimeters.
- `c` stands for centimeters.
- `i` stands for inches.
- `p` stands for points.

If we don't follow the coordinate with one of these letters, the program assumes that the item is in pixels. Let's look at some of the canvas commands and see what they do. In the following commands, the `pathName` identifier refers to the canvas path name:

```
pathName create arc x1 y1 x2 y2  ?option value option value ...?
```

This creates an `arc` item on the canvas, with `x1 y1 x2 y2` specifying the coordinates of a rectangular region enclosing the oval that defines the arc. Command options in the above include `-extent`, `-fill` and `-outline`. For example, the command,

```
% set k [.c create arc 10 10 50 50 -fill red -outline blue -tags redArc]
```

creates an `arc` item inside canvas `.c` with `$k` giving the value of the ID. Its outline is drawn in blue. This arc is enclosed inside a rectangle with canvas coordinates `10 10 50 50` and is filled in with red. A tag, `redArc`, is also associated with the `arc`.

```
pathName itemconfigure tagOrId ?option value option value ...?
```

This command is similar to the `-configure` widget command, except that we can use it to modify only item-specific options for the item denoted by `tagOrId`, instead of modifying the whole canvas widget. For example,

```
% .c itemconfigure redArc -fill yellow
```

will change all the `fill` colors of items associated with tag `redArc` to yellow.

```
pathName type tagOrId
```

This will return the type of first item in the list of items referred to by `tagOrId`. For example:

```
% .c type redArc
arc
```

```
pathName bind tagOrId ?sequence? ?command?
```

This is just like the `bind` command, but instead of applying the sequence to the whole canvas, it just applies to the item specified by `tagOrId`. If `command` isn't given, it returns all the commands associated with the binding sequence `sequence` for canvas item `tagOrId`. If neither `sequence` nor `command` is given, all the sequences bound to the item are returned. For example,

```
% .c bind $k <Enter> ".c itemconfigure redArc -fill blue"
% .c bind redArc  <Leave> ".c itemconfigure redArc -fill red"
```

The first binding will fill in the item associated with `tagOrId` `$k` with blue, when the mouse enters the item. The second binding fills in all the items associated with tag `redArc` with red when the mouse leaves them.

Text and canvasses support so many commands that it would take much more than one chapter to explain them all. We strongly advise that you refer to the `canvas` and `text` man pages for the mastery of these two widgets. Here's a small example that shows a few of their features:

Try It Out - Text on Canvas

1. First we create the canvas and then some objects to display on it: an image of a teapot, a line of text over the image, another text object to exhort users to move the items around, and a rectangle. We pack the canvas so it will fill the window.

```
#!/usr/bin/wish -f

set c [canvas .c -width 300 -height 300 -relief sunken -bd 2]

set image [image create photo -file teapot.ppm -width 200 -height 200]
$c create image 150 150 -anchor center -image $image -tags item

$c create text 150 150 -text " Image Object"  -fill white

$c create text 10 10 -text " Move any Item \n using Mouse " -justify center \
                    -anchor nw -tags item  -fill red
$c create rectangle 200 10  250 40 -fill yellow -outline blue -tags item

pack .c
```

2. Next, we bind the canvas so that we can operate on the items shown on it. We'll define the `itemDragStart` and `dragItem` procedures next:

```
bind $c <1> "itemDragStart $c %x %y"
bind $c <B1-Motion> "dragItem $c %x %y"
```

3. For the procedure's benefit, we need to define two global variables, `lastX` and `lastY`.

```
global lastX lastY

# event handler for the <1> event
proc itemDragStart {c x y} {
    global lastX lastY
    set lastX [$c canvasx $x]
    set lastY [$c canvasy $y]
}
# event handler for the <B1-Motion> event
proc dragItem {c x y} {
    global lastX lastY
    set x [$c canvasx $x]
    set y [$c canvasy $y]
    $c move current [expr $x-$lastX] [expr $y-$lastY]
    set lastX $x
    set lastY $y
}
```

The program produces this output:

How It Works

It's really a very simple example. We created a few canvas item types and bound the mouse buttons so that the user could move them with the mouse. For example, the line,

```
$c create image 150 150 -anchor center -image $image -tags item
```

creates an image on the canvas at the canvas location (150, 150). This image is an object in its own right, so you can move it and make it react to the user by binding event handlers to the tag associated with the item. Like text, canvas supports many features, so it's very difficult to explain them comprehensively in a simple twenty-line example. We'll look at some more of canvas's features in the final applications.

Before we leave canvas objects, we'll mention a few of their properties:

- Canvas items can have event handlers attached to them.
- An item can have many tags associated with it, but will have one unique ID.
- If an item is a widget, it should be the child of the canvas that contains it.
- If items are widgets, you can configure them just as you would had they been outside the canvas. Embedding them within the canvas doesn't change their methods.
- As you place items on the canvas, you can stack them on top of one another, obscuring some of the items beneath them. You can change the stacking order using canvas `raise` and `lower` commands.

Finally, to make things simpler in the last example, we don't bind the procedures to the objects through tags, but directly through the canvas. If you look at the `dragItem` procedure, the line,

```
set x [$c canvasx $x]
```

sets the values of `x` to `canvasx` coordinate from the real screen coordinate `x`. The line,

```
$c move current [expr $x-$lastX] [expr $y-$lastY]
```

moves the current object under the mouse cursor (denoted by the index `current`) to a new location, from `lastX` to `x`. `lastX` was saved when the user event handler `itemDragStart` was invoked, through the binding:

```
bind $c <1> "itemDragStart $c %x %y"
```

Here, the bind means that when the user clicks on the canvas with mouse button 1 the `itemDragStart` event handler is invoked with arguments `canvas`, `%x` (the value of `x` at the mouse click) and `%y` (the value of `y` at the mouse click). We'll discuss bindings later in the chapter.

Images

Tk can display images of two built in types: photo and bitmap. The photo type can display `gif` and `ppm` / `pgm` files, while the bitmap format can display `xbm` files. The `image` command can be used to create images. The general format of the `image` command is,

```
image option ?arg arg ...?
```

where `option` can be used to create, delete and set such options as height, names, image type and so on. To explore the image command, we are going to develop an example based on the sliding block example that comes with the Tk distribution, but we are going to jazz-up the original example by using the image command.

Try It Out - Manipulating Images

1. First we create the image. Then we configure the frame which will hold the pieces of the image that will form the puzzle. This we pack with a little padding:

```
#!/usr/bin/wish -f

set image [image create photo -file mickey.gif -width 160 -height 160]

frame .frame -width 120 -height 120 -borderwidth 2 -relief sunken \
-bg grey
pack .frame -side top -pady 1c -padx 1c
```

2. Now we create the individual pieces of the puzzle. This involves fifteen loops of the code, which crops portions of the original image to fit on the buttons.

```
set order {3 1 6 2 5 7 15 13 4 11 8 9 14 10 12}
for {set i 0} {$i < 15} {set i [expr $i+1]} {
    set num [lindex $order $i]
    set xpos($num) [expr ($i%4)*.25]
    set ypos($num) [expr ($i/4)*.25]

    set x [expr $i%4]
    set y [expr $i/4]

    set butImage [image create photo image-${num} -width 40 -height 40]
    $butImage copy  $image  -from [expr round($x*40)] \
                                  [expr round($y*40)] \
                                  [expr round($x*40+40)] \
                                  [expr round($y*40+40)]
    button .frame.$num -relief raised -image $butImage \
                       -command "puzzleSwitch  $num" \
                       -highlightthickness 0
    place .frame.$num -relx $xpos($num) -rely $ypos($num) \
                      -relwidth .25 -relheight .25
}
```

3. Finally, we have the event handler that deals with the user's input. The two global variables are set to show that the initial space in the puzzle is at the bottom right-hand corner

```
set xpos(space) .75
set ypos(space) .75

proc puzzleSwitch { num} {
    global xpos ypos
    if {(($ypos($num) >= ($ypos(space) - .01))
            && ($ypos($num) <= ($ypos(space) + .01))
            && ($xpos($num) >= ($xpos(space) - .26))
            && ($xpos($num) <= ($xpos(space) + .26)))
            || (($xpos($num) >= ($xpos(space) - .01))
            && ($xpos($num) <= ($xpos(space) + .01))
            && ($ypos($num) >= ($ypos(space) - .26))
            && ($ypos($num) <= ($ypos(space) + .26)))} {
        set tmp $xpos(space)
        set xpos(space) $xpos($num)
        set xpos($num) $tmp
        set tmp $ypos(space)
        set ypos(space) $ypos($num)
        set ypos($num) $tmp
        place .frame.$num -relx $xpos($num) -rely $ypos($num)
    }
}
```

When you run the program, you'll get this fifteen piece image puzzle output:

How It Works

The first line in the program creates a photo image, using the `mickey.gif` file and assigns it to the variable `image`. Portions of this image are then copied on to the buttons with the `set butImage` line and those following in a `for` loop. The result is fifteen buttons with fifteen associated images, taken from the big image held in `$image`. The rest of the program deals with event handlers to arrange the buttons when the user clicks on them. We'll return to that part when we deal with geometry management.

The gist of the `puzzleSwitch` algorithm logic is based on the fact that: when the user clicks on a button, if the button is next to an empty space, the button and empty space will be swapped with each other. If you play with the 15-puzzle, you will notice that the piece that can take the place of the empty space will obey one of the following rules.

- It will have the same x position as that of empty space and its y position will be 0.25 units away (up or down) from the empty space. (The piece is on the same column as that of the empty space and it is directly above or below the empty space.)
- It will have the same y position as that of empty space and its x position is 0.25 units away (left or right) from the empty space. (The piece is on the same row as that of the empty space and it is directly to the left or right of the emtpy space.)

The algorithm above makes use of these properties to decide whether to switch the pieces with the empty space.

Buttons and labels support images as labels. Also, these labels can be embedded inside canvas and text widgets. Refer to the `bitmap`, `photo` and `image` man pages for more information on Tk's `image` support.

Menu

Traditionally, menus are used to provide users a set of choices in an application without changing much of the application's appearance. Menus give users convenient access to various features of the application without the user having to move away from the main window. Tk's menu command creates a widget that displays a list of entries in a separate toplevel window. Menu is not a container widget; it is a single widget with different objects embedded in it.

Menus can have 3 types of entries embedded inside them:

- command entries, to run commands
- radio entries, to select one of many choices
- option entries, to select one or more choices from a group of options

Menus can also hold other menus in a recursive way, by using cascade entries.

Menu entries can be displayed with up to three separate fields. One of these may be a label (in the form of text), a bitmap, or an image using the `-label`, `-bitmap` or `-image` options respectively. A second field may use the `-accelerator` option to specify an accelerator sequence next to the label. The `accelerator` describes a key sequence that is used to invoke a particular entry associated with a menu entry. A third option is an indicator that radio and option entries display to the left of the label. Note that Tk does not automatically create a key binding when the `-accelerator` option is specified. The binding should be explicitly set using the bind command for the sequence to take effect - setting the `-accellerator` simply displays the key combination in the menu.

Menu entries can be configured with different options, such as foreground and background colors, and fonts using the `entryconfigure` option of the `widget` command. Entries can also be disabled using the `-state` option. If a menu entry is disabled, it will not respond to the user action.

Tk menus are very flexible. You can enable the `-tearoff` option of the menu so that the user can tear the menu off from the menu bar and use it as a toplevel window. You can also specify commands that can get called when a menu gets posted or torn off.

Menus are indexed using either their position numerically in the menu, their label , or "last" and "end" tags. Menus can be posted programmatically by calling the post and unpost menu commands. Tk's documentation refers to menus as being posted, as to say 'pulled down' or 'popped up' only describes the behaviour of certain menus on certain platforms. Posting is a more generic term.

Each toplevel widget in Tk can have one menu widget act as the default menu bar for that window. A menu bar is a list of menus arranged side by side in a frame. Menu bars can be attached using the `-menu` widget option associated with toplevel windows.

The Tk library provides a `<<MenuSelect>>` virtual event that will get triggered whenever a menu or one of its entries become active. The menu command provides lots of options; for a complete list of options, please refer to the `menu` command manual page.

The menu system was overhauled in Tk version 4.0, and many improvements were made in Tk version 8.0. Prior to Tk 8.0, users had to use functions such as:

`tk_menuBar frame ?menu menu ...`

`tk_bindForTraversal arg arg ..`

to create menu bars. These functions are deprecated and have no effect in Tk versions greater than 4.0

Try It Out - Menus

Let's look at an example that illustrates most of the menu command features. This example will make use of the text widget features. Using the menus, we will change background color and the properties of the font that is being used to display the text. We will also create a menu to insert bitmap images inside the text widget.

1. First, we will create the main window components, including a text widget, with an associated scrollbar, and a status widget, to display menu traversal and error messages. We arrange these widgets on the screen using the grid command. We will also create a new font named `myFont`. We will use the menu to manipulate the font attributes so that the text in the text widget will change its appearance.

```
wm title . "Menu demonstration"
wm iconname . "Menu demo"

# create the basic UI
scrollbar .yscroll -orient vertical -command ".text yview"
font create myfont -family Courier -size 10 -weight bold -slant italic \
    -underline 1
text .text -height 10 -width 40 -bg white -yscrollcommand ".yscroll set" -font myfont
label .msg -relief sunken -bd 2 -textvariable message -anchor w -font "Helvetica 10"
.text insert end "Menu Demonstration!"

# manage the widgets using the grid geometry manager.
grid .text -row 0 -column 0  -sticky "news"
grid .yscroll -row 0 -column 1 -sticky "ns"
grid .msg -row 1 -columnspan 2 -sticky "ew"

grid columnconfigure . 0 -weight 1
grid rowconfigure . 0 -weight 1
```

2. Next, we will develop callback functions, which will be associated with the menu entries. The `SetBg` procedure will change the background color of the text. `ConfigureFont` will change the attributes of `myFont`. `InsertImage` will insert the named bitmap into the text buffer. The `InsertImage` procedure has a side effect: If the named bitmap already exists in the text buffer, it will get deleted and a new bitmap will be inserted. The `OpenFile` procedure will prompt the user for a file and if the user selects a file, its contents will be displayed in the text widget.

```
# procedure to set text background color
proc SetBg {} {
    global background
    .text configure -bg $background
}

# procedure to configure the previously created font.

proc ConfigureFont {} {
    global bold italic underline
    expr {$bold ? [set weight bold]: [set weight normal]}
    expr {$italic? [set slant italic]: [set slant roman]}
    expr {$underline? [set underline 1]: [set underline 0]}
    font configure myfont -weight $weight -slant $slant -underline $underline
}

# Procedure to insert images in the text widget

proc InsertImage {image} {
    catch {destroy .text.$image}
    label .text.$image -bitmap $image
    .text window create end -window .text.$image
}

# Callback for open menubutton

proc OpenFile {} {
    global message
    set file [tk_getOpenFile]
    if {$file == ""}  {
        set message "No file selected..."
        return;
    }
    .text delete 0.0 end
    set fd [open $file "r"]
    while {[eof $fd] != 1} {
        gets $fd line
        .text insert end $line
        puts $line
        update idletasks
    }
    close $fd
}
```

3. Next, we will focus on the menu widget and its components. First, we will create a menu that will become the menu bar for the toplevel window.

```
# create toplevel menu

menu .menu -tearoff 0  -type menubar

# Create File menu

set m .menu.file
```

4. We will add a `File` submenu with open and exit entries. The open entry will prompt the user with an open file dialog. If the user chooses a file, that file will be displayed in the text widget using the `OpenFile` procedure. The `exit` menu entry is used to exit the application. As you can see, Tk does not create a default global binding for the menu entry just by using the `-accelerator` menu entry option. We have to explicitly create the binding in order for the accelerator to take effect.

```
menu $m -tearoff 0
.menu add cascade -label "File" -menu $m -underline 0
set modifier Meta
$m add command -label "Open..." -accelerator $modifier+o -command "OpenFile" -
underline 0 -command OpenFile
bind . <$modifier-o> "OpenFile"
$m add separator
$m add command -label "Exit..." -accelerator $modifier+x -command "exit" -underline 0
bind . <$modifier-x> "exit"
```

5. We next add an **Option** submenu to the main menu. This submenu contains **Background** and **Font** cascade menus. A background cascaded menu contains a group of radio buttons to change the background color of the text widget. The **Font** cascade menu provides a group of check buttons to manipulate `myfont` menu attributes:

```
#
# Create options menu
#
set m .menu.options
menu $m -tearoff 1
.menu add cascade -label "Options" -menu $m -underline 0
$m add cascade -label "Background" -menu .menu.options.bg -underline 0
$m add cascade -label "Font" -menu  .menu.options.font -underline 0

#
# create Radio button cascade menu
#

set m .menu.options.bg
menu $m -tearoff 0
$m add radio  -label "Red" -background red -variable background -value red \
    -command SetBg
$m add radio  -label "Yellow" -background yellow -variable background \
    -value yellow -command SetBg
$m add radio  -label "Blue" -background blue -variable background -value blue \
    -command SetBg
$m add radio  -label "White" -background white -variable background -value white \
    -command SetBg
$m invoke 3

#
# Insert option button cascade Menu
#

set m .menu.options.font
menu $m -tearoff 0
$m add check -label "Bold" -variable bold -command ConfigureFont
$m add check -label "Italic" -variable italic -command ConfigureFont
$m add check -label "underline" -variable underline -command ConfigureFont
$m invoke 3
```

As you can see from the above code, the entries in a menu can be configured to have different backgrounds and foregrounds, as well as other standard widget options.

6. Next, we will proceed to add yet another cascade entry to the main menu to insert bitmaps into the text widget. As explained earlier, these bitmap entry commands have a side effect - that only one instance of these bitmaps can be present in the text widget at any given time.

```
#
# Create insert menu option
#
set m .menu.insert
menu $m -tearoff 0
.menu add cascade -label "Insert" -menu $m -underline 0
foreach i {info questhead error} {
    $m add command -bitmap $i -command "puts {You invoked the $i bitmap}"\
         -hidemargin 1 -command "InsertImage $i"
}
$m entryconfigure 2 -columnbreak 1
```

One thing to observe from the above code snippet is that entries in a menu can be arranged in a tabular fashion using the `entryconfigure` command with the `-columnbreak` option.

7. Finally, we will attach the menu to the toplevel widget to make it the default menu bar. We also make use of the `<<MenuSelect>>` virtual event, which gets fired when any menu or its entries are selected. The `<<MenuSelect>>` virtual event will display a message in the message label, which indicates that a particular entry has been selected:

```
#
# Attach the menu to the toplevel menu
#
. configure -menu .menu


#
#  Bind  global tags
#

bind Menu <<MenuSelect>> {
    global message
    if {[catch {%W entrycget active -label} label]} {
        set label "    "
    }
    set message "You have selected $label..."
}
```

8. When you run the above example using the following command:

```
$ wish menu.tcl
```

you will see:

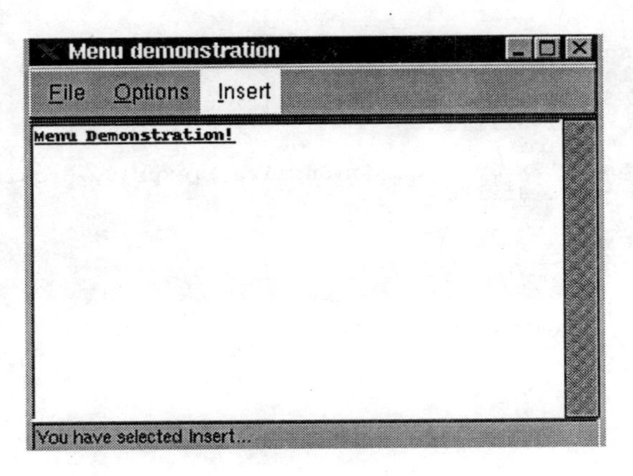

MenuButton

Menu buttons are like normal buttons with menus associated with them. They are very useful in graphical user interfaces to provide a set of choices grouped together by one button. Unlike menu bars, which usually have more than one cascade menu associated with them, menu buttons have only one menu associated. There is only one menu bar associated with a top level window but menu buttons can be embedded anywhere in the user interface.

Menu buttons can also be organized into groups to make menu bars, which can be placed anywhere inside a user interface (unlike top level menus). These can be used to build toolbars and similar functionality into your user interfaces. Usually, menu buttons can also be configured to behave like an option menu by setting the `-indicator` option. The menu button command syntax is as follows:

`menubutton pathName ?options?`

Try It Out - MenuButtons

To illustrate MenuButtons' features, we will create a simple application that draws circles and rectangles on a canvas with a specified fill color. First, we will develop a utility procedure that will draw a circle or a rectangle on the canvas. It uses 3 global variables: `x`, `y` and `sqsize`. `x` - `y` co-ordinates are used to specify where on the canvas the object needs to be drawn. `Sqsize` is used either as the diameter or the side of the square.

1. Let's start off with the basics needed to draw circles and squares.

```
wm title . "Menubutton demonstration"
wm iconname . "Menubutton demo"
#
# Initial parameters to draw circles and squares
#
set x 50
set y 50
set sqsize 30
#
# procedure to draw canvas objects
#
proc AddObject {type} {
    global x y sqsize sqsize  fillc
    if {$type == "circle"} {
        .c create oval $x $y [expr $x+$sqsize] [expr $y+$sqsize] \
            -tags item -fill $fillc
    } elseif {$type == "square"} {
        .c create rectangle $x $y [expr $x+$sqsize] [expr $y+$sqsize] \
            -tags item -fill $fillc
    }
    incr x 10
    incr y 10
}
```

2. Next, we create a canvas with a frame, menu button and a dismiss button. The frame widget will hold the menu and dismiss buttons. We pack all the elements to create the main user interface.

```
# create the basic User Interface canvas, 2 menu buttons and a dismiss button
set c [canvas .c -width 200 -height 200 -bd 2 -relief ridge]

frame .f -bd 2

menubutton .f.m1 -menu .f.m1.menu -text "Draw" -relief raised -underline 0 \
    -direction left
button .f.exit -text "Dismiss" -command "exit"

# manage the widgets using the grid geometry manager.
pack .c -side top -fill both -expand yes
pack .f -side top -fill x -expand yes

pack .f.m1 .f.exit -side left  -expand 1
```

3. Finally, we add a menu to the menu button. We create a menu and add three entries to it: two command entries to draw circle and square objects, and a cascade widget for fill color selection.

```
set m .f.m1.menu
menu $m -tearoff 0

$m add command -label "Circle" -command "AddObject circle" -accelerator "Meta-c"
bind . <Meta-c> "AddObject circle"
$m add command -label "Square" -command "AddObject square" -accelerator "Meta-s"
bind . <Meta-s> "AddObject square"
$m add separator
$m add cascade -label "Fill Color.." -menu .f.m1.cascade

set m  .f.m1.cascade
menu $m -tearoff 0
$m add radio  -label "Red" -background red -variable background -value red \
    -command "set fillc red"
$m add radio  -label "Yellow" -background yellow -variable background \
    -value yellow -command "set fillc yellow"
$m add radio  -label "Blue" -background blue -variable background -value blue \
    -command "set fillc blue"
$m add radio  -label "White" -background white -variable background -value white \
    -command "set fillc white"
$m invoke 1
```

As you can see from the above code, we have not only added the accelerators to the menu entries, we also have created the bindings explicitly using the bind command.

Popup Menu

Tk also supports popup menus. Unlike menubuttons and menubars, which provide static menus, popup menus are used to provide context sensitive menu system. For example, if you are designing a text editor, when the user selects a block of text and clicks the right mouse button, you can programmatically create a menu with items such as: "Spell...", "Format...", "Copy", "Delete", etc. Popup menus help facilitate such tasks. Popup menus are very helpful in associating menus to any type of widgets, such as text and canvas widgets. Popup menus don't have any menubuttons associated with them. They are plain menus that get posted programmatically by associating a binding to a specific widget and invoking the `tk_popup` command in the event handler of that binding. Since the menus are posted dynamically, the entries inside a popup menu can be created dynamically to display only relevant items.

The general creation format of an popup menu is

tk_popup menu x y ?entry?

where menu is the menu that needs to be posted, x and y specify the co-ordinates, and entry gives the index of an entry in menu. The menu will be positioned so that the entry is positioned over the given point. Let's build some popup menus.

Try It Out - Popup Menus

1. First, create a menu and add a binding to the toplevel window associated with the menu so that the menu will get posted when the user clicks on the window using the third mouse button.

```
set w .menu
catch {destroy $w}
menu $w
bind . <Button-3> {
    tk_popup .menu %X %Y
}
```

2. The rest of the example creates menu entries to show that popup menus have exactly the same capabilities as those of regular menus.

```
# Add menu entries

$w add command -label "Print hello" \
       -command {puts stdout "Hello"} -underline 6

$w add command -label "Red" -background red

# Add a  Cascade menu

set m $w.cascade

$w add cascade -label "Cascades" -menu $m -underline 0
menu $m -tearoff 0
$m add cascade -label "Check buttons" \
       -menu $w.cascade.check -underline 0
set m $w.cascade.check
menu $m -tearoff 0
$m add check -label "Oil checked" -variable oil
$m add check -label "Transmission checked" -variable trans
$m add check -label "Brakes checked" -variable brakes
$m add check -label "Lights checked" -variable lights
$m add separator
$m invoke 1
$m invoke 3

$m add cascade -label "Radio buttons" \
       -menu $w.cascade.radio -underline 0
set m $w.cascade.radio
menu $m -tearoff 0
```

```
$m add radio -label "10 point" -variable pointSize -value 10
$m add radio -label "14 point" -variable pointSize -value 14
$m add radio -label "18 point" -variable pointSize -value 18
$m add radio -label "24 point" -variable pointSize -value 24
$m add radio -label "32 point" -variable pointSize -value 32
$m add sep
$m add radio -label "Roman" -variable style -value roman
$m add radio -label "Bold" -variable style -value bold
$m add radio -label "Italic" -variable style -value italic
$m invoke 1
$m invoke 7
```

When you run the above example, using the command "`wish popup.tk`". You will see:

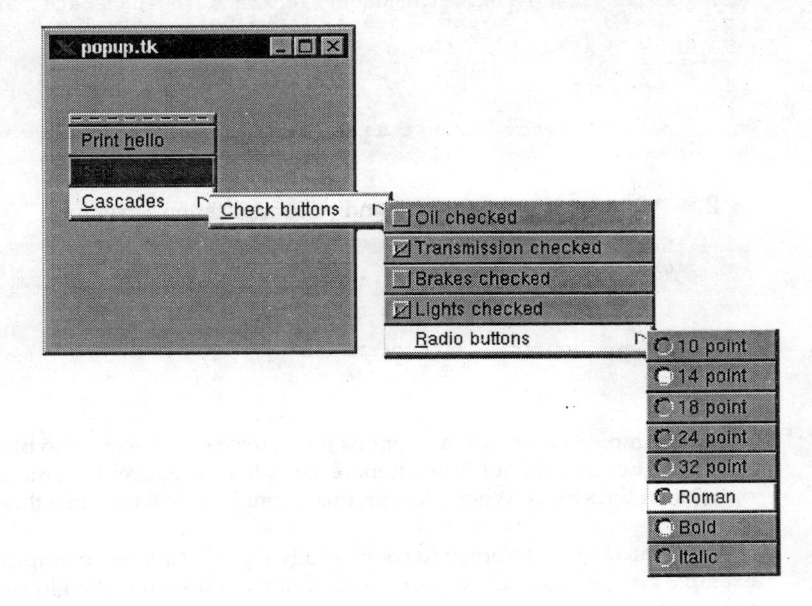

Option Menus

Tk's option menu is written completely in Tk to emulate the Motif option button and has the following syntax:

`tk_optionMenu w varName value ?value value...?`

The `tk_optionMenu` command creates an options menu button w and associates a menu with it. Together, the menu button and the menu allow the user to select one of the values given by the `value` arguments. The current value will be stored in the global variable `varName`, which users can use to manipulate the options button. Calling `tk_optionMenu` returns the menu associated with the options button.

Let's use option buttons to re-implement our earlier buttons example:

Try It Out - Menu Options

1. We set the global variable `state` equal to 1, create a check button and an options menu. These are packed side by side:

```
#!/usr/bin/wish -f

set state 1

checkbutton .lan -text "Language" -command {changeState} -relief flat \
            -variable state  -onvalue 1 -offvalue 0
set optMenu [tk_optionMenu .opt lang Tcl C Lisp C++]

pack .lan .opt -side left

# now make C As the default using lang variable
set lang C++
```

2. We need a procedure to handle the application's event:

```
proc changeState {} {
    global state
    if $state {
        .opt config -state normal
    } else {
        .opt config -state disabled
    }
}
```

In this example, we've used an options menu instead of three radio buttons. This example works the same way as `buttons.tk`, but is much more terse. It also reduces the amount of space needed to display the options on the screen. When you run this example, it will look like this:

If you wanted to, as before, you could add two push buttons, to output the value of the selection. This example also shows that we can control option menus using the global variable with which they are associated. The line,

```
set lang C++
```

sets the selection to C++ by setting the variable.

Dialogs

Dialogs are used extensively in a user interface design cycle. Tk provides a custom dialog called `tk_dialog`. It's very simple, but can be used in many clever ways to implement most tasks. `tk_dialog` has the syntax.

```
tk_dialog window title text bitmap default string string ..
```

This will create a modal dialog with title `title`, message text `text` and with the specified bitmap inside. It will also create buttons with titles given by the `string` arguments. When the user presses one of the buttons, `tk_dialog` will return that button number and then destroy itself.

Let's look at a simple example:

```
#!/usr/bin/wish -f

wm withdraw .

set i [tk_dialog .info  "Info" "Simple Info Dialog" info  0 Ok Cancel]
if {$i==0} {
    puts "Ok Button Pressed"
} else {
    puts "Cancel Button Pressed"
}
exit
```

The first line unmaps the default toplevel window, created by `wish`. This was necessary because `tk_dialog` creates a toplevel window itself and we don't want to have two windows popping up in this simple example. The next line creates a modal dialog `.info` with title Info, message Simple Info Dialog and adds in a built in `info` bitmap. It also creates two buttons, Ok and Cancel, and makes button number 0 (Ok) the default.

Just now, while we were explaining the dialog, we used the word *modal*. What's that? It means that the user's range of choices is restricted. The user won't be able to do anything with the application unless they first respond to the dialog by clicking either Ok or Cancel. Once the user has clicked on one of these buttons, control passes back to the application, where `i` is set depending upon the button the user invoked.

We can achieve modal interactions using the `grab` and `tkwait` commands. Take a look at the man pages or Tk books for more information on these topics.

Tk's Built-in Dialogs

In addition to providing the tk_dialog command, Tk also provides many utility dialog procedures. Most GUI-based applications have lots of common functionality, such as prompting users for input or output files, color choices, etc. Tk provides utility dialog boxes for these operations. Also, these built-in dialogues are written in such a way that they have the native look and feel of whichever operating system the Tcl script is run on. We will explore the utility dialogs in this section. These utility dialogs are not Tk's built-in commands, but rather utility scripts that provide a specific dialog functionality

Color Chooser

`tk_chooseColor ?option value ...?`

Most GUI-based applications provide their users ways to customize the look feel of the application using color and font choices. Humans are used to using descriptive names for colors, but underneath, most graphic systems deal with color using different schemes such as RGB or CMYK. RGB is a Red, Green and Blue color scheme. Any color in the system can be represented using a combination of these three colors.

Tk describes colors in a similar way to HTML - if you've programmed web pages before, you may be familiar with the notation. There is also a large number of valid color names which directly refer to specific color values. However, if you want to control Tk's colors more precisely, you'll have to become familiar with the way it represents them internally.

All colors in Tk are represented as hexadecimal integers. You can use various lengths of hex number, either three digits, six digits, nine or twelve. For example, you could use six digit hex numbers between #000000 and #ffffff. Each pair of digits represents the level of red, green, or blue, in that order. So #ff9900, for example, would represent a red value of #ff, a green value of #99, and a blue value of #00. In fact, the resulting color would be a shade of orange. In this system, #000000 is black and #ffffff is white. Values such as #a5a5a5, where all three components are the same, will lead to shades of gray. Any other value will be a color of some sort.

The other lengths of hex number acceptable to Tk are of course divided into three equal length hex numbers to form the three components, in exactly the same way as for the six digit example.

`tk_chooseColor` dialog provides a simple way to choose a color using the RGB color scheme. This dialog also provides a way to inquire about the RGB values for a given color by name. The procedure `tk_chooseColor` pops up a dialog box for the user to select a color. The following option-value pairs are possible as command line arguments:

`-initialcolor color`	Specifies the color to display in the color dialog when it pops up. `color` must be in a form acceptable to the `Tk_GetColor` function, for example `red` or `#ff0000`. (`#ff0000` is the RGB equivalent of red.)
`-parent window`	Makes `window` the logical parent of the color dialog. The color dialog is displayed on top of its parent window.
`-title titleString`	Specifies a string to display as the title of the dialog box. If this option is not specified, a default title will be displayed.

If the user selects a color, `tk_chooseColor` will return the name of the color in a form acceptable to Tk widget commands. If the user cancels the operation, both commands will return the empty string.

The following scripts illustrate the use of `tk_chooseColor` dialog box:

```
#
# tk_chooseColor demo
#

label .l -text "Set my background color:"
button .b -text "Choose Color..." -command ".l config -bg \[tk_chooseColor\]"
pack .l .b -side left -padx 10
```

When you run the above script and click on the "Choose Color..." button you will see:

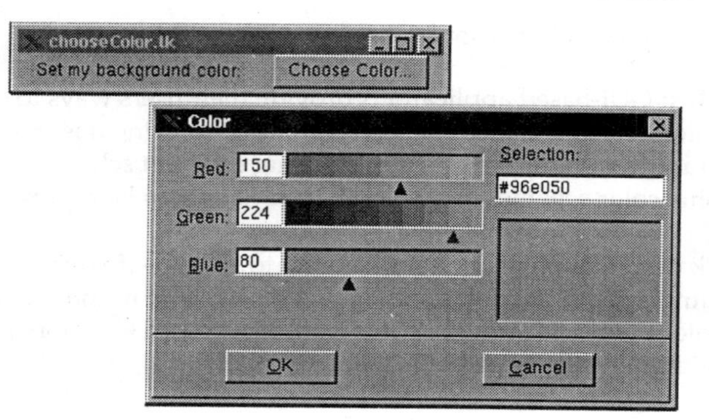

Get Open/Save Files

`tk_getOpenFile` and `tk_getSaveFile` are convenience functions to prompt the user for input or output file selection, respectively. In most GUI-based operating systems, all applications provide same dialog boxes for selecting input and output files. Tk makes this functionality available to all Tk-based applications by providing these convenience functions. These dialog boxes have native look, feel and behavior. The dialog boxes handle most the error conditions so that the programmer does not have to do much other than create and initialize these dialogs. They provide interfaces so that developers can specify filters to select only those files matching certain patterns. `Tk_getOpenFile` command is usually associated with the "Open" command in the File menu and `tk_getSaveFile` is usually associated with the "Save as..." command.

If the user enters a file that already exists, the dialog box prompts the user for confirmation as to whether or not the existing file should be overwritten. The syntax of these commands is as follows:

```
tk_getOpenFile ?option value ...?
tk_getSaveFile ?option value ...?
```

For a complete list of options to these commands, refer to the `tk_getOpenFile` manual page.

The following example illustrates the use of these commands:

```
# tk_getOpenFile demo
# tk_getSaveFile demo

label .o -text "File to open:"
entry .oe -textvariable open
set types {
    {{Text Files}       {.txt}    }
    {{TCL Scripts}      {.tcl}    }
    {{C Source Files}   {.c}      TEXT}
    {{GIF Files}        {.gif}         }
    {{GIF Files}        {}        GIFF}
    {{All Files}        *              }}

button .ob -text "Open..." -command "set open \[tk_getOpenFile -filetypes \$types \]"

label .s -text "File to save:"
entry .se -textvariable save
button .sb -text "Save..." -command "set save \[tk_getSaveFile\]"

# Create a dismiss button

button .b -text "Dismiss" -command "exit"

# Manage the widgets

grid .o -row 0 -column 0 -sticky e -padx 10
grid .oe -row 0 -column 1 -padx 10
grid .ob -row 0 -column 2 -padx 10
grid .s -row 1 -column 0 -sticky e -padx 10
grid .se -row 1 -column 1 -padx 10
grid .sb -row 1 -column 2 -padx 10
grid .b -row 2 -pady 10
```

As you can see from the code, these dialog routines have a way of specifying file filters using patterns. When you run the above example and click on Open, you will see:

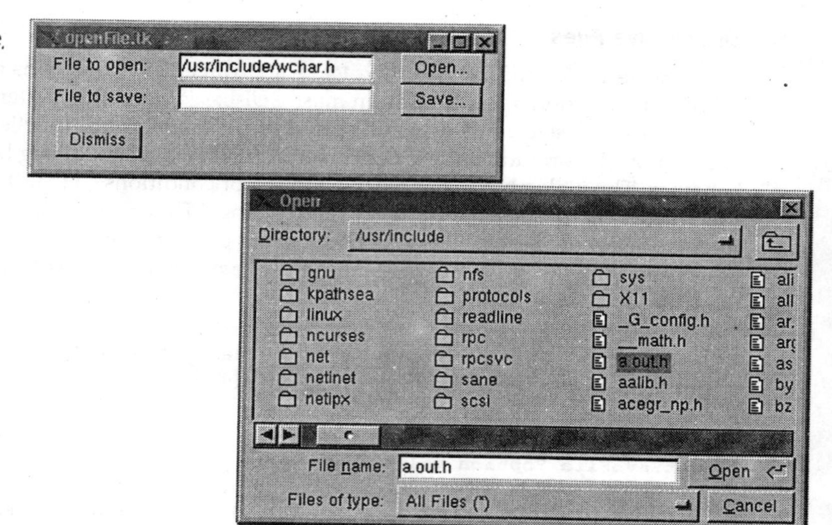

Color Schemes

When you create new widgets using Tk widget commands in Tk4.0 and later, all the widgets have a black foreground color and a gray background. So, if you create a complete application (like most of the examples above) that application will have a gray background and a black foreground. What if you wanted to create an application with a light blue background? One way to accomplish this is to configure all the created widgets' backgrounds to light blue. This will make the application code bloated and unreadable, however, since most of the commands in the code will be configuration commands – obscuring the application logic. To solve this problem, Tk provides a convenient way of globally changing the color scheme of the application. The following commands are used to set overall color scheme for any application

```
tk_setPalette background
tk_setPalette name value ?name value ...?
tk_bisque
```

If `tk_setPalette` is invoked with one argument, then that argument is taken as the default background color for all widgets and `Tk_setPalette` will compute the color palette using this color. For example, the following commands

```
tk_setPalette steelblue
button .b -text "Linux is cool!"
pack .b
```

will create a button and display it in a steel blue background. It will also set the background color of any future widgets in the same application to steel blue.

Alternatively, the arguments to `tk_setPalette` may consist of any number of name-value pairs, where the first argument of the pair is the name of an option in the Tk option database and the second argument is the new value to use for that option. The following option database names can be specified currently.

activeBackground	disabledForeground	foreground
highlightColor	highlightBackground	insertBackground
selectBackground background	selectColoractiveForeground	selectForeground
troughColor		

Refer to the `options(n)` manual page on the option database description. `tk_setPalette` tries to compute reasonable defaults for any options that you don't specify. You can specify options other than the above ones and Tk will change those options on widgets as well.

The procedure `tk_bisque` is provided for backward compatibility: it restores the application's colors to the light brown ("bisque") color scheme used in Tk 3.6 and earlier versions.

Fonts

If you have ever programmed using Xlib or Motif on an X window system you know fonts are one of the murkier areas of X. You have to specify font names in X Logical Font Description (XLFD) structures. For example, in applications created with pre-Tk8.0 versions, if a button had to be created with a specific font, the command would look something like this:

```
Button .b -text  "Hello" -font -font -*-Courier-Bold-O-Normal--*-120-*-*-*-*-*-*
```

We actually met this notation earlier, but we're going to see how we can get around this ugly format now. The reason X was designed this way was to adhere to the requirement that X client applications must be portable across server implementations, with very different file systems, naming conventions and font libraries. X clients must also be able to dynamically determine the fonts available on any given server, so that understandable information can be presented to the user and intelligent fallbacks can be chosen. XLFD provides an adequate set of typographic font properties, such as `FOUNDRY`, `FAMILY_NAME`, `WEIGH_NAME`, `SLANT`, etc. To learn more about XLFD refer to its specification in the X Window System documentation or play with the `xfontsel` command on your Linux box.

Even though XLFD is extremely powerful and flexible, it is not simple and intuitive. As in the case of colors, humans tend to associate simple names with fonts such as "Helvetica 12 point italic". Porting Tk to other non-X platforms introduced another complexity because other windowing systems do not use XLFD, so the users were forced to learn XLFD. In addition, XLFD does not support a way of creating fonts by name.

Tk 8.0 introduced a new mechanism to deal with fonts, using the `font` command. New named fonts can be created using human readable metrics. Tk internally will take care of translating these fonts to system-specific interfaces. One advantage of the new `font` command is that it gives a platform-independent way of specifying fonts. It also provides a way to associate names with created fonts. Font command syntax is as follows:

```
font create ?fontname? ?option value ...?
font configure fontname ?option? ?value option value ...?
```

The `font` command takes options such as `-family`, `-size -slant`, etc. For a complete list of font command options, take a look at the `font` manual page.

For example, you can create a font called `myfont` using this command:

```
font create myfont -family Courier -size 20 -weight bold -slant italic\
        -underline 1 -overstrike 1
```

Once the font is created, you can use that font name to specify a value for a `-font` widget option. After creating the font, if you run the following code using wish,

```
button .b -text "Hello World!" -font myfont
pack .b
```

You should see:

Bindings

We've said that once we've created widgets, we can attach event handlers to them to make them respond to the user. For example, in the final 'Hello World' program, we attached an event handler to the button:

```
bind .b <Control-Button-1> {puts "Help!"}
```

We use the `bind` command to attach all these event interactions with the widgets. The `bind` command associates Tcl scripts with X events and is very powerful. Its general syntax is:

```
bind tag
bind tag sequence
bind tag sequence script
bind tag sequence +script
```

The tag argument determines which window(s) the binding applies to. If tag begins with a dot, as in .a.b.c, then it must be the path name for a window; otherwise, it may be an arbitrary string. Each window has an associated list of tags, and a binding applies to a particular window. If its tag is among those specified for the window, the default binding tags provide the following behavior:

- If tag is the name of an internal window, the binding applies to that window.
- If tag is the name of a top level window, the binding applies to the top level window and all its internal windows.
- If tag is the name of a class of widgets, such as button, the binding applies to all widgets in that class.
- If tag has the value all, the binding applies to all windows in the application.

For example, let's see what happens if we invoke bind on the button class:

```
% bind Button
<Key-space> <ButtonRelease-1> <Button-1> <Leave> <Enter>
```

The result says that there are bindings for these five event sequences in the button class. Let's experiment further and see what happens when we invoke the second form of bind command on one of these bindings:

```
% bind Button <Key-space>
    tkButtonInvoke %W
```

The result says that <Key-space> binding on the button widget class (all the push buttons belong to this button class) will invoke the Tcl script tkButtonInvoke with the button path as the argument.

We can also use class names when we associate the binding. For example:

```
% bind Button <Control-Button-1> {puts "Help!"}
```

This will set the <Control-Button-1> binding on all the button widgets in the application. It's possible for several bindings to match a given X event. If the bindings are associated with different tags, each of the bindings will be executed in order. By default, a widget class binding will be executed first if it exists, followed by a binding for the widget, a binding for its top level and, finally, an all binding if one exists for that event. We can use the bindtags command to change this order for a particular window, or to associate additional binding tags with the window.

When a binding matches particular sequence, the script associated with that binding will be invoked. While we're invoking the script, we can inform the bind command to pass some arguments to that script from the X event that invoked the binding. For this, we use special modifiers. For example, in the canvas example, we had a binding:

```
bind $c <1> "itemDragStart $c %x %y"
```

There, we informed bind that, while invoking the itemDragStart command, it should pass $c, %x and %y, which bind replaces with the x and y coordinates of the X event structure. The bind command supports lots of substitution parameters; for a complete listing, refer to the bind man page.

BindTags

As described above, the bind command is used to associate an action with a binding. When creating an association with the bind command, a tag is specified. The tag argument specifies which windows the binding applies to. Usually, tag is the name of the widget, the name of the widget class, the keyword all or any other text string. Each window has an associated list of tags, and a binding applies to a particular window if its tag is among those specified for the window. When an event occurs in a window, it is applied to each of the window's tags in order; for each tag, the most specific binding that matches the given tag and event is executed. For example, after executing the following code snippet in the wish shell:

```
bind . <F1> "puts Toplevel"
entry .e
pack .e
bind .e <F1> "puts Entry"
```

If you press the *F1* key inside the entry widget, you will see the strings "Entry" and "Toplevel" printed in that order, because if you invoke the bindtags command on .e the result will be: .e Entry . all, meaning that when an event is triggered on .e, first it is checked in the .e tag and later in the toplevel that includes the entry. What if you want to make the toplevel binding fire before the entry's? You can use the bindtags command to change the order:

```
Bindtags .e {. .e Entry all}
```

By default, each window has four binding tags consisting of the following, in order:

- the name of the window
- the window's class name
- the name of the window's nearest top level ancestor
- all

Toplevel windows have only three tags by default, since the toplevel name is the same as that of the window.

The bindtags command can be used to introduce arbitrary additional binding tags for a window. In fact this function of bindtags accomplishes many things. It aids in creating a binding once and and associating with as many widgets as needed by simply inserting the binding tag in the widget's bind tags list. Second it allows widgets to have more than the standard 4 binding tags. Tags aid in identifying an action by name rather than a key sequence. The following example illustrates a practical use for bindtags.

```
set count 0
button .b -text "Tick(ms)"
label .ticker -textvariable count
pack .b .ticker

bind timer <ButtonPress-1> {
    set count 0
    StartTimer %W
}

bind timer <ButtonRelease-1> {
    StopTimer %W
}

proc StartTimer { widget } {
    global pending count
    incr count 200
    set pending [after 200 [list StartTimer $widget]]
}

proc StopTimer { widget } {
    global pending
    after cancel $pending
}

bindtags .b [linsert [bindtags .b] 0  timer]
```

In the above example we have first created a simple user interface with a button and a label to display timer ticks. Next we have created a binding with a tag `timer`. We have added two key sequences to the tag timer. The first sequence `<ButtonPress-1>`, starts the timer and `<ButtonRelease-1>` stops the timer. The code is pretty simple to understand. The point to observe here is the use of `bindtags`. We have easily added these key-sequences to the button .b in a single line. Without the `bindtag` command, we would have to do something like:

```
bind .b  <ButtonPress-1> "+{set count 0; StartTimer %W}"
```

And the same for the binding `<ButtonRelease-1>`. Also these bindings do not really imply what we are trying to achieve. Using the `bindtag` command we have identified these sequences with a name `timer`. If we create another button to do another timer, all we have to do is to invoke `bindtags` command on that button and insert the binding.

Geometry Management

After we've created the widgets and bound the event handlers using `bind`, we need to arrange the widgets on the screen in a way that makes the GUI meaningful and useful. Geometry managers perform this job. Tk currently supports three explicit geometry managers:

- Packer, using the `pack` command
- Placer, using the `place` command
- Table or grid manager, using the `grid` command

Packer

We use the pack command to arrange the slave widgets of a master window or widget in order around the edges of the master. The syntax of the pack command is one of these forms:

```
pack option arg ?arg ...?
pack slave ?slave ...? ?options?
pack configure slave ?slave ...? ?options?
```

Let's look at an example and explore some of the pack options:

```
#!/usr/bin/wish -f

foreach i  {1 2 3 4 } {
    button .b$i -text "Btn $i"
    pack .b$i -side left -padx 2m -pady 1m
}
```

This will produce the following output:

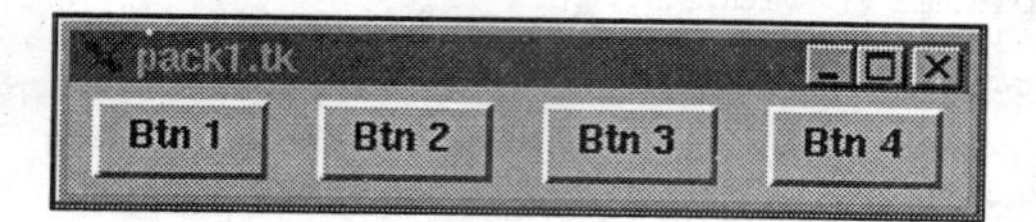

Here, all the buttons are packed to the left of each other, with a horizontal space of two millimeters between each of them and with a space of one millimeter vertically with the master's boundary.

One more pack sequence:

```
#!/usr/bin/wish -f

foreach i  {1 2 3 4 } {
    button .b$i -text "Btn $i"
    pack .b$i -side left -ipadx 2m -ipady 1m
}
```

In the examples, -ipadx specifies that the slaves be internally padded with two millimeters horizontally. Internal padding causes the slave (button) to expand to fill the extra space created.

> **There are many more combinations of the pack command. Refer to the pack man page and Ousterhout's *Tcl and the Tk Toolkit*, Addison-Wesley (ISBN-0-201-63337-X) for more information.**

Placer

Placer geometry manager is used for fixed placement of windows, where you specify the exact size and location of one window, the slave, within another window, the master. We'll use the image example to explain the placer geometry manager. The following code fragment shows how the buttons are created in the puzzle.

```
set order {3 1 6 2 5 7 15 13 4 11 8 9 14 10 12}
for {set i 0} {$i < 15} {set i [expr $i+1]} {
    set num [lindex $order $i]
    set xpos($num) [expr ($i%4)*.25]
    set ypos($num) [expr ($i/4)*.25]

    set x [expr $i%4]
    set y [expr $i/4]
    set butImage [image create photo image-${num} -width 40 -height 40]
    $butImage copy  $image  -from [expr round($x*40)] \
                                  [expr round($y*40)] \
                                  [expr round($x*40+40)] \
                                  [expr round($y*40+40)]
    button .frame.$num -relief raised -image $butImage \
                       -command "puzzleSwitch  $num" \
                       -highlightthickness 0
    place .frame.$num -relx $xpos($num) -rely $ypos($num) \
                      -relwidth .25 -relheight .25
}
```

This loop creates buttons and places them relative to the master, `.frame`. Here, `-relx 0` is the left edge of the master, while `-relx 1` is the right edge of the master and similarly for `-rely 0` and `-rely 1`. Now if you decipher the loop code, you'll see how all the buttons are arranged to form the puzzle.

Grid

The `grid` geometry manager arranges widgets (slaves) in rows and columns inside another window, called the **geometry master**. `grid` is a very powerful geometry manager; using it, we can create complex layouts with ease. Let's see just see how simple it is to create an entry for personnel information using ten lines of Tk code:

```
#!/usr/bin/wish -f

set row 0
foreach item {name email address phone} {
  label .$item-label -text "${item}:"
  entry .$item-entry  -width 20
  grid .$item-label -row $row -column 0 -sticky e
  grid .$item-entry -row $row -column 1 -columnspan 2 -sticky "ew"
  incr row
}

grid columnconfigure . 1 -weight 1
```

If you run this program, you'll see the output like this:

Here the slaves `.$item-label` and `.$item-entry` are arranged in the master, using the `-row $row` and `-column` options. You can also specify row and column span options for the slave using `-rowspan` and `-columnspan` options. These options will span the slaves to occupy span number of rows or columns or both. The line,

```
grid .$item-entry -row $row -column 1 -columnspan 2 -sticky "ew"
```

specifies that the `entry` widget will occupy two columns and `-sticky "ew"` implies that the slave will stretch from east to west in the parcel space available for it. If you just specify one letter in the `-sticky` option, it behaves as an anchoring option. The last line,

```
grid columnconfigure . 1 -weight 1
```

specifies that if the master (`.`) is resized horizontally, then column 1 should get the resized portion.

As we've developed these examples, we've made much use of the grid geometry manager. This is because it makes it so much easier to design and understand layouts. It's been in Tk since version `4.1`.

Focus and Navigation

When you have multiple toplevel windows on your computer screen and you press a key, which one of the windows will receive the `KeyPress` event? The answer is the toplevel window with the focus. So focus determines the target of the keyboard input. Toplevel window focus management is done automatically by the window manager. For example, some window managers automatically set the input focus to a toplevel window whenever the mouse enters it; others redirect the input focus only when the user clicks on a window. Usually, the window manager will set the focus only to toplevel windows, leaving it up to the application to redirect the focus among the children of the toplevel.

Tk provides two application level focus models. `Implicit`, which sets the focus to the widget the mouse is currently on, and `explicit`, where the user must either explicitly click on the widget or navigate to that widget using the keyboard. By default, tab keys are used to navigate focus between widgets in an explicit model.

Tk remembers one focus window for each toplevel (the most recent descendant of that toplevel to receive the focus); when the window manager gives the focus to a toplevel, Tk automatically redirects it to the remembered window. Within a toplevel, by default, Tk uses an explicit focus model. Moving the mouse within a toplevel does not normally change the focus; the focus changes only when a widget decides explicitly to claim the focus (e.g., because of a button click), or when the user types a key, such as *Tab*, that moves the focus.

The focus command syntax is as follows:

```
focus
focus window
focus option ?arg arg ...?
```

For a complete list of the focus command's usage, refer to focus manual page.

Once the application or any of its toplevel windows gets focus, the Tcl procedure tk_focusFollowsMouse may be invoked to create an implicit focus model. It reconfigures Tk so that the focus is set to a window whenever the mouse enters it. For example, the following example will instruct the window manager to give focus to whichever component the mouse is on, once the application toplevel gets the focus. If you run the following example, you will notice the buttons get focus as soon as the mouse is moved over them without a mouse click.

```
tk_focusFollowsMouse

button .b1  -text "Button 1"
button .b2  -text "button 2"
button .b3  -text "button 3"

pack .b1 .b2 .b3 -side left -padx 10
```

The Tcl procedures tk_focusNext and tk_focusPrev implement a focus order among the children of a toplevel; among other things, these are used in the default bindings for *Tab* and *Shift-Tab*.

The syntax of the tk_focusNext and tk_focusPrev commands is as follows:

```
tk_focusNext window
tk_focusPrev window
```

tk_focusNext is a utility procedure used for keyboard traversal. It returns the "next" window after window in focus order. The focus order is determined by the stacking order of windows and the structure of the window hierarchy. Among siblings, the focus order is the same as the stacking order, with the lowest window being first. If a window has children, the window is visited first, followed by its children (recursively), and then by its next sibling. Toplevel windows other than window are skipped, so that tk_focusNext never returns a window in a different toplevel from window.

After computing the next window, tk_focusNext examines the window's -takefocus option, to see whether it should be skipped. If so, tk_focusNext continues on to the next window in the focus order, until it eventually finds a window that will accept the focus or returns back to window.

The tk_focusPrev command is similar to tk_focusNext, except that it returns the window just before the window in the focus order.

The following example illustrates how a widget can avoid the focus by specifying the -takefocus 0 option. When you run the example, the "skip focus" button does not take focus, even though the mouse is on it.

```
tk_focusFollowsMouse

button .b1  -text "Button 1"
button .b2  -text "skip focus" -takefocus 0
button .b3  -text "button 3"

pack .b1 .b2 .b3 -side left -padx 10
```

Option Database

Just as in Motif or Xt, every widget in Tk has a **class** which can be retrieved using the command:

```
winfo class widget-path-name
```

These class names are used to specify application defaults and class bindings for the widget. Tk uses a special database, called the **option database**, to store and retrieve application resources. For example, in the very first program, we used the line:

```
option add *b.activeForeground brown
```

This informed the option database that buttons with names `.b` (it can have any parent) should have a brown `activeForeground` color. We could have specified the button class instead and still had the same effect:

```
option add *Button.activeForeground brown
```

The reason these commands change `activeForeground` is that, when Tk creates a widget, after setting the command line it searches the option database to set the appropriate resources. If it finds a match to the resource, it will use that option, otherwise it will use a default value.

The `option` command does the same things as an X resource file. In fact, we can store all the resources in a file and let the `option` command read the file, just as we did with `hello4.tk` program. We can also use the `option` command to query the options stored, using the syntax:

```
option get window name class
```

The option database is very versatile, much more so than the simple `.Xdefaults` file. We can use it to simulate the same application default loading mechanism that is supported by any Xt-based application. For example, before the application is loaded, the defaults file can be located in the directories specified by X Windows environment variables, like `XFILESEARCHPATH`, `XAPPLRESDIR`, `XUSERFILESEARCHPATH` and `XENVIRONMENT`.

We can now assign priorities to the application defaults file found in those directories while reading them into the application using the `option readfile ...` command. The code for this emulation would look something like this:

```
global env
if [info exists env(XFILESEARCHPATH)] {
   look for the app-defaults file in XFILESEARCHPATH dir
   load the file with priority 1
   } else {
   look in one of {/usr/lib/X11/app-defaults, /usr/openwin/lib/app-defaults,
/usr/lib/app-defaults..} directories and load the file with priority 1
   }
   if [info exists env(XUSERFILESEARCHPATH)] {
      look for the app-defaults file in XUSERFILESEARCHPATH dir
      load the file with priority 2 over riding XFILESEARCHPATH priority
       } elseif [info exists env(XAPPLRESDIR)] {
             look for the app-defaults file in XAPPLRESDIR dir
      load the file with priority 2 over riding XFILESEARCHPATH priority
       } elseif
```

```
         load app defaults file if exists from current dir with priority 2
      }
   if [ the defaults exist in .Xdefaults ] {
      load them with priority 3   }
         if [info exists env(XENVIRONMENT)] {
  load the file XENVIRONMENT as the app defaults file with second-highest priority
   }
   finally load command-line options with the highest priority
```

Inter-application Communication

Tk provides a very powerful mechanism for two applications which share the same display server (though they can be on different screens) to communicate with each other, using the `send` command. For example, application `A` can send application `B` (i.e. with Tcl interpreter name `B`) a command to output the string. `"hello"`:

```
send B [list puts "hello"]
```

Application `B` will receive this command and executes the `puts "hello"` command. For more information on this, refer to the `send` man page.

Selection

Imagine the scenario where a user is operating on a desktop with multiple xterms. The user highlights a selection of text in one xterm, using the left mouse button, and then pastes the selection in another xterm, using the middle button. There are a lot of things going on under the covers during this transaction:

When the user decides to select something in an xterm, the xterm must first of all figure out what information is being selected and then it should become the selection owner. Being the selection owner means that when another application decides to request the selection, the owner should convert the selection to the type specified by the requested application. A client wishing to obtain the selection in a particular format requests the selection from the selection owner. All of these co-operative interactions between X clients is described in the X Inter-Client Communication Conventions Manual (ICCCM)..

`Selection` can be of many types. `PRIMARY`, `SECONDARY` and `CLIPBOARD`. by default, the `PRIMARY` selection named `XA_PRIMARY`, is used by all the clients. A `SECONDARY` selection named `XA_SECONDARY` is used when applications need more than one selection. The `CLIPBOARD` selection is usually used to hold deleted data.

Selection command provides a Tcl interface to the X selection mechanism and implements the full selection functionality described in the X Inter-Client Communication Conventions Manual (ICCCM). The following example shows selection manipulation. It creates a new slave Tk interpreter, with a text widget. It automatically selects the text inside the text using the `sel` tag of text. Using the `sel` tag of the text command will make the selection by default `PRIMARY`. So, when the slave interpreter calls the `selection` own, it is owning the primary selection. The master interpreter then retrieves the selection and outputs it to the `stdout`.

```
#!wish
interp create foo

foo eval {
    load {} Tk
    text .t
    pack .t
    .t insert end "Hello World!"
    .t tag add sel  0.0 end
```

```
    selection own
    .t insert end "\n"
#   .t insert end "[selection get -selection SECONDARY]"
    .t insert end "[selection get ]"

}
puts "[selection get]"
```

If the commented line in the above example is uncommented, the application will output an error because there is no secondary selection. A selection owner can also reject selection retrievals by any other application or component.

Clipboard

In X, `CLIPBOARD` is another type of selection mechanism. The `CLIPBOARD` selection can be used to hold deleted data. For example, a client can place deleted data to the clipboard and exit. Another client can still retrieve the deleted selection from the clipboard, even thought the original client no longer exists. This is not possible with `PRIMARY` and `SECONDARY` selection types, because when a client requests `PRIMARY` or `SECONDARY` selection, the owner will be sent a request. If the owner no longer exists, then the selection request will fail.

The `clipboard` command provides a Tcl interface to the Tk clipboard, which stores data for later retrieval, using the `selection` mechanism. `Tk_clipboard` is not the same as the system clipboard that you see on various operating systems. `Tk_clipboard` is designed to hold deleted data between applications developed using Tk toolkit. In order to copy data into the clipboard, `clipboard clear` must be called, followed by a sequence of one or more calls to `clipboard append`. The following command illustrates the use of the `clipboard` command

```
#!wish
interp create foo

foo eval {
   load {} Tk
   clipboard clear
   clipboard append -type STRING "Clipboard Data"
}
      interp delete foo
puts "[selection get -selection CLIPBOARD]"
```

The above example creates a new Tk interpreter called `foo`. `foo` appends data to the clipboard. The master interpreter deletes the slave interpreter and retrieves the data from the clipboard. As you can see, even though the slave does not exist, the selection can still be retrieved.

Window Manager

Tk provides the wm command so that windows can communicate with the window manager. Window manager functions typically include, managing the keyboard focus between application windows, setting up toplevel window properties, allocating colormaps to windows, positioning toplevel windows on the screen, etc. Since window manager only deals with the toplevel windows of any application and leaves the internal window management to the application, wm command arguments must be toplevel windows. The kinds of functions that a client can request from the window manager include the following:

- iconifying and de-iconifying of a toplevel windows;
- positioning toplevel windows at a particular point on the screen;
- requesting the initial sizes of toplevel windows;
- setting the titles of toplevel windows;
- setting the focus model of an application;
- requesting the height and width of a toplevel window;
- overriding the default window manager decorations, etc. For example:

Using the wm command, one can query the state of a toplevel window in an application as follows:

```
% wm iconify .
% puts "[wm state .]"
iconic
```

Users can also set up window manager protocols on a toplevel window. For example, we can set up a handler on a toplevel window that will get called when the window receives focus or when the window gets deleted.

```
% wm protocol . WM_TAKE_FOCUS {puts "window . got foucs"}
% wm protocol . WM_DELETE_WINDOW {puts "window . is being deleted"; exit}
```

When run, the above code snippet will output "`window . got focus`" when the toplevel window "`.`" gets focus and the string "`window . is being deleted`" when the toplevel window "`.`" is deleted using the window manager delete button.

wm commands can also be used to set or query the title of a toplevel window using the command

```
wm title ?newtitle?.
```

A client can also request that a window manager not decorate a toplevel window. When the client makes such a request, the window manager will not display the iconify, deiconify or resize buttons on the window manager frame of the requested toplevel. The following code snippet requests the window manager to not add any decorations to the toplevel window `.t`

```
toplevel .t
wm withdraw .t
wm transient .t .
wm deiconify .t
```

When run, you will see the following output:

Actually the above code snippet shows more than one functionality of the window manager command. The application first requests the window manager to withdraw the toplevel window, it then asks the window manager to remove the minimize/maximize decorations for the toplevel window and finally it asks the window manager to map the window back to screen.

Dynamic/Static Loading

In the previous sections, we created new interpreters and loaded Tk statically. There are two ways in which interpreters can load the Tk toolkit—statically and dynamically, using the `load` command. For static loading, the executable should be preloaded with Tk. For example, the following code:

```
interp create debugInterp

debugInterp eval {
    load {} Tk
    text .t
    pack .t
    update
}

proc debug {interp args} {
    debugInterp eval [list  .t insert end "$args"]
}

debug . "hello world!"
```

statically loads the Tk executable to a newly created interpreter. The example also shows how to communicate between interpreters. The master interpreter creates a `debug` routine, which communicates with `debugInterp` to display debugging information.

So, how do we load a Tk interpreter dynamically into a `tclsh` application? The following examples illustrate how:

```
interp create debugInterp

debugInterp eval {
    load /usr/local/tk8.2b3/unix/libtk8.2.so Tk
    text .t
    pack .t
    update
}

proc debug {interp args} {
    debugInterp eval [list  .t insert end "$args"]
}

debug . "hello world!"
vwait foob
```

The above code assumes that you have compiled the Tcl/Tk distributions so that they are dynamically-loadable and the Tk dynamic library `libtk8.2.so` is located in `/usr/local/tk8.2b3/unix/` directory. As you can see from the above code, `tclsh` creates a new interpreter and loads Tk dynamically into the newly-created interpreter and the master interpreter enters the event loop using the `vwait` command. If the master interpreter did not enter the event loop, the application exits without warning. If you run the above code using this command:

```
Tclsh8.0 dynamicLoad.tk
```

the Tk interpreter will get loaded dynamically!

Safe Tk

Suppose you download a Tcl script from the network and execute it. If the script is malicious, it can do a lot of damage to your system. For example, it can delete all of your files, or transfer files to another computer. How do you ensure that these untrusted scripts do not do any damage? In 1994, Marshall and Rose created Safe-Tcl, which was originally conceived as a mechanism to allow email messages to contain Tcl scripts that would execute on the receiver's computer. Safe-Tcl was incorporated into the core code in Tcl version 7.5.

The goal of Safe-Tcl is to create a sandbox that allows users to safely execute untrusted Tcl scripts in the sandbox without having to worry about any side effects

Safe interpreters have a restricted command set. The following commands are hidden in a safe interpreter.

`cd`	`exec`	`exit`	`fconfigure`
`glob`	`load`	`open`	`socket`
`source`	`vwait`	`pwd`	`file`

The `safe base` Tcl manual page will describe how to create these safe interpreters. Sometimes, it might be necessary to give the newly-created safe interpreter some restricted access; for example, it might be allowed to open files in a particular directory. Safe-Tcl provides mechanisms for allowing such restricted access. Interpreters created with the `::safe::interpCreate` command give mediated access to potentially dangerous functionality through untrusted scripts by using the alias mechanism. Thus, Safe-Tcl is a mechanism for executing untrusted Tcl scripts safely and for providing mediated access by such scripts to potentially dangerous functionality.

Just like Safe-Tcl, it is necessary to create sandboxes to execute untrusted Tk scripts. For example, you don't want the Tk applet to delete all of your toplevel windows or to steal your X selection. Safe Tk adds the ability to configure the interpreter for safe Tk operations and load the Tk into safe interpreters. By default, you can't load Tk into a safe interpreter, because the safe interpreter does not allow load commands. Safe Tk also isolates the untrusted Tk scripts to be executed in a sandbox so that no damage can be done

The `::safe::loadTk` command initializes the required data structures in the named safe interpreter and then loads Tk into it. The command returns the name of the safe interpreter. `::safe::loadTk` adds the value of `tk_library` taken from the master interpreter to the virtual access path of the safe interpreter, so that auto-loading will work in the safe interpreter.

The following examples illustrate that you cannot load Tk into a safe interpreter unless you use the `::safe::loadTk` command

```
::safe::interpCreate  safeInterp

::safe::interpAddToAccessPath safeInterp /tmp

::safe::loadTk safeInterp

interp create -safe safeInterp2

puts " 1 -> [interp hidden safeInterp]"
puts " 2 -> [interp hidden safeInterp2]"

puts " 1 -> [interp aliases safeInterp]"
puts " 2 -> [interp aliases safeInterp2]"

safeInterp eval {
    text .t
    pack .t
    update
}

safeInterp2 eval {
     load {} Tk
 }
```

When you run the above script, you will see the following error message,

```
$ wish safeInterp.tk
 1 -> file socket send open pwd glob exec encoding clipboard load fconfigure source
exit toplevel wm grab menu selection tk bell cd
 2 -> file socket open pwd glob exec encoding load fconfigure source exit cd
 1 -> file load sourte exit encoding
 2 ->
Error in startup script: invalid command name "safeInterp2"
    while executing
"safeInterp2 eval {
     load {} Tk
 }"
    (file "safeInterp.tk" line 26)
```

informing you that you cannot load Tk into a safe interpreter, which is not created using the `::safe::createInterp` command. If you want to see how safe interpreters are used, take a look at the `safeDebug.tk` example in the distribution.

A Mega-Widget

We have now seen how to use various widget commands to create applications. Sometimes, people find a need to display their information in ways that require new types of widgets, such as panes, spreadsheets, notebooks, spinboxes, etc. Although the Tk team at Scriptics is planning to add these widgets to the core, as of this writing, they have not been added. So the question is: How does one go about creating custom widgets?

There are two ways to do this. One way is to use Tcl and Tk's C extension API, also known as TEA. The other way to do it is to use pure Tcl and existing Tk widgets. Since we have not yet discussed Tcl and Tk's C API, and it would in fact merit far more coverage than we can give it here, let's just go ahead and use pure Tcl and existing Tk widgets to create a MegaWidget. The MegaWidget that we are going to create is a tree widget. As of now, Tk does not have a built-in tree widget. This widget example is by no means complete, but it is quite useful and will steer you in the right direction

> **The rendering algorithm and some of the interface ideas in this example are taken from GPLed `comp.lang.tcl` posts. None of the other implementations that I have encountered have the flexibility of this package/namespace-based implementation.**

We will use Tcl's package and namespace mechanisms to encapsulate our tree widget into an abstract data structure. Next, the question is what kind of widget and configuration commands should we provide for this tree widget? Configuration-wise, we should provide most of the standard configuration options such as `-font`, `- backgroundcolor`, and some more tree-specific configuration options. Since tree widget supports hierarchies, we should provide methods such as `additem`, `delitem`, `config`, `setselection`, `getselection`, etc. So, let's just go ahead and define the tree widget package as follows.

```
#
#       Sample tree mega-widget.Can be used to display hierachies. The clients
#       who use this package need to specify parent and tail procedures for any
#       element of the tree hierarchy. All the nodes that get stored inside the
#       tree are complete path names separated by '/'. The toplevel node is
#       always /
#

package provide tree 1.0

namespace eval tree {
   variable tree

    #
    # default font setup
    #

    switch $tcl_platform(platform) {
       unix {
     set tree(font) \
         -adobe-helvetica-medium-r-normal-*-11-80-100-100-p-56-iso8859-1
       }
       windows {
     set tree(font) \
         -adobe-helvetica-medium-r-normal-*-14-100-100-100-p-76-iso8859-1
       }
    }

    #
    # Bitmaps used to show which parts of the tree can be opened/closed
    #

    set maskdata "#define solid_width 9\n#define solid_height 9"
    append maskdata {
```

```
        static unsigned char solid_bits[] = {
     0xff, 0x01, 0xff, 0x01, 0xff, 0x01, 0xff, 0x01, 0xff, 0x01, 0xff, 0x01,
     0xff, 0x01, 0xff, 0x01, 0xff, 0x01
        };
    }
    set data "#define open_width 9\n#define open_height 9"
    append data {
        static unsigned char open_bits[] = {
     0xff, 0x01, 0x01, 0x01, 0x01, 0x01, 0x01, 0x01, 0x7d, 0x01, 0x01, 0x01,
     0x01, 0x01, 0x01, 0x01, 0xff, 0x01
        };
    }

    set tree(openbm) [image create bitmap openbm -data $data \
            -maskdata $maskdata \
            -foreground black -background white]

    set data "#define closed_width 9\n#define closed_height 9"
    append data {
        static unsigned char closed_bits[] = {
     0xff, 0x01, 0x01, 0x01, 0x11, 0x01, 0x11, 0x01, 0x7d, 0x01, 0x11, 0x01,
     0x11, 0x01, 0x01, 0x01, 0xff, 0x01
        };
    }
    set tree(closedbm) [image create bitmap closedbm -data $data \
              -maskdata $maskdata \
              -foreground black -background white]

     namespace export create additem delitem config setselection getselection
     namespace export openbranch closebranch labelat
}
```

As shown above, tree widget exports one package variable called `tree`, as well as methods, such as `additem`, `delitem`, `config`, `setselection` etc. a tree package variable is used to hold instance information of all the trees created. As you can see from the above code, `tree` also creates some images to display open and closed branches and stores them inside the tree data structure.

Our next step is to define the widget commands. First, we will define the `tree::create` command. This command basically parses the configuration options and creates a canvas with the pathname specified by the `create` command. The `create` command also looks for `-parent` and `-tail` widget creation options. These options are procedures specified by the client, so that the tree command can determine the parent and tail of any of its nodes. Tail is basically the end part of the node name. For example, suppose the node is named `a/b/c`. The `tail` on this command will return `c` (presuming the character '`/`' is used as a path separator). The `parent` command will return `/a/b`. The tree mega-widget enforces '`/`' to be the path separator and all nodes are represented with absolute paths.

The philosophy behind these `-parent` and `-tail` option commands is to allow the tree to display any hierarchical information, and not just directory structures. The create command also initializes variables, such as `selection` and `selidx` which are the currently the selected node and its tag. The `create` command arranges the tree to be redrawn at a later time.

```
# tree::create --
#
#   Create a new tree widget. Canvas is used to emulate a tree
#   widget. Initialized all the tree specific data structures. $args become
#   the configuration arguments to the canvas widget from which the tree is
#   constructed.  #

# Arguments:
#    -paren   proc
#
#      sets the parent procedure provided by the application. tree
#      widget will use this procedure to determine the parent of an
#      element. This procedure will be called with the node as an
#      argument
#
#   -tail    proc  [Given a complete path this proc will give the end-element
#                        name]
#
# Results:    A tree widget with the path $w is created.
#

proc tree::create {w args} {
   variable tree
   set newArgs {}

   for {set i 0} {$i < [llength $args]} {incr i} {
      set arg [lindex $args $i]
      switch -glob -- $arg {
    -paren* {set tree($w:parenproc) [lindex $args [expr $i +1]]; incr i}
    -tail* {set tree($w:tailproc) [lindex $args [expr $i +1]]; incr i}
    default {lappend newArgs $arg}
    }
      }

   if ![info exists tree($w:parenproc)] {
      set tree($w:parenproc) parent
   }

   if ![info exists tree($w:tailproc)] {
      set tree($w:tailproc) tail
   }

  eval canvas $w -bg white $newArgs
  bind $w <Destroy> "tree::delitem $w /"
  tree::DfltConfig $w /
  tree::BuildWhenIdle $w
  set tree($w:selection) {}
  set tree($w:selidx) {}
}
```

When the tree is created, a root node by the name of / is automatically created. Every time a new node is added, the nodes are initialized with some default configuration, including, for example, the children associated with the node, whether the node should be displayed open, the icon and tags associated with the node. `tree::DfltConfig` is for node initialization.

```
# tree::DfltConfig  --
#
#   Internal fuction used to initial the attributes associated with an item/node.
Usually called when an item is added into the tree
#
#  Arguments:
#    wid   tree widget
#    node  complete path of the new node
#
#  Results:
#    Initializes the attributes associated with a node.

proc tree::DfltConfig {wid node} {
  variable tree
  set tree($wid:$node:children) {}
  set tree($wid:$node:open) 0
  set tree($wid:$node:icon) {}
  set tree($wid:$node:tags) {}
}
```

Just like any other Tk widget, tree widget should support the `-config` widget method. Tree widget supports this using the `tree::config` class method.

```
# tree::config --
#
#   Fuction to set tree widget configuration options.
#
#  Arguments:
#   args  any valid configuration option a canvas widget takes
#
#  Results:
#   Configures the underlying canvas widget with the options
#

proc tree::config {wid args} {
variable tree
    set newArgs {}
    for {set i 0} {$i < [llength $args]} {incr i} {
      set arg [lindex $args $i]
      switch -glob -- $arg {
    -paren* {set tree($w:parenproc) [lindex $args [expr $i +1]]; incr i}
    -tail* {set tree($w:tailproc) [lindex $args [expr $i +1]]; incr i}
    default {lappend newArgs $arg}
    }
      }
  eval $wid config $newArgs
}
```

Now that we are done with the creation and configuration of tree widget, the next step is to add an item. This routine makes sure that a duplicate item is not added to the tree. It finds out the parent of the new item and adds it into its children. The routine also parses the item tags, such as `-image` and `-tags` and sets the attributes of the item. The `-image` option is used to display an icon next to the item while rendering. The `-tags` option attaches tags to the newly added item. The `additem` routine also arranges the tree widget to be drawn when the application is not busy:

```
#  tree::additem --
#
#       Called to add a new node to the tree.
#
#  Arguments:
#       wid    tree widget
#       node   complete path name of the node (path is separated by /)
#       args   can be -image val, -tags {taglist} to identify the item
#
#  Results:
#       Adds the new item and configures the new item
#

proc tree::additem {wid node args} {
  variable tree
   set parent [$tree($wid:parenproc) $node]
   set n [eval $tree($wid:tailproc) $node]
  if {![info exists tree($wid:$parent:open)]} {
    error "parent item \"$parent\" is missing"
  }
  set i [lsearch -exact $tree($wid:$parent:children) $n]
  if {$i>=0} {
     return
  }
  lappend tree($wid:$parent:children) $n
  set tree($wid:$parent:children) [lsort $tree($wid:$parent:children)]
  tree::DfltConfig $wid $node
  foreach {op arg} $args {
    switch -exact -- $op {
      -image {set tree($wid:$node:icon) $arg}
      -tags {set tree($wid:$node:tags) $arg}
    }
  }
  tree::BuildWhenIdle $wid
}
```

Deleting an item does the opposite of `additem` and removes the item from the tree data structure and from its parent's children list. It also arranges the tree widget to be drawn at a later time:

```
#  tree::delitem  --
#
#   Deletes the specified item from the widget
#
#  Arguments:
#   wid   tree widget
#   node  complete path of the node
#
#  Results:
#   If the node exists, it will be deleted.
#

proc tree::delitem {wid node} {
  variable tree
  if {![info exists tree($wid:$node:open)]} return
  if {[string compare $node /]==0} {
    # delete the whole widget
    catch {destroy $wid}
    foreach t [array names tree $wid:*] {
      unset tree($t)
    }
  }
  foreach c $tree($wid:$node:children) {
    catch {tree::delitem $wid $node/$c}
  }
  unset tree($wid:$node:open)
  unset tree($wid:$node:children)
  unset tree($wid:$node:icon)
  set parent [$tree($wid:parenproc) $node]
   set n [eval $tree($wid:tailproc) $node]
  set i [lsearch -exact $tree($wid:$parent:children) $n]
  if {$i>=0} {
    set tree($wid:$parent:children) [lreplace $tree($wid:$parent:children) $i $i]
  }
  tree::BuildWhenIdle $wid
}
```

The user has control over which node in the item can be assigned as a selection. `setselection` and `getselection` routines are used to accomplish the job. The selection object is drawn with a highlighted background:

```
 tree::setselection  --
#
#   Makes the given node as the currently selected node.
#
#  Arguments:
#   wid - tree widget
#   node - complete path of the one of nodes
#
#  Results:
#   The given node will be selected
#

proc tree::setselection {wid node} {
  variable tree
  set tree($wid:selection) $node
  tree::DrawSelection $wid
}
```

```
#  tree::getselection  --
#
#   Get the currently selected tree node
#
#  Arguments:
#   wid - tree widget
#
#  Results:
#   If a node is currently selected it will be returned otherwise NULL
#

proc tree::getselection wid {
  variable tree
  return $tree($wid:selection)
}
```

The next task is building/rendering the tree. The algorithm recursively calls each node to draw itself and its children. After the tree is drawn, it will set the scroll region so that when the tree widget is associated with scrollbars it will behave properly. It also draws the current selection:

```
#  tree::Build --
#
#   Internal function to rebuild the tree
#
#  Arguments:
#   wid -  tree widgets
#
#  Results:
#
#     This routine has no complex logic in it. Deletes all the current items
#    on the canvas associated with the tree and re-builds the tree.  #
#
#

proc tree::Build wid {
  variable tree
  $wid delete all
  catch {unset tree($wid:buildpending)}
  set tree($wid:y) 30
  tree::BuildNode $wid / 10
  $wid config -scrollregion [$wid bbox all]
  tree::DrawSelection $wid
}
```

The meat of the tree drawing algorithm is `BuildNode`. It is a basic tree-drawing algorithm that draws the parent and each of its children if the open attribute of the parent node is set. If the open attribute of any of the child nodes is set, `BuildNode` will be called recursively to display its children. The rendering algorithm should be pretty self-explanatory:

```
#  tree::BuildNode --
#
#   Function called by tree::build to incrementally build each node
#
#  Arguments:
#   wid - tree widget
#       node - complete path of the node
#   in - the starting x-cordinate
#
#  Results:
#   The node gets drawn
#
```

```
proc tree::BuildNode {wid node in} {
  variable tree
  if {$node=="/"} {
    set vx {}
  } else {
    set vx $node
  }
  set start [expr $tree($wid:y)-10]
  foreach c $tree($wid:$node:children) {
    set y $tree($wid:y)
    incr tree($wid:y) 17
    $wid create line $in $y [expr $in+10] $y -fill gray50
    set icon $tree($wid:$vx/$c:icon)
    set taglist x
    foreach tag $tree($wid:$vx/$c:tags) {
      lappend taglist $tag
    }
    set x [expr $in+12]
    if {[string length $icon]>0} {
      set k [$wid create image $x $y -image $icon -anchor w -tags $taglist]
      incr x 20
      set tree($wid:tag:$k) $vx/$c
    }
    set j [$wid create text $x $y -text $c -font $tree(font) \
                              -anchor w -tags $taglist]
    set tree($wid:tag:$j) $vx/$c
    set tree($wid:$vx/$c:tag) $j
    if {[string length $tree($wid:$vx/$c:children)]} {
      if {$tree($wid:$vx/$c:open)} {
         set j [$wid create image $in $y -image $tree(openbm)]
         $wid bind $j <1> "set tree::tree($wid:$vx/$c:open) 0; tree::Build $wid"
         tree::BuildLayer $wid $vx/$c [expr $in+18]
      } else {
         set j [$wid create image $in $y -image $tree(closedbm)]
         $wid bind $j <1> "set tree::tree($wid:$vx/$c:open) 1; tree::Build $wid"
      }
    }
  }
  set j [$wid create line $in $start $in [expr $y+1] -fill gray50 ]
  $wid lower $j
}
```

Now, after the tree gets displayed, if the user chooses to open any of the branches by clicking the '+' image next to a node then the following openbranch routine will arrange to redraw the tree by displaying the node's children:

```
#  tree::openbranch --
#
#       A callback that gets called to open a node to show its children
#
#  Arguments:
#       wid - tree widget
#       node - the node whose children should be shown
#
#  Results:
#       The children of the node will be drawn
#

proc tree::openbranch {wid node} {
  variable tree
  if {[info exists tree($wid:$node:open)] && $tree($wid:$node:open)==0
      && [info exists tree($wid:$node:children)]
      && [string length $tree($wid:$node:children)]>0} {
    set tree($wid:$node:open) 1
    tree::Build $wid
  }
}
```

Similarly, when the user clicks on the '-' image next to a node, the `closebranch` routine will arrange the tree to be redrawn by closing the branch and undisplaying the children:

```
# tree::closebranch   --
#
#        The opposite of open branch, see above
#
#  Arguments:
#
#
#  Results:
#

proc tree::closebranch {wid node} {
  variable tree
  if {[info exists tree($wid:$node:open)] && $tree($wid:$node:open)==1} {
    set tree($wid:$node:open) 0
    tree::Build $wid
  }
}
```

The `DrawSelection` routine will highlight the currently selected node.

```
#  tree::DrawSelection --
#
#        Highlights the current selection
#
#  Arguments:
#        wid - tree widget
#
#  Results:
#        The current selection will be high-lighted with skyblue
#

proc tree::DrawSelection wid {
  variable tree
  if {[string length $tree($wid:selidx)]} {
    $wid delete $tree($wid:selidx)
  }
  set node $tree($wid:selection)
  if {[string length $node]==0} return
  if {![info exists tree($wid:$node:tag)]} return
  set bbox [$wid bbox $tree($wid:$node:tag)]
  if {[llength $bbox]==4} {
    set i [eval $wid create rectangle $bbox -fill skyblue -outline {{}}]
    set tree($wid:selidx) $i
    $wid lower $i
  } else {
    set tree($wid:selidx) {}
  }
}
```

The `BuildWhenIdle` routine is used to minimize the drawing refreshes by collecting all the redraw routines and arranging an event handler to draw the tree.

```
#  tree::BuildWhenIdle --
#
#       Function to reduce the number redraws of the tree. When a redraw is not
#       immediately warranted this function gets called
#
#  Arguments:
#       wid   - tree wiget
#
#  Results:
#       Set the tree widget to be redrawn in future.
#

proc tree::BuildWhenIdle wid {
  variable tree
  if {![info exists tree($wid:buildpending)]} {
    set tree($wid:buildpending) 1
    after idle "tree::Build $wid"
  }
}
```

Finally, the `tree::labelat` routine will return the node at a given `x` and `y` widget position. The magic is to use the canvas built-in commands:

```
#  tree::labelat --
#
#       Returns the tree node closest to  x,y co-ordinates
#
#  Arguments:
#       wid       tree widget
#       x,y       co-ordinates
#
#  Results:
#       The node closest to x,y will be returned.

proc tree::labelat {wid x y} {
  set x [$wid canvasx $x]
  set y [$wid canvasy $y]
  variable tree
  foreach m [$wid find overlapping $x $y $x $y] {
    if {[info exists tree($wid:tag:$m)]} {
      return $tree($wid:tag:$m)
    }
  }
  return ""
}
```

Since the underlying widget for the tree is canvas, this tree widget will support all the canvas binding commands with the same syntax.

Package File Generation

Now that we have defined and tree mega-widget, how do we use it? Before we dive into developing a new application using the tree widget, we have to generate a pkgIndex file for the tree widget. To do this, copy the tree.tcl file into /usr/local/lib/tcl and run the following command in a wish shell:

```
$ wish
% cd /usr/local/lib/tcl
% pkg_mkIndex . tree.tcl
```

This command will create a pkgIndex.tcl file in the /usr/local/lib/tcl directory. Make sure that there is no prior pkgIndex.tcl file before you create it, because tcl will clobber it.

Once you have generated pkgIndex.tcl file, you need to instruct your application that you want to use the tree widget by appending /usr/local/lib/tcl to the auto_loadpath by adding the following lines:

```
Lappend auto_path /usr/local/lib/tcl
Package require tree
```

An Application Using the Tree Mega-Widget

Let's use our tree package and develop a simple application. The application we are going to develop will display the root system file hierarchy.

We first inform the application of the location of the package file and use it to load the tree package:

```
#!/usr/local/bin/wish
#
# Simple application showing the use of tree mega widget
#
lappend auto_path /usr/local/lib/tk
package require tree
```

Now we have to inform the tree widget on parent and tail routines. By default, they are normal file dirname and tail routines, because we are displaying a root file system:

```
#
# Create utility procs that tree wiget uses to query parent
# and tail components of a node
#
proc parent {item} {
   return [file dirname $item]
}
proc tail {item} {
   return [file tail $item]
}
```

We create images to display directory and file images:

```
# Create imanges that we use to display directory and a normal file
#

image create photo idir -data {
    R0lGODdhEAAQAPIAAAAAAHh4eLi4uPj4APj4+P///wAAAAAAACwAAAAAEAAQAAADPVi63P4w
    LkKCtTTnUsXwQqBtAfh910UU4ugGAEucpgnLNY3Gop7folwNOBOeiEYQ0acDpp6pGAFArVqt
    hQQAO///
}
image create photo ifile -data {
    R0lGODdhEAAQAPIAAAAAAHh4eLi4uPj4+P///wAAAAAAAAAAACwAAAAAEAAQAAADPkixzPOD
    yADrWE8qC8WN0+BZAmBq1GMOqwigXFXCrGk/cxjjr27fLtout6n9eMIYMTXsFZsogXRKJf6u
    P0kCADv/
}
```

Next, we create a routine that dynamically adds the children of the node if the node happens to be the directory when the user double clicks on the item

```
#
# Dynamically add entries to the tree widget
#
proc AddDir {wid dir} {
    if ![file isdirectory $dir ] {
        return;
    }
    foreach file [exec ls $dir] {
        set file [file join $dir $file]
        if [file isdirectory $file] {
            tree::additem $wid [file join $dir $file] -image idir
        } else {
            tree::additem $wid [file join $dir $file] -image ifile
        }
    }
}
```

The main process creates the tree and sets up the double click bindings for the tree widget. It also adds the toplevel node to the tree.

```
#
# main proc
#
#
# Create tree wiget and set up bindings
#
tree::create .t -width 150 -height 400

#
# open a node when gets double clicked.
#
.t bind x <Double-1> {
    puts "Called"
    set child [tree::labelat %W %x %y]
    AddDir %W $child
    tree::openbranch %W $child
}


AddDir .t /

# mange the wiget

pack .t -fill both -expand 1
update
```

When you run the program you should see something similar to the following:

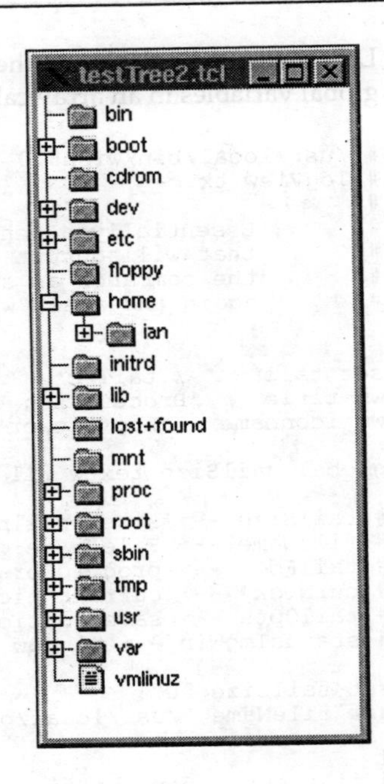

Tk Process Log Viewer

Now that we have seen how to create a mega-widget, how about creating an application using Tcl 8.0's new features, such as the event mechanism? More often than not, Linux users find themselves running the 'tail -f' or 'find / -print' command every day. So why don't we develop an application to display the outputs of those commands in a text window? We will also create shortcuts (nicks) to the commands they run, so that they can re-run them by clicking on the shortcut.

This application supports two types of logs – file logs and command logs. File logs are 'tail -f filename' type commands and command logs are 'find / -print'. For file log outputs, the user will specify a filename and a nick (shortcut). A command of the type tail -f filename will be constructed and associated with the given nick. For command logs, the user has to specify the entire command name and nickname.

Let's call this application "Tk Process Log Viewer". So, what do we need to build such an application? User interface wise, we need a menu bar for process commands, a text widget to display the output, a status bar to display error messages, a couple of entry boxes to specify commands and their nicknames, and an option button to display currently-available nicks. We also need a stop button to stop the current view process, and a delete button in the menu bar to delete any unwanted shortcuts (nicks).

Let's just start by declaring the global variables that we will use to build the application. We store all these global variables in an array called `tailOpts`.

```
#!/usr/local/bin/wish8.0
# logView.tk  --
#
#       Essentially a general purpose GUI wrapper to tail, gui and any commands
#       that will output data continuosly. This GUI has the ability to record
#       the commands as smart buttons, so that you can re-run the same commands
#       again and again without having to retype


set tailRc "~/.tailrc"
wm title .  "Process Log Viewer"
wm iconname . "Log Viewer"

global tailSize textw fileName tailFd curNick tailOpts statusImgWin

# tailSize --> size in lines of tail output to display
# fileName --> File name: variable
# tailFd   --> proc fd or file fd of current tail process
# curNick  --> current nick being shown; nick essentially a shortcut to a cmd.
# tailOpts --> saved options
# statusImgWin --> window showing what kind of error it is!

set tailSize 20
set fileName "/usr/local/processlog/logView.tk";     #include your own path here

#
# file types for the file selection dialog box.
#

set tailOpts(types) {
   {"All files"                    *}
   {"Text files"                   {.txt .doc}         }
   {"Text files"                   {}             TEXT}

   {"Tcl Scripts"                  {.tcl}         TEXT}
   {"C Source Files"               {.c .h}             }
   {"All Source Files"             {.tcl .c .h}        }
   {"Image Files"                  {.gif}              }
   {"Image Files"                  {.jpeg .jpg}        }
   {"Image Files"                  ""      {GIFF JPEG}}
}
set tailOpts(wins) {}
```

Next, we will build the user interface. First, the menu bar with **File** and **Edit** commands. The **File** menu will support the addition of new command nicks through an "Add New…" command button. The **File** menu will also contain an exit button to exit the application. The **Edit** menu will contain "Delete Nicks" button to edit the current nicks.

```
proc BuildTailGui {w} {
    global tailSize textw fileName tailFd curNick tailOpts statusImgWin
    global viewOptMenu

    if {$w == "."} {
      set w "";
    }

    #
    # Build Menu for file
    #

    menu $w.menu -tearoff 0
```

```
# File menu
set m $w.menu.file
menu $m -tearoff 0
$w.menu add cascade -label "File" -menu $m -underline 0
$m add command -label "Add New ..." -command {AddNew} -underline 0
$m add command -label "Exit" -command {exit} -underline 0

# Edit Menu

set m $w.menu.edit
menu $m -tearoff 0
$w.menu add cascade -label "Edit" -menu $m -underline 0
$m add command -label "Delete Nicks.." -command {DeleteNicks} -underline 0

# Help Menu
set m $w.menu.help
menu $m -tearoff 0
$w.menu add cascade -label "Help" -menu $m -underline 0
$m add command -label "About..." -underline 0 -command {
    tk_messageBox -parent . -title "Process Log Viewer" -type \
    ok -message    "Tk Tail Tool \nby Krishna Vedati(kvedati@yahoo.com)"
}
```

The routine then adds a text widget to display the output of any log process and a status bar to display error and informational messages.

Next, the routine builds rows of widgets. The first row will enable users to add file type nicks to the application. The second row will enable users to add command-type nicks. The last row contains a stop button to stop the current log process and an option button to quickly choose a short cut.

```
#
# Create status/error message window
#

frame $w.status  -relief sunken -bd 2
set statusImgWin [label $w.status.flag -bitmap info]
label $w.status.lab -textvariable statusText -anchor w -bg "wheat"
pack $w.status.flag -side left
pack $w.status.lab -side left -fill both -expand 1

#
# File name: entry panel
#

frame $w.file
label $w.file.label -text "File name:" -width 13 -anchor w
entry $w.file.entry -width 30 -textvariable fileName
button $w.file.choose -text "..." -command \
   "set fileName \[tk_getOpenFile -filetypes \$tailOpts(types) \
    -parent \[winfo toplevel $w.file\]\];"

button $w.file.button -text "Tail File" \
  -command "AddToView  file \$fileName"
pack $w.file.label $w.file.entry -side left
pack $w.file.choose -side left -pady 5 -padx 10
pack $w.file.button -side left -pady 5 -padx 10
bind $w.file.entry <Return> " AddToView  file \$fileName"
focus $w.file.entry

#
# Command entry panel
#
```

```
    frame $w.fileC
    label $w.fileC.cLabel -text "Command:" -width 13 -anchor w
    entry $w.fileC.cEntry -width 40 -textvariable command
    label $w.fileC.nLabel -text "Nick:" -anchor w
    entry $w.fileC.nEntry -width 15 -textvariable nick
    button $w.fileC.add -text "Add" -command "AddToView \"command\"\
        \$command \$nick;"
    pack $w.fileC.cLabel $w.fileC.cEntry -side left
    pack $w.fileC.nLabel -side left -pady 5 -padx 10
    pack $w.fileC.nEntry -side left -pady 5 -padx 5
    pack $w.fileC.add -side left -pady 5 -padx 5

    # Option Menu command panel

    frame $w.optF
    label $w.optF.label -text "View:" -width 12 -anchor w
    set viewOptMenu [tk_optionMenu $w.optF.optB curNick " "]
    button $w.optF.stop -text "Stop" -command Stop

    pack $w.optF.label -side left
    pack $w.optF.optB -side left -pady 5
    pack $w.optF.stop -side left -pady 5

    # create text widget
    frame $w.textf -bg red
    text $w.textf.text -height [expr $tailSize] -xscrollcommand \
       "$w.textf.scrollh set" -yscrollcommand "$w.textf.scrollv set" -bg lightblue
    set textw $w.textf.text
    scrollbar $w.textf.scrollh -orient horizontal -command "$w.textf.text xview"
    scrollbar $w.textf.scrollv -orient vertical -command "$w.textf.text yview"

    pack $w.textf.scrollv -side right -fill y -expand 1
    pack $w.textf.scrollh -side bottom -fill x -expand 1
    pack $w.textf.text -fill x -fill y -expand 1


    # pack all the frames
    [winfo toplevel $w.textf] configure -menu $w.menu
    pack $w.status -side bottom -fill x -pady 2m
    pack $w.file -side top -fill x -expand 1
    pack $w.fileC -side top -fill x -expand 1
    pack $w.optF -side top -fill x -expand 1
    pack $w.textf -side top -fill x -fill y -expand 1

}
```

Once the user sets up a command or a file-type nick, the `TailFile` method will get called. This method makes sure that the specified file exists. It creates the command and opens it as a process. Then, it binds a read event to the file descriptor and returns. The read event will call `TailUpdate` every time the file identifier associated with the process is readable:

```
#  TailFile --
#
#       Show the tail of the request file.
#
#  Arguments:
#       file name to be tailed.
#
#  Results:
#       The tail of the file is shown in the window.
#

proc TailFile { type file {nick ""}} {
   global tailSize tailFd  textw curNick
```

```
    set w $textw
    catch {
        fileevent $tailFd readable {}
        close $tailFd
        update
    }
    $w delete 1.0 end

    if {$type == ""} {
        $w insert end "Illegal type...";
        return
    }
    if {$type == "file"} {
        if {$file == ""} {
            $w insert end "please specify a valid filename..."
            return
        }
        if ![file exists $file] {
            DeleteFromView $file
            $w insert end "file $file does not exist..."
            return
        }
        set nick $file
    } elseif {$type == "command"} {
        if {$file == ""} {
            $w insert end "please specify a command..."
            return
        }
    }

    if {$type == "file"} {
        set tailFd [open "|tail -f $file" r]
        wm title [winfo toplevel $w] "Tail tool \[tail -f $file\]"
    } elseif {$type == "command"} {
        if [catch {set tailFd [open "|$file" r]}] {
            SetStatus error  "can't execute command $file..."
            DeleteFromView $nick
            set curNick ""
            return
        }

        wm title [winfo toplevel $w] "Tail tool \[tail |$file\]"
    }
    fconfigure $tailFd -blocking 0
    set lines 0
    fileevent $tailFd readable "TailUpdate \$tailFd"
}
```

The `TailUpdate` procedure gets called as part of the event handler on the current log process read status. When this procedure gets called, it collects the output from the process and inserts it into the text widget. It also makes sure that at any given time, no more than `$tailSize` lines are shown in the text window:

```
proc TailUpdate {fileFd} {
   global textw curNick
   global tailSize tailFd

   set w $textw
   if [eof $tailFd] {
      fileevent $tailFd readable {}
      $w insert end "Tailing \"$curNick\" done..."
      return
   }

   set line [gets $tailFd]

   $w insert end $line
   $w insert end "\n"

   set lines [lindex [split [$w index end] .] 0]
   if {$lines == [expr $tailSize+1]} {
      $w delete 1.0 2.0
   }
   $w yview moveto 1.0
}
```

The `Stop` call-back is used to stop the current `logProcess`.

```
#
# Stop the current tailing process
#

proc Stop {} {
   global tailFd
   set pid [pid $tailFd]
   catch {exec kill -9 $pid}
}
```

The `AddNew` procedure gets called every time the user adds a new shortcut through the **File** menu's **Add New..** menu command. It creates a simple GUI for the user to create a new command nick.

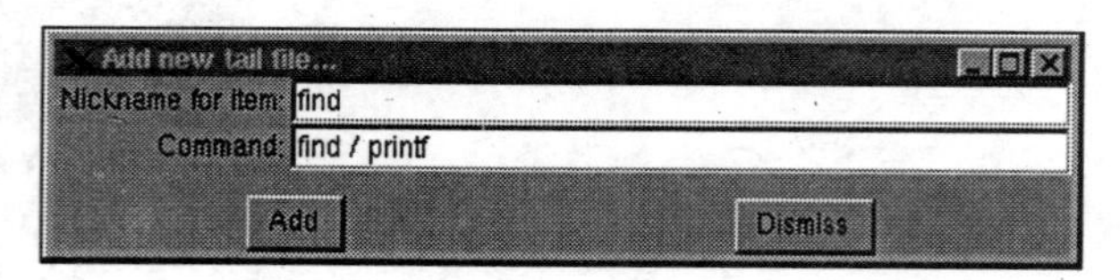


```
#  AddNew --
#       Add a new tail file to the system
#
#  Arguments:
#       none.
#
#  Results:
#

proc AddNew {args} {
   toplevel .addnew
   set w .addnew
   wm title $w "Add new tail file..."
```

```
   frame  $w.top
   frame $w.sep -bd 2  -relief ridge
   frame $w.bot

   set k $w.top

   label $k.name -text "Nickname for item:"
   label $k.command -text "Command:"

   grid $k.name -row 0 -column 0 -sticky e
   grid $k.command -row 1 -column 0 -sticky e

   entry $k.nameE -textvariable nameE -width 40
   entry $k.commandE -textvariable commandE -width 50

   grid $k.nameE -row 0 -column 1 -sticky ew
   grid $k.commandE -row 1 -column 1 -sticky ew

   grid columnconfigure $k 1 -weight 1
   grid propagate $k 1

   pack $w.top  -side top -fill both -expand 1
   pack $w.sep -side top -fill x -expand 1 -pady 5
   pack $w.bot -side top -fill x -expand 1


   button $w.bot.apply -text "Add" -command "AddToView \"command\"  \"\$commandE\"
\"\$nameE\""
   button $w.bot.dismiss -text "Dismiss" -command {destroy .addnew}
   pack $w.bot.apply $w.bot.dismiss -side left -expand  1
   PositionWindow $w
}
```

The `SetStatus` procedure is used to set GUI status messages in the status window. It's a general purpose routine to display both error and informational messages. If a type error occurs, then an error bitmap will be displayed in the status window:

```
proc SetStatus {type text {timer 5000}} {
   global statusText  statusImgWin
   set statusText $text
   after $timer "set statusText \"\""
   $statusImgWin config -bitmap $type
   after $timer "$statusImgWin config -bitmap \"\""
}
```

The `AddToView` command will add a nick to the option button. Before it adds the item to the option menu, it makes sure that the user had supplied the required information:

```
proc AddToView  {type command {nick ""}}  {
   global tailOpts  viewOptMenu


    catch {Stop}
   if {$type == "file"} {
      set nick $command
      if {$command == ""} {
         SetStatus error "Please supply File name..."
      }
   } elseif  {$type == "command"} {
      if {($nick == "") || ($command == "") } {
         SetStatus error "Please supply both nick and command names..."
         return
      }
   }
```

```
    set l [list  "$type" "$nick" "$command"]
    if ![info exists tailOpts(wins)] {
       set tailOpts $l
       return
    } else {
       foreach item $tailOpts(wins) {
          if {$nick == [lindex $item 1]} {
             if {$type == "file"} {
                SetStatus info "File $nick is all ready in the tail list...."
             } else {
                SetStatus info "Nick $nick is all ready in the tail list...."
             }
             return;
          }
       }
       lappend tailOpts(wins) $l
    }

   UpdateOptionMenu
   $viewOptMenu invoke end
}
```

The `DeleteNicks` routine will create a simple listbox-based user interface for the user to delete the nicks.

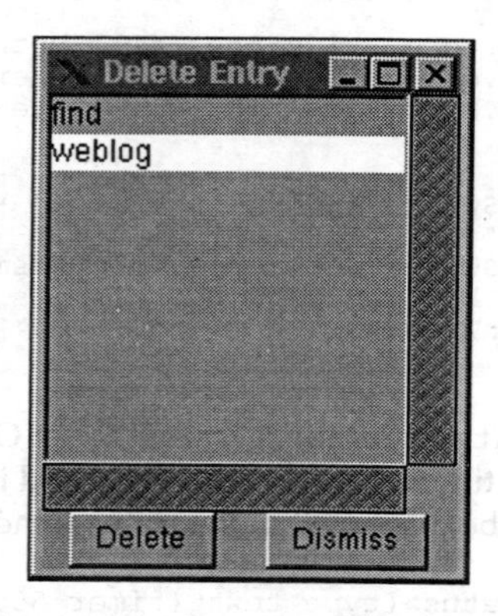


```
proc DeleteNicks {} {
   global   tailOpts

   if ![info exists tailOpts(wins)] {
      SetStatus info "No entries to delete..."
      return;
   }
   if {$tailOpts(wins) == {}} {
      SetStatus info "No entries to delete..."
      return;
   }
    catch {destroy .delent}
   toplevel .delent
   set w .delent
   wm title $w "Delete Entry"

   scrollbar $w.h -orient horizontal -command "$w.list xview"
   scrollbar $w.v -orient vertical -command "$w.list yview"
   listbox $w.l -selectmode single -width 20 -height 10 \
         -setgrid 1 -xscroll "$w.h set" -yscroll "$w.v set"

    frame $w.buts
    button $w.buts.d -text "Delete" -command {
```

```
        set index [.delent.l curselection ];
        if {$index == ""} {return}
        set sel [.delent.l get $index ];
        puts "sel $sel ; index $index"
        DeleteFromView $sel;
        .delent.l  delete $index
    }

    button $w.buts.dismiss -text "Dismiss" -command "destroy $w"

    grid $w.l -row 0 -column 0 -columnspan 2 -sticky "news"
    grid $w.v -row 0 -column 2 -sticky "ns"
    grid $w.h -row 1 -column 0 -columnspan 2 -sticky "we"
    grid $w.buts -row 2 -column 0 -columnspan 3

    pack $w.buts.d $w.buts.dismiss -side left -padx 10

   foreach ent $tailOpts(wins) {
     $w.l insert end [lindex $ent 1]
   }

    PositionWindow $w
}
```

The `DeleteFromView` routine is an internal routine that removes the specified nick from the data structures and updates the `optionbutton`:

```
proc DeleteFromView {nick} {
   global tailOpts

    if {$nick == ""} {
        return
    }
   set newList {}
   if ![info exists tailOpts(wins)] {
      return
   }
   foreach item $tailOpts(wins) {
      if {$nick != [lindex $item 1]} {
         lappend newList $item
      }
   }
   set tailOpts(wins) $newList
   UpdateOptionMenu
}
```

The `PositionWindow` routine centers a toplevel dialogue box around its parent. It is used to map dialog boxes on the main window, instead of some far-away corner of the screen:

```
#
# PositionWindow  --
#
#       Position the toplevel window centered to its parent.
#
#  Arguments:
#       toplevel window.
#
#  Results:
#       Positions the window
#
```

```
proc PositionWindow {w} {
    set paren [winfo parent $w]
    wm iconify $w
    set parenConf [wm geometry $paren]
    set parenConf [split $parenConf {+ - x}]
    set winConf [split [wm geometry $w] {+ - x}]
    set X [expr [lindex $parenConf 2] + [lindex $parenConf 0]/2 - \
              [winfo reqwidth $w]/2]

    set Y [expr [lindex $parenConf 3] + [lindex $parenConf 1]/2 - \
              [winfo reqheigh $w]/2]
    wm geometry $w +$X+$Y
    wm deiconify $w
}
```

The `UpdateOptionMenu` command updates the nicks option menu widget with the current set of active nicks:

```
#   UpdateOptionMenu --
#
#
#
#   Arguments:
#
#
#   Results:
#

proc UpdateOptionMenu {} {
    global tailOpts curNick viewOptMenu

    $viewOptMenu delete 0 end
    if ![info exists tailOpts(wins)] {
        return
    }
    if {$tailOpts(wins) == {}} {
        set curNick ""
        return
    }
    foreach item $tailOpts(wins) {
        $viewOptMenu add command -label [lindex $item 1] -command "catch Stop; TailFile
\"[lindex $item 0]\" \"[lindex $item 2]\" \"[lindex $item 1]\" "
        set curNick [lindex $item 1]
    }
}
```

Finally, we map the main window:

```
wm withdraw .

toplevel .t

BuildTailGui .t
```

When you run this application, you should see the following:

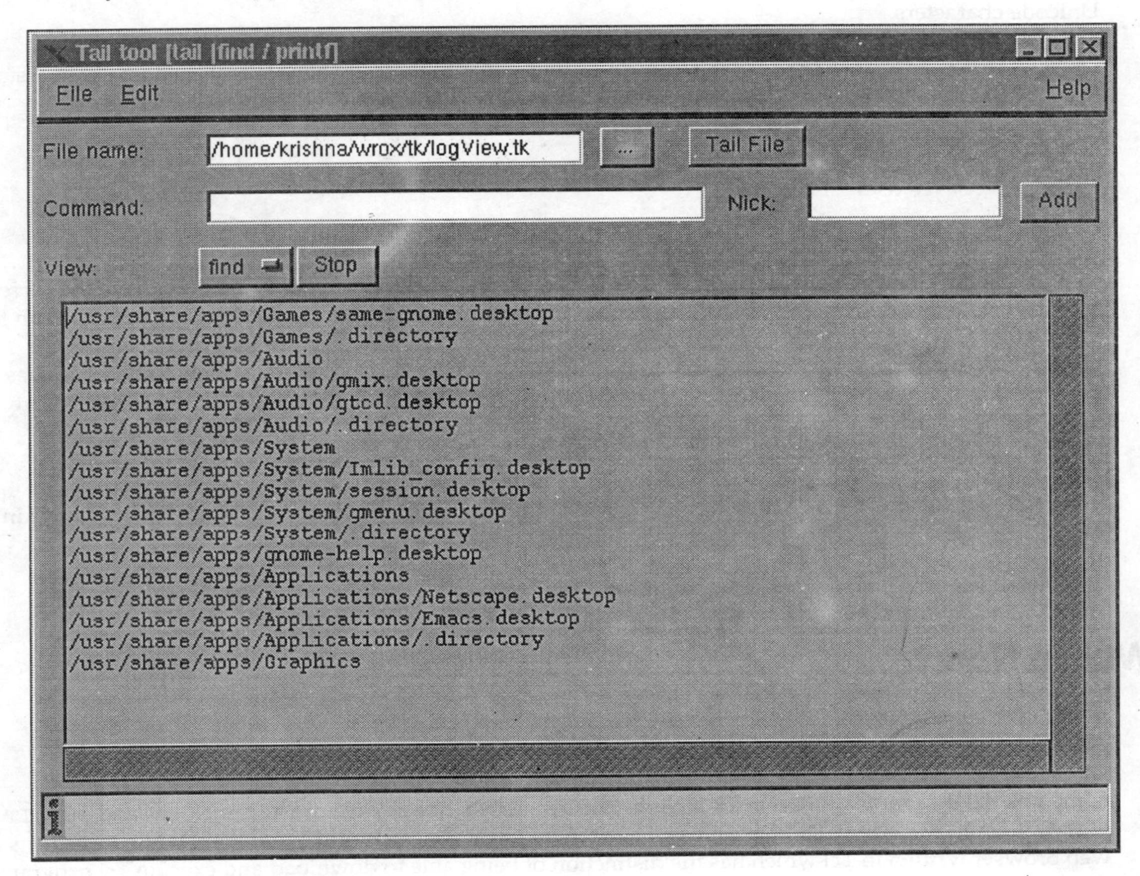

Internationalization

One thing we have not covered in this survey of Tk widgets is internationalization. Tcl8.1 has lots of new features such as Unicode support, functions to create and access message catalogs (so you can store the text of all your dialog boxes in multiple languages), support for different language encodings and generalized string manipulation. Beginning in Tcl 8.1, all Tcl string manipulation functions expect and return Unicode strings encoded in UTF-8 format. Because the use of Unicode/UTF-8 encoding is internal to Tcl, you should see no difference in Tcl 8.0 and 8.1 string handling in your scripts. In fact all the commands in Tcl8.1 onwards handle Unicode seemlessly. For example you can read a file that is encoded in `shiftjis` encoding into Tcl and the file read command automatically converts the `shiftjis` encoding to its UTF-8 encoding automatically.

```
set fd [open $file r]
fconfigure $fd -encoding shiftjis
set jstring [read $fd] close $fd
close $fd
```

Furthermore, the new regular expression implementation introduced in Tcl 8.1 handles the full range of Unicode characters.

Since all strings in Tcl are encoded in Unicode Tk widgets automatically handle any encoding conversions necessary to display the characters in a particular font. For example the following code snippet:

```
set str "\u592a\u9177"
??
% button .b -text $str
.b
% pack .b
```

should display Chinese transliteration of "Tcl" (*TAI-KU*) as the button label provided you have the correct X fonts installed to display this text. If the master font that you set for a widget doesn't contain a glyph for a particular Unicode character that you want to display, Tk attempts to locate a font that does. Where possible, Tk attempts to locate a font that matches as many characteristics of the widget's master font as possible (for example, weight, slant, etc.). Once Tk finds a suitable font, it displays the character in that font. In other words, the widget uses the master font for all characters it is capable of displaying, and alternative fonts only as needed.

Internationalization is a fascinating topic to cover. Unfortunately it requires more space than we have in this chapter. For an excellent introduction to internationalization in Tcl/Tk, read:

http://www.scriptics.com/services/support/howto/i18n.html

Where Now?

If you ever get stuck with Tk, as well as the `man` pages, there's always the Tk Widget Tour with its examples of how to use the Tk widget set. Run the program by typing `widget`.

Some notable programs written in Tk include `Xadmin`, `Exmh`, `ical`, `TkMan`, `TkElm`, `TkWWW` and `SurfIT`. `tkWWW` is an HTML editor, so you can use it to prepare pages for the World Wide Web, while `SurfIT` is a web browser written in Tcl which has the distinction of being able to download and execute Tcl programs directly from web pages. This, of course, can be a dangerous facility to allow with unknown hosts! `Ical` is an X based calendar program

At the time of writing this chapter, there are many things happening within the Tk community, so we'll round off with a brief survey of some notable projects.

Tix

Tix extends Tk with over 40 professional Motif look-and-feel widgets. Tix widgets are so powerful that they even give Motif 2.0 a run for its money. Check out Tix at http://www.xpi.com/tix/.

[incr Tk]

[incr Tcl] and [incr Tk] form an objected oriented extension to Tcl/Tk. Version 3.0 has recently been announced and is available at http://www.tcltk.com/itcl/. From their web pages:

"[incr Tcl] provides the extra language support needed to build large Tcl/Tk applications. It introduces the notion of objects, which act as building blocks for an application. Each object is a bag of data with a set of procedures or 'methods' that are used to manipulate it. Objects are organized into 'classes' with identical characteristics, and classes can inherit functionality from one another. This object-oriented paradigm adds another level of organization on top of the basic variable/procedure elements, and the resulting code is easier to understand and maintain.

[incr Tk] is a framework for building 'mega-widgets' using the [incr Tcl] object system. Mega-widgets are high-level widgets like a file browser or a tab notebook that act like simple Tk widgets but are themselves constructed using Tk widgets as component parts, without having to write any C code. In effect, a mega-widget looks and acts exactly like a Tk widget, but is considerably easier to implement."

BLT

The BLT-2.1 toolkit extends Tk by providing many new widgets, for example `blt_graph`, which is used to plot line and bar graphs and `blt_htext`, a hypertext widget and widgets for background execution. BLT homepage is http://www.tcltk.com/blt

Finally, comp.lang.tcl and comp.lang.tcl.announce are the best places to post Tk questions. Usually, people are quite friendly and somebody will always answer your questions. Before posting your questions to comp.lang.tcl, though, please read its frequently asked questions (FAQ) list, which is posted regularly to the news group.

Lots of Tk resources can be found on the web at Tcl's new home, scriptics corporation web page: http://www.scriptics.com/resource.

That about completes our survey of Tk. There is far more to Tk than this brief survey can do justice, as John Ousterhout intended Tcl/Tk to be an extensible and embeddable tool. Tcl commands and Tk widgets are written in C and you can code your own and add them in, or take advantage of the widget extensions available on the Internet. This is an advanced topic and space prevents us from covering it here, but it would be the way in which you would access a C program from your graphical Tcl/Tk front end. Please refer to John Ousterhout's book for details and, in the meantime, happy Tcl/Tk'ing!

Summary

In this chapter, we've rushed through the world of X windows programming.

After an overview of the thinking behind X Windows and the different ways in which this was implemented, we learned enough Tk to complement the Tcl that we learned in Chapter 15 and enable us to rapidly develop GUI front ends to our applications using Tk's rich widget set.

Next we're going to look at an exciting new way to program graphical applications in C - the GTK+ GNOME toolkit.

Programming GNOME using GTK+

This chapter is an introduction to an exciting development in the Linux world: GNOME. GNOME stands for the GNU Network Object Model Environment, which despite its complicated name, is a software project with a simple aim – to provide a user friendly, powerful user and development desktop environment that is based entirely on free, open source software. You'll find this chapter purposefully brief in its coverage, but you should be able to use the following pages as a starting point to program GNOME and then use the online documentation to fill in the details. In this chapter, we'll be looking at:

- An introduction to GNOME.
- The GNOME architecture.
- The GNOME desktop.
- The GTK+ widget set.
- GNOME widgets.
- An application for GNOME.

The GNOME project home page is at www.gnome.org where you can find out the latest news, browse complete online documentation and find a wealth of programming resources for GNOME.

GNOME is currently the default desktop system installed with the latest releases of the Red Hat and Debian distributions of Linux, but you can download the binaries and source code of GNOME compatible with most Linux and Unix systems from www.gnome.org.

An Introduction to GNOME

Perhaps the greatest difficulty with GNOME is understanding exactly what it is and what it does. To the average user it's easy to think of GNOME as just a collection of desktop tools, but as its name suggests, GNOME is a complete programming environment as well as a desktop, and its innovations go much further than an attractive user interface.

GNOME is a programming layer that sits between the low level X Window system and the high level Window Manager software, which gives the GUI programmer a wealth of powerful tools that Linux historically has been missing. Compatibility with programs not written for GNOME is not an issue as GNOME only adds resources. Specifically, GNOME addresses four key areas of problems encountered by UNIX developers:

- Lack of an integrated framework for building applications with a consistent user interface.
- Lack of inter-application communication.
- Lack of a standard for printing.
- Lack of a standard for session-management.

Before we look at how GNOME solves these problems, let's learn a little about the history of the project.

The GNOME project began in August 1997, initiated by amongst others, Peter Mattis and Spencer Kimball (programmers who worked on the GNU Image Manipulation Program, a.k.a The GIMP), Richard Stallman of the Free Software Foundation (FSF) and Erik Troan and Mark Ewing of Red Hat.

The impetus behind GNOME originally stemmed from frustrations over licensing problems in KDE, another Linux desktop project. KDE (the K Desktop Environment) is based on a widget toolkit called Qt written by TrollTech. Qt is not licensed under the GPL, and some felt that building a Linux desktop using a toolkit that was anything but GPL was a backward step for Linux whose tradition lies in non-proprietary, free (in the sense of 'with the freedom to use the software as you like') open source software.

Distancing themselves from KDE, the team of programmers began GNOME basing it around GTK+, a GPL toolkit having none of the restrictions of Qt. Within 18 months, GNOME version 1.0 was released.

KDE continues to grow with a large following in competition to GNOME. It's entirely a matter of personal taste which you prefer. If you're a hardened C++ hacker, then since it's Qt's native language, you might like KDE better. You can install both GNOME and KDE on a system - they happily coexist - and swap which one loads up by editing your X startup script. Find out more about KDE from the project's home page, www.kde.org.

The GNOME Architecture

The base toolkit in GNOME is GTK+ (the GIMP toolkit) originally written to simplify work on the GIMP. GTK+ is a well featured, object oriented, cross platform, language neutral toolkit used widely to create applications independently of GNOME. One of the reasons GTK+ was chosen as GNOME's toolkit was its support for many programming languages, including C, C++, TOM, PERL, Python, GUILE, ADA and many others. We'll stick to using C in this chapter, which is also the most popular language. GTK+ and GNOME are both written in C for many positive reasons, but object orientation has had to be forced into the implementation. The repercussions are small, but code is slightly less tidy than say, in a C++ implementation.

Toolkits like GTK+, Qt or Tk are collections of widgets – GUI objects like buttons, menus, dialog boxes etc – and general support functions.

GTK+ uses the GLIB (GIMP library) and GDK (GIMP Drawing Kit) set of libraries. GLIB defines datatypes and provides functions that deal with error handling and memory routines, and GDK is the platform dependent layer that sits between the native graphics API and GTK+. Thus porting GTK+ to other platforms should only require re-writing the GDK.

GNOME extends GTK+ by adding a separate layer of GNOME specific libraries and widgets which replace and enhance some of those provided by GTK+ in order to provide greater ease of programming and to encourage the developer into writing consistent user interfaces.

As an example, GNOME provides ready made dialog boxes, to which we simply add our text and specify which feedback buttons to provide. Thus, it's quick and easy to code any dialog box, and they have a uniform design across all GNOME applications.

Where both GTK+ and GNOME offer us routes for creating widgets, such as menus or toolbars, we'll only discuss the GNOME method, since it'll be invariably a more powerful option.

Let's summarize the major features of the GNOME architecture:

- Powerful, extensive widget set.
- GNOME Desktop front end featuring friendly, easy to use applications such as the panel, control center, file manager... etc.
- A custom implementation of the CORBA system called **ORBit** which allows software objects to communicate effectively.
- A framework called **Bonobo** allowing embedding of documents within applications, similar to Microsoft's Object Linking and Embedding (OLE). This would allow, for example, a spreadsheet to be embedded into a text document.
- A complete Internationalization system, including support for Unicode and Complex Text Processing necessary to display languages of the Middle East and South Asia.
- Printing framework.

GNOME is certainly comprehensive! Let's leave the complexities behind now and take a look at what we actually *see* – the desktop.

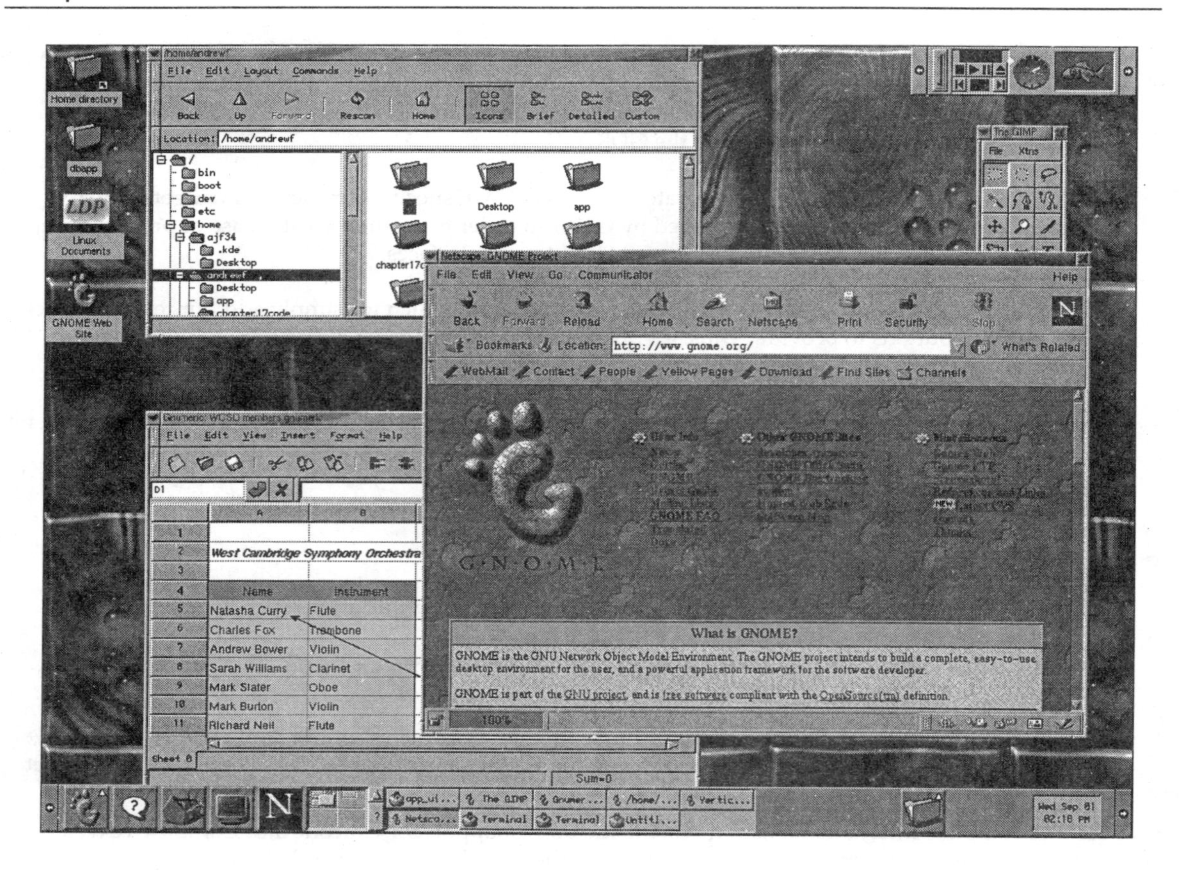

The GNOME Desktop

With GNOME and all the necessary libraries installed correctly (with **exec gnome-session** at the end of your X startup script, which may be called `~/.xinitrc`, `.xsession`, or `.Xclients` depending on your platform and configuration), we start up the desktop with the familiar command:

```
$ startx
```

By far the best way to familiarize yourself with the desktop is, of course, to use it! You'll soon see how well designed and user friendly it is, and how drastically it improves the usability of Linux.

At the heart of the GNOME desktop is the panel, a highly configurable taskbar. Independent panels can be placed on every edge of the screen, into which program shortcuts, menu shortcuts and small applications (applets) can be docked. Panels can be hidden by clicking on the outer arrows which slide the panel off the screen in a smooth, almost hypnotic animated fashion - guaranteed to provide hours of entertainment!

You are of course free to choose any window manager to use with GNOME, which controls the placement and appearance of windows on the screen, but several are more GNOME compliant than others. The most popular choices are "Enlightenment" and "IceWM". They are both fully GNOME compliant and have endless configuration options to customize the look of your desktop.

The file manager is a GNOME version of "mc", the midnight commander program. MS Windows users will feel at home with a tree display and full drag and drop functionality. We can easily copy, move, rename and change file ownerships and privileges.

Programming in GNOME using GTK+

Let's now move on to the exciting stuff – programming using GTK+! We'll build up our knowledge by looking at examples of the basic GTK+ widgets and then progress to the more complex widgets and finally use them to build a GNOME application.

Before we dive straight in, we should say a few things about data types we'll be using and the concept of widget hierarchy.

Datatypes

GLIB defines its own set of basic types, most of which are directly equivalent to the standard C types. This makes porting code to different platforms easier and in some cases, such as using `gpointer` instead of `void*`, it improves readability and understanding. Making sure we use these new types guarantees that our code will work even if the underlying implementation changes.

GLIB type	C type
gchar	char
gshort	short
glong	long
gint	int
gboolean	char
gpointer	void*

Widget Hierarchy

Widgets in GNOME/GTK+ are all members of a hierarchy, so that functions common to a set of widgets, such as `gtk_widget_show` need only be implemented once. To remove the need to duplicate code, new widgets are usually derived from existing widgets so that only the new features of the widget need to be written. Let's look at the widget hierarchy for the `GnomeApp` widget, the top level window widget, taken from the Gnome User Interface Library Reference Manual:

```
GtkObject
      +------GtkWidget
                 +------GtkContainer
                              +-----GtkBin
                                      +-----GtkWindow
                                                 +-----GnomeApp
```

This tells us that the GnomeApp widget is derived from the GtkWindow widget, which itself is derived from the GtkBin widget and so on. Thus we can apply GtkWindow, GtkBin, GtkContainer, GtkWidget and GtkObject functions to a GnomeApp widget because of its inheritance.

All widget creation functions, such as gnome_app_new return a GtkWidget pointer, the generic widget. This means that, if we want to call a GnomeApp specific function such as gnome_app_set_menus(GnomeApp *app, GtkMenuBar *menubar), then we use a macro (in this case GNOME_APP) to perform the cast from a GtkWidget type to a GnomeApp type. We can only do this because GnomeApp is derived from GtkWidget. In the case of an invalid cast, the compiler won't complain, but the GTK+ library will dump the error to the console when the program is run. GTK+ is very good at returning useful errors, to aid debugging. We'll see many examples of using macros for typecasting.

Let's put widgets aside for a moment and write our first GNOME program which will display a window.

Try It Out – Creating Windows

```
#include <gnome.h>

int main (int argc, char *argv[])
{
        GtkWidget *app;
        gnome_init ("example", "0.1", argc, argv);
        app = gnome_app_new ("example", "Window Title");
        gtk_widget_show (app);
        gtk_main ();
        return 0;
}
```

It is important to make sure that all of the GNOME and GTK+ libraries are correctly installed, and that the library path's correctly set before trying to compile any example code.

To make life easy, GNOME comes with a shell script called gnome-config that supplies the compiler with the correct flags required for compilation, and we append its output using single back quotes.

To compile the program gnome1.c you should type. (Note the back quotes and double dashes!)

```
$ gcc gnome1.c -o example1 `gnome-config --cflags --libs gnomeui`
```

Then run it from a terminal window within GNOME.

If you're having problems compiling, you can find details as well as solutions to common problems at www.gnome.org.

Up should pop an empty window, 200x200 pixels in size:

You can move, resize and close the window, but it doesn't return us to the shell prompt, because we haven't yet set up an exit handler.

How it works

Let's run through the code line by line. First we `#include gnome.h`, which takes care of all the necessary GNOME and GTK+ library definitions. In `main`, we declare a `GtkWidget` pointer `app` that will point to our window object and then we call `gnome_init`, the function that initializes the libraries, sets up session management and loads any user preferences. We pass to `gnome_init` the application `id`, in this case `"example"`, its version number, `"0.1"`, and the command line arguments as received by `main`. These are all used internally by GNOME.

Next we create our window by calling `gnome_app_new`. This function takes as arguments an application name, which can be different from the string supplied to `gnome_init` (also used internally) and the window title which in this case we imaginatively call `"window title"`, but can be left `NULL`. Don't be confused by the function's name; its purpose is to create a top level window not a 'new application', and we call `gnome_app_new` every time we want to create a new window. To make our window visible after creation, we call `gtk_widget_show`, and finally we relinquish control to GNOME using `gtk_main`, so that events, mouse clicks, button presses and so on, can be processed.

Once we've called `gtk_main` there's no way back – we have to use `callbacks` linking user events to functions in our program to perform any further actions. We'll see a couple of `callbacks` in action in the next example.

Try It Out – The Ubiquitous "Hello world"

Make the highlighted additions and changes to the first example:

```
#include <gnome.h>

static void button_clicked(GtkWidget *button, gpointer data)
 {
        char *string = data;
        g_print(string);
 }

int main (int argc, char *argv[])
{
        GtkWidget *app;
        GtkWidget *button;

        gnome_init ("example", "0.1", argc, argv);
        app = gnome_app_new ("example", "Window Title");

        button = gtk_button_new_with_label ("Hello,\n GNOME world!");

        gtk_signal_connect (GTK_OBJECT (app), "delete_event",
                                     GTK_SIGNAL_FUNC (gtk_main_quit),
                                     NULL);

        gtk_signal_connect (GTK_OBJECT (button), "clicked",
                                     GTK_SIGNAL_FUNC (button_clicked),
                                     "Ouch!\n");

        gnome_app_set_contents (GNOME_APP (app), button);
        gtk_widget_show_all (app);
        gtk_main ();
        return 0;
}
```

When you run the program, you'll see something similar to this:

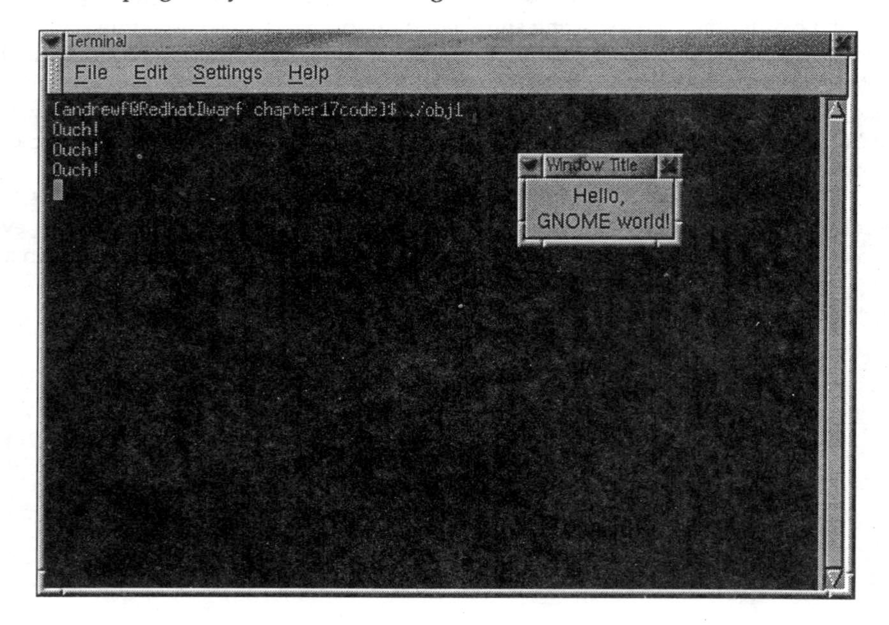

How it works

We've created a button widget with an embedded label widget using gtk_button_new_with_label and placed it in the window using gnome_app_set_contents, making use of the GNOME_APP macro to cast our GtkWidget pointer to a GnomeApp type.

We've also registered two callbacks, to output "Ouch!" each time the button is clicked, using the GLIB g_print function (generally used for debugging, as its output can be overridden unlike printf) and to call gtk_main_quit when the window is closed so that our program exits neatly.

We're ignoring return results from the GNOME functions here. In a production environment, 'industrial strength' applications would take care to check them!

Let's now look at these signal handlers in more detail.

Dealing With Signals and Callbacks

Every time the mouse moves, enters and leaves widgets, buttons are pressed, toggle buttons are toggled, menu items are selected and so on, a signal is sent to an application which can be passed to a callback function. (GNOME signals are quite distinct from the UNIX signals discussed in Chapter 10.) Applications aren't interested in most of these events, but sometimes they need to take action. A paint package might have to draw a line when the user clicks a mouse button, or a sound player might increase the output volume when a scale widget is adjusted. In GNOME/GTK+ we call gtk_signal_connect to connect signals with handler functions:

```
guint gtk_signal_connect (GtkObject *object , const gchar *name, GtkSignalFunc  func,
gpointer data)
```

It has four parameters which tell GNOME/GTK+ which widget the callback is associated with, the signal to be handled, the function to be called when the signal is sent and any arbitrary data to be given to the signal handling function. If we look back to the previous example, we can now understand the call:

```
gtk_signal_connect (GTK_OBJECT (button), "clicked",
                                          GTK_SIGNAL_FUNC (button_clicked),
                                          "Ouch!\n");
```

Which calls button_clicked every time the "clicked" signal occurs for the button widget, sending "Ouch!" as an argument. Notice that signals are referenced by strings in GTK+, not by constants as in normal signal handling, so that misspellings are caught at run-time in GTK+

Different widgets emit different signals, but signals emitted by buttons are:

Signal	Action
clicked	The button was clicked (both pressed and released).
pressed	The button was pressed down by the mouse.
released	The button was released.
enter	The mouse has moved over the button area.
leave	The mouse has moved out of the button area.

These are all the basics of programming the GNOME user interface. For the rest of the chapter we'll just be looking at more complicated widgets.

Don't be surprised to find many similarities between GTK+ and Tk. This is not a coincidence!

In the 'Hello world' example, the window shrank to enclose the button widget as you might expect. In fact, windows can only have one child widget and, if you tried to create and add a second button to the window, it would displace the first. You're probably thinking then, "How can I put more than one widget in a window?" This brings us to containers.

Containers

GTK+ is a container based toolkit, which means that widgets are positioned in windows only by specifying their parent container. Windows are single widget containers, and so GTK+ employs invisible **packing boxes**, which can hold multiple widgets to create window layouts. Packing boxes are simple beasts, come in horizontal and vertical form and are created with `gtk_hbox_new` and `gtk_vbox_new` respectively. To place widgets in these packing boxes, all we need to do is call `gtk_box_pack_start` for each widget and specify several formatting options.

This code fragment illustrates creating a vertical packing box and placing two label widgets inside:

```
GtkWidget *vbox, *label;
gboolean expand = FALSE;
gboolean fill = TRUE;
gint padding = 2;

vbox = gtk_vbox_new (homogeneous, spacing);

label = gtk_label_new ("This is the top label widget");
gtk_box_pack_start (GTK_BOX (vbox), label, expand, fill, padding);

label = gtk_label_new ("This is the bottom label widget");
gtk_box_pack_start  (GTK_BOX (vbox), label, FALSE, TRUE, 2);
```

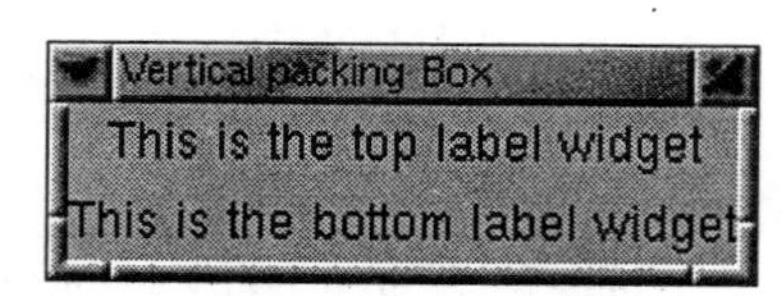

For the second label, we've used typical values for the `expand`, `fill` and `padding` attributes. This table explains their meanings.

Parameter	Type	Description
`homogeneous`	gboolean	Forces all widgets in the box to occupy the same area as the largest widget in the box.
`spacing`	gint	Determines the space between adjacent widgets.
`expand`	gboolean	Allows the packing box to expand to fill the remaining space. Ignored if homogenous flag is set.

Parameter	Type	Description
Fill	gboolean	Allows that particular widget to expand to fill the remaining space.
padding	gint	Determines the width of a frame surrounding the widget.

We'll now be using packing boxes in all our examples, starting with the next program to introduce some more button widgets:

Buttons

GTK+ provides four kinds of buttons, simple push buttons, toggle buttons, check boxes and radio buttons.

Button functionality in GNOME is essentially the same as in other GUIs. Push buttons are used to perform an action on clicking, toggle buttons and check boxes are buttons with an associated state – up or down – and radio buttons form a group of options from which only one can be selected.

Let's try out check boxes and radio buttons in the next example.

Try It Out – More Choices

1. First we declare the widgets and create an empty radio group using `GSList`:

```
#include <gnome.h>

int main (int argc, char *argv[])
{
GtkWidget *app;
        GtkWidget *button1, *button2;
        GtkWidget *radio1, *radio2, *radio3, *radio4;
        GtkWidget *vbox1, *vbox2;
        GtkWidget *hbox;
        GSList *group = NULL;

gnome_init ("example", "0.1", argc, argv);
        app = gnome_app_new ("example", "Music choices");
```

2. We give the window a border and create our packing boxes:

```
gtk_container_border_width (GTK_CONTAINER (app), 20);

        vbox1 = gtk_vbox_new (FALSE, 0);
        vbox2 = gtk_vbox_new (FALSE, 0);
        hbox =  gtk_hbox_new (FALSE, 0);
```

3. We add two check buttons to the first vertical packing box:

```
button1 = gtk_check_button_new_with_label( "Orchestra");
gtk_box_pack_start (GTK_BOX (vbox1), button1, FALSE, FALSE, 0);

button2 = gtk_check_button_new_with_label ("Conductor");
gtk_box_pack_start (GTK_BOX (vbox1), button2, FALSE, FALSE, 0);
```

4. And add four radio buttons to the second box, adding each new button to the group list:

```
radio1 = gtk_radio_button_new_with_label (group, "Strings");
gtk_box_pack_start (GTK_BOX (vbox2), radio1, FALSE, FALSE, 0);
group = gtk_radio_button_group (GTK_RADIO_BUTTON (radio1));

radio2 = gtk_radio_button_new_with_label (group, "Wind");
gtk_box_pack_start (GTK_BOX (vbox2), radio2, FALSE, FALSE, 0);
group = gtk_radio_button_group (GTK_RADIO_BUTTON (radio2));

radio3 = gtk_radio_button_new_with_label (group, "Brass");
gtk_box_pack_start (GTK_BOX (vbox2), radio3, FALSE, FALSE, 0);
group = gtk_radio_button_group (GTK_RADIO_BUTTON (radio3));

radio4 = gtk_radio_button_new_with_label (group, "Percussion");
gtk_box_pack_start (GTK_BOX (vbox2), radio4, FALSE, FALSE, 0);
group = gtk_radio_button_group (GTK_RADIO_BUTTON (radio4));
```

5. Lastly, we add an exit handler and put the packing boxes together:

```
        gtk_signal_connect (GTK_OBJECT (app), "delete_event",
                            GTK_SIGNAL_FUNC (gtk_main_quit),
                            NULL);

gtk_container_add (GTK_CONTAINER (hbox), vbox1);
        gtk_container_add (GTK_CONTAINER (hbox), vbox2);

        gnome_app_set_contents (GNOME_APP (app), hbox);

        gtk_widget_show_all (app);
        gtk_main ();
        return 0;
}
```

The packing box structure is shown in this diagram:

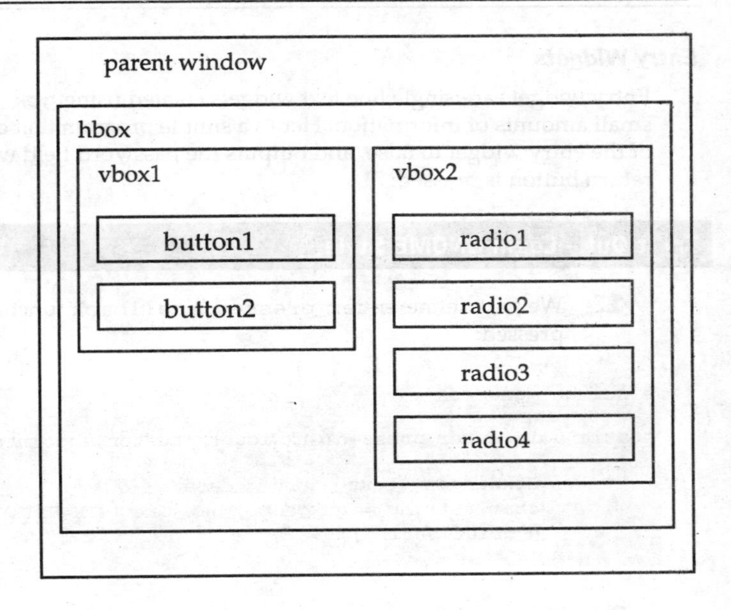

When run, the program displays this window:

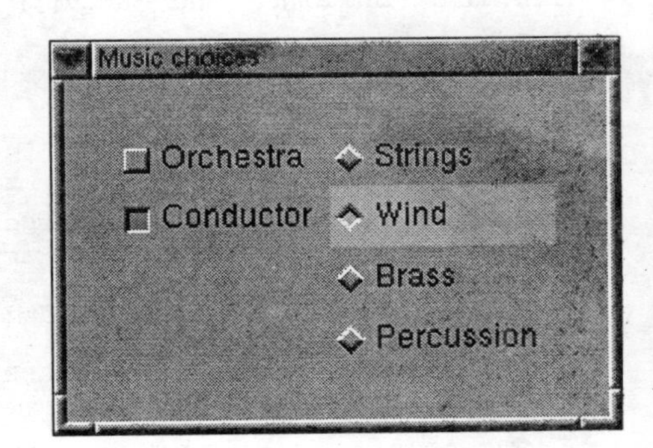

How it works

This is an unashamedly contrived example so that we can demonstrate new widgets and a nested packing box structure to create a window layout. We create two check boxes and add them to the first vertical packing box, `vbox1`. Their current state can be read by calling `gtk_toggle_get_state(button1)`, which returns a `gboolean`, indicating TRUE for pressed.

Creating radio buttons is very similar to check boxes, and all that we need to do extra is to specify a group the radio button belongs to and to update the group using `gtk_radio_button_group` after every new button creation. The first time a button is added to a group, the group should be NULL, as the group does not yet exist.

Radio buttons are derived from check buttons, which are derived from toggle buttons, so that we can use the same set of functions to read and modify their state and also use the same events. A full definition of relevant functions can be found in the GTK+ reference documentation available at www.gtk.org.

Entry Widgets

Entry widgets are single line text widgets created using `gtk_entry_new` and are commonly used to enter small amounts of information. Here's a simple program that creates a login window, sets the visibility flag of the entry widget to false, and outputs the password field when the `activate` signal occurs, when the return button is pressed:

Try It Out – Login GNOME Style

1. We first define `enter_pressed`, a `callback` function that gets called every time *return* is pressed:

```
#include <gnome.h>

static void enter_pressed(GtkWidget *button, gpointer data)
 {
         GtkWidget *text_entry = data;
         char *string = gtk_entry_get_text(GTK_ENTRY (text_entry));
         g_print(string);
 }
```

2. Next we define variables, initialize GNOME and create a horizontal packing box:

```
int main (int argc, char *argv[])
{
GtkWidget *app;
        GtkWidget *text_entry;
        GtkWidget *label;
        GtkWidget *hbox;
        gchar *text;

gnome_init ("example", "0.1", argc, argv);
        app = gnome_app_new ("example", "entry widget");

        gtk_container_border_width (GTK_CONTAINER (app), 5);

        hbox = gtk_hbox_new (FALSE, 0);
```

3. Now we create a label, set its alignment and add it to the packing box:

```
label = gtk_label_new("Password: ");
        gtk_misc_set_alignment (GTK_MISC (label), 0, 1.0);
        gtk_box_pack_start (GTK_BOX (hbox), label, FALSE, FALSE, 0);
```

4. Next we create the entry box and set its visibility to false, which makes its contents appear as asterisks:

```
        text_entry = gtk_entry_new();
        gtk_entry_set_visibility (GTK_ENTRY (text_entry), FALSE);
        gtk_box_pack_start (GTK_BOX (hbox), text_entry, FALSE, FALSE, 0);
```

5. Finally we set up the signal handlers, and place the packing box in the window:

```
        gtk_signal_connect (GTK_OBJECT (app), "delete_event",
        GTK_SIGNAL_FUNC (gtk_main_quit),
                                      NULL);

        gtk_signal_connect (GTK_OBJECT (text_entry), "activate",
                                    GTK_SIGNAL_FUNC (enter_pressed),
                                      text_entry);
gnome_app_set_contents( GNOME_APP (app), hbox);
        gtk_widget_show_all (app);
        gtk_main ();
        return 0;
}
```

When compiled and run, a window like this should appear:

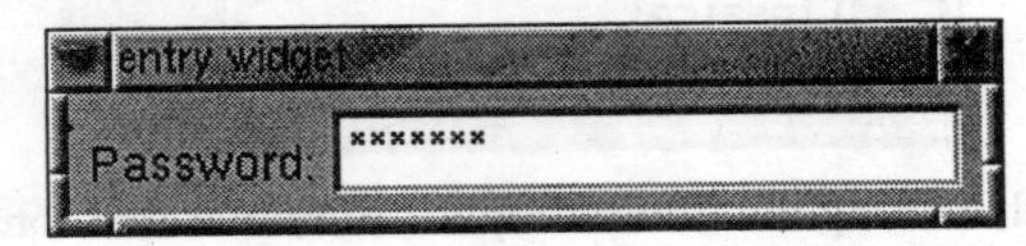

List Boxes and Combo Boxes

List box widgets hold a list of strings from which the user can select one or more, depending on the box's configuration. Combo boxes are entry widgets with an added pull down menu from which the user can select. Again, selection may be restricted to the items in the list depending on the widget's settings.

Here's a code fragment showing how to use them. The completed code is included in the source code bundle available from the Wrox web site.

```
listbox = gtk_list_new ();
gtk_list_set_selection_mode (GTK_LIST (listbox),
                                        GTK_SELECTION_MULTIPLE);

item = gtk_list_item_new_with_label ("Beethoven");
gtk_container_add (GTK_CONTAINER (listbox),item);

item = gtk_list_item_new_with_label ("Brahms");
gtk_container_add (GTK_CONTAINER (listbox),item);

item = gtk_list_item_new_with_label ("Bach");
gtk_container_add (GTK_CONTAINER (listbox),item);
gtk_box_pack_start (GTK_BOX (vbox), listbox, FALSE, FALSE, 0);

/* add items ad infintum */

label = gtk_label_new("Choose an era:");
gtk_misc_set_alignment (GTK_MISC (label), 0, 1.0);
gtk_box_pack_start (GTK_BOX (vbox), label, FALSE, FALSE, 0);
combolist = NULL;

combolist = g_list_append (combolist, "Renaissance");
combolist = g_list_append (combolist, "Baroque");
combolist = g_list_append (combolist, "Classical");
combolist = g_list_append (combolist, "Romantic");
combolist = g_list_append (combolist, "Impressionism");

combo = gtk_combo_new ();
gtk_combo_set_popdown_strings (GTK_COMBO(combo), combolist);
gtk_box_pack_start (GTK_BOX (vbox), combo, FALSE, FALSE, 0);
```

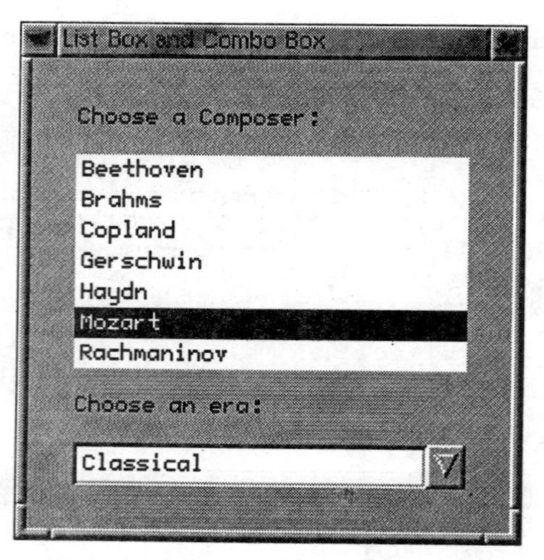

We have now arrived at describing the GNOME specific libraries that contain more complicated widgets that make the programmer's life easy. With plain GTK+ there is often a great deal of repetition in code, and it offers different approaches to common tasks like building menus, toolbars and dialog boxes. It's not that GTK+ is deficient in any way; it's just this flexibility that ensures its platform independence. As we'll see, if we use the GNOME libraries, then this gives our applications a great deal of extra functionality for low programming overheads.

Menus and Toolbars

GNOME lets us create menus and toolbars for our `GnomeApp` widgets that can be docked and undocked from the window. We just fill in arrays with the necessary information and call `gnome_app_create_menus` or `gnome_app_create_toolbar`.

The arrays are a list of structures that define the properties (type, string, `callback` pointer, accelerator key... etc) of each of the menu or toolbar items. For the details of this structure, consult the `libgnomeui` API reference manual. Most of the time, menu entries are very simple, and we can just use one of a set of macros provided by GNOME to create the structure for us. All common menu and toolbar options have a corresponding macro. Let's take a look at these.

Firstly there are the top level macros that create top level menus when passed an array that can contain any or all of the following `GnomeUIInfo` structures.

Menu	Macro
File	`GNOMEUIINFO_MENU_FILE_TREE` (tree)
Edit	`GNOMEUIINFO_MENU_EDIT_TREE` (tree)
View	`GNOMEUIINFO_MENU_VIEW_TREE` (tree)
Settings	`GNOMEUIINFO_MENU_SETTINGS_TREE` (tree)
Windows	`GNOMEUIINFO_MENU_WINDOWS_TREE` (tree)
Help	`GNOMEUIINFO_MENU_HELP_TREE` (tree)
Game	`GNOMEUIINFO_MENU_GAME_TREE` (tree)

Within the top level menu there are defined over thirty macros to create common menu items. The macros associate small images (pixmaps) and accelerator keys with each menu item. All we need to do is specify a `callback` function to be called when the item is selected and a data pointer to be passed to that function (`cb, data`). We'll list just a few here for later reference.

Top level menu	Menu Item	Macro
File	New	`GNOMEUIINFO_MENU_NEW_ITEM(label, hint, cb, data)`
	Open	`GNOMEUIINFO_MENU_OPEN_ITEM (cb, data)`
	Save	`GNOMEUIINFO_MENU_SAVE_ITEM (cb, data)`
	Print	`GNOMEUIINFO_MENU_PRINT_ITEM (cb, data)`
	Exit	`GNOMEUIINFO_MENU_EXIT_ITEM (cb, data)`
Edit	Cut	`GNOMEUIINFO_MENU_CUT_ITEM (cb, data)`
	Copy	`GNOMEUIINFO_MENU_COPY_ITEM (cb, data)`
	Paste	`GNOMEUIINFO_MENU_PASTE_ITEM (cb, data)`
Settings	Preferences	`GNOMEUIINFO_MENU_PREFERENCES_ITEM (cb, data)`
Help	About	`GNOMEUIINFO_MENU_ABOUT_ITEM (cb, data)`

Similarly for toolbars, we create an array using the `GNOMEUIINFO_ITEM_STOCK (label, tooltip, callback, stock_id)` macro, where `stock_id` is the id of a predefined icon that we want to use for that item. Again, the complete list of stock icons are listed in the `libgnomeui` reference pages.

There are also several special macros, including `GNOMEUIINFO_SEPARATOR` which creates a line that physically separates items and `GNOMEUIINFO_END` which denotes the end of the array.

Let's see how these arrays and macros work in practice.

Try It Out – Menus and Toolbars

1. We create a `callback` function to output text when an item is selected:

```
#include <gnome.h>

static void callback (GtkWidget *button, gpointer data)
{
        g_print ("Item Selected");
}
```

2. Now we create an array of two items to be placed in the file menu, an option that calls `callback` and an exit option:

```
GnomeUIInfo file_menu[] = {
        GNOMEUIINFO_ITEM_NONE ("A Menu Item","This is the statusbar info",
                                callback),
        GNOMEUIINFO_MENU_EXIT_ITEM(gtk_main_quit, NULL),
        GNOMEUIINFO_END
};
```

3. Then we create the menu structure with one top level menu, the file menu, that points to the array we've just created:

```
GnomeUIInfo menubar[] = {
        GNOMEUIINFO_MENU_FILE_TREE(file_menu),
        GNOMEUIINFO_END
};
```

4. Similarly for the toolbar, we create an array that holds two items, a print button and an exit button:

```
GnomeUIInfo toolbar[] = {
        GNOMEUIINFO_ITEM_STOCK("Print", "This is another tooltip",
                                callback,
                                GNOME_STOCK_PIXMAP_PRINT),
        GNOMEUIINFO_ITEM_STOCK("Exit", "Exit the application",
                                gtk_main_quit,
                                GNOME_STOCK_PIXMAP_EXIT),
        GNOMEUIINFO_END
};
```

5. Finally we create the menus and toolbar and add them to the window:

```
int main(int argc, char *argv[])
{
        GtkWidget *app;

        gnome_init ("example", "0.1", argc, argv);
        app = gnome_app_new ("example", "simple toolbar and menu");

        gnome_app_create_menus (GNOME_APP (app), menubar);
        gnome_app_create_toolbar (GNOME_APP (app), toolbar);

        gtk_widget_show_all (app);
        gtk_main ();
        return 0;
}
```

We'll see a small window with an embedded menu and toolbar which we can click, undock and drag around the screen. If we exit and reload, GNOME remembers their positions!

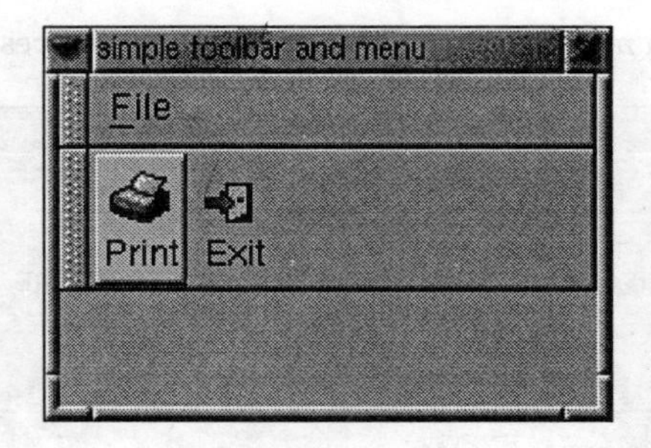

Dialog Boxes

When we need to create dialog boxes that display textual information to the user in GNOME, we call gnome_message_box_new and pass it the message text, type of dialog box we require and the buttons we want in the dialog box, all in a NULL terminated list. Next we bind the *clicked* signal of the dialog widget that we've just created to a handling function which is passed the button that the user pressed as an integer. Then all we need to do is call gtk_widget_show to display a non-modal box.

```
static void messagebox_clicked(GnomeDialog *dlg, gint button, gpointer data)
{
        switch (button)
        {
              case 1: /* user pressed apply*/
              return;
              case 0: /*user presser ok*/
              case 2: /*user pressed close */
              gnome_dialog_close(dlg);
        }
}

GtkWidget *dlg;

dlg = gnome_message_box_new ("This is the message text that appears in the dialog
box",
                                GNOME_MESSAGE_BOX_QUESTION,
                                GNOME_STOCK_BUTTON_OK,
                                GNOME_STOCK_BUTTON_APPLY,
                                GNOME_STOCK_BUTTON_CLOSE,
                                NULL);

gtk_signal_connect (GTK_OBJECT(dlg), "clicked",
     GTK_SIGNAL_FUNC(messagebox_clicked),
      NULL);

gtk_widget_show (dlg);
```

This creates a simple question message box, adds three buttons and responds to the user's clicks.

The Canvas Widget

The canvas widget is the most complicated and versatile of GNOME widgets and almost deserves a chapter to itself! The GNOME canvas is a high specification drawing widget designed to be a general purpose display engine for applications. It supports simple graphical objects such as lines and rectangles, and applications can define their own canvas items to provide greater sophistication.

The canvas supports two rendering back-ends, one based on `Xlib` for speed and efficiency and another based on `Libart` for a high quality, anti-aliased engine.

The canvas handles all drawing and redrawing of its items, so we never have to worry about buffering to prevent flicker. Best of all, since canvas items are widgets themselves, we can dynamically redefine their properties.

To create a canvas based on the `Xlib` engine, we write:

```
GtkWidget *canvas;

gtk_widget_push_visual(gdk_imlib_get_visual());
gtk_widget_push_colormap(gdk_imlib_get_colormap());
canvas = gnome_canvas_new();
gtk_widget_pop_visual();
gtk_widget_pop_colormap();
```

The `visual` and `colormap` functions must be called if we wish to place images in the canvas. `gnome_canvas_new` then creates our canvas.

Then we will need to call `gnome_canvas_pixels_per_unit` to set the conversion setting between canvas units and pixels.

When we create canvas items, we specify a group to which it becomes a member, so that we can apply global changes to a group, such as moving or hiding the entire group.

Creating canvas items involves calling `gnome_canvas_item` with a NULL terminated list of arguments. First in the list is its parent group, then a macro that defines the type of object we want to create (rectangle, line, ellipse... etc) and then its object dependent properties.

Let's see how to create a red rectangle, 100 x 100 canvas units in size

```
GnomeCanvasItem *item;

Item = gnome_canvas_item_new(gnome_canvas_root(canvas),
                                            GNOME_TYPE_CANVAS_RECT,
                                             "x1", 0.0,
                                             "y1", 0.0,
                                             "x2", 100.0,
                                             "y2", 100.0,
                                            "fill_color", "red",
                                           NULL);
```

We precede each property of the rectangle with a string of that property. Let's look at some of the common arguments of both rectangles and ellipses (GNOME_TYPE_CANVAS_RECT and GNOME_TYPE_CANVAS_ELLIPSE).

Argument	Type	Description
x1	double	Leftmost coordinate of rectangle or ellipse.
y1	double	Topmost coordinate of rectangle or ellipse.
x2	double	Rightmost coordinate of rectangle or ellipse.
y2	double	Bottommost coordinate of rectangle or ellipse.
fill_color	string	X color specification for fill color.
outline_color	string	X color specification for outline color.
width_pixels	uint	Width of outline in pixels. (Outline will not scaled when the canvas scale factor is changed.)
width_units	double	Width of outline in canvas units. (Outline will be scaled when the canvas scale factor is changed.)

We can use the same structure for both rectangles and ellipses, because ellipses are placed inside an invisible rectangular bounding box specified by the coordinates

An Application in GNOME

We've touched briefly on the main building blocks of a GNOME application, so let's consolidate our knowledge by bringing widgets together to create a small application.

Probably the most flexible and impressive widget in GNOME is the canvas, so let's create a graphical clock that demonstrates its power.

Requirements

We'll design a traditional analogue clock, so we'll need to read the machine's local time and convert that into coordinates for the clock hands. The hands will be canvas items that we'll update with new coordinates every second. We'll also put in a circular clock outline and dots that show the hour and minute positions around the clock.

Naturally we'll put in some appropriate menus and a toolbar and also a preference dialog box where we'll be able to hide the second hand and change the zoom factor of the canvas.

What do we Need to Code?

We need to code functions to perform:

- The creation of the user interface with a window, menus and toolbar.
- A redrawing routine for the clock hands.
- Preference box creation and handling.

Let's go ahead and start coding.

Try It Out – A GNOME Clock

1. As usual, we start out with `#include` files. We'll need functions from the time and math libraries for determining the coordinates of the clock hands:

```
#include <gnome.h>
#include <time.h>
#include <math.h>
```

2. Now we `#define` some constants for our clock:

```
#define CANVAS_SIZE 100.0
#define MIDDLE (CANVAS_SIZE/2.0)
#define SECOND_HAND_LENGTH 40.0
#define MINUTE_HAND_LENGTH 45.0
#define HOUR_HAND_LENGTH 20.0
#define DOT_RADIUS 45.0    /* distance from center of the clock to dots */
```

3. Next we initialize our global variables:

```
GtkWidget *canvas = NULL;
GnomeCanvasItem *second_hand = NULL;
GnomeCanvasItem *hand = NULL;
gboolean secondhand_is_visible = TRUE;
GnomeCanvasPoints *points, *second_hand_points;  /* the arrays that hold the hand
coordinates */
GtkWidget *clock_app;
```

4. Now the prototypes for our functions:

```
static void create_dots (int dots, GtkWidget *canvas);
static void change_canvas_scale (GtkAdjustment *adj, gfloat *value);
static void show_preference_dlg (void);
static void show_about_dlg (void);
static void apply_preferences (GnomePropertyBox *property_box, gint page_num,
                               GtkWidget *sh_checkbox);
static gint redraw (gpointer data);
```

5. Here we define three top level menus, `file`, `settings` and `help`, which hold an '`exit`', '`preferences`' and '`about`' option respectively. We link the '`preferences`' and '`about`' items to functions in our program to bring up the appropriate dialog box.

```
GnomeUIInfo file_menu[] = {
  GNOMEUIINFO_MENU_EXIT_ITEM(gtk_main_quit, NULL),
  GNOMEUIINFO_END
};

GnomeUIInfo help_menu[] = {
  GNOMEUIINFO_MENU_ABOUT_ITEM(show_about_dlg, NULL),
  GNOMEUIINFO_END
};

GnomeUIInfo settings_menu[] = {
  GNOMEUIINFO_MENU_PREFERENCES_ITEM(show_preference_dlg, NULL),
  GNOMEUIINFO_END
};
GnomeUIInfo menubar[] = {
  GNOMEUIINFO_MENU_FILE_TREE(file_menu),
  GNOMEUIINFO_MENU_SETTINGS_TREE(settings_menu),
  GNOMEUIINFO_MENU_HELP_TREE(help_menu),
  GNOMEUIINFO_END
};
```

6. Next we define the toolbar, which holds a single item, an `Exit` button:

```
GnomeUIInfo toolbar[] = {
  GNOMEUIINFO_ITEM_STOCK("Exit", "Exit the application",
                          gtk_main_quit,
                          GNOME_STOCK_PIXMAP_EXIT),
GNOMEUIINFO_END
};
```

7. Now we define a function that creates the dots that go round the outside of the clock. We'll call it sixty times, one for each minute, and this function will calculate that dot's position around the clock and create the `CanvasItem`:

```
static void create_dot( int dots, GtkWidget* canvas)
{
 double angle = dots * M_PI / (360.0/12);
 double x1, y1, x2, y2;
 double size;
 GnomeCanvasItem *dot;
```

8. Here we select the size of the dot based on where it appears in the clock. We make the dots that appear at the 12, 3, 6 and 9 o'clock positions the largest, followed by the multiples of five minutes:

```
    if ((dots % 15) == 0) {
        size = 2.0;
    }
     else if ((dots % 5) == 0) {
       size = 1.0;
    }
     else size = 0.5;

    x1 = MIDDLE - size + (DOT_RADIUS * sin (angle));
    y1 = MIDDLE - size + (DOT_RADIUS * cos (angle));
    x2 = MIDDLE + size + (DOT_RADIUS * sin (angle));
    y2 = MIDDLE + size + (DOT_RADIUS * cos (angle));

    dot = gnome_canvas_item_new(gnome_canvas_root (GNOME_CANVAS(canvas)),
                                        GNOME_TYPE_CANVAS_ELLIPSE,
                                        "x1", x1,
                                        "y1", y1,
                                        "x2", x2,
                                        "y2", y2,
                                        "fill_color", "red",
                                       NULL);
  }
```

9. Next is the heart of the application, the function that redraws, or more accurately, redefines the coordinates of the clock hands based on the current local time. For the minute and hour hand we actually use a single line object, defined with three points, so that we only need to redraw two canvas items every second, the second hand and the hour/minute hand:

```
static gint redraw (gpointer data)
{
  struct tm *tm_ptr;
  time_t the_time;
  float second_angle;
  float minute_angle;
  float hour_angle;

  time(&the_time);
  tm_ptr = localtime (&the_time); /* See chapter 4 for an explanation of the time
function */
  second_angle = tm_ptr->tm_sec * M_PI / 30.0; /* The angle the second hand makes with
the vertical */
```

10. We set up the second hand coordinate array to draw a line from the middle to the point on the clock:

```
  second_hand_points->coords[0] = MIDDLE;
  second_hand_points->coords[1] = MIDDLE;
  second_hand_points->coords[2] = MIDDLE + (SECOND_HAND_LENGTH*sin(second_angle));
  second_hand_points->coords[3] = MIDDLE -  (SECOND_HAND_LENGTH * cos (second_angle));
```

11. Next we calculate the appropriate angles for the hour and minute hands and use these to fill the coordinate array:

```
minute_angle = tm_ptr->tm_min * M_PI / 30.0;
hour_angle = (tm_ptr->tm_hour % 12) * M_PI / 6.0 +  (M_PI * tm_ptr->tm_min / 360.0);

points->coords[0] = MIDDLE + (HOUR_HAND_LENGTH * sin (hour_angle));
points->coords[1] = MIDDLE - (HOUR_HAND_LENGTH * cos (hour_angle));
points->coords[2] = MIDDLE;
points->coords[3] = MIDDLE;
points->coords[4] = MIDDLE + (MINUTE_HAND_LENGTH * sin (minute_angle));
points->coords[5] = MIDDLE - (MINUTE_HAND_LENGTH * cos (minute_angle));
```

12. We check if the hands have been created. If not, we create them, otherwise we give them their new set of coordinates:

```
if (hand == NULL) {

   hand = (gnome_canvas_item_new(gnome_canvas_root (GNOME_CANVAS (canvas)),
                                 GNOME_TYPE_CANVAS_LINE,
                                 "points",points,
                                 "fill_color", "blue",
                                 "width_units", 3.5,
                                 "cap_style", GDK_CAP_ROUND,
                                 "join_style", GDK_JOIN_ROUND,
                                 NULL));
   second_hand = (gnome_canvas_item_new(gnome_canvas_root (GNOME_CANVAS (canvas)),
                                 GNOME_TYPE_CANVAS_LINE,
                                 "points",second_hand_points,
                                 "fill_color", "white",
                                 "width_pixels", 2,
                                 NULL));
  }
 else
  gnome_canvas_item_set (hand, "points", points, NULL);
  gnome_canvas_item_set (second_hand, "points", second_hand_points, NULL);
 }
```

13. This function creates an `about` dialog box which appears when we click on about in the help menu:

```
static void show_about_dlg(void)
{
 GtkWidget *about;
  const gchar *authors[] = { "Andrew Froggatt", NULL };

  about = gnome_about_new("Gnome Clock", "0.1",
                          "Released under the GNU Public License",
                          authors,
                          ("A simple graphical clock for GNOME"),
                          NULL);
  gtk_widget_show (about);
}
```

14. Here we create our preference box in which we place a check box and slider widget. The GnomePropertyBox widget is derived from the GnomeDialog widget and has the extra functionality of an embedded notebook widget that provides separate 'pages' each with a tab that we can use to separate groups of widgets. GnomePropertyBox also defines two new signals: apply and help. apply is sent whenever the user clicks on ok or apply, and help is sent when the help button is clicked. We use the signals to provide a non-modal box.

```
static void show_preference_dlg(void)
{
  GtkWidget *preferencebox;
  GtkWidget *vbox, *hbox;
  GtkWidget *sh_checkbox;
  GtkObject *adj;
  GtkWidget *hscale;
  GtkWidget *label;

  preferencebox = gnome_property_box_new();

  vbox = gtk_vbox_new(FALSE, 2);
  hbox = gtk_hbox_new(FALSE, 0);

  sh_checkbox = gtk_check_button_new_with_label( "Second hand visible");
  gtk_toggle_button_set_state(GTK_TOGGLE_BUTTON (sh_checkbox),
                                  secondhand_is_visible);
  gtk_box_pack_start (GTK_BOX (vbox), sh_checkbox, FALSE, FALSE, 0);
```

15. We set up a signal handlers for the check box so that the ok and apply buttons become 'sensitive' (unshaded) when the check box is toggled:

```
  gtk_signal_connect_object (GTK_OBJECT(sh_checkbox), "toggled",
                                  GTK_SIGNAL_FUNC(gnome_property_box_changed),
                                  GTK_OBJECT(preferencebox));

  label = gtk_label_new("Clock zoom factor: ");
  gtk_misc_set_alignment (GTK_MISC (label), 1.0, 1.0);
  gtk_box_pack_start (GTK_BOX (hbox), label, FALSE, FALSE, 0);
```

16. Next we create a scale widget that will zoom our canvas and link two signal handlers to the value_changed signal called when a user has moved the scale widget:

```
  adj = gtk_adjustment_new (2.0, 0.1, 7.0, 1.0, 1.0, 1.0);  /* (default, min, max,
step, page, page size) */
  hscale = gtk_hscale_new (GTK_ADJUSTMENT (adj));

  gtk_signal_connect_object (GTK_OBJECT (adj), "value_changed",
                             GTK_SIGNAL_FUNC(gnome_property_box_changed),
                             GTK_OBJECT(preferencebox));

  gtk_signal_connect_object (GTK_OBJECT (adj), "value_changed",
                             GTK_SIGNAL_FUNC (change_canvas_scale),
                             &(GTK_ADJUSTMENT (adj)->value));

  gtk_signal_connect (GTK_OBJECT (preferencebox), "apply",
                          GTK_SIGNAL_FUNC(apply_preferences), sh_checkbox);

  gtk_box_pack_start (GTK_BOX (hbox), hscale, TRUE, TRUE, 0);
  gtk_box_pack_start (GTK_BOX (vbox), hbox, FALSE, FALSE, 0);
```

```
  gnome_dialog_set_parent(GNOME_DIALOG(preferencebox), GTK_WINDOW(clock_app));

  gnome_property_box_append_page(GNOME_PROPERTY_BOX(preferencebox),
                                 vbox,
                                 gtk_label_new("General"));

  gtk_widget_show_all(preferencebox);
}
```

17. Next is the function that gets called whenever the **ok** or **apply** buttons in the preference window are clicked. `page_num` refers to the current notebook page, to provide future support for a per-page **apply** button. The idea is that the **apply** signal is sent once for each notebook page, and once with a -1 `page_num`. We just reject any page other than -1. When we receive the -1 page, we make the second hand visible or invisible according to the status of the check box in the preferences dialog box. We update the global variable `secondhand_is_visible` so that the check box displays the correct state if the property box is closed and re-created. Note that the `GnomePropertyBox` widget takes care of closing the property window for us, when **ok** or **close** are clicked:

```
static void apply_preferences (GnomePropertyBox *property_box, gint page_num,
GtkWidget *sh_checkbox)
{
  if (page_num != -1)
       return;
  if (gtk_toggle_button_get_active(GTK_TOGGLE_BUTTON (sh_checkbox) ) == FALSE) {
   gnome_canvas_item_hide(second_hand);
   secondhand_is_visible = FALSE;
  }
   else {
   gnome_canvas_item_show(second_hand);
   secondhand_is_visible = TRUE;
  }
```

18. When the scale widget is moved, we update the canvas scale factor and adjust the size of the window so that the clock fits:

```
static void change_canvas_scale (GtkAdjustment *adj, gfloat *value)
{
   gnome_canvas_set_pixels_per_unit (GNOME_CANVAS (canvas),
                                     (double) *value);
   gtk_widget_set_usize(GTK_WIDGET (clock_app),
                        110 * (double) *value,
                        125 * (double) *value);
}
```

19. Finally we get to `main` where we do the usual initialization and creation of our widgets:

```
int main (int argc, char *argv[])
{

  GnomeCanvasItem *clock_outline;
  gint dots;

  gnome_init ("clock", "0.1", argc, argv);
  clock_app = gnome_app_new ("clock", "Gnome Clock");
```

```
  gtk_widget_set_usize (clock_app, CANVAS_SIZE, CANVAS_SIZE);
  gtk_widget_push_visual(gdk_imlib_get_visual());
  gtk_widget_push_colormap(gdk_imlib_get_colormap());
  canvas = gnome_canvas_new();
  gtk_widget_pop_visual();
  gtk_widget_pop_colormap();

  gnome_canvas_set_pixels_per_unit (GNOME_CANVAS (canvas), 2);
  second_hand_points = gnome_canvas_points_new(2);
  points = gnome_canvas_points_new(3);

  gtk_signal_connect (GTK_OBJECT (clock_app), "delete_event",
                      GTK_SIGNAL_FUNC (gtk_main_quit),
                      NULL);

  gtk_widget_set_usize(clock_app, 220, 300);


  gnome_app_set_contents (GNOME_APP (clock_app), canvas);
  gnome_app_create_menus (GNOME_APP (clock_app), menubar);
  gnome_app_create_toolbar (GNOME_APP (clock_app), toolbar);

  clock_outline = gnome_canvas_item_new (gnome_canvas_root(GNOME_CANVAS (canvas)),
                                         GNOME_TYPE_CANVAS_ELLIPSE,
                                         "x1", 0.0,
                                         "y1", 0.0,
                                         "x2", CANVAS_SIZE,
                                         "y2", CANVAS_SIZE,
                                         "outline_color", "yellow",
                                         "width_units", 4.0,
                                         NULL);
```

20. Here we create the sixty dots to mark out the minutes on our clock:

```
 for (dots = 0; dots < 60; dots++) {
   create_dot ( dots, canvas);
 }
```

21. This is the crucial function that calls redraw every 1000 milliseconds to update our clock:

```
  gtk_timeout_add(1000, redraw, canvas);

  redraw(canvas); /* make sure our hands are created before we display the clock */
  gtk_widget_show_all(clock_app);
  gtk_main();
 return 0;
}
```

That completes the code for creating the clock. When we've compiled and run the example, we should see our clock appear and start ticking:

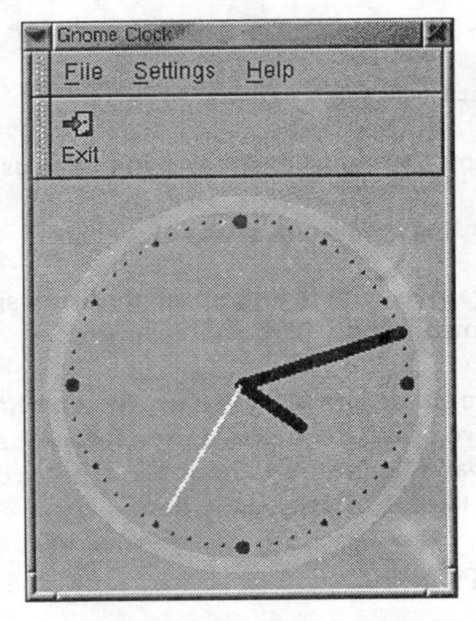

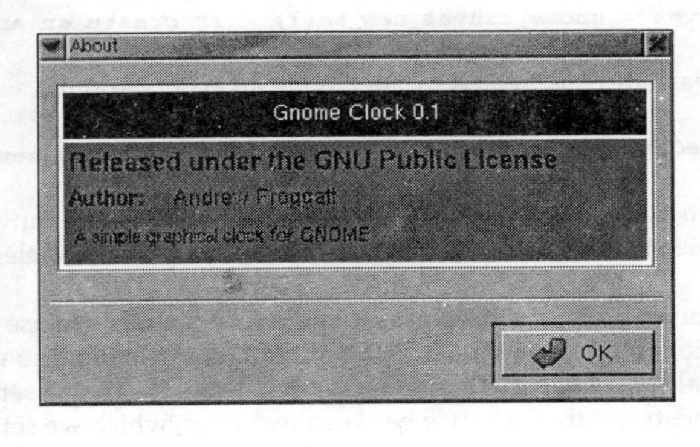

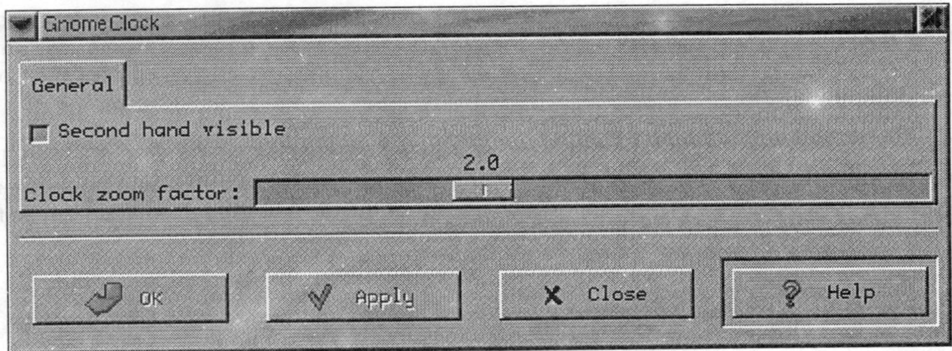

How it works

It may be lengthy, but it's essentially quite a simple example. The key to making the clock function is the `gtk_timeout_add` function, which calls `redraw` every second. In `redraw`, we calculate where the hands should point, set up the coordinate arrays and call `gnome_canvas_item_set` to update the canvas items.

The property dialog function takes a little explaining. We create a check box widget to toggle the visibility of the second hand and a scale widget that we link to the scale of the canvas. We handle changes in the state of the check box and scale widget in different ways. We wait until either the ok or apply buttons are pressed to update the visibility of the second hand, based on the check box state, but the canvas scale is changed immediately on alteration of the scale widget via the `value_changed` signal associated with scale widgets. This has the effect of instant zooming in and out as the scale widget is adjusted.

You might like to create an anti-aliased canvas instead to give a high quality clock, but beware! It can be resource intensive. All you need to do is change the canvas creation lines to read:

```
gtk_widget_push_visual(gdk_rgb_get_visual());
gtk_widget_push_colormap(gdk_rgb_get_cmap());
canvas = gnome_canvas_new_aa();    /* create an anti-aliased canvas */
```

Canvas lines are created by specifying an array of points, which we must create and initialize using:

```
GnomeCanvasPoints points = gnome_canvas_points_new (gint num_of_points)
```

where `num_of_points` is the number of points on the canvas we want to join up, so the array size is twice this size to hold the x coordinates in the even numbered elements and y in the odd elements.

Instead of having separate hour and minute hands, we use a single line that joins up the hour hand position to the center, then to the minute hand position, so we pass 3 to `gnome_canvas_points`. There is no real advantage in doing this, as opposed to creating a separate minute and hour hand, but it does demonstrates the join style between two lines, which we set to `GDK_JOIN_ROUND` here.

Before we finish, let's mention a few more of the canvas properties.

Canvas items and groups obey a stacking arrangement. Items created last are always on top, and to change the stacking order, you use the `gnome_canvas_item_lower` / `gnome_canvas_raise` functions. The canvas support text and images as well as simple items like lines, rectangles, ellipses and polygons Canvas items can have signal handlers attached to them

Ok, so what's next? We've reached the end of our whirlwind tour of GNOME now, and hopefully we've learnt enough about using widgets and programming methods in GNOME to be able to use the reference material on the web to create our own applications. Some of the most useful information can be found by examining the well documented header files usually found in `/usr/include/`.

CD Application in GNOME

You can find the source code to a GNOME front end to the CD database, where more widgets are used and explained, together with all the examples in this chapter on the Wrox web site, www.wrox.com.

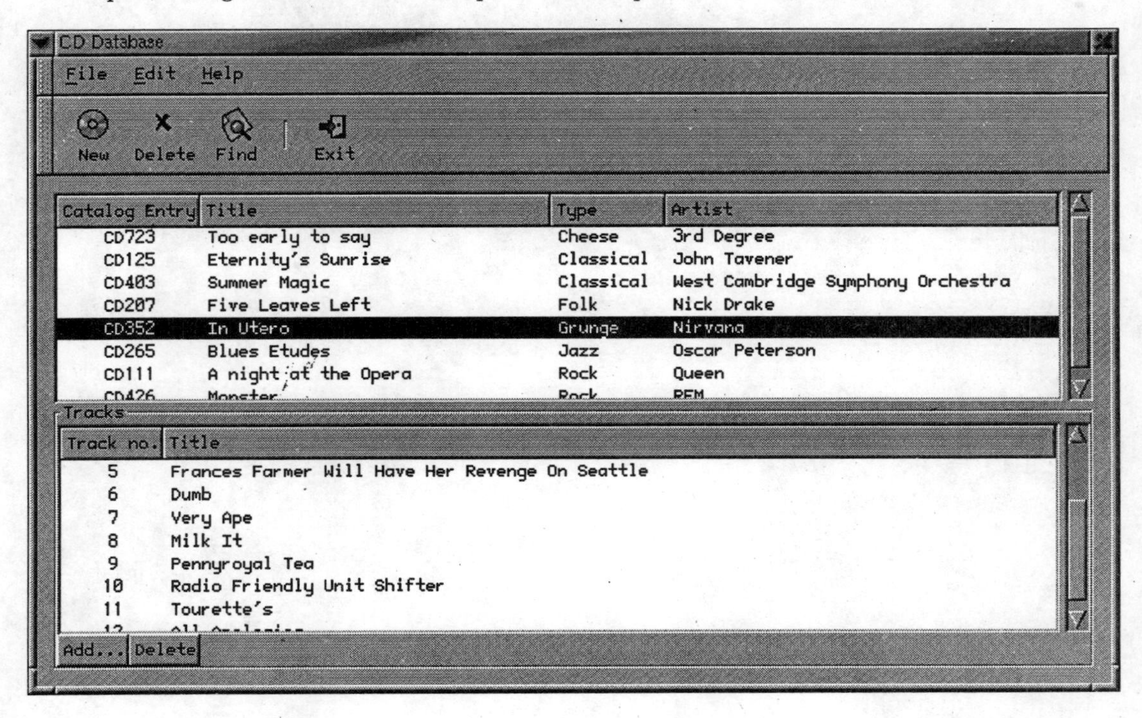

Of course there's never enough room to cover everything, and there's no question that we've only scratched the surface of GNOME. In some respects, a book should only cover the basics, because any detailed printed manuals at the current stage in GNOME's development will be soon out of date.

The GNOME community is busy and thriving. Currently around 300 programmers worldwide are regularly contributing to the cause. Maybe this chapter has fired your imagination enough for you to become one of them. Good luck, and happy GNOMEing!

Summary

In this chapter we've learnt what GNOME is and the basics of writing applications that take advantage of what GNOME has to offer.

We've seen the base toolkit, GTK+, and learnt how to use several of its widgets and also seen how to use the GNOME canvas.

The Perl Programming Language

Sitting in between shell and C, and influenced by many of the standard UNIX tools, Larry Wall's Perl programming language is ideally suited to text manipulation, CGI scripting and system administration tasks. However, as we will see, Perl is very extensible (you can even write graphical user interfaces in it using the PerlTk extensions). It would be fair to say that anything you can do in C, you can do in Perl, and probably much easier, too. Perl is particularly easy to learn, since it borrows elements from a whole host of programming languages and utilities which will probably be already familiar to you; C and shell programmers will feel particularly at home with it. sed, awk, Basic and Tcl programmers will not feel left out either.

One of the nicest features of Perl is that it provides a platform-independent UNIX-like abstraction layer on top of your operating system. What does this mean? Perl runs on a huge variety of platforms, including Windows, the Apple Macintosh, and, of course, anything that looks like UNIX. You can bring over all of the ideas about Linux programming we've seen so far, and Perl will implement them as well as it can on whatever we're running on. In effect, you can pretend any target operating system looks and behaves exactly like Linux does, which, as I'm sure you'll agree, is such a pleasant way of looking at things.

In this chapter, we'll be looking at how to write basic Perl scripts, carrying over what we've learnt so far into Perl. We can't deal with the whole of the Perl language in this chapter, but we'll examine the most useful and most commonly used areas, as well as how we'd implement our familiar CD database application in Perl.

An Introduction to Perl

Let's start off by looking at the basic features of the Perl language: variables, operators and functions, regular expressions and file input and output. There's a lot of information coming over the next few pages, and we won't really put it all together until the end. However, you should be familiar with all of the concepts coming up, so hopefully, it shouldn't be too heavy reading.

First , I suppose, we ought to check to make sure you've got a copy of Perl on your system. Most Linux distributions come with Perl these days, so you should be able to just type `perl -v` and get something like the following:

```
This is perl, version 5.005_03 built for i386-linux

Copyright 1987-1999, Larry Wall
```

```
Perl may be copied only under the terms of either the Artistic License or the GNU
General Public License, which may be found in the Perl 5.0 source kit.

Complete documentation for Perl, including FAQ lists, should be found on this system
using 'man perl' or 'perldoc perl'.  If you have access to the Internet, point your
browser at http://www.perl.com/, the Perl Home Page.
```

If that doesn't happen, check your path and your Linux package manager, if you have one, to see if you've actually got Perl installed; if not, you can get a recent copy from your Linux CD, the contrib or main sections of your Linux distributor's FTP site, or in source form from CPAN. (Which we'll describe later.) As it says, http://www.perl.com/ is the Perl Home Page, and contains a wealth of documentation, news and generally useful information about Perl.

Hello, Perl

First of all, let's see what a simple Perl program looks like, and how we run it. Here's our script, which we'll call `hello.pl`:

```
print "Hello, World\n";
```

Now, we could run this through the perl interpreter from the command line:

```
$ perl hello.pl
Hello, World
$
```

As expected, Perl says 'hello' and returns us to our shell prompt. Just like when we were writing shell scripts, we can use the `#!` convention to tell Linux where the interpreter is installed. Let's change `hello.pl` so that it looks like this:

```
#!/usr/bin/perl -w
# hello.pl, version 2
print "Hello, World\n";
```

(You might need to change the `#!/usr/bin/perl` to the actual location of your perl binary. Use `which perl`, or your shell's equivalent, to find out where it resides.)

Next, we need to make the file executable before we can run it:

```
$ chmod 755 hello.pl
```

Now we can run the file as we did with shell scripts:

```
$ ./hello.pl
```

Some things to note from this example:

1. Perl statements, like C statements, end with a semicolon. Also as in C, newlines in strings are represented by `\n`. All of the other string 'metacharacters' are borrowed wholesale from C.
2. Just like shell and Tcl, we're allowed to have comments starting with hashes. (Although, just like shell, `#!` has a special meaning.)
3. The "-w" in the first line is an option to the perl interpreter, which turns on extra warnings. This is highly recommended; although Perl allows us to get away with a lot of sloppy coding, our scripts will usually run more reliably if they pass the "-w" test.

Perl Variables

Perl has three variable types: scalars, arrays and hashes.

Scalars

Scalar variables are ordinary strings and numbers; these look and operate a lot like shell variables - we could rewrite our script, should we want to, like this:

```
$message = "Hello, World\n";
print $message;
```

C programmers might feel happier saying `print($message)`, and you can do that too. Perl is very relaxed about the need for braces around functions like `print`. Use this to increase readability, not decrease it. Similarly, unlike shell but like C, we can have spaces around the equals sign of an assignment statement if we want them. Note that unlike C, however, we don't need to allocate and deallocate space for our variables, nor do we need to declare them in advance; Perl takes care of all that, leaving you free to concentrate on getting the program written efficiently.

C programmers may also be happier using `printf` instead of `print`; Perl provides you with a `printf` function which works just like the C and shell functions of the same name. However, `print` is more efficient, so unless you need the formatting capabilities of `printf`, use `print` where you can.

Arrays

Arrays are the variable incarnation of **lists**, just like in Tcl. Instead of starting with a `$`, array variables are denoted by an `@`. Here's a simple list:

```
(1, 2, 3, 4)
```

and here's how we put it into a variable:

```
@mylist = (1, 2, 3, 4);
```

Now, what if we want to get things out of it again? Let's have a look at a simple list in operation, then we'll explain what's going on.

```
@message = ("\n", " ", "World", "Hello,");
print $message[3], $message[1], $message[2], $message[0];
```

OK, you know exactly what it's going to say, but how does it do it? The first thing to note is that we can have multiple parameters to `print` separated by commas. These actually form a **list**, but that's not the important part. (It'll get important later.)

Next, you'll have noted that our array is called `@message` but we referenced it with `$message[element]` This makes sense if you think about it from the point of view of "what you want" not "what you've got" - when we're pulling elements out one-by-one, we actually "want" scalar values from it, not arrays. (Don't be tricked into thinking that `$message` and `@message` refer to the same variable, though - they're independent; `$message` on its own doesn't refer to any elements in the array.)

Finally, the first array element is 0; fine if you're used to C, but possibly disturbing if you program BASIC, Pascal or sed/awk. You can change the number of the first array element array to 1 if you want, but the effects can be quite horrific, so it's best to leave it alone.

You may not want to grab individual elements, but rather a range or *array slice*. You can do this by giving a range of elements, and remembering that this time we do want a list, not a scalar:

```
@a = ("zero", "one", "two", "three", "four");
@b = @a[0,2..3]; # @b is ("zero", "two", three");

# Reducing it to one statement:
@b = ("zero", "one", "two", "three", "four")[0,2..3];
```

Perl automatically **flattens** lists; that is to say, lists cannot contain other lists, nor can arrays be multi-dimensional. (You can do that with references, but that's beyond the scope of this chapter; see the `perlref` and `perllol` manpages for more on how to do that.) This means that the following statements are equivalent:

```
@a = ("zero", "one", "two", "three", "four");

@a = ("zero", "one", ("two", "three"), "four");

@half = ("zero", "one", "two"); @half2 = ("three", "four");
@a = (@half, @half2);
```

You're also allowed to have lists on the left-hand side of an assignment, and in fact, this is a very useful thing to do:

```
($first, $last) = ("alpha", "omega");

@a = ("alpha", "omega") ; ($first, $last) = @a; # Same thing.
```

Things that are put on the left-hand side of an assignment are called "lvalues"; we say lists are 'lvaluable'. One really flash use of this is to swap the values of two variables without using a temporary variable. Here's the C programmer's way to do it:

```
$temp = $last;
$last = $first;
$first = $temp;
```

Whereas a native would say:

```
($first, $last) = ($last, $first);
```

Hashes

The final variable type we can have are **hashes**, also known as associative arrays. These allow you to store and retrieve data by keys, and the symbol for a hash is `%`. Hashes are very handy for representing relationships between data. Here's a simple hash in use to store and retrieve phone numbers:

```
%phonebook = ( "Bob" => "247305",
               "Phil" => "205832",
               "Sara" => "226010" );
```

We created our hash just like a list, but used the => operator (which is equivalent to a comma in most cases) to separate our key-value pairs. Now let's get at an entry:

```
print "Sara's phone number is ", $phonebook{"Sara"}, "\n";
print "Bob's phone number is ", $phonebook{Bob}, "\n";
```

Again we want a scalar, so we use the dollar sign. To signify which key we want to reference, we use braces rather than square brackets, and the second line illustrates the fact that we don't need to put quotes around the key. Be careful, though: hash keys, just like variable names, are case sensitive: `$phonebook{Bob}` is the same as `$phonebook{"Bob"}` but not the same as `$phonebook{bob}`. Once we've got this far, changing an entry in the hash is easy enough:

```
$phonebook{Bob} = "293028";
print "Bob's new number is ", $phonebook{Bob}, "\n";
```

Quoting and Substitution

Just like in shell scripting, variables inside double-quoted strings are substituted unless escaped with backslashes. We could rewrite our phonebook example like this:

```
%phonebook = ( "Bob" => "247305",
               "Phil" => "205832",
               "Sara" => "226010" );
print "Sara's phone number is $phonebook{Sara}\n";
print "Bob's phone number is $phonebook{Bob}\n";
```

(Don't put double-quoted strings inside double-quoted strings, obviously.)

As you might expect, as in the shell, single quotes don't cause substitution to happen or special characters like `\n` to work:

```
$myvar = "quoting";
print 'Take care when $myvar strings\n';
print "Take care when $myvar strings\n";
```

gives the following output:

```
Take care when $myvar strings\nTake care when quoting strings
```

As in Tcl, Perl converts between numbers and strings on demand:

```
print "4 bananas"+1; # Gives "5"
print "123" + "456"; # Gives "579"
```

Special Variables

Perl has a huge number of special variables, and we'll come across a few of them as we continue, but the most important three are these: `$_` is the default scalar for a lot of operations and functions. For instance, `print` with no arguments prints the value of `$_`. This can be really useful, but can also lead to code like this:

```
# Strip comment lines.
while (<>) { print unless /^#/ }
```

The variable `$_` was used three times there; once to get a line from standard input, (the <> or readline operator, which we'll cover later - but for the moment, remember what it does) once as the argument to `print`, and once to test against whether it started with a hash sign. (Again, we'll explain the tricky bit `/^#/` when we come to regular expressions later.). To a seasoned Perl programmer, this sort of code is bread-and-butter, but it can scare off newcomers. Don't omit `$_` in your own code unless your intention is clear.

There's also the `@ARGV` array, which contains the arguments to your program; Unlike in C, you don't get `argv[0]` as the name of your script. (That comes from `$0`.) Instead, `$ARGV[0]` is the first argument.

Finally, the `%ENV` hash allows you to inspect and change environment variables, as you would in shell programming, like this:

```
print $ENV{PATH}; # /usr/local/bin:/usr/bin...
print $ENV{EDITOR}; # vi
$ENV{EDITOR} = "emacs"; # change to emacs for the rest of the program.
```

Operators and Functions

In Perl, the ideas of 'function' and 'operator' aren't very clearly separated; some things you might think of as functions turn out to be operators, and vice versa. Because of this, we're not really going to make the distinction here. Let's use 'function' and 'operator' interchangeably.

Numeric Operators

What things can we do to numbers? Well, the first four are pretty guessable: +, -, * and / all do what you would expect, and can be combined with brackets in the usual way. Rules of precedence are pretty much the same as in C.

```
$a = (4*5)+3; # 23
$b = 1/(4+4); # 0.125
$c = 1/4+4; # 4.25
```

We can also use the remainder operator (also known as the *modulus* operator) `%`. However, be sure you're dealing with positive numbers when you use this; if you have `$a % -$b` the result is `($a % $b) - $a` which might not be what you expected. There's also the *exponentiation* operator, `**`.

```
$a = 17 % 5; # 17 into 5 goes 3 times remainder 2, so $a = 2
$a = 22 % -7; # 22 into 7 goes 3 times remainder 1, so $a = 1-7 = -6
$a = 2 ** 8; # 2 raised to the 8 is 256
```

For variables, we can use pre- and post-fix decrement and increment, (although these can operate differently on strings) as in C.

```
$a = 5; $b = 7;
$c = ++$a + $b; # $c is 6+7 = 13
```

Then there are the normal scientific functions: trigonometric `sin` and `cos`, `sqrt`, and `log` for square roots and natural logarithms, and so on. The 'perlop' and 'perlfunc' manpages will tell you all about these.

String Operators

One of the most common things we'll do to strings is to concatenate them, and we do this with the dot operator. Auto-conversion between numbers and strings takes place as normal:

```
$a = "foo" . "bar" . "baz" ; # Gives us "foobarbaz"
$a = "number " . 1 ;         # Gives "number 1"
$a = "1" . "2" ;             # Gives "12"
```

We might also want to repeat a string a given number of times. This is done with the cross, or x operator:

```
$a = "ba".("na"x4) ; # "bananananana"
$a = 1 x 3 ; # 111
```

The second example gives us a good reason not to confuse x and *.

Another common thing to do to a string is to remove the last character. The chop function removes the last character, no matter what it might be; chomp is more subtle, and removes the input record separator (usually a newline) from the end of the string. This is superb when you're reading input in from text files, where you don't want to blindly assume that the last character you read will be a newline. chop and chomp both return the new string and change the variable you gave them.

```
$a="bite me\n";
chomp($a); # $a is now "bite me"
chomp($a); # $a is still "bite me" since there's no newline
chop($a)   # $a is now "bite m"
```

If our strings are explicitly alphabetic, incrementing them works as you might expect - the ASCII value of the last character is increased, wrapping from 'z' or 'Z' to 'a'. If the strings start with a number, however, Perl will convert them to a numeral and the rest will be lost.

```
$a = "abc"; print ++$a; # Returns "abd"
$a = "azz"; print ++$a; # Returns "baa"
$a = "0 Goodbye Cruel World"; print ++$a; # Returns 1
```

As well as joining strings together, it's also very useful to split them up, which is done with the split function. You can split on a string or on a regular expression; if you give no arguments, it splits $_ on whitespace; you can give as an optional first argument, a pattern to split on, and as an optional second argument the text to split. Note that if you give a string to split on, you must also supply a pattern as the first argument; a common mistake is to omit the pattern but leave the text.

```
# Split $_ on whitespace
$_ = "one two three";
@a = split; # ("one", "two", "three")

$passwd="simon:x:500:500:Simon Cozens,,,:/home/simon:/bin/zsh";

@passwd= split ":", $passwd; # Split on a string.
# Can also write it like this:
@passwd= split /:/ $passwd; # Split on a regular expression.(Same thing)
($uid, $gid) = @passwd[2,3];

# More idiomatically:

($uid, $gid) = (split ":", $passwd)[2,3];
```

The exact opposite - converting a list to a string - can be done with join. Again, you can join things together with delimiters:

```
@mylist = ("one", "two", "three", "four");
$mystring = join "?", @mylist; # one?two?three?four
```

Anyone familiar with BASIC will know what `substr` does; it returns a substring from inside the string. You must supply two parameters: the string, and the offset. These two alone will get you everything from the offset to the end of the string. (A negative offset means 'count back from the end of the string': -1 is the last character, -2 the last but one, and so on.) Supplying another parameter, the length, will get you a maximum of that many characters.

```
$string="the glistening trophies";
print substr($string, 15); # trophies
print substr($string, -3); # ies
print substr($string, -18, 9); # listening
print substr($string, 4, 4); # glis
```

You can also use `substr` to modify a string, either by giving it another parameter:

```
substr($string, 7, 4, "tter"); # Returns "sten"
print $string;                 # the glittering trophies
```

(Note that this changes the string and returns what was in its place.) or, the more idiomatic way, by the assignment:

```
substr($string, 7, 4) ="tter"; # Functions as lvalues.
```

Let's quickly run through the final few functions since they're simple enough. `length` does what you expect: returns the length of a string. (You can't truncate a string by assigning to its length, though.) `reverse` returns the string in reverse. However, `reverse` is usually a list operation; it treats its parameters as a list, and returns the list in reverse order. If we feed it a string, though, it treats it as a one element list - which is the same in reverse order. To get what we expect, we need to force it into *scalar* operation, with the `scalar` keyword.

```
$a="Just Another Perl Hacker";
print length $a; # 24
print reverse $a; # list context - "Just Another Perl Hacker"
print scalar reverse $a; # "rekcaH lreP rehtonA tsuJ"
```

Finally `uc` and `lc` convert to upper and lower case, respectively, and `ucfirst` and `lcfirst` convert the first letter of the string to upper and lower case.

```
$zippy="YOW!! I am having FUN!!";
print uc($zippy); # YOW!! I AM HAVING FUN!!
print lc($zippy); # yow!! i am having fun!!
print ucfirst(lc($zippy)); # Yow!! i am having fun!!
print lcfirst(uc($zippy)); # yOW!! I AM HAVING FUN!!
```

Logical and Bitwise Operators

The ordinary bitwise operators `&`, (and) `|`, (or) `^` (xor) and `~` (not), as well as the bit shift operators >> and << all work on integers as you'd expect from C; You can even use the `0x` and `0` prefixes for hexadecimal and octal numbers.

```
0xF0 | 0x0F = 255 (0xFF)
0xAA ^ 0x10 = 186 (0xBA)
```

The logical operators `&&`, `||` and `!` also work as in C, but you can also use the English "and", "or" and "not". Because of Perl's short-circuit evaluation, these are often used as control structures:

```
risky_function()
  and print "Worked fine\n"
or print "Function didn't succeed\n";

# Also written as:
risky_function() && print "Worked fine\n"
|| print "Function didn't succeed\n";
```

You can also use `if` and `unless` in the same way:

```
print "Worked fine\n" if risky_function();
$a="Default value" unless $a;
```

You can obtain your true or false values either from scalars ("0" and undefined are false values - everything else is true) or from comparisons, of which there are many. You can compare numbers with the standard <, >, == (= is assignment; don't confuse the two.) and `!=`, but for strings you have to use a special set of comparisons: `lt` for lexicographically less, `gt` for greater, `eq` for equality, and `ne` for inequality.

Array Operations

We've seen most of the things we can do with scalars; that is, strings and numbers. What about arrays and lists?

One important thing you'll want to do with an array is to find the number of elements in it; you might think about using `length`, but this won't work. Instead, we have to evaluate the array in scalar context, like we did when reversing strings. Notice, however, that Perl doesn't support "sparse arrays"; the array is assumed to be filled with elements that are undefined.

```
@array = ("zero","one","two","three");
print scalar @array; # 4 elements in the array

$array[200] = "two hundred";
print scalar @array; # 201 elements; some of them are empty, though.
```

Perl also allows us to get at the index of the highest-numbered element. This is usually one less than the number of elements in the array, as we start counting from zero:

```
@array = ("zero","one","two","three");
print $#array; # 3
```

Next, we can take elements off the array. We can either think of it as an array in shell programming and `shift` the elements off the front of it, or as a stack, and `pop` elements off the end.

```
@array = ("zero","one","two","three");

print shift @array; # zero - array is now ("one","two","three")
print pop @array; # three - array is now ("one","two")
print shift @array; # one - array is now ("two")
print pop @array; # two - array is now ()
```

Similarly, we can put things back; either with `unshift` or `push`. We can put things on several elements at a time.

```
@array = ();
push @array, "two"; # array is now ("two")
unshift @array, "one"; # array is now ("one","two")
push @array, "three", "four"; # array is now ("one","two","three","four")
unshift @array, "minus one","zero";
print join ",", @array;
# minus one,zero,one,two,three,four
```

Now we can demonstrate the list use of `reverse`:

```
print join ",", reverse @array;
# four,three,two,one,zero,minus one
```

We can sort lists into ASCII order with `sort`;

```
@a = ("delta","alpha","charlie","bravo");
@b = sort @a; # ("alpha","bravo","charlie","delta");
```

You can also pick your own sort order by using the special 'BLOCK' form; Perl sets `$a` and `$b` to be the two values under comparison. In this case, for numerical values, we use the special comparison operator <=> which returns –1 if the left is bigger than the right, 0 if they are equal, and 1 if the right is bigger than the left.

```
@a = (5, 8, 3, 0, 1);
@b = sort {$a <=> $b} @a; #(0, 1, 3, 5, 8)
```

Hash Operations

Finally, we can do various things to hashes. The most magical is the `reverse` operation, which reverses the lookup tables:

```
%phonebook = ( "Bob" => "247305",
               "Phil" => "205832",
               "Sara" => "226010" );
%index = reverse %phonebook;
print $index{"226010"}; # Sara
```

You must be careful that you do not end up with two keys with the same value - one will get lost.
You can also extract a list of the keys and the values with the `keys` and `values` functions:

```
@names = keys %phonebook; # ("Bob", "Phil", "Sara")
@numbers = values %phonebook; # ("247305", "205832", "226010")
```

You can also get key-value pairs with `each`; every call to `each` returns a two-element list consisting of a new key and its value, until there are no more left.

```
while ( ($key, $value)  = each %phonebook ) {
        print "$key\'s phone number is $value\n";
}
```

Don't be fooled into thinking that the order you put items into a hash is the same as the order you'll get them out. Perl returns items in a seemingly random order - in fact, you can't guarantee that you'll get the same order twice.

Regular Expressions

Regular expressions (insiders call them "regexps") are one of Perl's greatest strengths. They allow for extremely powerful pattern matching and substitution, and are probably the biggest weapon in the Perl programmer's armory. Those familiar with `sed` and `awk` or `egrep` will know the general principles of regular expressions; Perl's regular expression engine encompasses and extends the `sed` model.

First, we'll look at how we use regular expressions to match strings, then we'll see how to substitute with them.

Matching

The most basic regular expression is just a piece of text we want to find inside a string. We traditionally enclose regexps in forward slashes, like this: `/regexp/`, and we "apply" a regexp to a variable or scalar using the syntax `$scalar =~ /regexp/` This functions as an operator which returns true if the match was successful. (There's also `!~` which is like `=~` only negated - returns true if the match failed.) So, let's see if our string contains "jaws":

```
$sea = "water sand Jaws swimmers";
print "Shark alert!" if $sea =~ /jaws/;
```

Well, that didn't print anything, because regular expressions are case sensitive by default; we can turn this off with the *modifier* 'i' like this:

```
print "Shark alert!" if $sea =~ /jaws/i;
```

Next, we can have special characters in our regexp: ^ stands for 'beginning of string' - that is, the expression we're trying to find must be the first thing in the string. Similarly, $ represents the end of the string; It should, for obvious reasons, come at the end of the regexp. If we tell you that `/regexp/` on its own tests the `$_` variable, we're now in a position to explain the confusing code we used to warn against implicit use of `$_` a few pages ago:

```
# Strip lines starting with a hash
while (<>) { print unless /^#/ }
```

To write it explicitly:

```
# Strip lines starting with a hash.
while ($_ = <>) { print $_ unless $_ =~ /^#/ }
```

In other words, while `$_` is true (i.e. contains something) after being set to the next line of standard input, we print the line unless the line starts with a hash sign.

Now we come up against the quantifiers: ? matches a character 0 or 1 times, that is, it states that the character it follows is optional in the match. * matches 0 or more times, just like in the shell. (However, be careful with that one: `/q*/` will **always** match, even if there are no "q"s in the string; it matched 0 times.) A + will match at least once. Here are some examples of quantifiers:

`/shoo?t/`	matches "shot" or "shoot".
`/sho+t/`	matches "shot" or "shoot" or "shooot" and so on but not "sht".
`/sho*t/`	matches "sht", "shot", "shoot" and so on.

The next set of special characters match different types of character: As well as all our usual metacharacters, `\t` for tab, `\n` for newline and so on, `\s` matches anything that looks like whitespace, `\w` matches a "word" (alphanumeric or "_") character, and `\d` matches a digit. These can be negated by capitalizing them: `\S` is a non-space, `\W` is a non-word, and `\D` is a non-digit. Furthermore, `.` matches anything at all. So:

`/push\s*chair/`	matches "push" then zero or more spaces or tabs, then "chair".
`/number\s*\d+\s/`	matches "number" then some optional whitespace, then one or more digits followed by a space.
`/^e.*d$/`	matches an "e" at the beginning of the line, then anything at all, and a "d" at the end of the line.
`/\S/`	matches a line that contains something other than just spaces.
`/\sPerl\s/`	matches the string "Perl" surrounded by space.

The last example is almost always better written as `/\bPerl\b/` - the 'word boundary' metacharacter matches non-word characters (allowing spaces, punctuation and so on) and the beginning or end of the string. Hence, `/\b\w+\b/` matches a 'word'.

What if we want to know what was matched? Well, if we place brackets around the part of the regular expression we're interested in, Perl will save it away for us. Just like sed, Perl will put the first bracketed expression into a variable caled `$1`, the next into `$2` and so on. From this we can get an insight into how the matching process works:

```
$test = "he said she said";
$test =~ /\b(\w+)\b/; # $1 is set to "he"
$test =~ /(sa.*d)/; # $1 is set to "said she said"
```

From the first example, Perl returns the first match it finds from the left, always. (This is called "eagerness".) From the second, Perl keeps matching from the first match it finds for as long as it can; it returns the first match it finds and seeks to make that as big a match as possible. (This is called "greed".) You can turn off greed by adding a `?` onto the quantifier - `/(sa.*?d)/` would have just matched "said". Helpfully, Perl also returns all the bracketed matches as a list if we're looking for a list:

```
$test = "he said she said";
@matches = $test =~ /\s*(\w+)\s*(\w+)\s*(\w+)\s*(\w+)/;
# @matches is ("he", "said", "she", "said");
# (Now you can see that split() actually splits on /\b/)
```

(Of course, this gets tedious for large operations; we'll see another way of doing this later.)
We can also use brackets to give options: `/(boy|girl)/` matches if the string contains either "boy" or "girl". If you don't want this match to populate a special variable, write it like this: `(?:boy|girl)`.
Finally, in this brief tour of regular expressions, we can define character classes - these are delimited by square brackets. For instance, `[a-z]` matches all lowercase letters, and `[aeiou]` matches lowercase vowels. You can put metacharacters inside character classes, and you can also negate character classes by placing a `^` at the beginning of the class: `[^a-zA-Z]` matches anything that is not a letter.

As you might expect, if you want to match any of these characters themselves, like `?`, `.`, `(`, `/` and so on, they must be escaped with a backslash. `/\.\s*\((.*?)\)/` matches a full stop, then zero or more spaces, then an open bracket, then copies text into a variable (we call these 'backreferences' for reasons which will very soon become apparent) until it comes to the next close bracket.

Substitution

After matching a string, we might want to substitute the match with some other text. This is done with the syntax: `s/regexp/replacement/`.

```
$test = "he said she said";
$test =~ s/said/did/; # Gives "he did she said"
```

As you can see, this finds the first match, replaces it, and then stops. Well, there's another modifier, "g", which applies the search-and-replace globally. (This goes for `sed` and even `vi` and `ed` too.)

```
$test = "he said she said";
$test =~ s/said/did/g; # Gives "he did she did"
```

You can use the "g" modifier in matches too, like this:

```
$test= "123 456 7 890";
@array = $test =~ /\b(\d+)\b/g; # (123, 456, 7, 890)
```

Of course, in the replacement text part of the substitution, match meta-characters don't have special meaning. You can't replace a match with 'any digit' or '0 or more "t"s', for instance. Replacement texts work like double-quoted strings, with variable substitution and so on. (Actually, so do regexps - you can put 'sub-regexps' in variables to make the expression tidier.) The really nice part about this is that the backreference variables, `$1`, `$2` and so on, are available here:

```
$test = "Swap this and that.";
$test =~ s/Swap (.*) and (.*)\./Swap $2 and $1./;
print $test; # "Swap that and this."
```

As a final example of regular expressions, let's extend our comment-stripper to remove comments in the middle of lines:

```
# Strip comments, version two.
while (<>) { s/#.*// ; print if /\S/ }
```

What does this do? Well, again we're bringing in a line and storing it in `$_`. Next, we replace a hash mark and everything that follows it with nothing at all. Then, if we've got anything left - that is, if there are is a non-blank character in there - we print the line. (Don't actually use this to remove comments from your Perl programs; firstly, it will remove half of any line which uses the `$#array` syntax or hash signs in strings or regexps, and, secondly, it's almost always better to leave the comments in.)

There are many, many more things you can do with regular expression matching, but this brief overview provides most of the common uses. Type `perldoc perlre` at the shell prompt to read the full documentation about matching.

Control Structures and Subroutines

We've seen, in passing, a few of the Perl control structures; `while`, the inline use of `if` and `unless`, and so the rest should be pretty easy:

Tests

Perl has, of course, a C-like `if-elsif-else` statement; the only difference is that you **must** wrap blocks in braces. That is, you can't say this:

```
if (/y(?:es)?/i)
        $answer = 1;
else
        $answer = 0;
```

Rather, you have to say

```
if (/y(?:es)?/i) {
        $answer = 1;
} else {
        $answer = 0
}
```

(Of course, in reality, you wouldn't write that anyway; you'd write something like `$answer = /y(?:es)/i;` instead.) Perl also allows you to use `unless` as the negative of `if` if it makes your code clearer.

Loops

We've seen a `while` loop, and you might have been able to guess that an `until` loop is available for the negative of `while`. There are also two types of `for` loop - the standard C one:

```
for ($i=0;$i<10;$i++) { print "Counter: $i\n";}
```

There's also the `foreach` loop, which iterates over a list, setting either `$_` or a variable, if one is given, to each element in turn. You can say either `foreach` or `for` to get `foreach` loops.

```
for $i (0..9) { print "Counter: $i\n"; } # As above.

foreach (@array) { print $_."\n"; } # Print each element of an array.
```

The interesting part is the way you can control loop flow: a `next` statement, like a `continue` in C, will immediately jump to the next iteration of a `while`-like or `for`-like loop. Here's another comment (and blank line) stripper:

```
while (<>) { next if /^#/; next unless /\S/; print }
```

`last`, on the other hand, finishes a loop altogether like C's `break`:

```
# Get the Subject of an email, then give up:
while (<>) {
        last if ($subj)=/^Subject: (.*)/;
}
print "Subject was $subj\n";
```

The little-used `redo` statement goes to the top of the loop again, without testing the conditional. This is useful if the input changes under your feet:

```
while (<>) {
        if (/\\\s*$/) { # Line ends with a backslash - continuation
                $_.=<>;
                redo;
        }
        ...
}
```

One thing you may miss, though, is the C switch (in other languages, case) statement. This is a common concern, and there are many ways to address it; the `perlsyn` and `perlfaq7` documentation discuss some solutions.

Statement Modifiers

As well as the ordinary C-style syntax for control structures, we can also apply a control structure to a single statement by means of a "statement modifier", or what I call an "inline" control structure. We've seen `if` and `unless` used in this way:

```
print "Operation successful" if all_ok();

$logfile = "output.log" unless $nologging;
```

You may also use `while`, `until`, and `for` as statement modifiers:

```
$input .= $_ while <>; # One (bad) way of concatenating a file

$cowscomehome=0;
main_loop() until $cowscomehome;

        print chr for (74, 117, 115, 116, 32, 65, 110, 111, 116, 104, 101,
        114, 32, 80, 101, 114, 108,32, 72, 97, 99, 107, 101, 114,);
```

Not many people use `for` like that, though.

Subroutines

We don't make a distinction between *functions* and *subroutines* in Perl; you can return a value from them if you want. Simple subroutines are declared like this:

```
sub greeting {
        print "Hello, world\n";
}
```

You can then use `greeting();` (or just `greeting;` if you know that Perl isn't going to try to interpret this as a string) to call the subroutine. Parameter passing is done through the `@_` array:

```
sub action {
        ($one, $two, $three) = @_;
        warn "Not enough parameters!"
            unless $one and $two and $three;
        print "The $one $two on the $three\n";
}

action("cat", "sat", "mat");
```

The warn function prints out an error message but allows your program to continue; there is also a die function which prints out an error message and stops the program immediately.

Since @_ is the default variable for array operations, as $_ is the default for scalars, it's traditional to use shift to get parameters:

```
sub greeting2 {
        $name = shift;
        print "Hello, $name\n";
}

greeting2("Robert");
greeting2("world");
```

You can return values using, predictably, the return function; you may return a scalar or a list - the wantarray function tells you what context the caller is expecting.

```
Sub mysub {
        # Do some stuff
        return unless defined wantarray; # void context, go home early
        if (wantarray) { # Want an array
              return @results;
        } else { # Just want a scalar
              return $summary
        }
        # Can't get here
}
```

Because of the way Perl scoping takes place, variables are usually 'global' - changes you make in subroutines affect the caller. If you want private variables, use the my function. Lexically scoped variables (often abbreviated to "lexical variables" in the Perl documentation) are declared with my, and cannot even be seen in subroutines called from the current one; they are truly private. If you want to scope something for the current subroutine and below, use dynamic global variables.

```
$myvar = "outside";
sub a { $myvar = "changed by a"; }
a();
print $myvar; # "changed by a";
$myvar = "outside";
sub b { my $myvar = "changed by b";
        print "In b: $myvar";
}
b(); #  "In b: changed by b"
print $myvar; # "outside"
```

File Input and Output

So far the only file input and output we've seen has been grabbing a line at a time from standard input. While this is fine for writing filters, perhaps, real applications need the ability to read from and write to other files as well.

File access in Perl is usually done through filehandles. When we said there were three variable types, we weren't exactly telling the truth; a filehandle is a very special type of variable. When the program starts, as you'd expect, there are three filehandles open: standard input, STDIN, standard output, STDOUT, and standard error, STDERR. We can write to these filehandles using a special form of print; indeed, 'print list' is just shorthand for 'print STDOUT list'

```
if ($statusok) {
        print STDOUT "Processed successfully.\n";
} else {
        print STDERR "An error occurred...\n";
}
```

Look carefully at that; there is no comma between the filehandle and the text to be output; the filehandle is not part of the list. There are two separate syntaxes to print, one with a filehandle and one without. It's very, very important not to confuse the two.

Now, we've also seen that we can read in a line from standard input, using <> - this is in turn a shorthand for `<STDIN>`. What about files from the filesystem, then? We can create a filehandle with the `open` function; just as in C, we give a filehandle and the filename, and state whether we're opening it for input or output. However, instead of assigning a mode number, we use shell-style syntax: `"filename"` (or `"<filename"`) to read from the file, `">filename"` to truncate or create the file and write to it, `">>filename"` to append to the file, and so on. (You can even open to and from pipes!) Here we read from a file, noting errors in a log file:

```
open LOG, ">error.log"
        or die "Can't write on error.log: $!";
# $! tells you why not.
print LOG "Error logging started.\n";
open INPUT, $inputfile;
while (<INPUT>) {
        next unless /\S/; # Skip blank lines.
        next if /^#/; # You know what this does.
        chomp;
        if (fictitious_error_generator($_)) {
              print LOG "Error processing $_\n";
        }
        do_something_with($_);
}
close LOG;
close INPUT;
```

Perl will close filehandles for you at the end of the program, but we close them here with the `close` function, just to be polite.

system()/``

Before we finish our tour of Perl, let's have a look at interacting with the system - that is, running external commands. There are two ways to do this: firstly `system()` which works in exactly the same way as the C construct, and backquotes (``) which work in the same way as the shell construct, apart from the way it handles newlines, keeping both sets of programmers happy.

There are, of course, significant differences between the two methods; `system()` suspends the running program and allows user interaction, but does not return the program's `STDOUT`; backquotes return the program's `STDOUT` and don't show it on the screen, so in interactive programs, the user may not be able to see any prompts. `system()` allows you to get at the return value of the executed program (divide the return value of `system()` by 256 or examine `$?`) whereas backquotes do not.

Basically, if you just want to run a program, use `system()` - if you want to know what it returned, use backquotes. Both of them use the shell to process the command line arguments, pipes, redirection and so on - with `system()` you can turn this facility off by splitting the call up into a list, rather than giving one parameter.

There is a temptation amongst some programmers - particularly those coming from shell scripting - to shell out for nearly everything. On the other hand, there are those who only shell out when absolutely necessary. Use whichever method keeps your code both tidy and efficient.

```
system("clear"); # Easiest way to clear screen.

$status = system("sendmail -q"); # Flush mail queue
# To avoid shell processing, use
# $status = system("sendmail","-q");
print STDERR "Something funny happened to sendmail: $?"
        unless $status==0;

$mail= `frm`;
if ($mail !~ /^You have no mail\./) {
        print "You have new mail:\n";
        print $mail;
        # $mail will contain newlines, so we don't need them.
}
```

A Full Example

Now we've got everything we need to write real, working Perl programs, let's see how we'd implement the shell version of the CD database. This is pretty much a straightforward translation of the shell script, with only one or two perl-like features. This also means we don't tidy up some of the less desirable features of that script - there's still the limitation that you can't have commas in track names, for instance. We'll see a full re-implementation of the database utility at the end of the chapter. In the meantime, you might want to compare this program with the one in chapter two line-by-line.

One thing we do change, however, is, instead of manipulating the data inside files, we'll read the files into arrays at the beginning of the program, and write them out again at the end. This avoids all that troublesome messing around with temporary files. (And gets over the Perl problem that we can't easily write to and read from a file at the same time.)

1. First, as in the shell script, we tell the kernel this is a Perl script, and we follow with our copyright notice:

```
#! /usr/bin/perl -w

# Perl translation of chapter 2's shell CD database
# Copyright (C) 1999 Wrox Press.

# This program is free software; you can redistribute it and/or modify
# it under the terms of the GNU General Public License as published by
# the Free Software Foundation; either version 2 of the License, or
# (at your option) any later version.

# This program is distributed in the hope that it will be useful,
# but WITHOUT ANY WARRANTY; without even the implied warranty of
# MERCHANTABILITY or FITNESS FOR A PARTICULAR PURPOSE. See the
# GNU General Public License for more details.

# You should have received a copy of the GNU General Public License
# along with this program; if not, write to the Free Software
# Foundation, Inc., 59 Temple Place, Suite 330, Boston, MA 02111-#1307  USA
```

2. Now the global variables as before. Notice the last line: we're setting the signal handler for an interrupt (*Ctrl-C* on the keyboard) to be a reference to a subroutine; we create what's called an 'anonymous subroutine reference' by putting what we want to achieve inside 'sub { }' and taking the return value. This subroutine reference calls the subroutine `tidy_up` to dump out the track and title arrays to files, and then exits. The `tidy_up` subroutine writes out the files in a similar way to the way we read them in. The only troublesome bit is the new-line processing; the files should have new-lines to separate records, but the array elements need not have new-lines in them. So, we chomp new-lines on the way in, and add them again on the way out.

```
$menu_choice="";
$title_file="title.cdb";
$tracks_file="tracks.cdb";
$temp_file="/tmp/cdb.$$";
$SIG{INT} = sub { tidy_up(); exit; } ;

sub read_in {
open TITLES, $title_file or die "Couldn't open $title_file : $!\n";
while (<TITLES>) { chomp; push @titles, $_ };
close TITLES;

open TRACKS, $tracks_file or die "Couldn't open $tracks_file : $!\n";
while (<TRACKS>) { chomp; push @tracks, $_ };
close TRACKS;
}

sub tidy_up {
# Die aborts with an error, and $! is the error message from open()
open TITLES, ">".$title_file or die "Couldn't write to $title_file : $!\n";
foreach (@titles) { print TITLES "$_\n"; }
close TITLES;

open TRACKS, ">".$tracks_file or die "Couldn't open $tracks_file : $!\n";
foreach (@tracks) { print TRACKS "$_\n"; }
close TRACKS;
}
```

3. Now our two little functions for getting keyboard input:

```
sub get_return {
        print "Press return ";
        <> # Get a line from STDIN, and ignore it.
}

sub get_confirm {
        print "Are you sure? ";
        while (1) {
                $_ = <>; # Get a reply into $_
                return 1 if (/^y(?:es)?$/i); # 1 is true, not 0
                if (/^no?$/i) {
                        print "Cancelled!\n";
                        return 0;
                }
                print "Please enter yes or no.\n";
        }
}
```

4. Now we display the main menu, and get a choice from the user. The `<<EOF` syntax is called a *here-document* and prints until it finds the word `EOF` or whatever delimiter string you choose.

```
sub set_menu_choice {
        print `clear`; # Shelling out to clear screen. Yuck.

        print <<EOF;
    a) Add new CD
    f) Find CD
    c) Count the CDs and tracks in the catalog
EOF

        if ($cdcatnum) {
                print "    l) List tracks on $cdtitle\n";
                print "    r) Remove $cdtitle\n";
                print "    u) Update track information for $cdtitle\n";
        }

        print "    q) Quit\n\n";
        print "Please enter choice then press return\n";
        chomp($menu_choice=<>);
        return
}
```

5. Then the one-liners as before to add new records to the arrays, and the subroutine to add track information.

```
sub insert_title {
        push @titles, (join "," , @_);
}

sub insert_track {
        push @tracks, (join "," , @_);
}

sub add_record_tracks {
        print "Enter track information for this CD\n";
        print "When no more tracks enter q\n";
        $cdtrack=1;
        $cdttitle="";
        while ($cdttitle ne "q") {
                print "Track $cdtrack, track title? ";
                chomp($cdttitle=<>);
                if ($cdttitle =~ /,/) {
                        print "Sorry, no commas allowed.\n";
                        redo;
                }
                if ($cdttitle and $cdttitle ne "q") {
                        insert_track($cdcatnum,$cdtrack,$cdttitle);
                        $cdtrack++;
                }
        }
}
```

6. Now we implement the `add_records` to add the record of a new CD to the database.

```
sub add_records {
        print "Enter catalog name ";
        chomp($cdcatnum=<>);
        $cdcatnum=~ s/,.*//; # Drop everything after a comma.

        print "Enter title ";
        chomp($cdtitle=<>);
        $cdtitle =~ s/,.*//;

        print "Enter type ";
        chomp($cdtype=<>);
        $cdtype =~ s/,.*//;

        print "Enter artist/composer ";
        chomp($cdac=<>);
        $cdac =~ s/,.*//;

        print "About to add a new entry\n";
        print "$cdcatnum $cdtitle $cdtype $cdac\n";

        if (get_confirm()) {
                insert_title($cdcatnum,$cdtitle,$cdtype,$cdac);
                add_record_tracks();
        } else {
                remove_records();
        }
}
```

7. Since we've got an array of lines, finding the CD is very simple; we could iterate through the array and pick out the matches. However, it's easier to use Perl's `grep` function which was intended for this very purpose.

```
sub find_cd {
        # $asklist is true if the first member of @_
        # (That is, the first parameter) is not "n"
        $asklist = ($_[0] ne "n");

        $cdcatnum="";
        print "Enter a string to search for in the CD titles ";
        chomp($searchstr=<>);
        return 0 unless $searchstr;

        # The \Q and \E metacharacters stop other metacharacters
        # from working, so question marks, asterisks and so on
        # in titles aren't dangerous.

        @matches = grep /\Q$searchstr\E/, @titles;
   if (scalar @matches == 0) {
        print "Sorry, nothing found.\n";
        get_return();
        return 0;
   } elsif   (scalar @matches != 1 ) {
       print "Sorry, not unique.\n";
       print "Found the following:\n";
       foreach (@matches)
           print "$_\n";
   }
   get_return();
   return 0;
}
```

```
($cdcatnum,$cdtitle,$cdtype,$cdac) =
    split "," , $matches[0];
unless ($cdcatnum) {
    print "Sorry, could not extract catalog field\n";
    get_return();
    return 0;
}
print "\nCatalog number: $cdcatnum\n";
print "Title: $cdtitle\n";
print "Type: $cdtype\n";
print "Artist/Composer: $cdac\n\n";
get_return();
if ($asklist) {
   print "View tracks for this CD? ";
   $_ = <>;
    if (/^y(?:es)?$/i) {
        print "\n";
        list_tracks();
        print "\n";
        }
}
return 1;
}
```

8. update_cd is nice and easy to implement, apart from the bit where we delete the old tracks from the array. We'll do this using another grep, but this time, we can negate the regular expression using !/regexp/.

```
sub update_cd {
        unless ($cdcatnum) {
                print "You must select a CD first\n";
                find_cd("n");
        }
        if ($cdcatnum) {
                print "Current tracks are :-\n";
                list_tracks();
                print "\nThis will re-enter the tracks for $cdtitle\n";
                if (get_confirm()) {
                        @tracks = grep !/^$cdcatnum,/, @tracks;
                        add_record_tracks();
                }
        }
}
```

9. Since it's all stored in arrays, counting the contents of the database is trivial.

```
sub count_cds {
        print "Found ".(scalar @titles)." CDs, ";
        print "with a total of ".(scalar @tracks)." tracks.\n";
        get_return();
}
```

10. We've seen how to use grep with a negated regexp to remove entries from an array; let's do this again:

```
sub remove_records {
        unless ($cdcatnum) {
                print "You must select a CD first\n";
                find_cd("n");
        }

        if ($cdcatnum) {
                print "You are about to delete $cdtitle\n";
                if (get_confirm()) {
                        @titles = grep !/^$cdcatnum,/, @titles;
                        @tracks = grep !/^$cdcatnum,/, @tracks;
                        @cdcatnum="";
                        print "Entry removed";
                }
                get_return();
        }
}
```

11. `list_tracks` requires a pager, so we need to write out a temporary file and shell out.

```
sub list_tracks {
        unless ($cdcatnum) {
                print "No CD selected yet.\n";
                return
        }
        open(TEMP, ">$temp_file")
             or die "Can't write to $temp_file: $!\n";
        @temp = grep /^$cdcatnum,/ , @tracks;
        if (scalar @temp == 0) {
                print "No tracks found for $cdtitle\n";
        } else {
                print TEMP "\n$cdtitle :-\n\n";
                foreach (@temp) {
                        s/^.*?,//; # Remove the first field
                        print TEMP $_."\n";
                }
                close TEMP;
                system("more $temp_file");
                unlink($temp_file); # Delete it.
        }
        get_return();
}
```

12. Now the main routine; we must remember to write out the arrays before exiting. We also make sure the files exist before reading from them, by creating them. Of course, we needn't have done it this way - the alternative is not to complain if the files do not exist, the arrays would be empty, and the files would be created when we leave.

```
# File tests work like shell
system("touch $title_file") unless ( -f $title_file );
system("touch $tracks_file") unless ( -f $tracks_file );

read_in();

system("clear");
print "\n\nMini CD manager\n";
sleep(3);
```

```
while (1) {
        set_menu_choice();
        if ($menu_choice =~ /a/i) { add_records(); }
        elsif ($menu_choice =~ /r/i) { remove_records(); }
        elsif ($menu_choice =~ /f/i) { find_cd("y"); }
        elsif ($menu_choice =~ /u/i) { update_cd(); }
        elsif ($menu_choice =~ /c/i) { count_cds(); }
        elsif ($menu_choice =~ /l/i) { list_tracks(); }
        elsif ($menu_choice =~ /b/i) {
                print "\n";
                foreach (@titles) {
                        print "$_\n";
                }
                print "\n";
                get_return();
        }
        elsif ($menu_choice =~ /q/i) { last; }
        else { print "Sorry, choice not recognized.\n"; }
}

tidy_up();
exit;
```

Perl on the Command Line

Now we've seen a full-blown Perl program, what about the little everyday uses of Perl? Well, like `sed` and `awk`, it's perfectly possible to use Perl as a filter for housekeeping tasks. Indeed, Perl provides quite a useful set of command line options to help us do this. Like we did with `-w` right at the beginning of the chapter, we can also put these on the `#!` line in our scripts.

The first option is `-e`; like `sed` and `awk`, this allows us to run a one line Perl script:

```
$ perl -e 'print "Hello, world\n";'
Hello, world
$
```

Similarly, we can provide Perl with a filename that it should take as standard input; we could rewrite our familiar comment-killer like this:

```
$ perl -e 'while(<>) { print unless /^#/ }' myfile
```

which would print out `myfile` without all the comment lines. However, looping through each line in a file is such a common operation that Perl provides a special syntax for it: `-n`

```
$ perl -n -e 'print unless /^#/' myfile
```

We could even do without the `print` - the `-p` flag acts as the following code:

```
while (<>) {
        ...
        print or die "-p destination: $!\n";
}
```

This is very useful for search-and-replace regular expressions: a line like `perl -p -e 's/foo/bar/g' file` will print out the file with every occurrence of "foo" changed to "bar". Now, let's go one further; let's say we do want to change, for instance, all references to "August" into "September" in a file. We'd normally have to collect the output into a temporary file, and then use `mv` to replace the old file with the temporary one. Not so in Perl. Perl supports the modification of files 'in place', using the `-i` option: `perl -p -i -e 's/August/September/g' myfile` is equivalent to this, in shell:

```
$ sed 's/August/September/g' myfile > tmpfile;
$ mv tmpfile myfile;
```

Want to take a backup of the original file? No problem! Just add a suffix to `-i`, like this: `perl -p -i.bak -e 's/August/September/g' myfile` changes the file, and saves a backup to `myfile.bak`. This is the way to build up very powerful filters and file editors with ease.

So, what other command-line magic can we achieve? We've seen `-w` to turn on additional warnings for your script. There's also `-c` to check the syntax of your program without running it, and `-d`, the debugger - a very powerful tool for tracking down problems with your scripts. Finally, how about this: tired of adding `"\n"` to all your `print` statements, and chomping your input? Turn on automatic line processing, with `-l`. This will automatically chomp anything coming into the script via the readline operator, and also adds `\n` to anything going out via `print` statements. Combine with `-p -e` for hours of fun!

Modules

If you're writing serious Perl programs, you will come to realize that a lot of the code you write has probably been written before; things like network programming, manipulating text or HTML, processing command line options, storing data in files, and so on. There may also be things you don't feel you can do within Perl, and need a C extension for.

Perl modules are the answer in both these situations: they provide for reusability of code, like libraries in C, and also allow interfacing with other languages. We won't go into a great deal of detail here about how to use modules or build your own modules, but try and give you a flavor of some of the things you can do with them.

CPAN

The main repository for Perl modules is called CPAN, the Comprehensive Perl Archive Network. As the name suggests, it's a set of mirrored archives for pretty much every Perl module you could think of. The entry point for CPAN is at http://www.cpan.org/ or at http://www.perl.com/CPAN/; these should direct you to your nearest mirror site. You can also download documentation, tutorials and the latest sources of Perl from CPAN, but what you'll want from it most often are the modules; look in the `/modules/by-category` subdirectory of your local mirror for a sorted list of modules, or the file `CPAN.html` in the main directory for descriptions of all the CPAN modules

Installing a Module

Having downloaded a module from CPAN, you can install it into your system as follows. We'll take the `Net::Telnet` module as an example. Assuming we've downloaded `Net-Telnet-3.01.tar.gz` from CPAN:

```
$ tar zxf Net-Telnet-3.01.tar.gz
$ cd Net-Telnet-3.01
$ perl Makefile.PL
Checking if your kit is complete...
Looks good
Writing Makefile for Net::Telnet
$ make install
```

The last step may need certain privileges to write to the Perl directories.

There is another way to install modules. The CPAN module by Andreas König which comes with your Perl distribution will guide you through installing them. Simply type:

```
$ perl -MCPAN -e shell
```

and follow the instructions. This can also be used for installing 'bundles' of modules, like `libwww`, which have many dependencies.

Documentation (perldoc)

All modules (including modules bundled with Perl, and the Perl language itself) should come with full documentation. This documentation is written in the POD (Plain Old Documentation) syntax, and can be read with the command `perldoc`. To read the documentation for the `Net::Telnet` module above, just type:

```
$ perldoc Net::Telnet
```

To find out more about the Perl language, start from `perldoc perl` and, if you're patient enough, work through all the pages that it points you to. `perldoc` also provides two very useful options: `-q` *keyword* will search through the extensive Perl FAQ for the specified keyword. For instance, `perldoc -q Y2K` will tell you about 'Year 2000 bug' compliance...etc. `-f` *function* brings up the section of the `perlfunc` page relating to the function in question. Try, for instance, `perldoc -f unshift`.

Networking

Right, let's see how these modules can actually help us. You'll need to download the relevant set of modules from CPAN.

LWP

The LWP (libwww-perl) is a suite of modules that cover web server and client operations. Let's assume we've got the whole bundle installed. We can now use the module `LWP::Simple` for simple operations. Let's get the HTML version of the day's news:

```
use LWP::Simple;
$news = get "http://news.bbc.co.uk/text_only.htm";
```

Now we can extract all the links from it, using the `HTML::LinkExtor` module found in the HTML-Parser library:

```
use HTML::LinkExtor;
$p = HTML::LinkExtor->new();
$p->parse($news);
@links = $p->links; # Array of all the links in the file
```

OK, maybe this isn't that clear to you, because we haven't introduced object orientated programming - however, just like C libraries, Perl modules can seriously simplify programming.

IO::Socket

Now, how about socket networking? Remember the C program to connect to a time server and get the time? Here's how we'd do it in Perl. The socket library, `IO::Socket`, is a standard module that should have come with your Perl distribution.

```
use IO::Socket;
$host = "localhost" unless ($host = shift);
$socket = IO::Socket::INET->new(
        PeerAddr => $host,
        PeerPort => "daytime")
or die "Couldn't connect to $host: $@";
$time = <$socket>; # Sockets act like filehandles.
print $time;
```

Of course, we could do it all with Perl's built in socket functions (`socket`, `connect`, `gethostbyname` and so on) but this way is a lot neater. Let the modules do the work.

Net modules

If you're using Perl to automate system tasks, you might find the `Net::` series of modules useful. The `Net::Telnet` module we installed earlier provides access to a telnet session, including automating connecting, logging in and executing commands; similarly, `Net::FTP` (from the libnet bundle) allows for FTP sessions to be done automatically. Here's how we'd get the MD5 module from CPAN:

```
use Net::FTP;
$ftp = Net::FTP->new("ftp.cpan.org") or die "Couldn't connect: $@\n";
$ftp->login("anonymous");
$ftp->cwd("/pub/modules/by-name/MD5/");
$ftp->get("MD5-1.7.tar.gz");
$ftp->quit();
```

There's also `Net::NNTP` (libnet) for news reading and posting, `Net::DNS` (Net-DNS) for DNS querying, `Net::POP3` (libnet) for fetching mail, `Net::Ping`, `Net::Whois` (Net-Whois), `Net::IRC` (Net-IRC) ...

Databases

There are a number of ways we can store and retrieve data in Perl; we've seen how to deal with flat-file databases. A more common method is the DBM system we saw in chapter 7. We can access DBMs by *tying* them to hashes. This means that the data in the hash will be linked to the data on the disk. We use the standard `AnyDBM_File` module as our interface to the GDBM libraries. (Note that `AnyDBM_File` can in fact access a number of DBM packages.)

```
use AnyDBM_File;
tie %database, "AnyDBM_File", "data.db";
```

```
# We can now use %database as a normal hash; any adding, deleting or
# modifying of keys will be reflected in the data file.

untie %database;
```

There are a number of similar modules to tie data structures to files. For instance, `DB_File` ties an array to a text file using the Berkeley DB library- in our CD database example, we could have used this instead of reading in and writing out the data files at the beginning and end of the program. `MLDBM` (Multi-level DBM) is a module used for storing complex data structures in a DBM, and we'll use this to implement our final version of the CD database.

Finally, using the DBI interface, one can store data in relational databases like MySQL, PostgreSQL, Oracle and Informix, and execute SQL queries and statements. The relevant modules are `DBI`, for the interface and `DBD::[Oracle,mysql...]` for the drivers for the individual databases.

The CD Database Revisited

Now we've seen what Perl can do, let's have a look at the CD database program as it would be written by a Perl native. There will be a few concepts in here (references and nested data structures for instance) that we haven't covered, but that's OK; don't worry too much if you don't understand everything here, you're not meant to - the idea is just to give you an impression of a 'real' Perl program.

1. First, we start with the comments as before:

```
#! /usr/bin/perl -w

# Perl translation of chapter 2's shell CD database
# Copyright (C) 1999 Wrox Press.

# This program is free software; you can redistribute it and/or modify
# it under the terms of the GNU General Public License as published by
# the Free Software Foundation; either version 2 of the License, or
# (at your option) any later version.

# This program is distributed in the hope that it will be useful,
# but WITHOUT ANY WARRANTY; without even the implied warranty of
# MERCHANTABILITY or FITNESS FOR A PARTICULAR PURPOSE.  See the
# GNU General Public License for more details.

# You should have received a copy of the GNU General Public License
# along with this program; if not, write to the Free Software
# Foundation, Inc., 59 Temple Place, Suite 330, Boston, MA  02111-#1307 USA
```

2. We'll place the whole of the program here, and flesh out the functions later:

```
use MLDBM qw(AnyDBM_File);
my $record;
tie(%tmp, "MLDBM", "cddb.db")
or die "Couldn't tie DB.\n"; # Scary complex hash contains the whole DB.
%database = %tmp; # Overcome a limitation in MLDBM. *sigh*

# Tidy up nicely
$SIG{INT} = sub { %tmp = %database; untie %tmp } ;
```

```
system("clear");
print "\n\nCD Database Manager\n\n";

while (1) {
        my $menu_choice = main_menu($record);
        if ($menu_choice eq "a") { $record = add_cd(); }
        elsif ($menu_choice eq "r") { remove_cd($record); undef $record; }
        elsif ($menu_choice eq "f") { $record = find_cd("y"); }
        elsif ($menu_choice eq "u") { update_cd($record); }
        elsif ($menu_choice eq "c") { count_cds(); }
        elsif ($menu_choice eq "l") { list_tracks($record); }
        elsif ($menu_choice =~ /q/i) { last; }
        else {
                print "Can't get here.\n";
        }
}

%tmp=%database;
untie %tmp;
```

3. Now we display the main menu and validate the choice:

```
sub main_menu {
    my $record = shift;
    my $choice;
    my $title = $database{$record}->{title} if $record;
    print <<EOF;

    Options :

       a) Add new CD
       f) Find CD
       c) Count CDs and tracks in the catalogue
    EOF
    if ($record) {
            print "    l) List tracks on $title\n";
            print "    r) Remove $title\n";
            print "    u) Update entry for $title\n";
    }
    print "   q) Quit\n";
    print "Your choice: ";
    while (1) {
            $choice=lc(<>);
            substr($choice,1)="";
            # Now, we see if the choice is contained in the string of
            # acceptable options, (Which includes l, r and u if we've
            # selecetd a record.) by using it as a regexp. Looks weird?
            return $choice if ("afcq".($record?"lru":"") =~ /$choice/);

            # If not, that's invalid
            print "Invalid choice.\nTry again: ";
    }
}
```

4. Let's tackle adding records to the database next. The database is actually quite a complicated hash; the keys are the catalog numbers, and the values are each themselves hashes. These hashes have keys "`title`", "`type`", "`artist`", and "`tracks`". That's why we used the funky-looking `$database{$record}->{title}` above - `$database{$record}` is a hash. (It's actually a *reference* to a hash; C programmers can think of them as pointers. For more about reference, look at the `perlref` documentation.) The `->{title}` syntax looks inside the hash reference and gets the value of the "`title`" key. The value of "tracks" is, of course, a reference to an array of tracks. Arrays inside hashes inside hashes; it takes a little getting used to.

```
sub add_cd {
        while(1) {
                print "Enter catalog number: ";
                chomp($record=<>);
                if (exists $database{$record}) {
                        print "Already exists. ";
                        print "Please enter a different number.\n";
                } else {
                        last;
                }
        }

        print "Enter title: ";
        chomp($title=<>);

        print "Enter type: ";
        chomp($type=<>);
        print "Enter artist/composer: ";
        chomp($artist=<>);

        $database{$record}= {
                "title" => $title,
                "type" => $type,
                "artist" => $artist
        };

        add_tracks($record);
        return $record; # Tell the main menu the new record number.
}
```

5. Now the subroutine to add the tracks; this is where we bring out the array reference.

```
sub add_tracks {
        my $record = shift;
        print "Enter track information for this CD\n";
        print "Enter a blank line to finish.\n\n";
        my $counter=0; my @tracks;
        while (1) {
                print ++$counter.": ";
                chomp($track=<>);
                if ($track) {
                        # @{...} means "interpret as an array"
                        push @{$database{$record}->{tracks}}, $track;
                } else {
                        last;
                }
        }
}
```

6. The code to find a CD is a bit complicated, since we need to look through all the values of `$database{$record}->{title}` for each value of `$record` in the hash. `grep` to the rescue again...

```
sub find_cd {
        $view = ($_[0] eq "y");

        print "Enter a string to search for: ";
        chomp($search=<>);

        # For each key, (record) add the key to the @found array if the
        # title field of that record contains the search string.
        @matches =  grep {$database{$_}->{title} =~/\Q$search\E/ }
                                keys %database;
```

```
        if (scalar @matches == 0) {
                print "Sorry, nothing found.\n";
                return;
        } elsif (scalar @matches != 1 ) {
                print "Sorry, not unique.\n";
                print "Found the following:\n";
                foreach (@matches) {
                        print $database{$_}->{title}."\n";
                }
                return;
        }
        $record=$matches[0];
        print "\n\nCatalog number: ".$record."\n";
        print "Title: ".$database{$record}->{title}."\n";
        print "Type: ".$database{$record}->{type}."\n";
        print "Artist/Composer: ".$database{$record}->{artist}."\n\n";

        if ($view) {
                print "Do you want to view tracks? ";
                $_ = <>;
                if (/^y(?:es)?$/i) {
                        print "\n";
                        list_tracks($record);
                        print "\n";
                }
        }
        return $record;
}
```

7. Once we've got this far, listing the tracks isn't difficult!

```
sub list_tracks {
        my $record = shift;
        foreach (@{$database{$record}->{tracks}}) {
                print $_."\n";
        }
}
```

8. Updating a CD just means removing the old tracks and adding a new set:

```
sub update_cd {
        my $record = shift;
        print "Current tracks are: \n";
        list_tracks($record);
        print "\nDo you want to reenter them?\n";
        if (($_ = <>) =~ /^y(?:es)?$/i) {
                # Remove the old entry from the hash
                delete $database{$record}->{tracks};
                add_tracks($record);
        } else {
                print "OK, canceling.\n"
        }
}
```

9. Similarly, removing a CD just means deleting its hash entry:

```
sub remove_cd {
        my $record = shift;
        print "\nDo you want to delete this CD?\n";
        if (($_ = <>) =~ /^y(?:es)?$/i) {
                delete $database{$record};
        } else {
```

```
                print "OK, cancelling.\n"
        }
}
```

10. Finally, counting the CDs is easy - it's just the number of keys in the hash. Counting the tracks, however, is a little more tricky; we evaluate the tracks array in scalar context for each of the keys in the database, and add the values together. (You could do this with `map()` but that would be less clear.)

```
sub count_cds {
        my $totaltracks=0;
        print "Found ".(scalar keys %database)." CDs and ";
        foreach (keys %database) {
                $totaltracks+= scalar @{$database{$_}->{tracks}};
        }
        print $totaltracks." tracks.\n";
}
```

Summary

In this chapter, we've seen how to use some features of the Perl programming language, examined some of the modules available for it and seen how our CD database application could be implemented in Perl.

Programming for the Internet: HTML

In this chapter, we're going to look at a way of programming graphical information. Rather than write programs that draw graphics and text, we'll specify what we want and use a separate program to view the specification.

We'll see how HTML, the language of the World Wide Web, is written and then set up a server so we can view our documents across a network using a client browser. Along the way, we'll cover:

- The history and nature of the World Wide Web
- HTML document structure
- Tags, tables, graphic images and anchors
- Client- and server-side clickable maps
- Tips for setting up servers and pages on the Web

What is the World Wide Web?

The World Wide Web, sometimes called simply **WWW** or **The Web**, started in 1989 at the CERN laboratory Geneva, when Tim Berners-Lee was investigating ways of disseminating information. In 1992, CERN placed the sample interface and protocol in the public domain. This was rapidly taken up by the Internet community and the Web was born.

There are three parts to the World Wide Web: a server, which holds documents and images; the network, which is used to transfer the information; and the client, a browser, which displays the information.

In this chapter, we'll be looking briefly at setting up a server (many implementations are freely available for several UNIX versions and other platforms), but mainly on how the information you wish to provide is defined.

Although the World Wide Web is generally associated with the Internet, there's no reason why you can't use exactly the same software on internal networks (so-called intranets) for providing information. Companies can and do set up internal WWW servers for providing internal information. As we'll see, this is easy to do and can provide information in an easy-to-use format.

Documents on the WWW are almost always hypertext documents, i.e. most documents are not complete in themselves, rather they link to other documents and may themselves be the target of other links.

For example, a company may provide a WWW site giving tourist information for the local area. This might consist of a single high-level page which provides many references to more detailed information on other pages. Since WWW documents exist on a computer, these links can be made 'live' and, when selected, take the user to a different page of information. This hypothetical tourist information service might also provide links to tourist information providers in neighboring regions, which, in turn, will probably reciprocate by providing links back to the original pages.

It's hard to explain the power and appeal of the World Wide Web. The only way is to experience it for yourself!

Terminology

Before we get started, we need to get some terminology clear. There are several different standards that are used in conjunction with the Web.

Many of these standards are defined in documents called **RFCs**. These are available in various places on the Internet, but if you can't find a site close to you that provides RFCs, you can obtain them from the machine ds.internic.net. If you have FTP access, you'll find the files in the subdirectory `rfc`; if you only have e-mail access, send mail to mailserv@ds.internic.net, leave the subject blank, and put the single word `help` in the body. The mail server will reply telling you how to request RFCs.

You can find other documents relating to the World Wide Web by following links from http://www.w3.org/, the home of the World Wide Web consortium. In the meantime, here are brief descriptions of some of the terms that you'll meet.

The HyperText Transfer Protocol (HTTP)

This is the protocol that is used to transfer information between the client and server computers.

Multimedia Internet Mail Extensions (MIME)

This started as an extension to Internet e-mail to allow transfer of information other than plain text. It has evolved considerably beyond that original aim and now defines the format of information being transferred over HTTP. Various MIME types and subtypes are defined that allow both client and server to understand the format of the information being transferred. You can find more information in RFC1521.

Standard Generalized Markup Language (SGML)

This is an international standard, ISO 8879:1986, for defining structured documents. It provides a standard way of specifying a structure for a document.

Document Type Definition (DTD)

This is a set of rules that define how SGML is applied to a particular document type.

HyperText Markup Language (HTML)

This is a particular application of SGML which defines the markup language used with WWW. It allows you to define the layout and the structure of a document. At the time of writing the current standard is HTML 4.0 (defined in W3C recommendation REC-html40 which can be found at http://www.w3.org/TR/REC-html40/, although an XHTML standard is expected to replace it when it is accepted as a recommendation.

HTML 4.0 specifies 3 DTDs, each of which varies in the numbers of tags supported. This is due to the fact that the current iteration of the HTML standard has been undoing a lot of the changes introduced in the two previous versions of the standard, 2.0 and 3.2. The HTML standards previously followed the lead of the two main browser vendors Netscape and Microsoft in the creation of new tags, by ratifying them. This has led to a pollution of the original purpose of HTML, which was to define only the structure of the document. Previous versions of the standard introduced purely stylistic elements, which should have remained separate. In the HTML 4.0 standard, many of the tags that define styles have been marked up for removal. These tags are known as deprecated. The three versions of the DTD have varying amounts of these tags already removed:

- Strict – only includes tags that haven't been deprecated, and don't appear in frameset documents
- Transitional – includes all tags, including those marked up for deprecation, but not those that appear in frameset documents
- Frameset – includes all tags included in the transitional DTD and the frameset ones as well

The reasoning behind the different versioning is so that people can still write documents viewable on older browsers, while taking advantage of HTML 4.0's new features.

In this chapter we will be using transitional HTML, so that you can create HTML documents viewable on pretty much all browsers.

Extensible Markup Language (XML)

Another language which has been derived from SGML. Although while HTML can be described as a single application of SGML, XML is actually a much simplified dialect of SGML. It was conceived as a way of trying to give some of the power and flexibility of SGML but without the complexity of SGML. It retains all of SGML's most commonly used features, and is, like SGML, a metalanguage – a language for describing other HTML like languages that are customized to a user's individual needs. It's real strength lies in it's ability to define structured data in a flexible, but human readable form. At a casual glance, an XML actually looks very like HTML, and was designed to be interoperable with it.

Cascading Style Sheets (CSS)

CSS is an internationalized standard which allows you to separate the style content out of an HTML document. There have been two versions of the standard to date, CSS1 came out on the 17th December 1996, a copy can be found at http://www.w3.org/TR/REC-CSS1. The most recent version of the standard is CSS2 which was released in May 1998, and the standard can be located at http://www.w3.org/TR/REC-CSS2.

Extensible Hypertext Markup Language (XHTML)

This is still a proposed recommendation (see http://www.w3.org/TR/1999/PR-xhtml1-19990824) which aims at defining HTML as an application of XML. In reality it means your pages will be little different from HTML 4.0, but it ensures that HTML pages written by the user have to conform to an HTML 4.0 DTD.

Uniform Resource Locator (URL)

This is a way of specifying a resource. This usually consists of a protocol name, a `:`, two `/` characters, a machine name and a path to a resource. If the path to the file is omitted, a default file will usually be returned.

To demonstrate with a couple of examples, a specification for FTP access to the document `rfc1866.txt`, which is stored on a machine with the name `ds.internic.net`, is ftp://ds.internic.net/rfc/rfc1866.txt, and you can find the Wrox Press WWW pages at http://www.wrox.com/.

Uniform Resource Identifier (URI)

A URI is a more general naming scheme for network resources and is intended to be a superset of the more protocol-specific URL naming scheme. You can find more information in RFC1734 and RFC1630.

Writing HTML

Before we look at HTML in detail, let's look at a very small HTML document, what it contains and how it appears in a browser.

Try It Out - A Simple HTML Document

Here's the source of a very simple HTML document:

```
<!DOCTYPE HTML PUBLIC "-//W3C//DTD HTML 4.0 Transitional//EN"
        "http://www.w3.org/TR/REC-html40/loose.dtd">

<HTML>
<HEAD>
<TITLE>A Simple HTML Document, html1.html</TITLE>
</HEAD>
<BODY>
<H1>This is a title</H1>
<P>
And here is some ordinary text.
</P>
</BODY>
</HTML>
```

If we use a WWW client program to view the file, what we see will vary slightly, depending on the client used. You can either open the file by specifying a URL of the form file:/directory/html1.html, or from the menu. Here's what Netscape Navigator for the X Window system shows when it loads this source file:

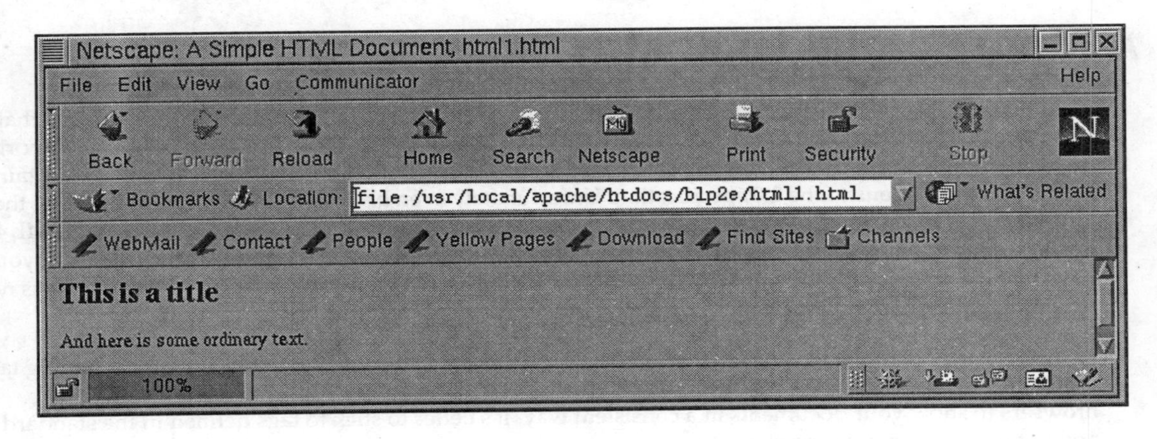

How It Works

As you can probably guess, the markup parts of HTML are enclosed in angle brackets, <>, and aren't displayed. Rather, they control how the remaining text is displayed.

The opening `<!DOCTYPE`... section defines that this is valid HTML 4.0 transitional. If your HTML doesn't conform to a particular standard, you should omit the `DOCTYPE` definition. Many HTML documents omit this specification. Using the latest and greatest features in browser X might be fun, but in general sticking to features not just in the HTML standard, but in older versions of the standard where possible, will allow a wider audience to view your HTML pages.

The rest of the document is enclosed in `<HTML> </HTML>` tags, which define the document as being HTML. Inside this, there are two further sections: a **head** and a **body**. Inside the head we have a **title**, which conventionally appears outside the rest of the text. In many browsers, it will appear as a title to the entire window.

Inside the body section, there is both a level 1 heading, delimited by `<H1></H1>`, and a paragraph, delimited by `<P></P>`. In many HTML documents you will see the `</P>` omitted. This used to be considered acceptable, but as HTML becomes more strictly defined the `</P>` should always be used to explicitly delimit paragraph sections. The plain text appears as is and may be wrapped to fit the width of the browser window. If you change the size of the window, the text will be reformatted to fit.

Notice how almost all HTML tags have a matched start and end tag and that tags are always closed in sequence, on a 'last opened - first closed' basis.

The markup tags are not case-sensitive, so `<TITLE>`, `<Title>` and `<title>` are all equivalent. The authors find it helpful to keep the tags in uppercase to help distinguish them from the rest of the document.

A More Formal Look at HTML

Now that we've seen the general form of an HTML document, let's look at the commonly used tags that are defined. The first format version of HTML was 2.0, and was rather basic, but is very widely supported by almost all browsers. At the time of writing, the latest version of the specification is 4.0, which contains many, many additions to the 2.0 specification. Unfortunately even browsers that claim to support all the latest features in version 4.0 occasionally miss out some minor features, but the core features of HTML 4.0 are well supported by most browsers. The more 'unusual' the feature you try and use, the more risk you have that it's support in different browsers will be missing, or not well implemented, so the display is not what you where hoping for.

Many browsers accept extensions to the standards. A browser presented with a document containing tags that it doesn't understand normally ignores them. In general, assuming you want a wide variety of browsers to show your documents in a consistent way, it's better to stick to tags defined in the standard and not use any browser-specific extensions.

HTML is a very important specification because it's machine-independent. You should be able to implement a basic HTML browser for just about any graphical display. There are even text-only HTML browsers, although, obviously, there's some compromise in what they can display. Non-graphical browsers are important for visually impaired people and (occasionally) for people with slow network connections.

You can author a formatted document in HTML and then distribute it to others with different computing platforms. They should still be able to view your document much as you wrote it. There have been various attempts to provide portable viewing of formatted documents in the past, but HTML is almost certainly the most successful yet, not least because you can author documents without purchasing specific software to do so.

Formally, an HTML document consists of characters as defined in standard ISO 10646. Characters in an HTML document consist either of text to be displayed or tags which control the display of information. Every tag starts with a < character, and ends with a > character. In between is case-insensitive text that defines the tag. Some tags contain further attributes (which *can* be case-sensitive) inside the < and > characters, in the form `attribute="value"`. Attributes control details of how the tag is to be interpreted.

Most tags are enclosures: there is a start tag, some enclosed text, and an end tag. End tags are always the same as the start tag, except that the tag name is preceded with a '/'. For example, `<H1>` is the start tag for a level one heading, and `</H1>` is the corresponding end tag. Tags can be nested, but end tags must always appear in the reverse order to the start tags. Thus `<H1> Heading <B> one </B> </H1>` is a valid sequence, but `<H1> Heading <B> one </H1> </B>` is not.

An HTML document consists of an HTML wrapper, that encloses the entire document, and two sections, a header and a body. Formal HTML authors may precede the HTML with a doctype specification, like this:

```
<!DOCTYPE HTML PUBLIC "-//W3C//DTD HTML 4.0 Transitional//EN"
        "http://www.w3.org/TR/REC-html40/loose.dtd">
```

The advent of XHTML means that the inclusion of a DTD will be mandatory for all HTML documents, so even though it isn't strictly necessary to include now, it's best to get used to using it.

All HTML documents must be enclosed in <HTML> and </HTML> tags. The HTML tag has several attributes that can be used, the only one that is generally useful is to specify a language using the ISO-639 language code. For English this is often omitted, but for other languages it is good to include it. Attributes are written using `attribute="value"` inside the tag, so a German HTML document should start with:

```
<HTML lang="de">
```

Inside the HTML wrapper tags, the first section we must define is the header. Although there are quite a few things that you can do inside the header section, it's almost always used solely for specifying a document title, using the <TITLE> tag.

The other section of an HTML page is the body, which contains the information you want on your page. It can be completely empty!

So, the minimum legal HTML document consists of:

```
<!DOCTYPE HTML PUBLIC "-//W3C//DTD HTML 4.0 Transitional//EN"
        "http://www.w3.org/TR/REC-html40/loose.dtd">
<HTML>
<HEAD>
<TITLE></TITLE>
</HEAD>
<BODY>
</BODY>
</HTML>
```

However, since this contains no title or displayable text it's not very useful!

As alluded to earlier almost all HTML browsers will accept HTML documents without the DOCTYPE specification, which is fortunate since rather too many documents on the Web seem to omit it. In some ways this is probably fortunate, because, sadly, very few of them conform to a published HTML standard. However this will all change in XHTML which requires the inclusion of a DTD to make the document format legal. We recommend you keep your HTML strictly legal, and include the DOCTYPE specification. Now that we have an overview of an HTML document, we can look in more detail at the tags that we can use.

HTML Tags

Let's look at the principal HTML tags.

Title

All HTML documents should have a title, defined within <TITLE></TITLE> tags in the head part of the document. This is usually shown outside the main displayed text, the contents of this tag is often stored as the text in a bookmark or favorite, so it's important to choose your words carefully. Titles like 'Home Page' don't mean much in a list of bookmarks.

Comments

Just like code, HTML documents can benefit from comments. An HTML comment looks like this,

```
<!-- this is a comment -->
```

where the ! and -- characters must be present exactly as indicated. It's safer not to use comments that extend across multiple lines, some early browsers don't handle them correctly.

Headings

Six levels of heading are defined, H1 through to H6. A top level header is H1. The text for the heading is enclosed between a start and an end tag, so a level two heading would look like this:

```
<H2>This is a heading 2</H2>
```

While previous HTML specifications added an ALIGN attribute to the HTML standard, this has since been deprecated in strict HTML 4.0 However, as the most 'visual' attribute of headings, we'll use it in a quick example. It takes the parameters left, right, center, or justify. Thus, we would specify a centered level three heading like this:

```
<H3 ALIGN="center">Centered level 3 heading</H3>
```

Text Formatting

Normally, all the body level text in an HTML document will be formatted as a continuous flow, disregarding any line breaks in the original source. This is generally a good thing because the originator doesn't know how wide the viewing page will be. The following tags allow additional control over formatting.

Tag	Description
 	This tag, which has no closing tag, causes the text flow to start on to the next line.
<P>	This tag, which is often used wrongly without a closing tag, causes a new paragraph to be started, usually after inserting a blank line. Note that <P><P> won't normally insert two blank lines. See the <PRE> tag (defined later) if you wish to force several blank lines in an HTML document.
<HR>	This tag causes a horizontal line to be drawn across the page.

Text Styles

A range of style tags are defined to allow control over the appearance of text.

<ADDRESS>This is my address</ADDRESS> formats the text in a form suitable for a postal mail address.

<B>This text is bold</B> sets the enclosed text into a bold font.

<BLOCKQUOTE>This text is a quote</BLOCKQUOTE> sets the enclosed text apart from the rest of the text, often by indenting it. Usually used for quotations.

<CITE>A citation</CITE> identifies citation text.

<CODE>Some source code</CODE> formats the enclosed text as a source code listing.

<EM>Emphasized text</EM> sets emphasized text. It's usually better to use bold or italic tags explicitly.

`<I>This text is in italics</I>` sets the enclosed text in an italicized font.

`<KBD>text typed by a user</KBD>` indicates text typed by a user, this is often a monospaced font.

`<PRE>Pre-formatted text</PRE>` prevents the browser from reformatting the enclosed text, so it appears on the browser the same as in the HTML source. You should use this sparingly; since you don't know the width or height of the browser's screen, you could inadvertently make the text very difficult for some users to view.

`<STRONG>This text is strong</STRONG>` sets the text to have strong emphasis.

`<SUB>This is subscript</SUB>` sets the enclosed text to a subscript.

`<SUP>and this is superscript</SUP>` sets the enclosed text to a superscript.

`<TT>Typewriter spacing</TT>` sets text into a monospaced font, as though it had been typed on a typewriter.

Normally `<B>`, `<I>`, `<PRE>` and `<CODE>` are sufficient for most general formatting needs, and also the ones most browsers display in a consistent manner.

Try It Out - Text Formatting

Now that we've seen some more tags, let's see what they look like in use. Remember that they may look different on browsers other than the one we used.

Here is some more HTML, showing some of the text formatting tags that we've just introduced:

```
<!DOCTYPE HTML PUBLIC "-//W3C//DTD HTML 4.0 Transitional//EN"
        "http://www.w3.org/TR/REC-html40/loose.dtd">
<HTML>
<HEAD>
<TITLE>Another Simple HTML Document, html2.html</TITLE>
</HEAD>
<BODY>
<H2>This is file html2.html</H2>
<P>
And here is some ordinary text.
<!— And here we have inserted a comment —>
<!— which takes two lines to type in —>
</P>
<H4>Heading level four</H4>
looks like the above.
<H5 ALIGN="center">This is a centered level five</H5>
heading, showing the extra ALIGN tag.
<P>
we can do quite a lot of typing, then put a break in here,<BR>so the text flow is
broken up.
</P><P>
If we didn't use the BR tag then text would just keep on flowing across the page. If
the user changes the width of the browser window then the text adjusts accordingly.
<HR>
Used sparingly a horizontal rule is a good separator.
```

```
</P><P>
Let us try some other changes. Here is some <B>bold</B> text, some <I>Italicized</I>
text and some <EM>emphasized</EM> text. A fixed width font is selected with TT like
<TT>this section</TT> of text.
</P><P>
If we would like to
include some code we can make it look like this:<BR>
<CODE>
#include &lt;stdio.h&gt;<BR>
int main() {<BR>

printf("Hello World\n");<BR>
}<BR>
</CODE>
</P><P>
Perhaps an easier way is to use the PRE
tag, like this:<BR>
<PRE>
#include &lt;stdio.h&gt;

int main() {
printf("Hello World\n");
}
</PRE>
</P><P>
Here is an example of an address:<BR>
<ADDRESS>
Mr. Postman Pat<BR>
7 Posty Lane,<BR>
Greendale<BR>
Lancashire<BR>
Great Britain<BR>
</ADDRESS>
</P><P>
This is a block quotation from<BR>
<CITE>Macbeth, by William Shakespeare</CITE>
<BLOCKQUOTE>
Is this a dagger which I see before me, The handle toward my hand? Come,
let me clutch thee:<BR>
I have thee not, and yet I see thee still.
</BLOCKQUOTE>
</P><P>
Which I consider an outstandingly good play.
</P>
</BODY>
</HTML>
```

When we view it with Netscape Navigator, we see:

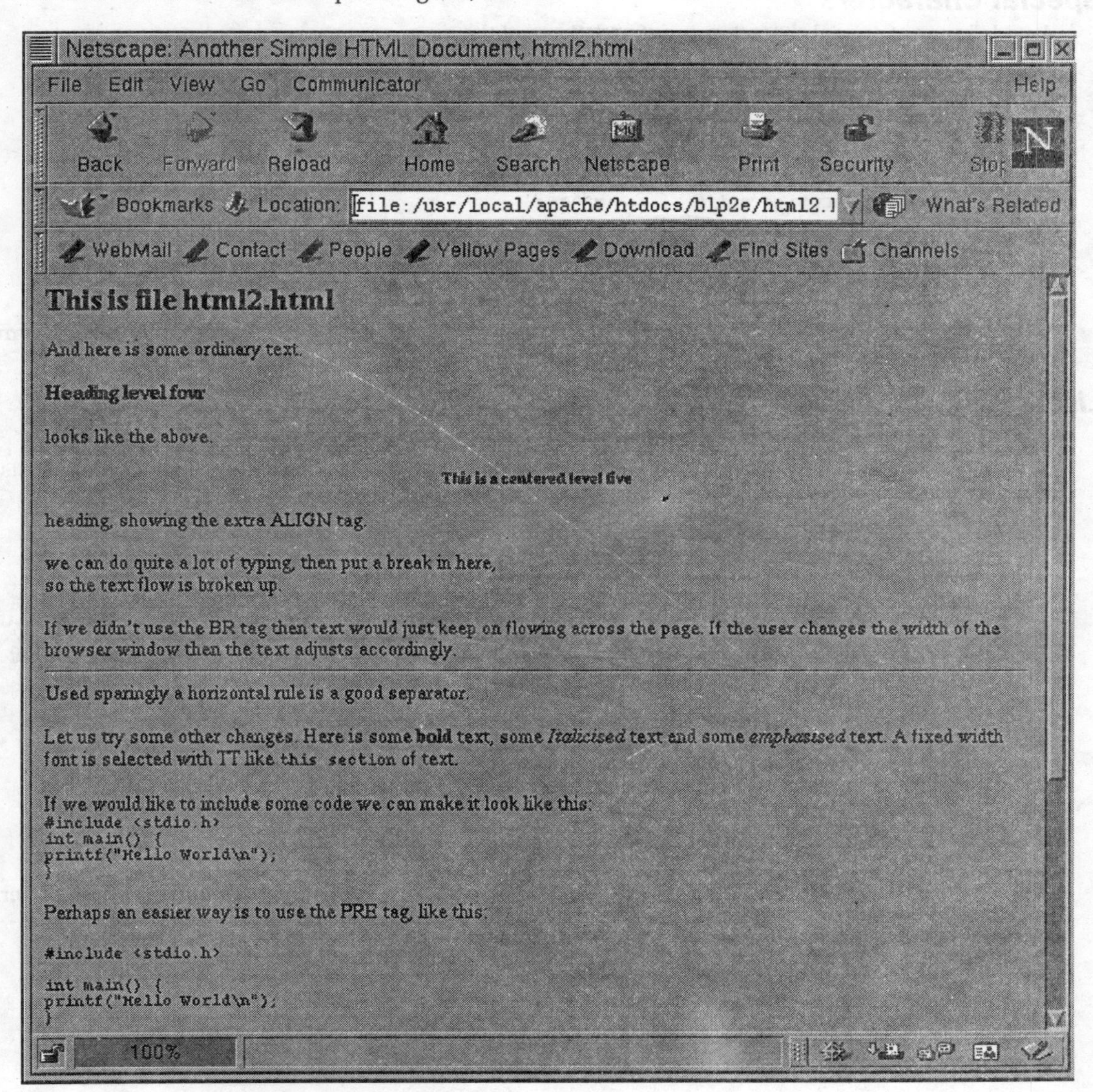

How It Works

This is simply an extension of the previous example. Notice that we're unable to use the < or > characters in the code fragments, since they are reserved for delimiting tags. We have to use a special syntax to define these characters.

Special Characters

A wide range of special characters is defined. Some of the more common ones are:

`<`	<
`>`	>
`&`	&
`"`	double quote, "
`©`	© symbol
`á`	a with acute accent, á
`æ`	an a-e ligature, æ
`ç`	c with a cedilla, ç
`ü`	u with an umlaut, ü

Many others can be specified with the HTML character codes, such as `@` for an ampersand, & symbol. See RFC1866 for a full list of the HTML coded character set

Lists

There is an important group of tags that you can use for providing lists. There are five types of list supported altogether, although three of them are very similar to one another. These are unordered lists, directory lists, and menus. The corresponding tags are:

- <UL> </UL>
- <DIR> </DIR>
- <MENU> </MENU>

Inside the list, each item is started with a list item, `<LI>` tag. Each item is usually marked with a bullet point, or similar symbol. Here's a simple unordered list:

```
<UL>
<LI>The first item
<LI>The second item
<LI>The last item
</UL>
```

Notice that the end tag `</LI>` may be omitted.

On many browsers, menu, directory and unordered lists look very similar, if not identical. If you prefer the items to be numbered, you can use an ordered list. This replaces the bullet mark with a sequential number and looks like this:

```
<OL>
<LI>The first item is 1
<LI>The second item is 2
<LI>The last item is 3
</OL>
```

The fifth form of list is the definition list. This is more suited to dictionary type entries, with a key word and some explanatory text. Unlike a single item list, there are pairs of tags: definition term `<DT>` and definition description `<DD>`. While the end tag of the definition list, `</DL>`, is required, both end tags `</DT>` and `</DD>` are optional. A definition list looks like this:

```
<DL>
<DT>Bush
<DD>A normal growing pattern for most Fuchsias<DT>Standard<DD>The main part of the
plant is raised on a single stem<DT>Basket
<DD>A group of fuchsias that look good in hanging baskets.
</DL>
```

Try It Out - Lists

Here's another example, containing lists:

```
<!DOCTYPE HTML PUBLIC "-//W3C//DTD HTML 4.0 Transitional//EN"
        "http://www.w3.org/TR/REC-html40/loose.dtd">
<HTML>
<HEAD>
<TITLE>Another Simple HTML Document, html3.html</TITLE>
</HEAD>
<BODY>
<UL>
<LI>This is entry number 1
<LI>This is entry number 2
<LI>This is entry number 3
<LI>This is entry number 4
</UL>
<OL>
<LI>This is entry number 1
<LI>This is entry number 2
<LI>This is entry number 3
<LI>This is entry number 4
</OL>
<H4>Fuchsia types</H4>
<DL>
<DT>Bush</DT>
<DD>A normal growing pattern for most Fuchsias.</DD>
<DT>Standard</DT>
<DD>The main part of the plant is raised on a single stem.</DD>
<DT>Basket</DT>
<DD>A group of fuchsias that look good in hanging baskets.</DD>
</DL>
</BODY>
</HTML>
```

The result is:

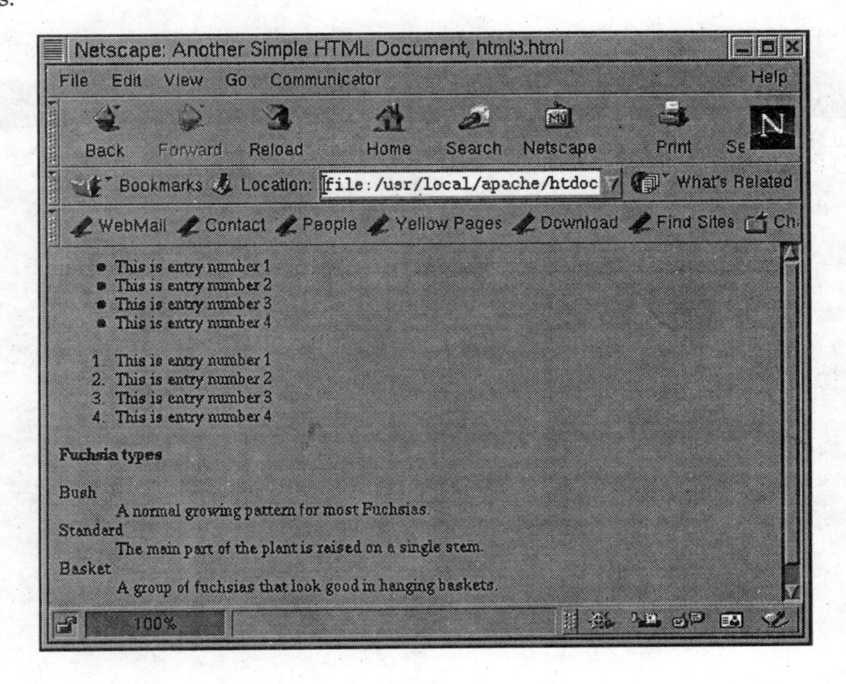

Images

All this formatting of text is quite nice, but adding some pictures is a big step forward. This is very easy to do: we simply use the `IMG` tag. This takes several attributes which control how the image appears.

The full tag, with attributes, is:

```
<IMG SRC="image URL" ALT="alternate text" ALIGN="top"|"middle"|"bottom"|"right"|"left"
WIDTH=n HEIGHT=n ISMAP>
```

The attributes separated with | characters are exclusive, i.e. `ALIGN` can only take one of the given values. `SRC` and `ALT` attributes are both required.

The `SRC` gives a reference to the source image file. This is commonly in GIF or JPEG format, although PNG (Portable Network Graphic) is also sometimes accepted. You should generally use the encoding method that gives the smallest file, which will depend on the type of image. You may need to experiment to determine which format gives the best resulting image in the smallest size. The image name can be either a simple file name, or a URL referring to a different location. Photographs are generally best done as JPEGs, and other images as GIFs.

The `ALT` provides some default text. This is used by browsers that cannot handle the graphic, where the user has turned image loading off, perhaps because they're connected via a slow linker while waiting for the image to download. You should include the `ALT` option with some sensible text.

The now deprecated `ALIGN` option takes one of the | separated strings and determines how subsequent text is aligned with the image.

`WIDTH` and `HEIGHT` provide clues for the browser about how much space, in pixels, to leave for the image. If the browser is loading images after text (a common setting for people with slow links), it allows the browser to lay out the text correctly before the image has been fetched.

The `ISMAP` option specifies that this is a mapped image, of which more later.

Try It Out - Adding an Image

Here's some HTML that inserts a picture of two of the authors' favorite beers:

```
<!DOCTYPE HTML PUBLIC "-//W3C//DTD HTML 4.0 Transitional//EN"
        "http://www.w3.org/TR/REC-html40/loose.dtd">

<HTML>
<HEAD>
<TITLE>Another Simple HTML Document, html4.html</TITLE>
</HEAD>
<BODY>
<H3>Black Sheep Ale</H3>
<IMG SRC="blac_s.jpg" ALT="Black Sheep Ale" ALIGN="left" HEIGHT=150
WIDTH=100>
<P>
Here is a picture of a bottle of Black Sheep Ale.
</P><P>
The culmination of five generations of brewing expertise.<P>
Brewed at Paul Theakston's Black Sheep Brewery in Masham, North
Yorkshire.<P>
And nowhere else.
</P>
<PRE>
```

```
</PRE>
<HR>
<H3>Spitfire</H3>
<IMG SRC="spit_s.jpg" ALT="Spitfire Bitter" ALIGN="right" HEIGHT=150
WIDTH=100>
<P>
Here is a picture of Spitfire Bitter.
</P><P>
This is a bottle conditioned bitter brewed at the Sheperd Neame brewery in
Kent.
</P><P>
Established in 1698 the bottle proclaims that it is Britain's oldest brewery.
</P>

</BODY>
</HTML>
```

What we see is:

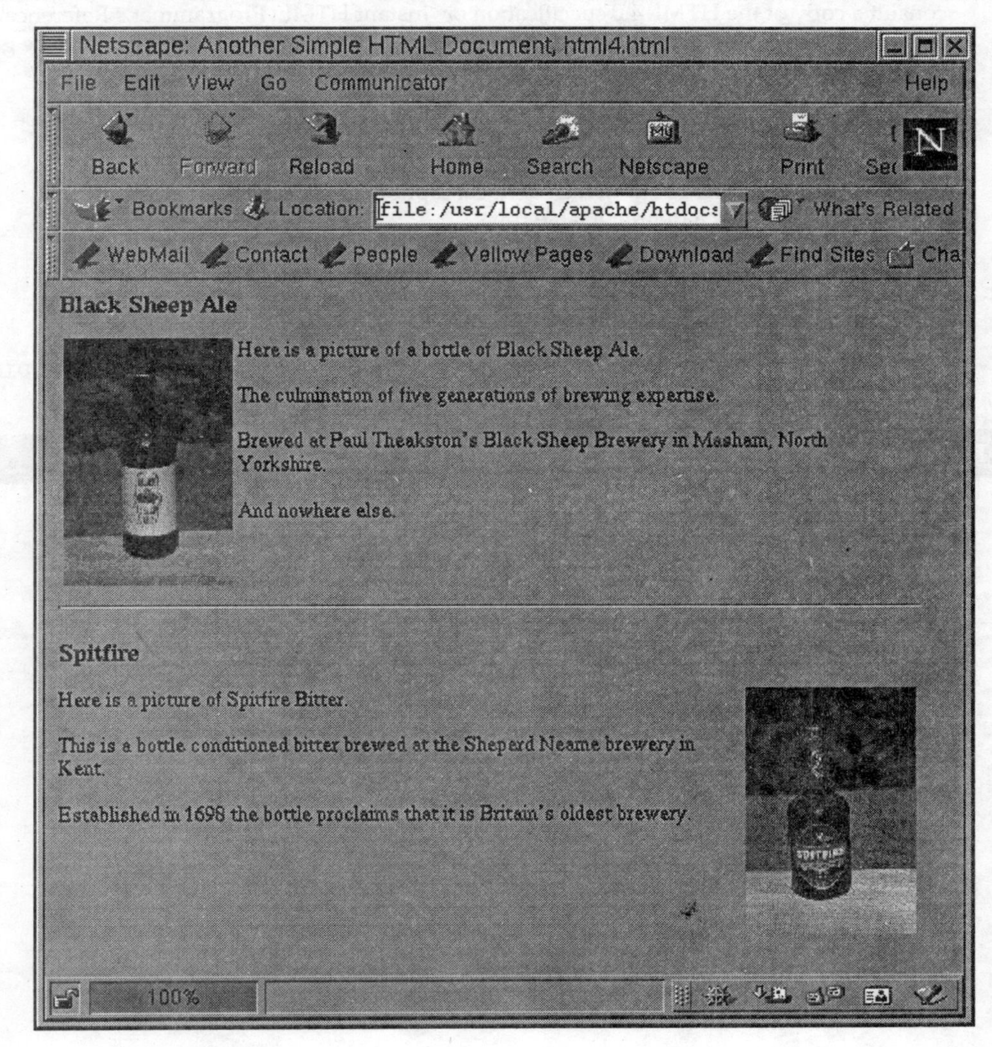

How It Works

The browser loads the text and image separately and places them together on the screen. In this case, the image is in JPEG format. Note how the ALIGN attribute changes the placing of the text following the image.

Tables

Tables were not in the original HTML definition, but are a very important method of formatting data. As well as using them for conventional tables, we can also sometimes use them with hidden border lines for controlling the placement of pictures and text.

Here, we present only the basic table attributes. If you need to use complex or nested tables you should consult a copy of the HTML 4.0 specification or "Instant HTML: Programmer's Reference", ISBN 1-861001-56-8, from Wrox Press. Tables are specified in terms of rows and columns. These can be grouped together to allow entries to span more than a single row or column.

A table is enclosed in <TABLE></TABLE> tags. You can use additional tags inside these that are only valid inside the table. These are:

<CAPTION> and </CAPTION> which define a caption for the table.
<TR> and </TR> which delimit a table row.
<TH> and </TH> which delimit a header for a table row or column.
<TD> and </TD> which delimit the data appearing inside a table cell.

These are only valid inside a table row.

The TABLE tag also takes several attributes, the most important of which are CELLPADDING and CELLSPACING, that control the width and separation of cells inside the table.

Try It Out - A Table

Here's a simple table:

```
<!DOCTYPE HTML PUBLIC "-//W3C//DTD HTML 4.0 Transitional//EN"
        "http://www.w3.org/TR/REC-html40/loose.dtd">
<HTML>
<HEAD>
<TITLE>Another Simple HTML Document, html5.html</TITLE>
</HEAD>
<BODY>
<TABLE CELLPADDING=5>
<CAPTION>A simple table</CAPTION>
<TR>
       <TD>flats</TD>
       <TD>houses</TD>
       <TD>shops</TD>
       <TD>factories</TD>
</TR>
<TR>
       <TD>small</TD>
       <TD>larger</TD>
       <TD>may be very big</TD>
       <TD>usually very large</TD>
</TR>
</TABLE>
</BODY>
</HTML>
```

What we see is:

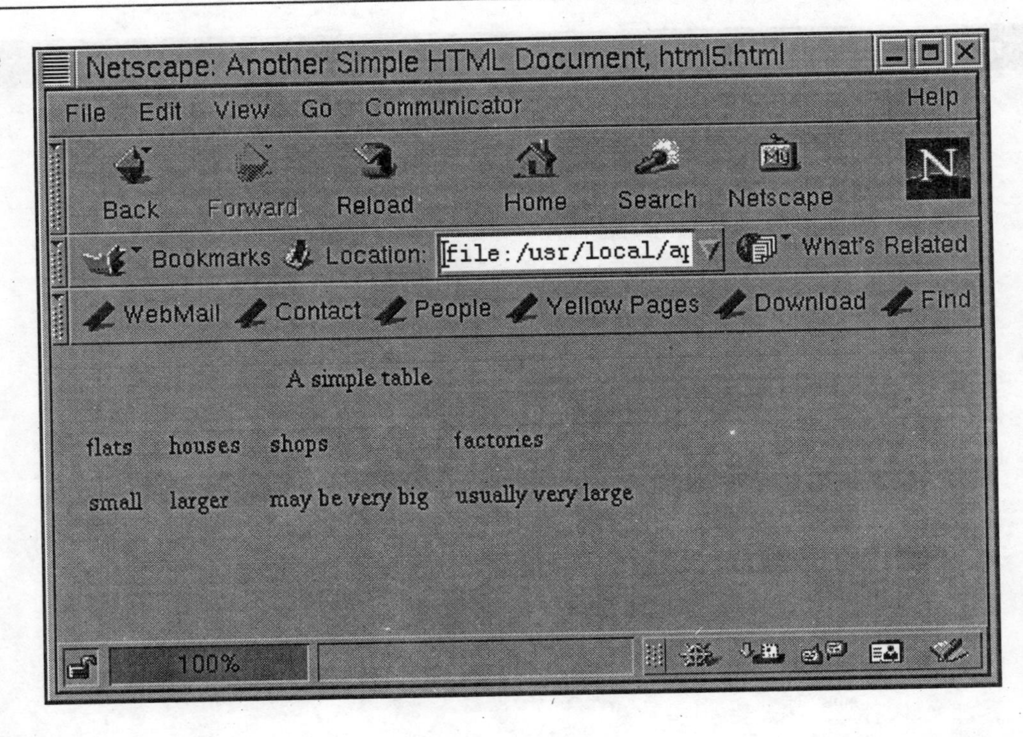

How It Works

Each row is started with a <TR> tag and should be closed with a </TR> tag. Each column in the table is separated with <TD> tags. These should be closed with a </TD> tag. Many documents omit the </TR> and </TD> tags, leaving the browser to determine from context where the rows and data should end. You should always put them.

The browser looks at the cells defined in the table and generates a table with the appropriate number of rows and columns. It also sizes the cells as required to fit the text inside them.

Try It Out - Another Table

Here's some HTML that generates a rather more complex table:

```
<!DOCTYPE HTML PUBLIC "-//W3C//DTD HTML 4.0 Transitional//EN"
        "http://www.w3.org/TR/REC-html40/loose.dtd">
<HTML>
<HEAD>
<TITLE>Another Simple HTML Document, html6.html</TITLE>
</HEAD>
<BODY>
<TABLE BORDER=2 CELLPADDING=15>
<CAPTION>HP printers in use</CAPTION>
<TR>
       <TH></TH>
       <TH COLSPAN=3>Inkjet</TH>
       <TH COLSPAN=2>Laser</TH>
</TR>
<TR>
<TH></TH>
       <TH>Original</TH>
       <TH>500</TH>
       <TH>600</TH>
       <TH>2p</TH>
       <TH>4m</TH>
</TR>
<TR>
       <TH>Software</TH>
       <TD>0</TD>
       <TD>2</TD>
       <TD>1</TD>
       <TD>0</TD>
       <TD>2</TD>
</TR>
<TR>
       <TH>Hardware</TH>
       <TD>1</TD>
       <TD>1</TD>
       <TD>0</TD>
       <TD>1</TD>
       <TD>0</TD>
</TR>
<TR>
       <TH>Sales</TH>
       <TD>0</TD>
       <TD>0</TD>
       <TD>0</TD>
       <TD>1</TD>
       <TD>1</TD>
</TR> <TR>
       <TH>Drawing</TH>
       <BR>Office
       <TD>0</TD>
       <TD>2</TD>
       <TD>0</TD>
       <TD>0</TD>
       <TD>0</TD>
</TR>
</TABLE>
</BODY>
</HTML>
```

What we see is:

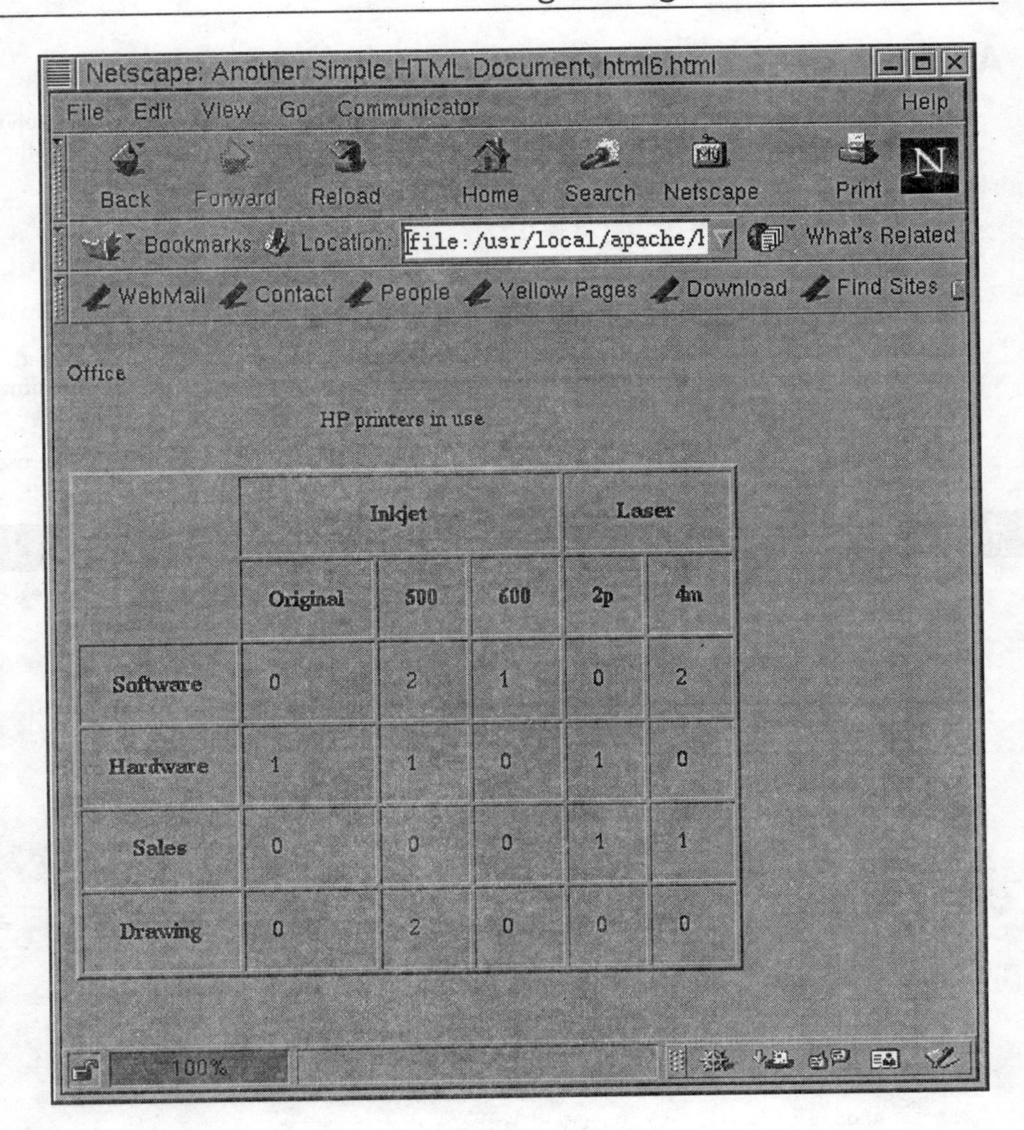

	Inkjet			Laser	
	Original	500	600	2p	4m
Software	0	2	1	0	2
Hardware	1	1	0	1	0
Sales	0	0	0	1	1
Drawing	0	2	0	0	0

How It Works

We add the `BORDER` attribute to the `<TABLE>` tag to specify borders round the cells and `CELLPADDING` to leave some space between the cell text and the border.

We use empty `<TH>` tags to skip columns where we don't wish to enter text. The `COLSPAN` attribute is used to allow the '`Inkjet`' and '`Laser`' labels to occupy multiple columns in the table. Notice also the `<BR>` tag to split '`Drawing Office`' across two lines.

Browsers normally default to fixed-width columns, however, in this example the browser has used variable-width columns.

Anchors or Hyperlinks

A very important part of the way World Wide Web documents work is the links between them. This feature is what gives HTML documents the power to create something as appealing as the World Wide Web.

The anchor tag is actually quite simple. It is:

```
<A NAME="where I am now" HREF="URL to go to"> some text</A>
```

The NAME attribute provides a way of naming the current location in a document. You may omit it.

The HREF is a hypertext reference, and provides a URL to go to when the link is activated. The character # in an HREF indicates that all characters after the # refer to an anchor NAME inside a document and all characters before the # are a URL referring to a document.

Any text between the start <A. . .> and end </A> anchor tags is highlighted. When the user selects the highlighted text, the browser moves to the URL specified in the HREF attribute.

Try It Out - Anchors

Here's a pair of HTML files that contain anchors allowing you to jump not only within each file, but also between them:

```
<!DOCTYPE HTML PUBLIC "-//W3C//DTD HTML 4.0 Transitional//EN"
        "http://www.w3.org/TR/REC-html40/loose.dtd">
<HTML>
<HEAD>
<TITLE>Another Simple HTML Document, html7.html</TITLE>
</HEAD>
<BODY>
<A NAME="top"></A>
<P>
Here is a simple document. It contains an anchor that allows you to jump to
<A HREF="html8.html"> html8.html</A> if you click on the highlighted text.
</P><P>
You can also jump to the <A NAME="bottom" HREF="html8.html#bottom"> bottom
of html8.html</A> if you wish.
</P>
</BODY>
</HTML>
```

```
<!DOCTYPE HTML PUBLIC "-//W3C//DTD HTML 4.0 Transitional//EN"
        "http://www.w3.org/TR/REC-html40/loose.dtd">

<HTML>
<HEAD>
<TITLE>Another Simple HTML Document, html8.html</TITLE>
</HEAD>
<BODY>
<A NAME="top"></A>
<P>
<H2>This is html8.html</H2>
Here is a simple document. It contains an anchor that allows you to jump to
the <A HREF="html7.html#bottom"> bottom
of html7.html</A> if you wish.
<P> We need to insert some text.</P>
<P> Quite a lot of text.</P>
<P> If we didn't, how could you tell which was <B>top</B> and which was
<B>bottom</B> of this document?</P>
<P> You can also <A HREF="#top"> jump to the top</A> of this document if you
wish</P>
```

```
<P> It might well all appear all on the same page.</P>
<P> Soon we will have enough text.</P>
<P> To prevent this fitting </P>
<P> on</P>
<P> a</P>
<P> single</P>
<P> page!</P>
<P> This is the bottom, but you can jump to the <A NAME="bottom"
HREF="#top">top</A> if you want, or back to <A HREF="html7.html">
html7.html</A> if you prefer!</P>
</BODY>
</HTML>
```

Here's a screen shot of part of `html8.html`, showing the highlighted links:

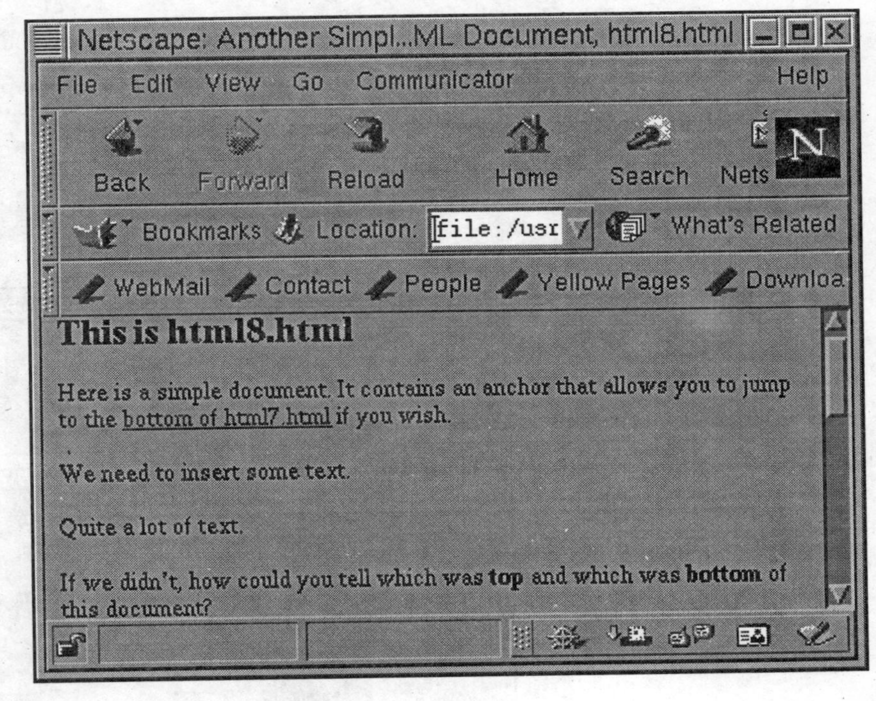

How It Works

This pair of HTML files demonstrates the use of the anchor tag, showing how locations in a document may be marked with `<A NAME=...>` tags and how other documents may be referenced with `<A HREF=...>` tags. Notice that all the tags used here use a relative URL, hence the absence of the machine name.

We also show how combining the two allows you specify a jump to a particular location in another document.

Combining Anchors and Images

It's very common to combine images and anchors, because clicking on an image is much more appealing than simple text. We do this by simply combining the anchor `<A>` and image `<IMG>` tags, like this:

Try It Out - Images as Anchors

Check out the following HTML:

```
<!DOCTYPE HTML PUBLIC "-//W3C//DTD HTML 4.0 Transitional//EN"
        "http://www.w3.org/TR/REC-html40/loose.dtd">
<HTML>
<HEAD>
<TITLE>Another Simple HTML Document, html9.html</TITLE>
</HEAD>
<BODY>
<A NAME="top"></A>
<H2>This is html9.html</H2>
Here is a simple document. It contains an anchor that allows you to jump by
clicking on a picture. Actually the HREF file "beer.html" doesn't exist,
but the browser does not discover this unless you click to take the hyper link.
<P> You can also <A HREF="beer.html"><IMG SRC="blac_s.jpg" ALIGN="MIDDLE"
ALT="jump to beer.html"></A> use images as
clickable items if you wish.</P>

<P> The end.</P>

</BODY>
</HTML>
```

What we see is:

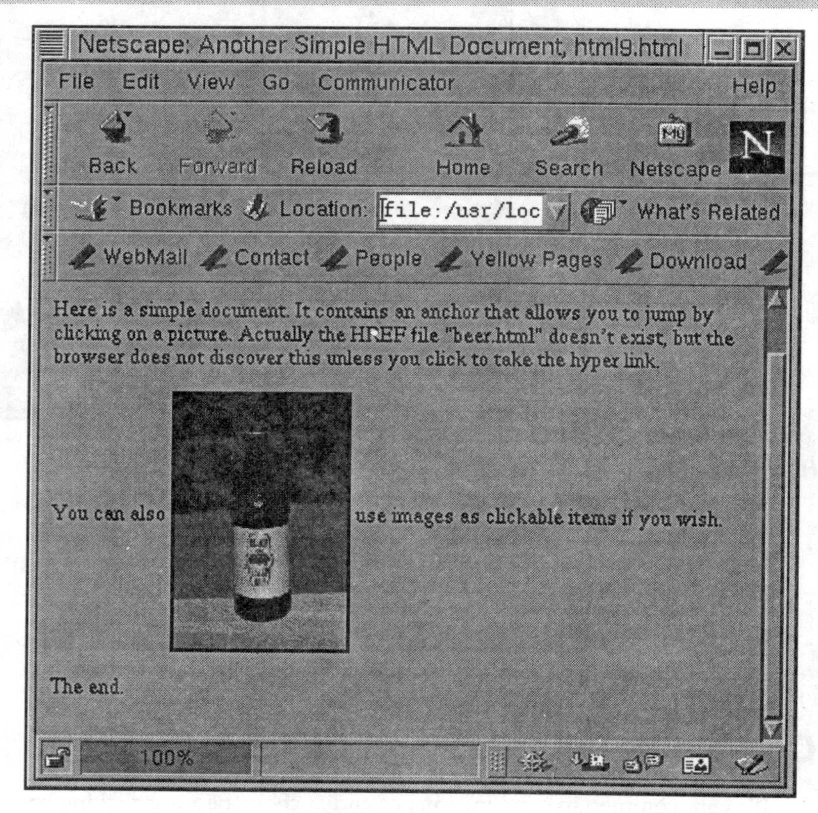

How It Works

Using the `<IMG>` tag inserts a picture into the anchor tag. Notice we also use an `ALT` attribute, so that people using browsers that are not displaying graphics for some reason can still see where the link is going and have the ability to select it. If the image is selected, the browser will attempt to load the URL specified in the link, `beer.html`.

The picture used here is large in proportion to the size of the text. In general, smaller pictures tend to look better, but this serves as an example.

Non-HTML URLs

So far, all our links have been to other HTML pages on the same machine, but, in fact, we can use lots of other URLs. The most popular is simply to reference a graphic file by writing an anchor such as:

```
<A HREF="picture.jpg">.
```

This causes a JPEG format picture to be returned when the link is selected.

We can configure servers that respond to requests from World Wide Web browsers to be aware of different file extensions and map them to the appropriate MIME file type for sending via the HTTP protocol.

The general scheme depends on where the document is being loaded from. If it's being fetched from a server, the server is responsible for deciding the MIME type and subtype of the file, which it then sends using the HTTP protocol before the actual data is sent. The browser is then responsible for determining how to process that MIME type and sub-type.

If a local file is being loaded, the browser must decide the MIME type and subtype, as well as how to process it.

A full discussion of mapping file extensions to MIME types is beyond the scope of this chapter; you should check your server and browser manuals for details of mapping extensions to MIME types. You can normally find these in files called `mime-types` and `mailcap`. By way of example, here's the `.mailcap` file for Netscape, which tells it that audio files are to be processed with the '`play`' command:

```
audio/* ; play %s
```

Other common URLs included in HTML pages include:

ftp://ftp.site.name/pub/filename. If this is selected, the browser is requested to start an FTP session to retrieve a file.

mailto:name@machine.com. If this is selected, the client is requested to start an e-mail session, with the address specified.

news:comp.os.linux.announce. If this is selected, the client is requested to start a news session to the appropriate newsgroup.

Anchors to Other Sites

The World Wide Web wouldn't be the resource it is if all machines could do was to serve local HTML pages. The power and the attraction of the World Wide Web is that pages can link to other resources on different machines. This is done using an absolute URL, of the form http://machine.name/file.html.

Try It Out - Links to Other Sites

Here's an example of a page using some less common URLs and some links to other sites:

```
<!DOCTYPE HTML PUBLIC "-//W3C//DTD HTML 4.0 Transitional//EN"
        "http://www.w3.org/TR/REC-html40/loose.dtd">
<HTML>
<HEAD>
<TITLE>Another Simple HTML Document, html10.html</TITLE>
</HEAD>
<BODY>
<H2>This is html10.html</H2>
This shows some less common URLs and links to remote machines.
<P> If you want to find out about some other WROX books we suggest you visit
their <A HREF="http://www.wrox.com/">home page</A>.</P>

<P> To send feedback on Wrox books you can email them at
their <A HREF="mailto:feedback@wrox.demon.co.uk">feedback address.</A></P>

<P> For more information about the World Wide Web, visit the <A
HREF="http://www.w3.org/">World Wide Web Consortium</A>. You will find many
specifications, draft specifications, lists of http servers, and lots of other helpful
files.</P>

<P> If you are just getting started with Linux, then you should subscribe to
the newsgroups</P>

<A HREF="news:comp.os.linux.announce"> comp.os.linux.announce</A>, and
<A HREF="news:comp.os.linux.answers"> comp.os.linux.answers</A>.
<P> Some people are not sure how Linux is</P>

<A HREF="english.au">pronounced</A>. Well now you know!
<P>
<HR>
</P>
<P>
<IMG SRC="pblinux.gif" ALT="Powered by Linux" ALIGN="middle">
This server is running on a Linux box. Be proud, be powered by Linux!
<HR>
<CITE>Many thanks to <A HREF="mailto:Alan.Cox@linux.org">Alan Cox</A> for
permission to use this graphic.</CITE>
</P> <P>
This page is &#169 Copyright Wrox Press.
</P>
</BODY>
</HTML>
```

When we view it we see:

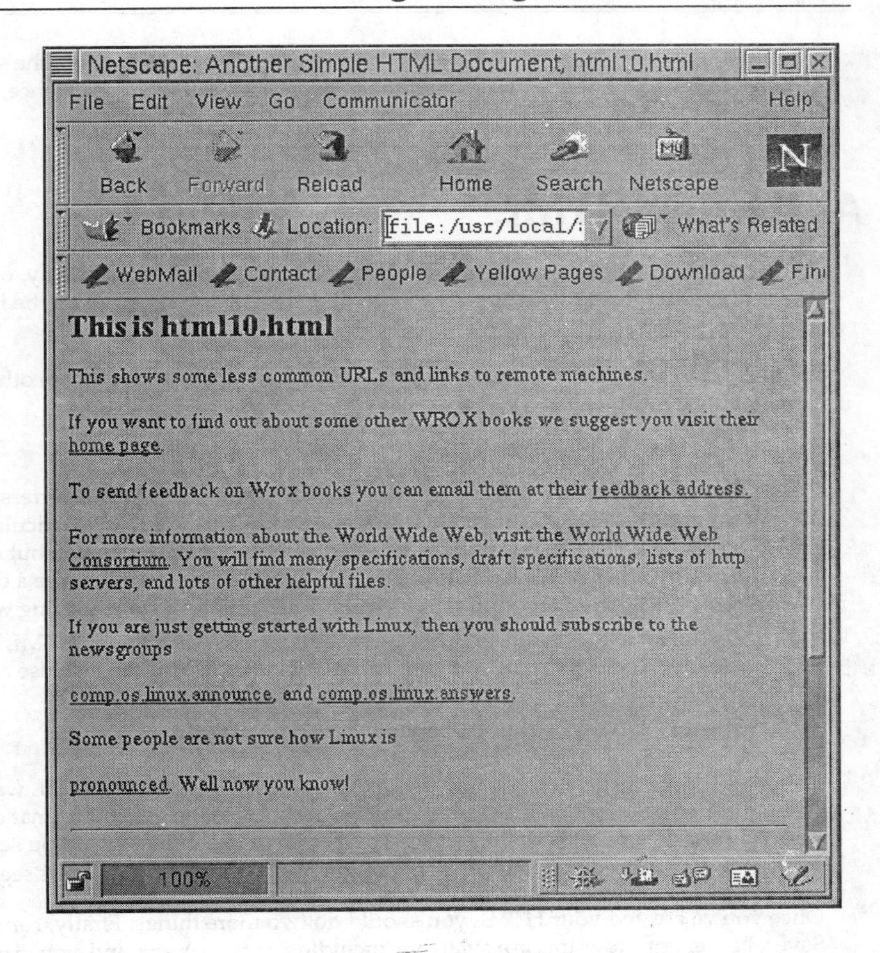

How It Works

This example shows a page combining absolute URLs and some other less common ones. Notice that the image has had the background color set transparent (a feature available in GIF files and supported by most viewers), so we can see no border around the picture. The Linux graphic originally appeared on http://www.linux.org.uk/; thanks to Alan.Cox@linux.org for permission to reuse it.

Other Things to do with Images

There are a few other tricks that we can play with graphics. A popular addition is to give pages a background. We do this by extending the `<BODY>` tag with the `BACKGROUND` attribute. You should keep your background image small and make sure it doesn't detract from your main text. A background tag looks like this:

```
<BODY BACKGROUND="background.gif">
```

You can set one of the colors in a GIF file to be transparent. This allows the background to show through, which often looks much cleaner than a square graphic put on a page.

Another feature of GIFs is that they allow you to store several images in the same GIF file. Some browsers understand this and will show each of the images in the GIF file in sequence, giving a simple animated image.

Authoring HTML

In this chapter, we've been writing HTML by simply typing it in. Certainly, once you have a reasonable grasp of HTML, it is quite easy to type it in directly. We simply input all the HTML in this chapter using the `emacs` editor.

If you start to write large amounts of HTML, you may wish to investigate other ways of generating it. The principal ways are:

- Type it in with a text editor.
- Use a converter to convert from an existing format. Several converters exist, including some that convert from HTML to another format, such as PostScript. Of particular interest is Linuxdoc-sgml. Like HTML, this is an SGML-defined structured document, but one that may be converted to many other formats, including HTML itself. If you want to write a document once, but reproduce it in many different formats, you should consider starting with Linuxdoc-sgml.
- Use a context-sensitive editor. Several editors exist that 'know' HTML and help you to chose tags and correctly structure your HTML document. You can also use an emacs HTML helper mode.
- Use a WYSIWYG editor that simply generates HTML.

Using a WYSIWYG generator could give you some problems. Since HTML was designed to accommodate many different viewers on different platforms, it specifies the general format of documents, but not normally the details, such as the font and point size to use. While what you see in your WYSIWYG generator may indeed be what *you* get, it might not be exactly what others see!

Once you've created your HTML you should do two more things. Firstly, run it though an HTML checker. Several excellent programs are available, including `html-check` and `weblint`. Secondly, you should test it on as many viewers (and platforms) as you can manage and check that each results in a reasonable image for the user.

That covers the principal parts of HTML, with the exception of forms (which we'll meet in the next chapter) and clickable maps, which we'll be covering later in this chapter.

Serving HTML Pages

So far, we have been writing HTML pages and simply loading them into a browser as files. This is fine as a way for a single person to view a document, but if you want a lot of people to view your work, you would have to send each of them their own copy.

A much better solution, and indeed the foundation of the World Wide Web, is the idea of transferring documents across networks as they are required. This allows users to browse (or surf if you prefer!) documents without having to request them in advance.

You can do this by setting up a server program running on a machine where all the documents are stored, allowing client programs to request these documents over the network.

Don't think that this has to be on the Internet to be useful; a company might decide that it offers a good way of distributing procedure documents, for example, rather than maintaining multiple paper copies which require tracking and updating. A single copy of the documents can be placed on a server on an internal LAN and viewed on any workstation connected to the LAN. Since both Linux and many HTML server programs are free, this can be a low cost solution.

Networked HTML Overview

The diagram below shows how clients can request HTML documents (along with images and other references files) stored on a server.

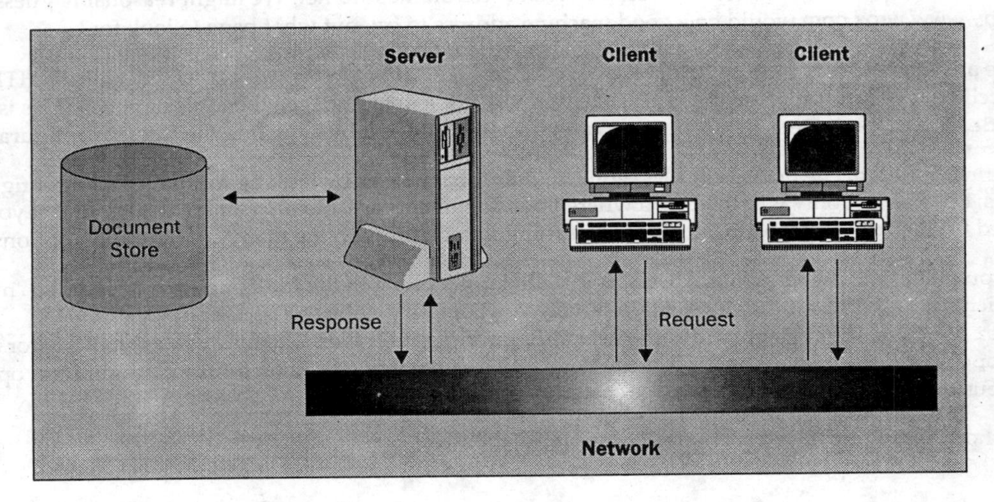

The browser program on the client machine generates a request across the network to the server. The server's HTTP daemon (the usual name for the server program on UNIX systems) processes the request, reads the documents from its document store and sends them back to the client as MIME encoded documents. All the data is transferred using the HTTP protocol, which runs on top of the underlying network protocols.

The system works in terms of requests and responses. The client requests a document and the server responds by sending the document, or an error if the document doesn't exist. Where a document consists of HTML text and images, the client is responsible for requesting the document and subsequently for asking for any additional files it requires, such as images included with `<IMG>` tags.

There's no 'conversation' as such between the client and the server. The server simply responds to requests as they happen and, apart from log files, keeps no record of any previous request from a particular client.

An HTTP daemon can serve many clients. It simply processes requests in the order in which it receives them. In fact, many implementations of the HTTP daemon use multiple processes to increase the throughput of requests and responses.

Setting up a Server

Many Linux distributions come with an HTTP server, normally the very popular (and free) Apache Server. Unless you have some very special reasons for wanting to use a different web server, this is an excellent server to use, though there are many others, many of them freely available.

Most Linux distributions will come with a web server included, usually Apache, and normally all you need to do is select it to be installed and run in your default configuration. It is that simple. If your distribution didn't have a web server, or you would like to install one from scratch, we suggest you use Apache from http://www.apache.org. It's free, excellent quality, very well documented on the web site, and easy to install.

One item that may need to be configured is a default page, which is served to a client when no page is specified. Suppose we wanted to look for Wrox Press on the Internet. We might reasonably guess that http://www.wrox.com would be a good machine address to try, but what page to look for?

The answer is to leave the page blank, so we try for a URL http://www.wrox.com/, i.e. with no HTML page specified. We can configure the HTTP daemon to serve a default page when this happens. This is normally `Index.html` or `index.html`, but you can normally change it by adjusting the `httpd` configuration files.

To find your Apache document files, you should probably start by looking for the Apache configuration files, because not only will it tell you where your documents are, but also where the log files if you ever need to track down problems. It's also interesting to look through the many configuration options.

If you don't know where your Apache is installed, try looking in the file `/etc/rc.d/init.d.httpd`, which may give you some clues. Alternatively you could try `/etc/httpd/conf` or `/usr/local/Apache/conf` directories for the configuration files. The files you are looking for are called `httpd.conf`, and `srm.conf`. To locate your actual document files, look for the configuration option `DocumentRoot` in the `srm.conf` file.

In short, setting up a web server on Linux is trivially easy!

Clickable Maps

These are images that take different actions, depending on which location inside the image is clicked on. There are two forms of clickable maps: server-side and client-side. We'll look briefly at both.

Server-side Maps

By including an `<IMG>` tag in an HTML page and using the `ISMAP` attribute, we tell the client that, when the map is clicked, the name of the map and the (x,y) location that was clicked must be sent to the server. Different servers will process the request in slightly different ways. The end result is the same: the (x,y) location on the map is translated to a URL, which is returned to the client as the next page to load.

We do this using a 'map' file on the server. The file defines certain regions of the picture as relating to different URLs. In general, you can use circles, rectangles and polygons. You can also specify a default URL if you wish.

There are two ways to generate a map file. The first method is to use a graphics program, such as **xv**, that can read in a graphics file and show you the coordinates of your pointer. You then write down each location in turn as you mark out the region you want to map to a URL. This method is fine for one or two simple maps, but rather tedious for anything more.

The second way is to look for a program that lets you mark out an image, writing a map file for you as you go. Several exist for various UNIX platforms. Here's a sample map file, in NCSA format, which relates different parts of the image to different URLs:

```
rect ovary.html 290,107 324,166
circle stigma.html 289,516 298,529
rect style.html 275,383 291,501
poly filament.html 183,366 109,491 120,496 186,375
poly filament.html 311,392 339,564 349,561 319,383
poly filament.html 264,396 261,541 268,536 271,397
circle anther.html 348,581 355,593
circle anther.html 266,550 277,556
circle anther.html 105,505 114,521
poly tube.html 287,158 328,168 328,208 314,183 280,176
poly sepals.html 325,230 315,186 200,160 232,204 325,237
poly sepals.html 332,233 371,264 403,334 406,371 422,372 424,323 375,246 329,227
poly corolla.html 211,205 348,249 403,366 343,399 159,344
```

Unfortunately, different UNIX servers implement maps in slightly different ways. Not only are there slight differences in the format of the map file, but the way it is accessed on the server can also vary. You should consult the appropriate manual for the server you are using.

On the Apache server, it's very easy. You simply put the map file in a subdirectory called maps in the main HTTP file directory and, in the client HTML document, specify an image file with an anchor, like this :

```
<A HREF="http://maps/fuchsia.map"><IMG ISMAP SRC="fuchsia.gif"></A>
```

Other servers require an additional configuration file to specify the location of the map file and also require a program, usually imagemap, to be stored in the cgi-bin directory of the server.

Client-side Maps

The client-side clickable map is a more recent form of clickable map and has a significant advantage over the server-side map in that all the processing load is on the client and clicking doesn't require transactions across the network.

To make a client-side map, we use an <IMG> tag with the USEMAP attribute, like this:

```
<A HREF="http:/fuchsia.map"><IMG SRC="fuchsia.gif" USEMAP="#fuchsiamap"></A>
```

Then, somewhere in the same HTML page, we include the actual map, in <MAP></MAP> tags, like this:

```
<MAP NAME="fuchsiamap">
<AREA SHAPE="rect" COORDS="290,107 324,166"  HREF="ovary.html">
...
<AREA SHAPE="poly" COORDS="325,230 315,186 200,160 232,204 325,237"
HREF="sepals.html">
</MAP>
```

Notice the order of the fields is slightly different in the client side map.

Server-side Includes

One final feature of pages served by **web server** programs is that they can be processed before they are returned to the client. This feature is called **server-side includes** and allows us to access information on the server at the time the page is served, rather than when the page was authored. Most server-side includes start with the sequence `<!—#` and end with the sequence —>.

All server-side includes have a directive and may also have an attribute. The directives are:

- `echo`, which allows access to environment variables. The usual variables that are available are:
  - `DATE_GMT`: the current date and time at Greenwich, UK. Now known as UTC time.
  - `DATE_LOCAL`: the local date and time
  - `LAST_MODIFIED`: the date and time when the current document was last updated.
- `include`, which allows an additional file to be inserted in the HTML file before it's returned to the client.
- `exec`, which inserts the output of a command into the HTML document before it's returned to the client.

Here's an example of a server-side include that would insert the date and time that the current document was last modified:

```
<!—#echo var="LAST_MODIFIED"—>
```

Not all servers can process server-side includes and, even if they can, they may be disabled or only certain directives accepted. Server-side includes cause problems for servers because they add an additional processing requirement. If server-side includes are enabled on all files, the `httpd` program must process every file it returns, looking for server-side directives, significantly adding to the processing load. Some servers permit server-side includes only on files with specific extensions, commonly `.shtml`.

The other problem, particularly with the `exec` directive, is that you are permitting others to run programs on your machine. Setting up a machine to serve HTML pages does open your machine to others, which is a reduction in security, but is generally reasonably safe since you're only returning a data stream. Allowing people to execute programs with `exec`, on the other hand, significantly compromises your security. For this reason, some commercial service providers don't allow `exec` in server-side includes.

Try It Out - Client-side Maps and Server-side Includes

Here's some HTML that shows both a client-side map and some server-side includes. Be careful when you're choosing the image to use as your map, because, to be useful, they must be displayed by the client. Very large images are only really acceptable when they're loaded locally.

```
<!DOCTYPE HTML PUBLIC "-//W3C//DTD HTML 4.0 Transitional//EN"
        "http://www.w3.org/TR/REC-html40/loose.dtd">
<HTML>
<HEAD>
<TITLE>Demonstration Page</TITLE>
</HEAD>
```

```
<BODY>
<H1><CENTER>This document is html11.html</CENTER></H1>
<P> This document was last modified on <!—#echo var="LAST_MODIFIED"—></P>

<P> It demonstrates server side includes, a client side map, and other links.</P>

<P>
<HR>
</P> <P> Here is a fortune, different just about every time this page is loaded!</P>

<PRE>

<!—#exec cgi="/cgi-bin/fortune"—>

</PRE>
<P>
<HR>
This is a clickable client side map.
</P>
<P> Try clicking on different parts of the fuchsia:</P>


<P>
<A><IMG SRC="fuchsia.gif" ALT="Fuschia" USEMAP="#fuschiamap">
</A>
</P>
<P>
<HR>
</P>
<P> If you want to find out about some other WROX books we suggest you visit
their <A HREF="http://www.wrox.com/">home page</A>.</P>

<P> For more information about the World Wide Web, visit the <A
HREF="http://www.w3.org/">World Wide Web Consortium</A>. You will find many
specifications, draft specifications, lists of httpd servers, and lots of other
helpful files. </P>

<P> If you are just getting started with Linux, then you should subscribe to
the newsgroups
<A HREF="news:comp.os.linux.announce"> comp.os.linux.announce</A>, and
<A HREF="news:comp.os.linux.answers"> comp.os.linux.answers</A>.</P>

<P> Some people are not sure how Linux is
<A HREF="english.au">pronounced</A>. Well now you know!</P>

<P>
<HR>
</P>
<P>
<IMG SRC="pblinux.gif" ALT="Powered by Linux" ALIGN="middle">
This server is powered by Linux!
<HR>
<CITE>Many thanks to <A HREF="mailto:Alan.Cox@linux.org">Alan Cox</A> for
permission to use this graphic.</CITE>
</P>
<P>
This page is &copy; Copyright Wrox Press.
</P>

<MAP NAME="fuschiamap">
<AREA SHAPE="rect" COORDS="290,107 324,166" HREF="ovary.html">
<AREA SHAPE="rect" COORDS="279,504 300,530" HREF="stigma.html">
<AREA SHAPE="rect" COORDS="275,383 291,501" HREF="style.html">
<AREA SHAPE="poly" COORDS="183,366 109,491 120,496 186,375" HREF="filament.html">
<AREA SHAPE="poly" COORDS="311,392 339,564 349,561 319,383" HREF="filament.html">
<AREA SHAPE="poly" COORDS="264,396 261,541 268,536 271,397" HREF="filament.html">
```

```
<AREA SHAPE="rect" COORDS="333,561 363,581" HREF="anther.html">
<AREA SHAPE="rect" COORDS="255,538 280,563" HREF="anther.html">
<AREA SHAPE="rect" COORDS="95,496 120,521" HREF="anther.html">
<AREA SHAPE="poly" COORDS="287,158 328,168 328,208 314,183 280,176" HREF="tube.html">
<AREA SHAPE="poly" COORDS="325,230 315,186 200,160 232,204 325,237"
HREF="sepals.html">
<AREA SHAPE="poly" COORDS="332,233 371,264 403,334 406,371 422,372 424,323 375,246
329,227" HREF="sepals.html">
<AREA SHAPE="poly" COORDS="211,205 348,249 403,366 343,399 159,344"
HREF="corolla.html">
</MAP>

</BODY>

</HTML>
```

The resulting page is:

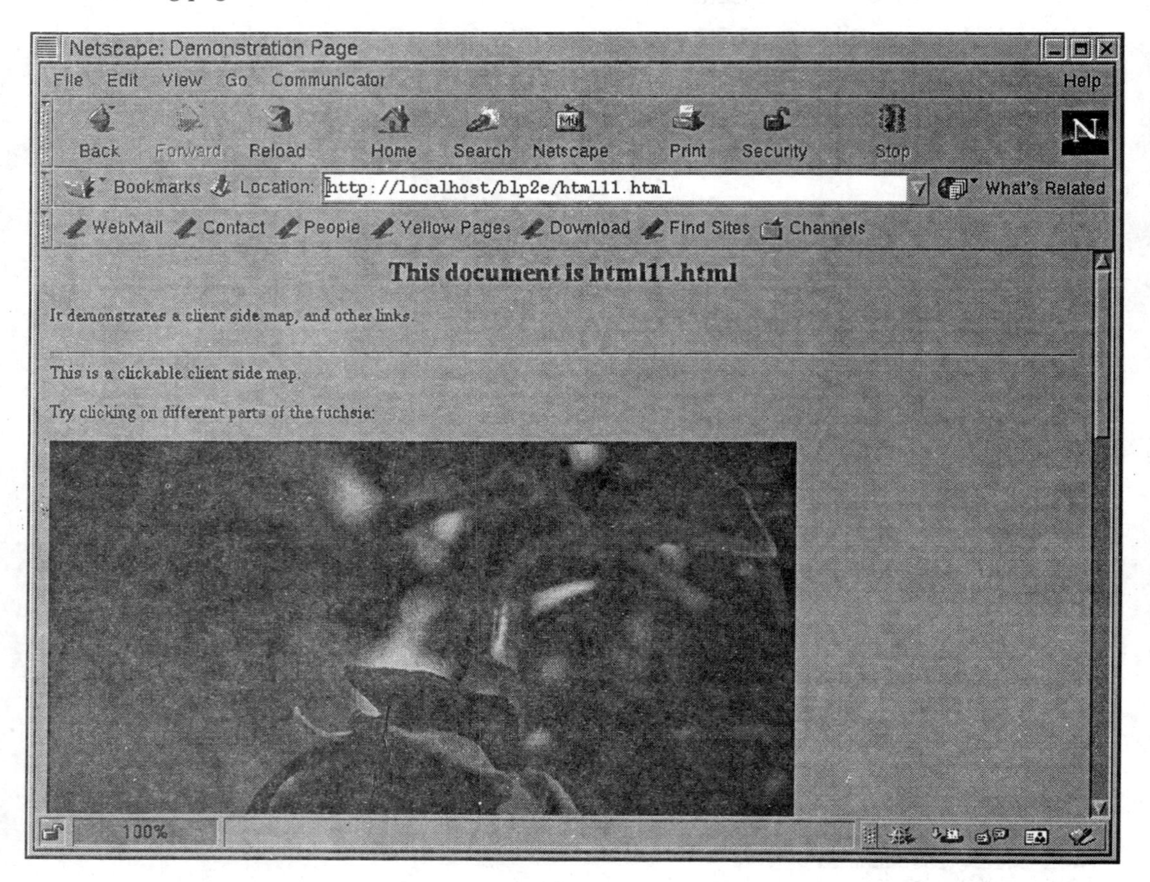

How It Works

The #echo server-side include inserts the current date and time of the file into the page.

The #exec server-side include executes the fortune program (actually the fortune program in the cgi-bin directory that was provided with the Apache server we got), and inserts its text into the page. We enclose this in <PRE></PRE> tags to preserve the formatting, which is important in many fortune cookies. Since this is invoked each time the page is fetched, and fortune returns a pseudo random fortune, this will change on virtually every request for the page.

Finally, the client-side map allows the user to click on different parts of the image.

Tips for Setting up WWW Pages

Lastly, here are some tips for setting up Web pages:

- Remember that documents can be linked. You don't need to include all the detail in a single document. Hide some detail behind hypertext links.
- Don't break your documents into many tiny pieces. If you split your documents up with too little information on each page they become fragmented and difficult to follow.
- Stick to the HTML standards. Just because your favorite browser has implemented some extension to the standard, it doesn't mean you have to use it. Not everybody will be using the same browser. Be conservative in what you expect browsers to support.
- Check your HTML. There are several very good HTML checkers freely available. Use them to make sure your HTML is correct.
- Take care with images. If you put very large graphics on your pages, people using slow modem links will experience much frustration waiting for the graphic to arrive. Remember a modem link is a lot slower than browsing on the server machine.
- Use the ALT attribute of the <IMG> tag. This allows people with non-graphical browsers (and those who have disabled graphics to speed up browsing) to view your pages. Remember that not everybody will be able to see the picture, and test the document without graphics on your machine to make sure it still looks all right.
- The title of a document is often used as a bookmark to refer to the location afterwards. Keep it succinct but accurate.

You can find many more hints, tips and rules in various style guides available on the Internet.

Summary

In this chapter, we've learned the basics of HTML, the markup language used to write pages that appear on the World Wide Web.

We've seen how to incorporate images on pages and how to link pages together, not just on a local site but across the Internet.

We have discussed checking your HTML to ensure that it's valid and viewable on a wide variety of platforms.

We saw some of the extra features that we can use when HTML pages are being delivered by a server, rather than read from a local file.

Finally, we gave you some basic tips about writing your own pages.

Internet Programming 2: CGI

In the last chapter, we saw how to set up HTML pages containing information that could be viewed both locally and across networks. While this is a very good way of publishing information, it is all essentially static information. To supply dynamic information we need to allow the user, through the web page, to interact with programs on the server in a dynamic way.

In this chapter, we'll learn how to allow the viewer to send information back to the server, and how the server can pass this information to programs, which can then respond to the client in a dynamic way. We are only going to look at server side processing, that is where code executes away from the client. We are also going to concentrate on stand alone server side programs, rather than scripts embedded in web pages, such as are used by PHP.

It is also possible to write client side programs, usually referred to as Dynamic HTML (DHTML), where scripts execute on the client, a topic we are not going to pursue here.

The interface specification that defines how information can be passed from browsers back to the server is called the **Common Gateway Interface**, usually abbreviated to **CGI**. The program accepting such information from a browser, commonly referred to as a **CGI program**, can process this information and use the HTTP protocol to send commands or dynamic documents back to the browser.

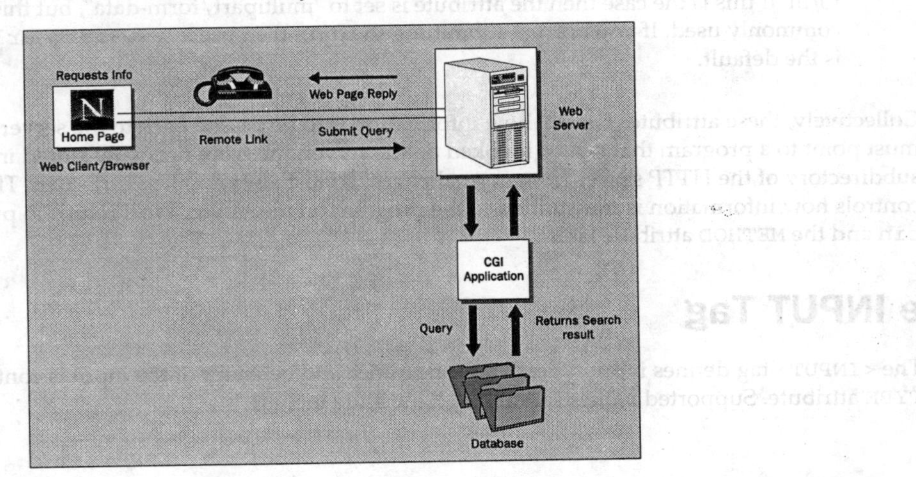

Before we can look at the CGI, we need to look at an HTML construct we haven't yet encountered, the FORM element.

FORM Elements

In the HTML that we've seen so far, all the tags have been concerned with controlling the way information is structured for display to the client, but haven't provided for any input from the browser, other than the selection of hypertext links.

We can set up fields that allow user input using the <FORM> tag. This is a composite tag. It can contain several other tags that are only valid inside a form. The <FORM> tag and its embedded tags, the form elements, have the following syntax:

```
<FORM ACTION= METHOD= ENCTYPE= >
  <INPUT NAME= TYPE= VALUE= SIZE= MAXLENGTH= CHECKED>
  <SELECT NAME= SIZE= MULTIPLE>
    <OPTION SELECTED VALUE= >
  </SELECT>
  <TEXTAREA NAME= ROWS= COLS= > </TEXTAREA>
</FORM>
```

In addition, we can also use the more common tags that we met in the last chapter inside the <FORM> tag. Notice that almost all the tags have a NAME attribute, which will be used by the server. We'll return to the processing of the NAME attribute when we look at general processing of forms by the server later in the chapter.

As you can see, <FORM> is a quite complex tag. Let's look at each element in turn.

The FORM Tag

The **<FORM>** tag starts an HTML form. It takes three attributes:

- The ACTION attribute specifies the URL of the program to invoke to process this form.
- The METHOD attribute takes either the value GET or the value POST.
- The ENCTYPE attribute is usually omitted, unless you wish to include a file to be sent with the form. If this is the case then the attribute is set to "multipart/form-data", but this is not commonly used. If you are just submitting the form then use x-www-form-urlencoded which is the default.

Collectively, these attributes control how information is to be passed back to the server. The ACTION value must point to a program that can be invoked on the server; these are normally stored in a separate subdirectory of the HTTP server from normal pages, almost always called cgi-bin. The METHOD attribute controls how information is transmitted to the program on the server. We'll return to programs in cgi-bin and the METHOD attribute later.

The INPUT Tag

The <INPUT> tag defines input types. The appearance and behavior of the input is controlled with the TYPE attribute. Supported values for the TYPE attribute include:

TEXT

When the TYPE attribute takes the value TEXT, the browser will display a single line box into which we can enter text. The NAME attribute gives the field a name, which will be used when the form is processed on the server. The SIZE attribute gives the size of the field on the web page; MAXLENGTH gives the maximum input size allowed. If this is larger than SIZE, the field will scroll to allow input. The VALUE attribute allows a default string to be entered in the field when it's first displayed.

Here's a fragment of HTML, illustrating the TEXT style of input:

```
Please enter your
<BR>
salutation: <INPUT TYPE=TEXT NAME=sal SIZE=5 MAXLENGTH=10 VALUE="Mr. ">
<BR>
first name: <INPUT TYPE=TEXT NAME=fname SIZE=20 MAXLENGTH=30>
<BR>
second name: <INPUT TYPE=TEXT NAME=sname SIZE=20 MAXLENGTH=30>
```

PASSWORD

The PASSWORD value is the same as the TEXT value, except that the contents of the field can't be seen in the browser. It's not very secure as a password, because the contents of the field are passed as plain text to the server, so anyone intercepting the transfer of the form information to the server will be able to read the password. However, it's useful to prevent other people from seeing what's being typed into the field.

Here's a fragment of HTML, illustrating the PASSWORD type:

```
Password: <INPUT TYPE=PASSWORD NAME=passwd SIZE=8>
```

HIDDEN

Setting TYPE=HIDDEN results in a text field that the user doesn't see on the browser screen and can't enter information into. This is used by server programs. Like the PASSWORD type, it's not very secure.

Here's a fragment of HTML, illustrating a HIDDEN field:

```
<INPUT TYPE=HIDDEN NAME=camefrom VALUE="foo/bar/baz.html">
```

CHECKBOX

The CHECKBOX type allows the user to select several of a number of options. Checkbox fields are grouped by specifying several of them with the same NAME attribute. The browser will allow the user to select from the set of checkbox fields having the same name.

The additional attribute CHECKED provides default selections. The VALUE attribute is used in returning the information to the server. To allow the user to see what's being selected, you should associate some text with each checkbox.

Here's a fragment of HTML, illustrating the CHECKBOX type of field. It shows the user a list of areas of the world and allows multiple selections:

```
<FORM ACTION="program" METHOD=POST>
<BR>
Please indicate which areas of the world you would like
to visit:<BR>
<INPUT TYPE=CHECKBOX NAME=cb VALUE="1">Asia<BR>
<INPUT TYPE=CHECKBOX NAME=cb VALUE="2" CHECKED>Africa<BR>
```

```
<INPUT TYPE=CHECKBOX NAME=cb VALUE="3">North America<BR>
<INPUT TYPE=CHECKBOX NAME=cb VALUE="4">South America<BR>
<INPUT TYPE=CHECKBOX NAME=cb VALUE="5">Antarctica<BR>
<INPUT TYPE=CHECKBOX NAME=cb VALUE="6">Europe<BR>
<INPUT TYPE=CHECKBOX NAME=cb VALUE="7" CHECKED>Australasia<BR>
</FORM>
```

RADIO

The RADIO type of <INPUT> tag is very similar to the CHECKBOX type, except that only one option may be chosen and only one of a set may be marked CHECKED. If no default is specified, the browser will make the first of the set checked when the radio buttons are first shown.

Here's a fragment of HTML, illustrating the RADIO type of field. It again shows the user a list of areas of the world, but, this time, allows only one to be selected:

```
<FORM ACTION="program" METHOD=POST>
<BR>
Please indicate in which area of the world you
live:<BR>
<INPUT TYPE="RADIO" NAME=cb VALUE="1">Asia<BR>
<INPUT TYPE="RADIO" NAME=cb VALUE="2">Africa<BR>
<INPUT TYPE="RADIO" NAME=cb VALUE="3" CHECKED>North America<BR>
<INPUT TYPE="RADIO" NAME=cb VALUE="4">South America<BR>
<INPUT TYPE="RADIO" NAME=cb VALUE="5">Antarctica<BR>
<INPUT TYPE="RADIO" NAME=cb VALUE="6">Europe<BR>
<INPUT TYPE="RADIO" NAME=cb VALUE="7">Australasia<BR>
</FORM>
```

IMAGE

The IMAGE type of <INPUT> tag allows the selection of an (x,y) coordinate from an image, giving a similar input type to image maps. It's very rarely used as image maps are almost always preferred, so we won't consider it further here.

SUBMIT

The SUBMIT type causes a button to be displayed by the browser. When this button is selected, the contents of the form are sent back to the server for processing. Almost all forms have a SUBMIT button, the label for which is given by the VALUE attribute.

Here's an example:

```
<INPUT TYPE=SUBMIT NAME=processnow VALUE="Submit Form">
```

RESET

TYPE=RESET also causes a button to be displayed by the browser. When this button is selected, the form elements are reset to the values displayed when the form was first loaded. This is done by the browser and doesn't cause any interaction with the server. The RESET type can also take a VALUE attribute. Here's an example:

```
Clear the form: <INPUT TYPE=RESET VALUE="Reset Form">
```

The SELECT Tag

The <SELECT> tag allows the user to select from a list of values. It has the attributes NAME, MULTIPLE and SIZE.

The NAME attribute, as usual, is used when information is returned to the server. The attribute MULTIPLE allows more than one option to be selected, but only one option can be seen at a time. It's not often used, because checkboxes are often a better choice. The SIZE attribute specifies the number of items that may be selected. The default is one and gives a selection list from which one element can be selected.

Each item in a <SELECT> tag is specified with an <OPTION> tag, with the attribute VALUE giving the value returned to the server when a selection is made. The optional attribute SELECTED specifies a default value.

An example of the SELECT tag is:

```
<SELECT NAME="Speed">
<OPTION VALUE="vslow">9600 or slower
<OPTION VALUE="slow">14400
<OPTION SELECTED VALUE="OK">28800
<OPTION VALUE="quick">better than 28000
</SELECT>
```

The TEXTAREA Tag

The <TEXTAREA> tag allows multiple input lines to be entered and returned to the server. In addition to the usual NAME attribute, it has ROWS and COLS attributes to specify the size of the area. Browsers usually take the ROWS and COLS to specify the visible size of the text area and add scroll bars to allow text input outside this area.

Here's an example of <TEXTAREA>:

```
Enter your address:<BR>
<TEXTAREA NAME="address" ROWS=5 COLS=50>
</TEXTAREA>
```

If text is entered between the opening and closing <TEXTAREA> tags, it appears as default text in the text area when the page is displayed.

A Sample Page

In preparation for the rest of the chapter and to summarize the last section, it's time for a Try It Out. Imagine, if you will, a virtual travel agent, where you ask for information on the various parts of the world you might like to visit, and give your modem speed (to determine the graphical content of the brochures). The part of the world you live in determines which branch of the company handles your request.

Try It Out - A Simple Query Form

1. Start with a basic HTML template, like the one below, and save it as `cgi1.html`.

```
<!DOCTYPE HTML PUBLIC "-//W3C//DTD HTML 4.0 Transitional//EN"
        "http://www.w3.org/TR/REC-html40/loose.dtd">
<HTML>
<HEAD>
<TITLE>A Simple HTML Form Document</TITLE>
</HEAD>
<BODY>
<H1>A demonstration of an HTML form</H1>
<P>

</P>
</BODY>
</HTML>
```

2. Now for the `FORM` element which fills the rest of the page. It starts with the `TEXT` and `PASSWORD` type elements:

```
<FORM ACTION="program" METHOD=GET>

Enter your name: <INPUT NAME=name TYPE=TEXT SIZE=20 MAXLENGTH=40>
and password: <INPUT NAME=passwd TYPE=PASSWORD SIZE=8 MAXLENGTH=8><BR>
<BR><BR>
```

3. For all the different parts of the world the customer might want to visit, we provide a series of checkboxes:

```
Please indicate which areas of the world you would like
to visit:<BR>
<INPUT TYPE="CHECKBOX" NAME=cb VALUE="1">Asia
<INPUT TYPE="CHECKBOX" NAME=cb VALUE="2">Africa
<INPUT TYPE="CHECKBOX" NAME=cb VALUE="3">North America
<INPUT TYPE="CHECKBOX" NAME=cb VALUE="4">South America
<INPUT TYPE="CHECKBOX" NAME=cb VALUE="5">Antarctica
<INPUT TYPE="CHECKBOX" NAME=cb VALUE="6">Europe
<INPUT TYPE="CHECKBOX" NAME=cb VALUE="7">Australasia
<BR><BR>
```

4. To save a little time, you can copy and modify the last section to use radio buttons to find out the customer's home continent:

```
Please indicate in which area of the world you
live:<BR>
<INPUT TYPE="RADIO" NAME=rb VALUE="1">Asia<BR>
<INPUT TYPE="RADIO" NAME=rb VALUE="2">Africa<BR>
<INPUT TYPE="RADIO" NAME=rb VALUE="3" CHECKED>North America<BR>
<INPUT TYPE="RADIO" NAME=rb VALUE="4">South America<BR>
<INPUT TYPE="RADIO" NAME=rb VALUE="5">Antarctica<BR>
<INPUT TYPE="RADIO" NAME=rb VALUE="6">Europe<BR>
<INPUT TYPE="RADIO" NAME=rb VALUE="7">Australasia<BR>
<BR><BR>
```

5. Now we use the `<SELECT>` tags for finding out the user's modem speed:

```
Please indicate your modem speed:
<SELECT NAME="Speed">
<OPTION value="none">No modem
<OPTION value="vslow">9600 or slower
<OPTION value="slow">14400
<OPTION SELECTED value="OK">28800
<OPTION value="quick">better than 28000
</SELECT>
<BR><BR>
```

6. Use the `TEXTAREA` input type for the customer's address:

```
Please enter your address:<BR>
<TEXTAREA NAME="address" ROWS=5 COLS=50>
</TEXTAREA>
<BR><BR>
```

7. Lastly, the **Submit** and **Reset** buttons and the closing `<FORM>` tag:

```
<INPUT TYPE=RESET VALUE="Clear fields">
<CENTER>
<INPUT TYPE=SUBMIT VALUE="Send Information">
</CENTER>
</FORM>
```

Having typed all this in, if you view the form in your web browser, you should see something like:

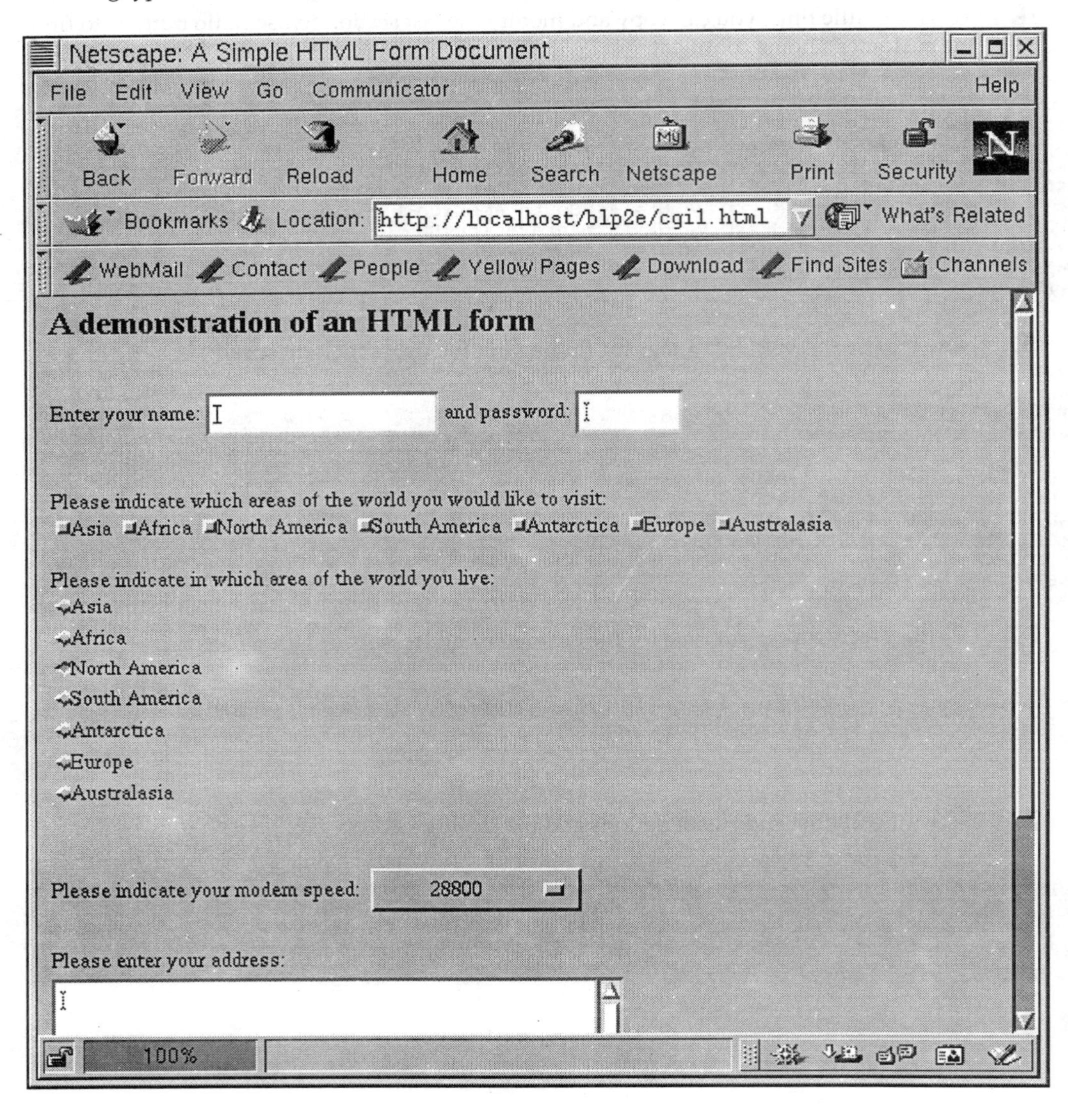

How It Works

The document starts with conventional HTML, just as we have seen before. We then start a form with the <FORM> tag. For now, we're not concerned with the ACTION and METHOD attributes.

We then ask the user to enter a name and password, using the TEXT and PASSWORD type <INPUT> tags. Since we didn't specify any line breaks, the text simply continues on the same line.

We then break the text with the <BR> tag, provide a prompt and use a CHECKBOX type of <INPUT> tag to allow the user to select multiple entries. We use the same NAME=cb field in each of the <INPUT> tags, to tell the browser that these entries should be grouped together.

After another paragraph break, we use a group of RADIO type <INPUT> tags to allow the user to select a single option. Again, we group them together by using the same NAME=rb for each of the buttons in group. We also use the CHECKED attribute to specify a default.

The modem speed element demonstrates a different type of selection, the SELECT type. The appearance of this element changes significantly depending on the platform the browser is running on. The one shown here is the OSF/Motif style SELECT.

We then use <TEXTAREA> tags to prompt the user for some free form information, in this case a postal address.

Finally, we provide a reset button for clearing the form to default values and a submit button for sending the information to the server. Note that the <CENTER> tag used here is depreciated in HTML 4, but serves our purpose, since we wish to stick to the basics of HTML, rather than getting involved in more complex issues such as style sheets and XHTML.

Sending Information to the WWW Server

Now that we've seen how to program a browser to allow the user to enter information and send it back to the server, we need to look at the other side of the system, how the information is transmitted to the server and how it's processed once there.

When the Submit button is selected, the browser encodes all the information in the form and sends it to the server using the HTTP protocol. The server software is then responsible for invoking the appropriate program on the server computer and passing the information to it. The program on the server is often called a CGI (or cgi-bin) program, since the interface between the WWW server software and the program is defined by the CGI specification. There are alternatives to invoking a separate program, common called 'in-process' handling. In-process handling is the purpose of the ISAPI interface to IIS, the NSAPI interface to Netscape server, and also they way Java servlets execute. At the end of this chapter we will see our own 'in-process' handling, where we see how to embed a Perl interpreter in the Apache web server, so we can write cgi Perl programs, without having to invoke Perl each time a cgi program needs executing.

Information Encoding

We've already met the ENCTYPE attribute of the <FORM> tag that specifies the encoding used to return information to the server. In HTML , this is normally omitted, as the default of application/x-www-form-urlencoded usually the encoding required.

When the data in a form is prepared for transmission to a server, a sequence of transformations is applied to encode the data:

The form field names and values are 'escaped'. This means that in each field and value pair, spaces are replaced with + characters. Non-alphanumeric characters are replaced by their hexadecimal digits, in the form %HH, where HH is the ASCII hex value of the character. Line breaks are encoded as %0D%0A.

The fields are listed in the order they appear in the form, with the name and value fields joined by an = character. The name/value field pairs are then joined together with & characters. The ; character is often accepted in place of the & character, although this is not part of the standard.

This encoding replaces the form information with a single stream of characters (with no whitespace) holding the all the information entered into the form.

Server Program

We now need to look at the programs on the server. These are normally stored in a subdirectory of the main HTTP server, called cgi-bin (since they are binary programs that implement the CGI interface). The program to be invoked is specified by the ACTION attribute of the <FORM> tag, like this:

```
<FORM ACTION="/cgi-bin/myprogram" METHOD=POST>
```

Security

A word of warning about security is appropriate at this point. When you allow people to send form information to your server, you're allowing them to specify some arbitrary data and pass it to a program they're invoking on your server. This is potentially a security problem. Depending on how the CGI program handles the data and if you allow it to invoke other programs, some people may find ways of starting programs you did not wish them to run. Look for the latest version of the WWW security FAQ and be very careful about allowing programs in cgi-bin to invoke any other programs.

For starters, here are a few tips on things to avoid:

- Don't trust the client. You have no control over which browser they're using and what it allows to be sent to your program.
- Don't use the shell or Perl eval statement in CGI programs, since it potentially allows an arbitrary string to be used to invoke a command shell.
- Be careful invoking other programs, especially using popen and system, which might allow the client to cause the wrong program to be invoked by clever use of the input data.

Having said that, there are many, many, Internet service providers offering WWW services allowing customers to write their own CGI programs, with very few scare stories about unauthorized access. You should be aware of the security problem, but don't let it stop you setting up a Web server!

Writing a Server-side CGI Program

There are almost no restrictions on what language you can use to write CGI programs. In this chapter, we'll mostly use C, but it's perfectly possible to write CGI programs using shell scripts, Tcl and possibly the most popular option, Perl.

A server program can receive information in three ways: through environment variables, from the command line and from the standard input. The method used is controlled by the `METHOD` attribute of the `<FORM>` tag.

Where `METHOD=GET`, the encoded form information is normally passed to the CGI program on the command line. This can cause problems on some systems where there may be a limit on the amount of such information that can be passed. Instead, for all but the simplest requests, many servers pass this information in the environment variable `QUERY_STRING` rather than the command line.

Where `METHOD=POST`, the form information is made available for reading on the standard input.

Historically, the `GET` method was used for forms that 'had no side effects', normally in forms implementing a query on the server, and the `POST` method for more complex forms that could result in changes on the server.

There's a special way of passing information to a CGI program without using a form at all. This is to append the information to the URL, separated by a `?` character. We'll see more of this later.

Environment Variables

Several important pieces of information are passed to the CGI program as **environment variables.** These are the same whatever the method of transferring the form data. The standard variables are:

Variable Name	Description
`SERVER_SOFTWARE`	Information about the server software that received the request and invoked the program.
`SERVER_NAME`	The server's hostname, or IP address.
`GATEWAY_INTERFACE`	The revision of the CGI specification that the server implements.
`SERVER_PROTOCOL`	The revision of the protocol used when the request was received from the client.
`SERVER_PORT`	The port on which the request was received. This is normally 80 for WWW servers.
`REQUEST_METHOD`	This is the method used to make the request, `GET` or `POST`.
`PATH_INFO`	Some additional information about the path to the CGI program.
`PATH_TRANSLATED`	The physical path to the CGI program.
`SCRIPT_NAME`	The name of the script being executed.

Table Continued on Following Page

Variable Name	Description
REMOTE_HOST	The name of the host computer the request came from.
REMOTE_ADDR	The IP address of the host the request came from.
AUTH_TYPE, REMOTE_USER	These are used where the server supports user authentication.
REMOTE_IDENT	The remote user name. This is not reliable and is rarely used.
CONTENT_TYPE	The content type of the information being transferred. This is usually application/x-wwwform-urlencoded.
CONTENT_LENGTH	The number of bytes of data being passed to the program. This should always be used in preference to looking for a null terminator or end of file when reading input where METHOD=POST.

The CONTENT_TYPE and CONTENT_LENGTH may not be set when METHOD=GET.

In addition, some servers may add further variables. These should start with HTTP_ to avoid clashes with names that may be added by later versions of the HTTP protocol and CGI specification.

The Apache server, and many others, also provide:

QUERY_STRING	This contains the information passed to the CGI program for METHOD=GET, or where the information was passed as part of the URL.

Putting it all Together

We now know almost enough to write our first CGI program, which will show the values of the environment variables when the client request was made. There are libraries that can do this for you, but it's instructive to show how it would be done by hand, since that will help you to understand the principles involved.

We don't yet quite understand how, after processing the information from the client, our CGI program can return a result to it. In actual fact the standard output of the cgi program is fed back to the browser, but before we can send HTML to the client we must send some HTTP header information. For now, it's enough to know that writing `Content-type: text/plain` and a blank line followed by the text you wish to display is sufficient for the browser to display simple text on the screen.

We'll use a shell program for this example, because that's the easiest method for the processing we need at this stage.

Try It Out - Our First CGI Program

1. We're going to write `cgi1.sh`, so we'll comment that into the header:

```
#!/bin/sh
# cgi1.sh
# A simple script for showing environment variable information passed to a CGI
program.
```

2. We start the output to the browser with the two lines that we were given above:

```
echo Content-type: text/plain
echo
```

3. Next, we want to display the arguments:

```
echo argv is "$*".
echo
```

4. Then we show the environment variables under which the CGI request was made, the meat of this first program:

```
echo SERVER_SOFTWARE=$SERVER_SOFTWARE
echo SERVER_NAME=$SERVER_NAME
echo GATEWAY_INTERFACE=$GATEWAY_INTERFACE
echo SERVER_PROTOCOL=$SERVER_PROTOCOL
echo SERVER_PORT=$SERVER_PORT
echo REQUEST_METHOD=$REQUEST_METHOD
echo PATH_INFO=$PATH_INFO
echo PATH_TRANSLATED=$PATH_TRANSLATED
echo SCRIPT_NAME=$SCRIPT_NAME
echo REMOTE_HOST=$REMOTE_HOST
echo REMOTE_ADDR=$REMOTE_ADDR
echo REMOTE_IDENT=$REMOTE_IDENT
echo QUERY_STRING=$QUERY_STRING
echo CONTENT_TYPE=$CONTENT_TYPE
echo CONTENT_LENGTH=$CONTENT_LENGTH
    exit 0
```

5. We need to change our HTML example page (let's call it `cgi2.html`) so that the request references our shell script. To do this, we just need to change the `ACTION` attribute, right after the HTML header:

```
<FORM ACTION="/cgi-bin/cgi1.sh" METHOD=POST>
```

6. Lastly, since we must access these scripts via our WWW server in order for the CGI program to be invoked correctly, we must now copy the files into the appropriate directories. For the `cgi1.sh` program, this should be in the `cgi-bin` subdirectory of the server setup, for the HTML it's with the other HTML files. We must also ensure the `cgi1.sh` program is executable.

We can now access our form via the server. When we press the Submit button on the form, this is what we see:

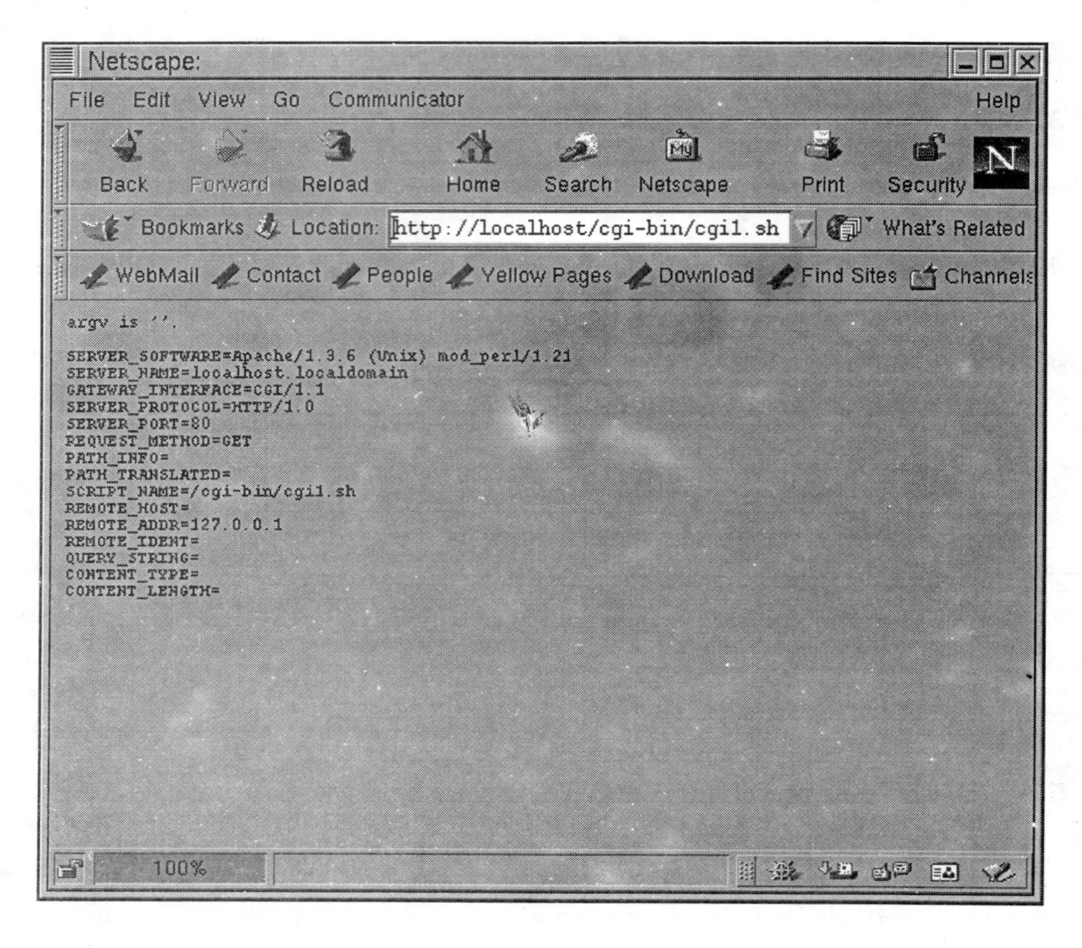

How It Works

When the user presses the `Submit` button, the form data is sent to the server which then invokes the `cgi1.sh` program. `cgi1.sh` uses the standard output to return data to the browser for it to display. Notice that `ACTION` has what appears to be an absolute path in it, but the server automatically prepends the location of the server files before invoking the program.

Note that we can't yet see any of the actual data from the elements on the form yet, just the environment in which the program was invoked.

We can now slightly extend the CGI script, to try and access the data being passed to the program. Since we used `METHOD=POST`, this data will appear on the standard input.

Try It Out - Reading the Data

Save a copy of cgi1.sh as cgi2.sh. We'll now make a very simple change to our script to read and return the input. Add the following code to the end of the script:

```
echo The data was:
read x
while [ "$x" != "" ]; do
    echo $x
    read x
done
```

We also change the ACTION attribute of our HTML form (call it cgi2.html) to reference the new CGI program, cgi2.sh.

When we submit the screen like this:

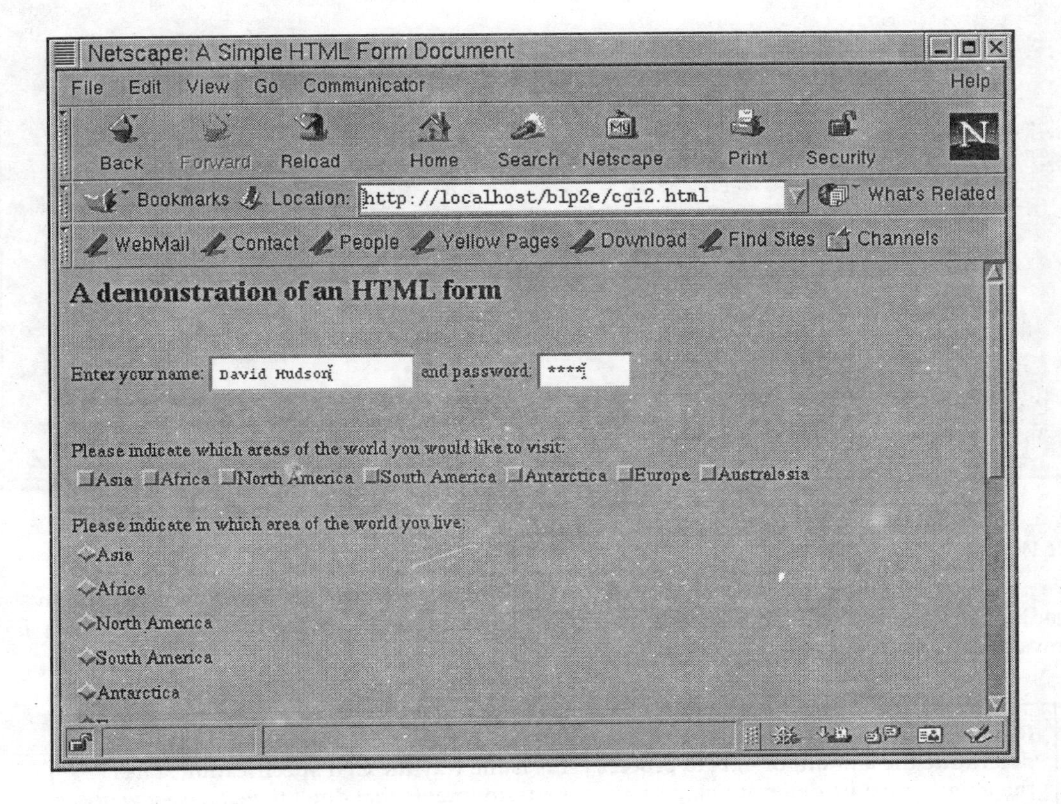

The output we get is:

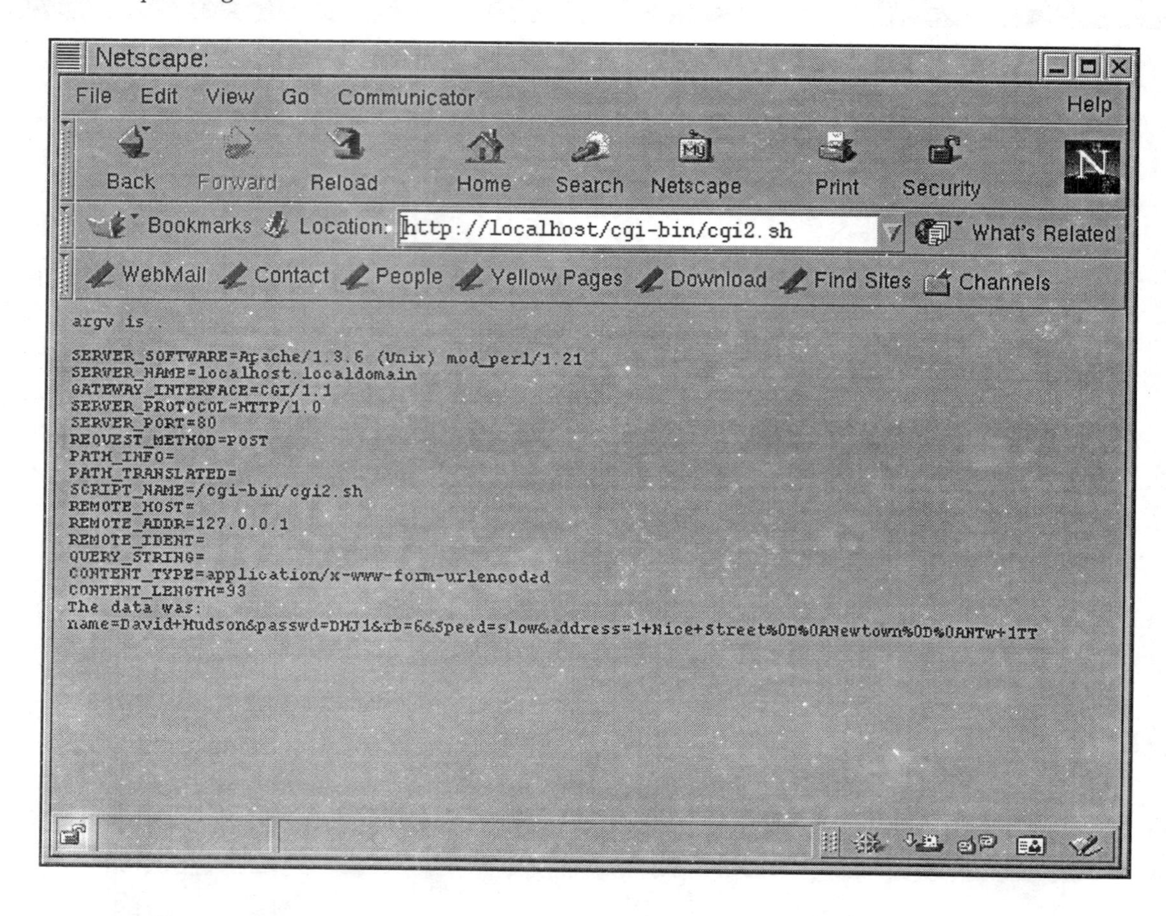

How It Works

We now read the entire standard input stream and return it to the browser. Remember that simply reading the standard input until it stops isn't an officially supported method of accessing the data. It does, however, serve our purposes here as an example.

> **Real programs should always use the `CONTENT_LENGTH` environment variable to determine the amount of data to process. This is the way the CGI specification states the length must be determined, perhaps for environments that don't have an easy way of detecting end-of-file on the standard input.**

There are two important things to notice in the information the CGI program received:

- The data has been encoded so that it forms a continuous string with no whitespace.
- There's no information about the checkbox part (where would you like to visit) of the form. This is because no boxes were checked, so the browser was free to omit that part of the data. This is an advantage in many ways, because it reduces the amount of data being transferred across the network, but it's important that form decoding software takes account of the possibility of empty fields being omitted. Browsers may arbitrarily suppress unused fields.

Try It Out - Using the GET Method

To complete our look at HTML forms, change the `METHOD` type to `GET` in our HTML sample, now `cgi3.html`. If we now invoke the form, the information is passed to `cgi2.sh` in a slightly different way, so we see:

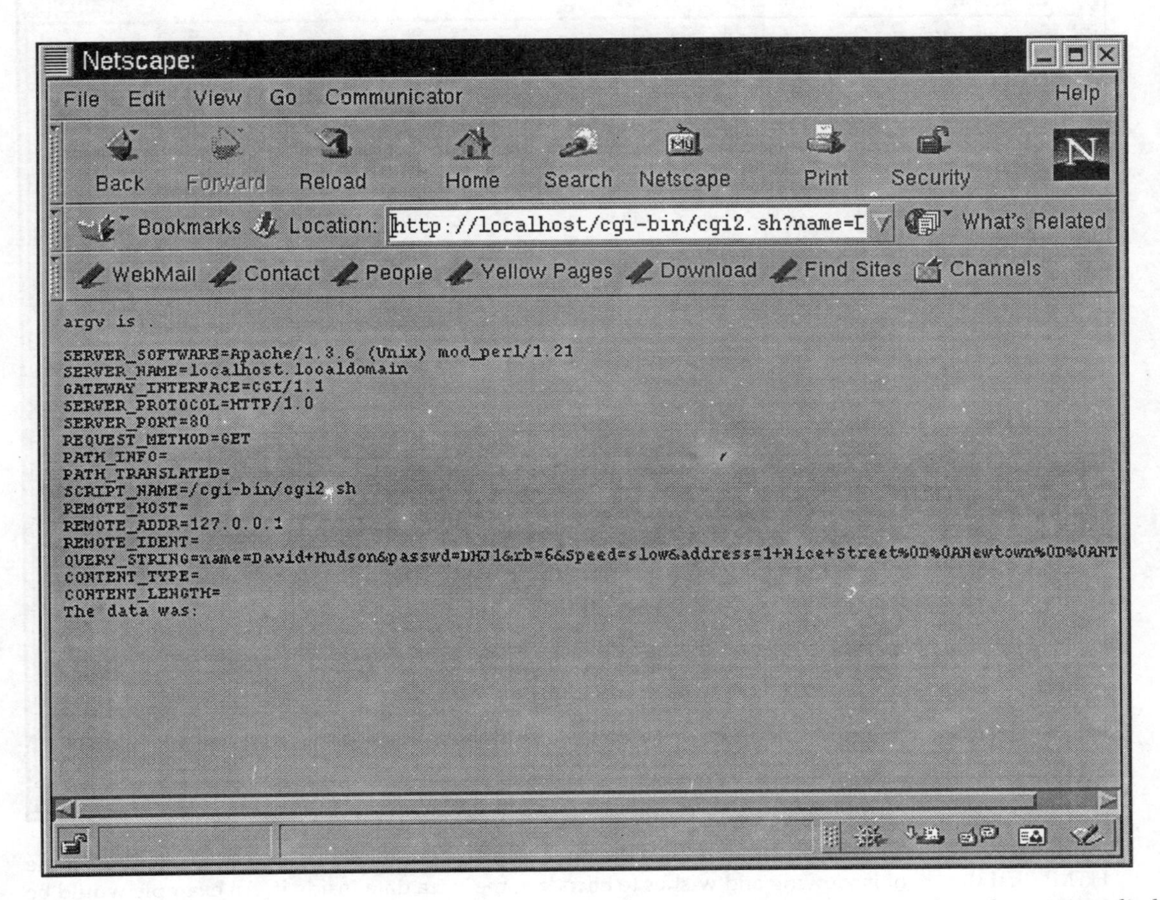

The information is encoded in the same way, but the `CONTENT_LENGTH` parameter is no longer supplied. It's now made available in the variable `QUERY_STRING`, not on the standard input. `METHOD=GET` is easier to process, but `METHOD=POST` is to be preferred for all but the simplest forms.

CGI Programs Using Extended URLs

Before we move on to decoding the data passed to the CGI program, we'll look at the remaining way of sending data to a CGI program: appending it to a URL. The server program separates the main part of the URL (the bit before the ?) and uses it as the program to invoke. It passes the remaining part of the URL as an argument to the program, as though it had come from a form.

Try It Out - A Query String

Invoke `cgi2.sh` again, this time using the URL:
`http://localhost/cgi-bin/cgi2.sh?Andrew+Stones=10`

Now the CGI program sees:

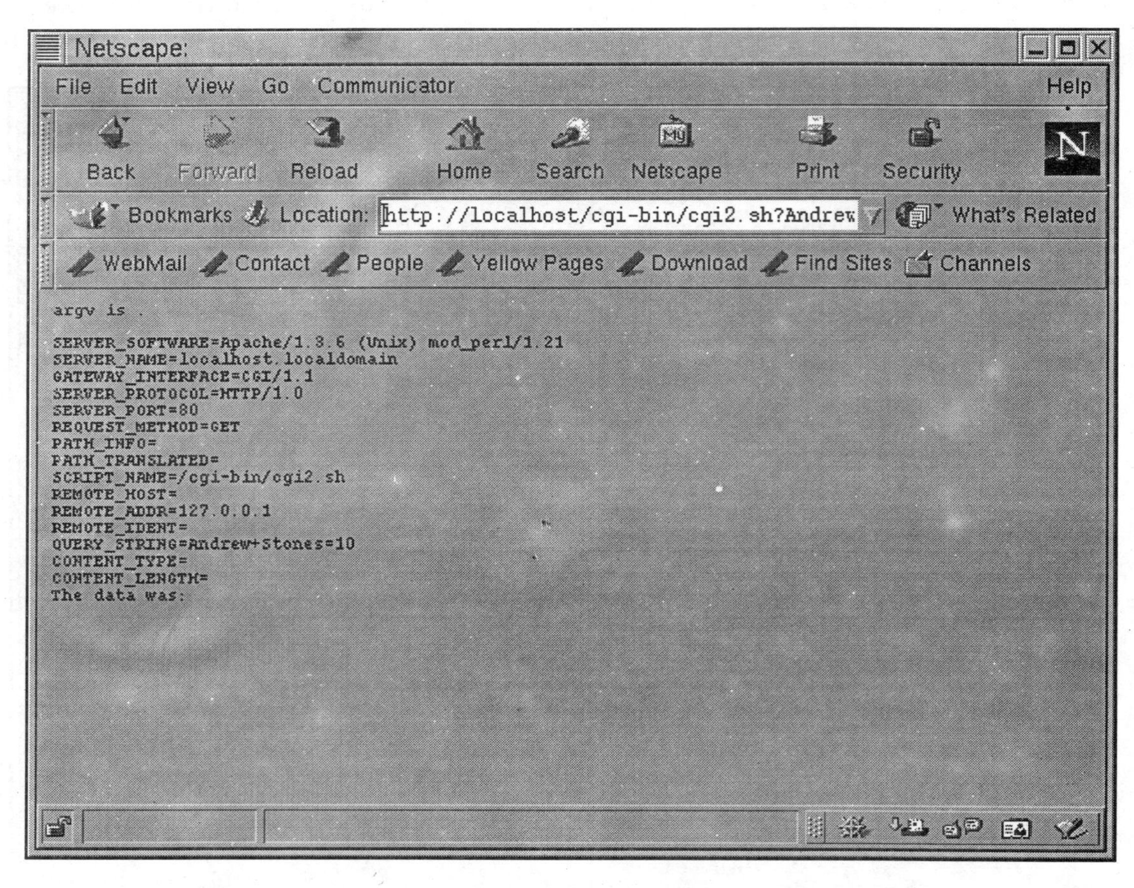

This method of passing information to CGI programs is often used where the server has generated the HTML that the client is viewing and wishes to encode some extra data inside it. An example would be Web pages that require user authentication. Since each request for a page is treated separately by the server, in theory, the user would have to enter their password every time a page was accessed. Instead, the user is given a special URL to access which encodes the user name and password or an authenticated pass key.

Suppose a user, Jenny Stones, with a password `secret` (obviously not a very worldly-wise user...), wishes to access the weather page of an online newspaper that asks her to register before she can have access. Rather than presenting her with a form that asks for her name and password, the page could ask her to enter a special URL of the format:

```
http://www.paper.com/cgi-bin/access?user=Jenny+Stones&passwd=secret&page=weather
```

Although this looks a bit cumbersome, it can be stored as a browser bookmark or shortcut and then accessed with a single selection. There is then no need to re-enter the name and password each time the page is accessed. It also saves Jenny Stones having to remember or write down the user name and password for all the online services to which she has access.

The drawback is that the password is stored as plain text, so this isn't a secure way of storing names and passwords or passing them across the network. In practice a feature called 'cookies' is often used to store a users access rights to a site, which saves them having to remember passwords. The drawback is that the cookie is stored by the browser on the local machine, so if you register at home, and get a cookie stored on your home PC, it's got going to help you access the site if you browse it from work on a different PCs. We will not be looking at cookies further in this chapter.

Decoding the Form Data

We've seen how to access the data returned by a form, so now we must decode it into a more usable format. This can be quite involved. However, when you've solved the problem once, you can reuse the decoding software again and again. There are already programs that decode form data available on the Internet, in a range of languages including Tcl, Perl, C and C++. Some of the examples are in the public domain, others have slightly more restrictive licenses.

Not to worry; we're going to decode the data using our own program. To do this, we need to perform the opposite of the encode and in the reverse order. Since we already know the encoding rules, it's just a case of writing the software to implement them. Let's call our first attempt `decode1.c`. To keep things simple, we will impose some fixed limits on the number and sizes or parameters we can process.

Try It Out - A CGI Decode Program in C

1. After adding in the standard headers and a couple of constants, we define a data structure, `name_value_st`, which can hold one field name and one value of that field. Then we declare the prototypes of the functions that we're going to use later.

```
#include <stdlib.h>
#include <stdio.h>
#include <string.h>

#define FIELD_LEN 250 /* how long each name or value can be */
#define NV_PAIRS 200  /* how many name=value pairs we can process */

typedef struct name_value_st {
    char name[FIELD_LEN + 1];
    char value[FIELD_LEN + 1];
} name_value;
```

```
name_value name_val_pairs[NV_PAIRS];

static int get_input(void);
static void send_error(char *error_text);
static void load_nv_pair(char *tmp_buffer, int nv_entry_number_to_load);
static char x2c(char *what);
static void unescape_url(char *url);
```

2. On its own, the `main` function doesn't do a great deal. It calls `get_input` to set the ball rolling by loading the `name_val_pairs` structure and sends the decoded information back to the client, starting with the `Content-type` and a blank line:

```
int main(int argc, char *argv[])
{
    int nv_entry_number = 0;

    if (!get_input()) {
        exit(EXIT_FAILURE);
    }

    printf("Content-type: text/plain\r\n");
    printf("\r\n");

    printf("Information decoded was:-\r\n\r\n");
    while(name_val_pairs[nv_entry_number].name[0] != '\0') {
        printf("Name=%s, Value=%s\r\n",
               name_val_pairs[nv_entry_number].name,
               name_val_pairs[nv_entry_number].value);
        nv_entry_number++;
    }
    printf("\r\n");
    exit(EXIT_SUCCESS);
}
```

3. Next, we define a function `get_input` that does just what it says. We need to discover whether the request is of type `POST` or `GET` and then copy the input to a data block called `ip_data`:

```
static int get_input(void)
{
    int nv_entry_number = 0;
    int got_data = 0;
    char *ip_data = 0;
    int ip_length = 0;
    char tmp_buffer[(FIELD_LEN * 2) + 2];
    int tmp_offset = 0;
    char *tmp_char_ptr;
    int chars_processed = 0;

    tmp_char_ptr = getenv("REQUEST_METHOD");
    if (tmp_char_ptr) {
      if (strcmp(tmp_char_ptr, "POST") == 0) {
                tmp_char_ptr = getenv("CONTENT_LENGTH");
                if (tmp_char_ptr) {
                    ip_length = atoi(tmp_char_ptr);
                    ip_data = malloc(ip_length + 1); /* allow for NULL character */
                    if (fread(ip_data, 1, ip_length, stdin) != ip_length) {
            send_error("Bad read from stdin");
            return(0);
            }
                ip_data[ip_length] = '\0';
                got_data = 1;
              }
      }
```

```
    }

    tmp_char_ptr = getenv("REQUEST_METHOD");
    if (tmp_char_ptr) {
      if (strcmp(getenv("REQUEST_METHOD"), "GET") == 0) {
         tmp_char_ptr = getenv("QUERY_STRING");
                 if (tmp_char_ptr) {
                    ip_length = strlen(tmp_char_ptr);
                    ip_data = malloc(ip_length + 1); /* allow for NULL character */
                    strcpy(ip_data, getenv("QUERY_STRING"));
                    ip_data[ip_length] = '\0';
                    got_data = 1;
                 }
      }
    }

    if (!got_data) {
         send_error("No data received");
         return(0);
    }

    if (ip_length <= 0) {
         send_error("Input length not > 0");
         return(0);
    }
```

4. By getting to this point, we know that we have the encoded data stored in `ip_data`. Next, we need to extract the `NAME` and `VALUE` components of the HTML submission and decode them individually. We know that `&` symbols represent the breaks between `NAME=VALUE` pairs, so we use them to split them up and pass the result to the function `load_nv_pair` to decode them one at a time.

```
    memset(name_val_pairs, '\0', sizeof(name_val_pairs));
    tmp_char_ptr = ip_data;
    while (chars_processed <= ip_length && nv_entry_number < NV_PAIRS) {

         /* copy a single name=value pair to a tmp buffer */
         tmp_offset = 0;
         while (*tmp_char_ptr &&
                *tmp_char_ptr != '&' &&
                tmp_offset < FIELD_LEN) {
              tmp_buffer[tmp_offset] = *tmp_char_ptr;
              tmp_offset++;
              tmp_char_ptr++;
              chars_processed++;
         }
         tmp_buffer[tmp_offset] = '\0';

         /* decode and load the pair */
         load_nv_pair(tmp_buffer, nv_entry_number);

         /* move on to the next name=value pair */
         tmp_char_ptr++;
         nv_entry_number++;
    }
    return(1);
}
```

5. You'll notice that we pass all errors to a function called `send_error`, which sends an error string back to the client. It's not too difficult, so we'll define it next:

```
static void send_error(char *error_text)
{
    printf("Content-type: text/plain\r\n");
    printf("\r\n");
    printf("Woops:- %s\r\n", error_text);
}
```

6. The actual decoding is handled by the function `load_nv_pair`, which we called in `get_input`. It breaks down the `NAME=VALUE` pairs further and places the `NAME` and `VALUE` into separate sections of our data structure and then calls another function, `unescape_url`, to continue the decoding.

```
/* Assumes name_val_pairs array is currently full of NULL characters */
static void load_nv_pair(char *tmp_buffer, int nv_entry)
{
    int chars_processed = 0;
    char *src_char_ptr;
    char *dest_char_ptr;

    /* get the part before the '=' sign */
    src_char_ptr = tmp_buffer;
    dest_char_ptr = name_val_pairs[nv_entry].name;
    while(*src_char_ptr &&
          *src_char_ptr != '=' &&
          chars_processed < FIELD_LEN) {

        /* Change a '+' to a ' ' */
        if (*src_char_ptr == '+') *dest_char_ptr = ' ';
        else *dest_char_ptr = *src_char_ptr;
        dest_char_ptr++;
        src_char_ptr++;
        chars_processed++;
    }

    /* skip the '=' character */
    if (*src_char_ptr == '=') {

        /* get the part after the '=' sign */
        src_char_ptr++;
        dest_char_ptr = name_val_pairs[nv_entry].value;
        chars_processed = 0;
        while(*src_char_ptr &&
              *src_char_ptr != '=' &&
              chars_processed < FIELD_LEN) {
```

```
            /* Change a '+' to a ' ' */
            if (*src_char_ptr == '+') *dest_char_ptr = ' ';
            else *dest_char_ptr = *src_char_ptr;
            dest_char_ptr++;
            src_char_ptr++;
            chars_processed++;
        }
    }

    /* Now need to decode %XX characters from the two fields */
    unescape_url(name_val_pairs[nv_entry].name);
    unescape_url(name_val_pairs[nv_entry].value);
}
```

7. The function `unescape_url` then decodes the special (non-alphanumeric) characters in the text from their `%HH` representation by running through the array and calling the function `x2c`:

```
/* this routine borrowed from the examples that come with the NCSA server */
static void unescape_url(char *url)
{
    int x,y;
    for (x=0,y=0; url[y]; ++x,++y) {
        if ((url[x] = url[y]) == '%') {
            url[x] = x2c(&url[y+1]);
            y += 2;
        }
    }
    url[x] = '\0';
}

/* this routine borrowed from the examples that come with the NCSA server */
static char x2c(char *what)
{
    register char digit;
    digit = (what[0] >= 'A' ? ((what[0] & 0xdf) - 'A')+10 : (what[0] - '0'));
    digit *= 16;
    digit += (what[1] >= 'A' ? ((what[1] & 0xdf) - 'A')+10 : (what[1] - '0'));
    return(digit);
}
```

We compile this program, copy it into the `cgi-bin` directory and change our HTML form so the `FORM ACTION` is now `/cgi-bin/decode1` and the `METHOD=POST`. This is now `cgi5.html`.

Here's the form information that we submit:

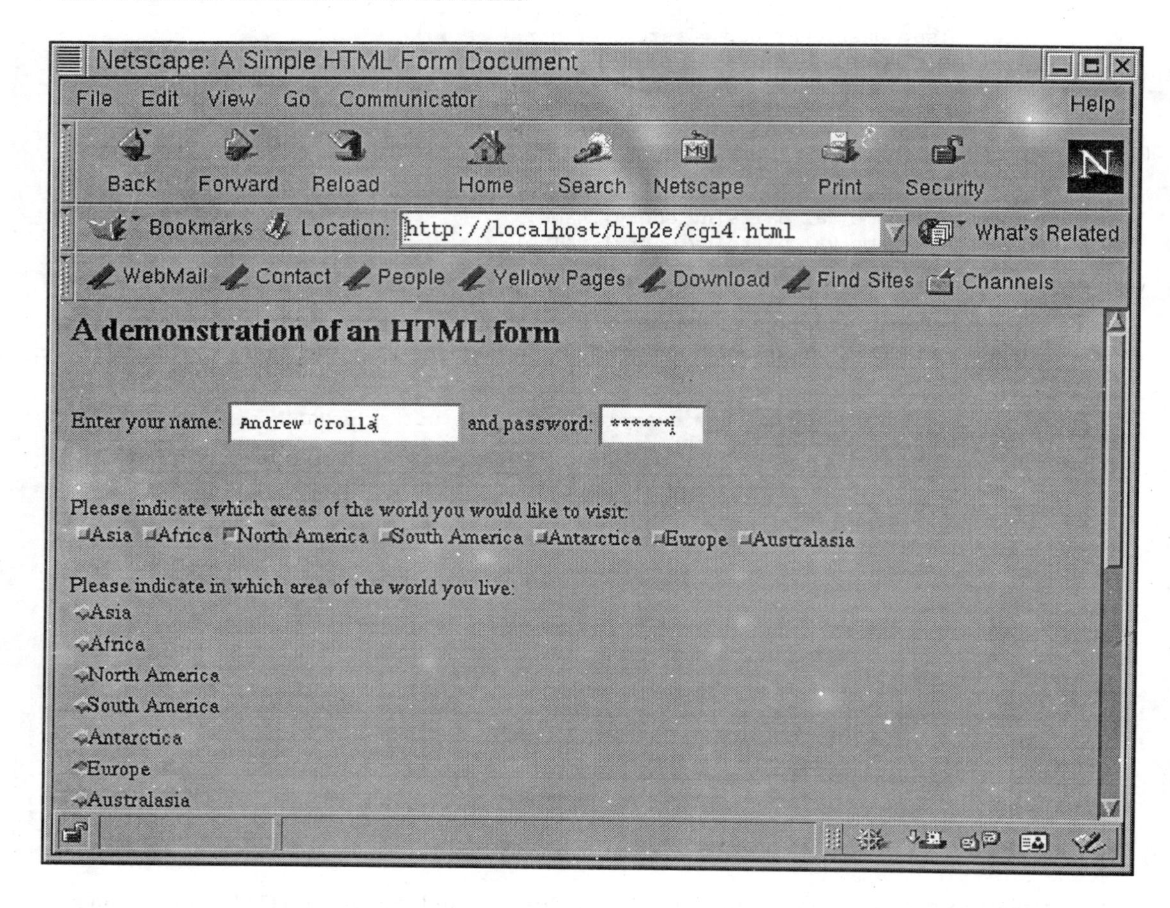

After submitting the form, we see:

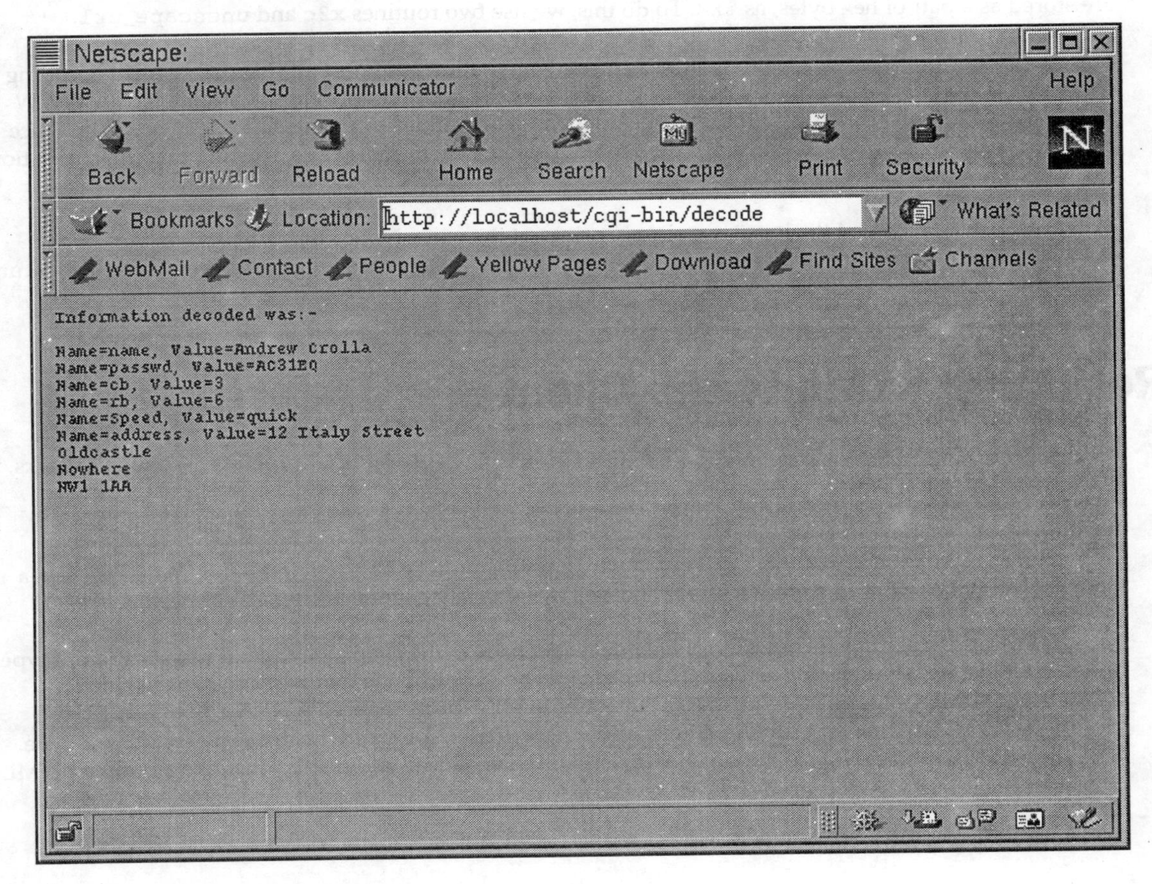

As you can see, the new line has been preserved.

How It Works

That was quite a large amount of C code, so let's segment it and look at how each piece works. We start by declaring a structure to hold each of the name/value pairs and then declare a global array to store them in. We impose some arbitrary limits on the sizes, because it makes the example rather easier to understand. A real-world program should perhaps use a linked list of nodes, each containing a pointer to a `malloced` area with the name and value in it, thus removing the arbitrary size restrictions.

We then call the routine `get_input` to load the `name_val_pairs` array. This takes several steps. First we check which method was used to post the data and transfer the data into some space pointed to by `ip_data`. Now the data is in a single place, we can use the same code to process both `GET` and `POST` methods.

The first stage is to break the single string so we can work on a single `name=value` string at a time. Remember that these are separated by `&` characters. We then call `load_nv_pair` once per name/value pair, which splits the pair by looking for the = character. It also replaces + characters with spaces.

Once the name and value strings have been separated, we can remove the special coding where characters are stored as a pair of hex bytes, as %XX. To do this, we use two routines x2c and unescape_url.

The x2c and unescape_url routines appear (usually verbatim) in almost all C and C++ form decoding software. As far as we can tell, they came originally from the examples provided with the NCSA WWW server. We've never seen a copyright message on them or any other comment claiming ownership. Since they are so widely distributed and solve the problem, we use them again here, trusting that the attribution to the NCSA server software is correct.

Now that we've processed the input, we simply print out the pairs. Notice that we precede our output with a Content-type line and blank line as before and that all lines are terminated with a carriage return and a new line.

Returning HTML to the Client

Until now, we've just been sending back plain text to the client from our CGI program. While this works, it doesn't look very attractive.

We'll now look at generating HTML, so that the CGI program's output looks more like a normal Web page. In fact, if we're careful, there's no reason why a user should be able to tell the difference between a static HTML page returned from the server and one dynamically generated by a CGI program.

Because the CGI program has full control over data sent back to the client, it can send many different types of data, not just text. It does this using the Content-type: control line that we saw earlier, which controls the MIME type and subtype that the client browser expects to receive. Rather than using the text/plain MIME type and subtype information that we used for text, we can use a text/html type. This allows us to send HTML to the client, which it will then decode and display just like a normal HTML page.

We could simply write code like this,

```
printf("<H1>A heading</H1>\r\n");
```

but it wouldn't be very elegant. A much better approach is to write some utility functions to cater for some of the lower level functionality that we need to send HTML tags to the client.

Here are some example lower level routines. The function html_content sends a string to the client to let it know that we'll be sending HTML to it:

```
static void html_content(void)
{
    printf("Content-type: text/html\r\n\r\n");
}
```

html_start then starts the HTML header section, sends a title string and starts the HTML body section:

```
static void html_start(const char *title)
{
    printf("<HTML>\r\n");
    printf("<HEAD>\r\n");
    printf("<TITLE>%s</TITLE>\r\n", title);
    printf("</HEAD>\r\n");
    printf("<BODY>\r\n");
}
```

We can use two more functions, `html_header` and `html_text`, simply as convenient utility routines to print header text of a specified level and ordinary body text, respectively.

```
static void html_header(int level, const char *header_text)
{
    if (level < 1 || level > 6) level = 6; /* force the level to a valid number */
    if (!header_text) return;
    printf("<H%d>%s</H%d>\r\n", level, header_text, level);
}

static void html_text(const char *text)
{
    printf("%s\r\n", text);
}
```

Finally, `html_end` terminates the HTML.

```
static void html_end(void)
{
    printf("</BODY>\r\n");
    printf("</HTML>\r\n");
}
```

Notice that we terminate all lines with both a carriage return and a newline character, rather than the more usual UNIX convention of terminating lines with a single newline character. A minimal CGI program could then consist of these routines; something as simple as:

```
html_content();
html_start("Example");
html_header(1, "Hello World");
html_text("Pleased to be here!");
html_end();
```

We can modify our earlier program to return HTML information rather than plain text by adding the five functions defined above to the end of our `decode1.c` program and making a few other changes. Call it `decode2.c`.

Try It Out - Returning HTML to the Client

1. Add the following function prototypes for the functions that we've just placed at the end. They can go after the ones that we've already defined:

```
static int get_input(void);
static void send_error(char *error_text);
static void load_nv_pair(char *tmp_buffer, int nv_entry_number_to_load);
static char x2c(char *what);
static void unescape_url(char *url);
static void html_content(void);
static void html_start(const char *title);
static void html_end(void);
static void html_header(int level, const char *header_text);
static void html_text(const char *text);
```

2. Most of the changes happen in the `main` function, since it deals with almost all the output. Basically, it's a matter of defining a buffer for the text to be stored in before it gets displayed in HTML format and then changing the output commands to make use of our new functions:

```
int main(int argc, char *argv[])
{
    char tmp_buffer[4096];
    int nv_entry_number = 0;

    if (!get_input()) {
            exit(EXIT_FAILURE);
    }

    html_content();
    html_start("Form decoding test");

    html_header(2, "Information decoded");
    while(name_val_pairs[nv_entry_number].name[0] != '\0') {
        sprintf(tmp_buffer, "Name=%s, Value=%s",
                name_val_pairs[nv_entry_number].name,
                name_val_pairs[nv_entry_number].value);
        html_text(tmp_buffer);
        html_text("<BR><BR>");
        nv_entry_number++;
    }
    html_end();
    exit(EXIT_SUCCESS);
}
```

3. The only other function that we need to change is `send_error`, the output from which must now also be in HTML format:

```
static void send_error(char *error_text)
{
    html_content();
    html_start("Woops");
    html_text(error_text);
    html_end();
}
```

After completing these changes (and changing the reference in the Web page, of course), we get the following output. Your hard-earned HTML expertise gives a slightly more professional look:

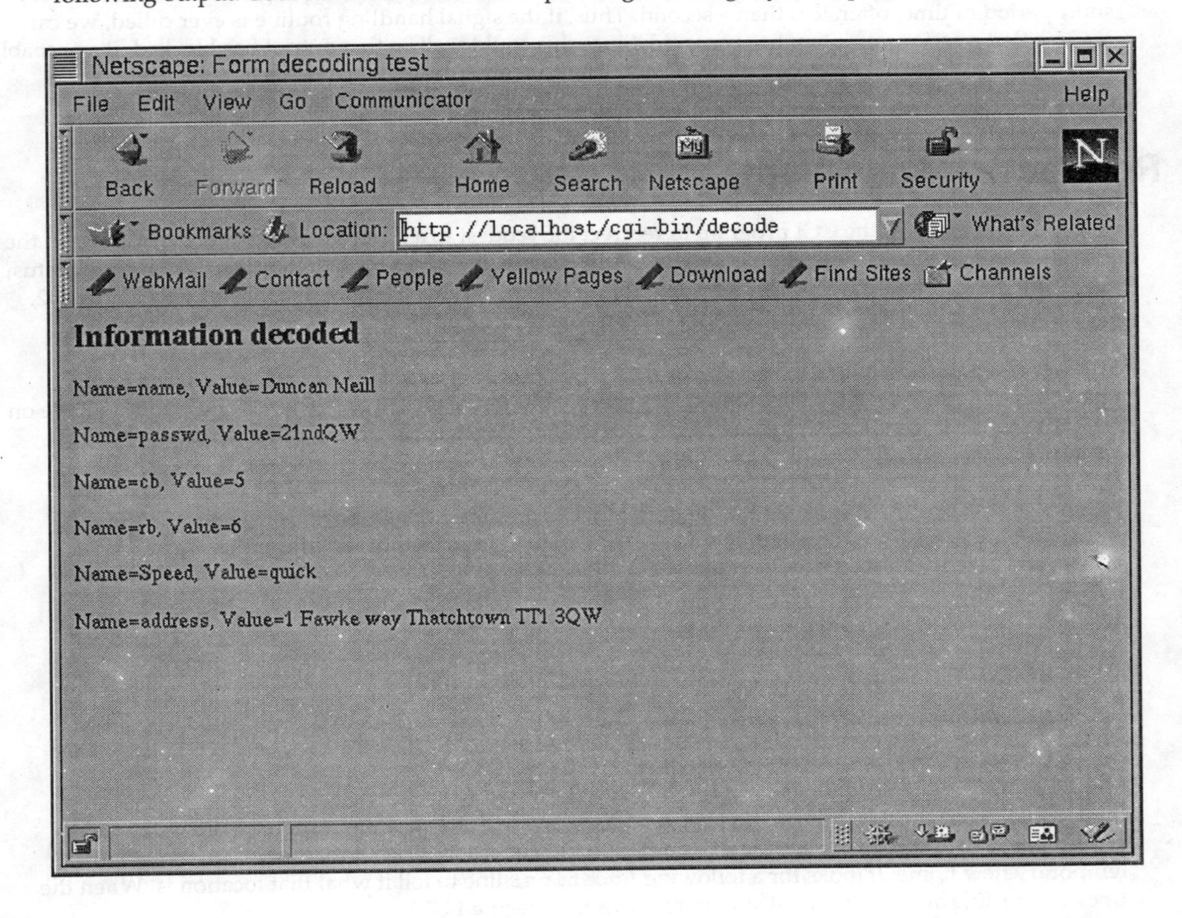

Tips and Tricks

Here are a few hints and tips that you may find useful in writing your own CGI programs.

Making Sure your CGI Program Exits

During the execution of your CGI program or when it's sending back its response to the client, the client could exit or the network may fail. If this happens, your program may get into a state where it's waiting to send output on the standard output that it can never complete. To avoid this, it's wise to ensure that there's a fail-safe way for the program to exit.

A good way of doing this is to trap the SIGALRM signal when the program starts, then, before doing any output, call alarm to generate a signal in, say, 30 seconds. Normally, a CGI program will run for a very short period of time, often less than a second. Thus, if the signal handling routine is ever called, we can assume that a serious problem has occurred. Since this could well be that output has blocked, it's probably best to just exit the CGI program, rather than trying to send error information back to the client. Alternatively, if the server system allows, we could use non-blocking I/O to avoid stalling.

Redirecting the Client

A common trick is for the CGI program to redirect the request to a different Web page, depending on the information that was passed. It does this by sending status messages back to the client. A range of status codes are defined, but only a very few are useful in CGI programs. Here we'll consider only status 302, which tells the client the page has temporarily moved.

Suppose we have a form that asks the user if they like jazz or classical music and, depending on the answer to the question, we wish to direct the user to different pages. If we generate the resulting page on the fly in the CGI program, we're now stuck with coding pages in programs, rather than using HTML files.

A much simpler solution is to ask the client to move to a different page. Suppose we decode the information in a CGI program and end up with a variable result that contains either jazz or classical. We can direct the client to the appropriate page like this:

```
printf("Status: 302\r\n");
if (strcmp(result, "jazz") == 0) {
    printf("Location: /jazz.html\r\n");
}
else {
    printf("Location: /class.html\r\n");
}
exit(EXIT_SUCCESS);
```

Notice that this is the first information we send back, so we don't start the response with a Content-type: line. When the client sees the Status: 302, it believes the URL it requested has moved to a temporary new home. It looks for a following Location: line to tell it what that location is. When the Location: line arrives the client simply requests the specified URL.

Dynamic Graphics

Many WWW pages have an access or hits counter. Since, in general, these appear on pages consisting of normal HTML, how does the up-to-date graphical access counter get there?

Often, the answer is to use an <IMG> tag, but to specify the SRC (usually a .gif or .jpg file) as a cgi-bin program. When the client accesses the base HTML page, it finds the <IMG> tag and tries to fetch the image specified. By making the cgi-bin program one that can generate images on the fly, a dynamic image can be returned.

A full discussion of this is beyond the scope of this chapter, but if you wish to investigate this further, you should search for a graphics library called gd, which lets you generate graphics from code.

Hiding Context Information

Often, a server would like to pass information between one form and the next. This might be a user's name, a customer code, or some other information.

Since each form is processed completely separately from any other form, we need to 'hide' information inside the form. We can do this using the hidden fields that we met earlier in the chapter, or by appending information to the URL after a ? character.

By declaring one or more hidden fields and giving them a default value when a CGI-generated HTML form is sent to the client, we can hide the information in the form in a way not immediately visible to the user. When the user has finished with the form and sends it back to the server, the CGI program can use the values of the hidden fields to extract the context information.

Notice that the fields are hidden, not secret. The user can still view the information by viewing the source to the HTML. Hidden fields are not a good place to hide secret passwords!

Data appended to a URL after a ? character is treated as though the user used a form with METHOD=GET. The CGI program can then decode the additional information and use it as context information. We'll demonstrate this in the following example application.

An Application

This is what you've been waiting for; we're now going to see how we can adapt our database application to be accessible over the Web. In this example, we're only going to implement read access to the database. This allows us to demonstrate the principle of accessing the database through a CGI script, but keeps the application reasonably simple. You could extend it to allow the database to be updated if you wished.

We'll start with the application that we developed in Chapter 7, using the dbm database, but replacing the app_ui.c file with a new front end, app_html.c. We'll also use the HTML functions that we wrote earlier in the chapter.

Try It Out - An HTML Database Interface

1. This is the full listing of the program app_html.c. The main function starts the database and then calls one of the other two functions, depending on whether a CD catalog number is specified on the URL command line:

```
#include <stdio.h>
#include <string.h>

#include "cd_data.h"
#include "html.h"

const char *title = "HTML CD Database";
const char *req_one_entry = "CAT";
```

```
void process_no_entry(void);
void process_cat(const char *option, const char *title);
void space_to_plus(char *str);

int main(int argc, char *argv[])
{
    if (!database_initialise(0)) {
        html_content();
        html_start(title);
        html_text("Sorry, database could not initialize");
        html_text("<BR><BR>");
        html_text("Please mail <AHREF=\"mailto:webmaster@anyhost.com\">
                                webmaster</A> for assistance");
        html_end();
        exit(EXIT_SUCCESS);
    }
    if (!get_input()) {
        database_close();
        html_content();
        html_start(title);
        html_text("Sorry, METHOD not POST or GET");
        html_text("Please mail <AHREF=\"mailto:webmaster@anyhost.com\">
                                webmaster</A> for assistance");
        html_end();
        exit(EXIT_SUCCESS);
    }
    html_content();
    html_start(title);
```

2. If there was a legitimate query string, display the tracks for that CD. Otherwise, list all the CDs in the database:

```
    if (strcmp(name_val_pairs[0].name, req_one_entry) == 0) {
        process_cat(name_val_pairs[0].name, name_val_pairs[0].value);
    }
    else {
        process_no_entry();
    }
    html_end();
    database_close();
    exit(EXIT_SUCCESS);
}
```

3. If we get here, no entry has been selected. Show a standard screen, listing all the CDs in the database:

```
void process_no_entry(void)
{
    char tmp_buffer[120];
    char tmp2_buffer[120];
    cdc_entry item_found;
    int first_call = 1;
    int items_found = 1;

    html_header(1, "CD database listing");
    html_text("Select a title to show the tracks");
    html_text("<BR><BR><HR><BR><BR>");

    while(items_found) {
        item_found = search_cdc_entry("", &first_call);
        if (item_found.catalog[0] == '\0') {
            items_found = 0;
        }
```

```
        else {
            sprintf(tmp_buffer, "Catalog: %s", item_found.catalog);
            html_text(tmp_buffer);
            html_text("<BR><BR>");
            strcpy(tmp2_buffer, item_found.catalog);
            space_to_plus(tmp2_buffer);
            sprintf(tmp_buffer, "Title: <A HREF=\"/cgi-bin/cddb/cdhtml?CAT=%s\">
                               %s</A>", tmp2_buffer, item_found.title);
            html_text(tmp_buffer);
            html_text("<BR><BR>");
            sprintf(tmp_buffer, "Type: %s", item_found.type);
            html_text(tmp_buffer);
            html_text("<BR><BR>");
            sprintf(tmp_buffer, "Artist: %s", item_found.artist);
            html_text(tmp_buffer);
            html_text("<BR><BR><HR><BR><BR>");
        }
    }
}
```

4. If we get here, the additional parameters have already been parsed:

```
void process_cat(const char *name_type, const char *cat_title)
{
    char tmp_buffer[120];
    cdc_entry cdc_item_found;
    cdt_entry cdt_item_found;
    int first = 1;
    int track_no = 1;

    if (strcmp(name_type, req_one_entry) == 0) {
```

5. This code shows a screen with one entry, defined by `cat_title`:

```
        html_header(1, "CD catalog entry");
        html_text("<BR><BR>");
        html_text("Return to: <A HREF=\"/cgi-bin/cddb/cdhtml\">list</A>");
        html_text("<BR><BR>");
        html_text("<HR>");

        cdc_item_found = search_cdc_entry(cat_title, &first);
        if (cdc_item_found.catalog[0] == '\0') {
            html_text("Sorry, couldn't find item ");
            html_text(cat_title);
        }
        else {
            sprintf(tmp_buffer, "Catalog: %s", cdc_item_found.catalog);
            html_text(tmp_buffer);
            html_text("<BR><BR>");
            sprintf(tmp_buffer, "Title: %s", cdc_item_found.title);
            html_text(tmp_buffer);
            html_text("<BR><BR>");
            sprintf(tmp_buffer, "Type: %s", cdc_item_found.type);
            html_text(tmp_buffer);
            html_text("<BR><BR>");
            sprintf(tmp_buffer, "Artist: %s", cdc_item_found.artist);
            html_text(tmp_buffer);
            html_text("<BR><BR>");
            html_text("<OL>");
            cdt_item_found = get_cdt_entry(cdc_item_found.catalog, track_no);
            while(cdt_item_found.catalog[0] != '\0') {
```

```
                sprintf(tmp_buffer, "<LI> %s", cdt_item_found.track_txt);
                html_text(tmp_buffer);
                track_no++;
                cdt_item_found = get_cdt_entry(cdc_item_found.catalog,track_no);
            }
            html_text("</OL>");
            html_text("<HR>");
        }
    }
}
```

6. This short function lives up to its name by accepting a string and changing any occurrence of the space character to a + symbol:

```
void space_to_plus(char *str)
{
    while (*str) {
        if (*str == ' ') *str = '+';
        str++;
    }
}
```

How It Works

The first part of the process is to check that the database will initialize. If this fails, we print some simple HTML to allow the user to mail the Webmaster at the site to report the problem. We then check to see whether there was a query string whose first component name is `req_one_entry` (which is set to be the string `CAT`). If there was, we call the routine `process_cat` to print out the tracks for a single entry. Otherwise, we call `process_no_entry` to list the known CDs in the database.

Information on a particular CD is given by the `process_cat` function, which we'll look at first, since it's slightly simpler. First, we send some HTML to add an anchor so the user can click to get back to the list of CDs. We then call the routine that we developed in Chapter 7, `search_cdc_entry`, to retrieve the information for the CD and send some more HTML to display the entry. After the header information, we use `search_cdt_entry` to scan the tracks. We list the tracks, using HTML to generate an ordered list, which gives us numbered entries.

If no catalog entry is selected, the function `process_no_entry` is invoked and it displays the standard screen which lists all the CDs in the database. The function searches the database using a blank string so that all the CDs are found. We then display them using HTML.

The 'clever' part is in the lines:

```
strcpy(tmp2_buffer, item_found.catalog);
space_to_plus(tmp2_buffer);
sprintf(tmp_buffer, "Title: <A HREF=\"/cgi-bin/cddb/cdhtml?CAT=%s\">%s</A>",
tmp2_buffer, item_found.title);
```

These create a copy of the catalog entry, but with spaces changed to + characters (as required by the standard rules for encoding `x-www-form-encoded` form data). We then generate an anchor line containing both the catalog name (to display on the screen) and the encoded version, so selecting the link calls the program `cgi-bin/cddb/cdhtml?CAT=CDA66374`. Remember that this invokes the `cdhtml` program, but passes `CAT=CDA66374` in the environment variable `QUERY_STRING`. The program detects this, decodes it and uses it to select the `process_cat` function, with the name set to `CAT` and the value set to `CDA66374`, which it can then use to find and display the track information.

To create the full application, we've still got a little more work to do. For a start, we need to define all the functions that we used in app_html.c. Create a file called html.c and start it like this:

```
#include <stdlib.h>
#include <stdio.h>
#include <string.h>

#include "html.h"

name_value name_val_pairs[NV_PAIRS];
```

Then add in all the functions (except main, of course) that we defined in our decode3.c program. The remaining things we need are the two header files that we've included in our source code files, html.h and cd_data.h, and the additional source code file, cd_access.c.

html.h looks like this,

```
#define FIELD_LEN 250 /* how long can each name or value be */
#define NV_PAIRS 200 /* how many name=value pairs can we process */

/* This structure can hold one field name and one value of that field  */
typedef struct name_value_st {
    char name[FIELD_LEN + 1];
    char value[FIELD_LEN + 1];
} name_value;

extern name_value name_val_pairs[NV_PAIRS];


int get_input(void);
void send_error(char *error_text);
void load_nv_pair(char *tmp_buffer, int nv_entry_number_to_load);
char x2c(char *what);
void unescape_url(char *url);

void html_content(void);
void html_start(const char *title);
void html_end(void);
void html_header(int level, const char *header_text);
void html_text(const char *text);
```

but the other two need no effort at all since, in an excellent example of code reuse, they're exactly the same as the files with the same names that we used back in Chapter 7. To put everything together, we can use a short makefile:

```
all:    cdhtml


.c.o:
        gcc -g -c $?

html.o: html.c html.h
        gcc -g -c html.c

app_html.o: app_html.c cd_data.h html.h
        gcc -g -c app_html.c

cd_access.o: cd_access.c cd_data.h
        gcc -I/usr/include/db1 -g -c cd_access.c

cdhtml: app_html.o cd_access.o html.o
        gcc -o cdhtml -pedantic -g app_html.o cd_access.o \
html.o -ldb
```

```
install: cdhtml
	-echo Depending on your setup, you need to do something like...
	-echo cp cdhtml /usr/local/apache/cgi-bin/cddb
	-echo cp cdc_data.db /usr/local/apache/cgi-bin/cddb
	-echo cp cdt_data.db /usr/local/apache/cgi-bin/cddb
```

After we compile the program with `make`, we need to move it into the `cgi-bin` directory (don't forget the database `cdc_data` files from the earlier version of the application!) and we can access it using the URL http:localhost/cgi-bin/cddb/cdhtml.

This gives us a list of CDs, like this:

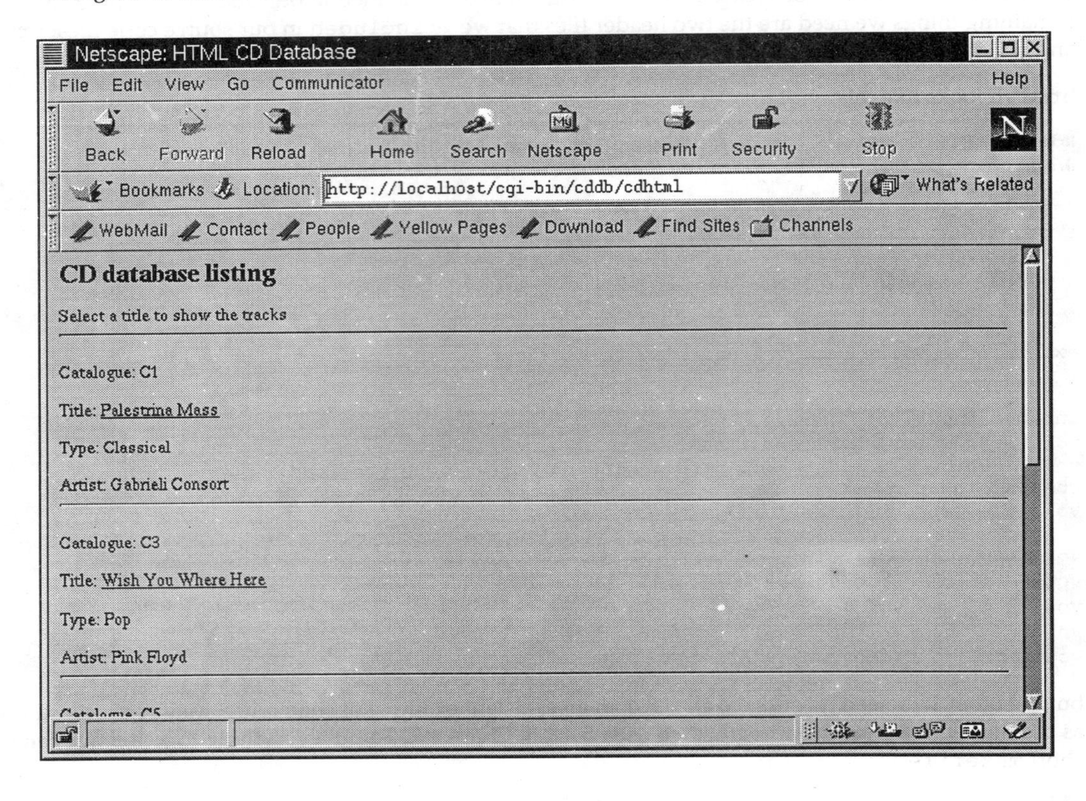

If we then click one of the highlighted links, we access the same executable, but this time with an appended query string. What we see are the tracks of the selected CD:

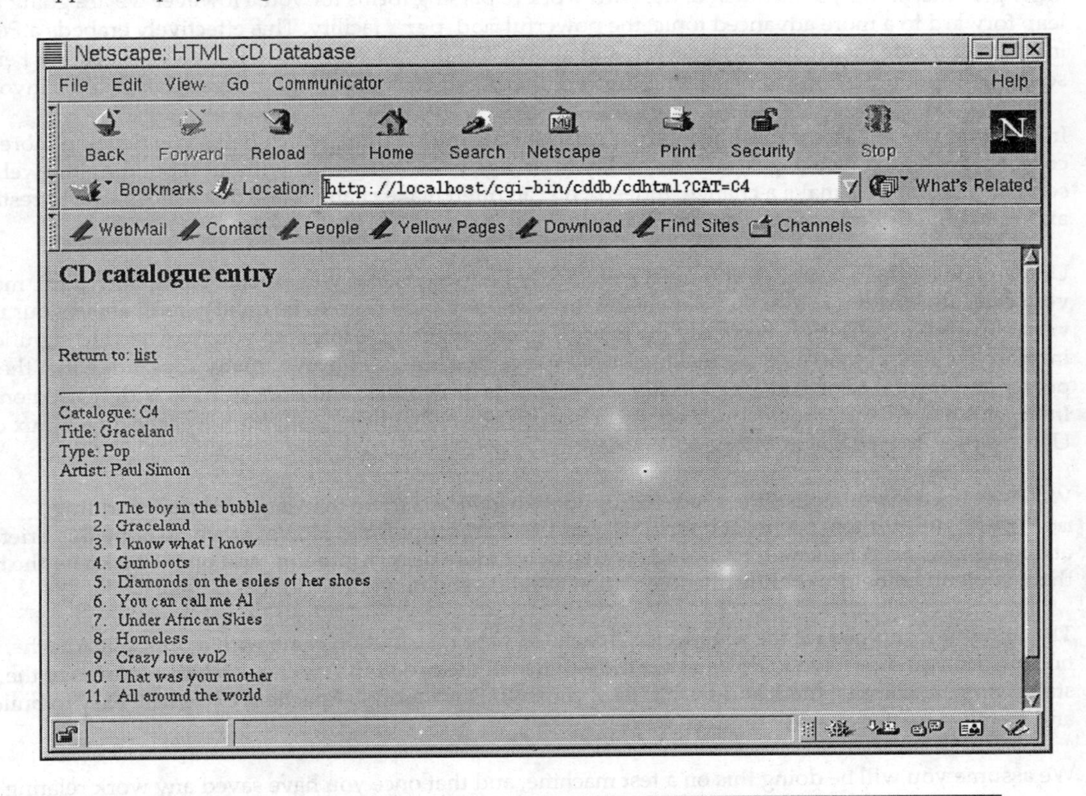

The `cdc_` and `cdt_` files that you've copied to the `/cgi-bin/cddb` directory must have read/write privileges set for everyone. Though `cdhtml` is read-only, the (unchanged) `cd_access.c` routines that open the database need to open the files for reading and writing.

If the thought of typing in all that code doesn't appeal to you, remember that the listings for this and all the other examples in the book are available from the Wrox Press Web site.

Perl

No book containing information about writing programs for a Linux-based Apache web server would be complete without a mention of Perl. Although we have generally stuck to using C, to be consistent with the main theme of this book, Perl is probably the most commonly used language for writing cgi programs on Linux and UNIX systems.

There are many Perl modules associated with writing cgi programs in Perl, most notably `CGI.pm`, which, amongst other things, does much of the hard work of parsing forms for you. However we are going to leap forward to a more advanced topic, the powerful `mod_perl` facility. This effectively embeds a Perl interpreter inside the Apache web server, and allows it to process requests that involve executing Perl scripts without the overhead of starting the Perl interpreter each time a cgi program needs to be invoked.

In addition you get access to some internal Apache state information, which helps you develop more complex generated web pages, and the ability to change your Perl scripts without rebuilding the web server each time you make a change. Indeed you can often make changes and just ask Apache to restart and re-load your Perl scripts next time it is idle.

Unfortunately, there is a price you must pay. Firstly Perl scripts that you execute using `mod_perl` must be very carefully written - since they run inside the web server you need to be quite careful about your use of variables and initialization. Secondly the process sizes can get quite large, so you may need to significantly increase the memory on a server making heavy use of `mod_perl`. However many sites judge that the power and flexibility of `mod_perl` vastly outweighs its drawbacks, and `mod_perl` is widely used on the Internet. You can even move your `mod_perl` scripts, normally unchanged, from Apache on a Linux or UNIX server, to Apache on Microsoft Windows.

We don't have anything like the space in this book to give you more than a quick taste of adding `mod_perl` support to Apache, and writing your first Perl script for it. However we do hope this brief look at a more advanced topic will encourage you to delve more deeply into this, and once you know the basics there is plenty of helpful online documentation to guide you on your way.

The first thing you need is the sources for Apache. If your distribution came with a pre-built Apache, but no sources, you may have to do what we did - uninstall the pre-built Apache, fetch the sources of the latest stable version, compile them and install them yourself. Don't worry, Apache is extremely easy to build and install, a matter of a few minutes work.

We assume you will be doing this on a test machine, and that once you have saved any work relating to your existing Apache web server, you have removed it and are starting from a clean install. If your Linux distribution came with Apache and `mod_perl` ready built you are in luck, and can skip these steps. Otherwise the safest course is to remove any web server that came with your distribution, and rebuilt Apache from the sources, so we can link in the `mod_perl` additions. Don't worry, it's very easy.

First go to http://www.apache.org and fetch the latest sources, usually they are in a gzip-ed tar file with the version number included. Download this file to a convenient directory, unzip and untar it. Read the `INSTALL` file that contains the instructions. If you want to install Apache in `/usr/local/apache`, a common location, `./configure --prefix=/usr/local/apache` is the first step, then you run `make`. If all looks well `su` to become root, and run `make install`. You then start your web server with the command `/usr/local/apache/bin/apachectr start` and away you go. We did say it wasn't hard!

Once you have Apache running from sources that you have built yourself, you are ready to install `mod_perl`. At the time of writing this is slightly more tricky, but not particularly difficult.

Assuming you already have Perl installed, but no additional modules, the first step in getting mod_perl working is to fetch additional modules from CPAN, the Comprehensive Perl Archive Network, which you can find at http://www.cpan.org. The minor inconvenience with mod_perl is that it relies on a large number of other modules, so each time you try installing mod_perl, it tends to complain you need a different module installing first. But then again, you should be impressed at how much re-use is possible with Perl modules, so it's not all bad news! It gets more frustrating when some of those modules themselves require further modules. In the words of "The Hitch Hiker's Guide to the Galaxy" by Douglas Adams, Don't Panic. There is an easy solution, and that solution is the CPAN Perl module.

Stage one is to fetch the FTP module. At the time of writing this is part of the libnet module. FTP to http://www.cpan.org, and fetch a copy into an empty directory and extract the files. Then you need just four commands to get it installed:

```
perl Makefile.PL
make
make test
make install
```

Well strictly speaking you could omit the make test, but better safe than sorry. Now you have a Perl module that can 'do' FTP for you. As it happens it can also do SMTP, NNTP and several other protocols, but FTP is the one that interests us right now.

Stage two is to install Andreas König's truly wonderful CPAN module. You configure this module once to tell it which CPAN sites are good download locations from your site, then it can take care of fetching modules from CPAN for you, working out dependant modules, fetching them as well, and installing them all in one go.

Repeat the steps for CPAN that you followed for libnet, except this time CPAN will ask you some questions. Don't worry, they are nice easy ones like 'where can I make a directory to work in' and 'tell me which continent you are on'. Nothing too difficult.

Once you have CPAN installed, it's time for stage three, the Apache module bundle.

Since the CPAN module will need access to the Internet, but sometimes has to do some work in between, if you are on a dial-up link that has an automatic timeout, you may need to take some steps to keep the dial-up link alive. A simple ping -i15 www.perl.com will do the trick, just remember to kill it off once CPAN has finished it's magic, and allow the dialup link to drop.

Start the CPAN module in interactive mode, with the command

```
perl -MCPAN -e shell
```

Perl will start, and you will be given an interactive cpan> prompt.

Enter the command

```
install Bundle::Apache
```

Then sit back and watch in amazement as all the hard work is done for you!

Don't worry if the final steps of installing mod_perl fail - we are going to run them again anyway, because we want to specify some extra options.

Once CPAN has finished, enter exit to return to the shell prompt.

Stage four (don't worry we are getting there) is to re-fetch by hand the mod_perl module from CPAN, because we want different options from the defaults that the CPAN module gave us. As before unpack it, but this time we want some extra command line options when we configure it.

```
perl Makefile.PL EVERYTHING=1 APACHE_PREFIX=/usr/local/apache
```

This means we want all mod_perl options, and our Apache web server is installed in /usr/local/apache. If yours is elsewhere you need to adjust the instructions as appropriate. Almost immediately you will be prompted for the source directory where you built Apache, type this in, you need to include the final /src part of the tree. We built Apache in a local directory, so the answer on this author's machine was /home/rick/apache/src/apache_1.3.9/src.

The version number may well have increased by the time you get to read this.

You will then be asked questions about allowing Apache to be rebuilt. You probably want to answer yes to all these questions. Then we run make, to rebuild our httpd binary, which will be built in the Apache src directory.

When the compile steps have completed, you can run make test to test that you have built a mod_perl enabled Apache server. It will run a special httpd using a different configuration file on a separate port, so it will not conflict with any existing web server running on the machine. Now it's possible that the test will fail. It did for us! At least this seemed to have been a problem with the testing itself, not the newly built httpd, so we kept going without further problems.

Now we have an httpd program built with mod_perl support, the final stage is to install and configure it, then we will be ready to write a test Perl module.

You can run make install, but our personal preference is to do this final step by hand, so that's what we will describe here.

Change into the /usr/local/apache directory, and su to become root.

If your web server is already running, stop it using the command

```
/usr/local/apache/bin/apachectr stop
```

Make a copy of the existing bin/httpd and conf/httpd.conf files, just in case.

Now overwrite the bin/httpd file with the one you just built in the apache/src directory. You should notice that the new httpd file is much larger than the old file.

There is just one thing left to do before we write our simple Perl module, which is to update the Apache configuration with some Perl additions.

Now there are several ways to do this, and what we are going to describe here is not the most efficient, in terms of execution, way of doing this. However, it is probably the simplest way, and quite sufficient for learning about mod_perl.

Edit `httpd.conf` (remember to take a copy first). At a convenient location in the file, add some additional lines:

```
PerlFreshRestart On
<Location /blp-hello-perl>
        SetHandler perl-script
        PerlHandler Apache::Hello
</Location>
```

The `PerlFreshRestart On` tells Apache that when it is restarted, it should reload any Perl scripts. This is an option you need if you are debugging Perl scripts.

The next section, that looks a little like a section in an HTML document, is telling Apache that when it is asked for a document `blp-hello-perl`, it needs to use the Perl script handler, and the Perl script it should invoke is `Hello`, in the module Apache.

Now we stop and start Apache, to let it re-read the configuration file:

```
/usr/local/apache/bin/apachectr stop
/usr/local/apache/bin/apachectr start
```

Now we have our Apache server with an embedded Perl interpreter, and we have configured it to invoke a Perl script when we ask for a document called `blp-hello-perl`. It's time to Try it Out.

Try It Out – A mod_perl Module.

The file we are going to create is: `/usr/local/apache/lib/perl/Apache/Hello.pm`

The directory `lib/perl` under the standard Apache install directory is one place `mod_perl` in Apache looks for Perl scripts. If you need to put it somewhere else, you need to add to the `httpd.conf` file an extra line `PerlSetEnv PERL5LIB` *`<comma separated list of places to look>`*. The additional `Apache` directory is because we are going to put our file in package call `Apache`. Here is our very first Perl module:

```
package Apache::Hello;

use strict;
use Apache::Constants ':common';

sub handler {
    my $r = shift;
    my $user_agent = $r->header_in('User-Agent');

    $r->content_type('text/html');
    $r->send_http_header;
    my $host = $r->get_remote_host;
    $r->print(<<END);
<HTML>
<HEAD>
<TITLE>HELLO</TITLE>
</HEAD>
<BODY>
<BR>
END
```

```
    $r->print("Hello $host with browser $user_agent \n\r<BR><BR>Welcome to Apache
running mod_perl\r\n");
    $r->print("</BODY>\r\n</HTML>\r\n");

    return OK;
}

1;
```

How it works

We declare that we are a file `Hello` in module `Apache`. Then we turn on the `strict` option, always a good idea, and declare that we wish to use the common constants in the `Apache` module.

We declare a subroutine `handler` which is a special name that Apache knows to invoke, to generate output for a web page.

The line `my $r = shift;` gets us a variable `r`, containing the request object. This object has all the common routines we need to call to generate our page from Perl.

We then get the user agent which will have been passed in the HTTP request, sent the content type, send a predefined HTTP header and get the remote host name.

The final lines are simple Perl to generate a very basic HTML page which is returned to the browser simply by calling the print method of the requester object.

Well that's all the hard work done, there is just one thing left to do - testing, and perhaps some debugging too.

Fire up your web browser, and point it at http://localhost/blp-hello-perl.

If all when well, you should see:

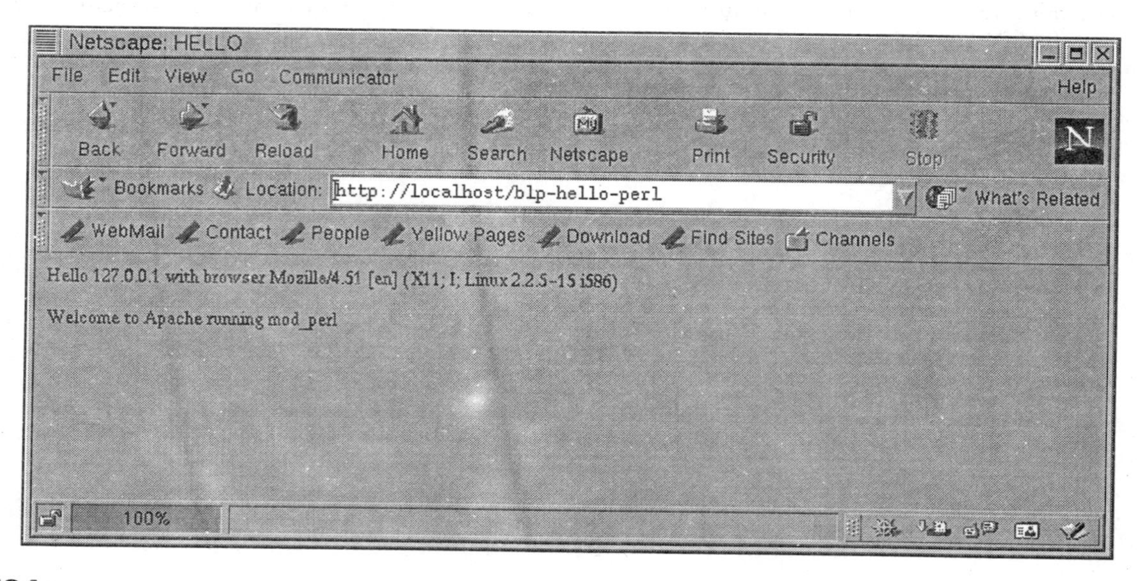

However if it doesn't work first time, don't worry. The first thing to try is a request to http://localhost/index.html. You should get the standard installation screen, telling you Apache is running OK. Assuming that worked, you should find the log files in `/usr/local/apache/logs` have some pretty good clues as to what went wrong.

Unfortunately this very brief taster of `mod_perl` is all we have room for here. However there is a huge amount of information available on the web, just follow the links from http::/www.apache.org, and if you get serious with Apache modules, you may want to look out for other books on Apache modules.

Summary

This chapter has shown you how to create dynamic, interactive Web pages. A faster changing subject you're unlikely to come across, so there are ever-improving methods of displaying information on the Web. We hope this has given you the basis (in theory and application) to write your own simple CGI applications in C.

To recap, in this chapter we've covered:

- The HTML to create forms for entering client-side information
- Encoding these forms for transmission
- The subsequent decoding using Perl or C
- Dynamically creating HTML pages with the CGI program's response
- CGI tips and tricks
- Using the CGI program to access our server database.
- A brief glance at an advanced topic, `mod_perl`, for embedding a Perl interpreter in the Apache web server.

Device Drivers

Up until now we've been concentrating on writing application code. We've looked at the libraries available to application programmers which allow them to access hardware and devices attached to the machine - file systems, memory, network connections, and so on. All of these libraries allow our applications to make demands on the **kernel** - the core of the operating system.

To round off this book, we're going to take a look at the kernel from the other side. In order to fulfil those demands from applications, the kernel relies upon **device drivers** to talk to all the different types of device it might encounter. This enables the kernel to present a uniform interface to applications, regardless of the underlying technology. The file system is an obvious example - we can use the same commands to operate on files, whether the files are stored on an IDE hard drive, a SCSI drive, a CD-ROM, a floppy, or even a RAM disk. This shows device drivers at work.

Writing device code, while it is not necessarily more difficult than writing application code, requires us to learn some new libraries, and consider some different sorts of problems, that we have not encountered in application space. We'll be writing code that forms part of the kernel itself, so while in application space the kernel provides a safety net for your mistakes, in kernel space there is no safety net. Kernel code has the power to monopolize control of the computer, preventing any other processes from executing, so we will have to write code which doesn't abuse that power, and behave as a good neighbour to other processes.

In writing kernel modules for Linux, we have the immense advantage that the entire body of kernel source code is available for us to look at, modify, and reuse in our own code. Throughout this chapter we'll point you to the source code of various header files and modules for further information. It is impossible to overemphasize the importance of the source code, as a source of information, good coding advice, and of ideas.

The focus of the following chapter will be Intel's x86 architecture, although the accompanying modules have also been tested on a Compaq Alpha, so they are known to be reasonably portable. Other differences exist between these two platforms and others, which we will try and outline more extensively in the section on portability later. That being said, the majority of the code will work on other architectures and we will do our best to clearly mention what parts are platform dependent (mainly due to differences in the hardware architecture) as we come across them. Thankfully, in recent years portability has become a great focus of kernel development and almost all of the kernel driver API is indeed very portable. Some code will never be completely portable, but if nothing is stated about portability in a section, it should work regardless of what particular machine you are working with.

Devices

So what is exactly is a device? It can be just about any part of a computer, either directly built into the core of it or as an add-on peripheral such as a SCSI controller, extra serial ports, network adapter and much more. Usually we are concerned with the latter when writing new device drivers – adding support for that flashy new adapter you just bought.

Device drivers are the software that controls the device and exports a usable interface that allows other programs to interact with this particular device. A device driver doesn't necessarily control a physical hardware peripheral. An example of this is `/dev/random` (spits out random data, more on this later) and `/dev/vcs0` (current virtual console). These devices have no connection to real hardware, but are a way of getting data from the kernel to applications and are usually named **software devices**.

Device drivers are a layer between the kernel and the hardware that it controls. As such it is a very useful abstraction, since it greatly simplifies the kernel: instead of having the kernel talk to each device itself it exports a well defined interface and leaves this task to the individual device drivers. This also means that the kernel proper can be (and is) written without knowledge of the various different devices that will be developed later on, as long as they can be accommodated within the framework of the defined models. So, for example, adding support for a new file system to the Linux kernel doesn't require a total rewrite and can be done relatively easily and with reuse of existing code. The file system, for example, is split into a generic virtual file system, VFS, that the specific file systems register themselves with. All the major parts of the kernel are designed this way – the CD-ROM subsystem, the SCSI layer, and others. This provides a good level of modularity and eases the development of new device drivers.

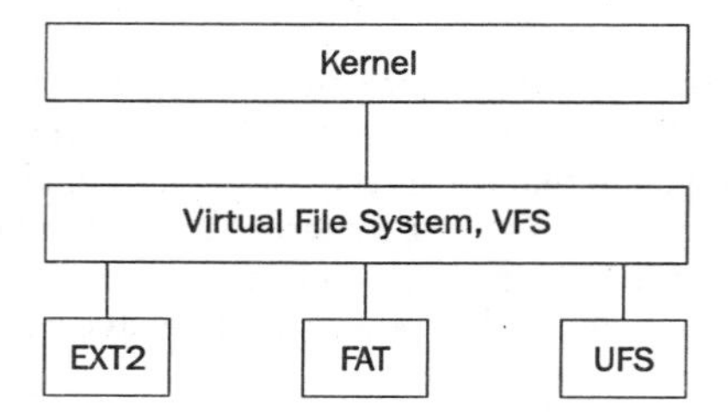

Device Classes

Device drivers can be split up into different classes according to their behavior. The two basic types are character and block oriented devices. **Character devices** are read byte by byte sequentially and access to them is not cached by the buffer system. Imagine how data or audio is read of a tape in a continuous stream – this is how character devices serve data. **Block devices**, on the other hand, allow random access, are read in multiples of their block size, and access to them goes through the buffer cache system. In contrast to other UNIX flavours, the Linux kernel does allow data that is not a multiple of the device block size to be read and so that difference is purely academic.

Most device drivers are accessed through the file system; an exception is network devices that have no file entries on Linux like on some other UNIX variants. /dev is populated with the device special files and its contents look almost like any other directory.

```
$ ls -l /dev
...
brw-rw----    1 root     disk        22,    1 May  5  1998 hdc1
crw-rw----    1 root     daemon       6,    0 May  5  1998 lp0
...
$
```

One of the things that make these different from regular files are the c and b "flags", which classify the device as either a *character* or *block* device, respectively. The distinction between these two types of devices is clear in this example: It would not make any sense to allow random access to a printer, for instance, while being able to copy a file from a disk without resorting to reading the entire hard drive from the beginning is essential. Device special files do not have to be located in the /dev directory, but this is tradition and keeps the system orderly. Some UNIX systems contain directories under /dev for the disk subsystem, for example, but Linux generally just has one big, messy directory.

The numbers following the owner and group of the special file, respectively indicate the major and minor number of the device. The **major number** indicates a specific device and the minor an instance within the device. In the example listing of /dev above, hdc1 has major 22 and minor 1. Major 22 is the official number for the secondary IDE controller and the IDE subsystem identifies partitions on the master and slave device according to the minor number. In fact, you could choose any name you wish for the special files; the kernel only cares about the type and the major.

New special files are created with the mknod system call, which can be invoked by the utility of the same name. The syntax for mknod is:

```
mknod name type major minor.
```

So to create the above lp0 entry, you would have to be root and type:

```
# mknod /dev/lp0 c 6 0
#
```

You can create them anywhere, as long as the hosting file systems support it. Most of the arguments are self-explanatory, so we will just mention that type corresponds to the class of the device – b for block devices and c for character devices. More information can be found in the man page for mknod.

User and Kernel Space

The first thing to come to grips with is the difference between programming device drivers and writing normal user space applications. Linux operates in two modes, **user-mode** and **supervisor-mode**. We will call the latter **kernel-mode** from know on, since this is the descriptive explanation of what is really going on. This reflects a change in the way the processor actually handles instructions - it supports these two execution modes internally. Intel's x86 (x >= 3) names its execution modes Ring 0, 1, 2, and 3, with Ring 0 being the most privileged mode and vice versa. In Linux, Ring 0 signifies kernel-mode execution and Ring 3 user-mode – the other modes are unused. Other architectures have similar features, but name their execution modes differently. We won't bore you with the tedious hardware details, but the gist of it is that the mode a process operates in places certain restrictions on what it is allowed to do. Processes running in user-space are, among other things, not allowed to directly access hardware and execute certain instructions.

When you are writing an ordinary program you use certain functions that you take for granted, such as `printf` and `strcpy`. These are part of the standard C library, `libc`, and have defined prototypes in appropriate header files. User space applications are (usually) linked against `libc` and these symbols are resolved at run time. Kernel modules, on the other hand, are linked against the kernel and are therefore restricted to using the functions that it exports. A device driver built as a kernel module is not run in the ordinary sense and so module symbols are resolved when you attempt to load the module into the kernel.

There are several issues concerning good practice when writing kernel level code that you should be aware of. Below are some of the rules to live by – some are black and white while others leave room for interpretation.

- Don't use floating-point arithmetic. The kernel does not save the processor's FP states when switching modes so if you do you have to save the state yourself. There is usually no good reason to do so.
- Don't busy wait in your driver. A user space application can never completely monopolize the CPU, but a loop spinning for a second inside the kernel will appear to hang the system during that time and prevent any real work from being done.
- Don't try to be too clever. Debugging, as we will see later, is much harder in kernel space and drivers often need precise timing when dealing with hardware – even adding a print statement might mess up the timing and hide an obscure bug. Keep the code as clean and comprehensible as possible.

What Goes Where?

You will also need to decide what to implement as a module and what to keep in user space. The general consensus is that if you can code it in user space, don't do it in kernel space! There are several reasons why this is excellent advice; mistakes happen, but an error in user space dumps core while the kernel might hang completely. Bloating the kernel space with unnecessary code is not good practice, either. Providing the necessary hooks in a kernel module for an application to use will often yield the best result when speed or timing is not too essential and critical. It will also give you the advantage of having the standard user space libraries available to link with.

Building Modules

Compiling a kernel module is no more difficult than what you are used to with ordinary applications. The examples that accompany this book are all supplied with `makefiles` for you to inspect. The basic procedure for compiling a kernel module is something in the order of:

```
gcc -D__KERNEL__ -D__SMP__ -DMODULE -DMODVERSIONS -I/usr/src/linux/include -Wall
                    -O2 -o module.o -c module.c
```

If you have never paid much attention to a kernel build this may look at bit overwhelming. Most of the above defines can be handled directly from within the module by reading the settings from the kernel. Let's look at what each of them does.

`__KERNEL__`	Not all kernel header files are only used by the kernel itself. Some user space applications include them, but parts of them are kernel specific and thus need to be hidden from user space. Code that will be inserted into the kernel has to define `__KERNEL__` to see the whole thing.
`__SMP__`	The kernel can be compiled for either SMP (Symmetric Multi Processor, systems having more than one CPU) or UP (Uni Processor) machines. A module that will be inserted in an SMP kernel must define `__SMP__`.
`MODULE`	Must be defined for code that is compiled as a kernel module.
`MODVERSIONS`	A safe guard against kernel and module incompatibilities. A more comprehensive explanation follows below.

The rest of the `gcc` command line options are not kernel specific and you have probably seen them used before. The `-O` switch tells `gcc` how much optimization to perform at compile-time. Kernel modules must be compiled with an optimization level of `O2` or higher to use functions that are inlined by the kernel, such as `outb`. Levels higher than `O2` may work, but we don't recommend them. All warnings are turned on, as this is good practice for any kind of program, not just kernel modules.

`/usr/src/linux` is the preferred place to keep your linux kernel tree, but it is not a requirement and you can store it anywhere you want. The `-I` (include path) option given to `gcc` above tells it to include this path when searching for includes. Header files that are specific to the kernel are located in the `include/` directory of the kernel tree, so when we write

```
#include <linux/module.h>
```

we are including the file `/usr/src/linux/include/linux/module.h`. There are two directories of importance inside the `include/` directory, one of them being `linux/` and the other `asm/`. The former contains platform independent files, while the latter is a symbolic link to `asm-`*`arch`*`/` where *arch* is `i386` or `alpha`, for example. This link is created when configuring and building the kernel and symbolic links to both include directories are made to `/usr/include/linux` and `/usr/include/asm`, correspondingly.

The `MODVERSIONS` define is used on kernels running with function versioning. This is a measure used to prevent modules from being loaded into an incompatible kernel, which could either cause malfunctioning or kernel crashes in the worst cases. When modules are compiled, they are built against the current kernel version you are running at the time and can usually only be loaded on exactly that version. A kernel running with versioning will suffix exported functions with checksum information based on the interface that it exports.

This provides a secure way of knowing that the underlying API has not changed since the module was build. You can check whether you are running a versioned kernel by inspecting /proc/ksyms, which contains the symbols exported on the running kernel. If the exported functions have a suffix similar to _Rxxxxxx, versioning is enabled. This will look something like:

```
$ cat /proc/ksyms
...
c0115728 printk_Rsmp_1b7d4074
c01d3ed0 sprintf_Rsmp_3c2c5af5
...
$
```

The actual function names of the above are printk and sprintf. The listing shows that we're currently running an SMP kernel with module versioning enabled. To be able to resolve these names, a module must include the linux/modversions.h file.

Name space is another issue that you may not have paid particular attention to before, unless you have worked with a big project. When you do kernel development, you should be careful about polluting the global kernel name space. An excellent way to avoid clashes, which is adopted by the vast majority of the kernel developers, is to prefix exported functions with the name of your driver. Still, only exporting functions and variables that are going to be used by other drivers is the best practice and should be used along with it. Declaring global variables and functions static achieves this beautifully, but has other side effects. Other variables and functions are explicitly exported with the macro EXPORT_SYMBOL, which adds them to the kernels global symbol table. You generally only need to worry about this if you plan on splitting your driver across several modules or otherwise expose internals for others to use. Of course, keeping global name space pollution to a minimum is always a good idea. The syntax is straightforward:

EXPORT_SYMBOL(name)	Export the variable or function name.
EXPORT_SYMBOL_NOVERS(name)	Export the variable or function name, but don't include module versioning even if defined.
EXPORT_NO_SYMBOLS	Don't export any symbols.

The declarations must be made outside of any functions – in an include file, bottom of module, or similar. The macros are defined in linux/module.h if you are curious. EXPORT_SYMTAB must be defined prior to using any of these macros.

Data Types

Linux runs on a lot of different architectures, some 32-bit and some 64-bit. Some efforts have been made to even allow Linux to run on 16-bit hardware and who knows what will happen in the future. Therefore it is important not to make assumptions about the size of a given type of variable. Linux defines standard types that have a given size on any platform.

__u8, ..., __u64	Unsigned and signed variables between char and 64-bit long in size.
__s8, ..., __s64	

If you need a specifically sized variable, use one of the above types. They also look much nicer in the code and make it more readable when you browse the driver source a couple of months later. There are also the special types that are passed to driver entry points, for example.

```
ssize_t schar_read(…, size_t count, loff_t *offset)
```

ssize_t and size_t are examples of types that serve a specific purpose within the kernel – we'll look at exactly what purpose later. Usually these types are acted upon directly and you therefore need not worry too much about the particular size. The various types are described in linux/types.h and asm/posix_types.h so look them up if you need a hint as to what size they are typedefed to. When you do need to assign them to the compiler's integral types, remember to use an appropriate cast. gcc is quite picky about size mismatches and will warn you about possible problems.

Try It Out - A Kernel Module

Now is an excellent time to dive in and create our very first module. In keeping with past tradition, "hello, kernel" seems like the thing to do - don't worry, it's the last time we'll revisit this bit of programming history in this book.

1. Let's start off with the following file, hello.c:

```
#include <linux/module.h>

#if defined(CONFIG_SMP)
#define __SMP__
#endif

#if defined(CONFIG_MODVERSIONS)
#define MODVERSIONS
#include <linux/modversions.h>
#endif

#include <linux/kernel.h>

int init_module(void)
{
        printk(KERN_DEBUG "Hello, kernel!\n");
        return 0;
}

void cleanup_module(void)
{
        printk(KERN_DEBUG "Good-bye, kernel!\n");
}
```

The kernel equivalent of printf is printk. They are similar in usage, but the latter does not support printing of floating point. The KERN_DEBUG define given to printk sets the priority of the printed message. The possible values are defined by linux/kernel.h as follows:

```
#define KERN_EMERG          "<0>"    /* system is unusable */
#define KERN_ALERT          "<1>"    /* action must be taken immediately  */
#define KERN_CRIT           "<2>"    /* critical conditions */
#define KERN_ERR            "<3>"    /* error conditions */
#define KERN_WARNING        "<4>"    /* warning conditions */
#define KERN_NOTICE         "<5>"    /* normal but significant condition */
#define KERN_INFO           "<6>"    /* informational */
#define KERN_DEBUG          "<7>"    /* debug-level messages */
```

So we could have written

```
printk("<7>Hello, kernel!\n");
```

instead, but we think you will agree that using the predefined levels makes the code easier to read. The log level setting controls what messages will actually get printed on the console and / or appended to the syslog. This is controlled by `syslogd` and can usually be setup in `/etc/syslog.conf`. As it is written you will probably not be able to see the messages directly. Instead they are stored in the kernel buffer allocated for these kinds of messages. The program `dmesg` will show you what is currently stored in there (lots of messages from your last boot, most likely).
Apart from `printk`, though, there shouldn't be anything too unfamiliar here - we'll look at what's new in a moment. For now, let's compile the module, with this command in the directory where you created the `hello.c` file:

```
$ gcc -D__KERNEL__ -I/usr/src/linux/include -DMODULE -Wall -O2 -c hello.c -o hello.o
$
```

2. Now let's try and insert the module into the kernel. Modules are loaded with the `insmod` (insert module) command, usually found in `/sbin/`. You must be root to insert and remove a module, as this would otherwise be a serious security breach if anybody were allowed to meddle with the kernel! Make sure that you are root and try the module out:

```
# insmod hello.o
#
```

3. No error messages so far, so how do we verify that the module has been inserted successfully? We can check the very end of the `dmesg` readout of the kernel buffer with this command:

```
# dmesg | tail -n1
Hello, kernel!
#
```

We can see the message from our module there in the kernel buffer. To prove that the module is loaded, `lsmod` (list modules) can be run. It lists the modules that are currently inserted.

```
# lsmod
Module                  Size  Used by
...
hello                    176   0  (unused)
...
#
```

4. Not surprisingly, `hello` is listed with the other modules. `lsmod` also lists the size and usage count of each loaded module. We will get into usage counts a little later. For now, lets get rid of the `hello` module again. The `rmmod` (remove module) command will detach a module from the kernel.

```
# rmmod hello
# dmesg | tail -n1
Good-bye, kernel!
#
```

How It Works

A couple of new things were introduced here. `linux/module.h` includes another header file (among others) called `linux/config.h` which contains the options selected at the kernel compile time, as `defines`. This is especially convenient for us, since we can be sure that if the kernel is compiled for SMP, `CONFIG_SMP` will be defined and we can define `__SMP__` appropriately. The same thing goes for `CONFIG_MODVERSIONS`; if that is configured we define `MODVERSIONS` and include `linux/modversions.h` to gain access to the versioning information.

As we saw, a little message is printed to the kernel buffer when the module is loaded and unloaded. The two functions we defined to perform this are the only ones that are actually needed to complete a module. `init_module` is called at load time and is responsible for setting up internal data structures, initialize the hardware, and perform any other tasks that need to be done before the device is invoked for the first time. Since the above is only a simple framework, no real work is done. Most things work both ways, and so `cleanup_module` takes care of shutting down the device and releasing any resources that the device may have occupied.

And that's it: we've built a module, and successfully inserted it into the kernel. Now we've overcome our fear of the Linux kernel, we can get on to something a little more substantial.

Character devices

While the `hello` module above is about as simple as you can get, it doesn't really do anything interesting. Once it is loaded you cannot interact with it and it does not export any useful functions to user space applications. As a first step beyond, let's look at a sample framework for a character driven driver.

Character devices have to register themselves with the kernel, and provide it with the information that enables the kernel to invoke the correct functions when applications wish to interact with the device. `register_chrdev` takes care of this and is invoked with the following syntax :

```
int register_chrdev(unsigned int major, const char *name, struct file_operations
*fops)
```

The return value is negative in case of failure, and non-negative (either a positive integer or zero) on success, which is the case with the majority of the kernel functions. Calling the function with zero as `major` provides dynamic major number assignment. In this case, the device is registered with the next available major number and this is returned. Using dynamic assignment is not hard, but in order to access devices you need to create the correct special files if the major has changed since the last time you loaded the module. Because of this, we will use a series of reserved major numbers in this book Majors 42 and 120-127 are set aside for local devices and thus not to be used by production modules. Consult `Documentation/devices.txt` for more information, including how to acquire an official number if you ever need one.

The second parameter, `name`, is only used for registration with `/proc/devices`. It is simply the name that will show up there, nothing more. The final parameter, the file operations structure, is the most interesting. It defines how the driver communicates with the outside world; specifically what functions it handles itself and what the kernel defaults take care of. The structure is defined in `linux/fs.h` and is a series of pointers to functions. This concept is used in numerous places in the kernel and provides a form of abstraction between the different layers and how they interact.

File Operations

Access to devices goes through the file system, as we saw in the first section on special files. This is independent of the type of device – be it directly related to file systems (a hard disk driver, for example) or totally unrelated - a parallel port driver, perhaps. Device drivers therefore need to register a set of file operations that define the specific implementation that they offer. Below is the current file operations structure with the prototypes defined. All of the possible function types are listed, although no one single module will normally need to define them all. You'll recognise the names of most of these functions as mirroring the low-level device access functions we met back in chapter three. These functions are actually where those low-level calls end up, once the kernel has identified the device which needs to be contacted to fulfil that request.

```
struct file_operations {
loff_t (*llseek) (struct file *, loff_t, int);
ssize_t (*read) (struct file *, char *, size_t, loff_t *);
ssize_t (*write) (struct file *, const char *, size_t, loff_t *);
int (*readdir) (struct file *, void *, filldir_t);
unsigned int (*poll) (struct file *, struct poll_table_struct *);
int (*ioctl) (struct inode *, struct file *, unsigned int, unsigned long);
int (*mmap) (struct file *, struct vm_area_struct *);
int (*open) (struct inode *, struct file *);
int (*flush) (struct file *);
int (*release) (struct inode *, struct file *);
int (*fsync) (struct file *, struct entry *);
int (*fasync) (int, struct file *, int);
int (*check_media_change) (kdev_t dev);
int (*revalidate) (kdev_t dev);
int (*lock) (struct file *, int, struct file_lock *);
}
```

Your driver can provide any combination of these functions in order to represent the functionality of its device to the kernel. Let's look at what the available functions are:

`llseek`	`llseek`, or `lseek` as it is known in user space, changes the position within the file structure. Specifically `file->f_pos` is modified; we will look at this later when discussing the file structure. On success, it returns the new position, while failure is identified with a negative return value.
`read`	`read` is seen from the application point of view, so `read` actually writes data back to user space. The return value, if positive, is the number of bytes read. Negative return values indicate an error.
`write`	`write` feeds data to the device and is equivalent to read with respect to return values.
`readdir`	`readdir` is strictly used by file systems to look up the contents of a directory.
`poll`	`poll` allows an application to be notified of given events from the device. `select`, the equivalent in BSD UNIX, is deprecated in Linux and `poll` should be used instead.
`ioctl`	`ioctl`, or I/O control, allows applications to control the behavior or get data from the device with the `ioctl` system call.

mmap	mmap implements memory mapping of the devices address space to user space. This can be used to provide direct access to an internal buffer or peripheral device memory space.
open	open is called when the device is opened by an application. This is the only function that is default implemented for both character and block devices, so you can leave this undefined if you don't need or care to know when the device is opened.
flush	flush, naturally, flushes the buffered data. As character devices aren't buffered this entry only makes sense for block devices.
release	release is called when the device is closed.
fsync	fsync synchronizes the in-memory state with that on disc, writing out all dirty data in the output buffer. It must not return until it's finished. This entry is also only relevant to block devices.
fasync	fasync is called when an application changes the behavior with fcntl.
check_media_change	check_media_change examines whether the media has changed since it was last accessed. Therefore it only makes sense to block devices handling removable media (such as CD-ROMs and floppies).
revalidate	revalidate and check_media_change are closely related. If a disc change has been detected, revalidate should update internal device information, if needed. revalidate also only makes sense for removable block devices.
lock	lock enables a user to lock a file. Only really makes sense for file systems.

A single device will probably never have to define all of the above methods. It is completely up to you to define the operations that make sense for your device and set the others to NULL.

When the character device is registered with the kernel, its file_operations structure and name is added to the global chrdevs array of device_struct structures where the major number indexes it. This is called the character device switch table.

```
struct device_struct {
   const char *name;
   struct file_operations *fops;
};
```

So by looking up chrdevs[YOUR_MAJOR]->fops, the kernel knows how to talk to the device and what entry points it supports.

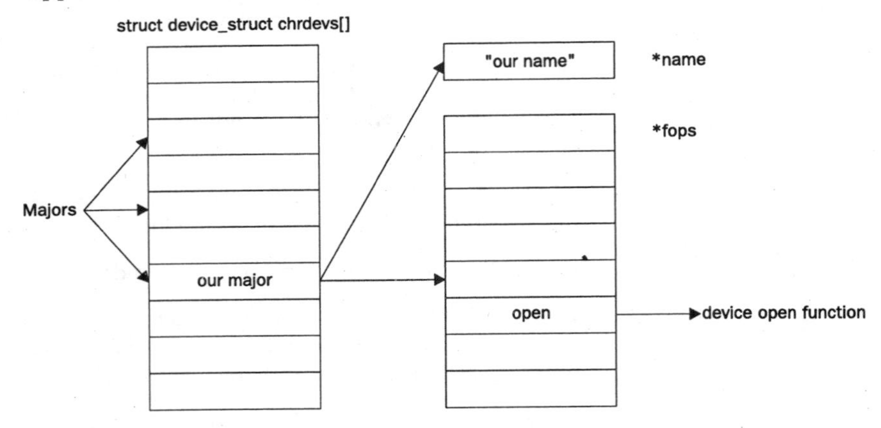

A Sample Driver, Schar

Let's take a look at a sample character device driver, which we'll call Schar. This driver implements reading and writing in its own fake way, by pretending to serve data from a device that is polled at a constant interval. The polling mechanism is managed by kernel timers, which we will explain fully in the next section.

Schar.c starts out with forwarding declarations of the functions that define our implementation of the file_operations structure. Then we fill it out.

```
/* forward declarations for _fops */
static ssize_t schar_read(struct file *file, char *buf, size_t count, loff_t *offset);
static ssize_t schar_write(struct file *file, const char *buf, size_t count, loff_t
*offset);
static unsigned int schar_poll(struct file *file, poll_table *wait);
static int schar_ioctl(struct inode *inode, struct file *file, unsigned int cmd,
unsigned long arg);
static int schar_mmap(struct file *file, struct vm_area_struct *vma);
static int schar_open(struct inode *inode, struct file *file);
static int schar_release(struct inode *inode, struct file *file);

static struct file_operations schar_fops = {
	NULL,			/* llseek */
	schar_read,
	schar_write,
	NULL,			/* readdir */
	schar_poll,
	schar_ioctl,
	NULL,			/* mmap */
	schar_open,
	NULL,			/* flush */
	schar_release,
	NULL,			/* fsync */
	NULL,			/* fasync */
	NULL			/* lock */
};
```

Some prefer the `file_operations` structure to appear at the beginning of the module, while others like it at the bottom. The latter approach would spare us from putting function prototypes at the beginning of the file. It is purely a matter of taste. Don't worry about some of the include files, we'll cross those bridges along the way.

The MSG macro

Before we dive deeper into `Schar's` sources, we need to introduce the `MSG` macro we use throughout this chapter. It is an alternative way to print debugging statements that can prove quite handy. Instead of sprinkling the code with ugly `#ifdef` statements, we put the definition of `MSG` in the `schar.h`:

```
#define DEBUG

#ifdef DEBUG
#define MSG(string, args...) printk(KERN_DEBUG "schar:" string, ##args)
#else
#define MSG(string, args...)
#endif
```

It keeps the code looking clean and prefixes every statement with the module name. You could also easily define a bitmask of events and get finely controlled logging, if you wish. Schar is very simple, so logging everything makes sense. Undefining `DEBUG` would effectively make `MSG` a no-op. Sometimes it would be advantageous to include even more information in the debug statement, especially for larger device driver projects. We might want to include line and file information to quickly be able to locate a specific message within the source. This could look something like this:

```
#define MSG(string, args…) printk(KERN_DEBUG \
"schar:__FILE__-__LINE__:" string, ##args)
```

It's up to you which one you prefer, all of the modules shown in this book use the former because their complexity does not warrant the extra information.

Registering the Device

As with the `hello` module, `Schar` naturally also has an `init_module` entry point. It does a lot of different things - allocating memory, initializing timers and variables, and so on, but for the time being we will stick to looking at the device registration.

```
int init_module(void)
{
   int res;

   if (schar_name == NULL)
      schar_name = "schar";

   /* register device with kernel */
   res = register_chrdev(SCHAR_MAJOR, schar_name, &schar_fops);
   if (res) {
      MSG("can't register device with kernel\n");
      return res;
   }
}
```

`schar_name` can be passed in to the module as a parameter - we'll see how later on. For now, we check to see if a name has been specified, and if not, set it to a default.

`SCHAR_MAJOR` is defined in `schar.h` and is set to 42, which as we said before is one of the reserved major numbers. It doesn't matter what number you choose as long as it is not being used by any other active devices. Choosing one of the reserved majors is always safe for experimenting on your own.

```
#define SCHAR_MAJOR        42
```

We could also have used dynamic assignment of majors instead. The advantage of that approach would be that we don't have to know anything about what majors are available. The downside, at least in this context, is that we would have to create new device special files for using the module every time we load it (provided that the major returned isn't the same all the time). For this reason, we will stick to static majors. A sample implementation of dynamic registration could be easily implemented and would look something like this:

```
int major = 0, res;

res = register_chrdev(major, schar, &schar_fops);
if (res < 0) {
   MSG("can't register device with kernel\n");
   return res;
} else {
   major = res;
   MSG("device registered with major %d\n" , major);
}
```

All the sample devices in this chapter use static major numbers, and switching to dynamic assignment is left as an exercise to the reader.

After a successful call to `register_chrdev`, the device is registered with the kernel and the given file operations structure is added to the character switch table. The device should also show up in `/proc/devices` in the character device section.

Module Usage Count

The kernel needs to keep track of usage information for each module loaded in the system. If it didn't, how else would it know when it was safe to remove a module? We certainly don't want a hard disk driver module to be removed while you were copying files to it – that would wreak havoc on the disk and leave the file system in an unreliable state.

There are two macros that modify the usage count, `MOD_INC_USE_COUNT` and `MOD_DEC_USE_COUNT`. The former increments the count by one while the latter decrements it. It is up to the driver rogrammer to maintain a usage count that at the same time protects the module from being unloaded unexpectedly while making certain that the module can be safely removed when it is unused. The kernel will only allow unloading of modules with a usage count of zero. The `MOD_IN_USE` macro evaluates to the current usage count, but is hardly ever needed since the kernel checks it itself before attempting to remove the module.

Open and Release

The module is now loaded and sits idle on your system, until someone opens the associated device. When the device is opened by a process, `schar_open` is invoked. Here the module usage count is incremented to prevent removal of the device while it is busy.

```
static int schar_open(struct inode *inode, struct file *file)
{
   /* increment usage count */
   MOD_INC_USE_COUNT;
```

this tells the Kernel that the module is now being used by one more process. If a user executes an `rmmod module_name`, the kernel returns -EBUSY for modules that have a usage count bigger than zero (i.e. they are in use). Therefore it is the module's own responsibility to keep the usage count up to date. We increase the usage count by one in `schar_open` which protects the module from being unloaded while a process has it opened. When a process closes the device we decrement the usage count to keep it in balance.

The `file` argument passed to `schar_open` is the in-kernel description of the file descriptor returned to applications. The `file` structure contains information about the mode the device is opened in. This code snippet tests whether the device is being opened for read or not, for example.

```
   if (file->f_mode & FMODE_READ) {
      MSG("opened for reading\n");
   ...
```

It also includes information on where the next read should be initiated and much more. The following parts are all that are relevant to this module (and most others, in fact).

```
struct file {
...
mode_t          f_mode;
loff_t          f_pos;
unsigned int    f_flags;
...
};
```

`f_mode` is the mode the device is opened in, either for reading, writing or both. `f_flags` provides more information, some of which is relevant to device modules, such as `O_NONBLOCK` or `O_NDELAY` for example. These flags are the ones given to the `open` call from the user space application and control the behavior of the device on read and write. You can find all the related information in `asm/fcntl.h`. `f_pos` is the position from which the next read or write operation will be performed.

Back to `schar_open`, and the next step is to set up the timer – we will look at this in the next section. `schar_open` ends up by printing the major and minor number of the opened device, extracted from the inode passed to it. Right now we have no real use for this, but later on we will examine modules that use this information to differentiate between different instances of the driver. Inodes, which we met in chapter three, identify files on disk and in memory and contain such information as owner, access time, size, type of file system, and much more. The `stat` system call gets its information by extracting it from the inode, so running `stat` on a file should give you some clue as to what data the inode provides (that are relevant outside the kernel). Look up the detailed information in `linux/fs.h` – note how the file system type is defined in the union u. Linux supports a lot of file systems!

`schar_release` does nothing more than decrement the usage count by 1. There is nothing else to be done, since `Schar` does not keep any memory `malloc`'ed on a per-open basis, and has no other state information that needs to be updated.

```
static int schar_release(struct inode *inode, struct file *file)
{
        MOD_DEC_USE_COUNT;
        MSG("schar_release\n");
        return 0;
}
```

Reading the Device

`schar_read` pretends to read data from the device - in fact it reads it from an internal data queue - and pass it back to user space. `Schar` keeps a global variable that keeps track of the data queue; when data is available, `schar_pool` holds the number of bytes that are in surplus. This means that if `schar_read` is invoked while `schar_pool` is zero or negative, reading processes must be made inactive until data is available.

```
static ssize_t schar_read(struct file *file, char *buf, size_t count,
          loff_t *offset)
{

   /* if less data than requested is here, put process to sleep */
   while (count > schar_pool) {
      MSG("putting process with pid %u to sleep\n", current->pid);
      /* go to sleep, but wake up on signals */
      interruptible_sleep_on(&schar_wq);
      if (signal_pending(current)) {
         MSG("pid %u got signal\n", (unsigned)current->pid);
         /* tell vfs about the signal */
         return -EINTR;
      }
   }

   /* copy the data from our buffer */
   if (copy_to_user(buf, schar_buffer, count))
      return -EFAULT;

   schar_pool -= count;
   schar_data_read += count;

   MSG("want to read %u bytes, %ld bytes in queue\n", (unsigned)count,
                         schar_pool);

   /* return data written */
   file->f_pos += count;
   return count;
}
```

This may seem a little daunting, but let's take it step by step. `count` is the amount of data that the reading process requested. If `count` is bigger than `schar_pool`, the read cannot be satisfied and we must put the reading process on hold until the requested data is available. `interruptible_sleep_on` changes the state of the process and adds it to the `schar_wq` wait queue. We'll look at wait queues in a moment - they provide a way for us to set the process reading the device to a non-running state, and let the scheduler select a new process for execution. The data is served from our internal buffer and copied back to the application with the aid of `copy_to_user`, a concept that will also be detailed later on.

At the end of schar_read we subtract count bytes from our pool, schar_length, and return the number of bytes read. In this case we just return count, since we pretend to have written exactly as much data to the application as it asked for. This works fine with dd, for example, since we can instruct it to request exactly the number of bytes we want. Try running cp on Schar later, and you will see what we mean – on our system, cp asks for data in blocks of 4 Kb and keeps going until 0 bytes read is returned. So you can feed Schar as much as you want, cp just keeps asking for more.

Don't worry if a lot of schar_read doesn't make much sense for now. We will look at each aspect of it one at a time in the following sections.

The current Task

There are several mentions of the current macro in schar_read. It is a macro that represents the currently running process in the form of a task structure. This means that the current we act upon in schar_read is the process that is currently reading from the device. A task structure has many elements – the complete listing can be found in linux/sched.h, but lets take a look at some of the fields we used here, directly or indirectly:

```
struct task_struct {
   volatile long state;
   ...
   int sigpending;
   ...
   pid_t pid;
   ...
   sigset_t signal, blocked;
   ...
};
```

As you can see, all the tasks in the system are linked in a doubly linked list. state signifies the current state of the process, i.e. whether it is running, stopped, or currently swapping. We'll look more at this in the discussion of wait queues. pid is self explanatory – the program id of the process. signal holds information regarding any signals sent to the process and blocked is a mask of signals that the process itself decided to block out. Finally, sigpending holds information on whether the process was sent an unblocked signal and is the variable checked by signal_pending. So if signal_pending returns true, we notify the VFS and let it restart the transfer.

Wait Queues

We're using wait queues to let the current task be put to sleep when no data is available and then wake it up when new data is copied to Schar. This frees up the system and allows it to run other processes. The scheduler will not consider the task until we wake it up again – which we'll do when the condition it sleeps on has been fulfilled. As we said, this gives our kernel code considerable power over user space applications which access it.

schar_read used this technique, and we'll see it again later, but let's take a more formal look at the implementation.

```
struct wait_queue {
   struct task_struct *task;
   struct wait_queue *next;
};
```

There's not much to say about the definition, it explains itself. `task` contains relevant state information in the task structure about the process being put to sleep and `next` is a pointer to the next entry in the wait queue. With that in mind, it should be obvious that you can have as many processes sleeping on a wait queue as you want. How do we put the processes to sleep?

```
void interruptible_sleep_on(struct wait_queue **p)
long interruptible_sleep_on_timeout(struct wait_queue **p, long timeout)
```

These macros put the process to sleep with a state, but allow it to wake on signals. The `_timeout` variant calls `schedule_timeout` internally and thus enables the callee to let the process wake on its own when it expires. We'll discuss how the timeout is specified later on when we come to timers.

```
void sleep_on(struct wait_queue **p)
long sleep_on_timeout(struct wait_queue **p, long timeout)
```

The semantics of these two are exactly the same as the functions above, except that the state is set to `TASK_UNINTERRUPTIBLE`.

If you wish to peek more at the internals, they can be found in `kernel/sched.c`.

Sooner or later a sleeping process must be brought to life, one way or another.

```
wake_up_interruptible(struct wait_queue **p)
wake_up(struct wait_queue **p)
```

Both of these are macros that expand to `__wake_up`. The former only wakes interruptible sleepers, while the latter wakes both. However, processes that were explicitly stopped (sent a `SIGSTOP`, for example) will not be awakened.

`Schar` puts readers to sleep on its wait queue, when it has no data to serve. A timer will wake them up, as would a writer, when enough data is available to satisfy the request.

```
interruptible_sleep_on(&schar_wq);
if (signal_pending(current))
        return -EINTR;
```

This structure is seen in many places throughout the kernel; we put the `current` process to sleep, but allow it to wake up in case it is sent a signal. When `interruptible_sleep_on` returns, the process has been awakened either by an explicit call to `wake_up_interruptible` or because it received a signal. If the latter is the case, `signal_pending` returns 1 and we instruct the VFS to restart the read by returning `-EINTR` to signify an interrupted call. If we had simply used `sleep_on` to put the process to sleep, it would sleep uninterruptibly while waiting for data and not even a `SIGKILL` would annihilate it.

As mentioned before, we wake the readers in the timer handler and `schar_write`.

```
wake_up_interruptible(&schar_wq);
```

This wakes up all the readers sleeping on the queue. Whether that is the appropriate behavior or not, depends on the situation – we may only be able to satisfy one read, so should we wake all the readers and let them race for the data? `Schar` could keep a per-device-open wait queue to solve the problem. Since that would not introduce any new concepts that exercise is left to the interested reader. Having per-device data is an interesting and useful concept by itself and will be demonstrated with the `Iomap` module later.

Writing to the Device

schar_write is much simpler by comparison, as it increments schar_pool by count and modifies file->f_pos to signify how much data was written to the device. The reason this is so much simpler than the read operation is that Schar doesn't care about finding something to do with the data, it'll take as much as we throw at it. The only thing we need to do apart from this is wake up any readers, since there might be enough data available now to satisfy their read. The implementation looks like this:

```
static ssize_t schar_write(struct file *file, const char *buf,
   size_t count, off_t *offset)
{
   schar_pool += count;
   schar_data_written += count;

   /* if we were really writing - modify the file position to
      reflect the amount of data written */
   file->f_pos += count;
   if (copy_from_user(schar_buffer, buf, count))
      return -EFAULT;

   /* wake up reading processes, if any */
   if (schar_pool > 0) {
      wake_up_interruptible(&schar_wq);
      wake_up_interruptible(&schar_poll_read);
   }

   MSG("trying to write %u bytes, %ld bytes in queue now\n",
       (unsigned)count, schar_pool);

   /* return data written */
   return count;
}
```

Non-blocking Reads

Drivers that serve data should differentiate between blocking and non-blocking opens. If not enough data is available to satisfy a request, we ordinarily put the process to sleep and wake it once enough data is available. When the device is opened non-blocking, we should instead supply as much data as we can and return immediately without putting the process to sleep. We acheive this by adding the following to the schar_read function:

```
static ssize_t schar_read(struct file *file, char *buf, size_t count,
         loff_t *offset)
...
   while (count > schar_pool) {
      /* if the device is opened non blocking satisfy what we
         can of the request and don't put the process to sleep. */
      if (file->f_flags & O_NONBLOCK) {
         if (schar_pool > 0) {
            file->f_pos += schar_pool;
         if (copy_to_user(buf, schar_buffer, schar_pool))
            return -EFAULT;
         count = schar_length;
         schar_pool = 0;
         return count;
      } else {
         return -EAGAIN;
      }
```

```
            MSG("putting process with pid %u to sleep\n", current->pid);
            /* go to sleep, but wake up on signals */
            interruptible_sleep_on(&schar_wq);
            if (signal_pending(current)) {
               MSG("pid %u got signal\n", (unsigned)current->pid);
               /* tell vfs about the signal */
               return -EINTR;
            }
         }
   }
   ...
   }
```

`schar_read` checks `f_flags` in order to detect with what method the device was opened. If the application requested more data than what is currently in our pool, we return what is there, but if the pool is empty we return `-EAGAIN`. This is a hint to the reading processes that it should try its request again later.

A device driver that only implements `read` and `write` is a bit boring. The file operation structure contains many other entry points – now let's implement some of these in Schar or at least explain why some of them work without even writing an explicit function in the driver to handle it.

Seeking

Schar does not implement its own seeking function and therefore relies on the default implementation in the kernel. The default implementation is invoked if a `NULL` is registered for `llseek` in the file operations structure passed to `register_chrdev`. The kernel version can be found in `fs/read_write.c` as `default_llseek` and provides `SEEK_SET`, `SEEK_CUR` and `SEEK_END` functionality. These macros, when used with `llseek`, change the value of `file->f_pos`, the position in the file stream from which the next byte will be read. In case you want to handle the seeking yourself – if the specific device does not support seeking relative to the end, for example – you will have to provide your own `llseek` implementation. This is a typical example:

```
loff_t own_llseek(struct file *file, loff_t offset, int mode)
{
   switch (mode) {
      case 0:                                    /* SEEK_SET */
         file->f_pos = offset;
         return file->f_pos;
      case 1:                                    /* SEEK_CUR */
         file->f_pos += offset;
         return file->f_pos;
      case 2:                                    /* SEEK_END */
         return -EINVAL;
      default:                                   /* cannot happen */
         return -EINVAL;
   }
}
```

If seeking does not make sense for the device at all, an `llseek` function will have to be defined to prevent seeking. In that case `-ESPIPE` should simply be returned, which is means "Illegal seek" in this respect.

```
loff_t own_llseek(struct file *file, loff_t offset, int mode)
{
      /* illegal seek */
      return -ESPIPE;
}
```

ioctl

Sometimes it can be useful to change or get the parameters from a running driver, instead of reconfiguring it and running a new compile. For some devices this is not even an option if it is constantly in use and thus cannot be removed from the system. `ioctl` is an entry point in the driver that will let you either set or retrieve settings while it is still running.

Every device in the kernel has a (somewhat) unique `ioctl` base number associated with them along with a range of commands. For example, the SCSI generic layer has `ioctl` base number 0x22 and the whole sub range of 0x00-0xff assigned to it. Sometimes only a part of the sub range is used as most devices won't need to support 256 commands. An `ioctl` command consists of an upper 16-bit base and a lower 16-bit command and so the first SCSI generic command would be 0x2200. The `ioctl` base numbers are documented in `Documentation/ioctl-number.txt` although it is not quite up to date as of this writing. The file also includes instructions as to how to request a suitable range for your own device. We selected an available base number for `Schar` – 0xbb. The lower level implementation is somewhat more complex than that. Ignorance is bliss, but if you are really interested look at the definitions in `asm/ioctl.h`.

Linux distinguishes between four types of `ioctl` function calls; direct commands, read, write, or read and write. This is defined by the way the identifiers are written in the module. The different types are defined as follows:

`_IO(base, command)`	Define the selected command. No data is transferred to or from the application issuing the `ioctl`. An `_IO` `ioctl` can still return an integer as long as it is positive (and thus not interpreted as an error).
`_IOR(base, command, size)`	A reading `ioctl`, as seen from the application. `size` is the size of the argument to be transferred back.
`_IOW(base, command, size)`	A writing `ioctl`, as seen from the application. `size` is the size of the argument to be transferred from user space.
`_IOWR(base, command, size)`	A reading and writing `ioctl`. As usual, `size` indicates the size of the argument to be transferred back and forth.

In addition, macros are provided to check the validity of the command sent. The kernel side encoding splits the bit field into a direction, size, and command section. The information can be extracted with the following macros.

`_IOC_DIR(command)`	The direction of the command, either `_IOC_NONE`, `_IOC_WRITE`, or `_IOC_READ` corresponding to the the types mentioned above. For `_IOWR`, the value is `_IOC_WRITE` OR'ed with `_IOC_READ`.
`_IOC_TYPE(command)`	The `ioctl` base number part of the field, 0xbb for `Schar`.
`_IOC_NR(command)`	The command part of the field.
`_IOC_SIZE(command)`	The size of the argument, if any.

The `ioctl` function itself is defined in the `file_operations` structure supplied when registering the module. `schar.h` defines the supported commands.

```
#define SCHAR_IOCTL_BASE          0xbb
#define SCHAR_TOGGLE_DEBUG        _IO(SCHAR_IOCTL_BASE, 0)
#define SCHAR_GET_POOL            _IOR(SCHAR_IOCTL_BASE, 1, unsigned long)
#define SCHAR_EX_TIMER_DELAY      _IOWR(SCHAR_IOCTL_BASE, 5, unsigned long)
```

The base number is sufficiently far away from anything else out there, so we shouldn't get any conflicts. These are the three different types that exist in `Schar`. `SCHAR_TOGGLE_DEBUG` toggles whether debug messages should be printed or not. No parameter is specified, hence the `_IO` type. `SCHAR_GET_POOL` returns the number of bytes currently residing in the pool and finally `SCHAR_EX_TIMER_DELAY` sets the number of jiffies between each timer delay and returns the old setting. Jiffies are a time measurement within the kernel and will be covered shortly.

The `schar_ioctl` function consists almost solely of a switch statement supporting the different commands.

```
static int schar_ioctl(struct inode *inode, struct file *file,
                       unsigned int cmd, unsigned long arg)
{
   /* make sure that the command is really one of schar's */
   if (_IOC_TYPE(cmd) != SCHAR_IOCTL_BASE)
      return -ENOTTY;

   switch (cmd) {
      case SCHAR_TOGGLE_DEBUG: {
         schar_debug = !schar_debug;
         return 0;
      }
      case SCHAR_GET_POOL: {
         if (put_user(schar_pool, (unsigned long *)arg))
            return -EFAULT;
         break;
      }
      case SCHAR_EX_TIMER_DELAY: {
         unsigned long tmp = schar_timer_delay;
         if (!capable(CAP_SYS_ADMIN))
            return -EACCES;
         if (get_user(schar_timer_delay,
```

```
                (unsigned long *)arg))
            return -EFAULT;
        if (put_user(tmp, (unsigned long *)arg))
            return -EFAULT;
        break;
    }
    default: {
        MSG("ioctl: no such command\n");
        return -ENOTTY;
    }
  }
  /* to keep gcc happy */
  return 0;
}
```

The implementation hopefully speaks for itself if you have used the `ioctl` system call before. We will look at the two calls which we've not met before - `get_user` and `put_user` - a little later. For now it should suffice to say that they copy data back and forth between user space and kernel space. The `default` case catches any commands that `Schar` does not support. `-ENOTTY` is the appropriate return value for unsupported commands. This might seem a bit odd, since this historically meant "Not a typewriter" and dates back to the days when the only devices were TTY's. Today this translates to "Inappropriate ioctl for device" when it is returned for an `ioctl` call.

Checking User Rights

`Ioctl`'s are available for use by anyone who has access to open the device. Depending on what operations should be performed access should not be permitted to all users. `SCHAR_EX_TIMER_DELAY` checks whether the user who opened the device is the super user, since setting too low a timeout will expire the timer too quickly and thus effectively prevent the machine from doing any useful work. Linux has a lot of different capability personalities defined, the most significant in this case being `CAP_SYS_ADMIN`. The various `CAP_` defines are located in `linux/capability.h` with comments regarding the operations permitted.

`int capable(int cap)`

The check is performed by `capable` which returns 1 if the user has the particular capability and 0 otherwise. The use of capabilities is not restricted to `ioctl`s alone, but they are most frequently used there.

poll

`poll` provides a way for a process to sleep on the device waiting for a certain event to take place. This is not to be confused with a repeated check for status as this is not what happens here. Using the `poll` system call is an efficient way of waiting for events to occur without resorting to busy looping. `Schar` implements `poll` somewhat, as much as it makes sense in our case anyway. The implementation of `poll` is very simple. Since a write to `Schar` will always succeed, we only need to test for reads. An `schar_poll_read` wait queue is introduced, and if our pool of data is empty a `poll` for read will sleep until data is available.

```
static unsigned int schar_poll(struct file *file,
                               poll_table *wait)
{
    unsigned int mask = 0;

    poll_wait(file, &schar_poll_read, wait);

    /* if the pool contains data, a read will succeed */
    if (schar_pool > 0)
        mask |= POLLIN | POLLRDNORM;

    /* a write always succeeds */
    mask |= POLLOUT | POLLWRNORM;

    return mask;
}
```

This is all it takes for `Schar`! If `Schar` kept an upper limit on the size of the pool, a `schar_poll_write` could easily be added and a similar check could be made for `POLLOUT`. The header file `asm/poll.h` contains the possible `poll` masks – We will cover the standard ones here.

POLLIN POLLRDNORM	The device can supply data on a succeeding read without blocking.
POLLOUT POLLWRNORM	The device can accept data on a succeeding write without blocking.
POLLERR	An error occurred.

If you have ever used `poll` for user space applications, you should be familiar with these as they are similar when seen from the kernel.

Try it out – reading and writing to Schar

Okay, we've covered the basics of `Schar` - we'll come on to the timer and memory functionality soon. But before we do, let's try it out. You can download the source code for `Schar` from the Wrox Press website, www.wrox.com. You can extract the archive anywhere on your system. `Schar` is located in `modules/schar`.

1. The first thing we need to do is create an appropriate special file for `Schar`. Recall from earlier that `mknod` is the command that does just that. We need to create a character special file with a major number of 42 and a minor of 0.

```
# mknod /dev/schar c 42 0
#
```

2. Go to the source of the `Schar` module and type `make` inside the directory. The compile should complete without errors or warnings. The finished module then resides in the same directory as `schar.o`. Insert the module.

```
# insmod schar.o
#
```

The device should now be registered with the kernel and ready to serve. Verify this by examining the /proc/devices file as explained above or type dmesg and notice how Schar welcomes us at the end.

```
$ dmesg | tail -n1
schar: module loaded
$
```

3. Now lets copy a file to Schar and see what happens. You can choose any file you'd like, but try a small text file if you have one handy, or can create one for the purpose. It would be a good idea to have a separate terminal window open to repeatedly run dmesg to follow Schar's output. Here we list the output from dmesg below each command.

If cp asks you if its okay to overwrite /dev/schar, just say yes.

```
$ cp small_file /dev/schar
schar: opened for writing
schar: major: 42 minor: 0
schar: trying to write 4096 bytes, 4096 bytes in queue now
schar: trying to write 4096 bytes, 8192 bytes in queue now
schar: trying to write 3241 bytes, 11433 bytes in queue now
schar: release
```

First we go through schar_open which is responsible for the first two lines of output. Then schar_write is entered and the 11433 byte file we copied to the device is written in chunks of 4096 bytes at the time. When the write has finished, schar_release is entered and the write of the file is completed.

4. Data is now available to be read from Schar, so lets copy some it back.

```
$ cp /dev/schar out_file
schar: opened for reading
schar: major: 42 minor: 0
schar: want to read 4096 bytes, 7337 bytes in queue
schar: want to read 4096 bytes, 3241 bytes in queue
schar: putting process with pid 757 to sleep
schar: pid 757 got signal
```

Again schar_open is the entry point, but this time schar_read is entered next. Data is read in chunks of 4096 bytes again – we can satisfy two reads of 4Kb before the pool contains less that what cp asks for. This is where we put the reader (cp) to sleep until more data becomes available. We got impatient and ended the read with a *Ctrl-C* which sent a signal to the process, hence the last line of output.

It is important to note that the 4Kb chunks we serve data in above is not an Schar limit, but rather the design of cp. We could just as well serve data in 1 byte or 16Kb chunks instead.

So, we can write data to Schar, and read data back. Let's now try and play with some of the other functions we included.

Try it out – ioctl

1. Make sure that the Schar module is built and loaded. Create a file called schar_ioctl.c in the directory containing the sources to Schar.

```
#include <stdio.h>
#include <fcntl.h>
#include <sys/ioctl.h>

#include "schar.h"

int main(int argc, char *argv[])
{
        int fd = open("/dev/schar", O_RDWR);

        /* complain if the open failed */
        if (fd == -1) {
                perror("open");
                return 1;
        }

        /* complain if the ioctl call failed */
        if (ioctl(fd, SCHAR_TOGGLE_DEBUG) == -1) {
                perror("ioctl");
                return 2;
        }

        printf("Schar debug toggled\n");

        return 0;
}
```

2. Compile the program and execute it with the following two lines:

```
$ cc -o schar_ioctl schar_ioctl.c
$ ./schar_ioctl
Schar debug toggled
$
```

3. If Schar was loaded with debugging enabled (as it defaults to), it should now stop printing informative messages about opens, reads, and such. Try the copy commands we used earlier, and check dmesg. You should see debgging output is no longer arriving in the kernel buffer.

Module Parameters

Linux provides an easy way to add parameter options for modules, which can be supplied at module load time with either modprobe or insmod. Schar has most of its user definable parameters set up this way.

```
MODULE_PARM(variable, type)
```

variable is the variable parameter set and type is a string compromising the length and type of the parameter. They can be placed anywhere in the module outside of functions, but are usually placed after the global variable declarations near the top. Lets look at an example from Schar.

```
MODULE_PARM(schar_debug, "1b");
```

The type string "1b" signifies that this is a byte value of length 1. The length can also be supplied with both a minimum and maximum size; "5-10b" would then mean that schar_debug was a byte size array with a minimum of 5 and a maximum of 10 items. If no length argument is given, a length of 1 is assumed. Four other types are defined besides byte size.

h	short
i	int
l	long
s	string

It is also possible to supply a descriptive text of the various module parameters. This information can be extracted with modinfo and gives the user a chance to see what parameters are supported without diving into the actual source of the module.

```
MODULE_PARM_DESC(schar_debug, "Enable debugging messages");
```

The above line is used to describe the meaning of the schar_debug variable exported prior with MODULE_PARM declaration. Finally, a general description and author field can be filled out.

```
MODULE_DESCRIPTION("Sample character driver");
MODULE_AUTHOR("Jens Axboe");
```

modinfo supports several options that let you extract the information you need. Beware that modutils-2.1.121 has a bug will cause it to continuously loop while printing the information so getting a newer version is recommended.

Try it out – modinfo

Let's try it out and list some of the module parameter information stored in a compiled Schar module. Make sure that you are in the directory containing the built Schar module:

```
$ modinfo -p schar.o
schar_name string, description "Name of device"
schar_debug byte, description "Enable debugging messages"
schar_inc int, description "Byte increase in pool per timer fire"
schar_timer_delay long, description "Timer ticks between timer fire"
schar_pool_min long, description "Timer fill pool minimum in bytes"
```

The -p parameter asks modinfo to print information about the parameter that the module can be fed at load time – its name, type, and a description of the option.

proc file system interface

The proc file system works much like a real file system, in that it is mounted and reading or writing is accomplished by using standard file utilities. The data read from a file is generated on the fly by the module or kernel and can provide run time statistics and other relevant information. Writeable files can be used to change configuration or behavior of the driver. Adding a proc file system entry to Schar thus allows users to retrieve information from the running module, without having to issue ioctl commands through a program.

Sysctl

The best place to register an entry is under the `/proc/sys` directory. Then entries can be retrieved with either `cat`, for example, or the `sysctl` system call. Devices should register themselves under the `dev/` directory and this is exactly what `Schar` does – it creates an `Schar` subdirectory and an entry called `0` inside it. The entries are defined in an array of `ctl_table` structures stacked on top of each other until the chain is complete. The `root` (`/proc/sys/dev`) is set up with `/proc/sys/dev/schar` as a directory entry child and finally `/proc/sys/dev/char/0` is added. Here's the code from `Schar.c`:

```
/* sysctl entries */
static char schar_proc_string[SCHAR_MAX_SYSCTL];
static struct ctl_table_header *schar_root_header = NULL;
static int schar_read_proc(ctl_table *ctl, int write, struct file *file,
          void *buffer, size_t *lenp);

static ctl_table schar_sysctl_table[] = {
   { DEV_SCHAR_ENTRY,                  /* binary id */
     "0",                              /* name */
     &schar_proc_string,               /* data */
     SCHAR_MAX_SYSCTL,                 /* max size of output */
     0644,                             /* mode */
     0,                                /* child - none */
     &schar_read_proc },               /* set up text */
   { 0 }
};

static ctl_table schar_dir[] = {
   { DEV_SCHAR,                        /* /proc/dev/schar */
     "schar",                          /* name */
     NULL,
     0,
     0555,
     schar_sysctl_table },             /* the child */
   { 0 }
};

static ctl_table schar_root_dir[] = {
   { CTL_DEV,                          /* /proc/dev */
     "dev",                            /* name */
     NULL,
     0,
     0555,
     schar_dir },                      /* the child */
   { 0 }
};
```

`DEV_SCHAR_ENTRY` is the binary ID used when issuing a `sysctl` system call and should be unique. `schar_proc_string` is the data returned to reading processes and is no longer than `SCHAR_MAX_SYSCTL` bytes in length. The implementation is very simple and merely consists of copying the statistics generated to a dedicated buffer – `schar_proc_string` – that is generated by `schar_read_proc` when the read takes place.

Once the appropriate tables have been set up, the entry is registered with the proc file system. A `ctl_table_header` is returned or 0 in the unlikely scenario that no memory was available.

```
schar_root_header = register_sysctl_table(schar_root_dir, 0);
schar_root_dir->child->de->fill_inode = &schar_fill_inode;
```

The last line sets up the `fill_inode`. Upon entering and leaving the `/proc/sys/dev/schar` directory the assigned function, `schar_fill_inode`, increments or decrements the module usage count. A `fill` argument is passed to the function indicating whether the inode associated with the directory is busy or not. By incrementing the usage count the module cannot be removed until no one is accessing the directory, which would otherwise generate a kernel fault (also known as an `Oops`, we will look at these in the section on debugging).

`proc_dostring` does the rest of the job for us, copying the data to user space and modifying the file position. The arguments remain untouched and are simply passed along.

```
return proc_dostring(ctl, write, file, buffer, lenp);
```

`Schar` is not very careful with regards to `proc` or `sysctl` support in the kernel. If this was a production module, the implementation should be protected by adding the necessary define checks. Something in the order of

```
#ifdef CONFIG_SYSCTL
...
#endif
```

around the relevant pieces of code. Otherwise the module would fail to compile on a kernel build without `sysctl` support, albeit that is an extremely rare scenario.

Writable Entries

The entry registered by `Schar` only provides information to the user and as such is read only. The mode set up does permit writing, however, and in that case the written string is merely printed to the logs.

```
if (write) {
    char *tmp = (char *) get_free_page(GFP_KERNEL);
    MSG("proc: someone wrote %u bytes\n", *lenp);
    if (tmp) {
        if (!copy_from_user(tmp, buffer, *lenp))
          MSG("proc: %s", tmp);
        free_page((unsigned long)tmp);
        file->f_pos += *lenp;
    }
    return 0;
}
```

A write argument is passed to the registered handler indicating whether the access was for reading or writing. In the latter case, the data is copied to us and printed.

It should not be hard to add a function to parse the input and change the configuration appropriately. Another alternative is to create numerous entries each holding one of `Schar`'s configuration options (much like the other `/proc/sys` entries) and thus provide the possibility of simply echoing changes directly to the separate files. It would then even be possible to use `proc_dostring` for both input and output. The `sysctl` abstraction does lend itself more in this direction, but having learned of both it should provide you with the necessary tools to further pursue the `proc` file systems. Besides, it is a two-for-one deal, since registering a `sysctl` table also takes care of setting up the `proc` file system entry. `kernel/sysctl.c` is a great place to look for more information.

How Schar Behaves

`Schar` keeps an internal count of how many bytes are either in surplus or in demand in the `schar_pool` variable. A negative value means that a reader is currently starved of `schar_pool` bytes, while a positive value signifies the opposite. Writing to the device will add the bytes written to the pool for later consumption. `Schar` keeps a kernel timer running that adds `SCHAR_INC` bytes to `schar_pool` at `SCHAR_TIMER_DELAY` intervals while a reader is waiting for data. A write to the device will always succeed, but if a reader requests more data than what is currently in the pool it is added to `Schar`'s wait queue and woken up every time the timer handler runs. It prints relevant information to the logs, so give it a try to get a feel for how the internals work.

`Schar` keeps a free page of memory as an internal buffer and copies read and written data to and from there. It serves no particular purpose other than to demonstrate how data is moved between kernel and user space – a concept we will look at much more closely later.

While `Schar` is useless by itself, it exposes the basic skeleton for a character driven device driver. We used a kernel timer to feed the pool to emulate the feel of a polled device. Polling is needed if the device is unable to provide feedback to the driver in the form of interrupts, a concept we will look at later when looking at interrupt driven character drivers.

Review

In this section we looked at how character devices register themselves in the kernel device switch table with the `register_chrdev` function. They passed a `file_operations` structure to this function that defined what access methods we provide in this driver. The module usage count makes sure that a driver is not unloaded while it is busy and is modified with the `MOD_INC_USE_COUNT` and `MOD_DEC_USE_COUNT` macros.

We looked at how `Schar` implements read and write operations and can put the current process to sleep and wake it up at will using wait queues. This is an important concept and is used in just about every character device driver.

Then we looked at which visible entry points the driver provides besides just read and write. The first one was seeking through `llseek` which turned out to be active even if we haven't written an implementation in the module. We looked at how disabling seeks could be accomplished by writing a basically empty implementation that merely returned `-ESPIPE`.

Next up was `ioctl`, IO Control, commands. We saw how calls were split up in two parts, a base number and a command. The implementation in `Schar` was basically just a switch statement and `-ENOTTY` was returned for unknown commands. Not all `ioctl` calls should be available to all users. Specific capabilities could be checked with the `capable` function.

`poll` provided a way for a reading process to sleep while data becomes available. The implementation in `Schar` only looked at reading processes, since it always accepts data from writers. Although only reads could be tested for in `Schar`, the other poll masks were also shown.

Finally we took a quick look at specifying module parameters before moving on to the `proc` file system setup in Schar. We went all the way and provided a `sysctl` entry that could be reached both by reading entries in `/proc/sys/dev/schar` and through the `sysctl` system call.

Finally we had a quick explanation of how `Schar` behaves when data is copied to and from the device. You should compile the module yourself and give it a go to fully understand what it does and how.

Time and Jiffies

The kernel keeps track of time passing in the global `jiffies` variable. You may consider this the kernel's heartbeat, since for every timer tick that goes by `jiffies` is incremented by one. The `define HZ` controls the rate of the ticks and can be modified at your will in `<asm/param.h>`. Beware that changing this will require a recompile of existing modules (and the kernel, of course) and will break applications that depend on its default value. Every platform, except the Alpha, sets this to 100; that gives us a heartbeat rate of one every 10 milliseconds. Increasing the value may give you better interactive performance at the expense of spending more time in the scheduler, but leaving it at 100 is probably a safe bet. Every now and then discussions arise, debating whether `HZ` should be changed since it has stayed the same since Linux was first introduced. So far it is not conclusive if increasing it will give better performance on today's faster processors

You might end up programming devices where you want to detect whether an operation was completed within a given amount of time or not. Some devices do not support raising interrupts upon completion and thus must be handled via some form of polling for status. This is usually only the case with old or badly designed hardware; modern devices should support some kind of event notification. Busy looping should never be considered good device driver programming practice. If you do need to resort to these dirty measures, make sure that it only runs in the odd case, i.e. during device probing or similar instances. In these cases the most used construct is a variant of the following:

```
unsigned long timeout = jiffies + PROBE_TIMEOUT;
do {
   do_command(PROBE);
   stat = get_status();
} while (stat == BUSY && time_before(jiffies, timeout));

if (time_after_eq(jiffies, timeout))
   printk("operation timed out.\n");
```

Now you might be wondering what the `time_before` and `time_after_eq` functions do and why we didn't just compare `timeout` and `jiffies` directly. Well, Linux is such a stable operating system that it is not that unusual to have machines running a very long time between reboots. Given that `jiffies` is defined to be an unsigned long it will wrap eventually and start ticking from zero again. If timeout wraps when `jiffies` and `PROBE_TIMEOUT` are added, a simple test of:

```
do {
   do_command(PROBE);
   stat = get_status();
while (stat == BUSY && (jiffies < timeout));
```

would cause the loop to exit prematurely. Clearly this isn't intended and keeping track of wraps ourselves, albeit not that difficult, shouldn't be something that the driver writer should be bothered with. For this reason, these four macros can do the job for us safely:

`time_before(jiffies, x)`	wrap safe `jiffies < x`
`time_after(jiffies, x)`	wrap safe `jiffies > x`
`time_before_eq(jiffies, x)`	wrap safe `jiffies <= x`
`time_after_eq(jiffies, x)`	wrap safe `jiffies >= x`

The macros are not only useful when doing direct tests like the above where the possibility of a wrap is miniscule, but also when testing for much larger values in drivers where packets are queued and then only tested for timeouts much later. That could be in a SCSI or network adapter driver code, for example. The macros are defined in `linux/timer.h`.

On the issue of portability and time-outs using `jiffies` – never assume that `HZ` equals 100. This is already a false assumption on Alpha architectures, which define it as 1024 and rtLinux (Real Time Linux) that uses 10,000. Users are free to select any value they please and changing `HZ` is as easy as modifying `asm/param.h` and recompiling. Therefore make sure that constructs like the above define `PROBE_TIMEOUT` in terms of `HZ` and not a tick value alone.

Small Delays

At times you need a finer control over time than that which `HZ` provides. Remember that `HZ` is 100 on most platforms, which will only give you an approximate resolution of 0.01 seconds. That may not seem like much, but for most hardware this is an extremely long period of time. In case you need finer resolution, `udelay` can provide up to microsecond precision.

```
/* delay for 0.5 milliseconds */
udelay(500);
```

`udelay` uses the `BogoMIPS` rating calculated at boot time and while you can not rely on precisely microsecond resolution, it does get fairly close. You may have wondered what the `BogoMIPS` rating shown at boot means and what it is used for – it is a calibration loop run at boot that measures a loops per second speed. As such it isn't directly related to hardware speed (hence `BogoMIPS`, for bogus), but it does provide a way to somewhat accurately offer delay operations for `udelay` and friends. Never use `udelay` for more than a millisecond or two as this can cause overflow on machines with high `BogoMIPS` ratings. In fact, be very certain that you really do need to delay like this! If you do need to pause for longer than this, either loop a specified amount of times and `udelay` a millisecond each time, like this:

```
/* delay for 10 milliseconds */
int i;
for (i = 0; i < 10; i++)
   udelay(1000);
```

Or you can use `mdelay`, which is a macro that does exactly that for you.

```
/* delay for 10 milliseconds */
mdelay(10);
```

Timers

Kernel timers are an excellent way of keeping track of time in your driver. Instead of looping and busy waiting for a certain amount of time to expire, you should take advantage of the available timer functions. As we have seen above, timers can also be used to poll a device at a constant interval. Timers are implemented as a doubly linked list with the following format:

```
struct timer_list {
   struct timer_list *next;
   struct timer_list *prev;
   unsigned long expires;
   unsigned long data;
   void (*function)(unsigned long);
};
```

You can find this definition in `linux/timer.h`. For the sake of simplicity, you will never have to touch the `*next` and `*prev` pointers; in fact you should not. The kernel uses these internally and does that for us. The interesting parts can be found in `kernel/sched.c`. `add_timer` takes care of acquiring the necessary locks and then calls `internal_add_timer`. This keeps the interface simple for us and we do not actually have to be concerned with the inner workings of `internal_add_timer`. The different locking schemes will be introduced later, when the issues of SMP and reentrant code are discussed.

`init_timer` does exactly what the name hints at – initializes the timer for use. In reality it merely updates `next` and `prev` to be null pointers so that timers added twice won't go unnoticed. This is also the technique used in `Schar`'s `open` procedure to detect whether the internal timer was already set up. Let's take a closer look at the code from `Schar` that shows how timers are used in that context. The timer is initialized as follows:

```
static struct timer_list schar_timer;
```

This code, from `init_module`, just prepares the timer for later use.

```
init_timer(&schar_timer);
```

`schar_open` then sets it up, provided that is hasn't already been set up by another reader.

```
if (!timer_pending(&schar_timer)) {
   schar_timer.function = &schar_timer_handler;
   mod_timer(&schar_timer, SCHAR_TIMER_DELAY);
}
```

Most important is the `timer_handler` function, a reference to which is passed to `schar_timer`'s `function` value.

```
static void schar_timer_handler(unsigned long data)
{
    /* setup timer again */
    if (schar_pool < schar_pool_min) {
        schar_pool += SCHAR_INC;
        schar_timer.expires = jiffies + schar_timer_delay;
        schar_timer.function = &schar_timer_handler;
        add_timer(&schar_timer);
        MSG("setting timer up again, %ld data now\n", schar_pool);
    }

    /* if the module is in use, we most likely have a reader waiting for
       data. wake up any processes that are waiting for data. */
    if (MOD_IN_USE && schar_pool > 0) {
        wake_up_interruptible(&schar_wq);
        wake_up_interruptible(&schar_poll_read);
    }

    return;
}
```

The syntax is fairly straightforward so we won't explain it to death. `data` is not used in `Schar` at all, since we are only maintaining one timer with the handler. We could have added a timer for both readers and writers, and let the value of `data` signify either a `SCHAR_READER` or `SCHAR_WRITER` timer. There are many other uses for `data` – it is passed to `timer_handler` as an argument so you can use it anyway you please. It is also worth noting that `expires` is not relative to the current time – you need to add `jiffies` explicitly.

Timers are automatically deleted when they expire, but leaving them hanging after the module has been unloaded is an excellent way to hang the kernel. This also means that you can add the timer again from the handler itself. `cleanup_module` calls `timer_pending` to detect whether the timer has expired or not. It returns `true` if the timer hasn't fired yet and `false` otherwise. If the timer is still running, it is explicitly deleted by `del_timer`. Strictly speaking, this isn't really necessary since calling `del_timer` on a timer that has fired does no harm. We included it here merely for the sake of covering all the related timer functions.

If you need to update the timer to extend the timeout, `mod_timer` is your friend. So instead of doing

```
del_timer(&timer1);
timer1.expires = jiffies + new_value;
add_timer(&timer1);
```

you can do

```
mod_timer(&timer1, new_value);
```

and end up with the same result in a nicer way. If the timer had already expired by the time `mod_timer` is invoked, it acts just like `add_timer` and merely adds the timer again.

Try it out – The timer implementation in Schar

Schar periodically adds data to its internal pool by using a kernel timer. The interval can be adjusted either through an ioctl call or by modifying SCHAR_TIMER_DELAY in schar.h.

The timer is added when a reader opens the device and re-added from the timer handler as long as data is in demand.

```
$ cp /dev/schar out_file
schar: opened for reading
schar: major: 42 minor: 0
schar: putting process with pid 889 to sleep

schar: setting timer up again, 1024 data now
schar: putting process with pid 889 to sleep

schar: setting timer up again, 2048 data now
schar: putting process with pid 889 to sleep
schar: setting timer up again, 3072 data now
schar: putting process with pid 889 to sleep

schar: setting timer up again, 4096 data now
schar: want to read 4096 bytes, 0 bytes in queue
schar: putting process with pid 889 to sleep
```

SCHAR_INC bytes of data are added to the pool each time the handler runs – 1024 in this case. Every time the handler runs it wakes the reading process (or processes, if you have more than one running) in case we now have enough data to satisfy the read. When the pool contains 4096 bytes, cp can receive the first chunk of data and the procedure starts over again.

Giving up the Processor

Instead of looping and waiting for a certain amount of time to expire, it may be beneficial to suspend execution of the current process and resume later. Changing the state of the process and calling the scheduler can accomplish this. In the listing of the Linux task structure we examined earlier, the state field was introduced. It can be assigned to any of the following values:

TASK_RUNNING	The task was selected by the scheduler the last time it ran and is currently in a running state. This is the state of the current process when entering the driver.
TASK_INTERRUPTIBLE	The task is in a state of sleep, but can be woken up by signals.
TASK_UNINTERRUPTIBLE	The task is in a state of sleep and signals cannot wake it up. The process is probably waiting on an event to happen and it wouldn't make sense to let it wake before that event occurs.

There are a couple more than this, but they aren't relevant here. Look them up in linux/sched.h if you wish.

So before invoking the scheduler, `current->state` should be set to either `TASK_INTERRUPTIBLE` or `TASK_UNINTERRUPTIBLE`. Which one to use depends on what condition the process is waiting for. The latter should only be used if wouldn't make sense to let wake it up before what it requested is ready and putting it away in a uninterruptible state is the most logical choice. For most issues that is not the case – If you `grep` through the Linux sources you will find very few places that actually use `TASK_UNINTERRUPTIBLE`. One example, however, is if pages belonging to the process are being brought in from swap; we don't want the process to wake up until the task is completed.

A piece of code that demonstrates these principles could be:

```
current->state = TASK_INTERRUPTIBLE;
schedule();
```

Now the process gets tugged away and the scheduler runs. But how do we know when the process returns? If there are no other suitable processes to run, the same task will be selected to run again and we end up at the same place almost instantly. This is where `schedule_timeout` enters the picture – you call it instead of `schedule`, and it returns the number of `jiffies` left to be slept. The scheduler is guaranteed not to select the process for execution before the specified timeout has expired.

```
/* put the process away for a second */
current->state = TASK_INTERRUPTIBLE;
schedule_timeout(HZ);
```

The value signifies the number of jiffies the process should sleep before being run again. The inner workings of `schedule_timeout` are rather interesting – it is implemented with the aid of a kernel timer, and the `data` argument is the address of the current process. After the timer has been added, `schedule_timeout` calls `schedule` itself. The timer function simply does a wake up of the process with address data. If you are interested, look in `kernel/sched.c`.

Task Queues

We have looked at how timers can be used to wake up processes at a given point in the future. While timers are handy, it could also be useful to delay work to be executed later. This becomes particularly interesting when we deal with interrupt handling routines and bottom halves, which task queues are very closely related to. For now, let's stick to task queues and defer the discussion of interrupt handling to the next section.

```
struct tq_struct {
   struct tq_struct *next;        /* linked list of active bh's */
   unsigned long sync;            /* must be initialized to zero*/
   void (*routine)(void *);       /* function to call */
   void *data;                    /* argument to function */
};
```

The declaration is from `linux/tqueue.h`. As usual, you do not have to touch all the fields yourself. `*next` is used internally to keep the queued tasks in a linked list and `sync` makes sure that a task is not queued twice before being run. This would corrupt the linked list, so if you attempt to queue the task twice you will simply be ignored.

Some predefined task queues exist in the kernel, but let's first look at declaring your own queue.

```
DECLARE_TASK_QUEUE(q_task);
struct tq_struct q_run = { NULL, 0, (void *)q_task_handler,
                &q_task };
```

This is the definition of the structure in queues and is pretty much taken directly from the header file. The only real difference is that we define our own function to be called and activate the task queue from there. `DECLARE_TASK_QUEUE` is a macro that initializes the queue to `NULL`. `q_task` is where we queue the tasks, and `q_run` will run `q_task_handler` when the task queue is being consumed. Adding a process to the above queue is done with

```
queue_task(&q_run, &q_task);
```

`queue_task` can be called numerous times and when we are ready to execute the tasks on hold on the queue, `run_task_queue` is invoked. All the tasks queued on `q_task` are then consumed.

```
run_task_queue(&q_task);
```

The Predefined Task Queues

We won't talk any more about defining your own task queues, since the kernel provides a few for us to use and they will suffice for the most part. Therefore you hardly ever need to handle your own.

`tq_immediate`	Gets run as soon as possible. We'll talk more about it in the section on interrupt handling.
`tq_timer`	After each passing timer tick, `tq_timer` is run. This queue is the one the kernel uses for kernel timers internally.
`tq_scheduler`	Gets run every time the scheduler is invoked, if it contains any tasks.
`tq_disk`	Mostly used by the VFS and the block functions when dealing with requests.

The first three queues are clearly the most interesting and you should probably stay away from `tq_disk`, since it has a very specialized purpose. If we disregard `tq_disk`, We have placed them in order of how fast they will get executed after queuing (as a rule of thumb).

When you deal with the built-in task queues, you will never have to invoke `run_task_queue` on your own. Depending on which queue you use, you instead simply mark the queue after adding the task and it will be run automatically. Before we move on to looking at how to mark the queues for execution, let's take a very quick look at the implementation of bottom halves in Linux.

We will look closer at bottom halves in the section on interrupt handling, but since they are closely related to task queues it seems appropriate to use them as an example. Basically, interrupt handlers can be split in two parts – a top and bottom half. The former receives the interrupt and takes care of immediate, basic needs such as acknowledging it to the device. The bottom half runs later and is used to defer processing of the data received in the top half. This allows Linux to process more interrupts than a single interrupt handler can manage on its own.

In fact, task queues are implemented as bottom halves in Linux. As the different bottom halves are marked active, the kernel executes them with `do_bottom_half` from the scheduler. The kernel maintains a list of possible bottom halves in `linux/interrupt.h`. Here is a snippet:

```
enum {
        TIMER_BH = 0,
        CONSOLE_BH,
        TQUEUE_BH,
        ...
        IMMEDIATE_BH,
        ...
};
```

These are the older embedded bottom halves and are not directly available to modules since each of them serves a specialized purpose. If you look in the header file, you will notice that there isn't an entry for `tq_scheduler` because it does not need to be marked for execution. The first thing the scheduler does, is to check if `tq_scheduler` contains any tasks and executes them if it does. This also means that this queue is run every time the scheduler is invoked, which is dependent on many factors.

`tq_timer` is run on every timer tick if it contains any tasks and thus does not need to be marked as active either. This also means that task waiting on this queue are being run at interrupt time which places certain restrictions on what they can do. Functions that are being run at interrupt time must not block or sleep, for example. This may not sound like such a hard thing to achieve, but you must also bear in mind that the entire call path of such a function is included – so you must not call other functions that might block.

The last queue that should be considered for general use is `tq_immediate`. As the name implies, the queue is run extremely fast. It is generally intended to be used as a way of defering work for interrupt handlers and we will use it in the interrupt handling section.

`void init_bh(int nr, void (*routine)(void))`	Enable the handling of bottom half `nr` by function `routine`.
`void mark_bh(int nr)`	Mark the appropriate bit in `bh_active`, which will make the scheduler run the task queue when it is invoked.

`tq_immediate` is the only queue that must be explicitly marked, since its intended use is as a bottom half. When we get to interrupt handling, some examples on how to use task queues and bottom halves will be shown.

Review

We started out by looking at `jiffies`, the heart beat of the kernel. The standard kernel maintains a tick rate of 100 per second and increments `jiffies` by one each tick. Sooner or later `jiffies` wraps and starts ticking from zero again, which is why we covered four macros that aid the device writer in determining whether a certain timeout had passed or not. We showed how a process could be rescheduled, either with an explicit timeout value or just forcing the scheduler to run and pick a new process for execution (and in that case it might select the very same process again).

We also covered kernel timers and showed how they are used in `Schar` to invoke a specific timer handler at a given point in the future. Task queues were another way of deferring work to be done later, although they can't explicitly be invoked at a given time in the future and overall lend themselves more toward processing work immediately or running batches of jobs.

Memory Management

Before we deal with how to allocate memory properly in a driver, let us take a brief tour of memory management in general and how Linux handles it. You have probably come across the term virtual memory before and may have wondered just what precisely it covered. When you allocate memory in user space applications, you aren't handed a private section of the RAM in your machine. While this would be a way for an operating system to handle memory allocations, it would only allow you to run as many applications as your memory could hold in total. Linux does not work this way – it pretends that much more memory is available (hence the term virtual memory, it isn't actually real) and hands out virtual addresses to applications.

The mapping between virtual and physical addresses is kept in several structures, which comprise the page table. The page table consists of three levels – the page directory, page middle directory, and the page table entries each which of provide an offset of the virtual address. This is the lowest level of memory management, and the driver writer won't usually have to deal with the page table directly.

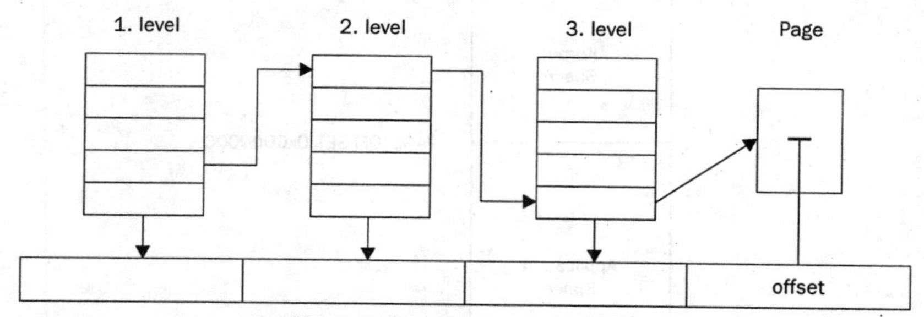

Virtual to physical address translation

Virtual Memory Areas

Above the page table reside the virtual memory areas. These are a map of contiguous virtual memory addresses, as handed out to an application.

```
struct vm_area_struct {
   ...
   unsigned long vm_start;
   unsigned long vm_end;
   ...
   pgprot_t vm_page_prot;
   ...
   struct vm_operations_struct *vm_ops;
   unsigned long vm_offset;
   struct file *vm_file;
   ...
};
```

This is a highly snipped version of the structure, you can find it in `linux/mm.h`. We will cover the members that we will actually need later on. `vm_start` and `vm_end` represent the beginning and end of the virtual memory area and `vm_page_prot` is the protection attributes assigned to it – whether it is shared, private, executable, and so forth. `vm_ops` is similar to the `file_operations` structure used with character and block devices and forms an analogous abstraction to operation on virtual memory areas. Finally `vm_offset` is the offset into the area and `vm_file` is used in correlation with memory mapping of files. We'll take a much closer look at this structure when we dissect the mmap functions of `Schar`.

The mappings made by a specific process can be seen in `/proc/<pid>/maps`. Each one corresponds to a separate `vm_area_struct` and the size, span, and protection associated with the mapping can be read from the `proc` entry, amongst other things.

Address Space

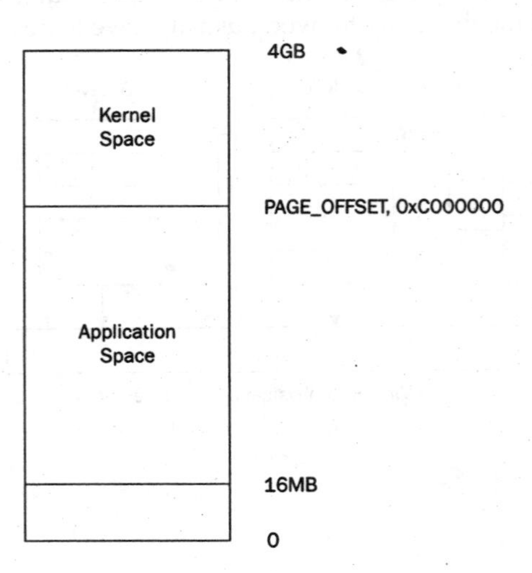

The entire addressable area of memory (4 Gb on 32-bit platforms) is split into two major areas – kernel space and user (or application) space. PAGE_OFFSET defines this split and is actually configurable in asm/page.h. The kernel space is located above the offset and user space is kept below. The default for PAGE_OFFSET on the Intel platform is 0xc0000000 and thus provides the kernel with approximately 1 GB of memory, leaving 3 GB for user space consumption. On the Intel platform, the virtual addresses seen from the kernel are therefore a direct offset from the physical address. This isn't always the case and primitives to convert between the two must thus be used.

Types of Memory Locations

There are three kinds of addresses that you need to be aware of as a device driver writer :

- **Physical**. This is the "real" address, the one that is used to index the memory bus on the motherboard.
- **Virtual**. Only the CPU and the kernel (via its page tables and TLB) knows about virtual addresses.
- **Bus**. All devices outside the CPU. On some platforms this is identical to the physical addresses.

Now, if you want to talk to an add-on card you can't hand it a virtual memory address and tell it to transfer X number of bytes to you. The card knows absolutely nothing about what addressing scheme the kernel and CPU has agreed upon since it does not have access to the page tables and thus can't make any sense of the memory address. Similarly, the kernel uses virtual addresses for everything and accessing bus memory varies from platform to platform. Linux therefore provides convenient macros and functions to convert the three types of addresses back and forth.

```
unsigned long virt_to_phys(void *address)
void *phys_to_virt(unsigned long address)

unsigned long virt_to_bus(void *address)
void *bus_to_virt(unsigned long address)
```

Talking to a peripheral device requires the translation back and forth between virtual addresses (that the kernel knows about) and bus addresses (what the devices know about). This is regardless of the type of bus the peripheral is installed in, be it PCI, ISA, or any other. Note that jumping through the extra hoops of converting addresses is only necessary when you explicitly need to pass a pointer to a memory area directly to the device. This is the case with DMA transfers, for example. In other situations you normally read the data from device I/O memory or I/O ports.

Getting Memory in Device Drivers

Memory is allocated in chunks of the PAGE_SIZE on the target machine. The Intel platform has a page size of 4 Kb whereas the Alpha uses 8 Kb sized pages and it is not a user configurable option. Keep in mind that the page size varies depending on the platform. There are many ways of allocating memory for driver usage, the lowest level one being a variant of :

`unsigned long __get_free_page(int gfp_mask)`	Allocate exactly one page of memory.

`gfp_mask` describes priority and attributes of the page we would like to get a hold of. The most commonly used ones in drivers are :

`GFP_ATOMIC`	Memory should be returned, if any is available, without going blocking or bringing in pages from swap.
`GFP_KERNEL`	Memory should be returned, if any is available, but the call may block if pages need to be swapped out.
`GFP_DMA`	The memory returned should be below the 16 MB mark and thus suitable as a DMA buffer. This flag is only needed on ISA peripherals, as these cannot address more memory than 16MB.

`GFP_ATOMIC` must always be specified if you wish to allocate memory at interrupt time, since it is guaranteed not to schedule out the current process if a suitable page is not available. ISA boards can only see up to 16 MB of memory and hence you must specify `GFP_DMA` if you are allocating a buffer for DMA transfers on an ISA peripheral. Depending on how much memory is installed and the level of internal fragmentation, memory allocated with `GFP_DMA` may not succeed. PCI devices do not suffer under this constraint and can use any memory returned by `__get_free_page` for DMA transfers.

`__get_free_page` is actually just a special case of `__get_free_pages`.

`unsigned long __get_free_pages(int gfp_mask, unsigned long order)`

`gfp_mask` has the same meaning, but `order` is a new concept. Pages can only be allocated in orders of 2, so the number of pages returned is 2^{order}. The `PAGE_SHIFT` define determines the software page size and is 12 on the Intel platform (2^{12} bytes is 4 Kb). An `order` of 0 returns one page of `PAGE_SIZE` bytes and so forth. The kernel keeps internal lists of the different orders up to 5 which limits the maximum order to that amount, giving you a maximum of 2^5 * 4 Kb == 128 Kb on the Intel platform.

You may have wondered why the functions are prefixed with __ and there is a perfectly good explanation for this. They are actually faster variants of `get_free_page` and `get_free_pages` respectively and the only difference lies in the fact that the __ versions don't clear the page before returning it. If you copy memory back to user space applications, it may be beneficial to clear the page of previous contents which could inadvertently contain sensitive information that should not be passed to another process. `__get_free_page` and friends are quicker and, if the memory allocated is only to be used internally, clearing the pages may not be needed.

It is extremely important to free memory once you are done using it. The kernel does not reap allocated pages when the module is unloaded and this makes it the module's complete responsibility to do its own memory management.

`void free_page(unsigned long addr)` `void free_pages(unsigned long addr, unsigned long order)`	Free the page(s) at memory location `addr`. You are expected to keep track of the size of allocated pages, since `free_pages` expect you to the supply it with the order you used when allocating the memory.

kmalloc

Allocation of memory with `get_free_page` and the likes is a bit troublesome and places a lot of the memory management work in the hands of the device driver. Depending on what you are aiming at using the memory for, a page oriented scheme might not be the most appropriate. Besides, it is not that often that the size requirement fits perfectly into the scheme of allocating pages in orders of two of the page size. This can lead to a lot of wasted memory. Linux provides `kmalloc` as an alternative, which lets you allocate memory any size you want.

```
void *kmalloc(size_t size, int flags)
```

`size` is the requested amount of memory and is rounded up to the nearest multiple of the page size. flags consist of a mask of priorities, just like with the `get_free_page` variants. The same size restrictions apply – you can only get up to 128 KB at the time. Trying to allocate more will get you an error in the log, saying "`kmalloc: Size (135168) too large`" for example.

```
void kfree(const void *addr)
```

`kfree` will free the memory previously allocated by `kmalloc`. If you are used to dynamically allocating memory in applications with malloc, you will feel right at home with `kmalloc`.

vmalloc

The third and final way to acquire memory is with `vmalloc`. While `get_free_page` and `kmalloc` both return memory that is physically contiguous, `vmalloc` provides memory that is contiguous in the virtual address space and thus serves a different purpose. It does so by allocating pages separately and manipulating the page tables.

```
void *vmalloc(unsigned long size)
void vfree(void *addr)
```

`vmalloc` allows you to allocate much larger arrays than `kmalloc`, but the returned memory can only be used from within the kernel. Regions passed to peripheral devices cannot be allocated with `vmalloc`, exactly because they are not contiguous in the physical address space. Virtual memory is only usable within the kernel / CPU context, where it can be looked up in the page tables.

`vmalloc` cannot be used at interrupt time either as it may sleep, since internally `kmalloc` is called without `GFP_ATOMIC` set. This should not pose a serious problem, as it would be abnormal to need more memory than `__get_free_pages` can provide inside an interrupt handler.

All things considered, `vmalloc` is most useful for internal storage. The RAM disk module, `Radimo`, shown in the block device section will provide an example of `vmalloc` usage.

Transferring Data Between User and Kernel Space

Applications running on the system can only access memory below the PAGE_OFFSET mark. This ensures that no process is allowed to overwrite memory areas managed by the kernel, which would seriously compromise system integrity, but at the same time poses problems regarding getting data back to user space. Processes running in the context of the kernel are allowed to access both regions of memory, but at the same time it must be verified that the location given by the process is within its virtual memory area.

```
int access_ok(int type, const void *addr,
              unsigned long size)
```

The above macro returns 1 if access of the desired type to/from the memory location addr of size bytes is permitted and 0 if not. type is either VERIFY_WRITE or VERIFY_READ, depending on the direction of the transfer. Every transfer taking place to and from user space must make sure that the location given is a valid one. The code to do so is architecture dependent and located in asm/uaccess.h.

The actual transfer of data is done by various functions, depending on the size of the transfer.

get_user(void *x, const void *addr)	Copy sizeof(addr) bytes from user space address addr to x.
put_user(void *x, const void *addr)	Copy sizeof(addr) bytes to user space to variable x from addr.

The type of the pointer given in addr must be known and cast if necessary, which is why there is no need for a size argument. The implementation is quite intricate and can be found in the above mentioned include file. Frequently they are used in implementing ioctl calls, since those often copy single value variables back and forth.

You may have wondered why the appropriate access_ok call was not included in Schar, for example. Often the check is omitted by mistake and the x_user functions therefore include the check. The return value is 0 if the copy was completed and -EFAULT in case of access violation.

__get_user(x, addr)

The versions prefixed with __ perform no checking. They are typically used when performing multiple single value copies where performing the access check several times is redundant.

```
char foo[2];
...
if (access_ok(VERIFY_WRITE, arg, 2*sizeof(*arg)) {
   __put_user(foo[0], arg);
   __put_user(foo[1], arg+1);
} else {
   return -EFAULT;
}
```

This is a trivial case, but the idea behind it should be clear. A third version of the x_user family also exists. Typically the return value is checked and -EFAULT is returned in the case of access violation and this lead to the introduction of the last variant.

```
void get_user_ret(x, addr, ret)
void put_user_ret(x, addr, ret)
```

The _ret versions return the value in ret for you in case of error – they don't return any error code back to you. This simplifies the programming of ioctl's and leads to such simple code as:

```
get_user_ret(tmp, (long *)arg, -EFAULT);
```

Moving more Data

Often more data needs to be copied than just single variables and it would be very inefficient and awkward to base the code on the primitives above. Linux provides the functions needed to transfer bigger amounts of data in one go. These are the ones that are used in Schar's read and write functions.

```
copy_to_user(void *to, void *from, unsigned long size)
copy_from_user(void *to, void *from, unsigned long size)
```

They copy size amount of bytes to and from the pointers specified. The return value is 0 in case of success and non-zero (in actual fact the amount not transferred) if access is not permitted, as copy_xx_user also calls access_ok internally. An example of the usage can be found in Schar.

```
if (copy_to_user(buf, schar_buffer, count))
    return -EFAULT;
```

As with get_user, non checking versions also exist and are prefixed in the same manner with __.

```
__copy_to_user(void *to, void *from, unsigned long size)
__copy_from_user(void *to, void *from, unsigned long size)
```

Finally, _ret variants are also available that return ret in case of access violations.

```
copy_to_user_ret(void *to, void *from, unsigned long size, int ret)
copy_from_user_ret(void *to, void *from, unsigned long size, int ret)
```

It should be noted that all of the above rely on being run in the context of a process. This means that using them from interrupt handlers and timer functions, for example, is strictly prohibited. In these situations the kernel functions are not working on behalf of a specific process and there is no way to know if current is related to you in any way. In these situations it is far more advisable to copy data to a buffer maintained by the driver and later move the data to user space. Or, as will be seen next, memory mapping of device driver buffers can be implemented and solve the problems without resorting to an extra copy.

Simple Memory Mapping

Instead of copying data back and forth between user and kernel space incessantly, at times it is more advantageous to simply provide the applications a way to continuously view in-device memory. The concept is called **memory mapping** and you may already have used it in applications to map entire files and read or write to them through pointers, instead of using the ordinary file oriented read or write. If not, Chapter 3 contains an explanation of what mmap is and how it is used in user space. In particular, many of the arguments are explained there and they map directly to what we are going to do here.

It is not always safe or possible to copy data directly to user space. The scheduler might schedule the process in question out, which would be fatal from an interrupt handler, for example. One possible solution is to maintain an internal buffer and have such functions write and read there and later copy the data to the appropriate place. That causes additional overhead since two copies of the same data have to be made, one to the internal buffer and an extra one to the application's memory area. However, if the driver implements the mmap driver entry point, a given application can directly obtain a viewpoint into the driver buffer and the need for a second copy is thus gone.

schar_mmap is added to the file_operations structure to declare that we support this operation. Let's look at the Schar implementation.

```
static int schar_mmap(struct file *file,
              struct vm_area_struct *vma)
{
   unsigned long size;

   /* mmap flags - could be read and write, also */
   MSG("mmap: %s\n", vma->vm_flags & VM_WRITE ? "write" :
       "read");

   /* we will not accept an offset into the page */
   if(vma->vm_offset != 0) {
      MSG("mmap: offset must be 0\n");
      return -EINVAL;
   }

   /* schar_buffer is only one page */
   size = vma->vm_end - vma->vm_start;
   if (size != PAGE_SIZE) {
      MSG("mmap: wanted %lu, but PAGE_SIZE is %lu\n",
         size, PAGE_SIZE);
      return -EINVAL;
   }

   /* remap user buffer */
   if (remap_page_range(vma->vm_start,
       virt_to_phys(schar_buffer),
       size, vma->vm_page_prot))
      return -EAGAIN;

   return 0;
}
```

We receive two arguments in the function – a file structure and the virtual memory area that will be associated with the mapping. As mentioned earlier, vm_start and vm_end signify the beginning and end of the mapping and the total size wanted can be deduced from the difference between the two. Schar's buffer is only one page long, which is why mappings bigger than that are rejected. vm_offset would be the offset into the buffer. In this case it wouldn't make much sense to allow an offset into a single page and schar_mmap rejects the mapping if one was specified.

The final step is the most important one. `remap_page_range` updates the page tables from the `vma->vm_start` memory location with `size` being the total length in bytes. The physical address is effectively mapped into the virtual address space.

```
remap_page_range(unsigned long from, unsigned long phys_addr,
                 unsigned long size, pgprot_t prot)
```

The return value is 0 in case of success and `-ENOMEM` if it failed. The `prot` argument specifies the protection associated with the area; `MAP_SHARED` for a shared area, `MAP_PRIVATE` for a private, etc. `Schar` passes it directly from the one given to `mmap` in the application.

The page, or pages, being mapped must be locked so as to not be considered for other use by the kernel. Every page present in the system has an entry in the `mem_map[]` array and we can look up the page allocated in there and set the necessary attributes.

`unsigned long MAP_NR(unsigned long page_addr)`	Return the index in mem_map for the page.

`Schar` allocates a page of memory and calls `mem_map_reserve` for the index returned by `MAP_NR`, which makes sure that `Schar` has the page completely to itself. The page is unlocked by `mem_map_unreserve` and freed in `cleanup_module` when the driver is unloaded. This order of operation is important, as `free_page` will not free a page that is reserved. The entire page structure along with all the different flags attributes can be found in `linux/mm.h`.

This was an example of how to access the kernel's virtual memory from user space by making `remap_page_range` do the work for us. In many cases, however, memory mapping from drivers allows access to the buffers on peripheral devices. The next section will introduce I/O memory and, among other things, will briefly touch upon how to do that.

I/O Memory

The last kind of address space we are going to look at is I/O memory. This can be both ISA memory below the 1 Mb boundary or high PCI memory, but we conceptually use the same access method for both. I/O memory is not memory in the ordinary sense, but rather ports or buffers mapped into that area. A peripheral may have a status port or onboard buffers that we would like to gain access to. The sample module `Iomap` gives a demonstration of these principles and can be used to read and write or memory map a region of I/O memory.

Where I/O memory is mapped to, depends highly on the platform in question. On the Intel platform simple pointer dereferencing can be used to access low memory, but it is not always in the physical address space and therefore must be remapped before we can get a hold of it.

```
void *ioremap(unsigned long offset, unsigned long size)
```

ioremap maps a physical memory location to a kernel pointer of the wanted size. Iomap uses it to remap the framebuffer of a graphics adapter (the main intended use for the module) to a virtual address we can access from within the driver. An Iomap device consists of:

```
struct Iomap {
   unsigned long base;
   unsigned long size;
   char *ptr;
}
```

Where base is the starting location of the frame buffer, size is the length of the buffer, and ptr is what ioremap returns. The base address can be determined from /proc/pci – provided you have a PCI or AGP adapter – it is the prefetchable location listed there:

```
$ cat /proc/pci
PCI devices found:
  Bus  1, device   0, function  0:
    VGA compatible controller: NVidia Unknown device (rev 17).
      Vendor id=10de. Device id=29.
      Medium devsel.  Fast back-to-back capable.   IRQ 16.  Master Capable.
Latency=64.   Min Gnt=5.Max Lat=1.
      Non-prefetchable 32 bit memory at 0xdf000000 [0xdf000000].
      Prefetchable 32 bit memory at 0xe2000000 [0xe2000008].
```

Find your graphics adapter among the different PCI devices in your system and locate the memory listed as prefetchable – as you can see, that would be 0xe2000000 on this system. Iomap can manage up to sixteen different mappings all set up through ioctl commands. We'll need this value when trying out Iomap a little later.

Once the region has been remapped, data can be read and written to. Iomap using byte size functions.

```
unsigned char *readb(void *addr)
unsigned char *writeb(unsigned char data, void *addr)
```

readb returns the byte read from addr and writeb writes data to specified location. The latter also returns what it wrote, if you need that functionality. In addition doubleword and long versions also exist.

```
unsigned short *readw(void *addr)
unsigned short *writew(unsigned short data, void *addr)
unsigned long *readl(void *addr)
unsigned long *writel(unsigned long data, void *addr)
```

If IOMAP_BYTE_WISE is defined, this is how Iomap reads and writes data. As one would expect, they are not that fast when doing copies of the megabyte size since that is not their intended use. When IOMAP_BYTE_WISE is not defined, Iomap utilizes other functions to copy data back and forth.

```
void *memcpy_fromio(void *to, const void *from, unsigned long size)
void *memcpy_toio(void *to, const void *from, unsigned long size)
```

They work exactly like memcpy, but operate on I/O memory instead. A memset version also exists that sets the entire region to a specific value.

```
void *memset_io(void *addr, int value, unsigned long size)
```

Iomap's read and write functions work basically just like Schar's, for example, so we are not going to list them here. Data is moved between user space and the remapped I/O memory through a kernel buffer and the file position is incremented.

At module cleanup time, the remapped regions must be undone. The pointer returned from ioremap is passed to iounmap to delete the mapping.

```
void iounmap(void *addr)
```

Portability

The data returned by the read and write functions is in little endian format, whether that is the native byte ordering on the target machine or not. This is the ordering used in PCI peripherals' configuration space, for example, and the above functions will byte swap the data if necessary. If data needs to be converted between the two data types, Linux includes the primitives to do so. The section on portability will look closer at that.

Assignment of Devices in Iomap

Iomap keeps a global array of the possible devices created, indexed by minor numbers. This is a widely used approach to managing multiple devices and is easy to work with. The global array, iomap_dev, holds pointers to all the potential accessed devices. In all the device entry points, the device being acted upon is extracted from the array.

```
Iomap *idev = iomap_dev[MINOR(inode->i_rdev)];
```

In the cases where an inode is not directly passed to the function, it can be extracted from the file structure. It contains a pointer to the dentry (directory entry) associated with the file, and the inode can be found in that structure.

```
Iomap *idev = iomap_dev[MINOR(file->f_dentry->d_inode->i_rdev)];
```

I/O Memory mmap

In addition to being read and written ordinarily, Iomap supports memory mapping of the remapped I/O memory. The actual remapping of pages is very similar to Schar, with the deviation that since actual physical pages are not being mapped no locking needs to be done. Remember that I/O memory is not real RAM and thus no entries exists for it in mem_map.

```
remap_page_range(vma->vm_start, idev->base, size,
                 vma->vm_page_prot)
```

As with Schar, remap_page_range is the heart of iomap_mmap. It does the hard work for us in setting up the page tables. The actual function doesn't require much code.

```
static int iomap_mmap(struct file *file, struct vm_area_struct *vma)
{
    Iomap *idev = iomap_dev[MINOR(file->f_dentry->d_inode->i_rdev)];
    unsigned long size;

    /* no such device */
    if (!idev->base)
        return -ENXIO;

    /* size must be a multiple of PAGE_SIZE */
    size = vma->vm_end - vma->vm_start;
    if (size % PAGE_SIZE)
        return -EINVAL;

    /* remap the range */
    if (remap_page_range(vma->vm_start, idev->base, size,
                vma->vm_page_prot))
        return -EAGAIN;

    MSG("region mmapped\n");
    return 0;
}
```

We start by finding the specific device in the `iomap_dev` array and check whether this particular device has been set up. If it hasn't, we return an appropriate error message. We also require that the range that is going to be remapped is a multiple of the page size and return an error. If all is in order, we call `remap_page_range` and let it do its job.

Try it out – the Iomap module

`Iomap`'s source is also included in the code download from the Wrox website. Go to the `modules/iomap` directory, where you should find the following files:

```
$ ls
iomap.c     iomap.h    iomap_setup.c     Makefile
```

1. As root, run make to build the `iomap` module, and make two special file entries, one with minor 0 and one with minor 1, then insert the module.

```
# make
# mknod /dev/iomap0 c 42 0
# mknod /dev/iomap1 c 42 1
# insmod iomap.o
iomap: module loaded
```

2. Now we are ready to take it for a spin. `Iomap` won't do anything on its own, so we need to set up two devices to experiment with. First you will need to dig up the base address of the frame buffer on your display adapter - examine `/proc/pci` as explained at the beginning of the I/O memory section. Recall that the address was 0xe200000 on this system. We will need this now when creating a small program that sets up the two devices through `ioctl` calls. Create a file called `iomap_setup.c` in the directory where the Iomap module sources are located, or edit the existing code, containing the following:

```
#include <stdio.h>
#include <fcntl.h>
#include <sys/ioctl.h>

#include "iomap.h"

#define BASE    0xe2000000

int main(int argc, char *argv[])
{
```

```
    int fd1 = open("/dev/iomap0", O_RDWR);
    int fd2 = open("/dev/iomap1", O_RDWR);
    Iomap dev1, dev2;

    if (fd1 == -1 || fd2 == -1) {
        perror("open");
        return 1;
    }

    /* setup first device */
    dev1.base = BASE;
    dev1.size = 512 * 1024;
    if (ioctl(fd1, IOMAP_SET, &dev1)) {
        perror("ioctl");
        return 2;
    }

    /* setup second device, offset the size of the first device */
    dev2.base = BASE + dev1.size;
    dev2.size = 512 * 1024;
    if (ioctl(fd2, IOMAP_SET, &dev2)) {
        perror("ioctl");
        return 3;
    }

    return 0;
}
```

As you'd expect, you should change `BASE` to point to your frame buffer address! Otherwise we might end up writing to another device in your system, which could be fatal. Compile and run the `iomap_setup` program, this should define the two devices that we are going to operate on.

```
$ cc -Wall -o iomap_setup iomap_setup.c
$ ./iomap_setup
iomap: setting up minor 0
iomap: setup: 0xe2000000 extending 0x80000 bytes
iomap: setting up minor 1
iomap: setup: 0xe2080000 extending 0x80000 bytes
```

3. We have now set up two devices, one mapping 0.5Mb from the start of the frame buffer and the other mapping 0.5Mb from the start of the first mapping. These map directly into the graphics memory of the display adapter and writing to them should cause a visible distortion on your screen. Before running the next few lines to try that out, make sure that you have X loaded and execute the commands from within a terminal there.

```
$ cp /dev/iomap1 /dev/iomap0
```

4. Now the effects of the above command should be apparent! The region on you monitor that corresponds to the mapping of the second device should now also appear at the top the screen, thus creating an odd looking X session. Continue the fun and fill the top of the monitor with garbage by copying random data to it:

```
$ dd if=/dev/random of=/dev/iomap0 bs=512 count=1024
```

I/O Ports

I/O ports are a phenomenon that is only seen on some platforms such as the x86 architecture. They can be either a status port on a peripheral device or the serial port that your mouse is connected to. Data is read and written to ports in sizes according to its width. Other platforms, the Alpha for example, don't have real ports but only I/O memory. Reading and writing to memory locations instead then achieves access to I/O data.

Linux supports a wide variety of functions to read and write to and from I/O ports. They are all variants of the same flavor and differ mainly in how wide a port they talk to. Note that this section deals with regular I/O ports, not I/O memory, which was covered above. The header file to browse for this section is `asm/io.h` - this is a very nasty file, consider yourself warned!

A driver ought to verify that a given port can be used. Another driver might already have grabbed the port we are looking for and we do not want to wreak havoc by outputting data that might confuse the device it handles.

```
int check_region(unsigned int from, unsigned long extent)
```

`from` is the port we are testing and `extent` is how wide it is counted in bytes. The return value is 0 on success or any other value if the port already taken. Once a proper port has been found, you can go ahead and request it.

```
void request_region(unsigned int from, unsigned long extent, const char *name)
void release_region(unsigned int from, unsigned long extent)
```

The parameters are almost alike – `name` is the one that shows up in `/proc/ioports` and should be considered a device label along the lines with the `/proc/devices` entry. Ports can be 8, 16, or 32-bit wide.

```
__u8  inb(unsigned int port)
__u16 inw(unsigned int port)
__u32 inl(unsigned int port)
```

The usage should be clear – they all read the respective size value from a port. The return value is the data read and, depending on what platform is used, different types fill the size requirement. The functions for writing to ports are similar.

```
void outb(__u8 data, unsigned int port)
void outw(__u16 data, unsigned int port)
void outl(__u32 data, unsigned int port)
```

Again, the typing is a bit loose because it varies from one platform to another. Typing is not the only problem with I/O ports, as some platforms don't have regular ports but emulate them by reading and writing to memory locations instead. We won't detail this any further here – your best bet is to study some of the drivers in the kernel.

In addition, Linux provides string versions that allow you to transfer more than one datum at the time efficiently.

```
void insb(unsigned int port, void *addr, unsigned long count)
void outsb(unsigned int port, void *addr, unsigned long count)
```

addr is the location in memory to transfer to or from and count is the number of units to transfer. Similar version exists for word and double word size transfers with the same naming convention as the single datum functions. They are very fast, much more efficient than building a loop around the inb, for example.

Portability

Not all platforms have regular I/O ports such as the Intel architecture, but implement them as a mapped region of regular memory. The above functions for talking to I/O ports are also not the only variants that exist as different platforms have differing needs. The data returned is in little endian format which might not be suitable and some big endian platforms provide variants that don't byte swap the result. Inspect asm/io.h from the various architectures if you are curious.

Interrupt Handling

Most real hardware does not rely on polling to control the data flow. Instead interrupts are used to signal the availability of data or other hardware conditions to the device driver and let it take the appropriate action. Writing an ISR (Interrupt Service Routine) is often surrounded by mysticism, but that can only be because people have not seen how easy it really is to do in Linux. There is nothing special about it, because Linux exports a very elegant and uncomplicated interface for registering interrupt handlers and (eventually) handling interrupts as they come in.

So what is an interrupt exactly? It is a way for a device to get the device drivers attention and tell it that the device needs to be serviced somehow. This could be to signal that data is available for transfer or that a previously queued command has now completed and the device is ready for a new one.

How interrupts are handled internally by Linux is very architecture dependent, since it all depends on what interrupt controller the platform is equipped with. If you are interested, you can find the necessary information in arch/<your arch>/kernel/irq.c, arch/i386/kernel/irq.c for example.

Interrupts that have no designated handler assigned to them, are simply acknowledged and ignored by Linux. You can find a listing of what handlers are installed on you system by listing the contents of /proc/interrupts:

```
          CPU0       CPU1
  0:   1368447    1341817   IO-APIC-edge  timer
  1:     47684      47510   IO-APIC-edge  keyboard
  2:         0          0         XT-PIC  cascade
  4:    181793     182240   IO-APIC-edge  serial
  5:    130943     130053   IO-APIC-edge  soundblaster
  ...
```

This is an incomplete listing of our system right now. The leftmost column is the interrupt number, then the numbers represent the number of times each CPU has handled the particular interrupt The last two items are the interrupt type, and finally the device that registered the handler. So the listing above reveals that CPU0 has handled 130943 interrupts from the soundblaster device and CPU1 took care of 130053. 0 is a special case – the timer interrupt (On the x86. Other platforms are different.) – and indicates the number of ticks since the system was booted. The fourth column here indicates how the interrupts are handled. This is not really important to us here and it should suffice to know that in a SMP environment the `IO-APIC` distributes the interrupts between the CPU's. `XT-PIC` is the standard interrupt controller.

Another file you might want to look at is `/proc/stat`. It contains, among other things, the total number of interrupts that have transpired. The line of interest to us now is `intr`, which has the following format: `intr total irq0 irq1 irq2 ...`, where total is the sum of all interrupts, `irq0` the sum of interrupt 0, and so forth. This file might come in handy, when you are experimenting with your first interrupt driven driver, since it also lists triggered interrupts that don't have a handler registered which `/proc/interrupts` doesn't.

Allocating an Interrupt

Now that we have looked at the interrupt statistics gathered in `/proc`, let's move on to how you can request your own IRQ. An explanation of the parameters follows below.

```
int request_irq(unsigned int irq,
      void (*handler)(int, void *, struct pt_regs *),
      unsigned long irqflags,
      const char *devname,
      void *dev_id)
```

`request_irq` returns 0 on success and failure is indicated by an appropriate negative error – most notably, `-EINVAL` is returned if the IRQ is out of range and `-EBUSY` if a shared handler was requested and the `irqflags` do not match with an already installed handler.

`irq`	The actual IRQ that you wish to handle.
`handler(int irq, void *dev_id, struct pt_regs *regs)`	When the interrupts occurs this is the function that gets called. This is the IRQ handler.
`irqflags`	This controls the behavior of the interrupt. We will look more at that later.
`devname`	The name that is listed in `/proc/interrupts`.
`dev_id`	Helps support sharing of interrupts. It is the one that is passed to the handler given and can thus be used if you need to pass it information. The IDE subsystem, for example, uses it to distinguish between the master and slave that it controls per interrupt.

The `irqflags` parameter is comprised of several possible combinations.

SA_INTERRUPT	A handler registered with this flag runs with all IRQ's disabled. Not setting it only disables the IRQ being serviced by the handler.
SA_SHIRQ	Enable the IRQ line to be shared between more than one device. The drivers must also agree on the rest of the `irqflags` mask and supply the proper `dev_id`, otherwise sharing is not allowed.
SA_SAMPLE_RANDOM	The Linux kernel keeps an internal entropy pool managed by the `random` device. If the device being managed by the handler does not interrupt at a fixed rate, it may be able to contribute to the randomness of this pool and the flag should be set. Naturally, this depends heavily on the actual hardware being driven.

The handler being registered receives three arguments when invoked. `irq` can only be considered useful if the handler manages more than one IRQ, otherwise you know what specific interrupt that occurred. `regs` contains the imagery of the CPU registers before the interrupt occurred. It is rarely useful, but find the definition in `asm/ptrace.h` if you are curious. The second argument is `dev_id`, which we already covered.

Unregistering an IRQ handler is done with `free_irq`. The arguments are similar to `request_irq` and need no further explanation.

```
void free_irq(unsigned int irq, void *dev_id)
```

Getting an Appropriate IRQ

Before you can register a handler to use with your driver you have to find out what IRQ to use. This is highly hardware dependent, both with regards to the type of peripheral device and the host bus, be it ISA, PCI, or SBUS (A host bus found on the SPARC). Regarding the former, some devices will let you read the configuration from a status port; others you may have to probe. If you are going to write a driver for a real piece of hardware you need the programming specifications from the vendor and they will tell you how to correctly retrieve the needed information.

The most prevalent bus types are ISA and PCI (at least on the Intel platform). Although efforts have been made to partially add plug-and-play capabilities to ISA devices, ISA was invented before plug-and-play was an issue and no real standard exists. Besides, we have probably all experienced how well that works... PCI devices provide a clean and standardized way to retrieve configuration information without resorting to nasty probing and guesswork. How to handle PCI devices is beyond the scope of this book. `linux/pci.h` is a good place to start if you want to deal with PCI and, as always, plenty of examples exist within the Linux sources. The rest of this section will only deal with legacy devices.

If the hardware allows you to retrieve the configuration directly, you will not have to do any probing yourself. As mentioned previously, this information is located in hardware device manuals and we can't say anything generic about that. Linux provides interrupt detection for devices that don't support nicer alternatives.

```
unsigned long probe_irq_on(void)
int probe_irq_off(unsigned long unused)
```

probe_irq_on initiates the probing sequence and probe_irq_off ends it. In between you should put code that will trigger an IRQ from the device and this will then be the return value from probe_irq_off. If more than one IRQ fired, probe_irq_off will return a negative value (in fact corresponding to the first triggered IRQ found, which could provide some hint). The probing sequence will typically look something like the below:

```
int irq;
unsigned long foo;

/* clear dangling interrupts */
probe_irq_off(probe_irq_on());

foo = probe_irq_on();

/* this should provoke an interrupt from the device */
outb(TRIGGER_IRQ, PORT);

irq = probe_irq_off(uu);

if (irq > 0)
   printk("irq %d detected\n", irq);
```

This is purely a theoretical example of how you might detect the IRQ used. The value returned by probe_irq_on is purely bogus and explains why probe_irq_off names it unused. The interesting part is what is returned after the probe – hopefully the interrupt you need.

The IRQ Handler

Once you have the available IRQ that you need, you need to write a handler to deal with the device interrupts. The job of the handler is to acknowledge the interrupt and service the device in some way. Typically some form of data is available and should be transferred from the device, or a state change occurred and the hardware wants to let us know about it. The handler runs either with all interrupts enabled except its own or no interrupts enabled depending on whether SA_INTERRUPT was specified, so any interrupts from the same device are lost until the handler has finished running. We'll see later how to deal with that issue.

The normal flow of execution is halted when an interrupt occurs – the kernel stops what it was currently doing and invokes the appropriate handler registered. Interrupt handlers are different from the normal driver entry points in that they run at interrupt time and as such are not running on behalf of a specific process. That means that the current process typically doesn't have any relation to the driver and it shouldn't be touched. This also includes any access to user space, such as copying data back and forth.

Interrupt handlers should finish as soon as possible, since you may otherwise miss another interrupt from the device. If you share the interrupt with another device, you are also preventing interrupts from there being serviced. Although it has been mentioned before, it is important to stress that you must not block at interrupt time. If you do, the scheduler may be invoked and this is not allowed. It will inform you of such an occurrence with "Scheduling in interrupt" on the console followed by an Oops. Nor are you allowed to sleep in the handler. In general, think carefully about how you interact with the rest of the system while running at interrupt time.

There is nothing special about interrupt handlers other than what is mentioned above, so we won't give detailed examples on how to write one. As with the probe example, here is a theoretical interrupt handler:

```
void our_intr(int irq, void *dev_id, struct pt_regs *regs)
{
   int status;

   printk("received interrupt %d\n", irq);

   /* reading status from board */
   inb(STATUS_PORT, status);

   /* we are sharing irq, check if it was our board */
   if (status & MY_IRQ_STAT)
      return;

   /* acknowledge IRQ */
   outb(STATUS_PORT, MY_ACK_IRQ);

   >transfer data from the device, if needed<

   /* schedule bottom half for execution */
   our_taskqueue.routine = (void *)(void *)our_bh;
   our_taskqueue.data = (void *)dev_id;
   queue_task(&our_taskqueue, &tq_immediate);
   mark_bh(IMMEDIATE_BH);

   return;
}
```

The first thing we do is check whether the IRQ was generated from the device the driver is managing by reading a status from a designated port on the hardware. This is one way of handling interrupt sharing. If the handler was controlling several instances of the same hardware device, we could have used `dev_id` to differentiate between them.

Bottom Halves

The above handler introduces a new concept, bottom halves. They were mentioned briefly in the section on task queues, but they deserve a little more attention. Instead of doing all the work in the actual interrupt handler, we declare a task queue and add it to the immediate queue (thus guaranteeing very swift execution). `our_bh` is the bottom half for this device and will be consumed by the immediate queue as soon as we return from the top half (the actual interrupt handler). The top half will most likely copy data from the device to an internal buffer and let the bottom half deal with necessary processing.

Whether keeping a separate bottom half is worth the effort, depends on how much time you need to spend in the top half and if the IRQ is shared or not. As soon as the interrupt handler returns from execution, the device IRQ reporting is enabled again. Bottom halves thus run with the device IRQ active and thereby allow the handler to service more interrupts than it otherwise would have been able to. Bottom halves are atomic with respect to each other, so you don't have to worry about being reentered. A top half, however, can be invoked while the bottom half is still executing. If a bottom half is marked while it is running it will be run again as soon as possible, but marking it twice will still only make it run once.

Often you need to share data between the two, since the bottom half is doing work for the top half. This requires some care. We will look more about atomicity and reentrancy in a dedicated section.

You don't have to use `tq_immediate`, but it is usually the one used simply because it is the quickest. Since the regular bottom halves are all predefined in the kernel, this is the replacement to use if you need it.

Reentrancy

One of the more important issues with device drivers is the issue of **reentrancy**. We have already discussed some of the issues loosely throughout the text, but only in passing and the issue clearly needs more attention than that. Imagine having your driver opened by several processes at once. Often a driver for a real device has to maintain several internal structures that are manipulated in a myriad of places. It goes without saying that the integrity of these structures must remain intact, so how do you make sure that two processes aren't modifying the same structure at the same time? The issue is even more important as SMP systems are becoming more prevalent and having two CPUs these days is not uncommon. Linux 2.0 solved this problem by guarding the entire kernel space with a big lock thus making sure that only one CPU was spending time in the kernel at the time. While this solution worked, it didn't scale very well as the number of CPU's increased.

During the 2.1 development cycle it became apparent that finer grained locking was needed if Linux was to conquer machines with more than two CPU's and do it well. So instead of having one big lock and having processes acquire it upon entering kernel space, new locking primitives were introduced. Important data structures inside the kernel are now guarded with a separate lock and having numerous processes executing inside the kernel is now possible. Sections of code that modify structures that can also be modified by others at the same time are called **critical sections** and this is the piece of code we need to protect against reentrancy.

As we mentioned earlier, a process running in kernel space can't be preempted on its own so you can be assured that `current` won't change beneath you – they have to give up execution. This was almost true. Actually, interrupts can come in at any time and will break the current flow of execution. Of course there is also the issue of putting processes to sleep and explicitly doing a schedule from within the driver – here we must also be prepared to handle the consequences of being reentered. Does this mean that you have to guard all variables? No, luckily only global structures share the same address space. Variables local to a function reside in the kernel stack for that process and are thus distinct to each accessing process.

```
int global;

int device_open(struct inode *inode, struct file *file)
{
   int local;

   printk("pid = %d : ", current->pid);
   printk("global = 0x%p, local = 0x%p\n", &global, &local);
   ...
}
```

The output of the above code in a module verifies that this is true, global variables are shared while local variables are different copies:

```
pid = 909 : global = 0xc18005fc, local = 0xc08d3f2c
pid = 910 : global = 0xc18005fc, local = 0xc098df2c
```

While having local variables residing in the kernel stack is a relief it also places certain constraints on what you can fit in that space. Linux 2.2 reserves approximately 7 Kb of kernel stack per process, which should be plentiful for most needs. Some of this is reserved for interrupt handling and the likes – you should be careful not to overstep this limit. Should you need more than approximately 6 Kb, you must allocate it dynamically.

The classic way of guarding yourself against reentrancy was to disable interrupts globally, do your work, and enable interrupts again. Interrupt handlers, and everything else that runs at interrupt time, work asynchronously with your driver and structures that are modified by these handlers need to be protected against being changed while you are working with them.

```
unsigned long flags;

/* save processor flags and disable interrupts */
save_flags(flags);
cli();

_read/modify structures, critical section_

restore_flags(flags);
```

While this still works, it disables interrupts across all CPU's and as such it is a slow and non-cooperative way of guarding yourself. If the target system is guaranteed to be UP (single CPU systems), this is all you need since only one CPU can be executing kernel code. Instructions are thus guaranteed to be serialized and are therefore atomic in respect to each other.

Disabling Single Interrupts

If you know that only your own interrupt handler modifies the internal structures, it can be considered overkill to disable all interrupts in the system. All you really need is to make sure that your own handler doesn't run while you are mucking around with them. In this case Linux provides functions to disable a single IRQ line.

```
void disable_irq(unsigned int irq);
void disable_irq_nosync(unsigned int irq);
void enable_irq(unsigned int irq);
```

The critical region can thus be placed between a `disable` and `enable` of the interrupt, and the top half will not be invoked if the interrupt line is raised. The difference between the regular `disable_irq` and the `_nosync` version is that the former guarantees that the specified IRQ is not running on any CPU before returning, while the latter will disable the specified interrupt and return even if a top half handler is still running.

Atomicity

Instructions are said to be atomic when you know there are executed in one go, i.e. you will not be interrupted until you are done. Disabling interrupts accomplishes this, as we saw above, since no one can interrupt us in the critical section. Linux also offers atomic primitives that act on variables without the need to lock everybody else out. They are defined in `asm/atomic.h`.

```
void atomic_add(int i, volatile atomic_t *v)
void atomic_sub(int i, volatile atomic_t *v)
void atomic_inc(volatile atomic_t *v)
void atomic_dec(volatile atomic_t *v)
int atomic_dec_and_test(volatile atomic_t *v)
```

As you can see these operate on the `atomic_t` type which is a structure containing only a counter member. What it contains doesn't really matter, since you should only access it via the `atomic_x` functions and macros. Only then are you insured atomicity. They are mainly used for keeping count for semaphores, but can be used any way you please.

Atomic operations are often needed to prevent race conditions. A race exists when a process decides to sleep on an event based on evaluating an expression non-atomically. `Schar` does not have such a construct, but it is common enough that we will give an example.

```
/* if device is busy, sleep */
if (device->stat & BUSY)
   sleep_on(&queue);
```

If the test for device busy is not atomic, the condition may become false after the test but before `sleep_on` is invoked. The process may sleep forever on the queue. Linux has some handy bit testing operations that are guaranteed to execute atomically.

`set_bit(int nr, volatile void *addr)`
`clear_bit(int nr, volatile void *addr)`
`test_bit(int nr, volatile void *addr)`
	Set, clear, or test the bit specified in `nr` from the bitmask at `addr`.

The above device busy test could then be implemented as:

```
/* if device is busy, sleep */
if (test_bit(BUSY, &device->stat)
   sleep_on(queue);
```

and be completely race safe. There are several others, including test-and-set operations as well, defined in `asm/bitops.h`.

Protecting Critical Sections

Going with the assumption that your modules are only going to be run on UP systems is clearly a very bad idea. Linux provides two variants of spin locks that can be used to protect structures against manipulation. On UP systems this defaults to the above construct of disabling interrupts with `cli`, while on SMP systems they only disable interrupts on the local CPU. The latter is sufficient as long as all the functions on your driver acquire the same spin lock before modifying shared structures.

Basic Spin Locks

Spin locks are one of the most basic locking primitives. A process trying to enter a critical region already protected by another process with a spin lock, will "spin", or loop, until the lock is released and can be acquired.

The different types of spin locks can be found in `asm/spinlock.h`. This is also the file to inspect if you are at all interested in how they are implemented differently in single and multiple CPU configurations. There are two basic types implemented in Linux.

```
spinlock_t our_lock = SPIN_LOCK_UNLOCKED;
unsigned long flags;

spin_lock(&our_lock);
spin_lock_irqsave(&our_lock, flags);
```

If the structures are not going to be modified at interrupt time, `spin_lock` is all you need. It provides safety from modification across CPU's, but doesn't disable interrupts even on the local CPU. This makes it faster than `spin_lock_irqsave`, which also provides assurance against interrupt handlers.

```
spin_unlock(&our_lock);
spin_unlock_irqrestore(&our_lock, flags);
```

These are the equivalent unlocking macros to be used when you're done modifying structures.

There are a lot more functions in `asm/spinlock.h`, including macros that allow you to test whether getting a lock will succeed before trying to acquire it, and others. If you need more functionality you can find the needed information in there.

Reader and Writer Locks

The above spin locks provide full locking and protect the code in between from being reentered for any purpose. It may also be useful to further differentiate access to structures; access with the purpose of only reading data, or write access. For this purpose Linux provides locks that allow you to acquire either read or write access, thus allowing multiple readers or a single writer to enter the critical region at the same time.

```
rwlock_t our_lock = RW_LOCK_UNLOCKED;
unsigned long flags;

read_lock(&our_lock);
read_lock_irqsave(&our_lock, flags);
write_lock(&our_lock);
write_lock_irqsave(&our_lock, flags);
```

The semantics are exactly the same as for basic spin locks, so we won't explain them further. Unlocking the region is provided by similar macros.

```
read_unlock(&our_lock);
read_unlock_irqrestore(&our_lock, flags);
write_unlock(&our_lock);
write_unlock_irqrestore(&our_lock, flags);
```

Now you know how to protect yourself effectively against the gruesome effects of reentrancy with basic spin locks and reader/writer spin locks. In a UP environment the non-IRQ versions all expand to no-ops (IRQ versions still disable interrupts, since they are handled as soon as they come in and therefore still run asynchronously) so you will not lose performance there, but the behavior on SMP systems is far more attractive than the basic `cli` construct.

Automated Locking

Most of the functions available to device drivers are protected internally by spin locks, courtesy of the kernel, and no extra locking is thus required. An example of such was given in the section on timers, where `add_timer` internally acquired the `timer_list` lock before manipulating the given timer structure. If the timer is local to the function no locking is needed and `internal_add_timer` could be called directly. However, it is recommended to always use the "safer" variants and this subsection is purely added in case you were wondering why no locking was used to maintain integrity of wait queue or timer lists in `Schar`, for example.

Block Devices

The second class of devices that are covered in this book is block devices. They are entirely different creatures than character drivers in that they don't serve bytes of data, but entire blocks instead. While character drivers are usually accessed directly from applications by reading and writing to them, block device accesses go through the buffer cache in the system.

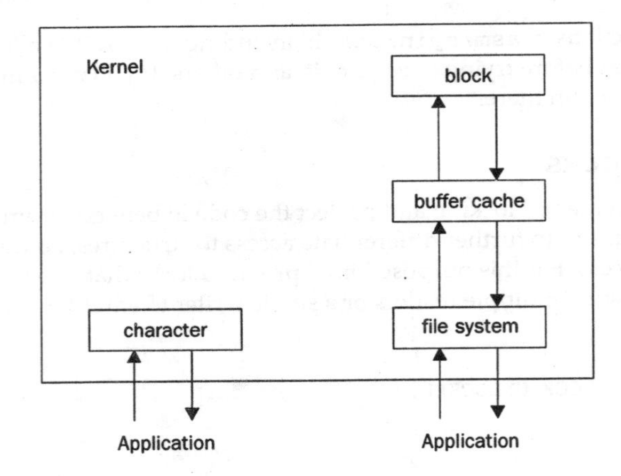

The illustration above is a half-truth since only reading and writing of blocks passes through the buffer cache. `open`, `close`, and `ioctl` have normal entry points, for example.

Block devices usually host file systems and can be accessed randomly by specifying which block to read or write. This is in contrast to character drivers, which only allow sequential, non-random access and thus cannot be used for providing file system storage.

Linux does not distinguish sharply between the two and even provides the same interface for both. When we were designing the first character driver, `Schar`, some of the elements of the `file_operations` structure did not lend themselves to a character oriented access scheme, exactly because the same one is used for both types of devices.

Radimo – A Simple RAM Disk Module

The best way to get a little familiar with the inner workings of block devices and the underlying system they depend on is to dig in with a working example. `Radimo` is RAM disk driver that will host a file system of varying size, depending on the available memory in the system.

At the heart of every block device driver is the request function. This is the one that receives the read and write requests and turns them into something that the device can comprehend. If we were to write an IDE driver, the request function would generate commands and send them to the controller to initiate the transfer of data in both directions. Several items, including the request function, need to be defined in a special order at the beginning of the module. The normal order of include files apply, but the items below must be defined before `<linux/blk.h>` is included.

`#define MAJOR_NR`	`RADIMO_MAJOR`	The major number of the device. This is mandatory.
`#define DEVICE_NAME`	`"radimo"`	The name of the device – may be omitted and is then set to "unknown". Serves no particular function other than providing a name to be printed in case of request errors.
`#define DEVICE_REQUEST`	`radimo_request`	The request function for the device. Is also mandatory.
`#define DEVICE_NR(device)`	`(MINOR(device))`	Used for partionable devices to enable them to use the minor number for partition selection.
`#define DEVICE_ON(device)` `#define DEVICE_OFF(device)`		Motorized devices can set this to the functions related to spinning the device up and down. When a request has ended, the block system will call the off function. `DEVICE_OFF` must be defined even as just an empty define, but `DEVICE_ON` can be omitted.

`#define DEVICE_NO_RANDOM`	If defined, the device will not contribute to system entropy. This is similar to `SA_SAMPLE_RANDOM` for interrupt handlers.

After having defined the above, `linux/blk.h` can be included.

Size Issues

There are two sector sizes associated with a block device, a hardware and software sector size. The former is how the data is arranged on the physical media controlled by the device while the latter is the arrangement within the device. By far the majority of devices have a hardware sector size of 512 bytes, although deviants such as MO-drives do exist and typically use 2048 byte sector sizes.

The respective sizes are set at initialization time in global arrays indexed by major number.

```
#define RADIMO_HARDS_SIZE              512
#define RADIMO_BLOCK_SIZE              1024
static int radimo_hard = RADIMO_HARDS_SIZE;
static int radimo_soft = RADIMO_BLOCK_SIZE;

...

hardsect_size[RADIMO_MAJOR] = &radimo_hard;
blksize_size[RADIMO_MAJOR] = &radimo_soft;
```

We go with the flow and use a hardware sector size of 512 bytes. It does not really matter, since `Radimo` stores data in a buffer internally. The software block size can be any value, with a couple of restrictions: it has to be equal to or bigger than the hardware sector size, a multiple of the hardware sector size, and smaller then the `PAGE_SIZE`. If you neglect to set either one, 512 is assumed for the hardware sector size and 1024 for the block size.

In addition to the sector sizes, the total size of the device is also kept in a global array. The size argument is given in Kb and lets the kernel return `-ENOSPC` (No space left on device) automatically.

```
blk_size[RADIMO_MAJOR] = &radimo_size;
```

It is interesting to note that if we kept several virtual devices (indexed by minor, for example) `radimo_size` and friends could be an array and thus get `[MAJOR][MINOR]` indexing. The actual definition of the various block related global structures reside in `drivers/block/ll_rw_blk.c` which also contains comments about them.

Registering a Block Device

Once the various defining is done, a file operations structure is set up.

```
static struct file_operations radimo_fops = {
    NULL,                       /* llseek */
    block_read,                 /* generic block read */
    block_write,                /* generic block write */
    NULL,                       /* readdir */
    NULL,                       /* poll */
    radimo_ioctl,
    NULL,                       /* mmap */
    radimo_open,
    NULL,                       /* flush */
    radimo_release,
    NULL,                       /* fsync */
    NULL,                       /* fasync */
    radimo_media_change,
    radimo_revalidate,
    NULL                        /* lock */
};
```

The file operations structure sets up our communications system. There is usually no need to define our own read and write functions as the defaults set up the request and call `ll_rw_block` which queues the requests for us to execute. The defaults can be found in `fs/block_dev.c` and `drivers/block/ll_rw_block.c`, but you don't really need to know the inner workings to be comfortable with block devices. We define our own `ioctl` function – for a block device to function properly with the standard file system utilities, there are some `ioctl` commands we have to support. We will look at them a little later. `open` and `release` serve the same purpose as with character devices and that just leaves `radimo_media_change`.

Finally the block device is registered much the same way as the character devices.

```
res = register_blkdev(RADIMO_MAJOR, "radimo", &radimo_fops);
if (res) {
    MSG(RADIMO_ERROR, "couldn't register block device\n");
    return res;
}
```

Media Change

Whenever a block device is being mounted, the defined `check_media_change` function is called to detect whether the medium has changed or not. Being a RAM disk driver this can never be the case, but we will play along and pretend it can happen anyway. Radimo sets up an internal timer that clears our storage every 60 seconds if the device is not busy. In addition, it invalidates any buffers that might be in the buffer cache in the system, forcing them to be re-read instead of being served from the cache. The buffers are in fact invalidated by the VFS when we return 1 to indicate a media change, but that won't happen until mount time. Buffers might still be cached if the user simply copied the device raw with `dd` or `cp`.

`revalidate` is closely related to the media change. If a change has occurred, `radimo_media_change` returns 1 to inform the VFS of the change. Next, the `revalidate` function is called to allow the device to perform whatever it needs to update its internal device information. There is no need to implement a speçific `revalidate` function if the necessary actions can be taken in the media change function. Nor does it matter what you return – the function is strictly called for your pleasure.

ioctl for Block Devices

Since block devices are used to host file systems, it seems only appropriate that all block devices should accept some standard `ioctl` commands. We looked at implementing `ioctl`'s earlier and you might want to skip back if you want to have your memory refreshed. `Radimo` implements the most common and standard ones.

BLKFLSBUF	**Block flush buffers.** Write out all dirty buffers currently residing in the buffer cache. `Radimo` does nothing more than call `fsync` to write the out dirty buffers andinvalidate them.
BLKGETSIZE	**Block get size.** Return the size of the device in units of 1024 bytes. The various file system related utilities (`fsck`, for instance) determine the total size by issuing this `ioctl`. If the device does not support this command, they will have to guess.
BLKSSZGET	**Block get sector size.** Return the software sector size of the block device.
BLKRAGET	**Block get read ahead.** Return the current read ahead value for the device.
BLKRASET	**Block set read ahead.** Set the read ahead value for the device.
BLKRRPART	**Block re-read partition table.** Called by `fdisk` when rewriting the partition table. `Radimo` is not partionable and does not support this command.

The implementation is fairly straightforward so we won't list it here. There are other standard commands for block devices – find them in `linux/fs.h` if you are interested. Radimo does not implement any device specific commands, but if it did they would naturally be enclosed within the same switch statement.

The Request Function

The `request` function is definitely the backbone of the block device. In contrast to character devices which receive a stream of data, block devices process requests instead. A request is either a read or a write and it is the job of the `request` function to either retrieve or store the data sent to it on the media it controls. Depending on the peripheral in question, the actions performed by the `request` function naturally differs a lot.

Requests are stored in lists of structures, each of which are of the type `struct request`. The function does not need to traverse the list itself, but instead accesses the request via the `CURRENT` macro (not to be confused with `current`, the process).

```
#define CURRENT (blk_dev[MAJOR_NR].current_request)
```

The definition resides in `linux/blk.h`. The structure of the request is as follows, with the irrelevant (to our discussion of the block system) parts left out – the ones used by `Radimo` will be expanded upon further when we look at its `request` function next.

CURRENT->	
`volatile int rq_status`	Status of the request, either `RQ_ACTIVE` or `RQ_INACTIVE` (the SCSI subsystem does use more, however). The kernel uses the status internally while finding an unused entry in the list of requests.
`kdev_t rq_dev`	The device the request is for. If the driver is managing several minors, information can be extracted from here by using the `MINOR` macro.
`int cmd`	The type of request, either `READ` or `WRITE`.
`int errors`	Can be used to maintain a per-request error status count.
`unsigned long sector, current_nr_sectors`	The starting sector and number of sectors that we should act upon.
`char *buffer`	Where we should read/write the data.
`struct buffer_head *bh;`	The buffer head associated with the request. We look a bit more at buffer heads in the section about the buffer cache.

These are the details of a request. `Radimo` stores the data in an array allocated with `vmalloc` at init time and serve requests by copying the data from `CURRENT->buffer` back and forth as instructed. The sectors are thus no more than an offset into the array. Request functions have a somewhat peculiar format – let's look at `Radimo`'s version and follow up with a few comments afterward.

```
void radimo_request(void)
{
  unsigned long offset, total;

radimo_begin:

  INIT_REQUEST;

  MSG(RADIMO_REQUEST, "%s sector %lu of %lu\n",
           CURRENT->cmd == READ ? "read" : "write",
           CURRENT->sector,
           CURRENT->current_nr_sectors);

  offset = CURRENT->sector * radimo_hard;
  total = CURRENT->current_nr_sectors * radimo_hard;

  /* access beyond end of the device */
  if (total+offset > radimo_size*1024) {
     /* error in request  */
     end_request(0);
     goto radimo_begin;
  }

  MSG(RADIMO_REQUEST, "offset = %lu, total = %lu\n", offset, total);
```

```
    if (CURRENT->cmd == READ) {
        memcpy(CURRENT->buffer, radimo_storage+offset, total);
    } else if (CURRENT->cmd == WRITE) {
        memcpy(radimo_storage+offset, CURRENT->buffer, total);
    } else {
        /* can't happen */
        MSG(RADIMO_ERROR, "cmd == %d is invalid\n", CURRENT->cmd);
        end_request(0);
    }

    /* successful */
    end_request(1);

    /* let INIT_REQUEST return when we are done */
    goto radimo_begin;
}
```

The macro `INIT_REQUEST` is responsible for quite a number of actions. First, it checks whether `CURRENT` contains a request and returns if it does not. Then it performs a validity check of the request (is it really for this device?) and if the proper locking of `CURRENT->bh` is in order. The first check also explains why we continuously loop around `INIT_REQUEST`; when we are done, it will return for us. The offset into our storage array is calculated by multiplying the supplied starting sector `CURRENT->sector` by our hardware sector size. The total amount of data to be transferred is found in a similar way by examining the total number of sectors that `CURRENT->current_nr_sectors` specifies. Data is then copied with a simple `memcpy` depending on what direction `CURRENT->cmd` contains.

`void end_request(int uptodate)`	Ends the CURRENT request.

An `uptodate` value of 1 indicates that the request was successfully fulfilled. `CURRENT` is then set to the next request. If that request is also for `Radimo`, control is handed back to us and `radimo_request` continues; if not, then another `request` function is brought to life.

If the request cannot be fulfilled (it could be beyond the end of the device, for example), `end_request` is invoked with a value of 0. This will generate an I/O error in the system logs, specifying the offending device and the sector that caused the error. Note that we only receive the request from the generic block read and write functions when it has already verified that the request does not exceed the boundaries. If `blk_size[RADIMO_MAJOR]` is set to `NULL` the simple check is bypassed when the request is created and a read error can be provoked by accessing beyond the end of the device:

```
radimo: read sector 4096 of 2
end_request: I/O error, dev 2a:00 (radimo), sector 4096
```

The info printed is the device major and minor numbers in hexadecimal and the `DEVICE_NAME` defined.

The Buffer Cache

Blocks of data written and read from block devices get cached in the buffer cache. This improves system performance, because if a process wants to read a block of data just read or written, it can be served directly from the buffer cache instead of issuing a new read from the media. Internally this cache is a doubly linked list of buffer head structures indexed by a hash table. Although it initially does not look like we touched a buffer head in `radimo_request`, `CURRENT->buffer` is merely a pointer to the data field inside the buffer head.

If you are running `Radimo` with `RADIMO_REQUEST` in the `MSG` mask, you can follow the requests as they are processed by the request function. Issuing a read of, say, the same 10 blocks twice will only cause them to be read once by `Radimo`; the second time the request is served from the buffer cache. The opposite can also be investigated – try writing some blocks to the device and notice how they are not processed immediately. The blocks reside in the buffer cache for some time before being flushed to the device. Even if `Radimo` did not copy the data sent to it to internal storage, the device would be fully functional while the buffers still resided in the cache. The ram disk module that comes with the kernel (drivers/block/rd.c) uses this principal. `Rd` does nothing to maintain internal storage, but instead marks the used buffers as locked and thus ensures that they stay in the buffer cache and not be put on the freelist. `Radimo` can emulate this behavior if `RADIMO_CHEAT_REQUEST` is defined.

The buffer head structure can be found in `linux/fs.h`. Going into details would be beyond the scope of this book, but lets take a look at the state flags since they are accessed indirectly by a couple of functions in `Radimo`.

`BH_Uptodate`	The data residing in the buffer is up to date with that on disk.
`BH_Dirty`	Data in the buffer has been modified and must be written out to disk.
`BH_Lock` `BH_Protected`	Buffer has been locked and cannot be put on the free list.
`BH_Req`	Unset if the buffer was invalidated.

`invalidate_buffers` is called when we wish to remove all references to the buffers associated with `Radimo` from the buffer cache. It clears all but `BH_Lock` and the buffers are then free to be reused.

Try it out – Radimo

`Radimo` is the final module included in the source code download. It's located, naturally, in the `modules/radimo` directory. As usual, you will need to compile and insert the module and create a corresponding special file before we can interact with the device.

```
# make
# mknod /dev/radimo b 42 0
# insmod radimo.o
radimo: loaded
radimo: sector size of 512, block size of 1024, total size = 2048Kb
```

The options printed can all be specified at load time by supplying the appropriate parameters to `insmod`. Browse back to the beginning of the `Radimo` section and find them or use `modinfo` to dig them out. The defaults will do fine for this session.

Now that the module is loaded, we are ready to create a file system on the device. Any type will do, but lets use `ext2` in this example.

```
# mke2fs /dev/radimo
# dmesg | tail -n1
radimo: ioctl: BLKGETSIZE
```

Since we implemented the `BLKGETSIZE` `ioctl` call in `Radimo`, `mke2fs` can obtain the complete size of the device on its own. Now you can mount the file system and copy files to and from it, just like you would on an ordinary hard drive.

```
# mount -t ext2 /dev/radimo /mnt/radimo
# cp /vmlinuz /mnt/radimo
```

There should be nothing new in that concept. `umount` the device and leave it alone for 60 seconds, `RADIMO_TIMER_DELAY` defined in `radimo.h`, to test the media change mechanism. Now try mounting it again.

```
# umount /dev/radimo; sleep 60
# mount -t ext2 /dev/radimo /mnt/radimo
mount: wrong fs type, bad option, bad superblock on /dev/radimo,
       or too many mounted file systems
# dmesg
radimo: media has changed
VFS: Disk change detected on device radimo(42,0)
radimo: revalidate
```

On the last mount our timer handler has run and set `media_changed` to 1. This causes `radimo_media_change` to return 1 to the VFS indicating a media change, VFS prints a message confirming this and then invokes `radimo_revalidate` to let the device do any handling it might need to perform on a disc change. The end result is that the mount fails.

Going Further

This was only meant as a short introduction to block devices, mainly the `request` function with related structures and `ioctl` calls. `Radimo` is a very simple driver and as such does not demonstrate how block device drivers handle a real hardware peripheral. Actual hardware typically relies on interrupts to control the flow of data and in those cases the request function cannot indicate whether the request completed successfully or not right away. The interrupt handler normally deals with this when the device has signaled the outcome of the operation. There are myriad examples of interrupt driven block drivers in the kernel for you to study, if you need a real case to study.

As block devices are used to host file systems, they normally support partition-based access. Linux offers generic partition support defined in the `partition` and `gendisk` structure defined in `linux/genhd.h`. The implementation can be found in `gendisk.c` in `drivers/block` where various drivers that utilize the support are also located. Adding partition support to `Radimo` should not pose any significant problems and would be a good exercise in getting familiar with the generic disk subsystem. That is left as an exercise to the reader!

Most block devices in the kernel belong to a specific class, such as SCSI, IDE or even CD-ROM drivers. While these can be considered ordinary block devices, Linux offers special interfaces for these that should be utilized. The readily available examples in the kernel along with the obtainable documentation found in Documentation/ or the Linux Documentation Project is an invaluable resource in this situation.

Debugging

Device drivers are no different from regular programs; they are almost never bug free.

Kernel level code does not segmentation fault in the ordinary sense and produce nice core dumps for you to examine and so doing postmortem debugging on device drivers is very different from regular debugging. Some people might tell you that the human mind is the best debugger there is, and they are right. In this case, all we can do is go back to the source and work it through step by step. The great thing about Linux is that you have the entire source code available – use it. Using a debugger can be invaluable, but make sure you end up fixing the real bug and not just adding band-aid for hiding the real problem.

Oops Tracing

One technique that is essential to master is Oops tracing. Most kernel bugs manifests themselves as NULL pointer dereferences and depending on where they happen, the kernel can often continue running. This is much like a segmentation fault in applications, but it does not generate a core file. The layout of Oops is highly processor specific and the rest of this section will look at how the x86 version looks. The procedure for decoding the dump is basically the same for other platforms and the information provided in this section will therefore be useful on non-Intel architectures as well. Let's dive into an Oops.

```
Unable to handle kernel paging request at virtual address 01380083
current >tss.cr3 = 06704000, %cr3 = 06704000
*pde = 00000000
Oops: 0000
CPU:    1
EIP:    0010:[<c0144040>]
EFLAGS: 00010202
eax: c0144000   ebx: 01380083   ecx: 00000005   edx: c64e8550
esi: c64e9c20   edi: c5f17f84   ebp: 00000000   esp: c5f17f3c
ds: 0018   es: 0018   ss: 0018
Process bash (pid: 390, process nr: 32, stackpage=c5f17000)
Stack: c5f17f84 c64e859c c64e859c fffffffe c012dfaf c64e8550 c64e9c20
       c5f17f84 00000000 c60dd004 00000001 c012e17a c64e9620 c5f17f84
       c60dd000 c60dd000 c5f16000 bffff6b0 c60dd002 00000002 000006b3
       c012e26c c60dd000 c64e9620
Call Trace: [<c012dfaf>] [<c012e17a>] [<c012e26c>] [<c012c232>] [<c0108be4>]
Code: 66 83 3b 00 74 4e 31 c9 8b 74 24 20 66 8b 4b 02 3b 4e 44 75
```

If this the first time you have come across an Oops, it might look at bit intimidating. It contains a dump of the processor registers at the time of the fault, a stack trace, a back trace of the function calls, and a listing of the machine code that caused the Oops. This information is useless if we can't map the addresses shown to actual function names. The tool ksymoops does this for us, among other things. It is conveniently located in the scripts/ksymoops sub directory of your kernel sources. Running the above Oops through ksymoops, will yield something like the text opposite.

```
Unable to handle kernel paging request at virtual address 01380083
current >tss.cr3 = 06704000, %cr3 = 06704000
*pde = 00000000
Oops: 0000
CPU:    1
EIP:    0010:[<c0144040>]
EFLAGS: 00010202
eax: c0144000   ebx: 01380083   ecx: 00000005   edx: c64e8550
esi: c64e9c20   edi: c5f17f84   ebp: 00000000   esp: c5f17f3c
ds: 0018   es: 0018   ss: 0018
Process bash (pid: 390, process nr: 32, stackpage=c5f17000)
Stack: c5f17f84 c64e859c c64e859c fffffffe c012dfaf c64e8550 c64e9c20
       c5f17f84 00000000 c60dd004 00000001 c012e17a c64e9620 c5f17f84
       c60dd000 c60dd000 c5f16000 bffff6b0 c60dd002 00000002 000006b3
       c012e26c c60dd000 c64e9620
Call Trace: [<c012dfaf>] [<c012e17a>] [<c012e26c>] [<c012c232>] [<c0108be4>]
Code: 66 83 3b 00 74 4e 31 c9 8b 74 24 20 66 8b 4b 02 3b 4e 44 75

>>EIP: c0144040 <proc_lookup+4c/e0>
Trace: c012dfaf <real_lookup+4b/74>
Trace: c012e17a <lookup_dentry+126/1f0>
Trace: c012e26c <__namei+28/58>
Trace: c012c232 <sys_newstat+2a/8c>
Trace: c0108be4 <system_call+34/38>
Code:  c0144040 <proc_lookup+4c/e0>          00000000 <_EIP>:
Code:  c0144040 <proc_lookup+4c/e0>             0:    66 83 3b 00      cmpw
$0x0,(%ebx)
Code:  c0144044 <proc_lookup+50/e0>             4:    74 4e            je     54
<_EIP+0x54> c0144094 <proc_lookup+a0/e0>
Code:  c0144046 <proc_lookup+52/e0>             6:    31 c9            xorl
%ecx,%ecx
Code:  c0144048 <proc_lookup+54/e0>             8:    8b 74 24 20      movl
0x20(%esp,1),%esi
Code:  c014404c <proc_lookup+58/e0>             c:    66 8b 4b 02      movw
0x2(%ebx),%cx
Code:  c0144050 <proc_lookup+5c/e0>            10:    3b 4e 44         cmpl
0x44(%esi),%ecx
Code:  c0144053 <proc_lookup+5f/e0>            13:    75 00            jne    15
<_EIP+0x15> c0144055 <proc_lookup+61/e0>
```

For `ksymoops` to resolve the addresses to function names, it needs the appropriate system map for the running kernel. During the kernel building process an updated file is placed in the root of your kernel source directory, usually `/usr/src/linux/System.map`. However, the file only contains entries for the files that are compiled in since it can not possibly know the memory location where a particular module will be loaded later. Getting the location of modularized code can be accomplished at load time by telling `insmod` to do so by adding the `-m` parameter. Exported symbols also show up in `/proc/ksyms`.

The call trace of this particular Oops goes from `system_call` through the listed functions and ends up in `proc_lookup` where the fault occurred. The trace lists functions according to the following format.

```
<function_name+offset/length>
```

The offset indicates where in the function the jump was made and length is the total length. The offending code is listed disassembled. At offset 0x4c into `proc_lookup` a `compare` was made against the `ebx` register and looking at the register dumps shows that it contains an invalid address. Now we need to locate the file that contains the function in question and find out what could be causing this. In this case it seems reasonable that `proc_lookup` would be a part of the `proc` file system and indeed the function is listed in `fs/proc/root.c`. The Makefile in the kernel allows you to run a `make fs/proc/root.s` and get an assembler listing containing debugging information. Open `root.s` in an editor, find `proc_lookup` and the offending operation, along with a line number in `root.c`. In this particular case, the dentry pointer passed to `proc_lookup` was completely bogus.

That was the easy part – now you have to find out how on earth that could have happened? It might be a valid thing to do and in that case a check should probably be added. However, it is far more plausible that the driver being created is at fault. In this case the Oops occurred while we were testing the `proc` implementation in `Schar`. The problem was that while someone was accessing the `proc` entry, the module was removed, and the directory entry associated with it was freed. Next time the entry was looked up, the dentry passed was no longer valid. `Schar` was fixed to increment its module usage count when the `proc` entry was busy and the problem was solved.

Debugging Modules

Unfortunately it is not possible to single step kernel code like ordinary applications, at least not right out of the box. The best way to go about debugging your own modules is to strategically add `printk` statements in troublesome areas and work your way down from there. Beware that obscure bugs may be hidden by a simple `printk` statement, either because it changes the timing or the alignment of data slightly. But try it and see what happens. If it hangs, find out where and print critical variables. An Oops can be decoded using the techniques demonstrated above and `ksymoops` includes `/proc/ksyms` by default and can thus also decode any functions exported by the modules loaded. During development it is advisable to export all possible functions and variables to make sure that `ksymoops` will catch them. The section on integrated debugging will explore further options.

The Magic Key

The most unfortunate bugs are the ones that crash the system completely. In these situations the Magic `SysRq` key, or System Attention Key (SAK), can be of great assistance. This handy feature was added during the 2.1 development cycle and you can enable the option when configuring the kernel. It doesn't add any overhead to normal system operation and it can be the only way to resolve a complete hang, so whether you are doing kernel development or not, always leave it enabled. You activate the different commands by pressing *Alt Sys Rq* and a command key. The different commands are documented in `Documentation/sysrq.txt` – here we will examine the *p* command. So go ahead and press *Alt Sys Rq p* :

```
SysRq: Show Regs

EIP: 0010:[<c0107cd0>] EFLAGS: 00003246
EAX: 0000001f EBX: c022a000 ECX: c022a000 EDX: c0255378
ESI: c0255300 EDI: c0106000 EBP: 000000a0 DS: 0018 ES: 0018
CR0: 8005003b CR2: 4000b000 CR3: 00101000
```

This is a listing of the processor state, complete with flags and registers. `EIP`, the instruction pointer, shows where the kernel is currently executing so you need to look up this value in the symbol map for your kernel. The closest matches for our kernel are

```
c0107c8c T cpu_idle
c0107ce4 T sys_idle
```

which reveals that the kernel was currently executing `cpu_idle`. If a driver gets stuck in an endless loop, *SAK p* will tell you exactly where, assuming that the scheduler is still running. The system might also be completely hung and in that case the SAK cannot help you.

Kernel Debugger – KDB

There is a way to debug a running kernel safely that has minimal impact on normal system operation. It does require patching of the kernel for the Intel platform, however, as the features are not yet included there – although they might be in the future. Some of the other platforms provide similar features without the need to patch the kernel. Snoop around in the kernel configuration or search the internet, if necessary.

The debugger can be invoked in different places. At boot you can pass the `kdb` parameter to lilo and the debugger will be started as soon as possible. During system operation, the debugger can be entered manually by pressing the *Pause* key and is invoked automatically when an Oops occurs. From within the debugger you can inspect and modify CPU registers and process variables, single step execution, set breakpoints, and much more.

The patch comes with quite a few man pages explaining how to use it so we won't go into detail here. The debugger is fairly simple to use, although it is not as pleasant to work with as `gdb` and does not provide the same degree of functionality. This is to be expected for a built-in debugger, but having said that it still is a very handy tool. Entering the debugger, setting a breakpoint, and then having the debugger automatically invoked when it is reached, provides an excellent way to single step your module without affecting general system performance that much.

Remote Debugging

After Chapter 9, we're familiar with `gdb` and how to use it with ordinary applications. With the `kgdb` kernel patches, a running kernel can be debugged over a serial line from `gdb` just like any other program. This approach requires two machines – a master, where the controlling `gdb` is run from, and a slave being debugged. A null-modem cable connects the two machines and it is probably a good idea to test the connection with Minicom or a similar terminal program to make sure that the link is fully functional and reliable.

After having patched the kernel on the slave, recompiled, and rebooted, the machine runs just like before until an accompanying debug script is invoked. A breakpoint is defined in the kernel and upon executing the script, the slave is halted and control passed to the master. From there you can use `gdb` like you are used to – the slave machine is resumed with "continue" and can be stopped with *Ctrl C* again or when it hits a breakpoint.

The `KDB` patches also offer serial line debugging, but if you have two machines set up, using the `kgdb` patches offers the advantage of providing the interface through the vastly more powerful `gdb`. Whether you need that extra functionality or not, is up to you.

General Notes on Debugging

While the various ways to debug the kernel differ in one way or another, they all have some points in common. Generally, you will have to be very careful with breakpoints. If you are using an integrated debugger, setting breakpoints in some of the keyboard handling is not a very good idea (for obvious reasons). Likewise with debugging via a network connection and enabling a breakpoint in the driver or somewhere in the network stack. It might work, and it might not – but be prepared to hit the big red switch and enjoy a cup of coffee while `fsck` runs! Some drivers rely on precise timing and single stepping those will probably not work either. This also applies to interrupt and timer handlers. Be prepared to handle crashes until you get the hang of kernel debugging and know where *not* to place breakpoints.

In our experience, having a dedicated machine for testing and debugging provides the most flexible solution. It does not have to be an expensive solution either; we have an old 486 hooked up to our main workstation that boots over the network and mounts its root file system through NFS. The test machine contains nothing more than a motherboard with little RAM, a network adapter, floppy, and a cheap graphics adapter. The development is kept on the workstation while trial runs and debugging is done on the test machine alone. If it happens to crash, a reboot takes only about half a minute with no file system check necessary and we can keep editing sources undisturbed on the workstation. Hook up a serial cable, and remote debugging the test machine is a cinch.

Portability

The device driver created should naturally run on as many platforms as possible. Luckily the exposed API is very portable, and the problems that arise are mainly due to platform differences. Most of the portability issues have been mentioned in the sections where most of the problems arise. This small section will look a little closer at some of these and introduce a few others.

Data Types

The small section located near the beginning of the chapter listed the __uXX and __sXX data types. It is always a good idea to use these when a specific size of variable is needed, since there is no guarantee that a `long` is the same size on all platforms, for example.

Endianess

Platforms like the Intel or Alpha use little-endian byte orientation, which means that the most and least significant byte values are swapped. Power PC and Sparc CPU's are some of the big endian platforms that Linux runs on, however, and they store the data in that order. This is how C views the world and what is easiest to read by humans. In most cases you do not need to worry about the target endianess, but if you are building or retrieving data with a specific orientation, converting between the two will be needed. For big endian `__BIG_ENDIAN_BITFIELD` is defined and `__LITTLE_ENDIAN_BITFIELD` for little endian platforms, so the relevant code can be placed inside define checks.

```
#if defined( __LITTLE_ENDIAN_BITFIELD)
   byteval = x >> 8;
#else
   byteval = x & 0xff;
#endif
```

Linux also provides primitives to ease the conversion of variables. These are defined in `linux/byteorder/generic.h` and come in many different flavors. Some of the most common (for Intel, at least) are:

`unsigned long cpu_to_be32(unsigned long x)` `unsigned short cpu_to_be16(unsigned short x)`	Convert the variable x from the CPU native ordering to big endian.
`unsigned long be32_to_cpu(unsigned long x)` `unsigned short be16_to_cpu(unsigned short x)`	Convert big endian variable x to CPU native ordering.

There are numerous other functions to satisfy the conversion of 16, 32, and 64-bit variables to either type byte ordering; they can all be found in the above mentioned include file.

Alignment

A piece of data is said to be properly aligned, when it resides at a memory address that a processor can access in an efficient manner. It is dependent on the type of the processor when it considers data to be unaligned and what happens when it is accessed; the consequences are either a slowdown in execution for the architecture that allows unaligned access or failure for one that does not.

`get_unaligned(ptr)` `put_unaligned(val, ptr)`	Access unaligned data.

If you need to access data that is known to be misaligned, use the above macros. They are defined in `<asm/unaligned.h>`. For the architectures that directly support unaligned access, they expand to general pointer dereferencing.

Other possible portability problems have been mentioned throughout the text where they belong and you should not encounter any that were not listed either here or there. Portable code is beautiful code, so keep it that way!

Continuing the Quest

We hope you will enjoy delving into kernel development. At times it may seem like an impossible task, given the size of the entire kernel source, but hopefully the following chapters will provide you with enough baggage and incentive to dig in deeper on your own. Reading this book is by no means a substitute for looking at the source your self. The source is, of course, also the only documentation that is always completely up-to-date! This is surely the most powerful aspect of Open Source projects to programmers, as the entire source is freely available for you to study. Documentation for the Linux kernel is scarce at best, which makes reading other people's drivers and kernel modifications the best resource to be had.

The road to full understanding of the Linux kernel and device drivers is steep and filled with obstacles along the way. We hope this short introduction will aid you in getting started and encourage you to continue the quest on your own. In spite of many frustrating nights looking for an obscure bug and pulling out hair in distress until we finally nailed it, or maybe even because of them, you should still feel compelled to continue hacking the sources and keep learning. Some of the kernel developers are extremely gifted and studying their work is well worth the time spent.

Perhaps the biggest obstacle to overcome for beginning kernel programmers is knowing where to find a specific piece of code in the kernel sources. Hopefully this text will give you a head start and provide a general overview of what goes on where in the kernel. When you get stuck in a particular section anyway, `grep` like you have never grepped before and find all the examples you can. As mentioned in the beginning, the kernel is evolving all the time and a hard copy text can thus never be completely up to date. When and if you find differences between what is written here and in the kernel, always trust the kernel.

Anatomy of the Kernel Source

linux		
	arch (architecture dependent code)	
	drivers	
		block (block devices)
		cdrom (generic drivers and uniform layer)
		char (character devices)
		macintosh
		misc (mostly parallel port)
		net (network drivers)
		pci (PCI subsystem)
		sbus (SBUS subsystem (SPARC))
		scsi (drivers and SCSI subsystem)
		sound (drivers and sound subsystem)
		video (mostly framebuffer drivers)
	fs (vfs and all other file systems)	
	include	
		asm (symlink to appropriate platform, e.g. asm-alpha)
		linux
	init (where it all begins)	
	ipc (Inter Process Communication)	
	kernel	
	lib (string functions, et al)	
	mm (the memory management subsystem)	
	modules	
	net (the network subsystem)	
	scripts (various useful tools)	

We have omitted large parts, but this is the basic structure of the kernel. You are encouraged to go look for yourself.

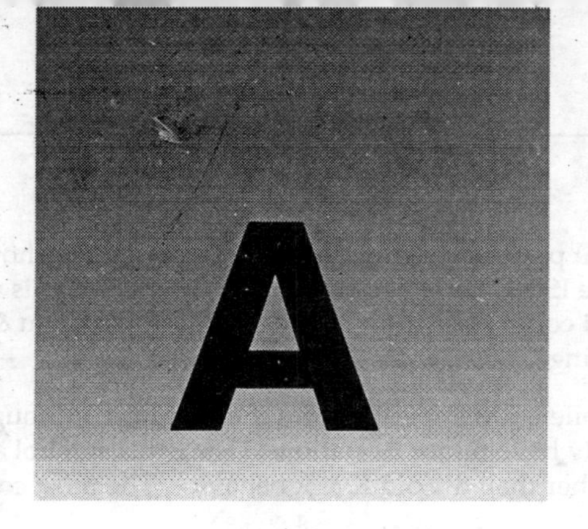

Portability

There are three main types of portability:

- Portability between different operating systems, either alternative implementations of UNIX or to completely different operating systems, such as OS-9, VMS or MS-DOS.
- Portability between different vendors' compilers, whether that means other C compilers or compatibility with being compiled as C++ code.
- Portability between different hardware, where word size, byte storage order and other differences can lead to problems.

We're not overly concerned in this book with portability between different operating systems, but the other types of portability are of interest here.

Portability has always been important in the UNIX world, because different versions of UNIX have been available on many different platforms. Until recently, Linux was only available for 80x86 class machines, but now Linux too is becoming available on other platforms, most notably the Motorola 68k series and the DEC Alpha processors.

In this appendix, we'll provide some hints, tips and general notes about portability to help you ensure your software is portable between different UNIX platforms and different versions of compilers.

Language Portability

First, we'll look at what steps you should take to ensure your code is portable between different versions of C compilers and different versions of UNIX.

Preprocessor Symbols

Several preprocessor symbols are used to indicate the type and conformity of the compiler. They're not defined in the usual way (in a header file), but are provided by the preprocessor or the compiler system. Their meanings are significant for portability.

__STDC__

Perhaps the most important preprocessor symbol is `__STDC__`. This should be defined by a compilation environment that meets the ISO C language standard. Historically, this was often used for moving code between older systems that could only compile the original Kernighan & Ritchie style C and newer systems tracking the evolving C standard.

These days, very few compilers differ greatly from the standard, although many compilers aren't validated and thus probably have minor deviations. Using this symbol allows you to isolate parts of the code that require ISO C rather than the old K & R behavior. The most common difference is in prototyping.

To use this symbol, you may write code like this:

```
#ifdef __STDC__
    int my_function(const char *mystring, const int a_value);
#else
    int my_function();
#endif
```

If you're using the GNU compiler `gcc`, use the `-ansi` switch to enable standard C compilation.

Some people have reported compilers that define `__STDC__` to 0, apparently to indicate they don't conform to the ISO C standard! If you do encounter this unusual behavior, you may have to switch to using `#if __STDC__`.

_XOPEN_SOURCE

If your code is compliant (or supposed to be) with the X/Open and POSIX standards, define `_XOPEN_SOURCE` before including any header files.

This define may modify the behavior of included files to bring them in line with the X/Open standard. You won't need the older define `_POSIX_SOURCE` if `_XOPEN_SOURCE` is defined.

Use it like this:

```
#define _XOPEN_SOURCE

#include <unistd.h>
...
```

Reserved Names

A number of names are reserved. The ISO C language, for example, reserves a list of words, but be wary of nonstandard compilers which may reserve some others too. The compiler reference manual will be the definitive source in these cases.

auto	break	case	char	const	continue	default
do	double	else	enum	extern	float	for
goto	if	int	long	register	return	short
signed	sizeof	static	struct	switch	typedef	union
unsigned	void	volatile	while			

In addition, it's probably wise to avoid any C++ keywords, should you later wish to convert your program from C to C++. Since, at the time of writing, the ANSI C++ standard is still evolving, it's impossible to give a complete list. However, as a minimum you should avoid:

asm	catch	class	delete
friend	inline	new	operator
private	protected	public	template
this	throw	try	virtual

Many other names are also reserved. In particular, all names starting with an underscore _ are reserved for the compiler to use. Names ending in `_t` are also reserved for use in POSIX header files. The rule is, never start a name with _ or end it with `_t`.

Once you start including header files, additional names become used, which can be quite a problem. Consider the following scenario. You have a file that compiles correctly. You then write a new function in the file, requiring an additional header file to be included. This new header file uses names that clash with your existing names, forcing you to rewrite some parts of the program code. The solution to this, of course, is to avoid all names reserved by any header file.

The names that are used by the different header files are listed here:

Header	Used Names
`ctype.h`	All names starting `is` or `to`.
`dirent.h`	All names starting `d_`.
`errno.h`	All names starting `E`, followed by a number or other uppercase letter.
`fnctl.h`	All names starting `l_`, `F_`, `O_` or `S_`.
`grp.h`	All names starting `gr_`.
`limits.h`	All names ending `_MAX`.
`locale.h`	All names starting `LC_`.
`pwd.h`	All names starting `pw_`.
`signal.h`	All names starting `sa_`, `SIG` or `SA_`.
`string.h`	All names starting `mem`, `str` or `wcs`.
`sys/stat.h`	All names starting `st_` or `S_`.
`sys/times.h`	All names starting `tms_`.
`termios.h`	All names starting `c_`, `V`, `I`, `O` or `TC`.

Limits

The header file `limits.h` defines many maximum values. Always use the values from the header, rather than inventing your own arbitrary ones. If you *do* need to define your own limits and expect your code to be used on many different systems, it may be worth adding some 'once only' code to check that the current system limits are the same as or better than any limits your program requires.

It's much better for a program to exit gracefully when you try and run it, explaining what limit is incompatible with the program, than to attempt to run but behave incorrectly.

Hardware Portability

Since UNIX, and now Linux, is available on a wide range of hardware, you should take steps to ensure you don't inadvertently write code that's restricted to a particular platform.

The C language is widely regarded as a portable language. It's suitable for a very diverse range of tasks, from low-level hardware access to higher level applications such as databases. It's also a very efficient language in that it can normally be translated by a compiler into machine code that will perform the required task efficiently, with little run-time overhead.

Unfortunately, that's not the whole story. There are many parts of C that aren't fully defined and can cause problems when C source code is moved between different systems. Perhaps the classic example of this is the size of an integer. For many years, UNIX programmers expected integers to be 32 bits wide and thus hold very large values, while MS-DOS programmers expected integers to be only 16 bits wide. Moving code from UNIX that assumed an integer could hold values bigger than 65,535 to MS-DOS could be a major undertaking.

In the authors' opinion, there are three different approaches to producing portable code:

- Write it on a single platform and worry about portability later. This certainly gets the initial code written more quickly, but it's quite likely that moving it to a different system will require significant rewriting and many new bugs will probably appear in the new code.
- Write it on one system, but take care to avoid non-portable features. If you need to use a feature that you know will cause portability problems, try to isolate it to a single file or function call. This approach means that some effort will almost certainly be required when the code is ported, but it shouldn't be extensive and major problems should be confined to small sections of the code that are known to require porting effort.
- Switch development between as many different platforms as possible and avoid any features that may be non-portable. This approach will probably result in the first version of your software taking a very, very long time to come to fruition and it will probably run slowly and still require effort to port to a system it hasn't been run on before. Nobody, not even a team of dedicated professionals, can catch every possible problem before it arises.

As you can perhaps guess, the authors favor the second approach. Here we list some common porting pitfalls, and suggest some things that can be done to avoid them.

Sizes

In C, the integer is defined to be the natural word size of the processor. This would be 16 bits on an 8086 and 32 bits on a 68030. The varying size of `int` is a common cause of problems. Not only could you find that your integer will take a different range of values on different machines, but trying to set or test bits in a integer can also cause problems.

For example, suppose we wish to set bit 2 (counting from 0) in an integer called `i`. The expression,

```
i |= 0x04;
```

will set the bit, regardless of how wide the integer `i` is.

Clearing the bit is less straightforward. An obvious answer is to write

```
i &= 0xfffb; /* Do not write this */
```

which will clear the bit if `i` is 16 bits wide. The problem arises if `i` is actually 32 bits wide, in which case we've cleared not only bit 2 but also the top 16 bits accidentally! The correct way to write this is:

```
i &= ~0x04;
```

This allows the compiler (which knows how wide an integer is) to first create the bit complement of `0x04`, using the ~ operator, and then mask `i` against it. This way, the mask will always have the correct number of bits in it.

Byte Order

Different processors arrange bytes in memory in a different order. A few processors even have instructions for changing the way they store bits in memory. There are two classes of processors.

Little-endian

In this class of processors, the least significant bits (LSBs) of variables are stored at the lowest addresses. The VAX and 80x86 classes are notable processors that access memory in this fashion.

Big-endian

In this class of processors, the most significant bits (MSBs) of variables are stored at the lowest addresses. The SPARC and 68k series of processors use memory in this fashion.

A very few processors allow you to select the 'endedness' at run time, but we won't consider that here.

You could face a number of problems when you're moving programs between these classes of processors, notably when you're passing parameters to functions. Avoid taking the address of function parameters. For example:

```
char z;
func(z);

func(char zz) {
    char *p, tmp;
    p = &zz; /* Not a good idea */
    tmp = zz;
    p = &tmp; /* much safer */
```

A more serious problem arises when you're transferring data between the different types of processors on disk or across a network. A full discussion is beyond the scope of this book, but if you're interested, you should consider the `htonl`, `htons`, `ntohl` and `ntohs` functions which convert between host and network byte ordering. You can find a more general set of routines in the XDR (external data representation) standard.

char

A surprising number of programs seem to depend for their correct operation on whether a character is signed (ranges from -127 to +128) or unsigned (ranges 0 to 256). Never assume either. If you require characters to be signed or unsigned, explicitly declare them as `signed char` or `unsigned char`. Problems can also occur with shorts and integers, but this seems to be much less common.

Union Packing

The way the compiler arranges fields inside a union isn't defined. Suppose you declare a union like this:

```
union baz {
    short bar_short;
    char bar_char;
} my_baz;
```

If you try and write code that stores values in one 'part' of the union and reads them from the other, the results are undefined. You can't use a union to change the type of a variable in a portable way.

```
my_baz.bar_short = 7;
if (my_baz.bar_char == 7) { /* No ! */
```

Structure Alignment

A similar problem occurs with structures.

```
struct foo {
    short bar_short;
    char bar_char;
} my_foo;
```

The size of `foo` will vary between processors, depending on how the compiler has added padding bytes between the members of the structure.

Another pitfall of structures is to try and compare them with the memcmp function. Using our foo structure again, you might write:

```
struct foo foo1;
struct foo foo2;

/* some code that manipulates the structures */

if (memcmp(foo1, foo2, sizeof(struct foo))) { /* No !*/
```

Don't do this. You're asking if every byte in structure foo1 is the same as in foo2, but because of padding there may be bytes in the structure that don't correspond to any of the members in the structure. If you need to compare two structures, you must explicitly compare every member. It is, however, acceptable to copy structures using normal assignment or memcpy, since this transfers all the members.

Pointer Sizes

A lot of older UNIX code assumes `sizeof(int) = sizeof(void *);`

Never assume that you can move pointers to integers and back. If you need an anonymous pointer, use a `void *`. Also, beware the qsort function, which has the prototype:

```
    void qsort(void *base, size_t num_el, size_t size_el,
            int (*compare)(const void *, const void *));
```

Suppose you want to compare two members of our foo structure. Don't write the compare function to accept a pair of pointers to foo structures. The prototype requires `void *`. Instead, write the compare function to accept two void pointers and then cast the pointers back using local variables, like this:

```
int compare(void *struct_one_ptr, void *struct_two_ptr)
{
    struct foo *foo1_ptr;
    struct foo *foo2_ptr;

    foo1_ptr = (struct foo *)struct_one_ptr;
    foo2_ptr = (struct foo *)struct_two_ptr;
...
```

Function Parameter Evaluation

The order in which function parameters are evaluated is undefined. If you write code such as,

```
func(a++, b=a+c);
```

you may have portability problems, because some compilers will evaluate a++ first and some b=a+c first. Also, take extreme care with macros that may have side effects when used in function arguments, or in particular parts of some expressions. For example, beware,

```
isdigit(*ptr++); /* No! */
```

since the function isdigit is often implemented as a macro.

Moving to C++

Today you may be writing your code in ISO C, but in a few years you may wish to come back, add some new features and at the same time update the code to be compiled as C++. As the C++ standard evolves, it's moving further and further away from C and moving C code to a C++ compiler consequently becomes harder. We've already seen some C++ keywords to avoid. In addition, there are some other features to avoid in C that will make a later move to C++ easier.

Always prototype. C++ requires prototypes; C just encourages it.

A C `func()` may take any number of arguments; in C++ it takes no parameters.

Global data must be declared exactly once in C++; C is more relaxed.

In C, a global `const` has external linkage; in C++ it has file linkage.

In C, a `struct` variable declaration requires the keyword `struct` before the structure name; in C++, it doesn't.

In C++, enumerations are more tightly type checked than in C, which considers them integers.

Use the Compiler

Most modern compilers are very good at offering warnings about doubtful code. Use the compiler options to turn those warnings on. If you are using `gcc`, you can use the `-Wall` option, which turns on all warnings. If you're about to port your code to a different environment, also consider `gcc`'s `-pedantic` option, which can be extremely pedantic indeed! It will help you find constructs in your code that may need reworking as part of the port. It's much easier to correct warnings from a compiler before moving the code than it is to try and test and correct a buggy program after porting.

If you are writing production code, you should consider using `-Wall` and ensuring that your compiles produce no warnings. This might seem a rather optimistic goal, since you will almost undoubtedly receive some warnings about constructs that are correct.

There are two things to remember. Firstly, the team that wrote the compiler probably knew a great deal about the finer points of the language. Secondly, if you start with clean compiles and continue keeping your compiles clean, you'll find it much easier to spot important warnings. It's very easy to become accustomed to a particular file generating a stream of warnings and miss the new and important warning that just appeared.

Programs are Read by People

Our final tips are all about remembering that code is read by people and is almost always read many more times than it is written. Most code is around for much longer that the original authors intend. Today's quick one-off might be next year's mission-critical application.

Take the time to use proper, meaningful variable names. Using `i` or `j` for a simple integer loop variable is perhaps acceptable, but all other variables should have more meaningful names.

Name functions in a consistent manner. For example, if you have a set of functions that get the state of particular options, name them in a consistent way, such as `get_option_baud()`, and `get_option_typeahead()`. This helps readers find related functions quickly and more easily.

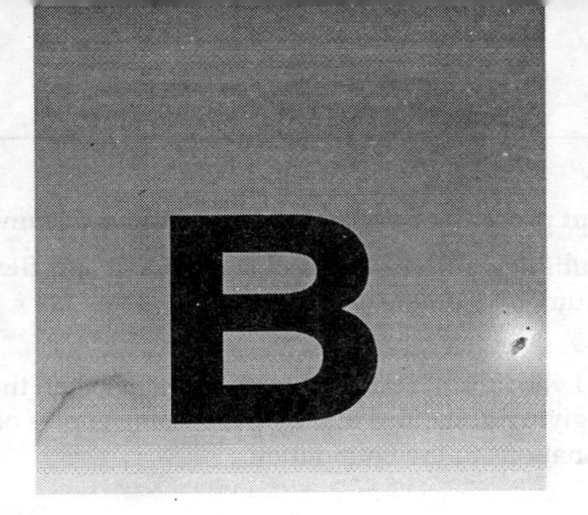

FSF and the GNU Project

To quote from the GNU Bulletin, "The Free Software Foundation is dedicated to eliminating restrictions on people's right to use, copy modify and redistribute computer programs."

The word free isn't about money. There's nothing wrong with paying to obtain a CD containing GNU software. Free refers to the freedom to have the source code, to learn how it works, to adapt it and to share it with others.

The Free Software Foundation (FSF) are putting together a complete software system, named **GNU**, which stands for **GNU's Not UNIX**. It's intended to be upwardly compatible with UNIX, while allowing access to the complete source code. The project isn't yet finished, but many parts are available and most Linux distributions rely on large parts of the GNU project.

The GNU Project

The major parts of the project are:

- The Hurd, a collection of server processes to run on a kernel called Mach, developed at CMU. The Hurd isn't yet complete, but the Linux kernel suffices quite nicely!
- The GNU C Library. Most Linux distributions use this. It's almost complete, but still being worked on.
- GNU EMACS. Arguably, the most configurable programming editor yet written. It can be difficult to learn, but persistence in mastering this editor will pay dividends in the end. It seems that work on EMACS will continue forever!
- GCC, the GNU C compiler. This actually consists of many parts and different front ends keep being added. Currently, work is proceeding on Pascal and CHILL (http://www.kvatro.no/telecom/chipsy/) front ends and is mostly complete. At the time of writing, it's not an ISO C certified compiler; the fact that certification costs a considerable amount of money is a drawback to a Foundation always short of spending power. However, GCC does track the standard closely and differences are mostly quite minor. GCC is also a C++ compiler.

- Ghostscript, a Postscript processor for viewing and printing documents.
- There are many other utilities, such as the **bash** shell, **bison** and **flex** (replacements for YACC and LEX), **make** and numerous others.

With few exceptions, the GNU versions of standard tools are better than the originals. You can help the Free Software Foundation by giving donations and by purchasing copies of their software, either directly or from vendors that make donations to the Foundation.

The GNU Public License

This is sometimes referred to as **copyleft**, or the **GPL**. Unlike other copyrights that restrict freedoms, this one enhances freedoms in a rather ingenious way.

Here's the full text of the license:

GNU GENERAL PUBLIC LICENSE

Version 2, June 1991

Copyright © 1989, 1991 Free Software Foundation, Inc., 675 Mass Ave, Cambridge, MA 02139, USA. Everyone is permitted to copy and distribute verbatim copies of this license document, but changing it is not allowed.

Preamble

The licenses for most software are designed to take away your freedom to share and change it. By contrast, the GNU General Public License is intended to guarantee your freedom to share and change free software--to make sure the software is free for all its users. This General Public License applies to most of the Free Software Foundation's software and to any other program whose authors commit to using it. (Some other Free Software Foundation software is covered by the GNU Library General Public License instead.) You can apply it to your programs, too.

When we speak of free software, we are referring to freedom, not price. Our General Public Licenses are designed to make sure that you have the freedom to distribute copies of free software (and charge for this service if you wish), that you receive source code or can get it if you want it, that you can change the software or use pieces of it in new free programs; and that you know you can do these things.

To protect your rights, we need to make restrictions that forbid anyone to deny you these rights or to ask you to surrender the rights. These restrictions translate to certain responsibilities for you if you distribute copies of the software, or if you modify it.

For example, if you distribute copies of such a program, whether gratis or for a fee, you must give the recipients all the rights that you have. You must make sure that they, too, receive or can get the source code. And you must show them these terms so they know their rights.
We protect your rights with two steps: (1) copyright the software, and (2) offer you this license which gives you legal permission to copy, distribute and/or modify the software.
Also, for each author's protection and ours, we want to make certain that everyone understands that there is no warranty for this free software. If the software is modified by someone else and passed on, we want its recipients to know that what they have is not the original, so that any problems introduced by others will not reflect on the original authors' reputations.
Finally, any free program is threatened constantly by software patents. We wish to avoid the danger that redistributors of a free program will individually obtain patent licenses, in effect making the program proprietary. To prevent this, we have made it clear that any patent must be licensed for everyone's free use or not licensed at all.
The precise terms and conditions for copying, distribution and modification follow.

GNU GENERAL PUBLIC LICENSE

TERMS AND CONDITIONS FOR COPYING, DISTRIBUTION AND MODIFICATION

1. This License applies to any program or other work which contains a notice placed by the copyright holder saying it may be distributed under the terms of this General Public License. The "Program", below, refers to any such program or work, and a "work based on the Program" means either the Program or any derivative work under copyright law: that is to say, a work containing the Program or a portion of it, either verbatim or with modifications and/or translated into another language. (Hereinafter, translation is included without limitation in the term "modification".) Each licensee is addressed as "you".
   Activities other than copying, distribution and modification are not covered by this License; they are outside its scope. The act of running the Program is not restricted, and the output from the Program is covered only if its contents constitute a work based on the Program (independent of having been made by running the Program). Whether that is true depends on what the Program does.
2. You may copy and distribute verbatim copies of the Program's source code as you receive it, in any medium, provided that you conspicuously and appropriately publish on each copy an appropriate copyright notice and disclaimer of warranty; keep intact all the notices that refer to this License and to the absence of any warranty; and give any other recipients of the Program a copy of this License along with the Program.
   You may charge a fee for the physical act of transferring a copy, and you may at your option offer warranty protection in exchange for a fee.
3. You may modify your copy or copies of the Program or any portion of it, thus forming a work based on the Program, and copy and distribute such modifications or work under the terms of Section 2 above, provided that you also meet all of these conditions:
   a. You must cause the modified files to carry prominent notices stating that you changed the files and the date of any change.
   b. You must cause any work that you distribute or publish, that in whole or in part contains or is derived from the Program or any part thereof, to be licensed as a whole at no charge to all third parties under the terms of this License.

c. If the modified program normally reads commands interactively when run, you must cause it, when started running for such interactive use in the most ordinary way, to print or display an announcement including an appropriate copyright notice and a notice that there is no warranty (or else, saying that you provide a warranty) and that users may redistribute the program under these conditions, and telling the user how to view a copy of this License. (Exception: if the Program itself is interactive but does not normally print such an announcement, your work based on the Program is not required to print an announcement.)

These requirements apply to the modified work as a whole. If identifiable sections of that work are not derived from the Program, and can be reasonably considered independent and separate works in themselves, then this License, and its terms, do not apply to those sections when you distribute them as separate works. But when you distribute the same sections as part of a whole which is a work based on the Program, the distribution of the whole must be on the terms of this License, whose permissions for other licensees extend to the entire whole, and thus to each and every part regardless of who wrote it.

Thus, it is not the intent of this section to claim rights or contest your rights to work written entirely by you; rather, the intent is to exercise the right to control the distribution of derivative or collective works based on the Program.

In addition, mere aggregation of another work not based on the Program with the Program (or with a work based on the Program) on a volume of a storage or distribution medium does not bring the other work under the scope of this License.

4. You may copy and distribute the Program (or a work based on it, under Section 3) in object code or executable form under the terms of Sections 2 and 3 above provided that you also do one of the following:
   a. Accompany it with the complete corresponding machine-readable source code, which must be distributed under the terms of Sections 2 and 3 above on a medium customarily used for software interchange; or,
   b. Accompany it with a written offer, valid for at least three years, to give any third party, for a charge no more than your cost of physically performing source distribution, a complete machine-readable copy of the corresponding source code, to be distributed under the terms of Sections 2 and 3 above on a medium customarily used for software interchange; or,
   c. Accompany it with the information you received as to the offer to distribute corresponding source code. (This alternative is allowed only for noncommercial distribution and only if you received the program in object code or executable form with such an offer, in accord with Subsection b above.)

The source code for a work means the preferred form of the work for making modifications to it. For an executable work, complete source code means all the source code for all modules it contains, plus any associated interface definition files, plus the scripts used to control compilation and installation of the executable. However, as a special exception, the source code distributed need not include anything that is normally distributed (in either source or binary form) with the major components (compiler, kernel, and so on) of the operating system on which the executable runs, unless that component itself accompanies the executable.

If distribution of executable or object code is made by offering access to copy from a designated place, then offering equivalent access to copy the source code from the same place counts as distribution of the source code, even though third parties are not compelled to copy the source along with the object code.

5. You may not copy, modify, sublicense, or distribute the Program except as expressly provided under this License. Any attempt otherwise to copy, modify, sublicense or distribute the Program is void, and will automatically terminate your rights under this License.
   However, parties who have received copies, or rights, from you under this License will not have their licenses terminated so long as such parties remain in full compliance.
6. You are not required to accept this License, since you have not signed it. However, nothing else grants you permission to modify or distribute the Program or its derivative works. These actions are prohibited by law if you do not accept this License. Therefore, by modifying or distributing the Program (or any work based on the Program), you indicate your acceptance of this License to do so, and all its terms and conditions for copying, distributing or modifying the Program or works based on it.
7. Each time you redistribute the Program (or any work based on the Program), the recipient automatically receives a license from the original licensor to copy, distribute or modify the Program subject to these terms and conditions. You may not impose any further restrictions on the recipients' exercise of the rights granted herein.
   You are not responsible for enforcing compliance by third parties to this License.
8. If, as a consequence of a court judgment or allegation of patent infringement or for any other reason (not limited to patent issues), conditions are imposed on you (whether by court order, agreement or otherwise) that contradict the conditions of this License, they do not excuse you from the conditions of this License. If you cannot distribute so as to satisfy simultaneously your obligations under this License and any other pertinent obligations, then as a consequence you may not distribute the Program at all. For example, if a patent license would not permit royalty-free redistribution of the Program by all those who receive copies directly or indirectly through you, then the only way you could satisfy both it and this License would be to refrain entirely from distribution of the Program.
   If any portion of this section is held invalid or unenforceable under any particular circumstance, the balance of the section is intended to apply and the section as a whole is intended to apply in other circumstances.
   It is not the purpose of this section to induce you to infringe any patents or other property right claims or to contest validity of any such claims; this section has the sole purpose of protecting the integrity of the free software distribution system, which is implemented by public license practices. Many people have made generous contributions to the wide range of software distributed through that system in reliance on consistent application of that system; it is up to the author/donor to decide if he or she is willing to distribute software through any other system and a licensee cannot impose that choice.
   This section is intended to make thoroughly clear what is believed to be a consequence of the rest of this License.
9. If the distribution and/or use of the Program is restricted in certain countries either by patents or by copyrighted interfaces, the original copyright holder who places the Program under this License may add an explicit geographical distribution limitation excluding those countries, so that distribution is permitted only in or among countries not thus excluded. In such case, this License incorporates the limitation as if written in the body of this License.

10. The Free Software Foundation may publish revised and/or new versions of the General Public License from time to time. Such new versions will be similar in spirit to the present version, but may differ in detail to address new problems or concerns.
    Each version is given a distinguishing version number. If the Program specifies a version number of this License which applies to it and "any later version", you have the option of following the terms and conditions either of that version or of any later version published by the Free Software Foundation. If the Program does not specify a version number of this License, you may choose any version ever published by the Free Software Foundation.
11. If you wish to incorporate parts of the Program into other free programs whose distribution conditions are different, write to the author to ask for permission. For software which is copyrighted by the Free Software Foundation, write to the Free Software Foundation; we sometimes make exceptions for this. Our decision will be guided by the two goals of preserving the free status of all derivatives of our free software and of promoting the sharing and reuse of software generally.

NO WARRANTY

12. BECAUSE THE PROGRAM IS LICENSED FREE OF CHARGE, THERE IS NO WARRANTY FOR THE PROGRAM, TO THE EXTENT PERMITTED BY APPLICABLE LAW. EXCEPT WHEN OTHERWISE STATED IN WRITING THE COPYRIGHT HOLDERS AND/OR OTHER PARTIES PROVIDE THE PROGRAM "AS IS" WITHOUT WARRANTY OF ANY KIND, EITHER EXPRESSED OR IMPLIED, INCLUDING, BUT NOT LIMITED TO, THE IMPLIED WARRANTIES OF MERCHANTABILITY AND FITNESS FOR A ARTICULAR PURPOSE. THE ENTIRE RISK AS TO THE QUALITY AND PERFORMANCE OF THE PROGRAM IS WITH YOU. SHOULD THE PROGRAM PROVE DEFECTIVE, YOU ASSUME THE COST OF ALL NECESSARY SERVICING, REPAIR OR CORRECTION.
13. IN NO EVENT UNLESS REQUIRED BY APPLICABLE LAW OR AGREED TO IN WRITING WILL ANY COPYRIGHT HOLDER, OR ANY OTHER PARTY WHO MAY MODIFY AND/OR REDISTRIBUTE THE PROGRAM AS PERMITTED ABOVE, BE LIABLE TO YOU FOR DAMAGES, INCLUDING ANY GENERAL, SPECIAL, INCIDENTAL OR CONSEQUENTIAL DAMAGES ARISING OUT OF THE USE OR INABILITY TO USE THE PROGRAM (INCLUDING BUT NOT LIMITED TO LOSS OF DATA OR DATA BEING RENDERED INACCURATE OR LOSSES SUSTAINED BY YOU OR THIRD PARTIES OR A FAILURE OF THE PROGRAM TO OPERATE WITH ANY OTHER PROGRAMS), EVEN IF SUCH HOLDER OR OTHER PARTY HAS BEEN ADVISED OF THE POSSIBILITY OF SUCH DAMAGES.

END OF TERMS AND CONDITIONS

Appendix: How to Apply These Terms to Your New Programs

If you develop a new program, and you want it to be of the greatest possible use to the public, the best way to achieve this is to make it free software which everyone can redistribute and change under these terms.
To do so, attach the following notices to the program. It is safest to attach them to the start of each source file to most effectively convey the exclusion of warranty; and each file should have at least the ``copyright'' line and a pointer to where the full notice is found.

<one line to give the program's name and a brief idea of what it does.>

Copyright ©19yy <name of author>

This program is free software; you can redistribute it and/or modify it under the terms of the GNU General Public License as published by the Free Software Foundation; either version 2 of the License, or (at your option) any later version.

This program is distributed in the hope that it will be useful, but
WITHOUT ANY WARRANTY; without even the implied warranty of
MERCHANTABILITY or FITNESS FOR A PARTICULAR PURPOSE. See the GNU General
Public License for more details.

You should have received a copy of the GNU General Public License along
with this program; if not, write to the Free Software Foundation, Inc.,
675 Mass Ave, Cambridge, MA 02139, USA.

Also add information on how to contact you by electronic and paper mail.

If the program is interactive, make it output a short notice like this when it
starts in an interactive mode:

```
Gnomovision version 69, Copyright © 19yy name of author
Gnomovision comes with ABSOLUTELY NO WARRANTY; for details type 'show w'
This is free software, and you are welcome to redsitribute it under certain
conditions; type 'show c' for details.
```

The hypothetical commands `show w' and `show c' should show the appropriate
parts of the General Public License. Of course, the commands you use may be
called something other than `show w' and `show c'; they could even be mouse-
clicks or menu items-whatever suits your program.
You should also get your employer (if you work as a programmer) or your
school, if any, to sign a ``copyright disclaimer'' for the program, if
necessary. Here is a sample; alter the names:

Yoyodyne, Inc., hereby disclaims all copyright interest in the program
`Gnomovision' (which makes passes at compilers) written by James Hacker.

<signature of Ty Coon>, 1 April 1989

Ty Coon, President of Vice

This General Public License does not permit incorporating your program into
proprietary programs. If your program is a subroutine library, you may
consider it more useful to permit linking proprietary applications with the
library. If this is what you want to do, use the GNU Library General Public
License instead of this License

Internet Resources

There are many, many resources on the Internet for Linux, UNIX and other related software. Here we suggest just a few places you might start looking. Since the Internet is such a dynamic resource, it seems certain some of the resources may have gone by the time you read this. Never fear! Use your favorite search engine to find new ones, or even ones that we've missed.

WWW Locations

Like the Web as a whole, the number of sites grows all the time. Try these starting points, follow the links, and see what you can find.

Linux Specific

Linux News

Current news about Linux can be found at the following sites:

http://www.slashdot.org/
http://www.freshmeat.net/
http://linuxtoday.com/
http://www.linuxworld.com/
http://www.linuxgazette.com/

Linux Kernel Resources

Alan Cox's Diary
http://www.linux.org.uk/diary

Linux Kernel Archives
http://www.kernel.org/

Linux-kernel mailing archive
http://www.uwsg.indiana.edu/hypermail/linux/kernel/index.html

KDB patches providing integrated debugging
http://reality.sgi.com/slurn_engr/

Linux Distribution Vendors

Debian Project
http://www.debian.org/

Red Hat
http://www.redhat.com/

ŞuSE
http://www.suse.com/

Caldera Inc.
http://www.caldera.com/

Other Linux Resources

Linux Software Map
http://www.execpc.com/lsm

Linux Documentation Project
http://www.linuxdoc.org/

The Linux Home Page
http://www.linux.org/

Linuxberg
http://www.linuxberg.com/

Linux v2 Information HQ
http://www.linuxhq.com/

The Linux Threads Library
http://pauillac.inria.fr/~xleroy/linuxthreads/

LINUX.ORG.UK
http://www.uk.linux.org/

Linux 2.0 Penguins
http://www.isc.tamu.edu/~lewing/linux/

GNOME Project homepage
http://www.gnome.org/

Linux packages in RPM format
http://rufus.w3.org/

Pacific HiTech Home Page
http://www.pht.com/

The Linux Midi + Sound Main Page
http://www.bright.net/~dlphilp/linuxsound/

Trusted Information Systems: Firewall Toolkit on Linux
http://www.pauck.de/marco/misc/misc.html

Linux International: Promoting Linux
http://www.li.org/

InfoMagic Main Index Page
http://www.infomagic.com/

The Cathedral and the Bazaar
http://www.tuxedo.org/~esr/writings/cathedral-bazaar/cathedral-bazaar.html/

StarOffice office productivity suite
http://www.sun.com/products/staroffice/

Applixware
http://www.applix.com/applixware/

Unix and General Programming

The GNU Project Homepage
http://www.gnu.org/

Cygnus
http://www.cygnus.com/

The Electronic Frontier Foundation
http://www.eff.org/

UK UNIX User Group Home Page
http://www.ukuug.org/

Troll Tech - Qt Multi-platform C++ GUI Framework
http://www.troll.no

UnixWorld Online Magazine Home Page
http://www.wcmh.com:80/uworld/

Walnut Creek CDROM Electronic Catalog
http://www.cdrom.com/

Association of C & C++ Users WWW
http://www.accu.org/ - mail membership@accu.org for more info

Tcl WWW Info
http://www.sco.com/Technology/tcl/Tcl.html

The X Consortium Homepage
http://www.x.org/

Andrew S. Tanenbaum (provides a reference to Minix, a tiny UNIX-like OS)
http://www.cs.vu.nl/~ast

Tcl/Tk Project at the Scriptics Corporation
http://www.scriptics.com/

Tcl Contributed Software Archive
http://www.neosoft.com/tcl/contributed_sources/

Perlmongers homepage
http://www.perl.org/

V: a Freeware Portable C++ GUI Framework for Windows and X
http://www.objectcentral.com/

The Hungry Programmers (writing a free Motif clone)
http://www.hungry.com

Sun User Group
http://www.sunukug.org/
http://www.european.org/

Unix freeware sources
http://linux.robinson.cam.ac.uk/linapps/linapps.html

The NetBSD Project
http://www.netbsd.org

The Jargon File: a Collection of Slang Terms Used by Computer Hackers
http://www.fwi.uva.nl/~mes/jargon

The Official fvwm Homepage
http://www.fvwm.org/

SAMBA Web Pages: Allows SMB Access to UNIX Files and Printers
http://samba.anu.edu.au/samba/

The Xfree Home Page
http://www.XFree86.org/

Xforms C++ GUI library
ftp://ftp.cs.ruu.nl/pub/XFORMS/

C++ Information
http://www.maths.warwick.ac.uk/c++
http://www.ocsltd.com/c++

HTML & HTTP Information

General

The World Wide Web Consortium: Information on W3C
http://www.w3.org/

The World Wide Web Consortium: Protocol Information
http://www.w3.org/Protocols/Overview.html

Beginner's Guide to HTML
http://www.ncsa.uiuc.edu/General/Internet/WWW/HTMLPrimer.html

Guides to Writing Style for HTML Documents
http://union.ncsa.uiuc.edu/HyperNews/get/www/html/guides.html

Tools for Aspiring Web Authors
http://www.nas.nasa.gov/NAS/WebWeavers/

Location of the `weblint` Program
http://www.khoral.com/staff/neilb/weblint.html

Internet Engineering Task Force: HTML Standards
http://www.ics.uci.edu/pub/ietf/html/

Style Guide for Online Hypertext
http://www.w3.org/hypertext/WWW/Provider/Style/Overview.html

Tools for WWW Providers
http://www.w3.org/Tools/Overview.html

Introduction to HTML
http://www.cwru.edu/help/introHTML/toc.html

Webmaster Reference Library™
http://www.webreference.com/

CGI

The Common Gateway Interface
http://hoohoo.ncsa.uiuc.edu/cgi/

Matt's Script Archive
http://worldwidemart.com/scripts/

GIFs on the FLY
http://www.unimelb.edu.au/fly/fly.html

Graphics Library for GIF Creation
http://www.starship.python.net/~richard/gdmodule/

Beginner's Guide to HTML and CGI scripting
http://www.demon.co.uk/dita/new2html.html

Web Developer's Virtual Library: CGI
http://www.charm.net/Vlib/Providers/CGI.html

CGI security: Pitfalls to Avoid for CGI Programmers
http://www.cerf.net/customer_service/unix-web/secure_s.htm

`cgihtml`: Library of CGI and HTML Routines Written in C
http://cgi.resourceindex.com/Programs_and_Scripts/C_and_C++/

Web Info

The World Wide Web Consortium: Information on W^{3}C
http://www.w3.org/

World Wide Web FAQ
http://www.boutell.com/openfaq/browsers/

HTTP Servers

World Wide Web Server Software - Lots of Servers Listed Here
http://www.w3.org.Servers.html

Apache HTTP Server Project
http://www.apache.org/

Status of the W^{3}C httpd
http://www.w3.org/hypertext/WWW/Daemon/Status.html

The NCSA httpd Home Page
http://hoohoo.ncsa.uiuc.edu/

An Overview of the WN Server
http://hopf.math.nwu.edu/docs/overview.html

Newsgroups

Usenet is always a good starting point.

General UNIX Groups

alt.unix.wizards
comp.sources.unix
comp.std.unix
comp.unix <various>
gnu.announce

Linux-specific Groups

comp.os.linux <various>

If you're running Linux and have Internet access then you should at least subscribe to comp.os.linux.announce and comp.os.linux.answers.

FTP Archive Sites

There are lots of archives. Some of the main ones are:

ftp://sunsite.unc.edu
ftp://tsx-11.mit.edu
ftp://prep.ai.mit.edu/pub/gnu

Remember, the main sites are always very busy, as is the Internet. If possible, use a mirror site closer to your location.

URLs for the Tools Mentioned in Chapter 9

ftp://sunsite.unc.edu/pub/Linux/devel/lang/c/

- `Checker-0.7.2.lsm`
- `Checker-0.7.2.tgz`
- `Checker-libs-0.7.2.tgz`
- `ElectricFence-2.0.5.lsm`
- `ElectricFence-2.0.5.tar.gz`
- `cflow-2.0.tar.gz`
- `cflow.lsm`
- `cxref-1.0.lsm`
- `cxref-1.0.tgz`
- `cxref-1.0.txt`
- `lclint-2.1a.common-mini.tar.gz`
- `lclint-2.1a.common.tar.gz`
- `lclint-2.1a.linux-a.out.tar.gz`
- `lclint-2.1a.linux-elf.tar.gz`
- `lclint-2.1a.lsm`
- `lclint-2.1a.src.tar.gz`

Note that version numbers will change. At the time of writing, the most current version of `lclint` is `lclint-2.4b`. Home site for the Larch (`lclint`) project is http://larch-www.lcs.mit.edu:8001/larch/lclint

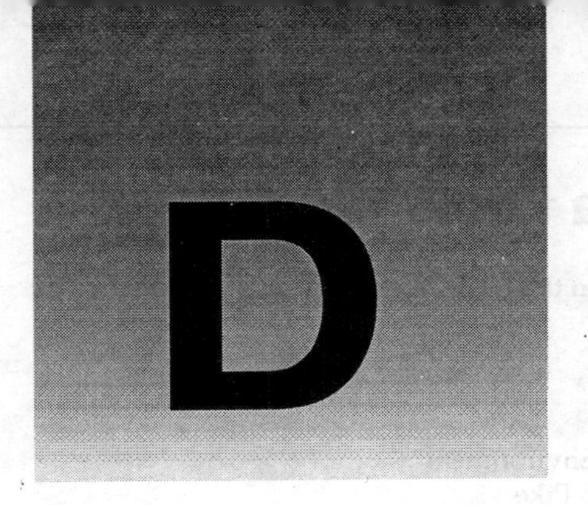

Bibliography

Standards

X/Open Single UNIX Specification
(Often referred to as Spec. 1170)
ISBN 1-85912-085-7
X/Open publications, +44 (0) 1993 708731
http://www.xopen.org/

IEEE Portable Operating System Interface for Computer Environments, POSIX
IEEE Std 1003.1-1988 C Language interface
ISBN 1-55937-003-3
IEEE, The Standards Office, 445 Hoes Lane, PO Box 1331,
Piscataway, NJ 08855-1331, USA
http://www.ieee.org

ISO C
ISO/IEC 9899:1990, Programming Languages, C
(Technically identical to ANSI standard ANS X3.159-1989, Programming Languages, C)

Other Documentation and Resources

Linux Manual Pages.
Linux HOWTO guides.
The many and various Linux CD-ROM distributions.

Books Worth a Look

Advanced Programming in the UNIX Environment
W. Richard Stevens
Addison-Wesley
ISBN 0-201-56317-7

The UNIX Programming Environment
Brian W. Kernighan & Rob Pike
Prentice-Hall
ISBN 0-13-937681-X

Linux Application Development
Michael K. Johnson & Erik W. Troan
Addison-Wesley
ISBN 0-201-30821-5

Writing Apache Modules with Perl and C
Lincoln Stein & Doug MacEachern
O'Reilly & Associates
ISBN 1-56592-567-X

Tcl and the Tk Toolkit
John K. Ousterhout
Addison-Wesley
ISBN 0-201-63337-X

Advanced UNIX Programming
Marc J. Rochkind
Prentice-Hall
ISBN 0-13-011800-1

X Window Systems Programming and Applications with Xt
Douglas A. Young
Prentice-Hall
ISBN 0-13-972167-3

Instant UNIX
Evans, Matthew & Stones
Wrox Press
ISBN 1-874416-65-6

The Design of the UNIX Operating System
Maurice J. Bach
Prentice-Hall
ISBN 0-13-201757-1

The UNIX system
S.R. Bourne
Addison-Wesley
ISBN 0-201-13791-7

Programming the UNIX system
M. R. M. Dunsmuir & G. J. Davies
Macmillan
ISBN 0-333-37156-9

Programming Perl
Larry Wall & Randal L. Schwartz
O'Reilly & Associates
ISBN 0-937175-64-1

Learning Perl
Randal L. Schwartz & Tom Christiansen
O'Reilly & Associates
ISBN 1-56592-284-0

Practical Programming in Tcl and Tk
Brent B. Welch
Prentice-Hall
ISBN 0-13-182007-9

POSIX Programmer's Guide
Donald Lewine
O'Reilly & Associates
ISBN 0-937175-73-0

The Korn shell
Morris I. Bolasky & David G. Korn
Prentice-Hall
ISBN 0-13-516972-0

Principles of Concurrent and Distributed Programming
M. Ben-Ari
Prentice-Hall
ISBN 013711821X

HTML The Definitive Guide
Chuck Muciano & Bill Kennedy
O'Reilly & Associates
ISBN

Spinning the Web
Andrew Ford
International Thomson Publishing
ISBN 1-850-32141-8

Managing Projects with make
Andrew Oram & Steve Talbott
O'Reilly & Associates
ISBN 0-937175-90-0

Managing Internet Information Services
Cricket Liu, Jerry Peek, Russ Jones, Bryan Buus & Adrian Nye
O'Reilly & Associates
ISBN 1-56592-062-7

Linux in a Nutshell
Jessica Perry Hekman
O'Reilly & Associates
1-56592-167-4

Exploring Expect
Don Libes
O'Reilly & Associates
ISBN 1-56592-090-2.

UNIX Network Programming
W Richard Stevens
Prentice-Hall
ISBN 0-13-949876-1

Operating System Concepts
Abraham Silberschatz & Peter Galvin
Addison-Wesley
ISBN 0-20-159113-8

The Magic Garden Explained
Berny Goodheart & James Cox
Prentice-Hall
ISBN 0-13-098138-9

Linux Device Drivers
Alessandro Rubini
O'Reilly & Associates
ISBN 1-56-592292-1

Open Sources
Chris DiBona, Sam Ockman & Mark Stone (eds)
O'Reilly and Associates
ISBN 1 56592 582 3

And Finally, Three Books to Read away from the Computer

Gödel, Escher, Bach: An Eternal Golden Braid
Douglas R. Hofstadter
Penguin Books
ISBN 0140055797

The Illuminatus! Trilogy
Robert Shea & Robert Anton Wilson
Dell
ISBN 0440539811

The Wasp Factory
Iain Banks
Abacus Fiction
ISBN 0-349-10177-9

Index

A

B

C

D

F

G

I

J

K

M

P

S

T

U

V

W

X

Z

Symbols

SPD/Wrox Reprints

ISBN	Title	Author	Price
Published Titles			
8173661448	ADO 2.6 Programmer's Reference, *720 Pages*	Sussman	400.00*
8173661464	ASP 3.0 Programmers Reference, *1,344 Pages*	Sussman	475.00
8173661499	Beginning Active Server Pages 3.0, *1,224 Pages*	Francis	600.00
8173663971	Beginning ASP.Net using VB.Net, *824 Pages*	Cornes	500.00*
8173664218	Beginning ASP.Net Using C#, *832 Pages*	Birdwell	550.00*
8173661502	Beginning ASP Databases, *868 Pages*	Blexrud	575.00
8173661510	Beginning ATL 3 COM Programming, *548 Pages*	Grimes	350.00
817366398X	Beginning C#, *1,036 Pages*	Bellinaso	650.00*
8173661529	Beginning Components for ASP, *868 Pages*	Anderson	575.00
8173664137	Beginning Databases with PostgreSQL, *592 Pages*	Matthew	400.00*
817366143X	Beginning E-Commerce with VB, ASP, SQL er 7.0 & MTS, *802 Pages*	Reynolds	550.00
8173661545	Beginning Java 2 – JDK 1.3 Edition, *1,272 Pages*	Horton	550.00
8173663998	Beginning Java Networking, *832 Pages*	Darby	550.00*
817366160X	Beginning Java Object, *696 Pages*	Barker	375.00*
8173661618	Beginning JavaScript, *1,052 Pages*	Wilton	475.00*
8173661561	Beginning Linux Programming Second Edition, *988 Pages*	Matthew	575.00*
8173661774	Beginning Perl, *704 Pages*	Cozens	425.00
8173661537	Beginning PHP 4, *804 Pages*	Wrox	575.00*
8173661669	Beginning SQL Programming, (BOOK/CD-ROM) *752 Pages*	Kauffman	575.00*
8173663181	Beginning SQL Server 2000 for Visual Basic Developers, *888 Pages*	Willis	525.00*
8173663467	Beginning SQL Server 2000 Programming, (BOOK/CD) *796 Pages*	Dewson	600.00*
817366420X	Beginning VB.NET Databases, *716 Pages*	Forgey	500.00*
8173664072	Beginning VB.NET, *868 Pages*	Crossland	525.00*
8173661626	Beginning Visual Basic 6 Database Programming, *880 Pages*	Connell	475.00
8173660417	Beginning Visual Basic 6, *920 Pages*	Wright	500.00
8173660409	Beginning Visual C++ 6, *1,216 Pages*	Horton	600.00
8173662088	Beginning WAP: WML and WMLScript, *676 Pages*	Wrox	425.00*
8173661642	Beginning XHTML, *768 Pages*	Wrox	400.00*
8173661650	Beginning XML Programming, *800 Pages*	Wrox	500.00
8173662215	C# Programming with the Public Beta, *416 Pages*	Harvey	300.00*
8173663041	C# Web Services, *628 Pages*	Banerjee	450.00*
8173663238	Data-Centric .NET Programing with C#, *812 Pages*	Ferracchiati	550.00*
8173664080	Early Adopter HailStorm (.NET My Services), *244 Pages*	Eisenberg	175.00*
8173664048	Early Adopter J2SE 1.4, *218 Pages*	Hart	175.00*
8173662940	Early Adopter JXTA, *312 Pages*	Li	225.00*
8173664005	Early Adopter VoiceXML, *328 Pages*	Andersson	250.00*
8173661707	Enterprise Application Architecture with VB, ASP, MTS, *816 Pages*	Moniz	425.00*
8173663874	Expert One-on-One Oracle, *1,328 Pages*	Kyte	675.00*
8173661758	Instant UML, *368 Pages*	Muller	300.00
8173661596	Introducing .NET, *474 pages*	Wrox	300.00*
817366174X	Implementing LDAP, *518 Pages*	Wilcox	375.00*
8173661766	Ivor Horton's Beginning C++ - The Complete Language, *1.000 Pages*	Horton	525.00
8173661685	Java Programmer's Reference, *1.252 Pages*	Palmer	450.00*
8173661855	JavaScript Programmer's Reference (BOOK/CD-ROM), *1004 Pages*	Wootton	500.00*
817366191X	A Preview of Active Server Pages+, *384 Pages*	Anderson	275.00*
817366322X	Oracle 9i Java Programming, *884 Pages*	Hólm	575.00*
8173664013	Professional .NET Framework, *760 Pages*	Gabriel	550.00*
8173661790	Professional Active Server Pages 3.0, *1,316 Pages*	Blexrud	650.00
817366157X	Professional Application Centre 2000, *432 Pages*	Homer	300.00*
8173664056	Professional ADO.NET, *746 Pages*	Dickinson	500.00*
8173664242	Professional ASP.Net Web Services, *792 Pages*	Basiura	550.00*

ISBN	Title	Author	Price
8173661634	Professional ASP Data Access, *1,340 Pages*	Anderson	625.00*
8173662959	Professional ASP XML, *920 Pages*	Baartse	525.00*
8173663483	Professional ASP.NET, *1,356 Pages*	Wrox	675.00*
8173662444	Professional BizTalk, *732 Pages*	Mohr	350.00*
8173663491	Professional C#, *1,348 Pages*	Wrox	675.00*
8173663505	Professional Commerce Server 2000, *1,126 Pages*	Wrox	575.00*
8173662967	Professional ColdFusion 5, *1,240 Pages*	Ambrose-Haynes	650.00*
8173661898	Professional DCOM Application Development, *496 Pages*	Pinnock	325.00
8173661901	Professional DCOM Programming, *592 Pages*	Grimes	375.00
8173664064	Professional ebXML Foundations, *724 Pages*	Chappell	550.00*
8173663513	Professional EJB, *1,200 Pages*	Wrox	675.00*
8173663157	Professional J2EE EAI, *958 Pages*	Juric	600.00*
8173662452	Professional J2EE Programming with BEA Web Logic Server, *538 Pages*	Gomez	300.00*
8173661022	Professional Java E-Commerce, *1,034 Pages*	Ashri	400.00*
8173661863	Professional Java Programming, *1,144 Pages*	Spell	475.00*
8173663009	Professional Java Server Programming 2/e - J2EE Version, *1,688 Pgs*	Allamaraju	675.00*
8173661804	Professional Java XML, *1,188 Pages*	Wrox	650.00*
8173661944	Professional Java XML Programming with Servlets & JSP, *804 Pages*	Myers	525.00*
8173661952	Professional JavaScript, *1,192 Pages*	McFarlane	650.00
8173662975	Professional Jini, *928 Pages*	Li	575.00*
8173661723	Professional JMS Programming, *800 Pages*	Wrox	350.00*
8173662118	Professional JSP, *940 Pages*	Avedal	500.00
8173661960	Professional Linux Deployment, *1,000 Pages*	Prasad	500.00
8173662002	Professional Linux Programming, *1,196 Pages*	Matthew	650.00*
8173661979	Professional MFC with Visual C++ 6, *1,248 Pages*	Blaszczak	625.00
8173331812	Professional Oracle8i Application Prog w/Java, PL/SQL and XML, *1,248 Pages*	Awai	575.00*
8173663696	Professional Perl Development, *750 Pages*	Wrox	450.00*
817366305X	Professional Perl Programming, *1,248 Pages*	Wrox	575.00*
8173663548	Professional PHP 4, *800 Pages*	Thomas	575.00*
8173662010	Professional PHP Programming, *856 Pages*	Castagnetto	600.00
8173662029	Professional Site Server 3.0 Commerce Edition, *786 Pages*	Tabini	500.00
8173662908	Professional Java SOAP, *546 Pages*	Bequet	350.00*
8173664099	Professional SQL Server 2000 Data Warehousing with Analysis Services, *708 Pages*	Bain	450.00*
8173662053	Professional SQL Server 2000 DTS (Data Transformation Services), *888 Pages*	Chaffin	525.00
8173663572	Professional SQL Server 2000 Database Design, *628 Pages*	Davidson	575.00*
8173662061	Professional SQL Server 2000 Programming, *1,428 Pages*	Vieira	750.00*
8173663556	Professional SQL Server 2000 XML, *622 Pages*	Burke	400.00*
8173664021	Professional VB.Net, *966 Pages*	Barwell	550.00*
8173662177	Professional Visual Basic 6 XML, *748 Pages*	Wrox	425.00
817366210X	Professional WAP, *858 Pages*	Wrox	500.00
8173663084	Professional Windows DNA: Building Distributed Web Applications with Visual Basic, COM+, MSMQ, SOAP and ASP, *1,016 Pages*	Blexrud	600.00*
8173663351	Professional Windows Forms, *708 Pages*	Bell	500.00*
8173663068	Professional XML Databases, *1,040 Pages*	Williams	600.00*
8173663122	Professional XML for .Net Developers, *754 Pages*	Dalvi	550.00*
8173662207	Professional XML, *1,200 Pages*	Birbeck	675.00
8173663076	Professional XSL, *800 Pages*	Wrox	500.00*
8173661731	VB.NET Programming with the Public Beta, *554 Pages*	Wrox	225.00*
817366224X	VBScript Programmer's Reference, *844 Pages*	Clark	475.00*
8173662290	XML Applications, *600 Pages*	Boumphrey	400.00
8173662223	XSLT Programmer's Reference, Second Edition, *984 Pages*	Kay	575.00*

ISBN	Title	Author	Price
	Forthcoming Titles		
March 2002			
817366238X	Early Adopter JSP Standard Tag Library, *200 Pages*	Wrox	175.00*
8173662304	Early Adopter XQuery, *200 Pages*	Wrox	175.00*
8173663033	Professional ASP.NET Server Controls, *1,000 Pages*	Wrox	650.00*
817366255X	Professional Java Servlets 2.3, *800 Pages*	Wrox	575.00*
8173662614	Professional Java Web Services, *800 Pages*	Wrox	575.00*
April 2002			
8173661154	ASP.NET Security, *600 Pages*	Seven	450.00*
8173661146	ASP.NET Website Programming, *500 Pages*	Wrox	375.00*
8173662134	Early Adopter .NET Compact Framework, *200 Pages*	Wrox	175.00*
8173662258	Early Adopter VSA, *200 Pages*	Wrox	175.00*
8173662355	Early Adopter J#, *200 Pages*	Sarang	175.00*
8173662274	Early Adopter Windows XP Instant Messaging Programming, *200 Pages*	Wrox	175.00*
8173662738	Beginning Oracle 9i Programming, *700 Pages*	Wrox	500.00*
8173661928	Professional Java Data, *1,360 Pages*	Betapudi	675.00*
8173662932	Professional Java Security, *544 Pages*	Garms	350.00*
8173661472	Professional VC++ .NET, *600 Pages*	Wrox	450.00*
8173661812	Professional VB.NET Transactions, *500 Pages*	Wrox	350.00*
May 2002			
8173661456	.NET Enterprise Development in C#: From Design to Deployment, *800 Pages*	Reynolds	575.00*
8173661553	.NET Enterprise Development in VB.Net: From Design to Deployment, *752 Pages*	Wrox	525.00*
8173660212	Beginning ASP.NET Databases, *600 Pages*	Kaufmann	450.00*
8173662827	Beginning MySQL, *500 Pages*	Matthew	350.00*
8173661383	C# Programmer's Reference, *450 Pages*	Palmer	325.00*
8173661693	VB.NET Class Design Handbook, *250 Pages*	Wrox	175.00*
8173661847	Visual Studio .NET Enterprise Edition, *700 Pages*	Sempf	500.00*
8173662436	Early Adopter Sun Java Web Services Pack, *200 Pages*	Wrox	175.00*
8173662460	Professional JSP Tag Libraries, *600 Pages*	Wrox	450.00*
8173661839	Professional Visual Basic Interoperability – COM and VB6 to .NET, *700 Pages*	Wrox	500.00*
8173661987	XML Application Development with MSXML 4.0, *800 Pages*	Livingstone	575.00*
	SPD/friends of ED Reprints		
Published Titles			
817366336X	Flash 5 Studio (BOOK/CD-ROM), *798 Pages*	Adnani	600.00*
8173662185	Foundation ActionScript, *512 Pages*	Bhangal	300.00*
8173662126	Foundation Flash 5, *646 Pages*	Bhangal	350.00*
8173663386	Foundation Dreamweaver UltraDev, *480 Pages*	Paddock	300.00*
	Forthcoming Titles		
February 2002			
8173664196	Director 8.5 Studio (BOOK/CD-ROM), *836 Pages*	Bauman	600.00*
8173663408	Foundation Director 8.5, *456 Pages*	Uttan	325.00*
8173664188	Foundation Photoshop 6 (Includes 8 Full Color Pages), *672 Pages*	Smith	425.00*
8173663416	Flash XML StudioLab, *512 Pages*	Tracey	375.00*
8173663459	Foundation Illustrator 10, *548 Pages*	Loader	400.00*
8173663939	Flash & Director, *516 Pages*	Gould	400.00*

- **Dates and Prices of forthcoming titles are tentative and subject to change without notice.**
- **New titles are denoted with *.**
- **All Prices are in Indian Rupees.**